Prisons and Prison Systems

Prisons and Prison Systems

A Global Encyclopedia

Mitchel P. Roth

GREENWOOD PRESS
Westport, Connecticut • London

Library of Congress Cataloging-in-Publication Data

Roth, Mitchel P., 1953–
  Prisons and prison systems : a global encyclopedia / Mitchel P. Roth.
    p. cm.
  Includes bibliographical references and index.
  ISBN 0–313–32856–0 (alk. paper)
  1. Prisons—Encyclopedias. 2. Imprisonment—Cross-cultural
studies—Encyclopedias. 3. Prisons—History—Encyclopedias. 4.
Prisoners—Biography—Encyclopedias. 5. Prisons—Officials and
employees—Biography—Encyclopedias. I. Title.
  HV8665.R67   2006
  365'.03—dc22   2005018722

British Library Cataloguing in Publication Data is available.

Library of Congress Catalog Card Number: 2005018722
ISBN 0–313–32856–0

First published in 2006

Greenwood Press, 88 Post Road West, Westport, CT 06881
An imprint of Greenwood Publishing Group, Inc.
www.greenwood.com

Printed in the United States of America

The paper used in this book complies with the
Permanent Paper Standard issued by the National
Information Standards Organization (Z39.48–1984).

10 9 8 7 6 5 4 3 2 1

Dedicated to Erica Roth
(born October 2, 2004)

Contents

Alphabetical List of Entries

Topical List of Entries

Prison Books and Films

Preface

As the countries of the world lock up more of their citizens each year, the dearth of reference works on international prisons and prison systems seems even more glaring. *Prisons and Prison Systems: A Global Encyclopedia* was conceived and written to help fill a void in prison reference books. This book is dedicated to offering the most current research available on all the prison systems in the world, past and present, as well as reference materials on famous and important prisons, prison reformers, famous prisoners, and prison architecture and architects. All topics are referenced with sources and cross-referenced to main entries in **bold face** type.

Historically, prison populations have been overwhelmingly made up of adult males, hence the concentration on adult male facilities over juvenile and women's prisons. All reference works are subject to limitations of content and length. This work is no exception. A deliberate decision was made to focus on correctional systems, personnel, reformers, prisoners, architecture, and legislation. Hence decisions were made to avoid issues such as the death penalty, death row, and executions. Likewise, an entire book could be devoted to prisoner-of-war camps, so these too have been excluded from the purview of this book. Including these topics would have required at least a second volume.

The author was responsible for including the Soviet Gulag and other types of labor camps but excluding the concentration camps of World War II, the prison camps of Yugoslavia's civil war, and Axis internment camps in the United States in the 1940s. Since these camps were devoted to single issues and specific individuals based on race, ethnicity, or religion, they had less in common with the traditional notion of imprisonment as a method of rehabilitation, penitence, or punishment. In contrast, the Soviet Gulag, like other prison systems, held a wide range of individuals, with no dominant race, religion, or ethnic group represented.

Several sources were indispensable to the writing of this book. The study of international prison systems was in its infancy when George W. Hale compiled and wrote his *Police and Prison Cyclopedia* in 1893. Although its major focus is on policing, Hale, a former police officer himself, does include valuable statistics and hard-to-find information on "foreign police departments and prisons," making it a valuable resource to prison scholars. Other pioneering works that should be considered by anyone researching the development of international corrections include criminologist John L. Gillin's 1931 book *Taming the Criminal: Adventures in Penology* and Negley K. Teeters's *World Penal Systems*. Written in 1944, Teeters's book offers valuable research on colonial and other Third World prisons and prison systems, as well as on pre-Socialist institutions in China, Cuba, Vietnam, and Korea prior to the emergence of their Communist governments.

In the modern era the research of Roy Walmsley, a consultant to the European Institute for Crime Prevention and Control (HEUNI), is a must for any researcher looking for statistics on prisons and prison systems. As research director of World Prison Brief Online, he has meticulously compiled a comprehensive database on the prison systems of the world that is an asset to anyone interested in international corrections. For more than thirty years Norman Johnston has been chronicling the history of prison architecture and design. Throughout the writing and researching of this reference work, I have never been farther than arm's reach from Johnston's comprehensive *Forms of Constraint* (2000) and Walmsley's World Prison Population List. Although I have never met either author, my hat's off to both of them.

This project could not have been completed in a timely fashion without the help of several individuals. Connie Alvarez and Jillian Harris were always there in the clutch to help with copying or providing this technophobe with computer assistance. Virginia Wilson demonstrated excellent research skills in collecting information on various Asian prison systems. Also meriting thanks is Doug Goldenberg-Hart, who put this project in my lap several years ago, and my current editor with Greenwood Press Steven Vetrano, who provided excellent suggestions for making this a better book.

Words alone cannot describe the support and love provided by my wife Ines Papandrea and the happiness she brought into my life with the birth of our daughter Erica, to whom this book is dedicated.

Introduction

The way a society treats its prisoners can tell you much about its culture. The prison system is in many respects an excellent prism through which to examine a particular culture. If a prison system is punitive, it might tell us that a particular society is tired of high crime rates. Or better yet it can convey whether or not a society respects human rights. One need look no further than the reports by **Amnesty International** or **Human Rights Watch** to find out which countries treat prisoners poorly. However, before making a rush to judgment, it is also important to consider the lot of the free citizens. Are they poorly fed, housed, and clothed as well? One common theme in the history of prisons and prison systems is the mistreatment of the other—those most marginalized in society. American prisons, for example, imprison minorities at a proportionately higher rate than the majority Caucasian populace. A number of countries, especially Australia, imprison a high proportion of their indigenous peoples. In nineteenth-century Peru, prison reformer **Mariano Felipe Paz Soldan** was even convinced that the country's large Indian population would enjoy solitary confinement and that working in a congregate setting would cure them of their "natural laziness." By examining the world's prisons and prison systems one can learn many lessons. Scholars and laypersons alike can examine race relations, politics, sociology, history, architecture, and other disciplines through the prism of the prison.

A number of scholars suggest that the modern prison is a product of the eighteenth-century Enlightenment. This has led many reference works on prisons and prison systems to give short shrift to the development of prisons and places of confinement prior to the 1700s. Although early prisons were rarely built expressly for the purpose of imprisonment, most cultures resorted to makeshift cages or dungeons to confine prisoners in existing structures. Since incarceration is so widely used as punishment in the world today, most readers would be surprised to find that imprisonment played a minor role in the punishment regimes of most countries before the nineteenth century.

Some of the world's most famous buildings, including **The Kremlin** and the **Tower** of London, have been used as prisons over the centuries. References to early prisons can be found in a number of ancient cultures. Several thousand years ago the Babylonians utilized places of incarceration, or *bit kili*, for debtors and petty criminals, as well as for convicts who were either slaves or foreigners. Classical Greece and Rome sporadically used a private prison, or *carcer privatus*, to detain debtors and individuals awaiting trial or execution. Ancient Athens had a prison called the *desmoterion*, or "the place of chains." Rome's Twelve Tables refers to a place of forced detention called the *ergastalum*. By the sixth century the Latin term *carcer* was used to refer to penitential confinement, and in the Middle Ages *carceres* were the special rooms monasteries dedicated for "delinquent clergy."

The Old Testament reports the use of imprisonment by Egyptians, Philistines, Assyrians, and Israelites. Jerusalem had at least three prisons at the time of Nebuchadnezzar, including *Beth ha-keli*, or "house of detention"; *Beth haasourim*, literally "house of chains"; and *Bor*, which was little more than an underground cistern.

No word conjures up the worst aspects of imprisonment more than *dungeon*. Derived from the Latin term *domgio*, referring to a precipice where a castle or fortress is built, the French adopted the term *donjon*, from which the more familiar English version, *dungeon*, was derived. Over time *dungeon* became synonymous for the inner sanctums and places of confinement in towers and castles built at high elevations. One of the earliest examples of subterranean chambers for prisoners was **Mamertine Prison** built in Rome in 64 B.C.E.

Early English jails can be found at least as far back as 1166 when King Henry II required that each sheriff establish a county jail in his shire. A number of towns used formidable **gatehouse prisons** located near the city gates. Except for nomenclature there was little distinction between jails, prisons, and other places of confinement until the eighteenth century. The original functions of prisons varied little. Most held individuals awaiting trial or punishment after adjudication. If the guilty did not die from whatever sentence awaited them, they were released and their debts to society were completed. Between the twelfth and fifteenth centuries pre-existing structures such as tower keeps, cellars, and dungeons held prisoners in various locations. Most of these facilities housed all prisoners in a single room, while a small number of buildings experimented with cellular confinement. According to one historian, early European hospitals, or **lazarettos**, provided the inspiration for modern "purpose-built" prison designs.

In the sixteenth and seventeenth centuries England opened a number of **houses of correction** known as **Bridewells**. Parliament ruled that every county should open one of these institutions to hold indigents and vagrants while inculcating them with the appropriate work ethic. In these facilities petty criminals and transient types were introduced to a number of tasks that could help support the institution, such as baking and milling. By the late 1500s Bridewells offered training and apprenticeships to poor freemen and women and to street children that included 25 different occupations. Amsterdam contributed its version of the house of correction, the **rasphouse**, in the sixteenth century as well. Sheriffs in medieval London utilized **gaols** (jails) known as **compters** to incarcerate misdemeanants such as debtors, drunks, and vagrants. Like other holding facilities of the era these institutions earned an unsavory reputation for charging prisoners fees for even their most basic needs.

An important step in the development of the prison was the use of cellular confinement. Some of the earliest examples of this were located in what is now Italy. In 1677 the Hospice of San Filippo was operating near Florence. One criminologist has described this institution as the "first practical attempt" to use 24-hour segregation "for the avowed purpose of correction and reformation." Others have credited the **San Michele Hospice** in Rome as being the inspiration for cellular confinement. Another major step in prison innovation was the rebuilding of the original house of correction in **Ghent** in the 1770s, replete with separate cells for prisoners. By adopting the regime made famous at Rome's San Michele Hospice and later by the **Auburn system**, prisoners were housed in a congregate setting by day and slept in separate cells at night.

When **transportation** of British convicts to the American colonies was abruptly interrupted in 1775, Britain's overcrowded prisons forced authorities to look for alternative detention facilities—they did not need to look far. Rather than build new prisons, penurious administrators turned to derelict warships and merchant vessels, or **convict hulks**, to confine prisoners. Great Britain was not the only country to experiment with penal colonies. France's **Devil's Island** was probably the best known. Operating the facility between 1852 and 1946, France adopted penal transportation just as Britain abandoned it in Australia. Islands have proven to be popular with prison planners. From **Van Diemen's Land** and **Norfolk Island** to the world's largest island, Australia, to America's **Alcatraz**, France's Devil's Island, and Italy's **Lipari** island, the planet's oceans have an enviable record for providing the ultimate in correctional security.

Following the American Civil War the former Southern states, as well as several others, turned to **convict leasing** to make up for the dearth of prison facilities and lack of financial resources. Like so many other experiments in penology **chain gangs** have gone in and out of fashion in the United States. Societies have used forced labor at least as far back as fifth-century B.C. Greece, when state-owned slaves were leased out to private mining operators. Convict labor was used during the Roman Empire and into the Middle Ages. But not until the age of the modern penitentiary did the convict-leasing system find an environment in which it could prosper. Nowhere was this truer than in the United States. Although colonial jails forced prisoners to work, not until the opening of Philadelphia's **Walnut Street Jail** in 1790 was prison labor placed at the disposal of outside contractors. In the post–Civil War American South the convict-leasing system was the result of a paucity of funding from the shattered Confederate states. Convict leasing diminished in popularity in the twentieth century, particularly in America, as a result of the growing clout of labor unions, who saw convict leasing as unfair business competition in a world of free labor.

England's **John Howard** was probably history's best-known prison reformer. In homage to Howard, prison reform societies have been named after him, and various reformers have been referred to as the John Howard of their respective countries: America's John Howard was **Thomas Eddy**, and the Prussian physician **Nicolaus Julius** was accorded the moniker the "German John Howard," for example.

In the early years of the nineteenth century the United States took the lead in creating the modern prison. American prison reformers championed two prison models. New York established the Auburn system, sometimes referred to as the congregate model. It allowed convicts to work in a congregate setting with other inmates by day but isolated them in individual cells at night. The **Pennsylvania sys-**

tem, in contrast, became known as the solitary system for its forced separation of prisoners "24/7" for their entire prison term. It was hoped that the Quaker-inspired Pennsylvania system would allow prisoners to reflect on their lives and at the same time learn the value of discipline and proper work habits. According to one early reformer, "The **Quakers** took up the cause of prison reform and made a religion of it." Most prison systems favored the Auburn system because it was cheaper to operate and its use of congregate labor made it more financially productive than the competing Pennsylvania system. Except for Pennsylvania and New Jersey's **Trenton State Prison,** all American prisons built in the nineteenth century adopted the Auburn model. However, the legacy of the Pennsylvania system was more pronounced in Europe and South America, where a number of prisons were built on this model. Worldwide, almost 300 prisons were inspired by **Eastern State Penitentiary**'s radial design.

A handful of other noteworthy prison designs emerged during the late eighteenth and early nineteenth centuries. Never as popular as the Auburn and Pennsylvania systems, the circular or semicircular **Panopticon** devised by **Jeremy Bentham** was copied by several countries and the United States. Although it allowed the continual observance of inmates, its unpopularity was in part a consequence of its waste of space as well as the prisoners' ability to easily follow the movements of guards.

Before the twentieth century a number of prisons employed "make-work" strategies to keep prisoners busy. Sometimes work was constructive and provided income for the prison facility; at other times the tasks was unconstructive and purely punitive. Great Britain introduced a number of such strategies, including the **treadmill,** the **crank,** and **oakum picking.** These tedious tasks were designed to "grind men good." Amsterdam, however, pioneered the use of such practices as early as the sixteenth century through the use of rasping. In so-called **rasphouses,** a type of **workhouse,** inmates were kept busy rasping or sawing up to 25 pounds of sawdust per day per inmate to produce powder for coloring merchandise. This could take between 10 and 15 hours per day, equivalent to the average workday in the free world at that time. Reformers such as John Howard saw rasping and other mindnumbing tasks combined with a heavy dose of religion as an effective avenue to reform. In the minds of the prison keepers hard labor helped rehabilitate inmates and at the same time enabled institutions such as houses of detention to remain selfsufficient.

The emergence of the modern prison in the nineteenth century was to a great extent an outcome of the growing sentiment against punishments of the day—brutal floggings, hangings, mutilations, and the like. A major step in the creation of modern prison systems was the formation of the **National Prison Congress** in 1870. International prison congresses on prison reform had been convened in Europe almost 25 years earlier, but little was achieved until the meeting held in Cincinnati, Ohio, in 1870. More than 130 delegates, including judges, wardens, prison chaplains, and governors, met and unanimously adopted a Declaration of Principles, which included increased emphasis on rehabilitation, education, religion, training, and most important, pushed for the widespread adoption of indeterminate sentencing and the end of political patronage.

The development of prisons and prison systems in the modern era has been fraught with experimentation. Many of these experiments have been undertaken by the prison-oriented American criminal justice system. For example, in the early nineteenth century **Thomas Mott Osborne** inaugurated the **Mutual Welfare League** at

Auburn Prison, an "anti-institutional" approach that experimented with offering prisoners the opportunity to achieve a modicum of self-respect by removing the constraints of the **silent system**. Great Britain embarked on the **Q Camp Experiment** in the prewar 1930s, which like the Mutual Welfare League, hinged on democratic incarceration and shared responsibility. In the 1980s and 1990s shock incarceration centers, better known as **boot camps**, were seen as a panacea for the growing juvenile crime rate. Demonstrating the cyclical nature of prison reform, the boot camp regimen had much in common with reformer **Zebulon Brockway**'s attempts to combine education, athletics, and military discipline as a pathway to reform. As with many other "get-tough" initiatives, there is little evidence that boot camps had much impact on recidivism. Beginning in the early 1900s Great Britain experimented with detention centers for youthful offenders known as **Borstals**, named after the village where the first one was located. Several studies have suggested that the Borstals and boot camps often resulted in high recidivism rates for their graduates. More countries have found better success through diversion of juveniles into noncustodial adjudication.

The twentieth century ushered in a new era in prisons and prison systems. It saw not only the closing of Devil's Island and the inauguration of the prison **big house** movement in America but also the creation of enormous work camps and the Soviet **Gulag**. By the 1980s the Soviet Union was sentencing 99 percent of its convicted criminals to these labor camps. The new century also witnessed the flowering of alternatives to cellular confinement, once the great panacea. **Probation** and **parole** became standard alternatives, as did work release and the suspended sentence. Beginning in the late 1980s **supermaximum prisons** revived some of the most discredited strategies of earlier prison regimes. It was hoped that keeping prisoners in their cells 24/7 and making communal dining rooms and exercise yards redundant would keep prisoners and staff safer.

Prisons can both appall and intrigue those who have never experienced life behind bars. As this book will demonstrate, prisons and prison systems have inspired great works of literature and important motion pictures, though often demonstrating the worst aspects of human behavior. Prisons have housed some of history's greatest criminals as well as some of its most cherished leaders. But despite dramatic change, much remains the same. Since the advent of the prison and cellular confinement, prison systems have been plagued with overcrowding and brutality. As more individuals are imprisoned than ever before in the United States and other nations, prisons have become big business—a business that will probably survive into the next millennium.

Sources: Deford, *Stone Walls*, 1962; Morris, *Prisons*, 1976; McKelvey, *American Prisons*, 1977; Salvatore and Aguirre, *The Birth of the Penitentiary in Latin America*, 1996; Roberts, *Reform and Retribution*, 1997; Christianson, *With Liberty for Some*, 1998; Morris and Rothman, eds., *The Oxford History of the Prison*, 1998; Johnston, *Forms of Constraint*, 2000.

Chronology

c. 1900 B.C.	References made to the "**Great Prison**" of ancient **Egypt**.
c. 500 B.C.	*Desmoterion*, or "the place of chains," described in Greek play by Aeschylus.
451 B.C.	Rome's Twelve Tables mention imprisonment for debt.
399 B.C.	Plato discusses imprisonment in his *Apology* and in the trial of Socrates.
64 B.C.	Rome's **Mamartine Prison** built beneath city sewer system.
428	Theodisian Code notes separation of prisoners by sex.
817	Meeting of Benedictine priors at Aix-la-Chapelle set standards for punishment and torture.
1066	King William I begins construction of **Tower of London**.
c.1100	**England** begins imprisoning debtors.
1166	Assize of Clarendon requires sheriffs to build jails in each county until the arrival of justice of the peace.
1200	Best-known early French prison in operation at the *Chatelet* in Mont-Saint Michel.
1298	Marco Polo imprisoned in Genoa.
1370	Groundwork laid for the **Bastille** in Paris.
1460s	**Antonio Averlino** describes a progressive prison regime in his *Treatise on Architecture*.
1495	Dungeons built under the **Kremlin**'s Trinity Tower.
1500s	Use of **galley servitude** popularized in **France**, **Spain**, and Italian states.
1539	**Lazaretto** of San Pancrazio, **Italy** designed.
1556	London **Bridewell** opened.

1575	Cervantes enslaved by Barbary pirates for five years.
1596	Amsterdam incorporates house of correction known as the **rasphuis**.
1601	John ("No Man is An Island") Donne imprisoned.
1627	**The Malefizhaus** built for sinners and witches in Bamberg, Germany.
1633	Italian scientist Galileo sentenced to house arrest.
1635	**Joseph Furttenbach** describes cellular confinement in his *Architectura Universalis*.
1660	John Bunyan sentenced to **Bedford Prison, County Gaol**.
1677	Hospice of San Filippo opened in Florence for delinquent boys.
1682	**William Penn**'s Code introduces important penal reform to Quaker colony of Pennsylvania.
1703	Author Daniel DeFoe sentenced to prison for libel.
1704	Pope Clement XI opens house of correction for criminal boys at **San Michele**.
1718–1722	**France** transports convicts to Louisiana.
1718	**England** begins **transportation** to America.
1720	English statute rules that **houses of correction** be used to house criminal offenders.
1734	**Iceland** introduces imprisonment (in Danish prisons) as punishment.
1757	**Benjamin Rush** advocates classification of prisoners.
1764	**Cesare Beccaria**'s *On Crimes and Punishment* published.
1769	London's **Newgate Prison** erected.
1771	**Iceland** opens prison in Reykjavik.
1773	**Walnut Street Jail** opens as local and county prison.
1773	**John Howard** appointed High Sheriff of Bedfordhsire.
1773	**John Howard** begins tour of British prisons.
1776	Britain ends **transportation** of convicts to America.
1776	**England** begins using **convict hulks** to house prisoners.
1776	**Belgium**'s **Vilvorde Prison** completed.
1779	English **Penitentiary Act of 1779**.
1785	**Francesco Milizia** distinguishes between civil and criminal architecture in *Principi di Archiettura Civile*.
1787	The **Pennsylvania Prison Society** is created.
1787	**England** resumes **transportation**, this time to Australian penal colonies.
1788	First British convicts arrive in **Australia**.
1789	Publication of **John Howard**'s *Account of the Principal Lazarettos in Europe*.
1790	**John Howard** dies from **"gaol fever"** in the Crimea.

1790	Philadelphia's **Walnut Street Jail** introduces the penitentiary and **Pennsylvania system** to America, when it becomes state penitentiary.
1790	**Jeremy Bentham**'s first plan for the **Panopticon** submitted to British Parliament.
1791	Bentham's *Panopticon Postscript* published.
1797	New York prison reformer **Thomas Eddy** oversees construction of **Newgate Prison** on the Hudson River.
1800	Virginia opens prison in Richmond based on panopticon design.
1809	**Dartmoor Prison** completed.
1815	First use of striped uniforms in American prisons.
1816	England's **Millbank Prison** opens.
1817–1819	New York's **Auburn Prison** receives its first prisoners.
1818	**Maidstone Prison** opens.
c.1820	**England** introduces **treadmill**.
1824	Early Italian reform prison opened in Padua in the Kingdom of Lombardy and Venice.
1825	New York's **Sing Sing Prison** accepts its first prisoners.
1825	**Switzerland**'s Geneva penitentiary completed.
1825	New York City opens house of refuge to handle juveniles.
1826	The Society for the Improvement of Prison Discipline publishes *Remarks on the Form and the Construction of Prisons with Appropriate Designs* in Great Britain.
1829	**Eastern State Penitentiary** receives its first prisoner.
1830	**Coldbath Fields Prison** opens.
1830s	**Australia** opens Berrima jail, one of its first professionally designed prisons.
1831	Magistrates Gustave de Beaumont and **Alexis de Tocqueville** visit American prisons.
1835	**Kingston Prison** opens, **Canada**'s first penitentiary.
1835	**Manuel Montesinos** becomes director of **Spain**'s Valencia Prison.
1836	**Eastern State Penitentiary** completed.
1836	**John Haviland**'s **Trenton State Prison** opens.
1836	Paris's **Petite Roquette Prison** completed.
1836	**Alexander Maconochie** arives in **Australia**.
1837	**Joshua Jebb** appointed England's first surveyor-general of prisons.
1838	The Haviland-designed **Tombs Prison** opens in New York City incorporating Egyptian revival motifs.
1840	**Alexander Maconochie** experiments with convict reform on **Norfolk Island**.

1841	Victoria Prison opens in **Hong Kong**.
1842	Great Britain opens **Pentonville Prison**, becoming one of the most copied prisons in the world.
1844	Construction begins at Berlin's **Moabit Prison** based on Pennsylvania system.
1844	**Reading County Gaol** opens.
1845	**Elizabeth Fry** dies.
1846	First international prison congress convenes in Frankfurt.
1847	Sweden's earliest departmental prison opens at Gavle.
1849	**Holloway Prison** opens.
1849	Novelist **Fyodor Dostoyevsky** sentenced to Siberian **gulag**.
1850	Early Spanish reform prison at Valladolid opens.
1851	Oslo, **Norway**, opens cellular prison.
1853	**Denmark's** Horsens Prison built on Auburn model.
1854	Sir **Walter Crofton** inaugurates **Irish system**, or **mark system**.
1861	**Spain** completes its first cell prison in Vitoria.
1867	**McNeil Island Territorial Prison** opens.
1870	First National Prison Association meets.
1870	**Declaration of Principles** adopted at National Prison Association meeting.
1870	Britain ends **transportation** of convicts to penal colonies.
1873	Opening of the Indiana Women's Prison, marks appearance of first seprate women's prison in the United States.
1876	**Elmira Reformatory** opens.
1876	Bogota, **Colombia**, opens model prison on Auburn plan.
1883	**Panopticon** in La Paz, Bolivia is first national prison for men.
1884	Prison reform in **Egypt** begins under the first director general of prisons.
1884	Three **panopticon** prisons open in Holland, at Arnhem, Haarlem, and Breda.
1885	Construction on **Uruguay's** first penitentiary begins.
1891	U.S. Congress approved Three Prisons Act leading to construction of three federal penitentiaries.
1891	**Wormwood Scrubs Prison** opens, considered first **telephone pole** style prison.
1896	Howard League Founded.
1898	**Fresnes-les-Rungis**, based on **telephone pole** plan, completed outside Paris.
1905	**England** opens its first **Borstal** in Rochester, Kent.
1906	**Leavenworth Federal Penitentiary** opens.
1907	Penal Reform League founded.
1914	**Thomas Mott Osborne** becomes warden of New York's **Sing Sing Prison**.

1918	Bertrand Russell imprisoned.
1921	**Howard Association** and Penal Reform League join forces to become the Howard League for Penal Reform.
1925	Opening of Illinois' **Stateville Prison** marks the construction of America's last **panopticon**-style prison.
1926	Cuba opens national prison on the Isle of Pines.
1929	America's Federal Bureau of Prisons organized.
1930	United States establishes Federal Bureau of Prisons.
1932	Publication of *I Am a Fugitive from a Georgia Chain Gang!*
1934	**Alcatraz** Prison opens.
1946	French penal colony of **Devil's Island** closed.
1948	World's first use of **boot camps** method of "shock incarceration" demonstrated in **England**.
1948	**England** outlaws penal servitude and hard labor.
1963	Weekend incarceration, a form of periodic detention, introduced in Auckland, **New Zealand**.
1963	Storied **Alcatraz** Prison closed.
1971	**Attica Prison** Riot results in 39 deaths.
1975	Publication of Michel Foucault's *Surveiller et punir: La Naissance de la prison,* or *Discipline and Punish: The Birth of the Prison.*
1982	English Borstals replaced by youth custody.
1983	Use of electronic monitoring inaugurated in Albuquerque, New Mexico.
1985	Marion County, Kentucky, the site of the modern world's first privately owned and operated prison for adult felons.
1990	**Australia**'s Borallon Prison becomes the nation's first privately managed prison.
1992	**England** opens its first privately managed prison at Wold's Prison, Humberside.
1994	American federal government opens its first **supermaximum prison** in Florence, Colorado.
2002	American prison population reaches 2,166,260.
2004	**Iraq**'s **Abu Ghraib Prison** scandal erupts.

Sources: Morris and Rothman, eds., *The Oxford History of the Prison*, 1995; Greg Newbold, "A Chronology of Correctional History," in *Journal of Criminal Justice Education* 10, no. 1 (Spring 1999), pp. 87–100; Johnston, *Forms of Constraint*, 2000.

Prisons and Prison Systems

A

ABKHAZIA. In 1992 this region within **Georgia** declared itself an independent state. Sporadic conflict has left the status of this region unresolved despite a treaty brokered by the Russian Federation in 1998. At last count Abkhanzia had two prison facilities. The central facility was Dranda Prison, which held 450 prisoners at the beginning of 2003. There is also a small colony settlement in the same area with 16 prisoners. Supplementing these facilities are six "temporary detention isolators," operated by police management. The most recent figures indicate a prison rate of 87 per 100,000 of the national population. Among the current schemes to update the prison regime are projects to improve light and ventilation and to train prisoners in computer skills.

Source: Walmsley, *Further Developments in the Prison Systems of Central and Eastern Europe*, 2003.

ABU GHRAIB PRISON. This Iraqi prison came to world prominence during the Iraqi prisoner abuse scandal involving coalition guards in 2003. Under Saddam Hussein's Baathist regime this location was known as a place of torture and executions. It has been estimated that 4,000 were executed there in 1984 alone. British contractors had built the prison complex in the 1960s. Under the Iraqi regime the prison was called Baghdad Central Confinement Facility (BCCF). Following the invasion by coalition forces the prison was renamed Abu Ghraib. Senior British advisors wanted to demolish the structure immediately but were overruled by U.S. authorities.

Located 32 kilometers west of Baghdad in the city of Abu Ghraib, the prison complex itself covers 280 acres and is surrounded by 24 guard towers. Inside the facility are five walled structures. The cells measured four meters by four meters and on average held forty prisoners. Under Hussein the prison was divided into open and closed wings, with the closed wings reserved exclusively for Shi'ites who were not permitted visitors or any contact outside the prison. As recently as 2001 it housed close to 15,000 inmates. Plans were underway to expand the prison when the coalition forces invaded in 2003.

Under U.S-led coalition forces the facility was renamed Baghdad Correctional Facility. In the aftermath of the invasion it held 7,000 detainees, some alleged criminals, others not. In April 2004 the U.S. television news magazine show *60 Minutes II* broke the story detailing the abuse and humiliation of Iraqi inmates.

By September 2004 the population of Abu Ghraib was down to 2,800 prisoners from a high of 10,000 at its peak of overcrowding in 2003. Plans are underway to reduce the population to 1,000 as new facilities are completed. Since January of 2004, when the prisoner abuse scandal broke, close to 7,500 prisoners have been exonerated and released. In a May 2004 speech at the U.S. Army War College in Pennsylvania, President George W. Bush announced plans to demolish the prison. However, interim Iraqi officials were opposed to this, and in June 2004 a U.S. military judge ruled that since the prison was a crime scene, it could not be destroyed. Recent revelations from guards previously stationed at **Guantanamo Bay** indicate that American interrogators at the prison learned how to terrorize prisoners with dogs. More than one year after the scandal was made public, Abu Ghraib continues to hold Iraqi prisoners.

Sources: Norimitsu Onishi, "Transforming a Prison with U.S. Image in Mind," *New York Times*, September 16, 2004, A13; Josh White, "Abu Ghraib Tactics Were First Used at Guantanamo," *Washington Post*, July 14, 2005, A01.

AFGHANISTAN. Following the end of the monarchy, government efforts have been directed toward rehabilitation programs and reform schools for juveniles. Prison labor has been widely used for supplying clothing and supplies for the military. Toward the end of the 1980s prisoners were encouraged to learn trades and craft-making skills. Prisoners were also allowed to keep much of the money earned through their training in stonemasonry, pottery making, and rug weaving.

During the Soviet occupation hundreds of thousands of prisoners passed through the gates of Pul-i-Charkhi Prison on the eastern fringe of Kabul, the site of almost daily executions. Following the 1979 invasion, the Soviets took advantage of the forbidding edifice built in the 1970s.

Prior to the Taliban era most cities and towns had jails, while larger population centers had prisons. According to established protocol family members and friends were expected to supply the prisoner with food. In cases where this was not possible, it was incumbent on the accuser to provide food. In towns fortunate enough to have posts of gendarmes, lockup rooms were available for prisoners awaiting sentencing. Government officials were expected to make routine inspections of detention facilities.

In 1992 anti-Communist forces overthrew the Soviet-supported Najibullah government and in the process freed thousands of political figures. Pul-i-Charkhi Prison would remain empty until the Taliban takeover in 1995. The prison was emptied once more in the wake of the Taliban capitulation in November 2001. Despite an ongoing attempt to reconstruct the nation's criminal justice system, human rights abuses continued through lack of resources. Human rights groups reported continued arbitrary arrests and poor prison conditions into 2002.

The former conditions may be ameliorated under a new regime, however. Under the new Karzai administration Kabul's prison is once more preparing for prisoners in 2003, although officials have pledged to honor human rights and avoid political prosecution. By 2003 the United Nations Office on Drugs and Crime was leading a $6 million penitentiary and judicial reform program, which included $200,000 to repair sanitation, water, and kitchen facilities at Pul-i-Charkhi. Formerly under the Interior Ministry, the program is now under the direction of the Justice Ministry.

On May 31, 2005 new legislation was passed to improve the country's deteriorating prisons. Recent evidence indicates that in 20 provinces inmates are housed in rented buildings that become quickly overcrowded. Some facilities have mud floors, poor food, and little in the way of medical services. As of June 2005, Afghanistan's 34 state jails held 6,000 prisoners. This does not take into account the thousands held in private prisons in provinces controlled by warlords and local military commanders. There are also an unknown number of detention facilities maintained by U.S.-led coalition forces. These typically hold "suspected" Taliban and Al-Qaeda supporters. At this writing, a lack of financial resources has prevented "any meaningful upgrade of penal facilities."

Sources: Kurian, ed., *World Encyclopedia of Police Forces and Penal Systems*, 1989 (henceforth *WEPP*); *Amnesty International Report*, 2003; Carlotta Gall, "Where Thousands Met Death, Prisoners Are Returning," *International Herald Tribune*, July 8, 2003, p. 2; Reuters Foundation, "Afghanistan: New Law to Promote International Standards in Prisons," June 15, 2005, www.alertnews.org/thenews/newsdesk, retrieved July 28, 2005.

AICHACH PRISON. One of the few prisons devoted exclusively to women in Nazi **Germany**, it was located near the Bavarian city of Augsburg. It received its first prisoners in 1909 and was most influenced by the **panopticon** design. Similar to other German prisons of the day, it housed inmates in either single or congregated cells. In 1935 it housed 443 prisoners representing most forms of criminal activity. By 1943 this number more than tripled, leading to prisoners housed four and five to a single cell. Prison conditions were not surprisingly atrocious as a result of the massive overcrowding and the tenor of the Nazi regime. Following liberation by U.S. forces in 1945, most of the prison staff was removed because of their Nazi Party affiliation.

Source: Wachsmann, *Hitler's Prisons*, 2004.

ALBANIA. In the early 1990s the Directorate of Prison Administration under the Ministry of Justice ran the Albanian prison system. As of 1994 the nation had 7 penal institutions capable of holding more than 1,200 prisoners. The overwhelming majority of prisoners are male. Several categories of prisoners are held in the prison system, including pre-trial detainees and juvenile offenders. Only the two high-security facilities are referred to as prisons; the others are considered penal institutions. Prison populations range from the smallest capacity at 62 to the highest at 350. The two high-security prisons are located at Tirana ('313') and Tepelena; those considered penal institutions are situated at Kavaja, Lezha, Lushnya, Savanda, and Tirana ('32'—open). However, an impressive reform effort in 2001 has led to five new prisons under construction at Rrogozhina, Peqin, Kruja, Lezha, and Fushe-Kruja.

As of late 1994, 1,077 prisoners were held in penal institutions, 13 percent of whom were pre-trial detainees. Most reports indicate that the prison population was only one third of what it had been prior to the revolution in 1991. Despite a rising incarceration rate in subsequent years, the prison population appears to be proportionately lower than that of other central and eastern European countries.

In eastern Europe few countries use single-cell detention. The same holds true in Albania. Here, the most crowded cells hold 10 prisoners. Some prisons, such as the Kavaja facility, have dormitory rooms holding more than 60 prisoners. Most of the prisons are in a neglected condition, having been built by the previous government to serve as hard labor camps. Located in remote areas, they are difficult to reach not only for prison visitors but for the staff as well. In 1994 suggestions were made to convert some former military camps to penal institutions.

Reports by human rights groups and other sources indicate that sanitary conditions are barely adequate, with few provisions for personal hygiene or washing clothes. By comparison, female accommodations, particularly at the Tirana prison are reportedly clean in comparison. A poor country, Albania allows prisoners to wear their own clothes, which are usually provided by their families. All prisoners have a separate place to sleep, usually consisting of mattress and pillow rather than a complete bed. When beds are available, they are usually uncomfortable old metal bunks from the earlier regime.

Although three meals are served each day, they are reportedly deficient in both quality and quantity of food. Families are allowed to supplement the poor rations. The larger prisons have a full-time doctor, nurses, and dentists, but medicine is reported in limited supply. Prisoners are permitted to send and receive 20 letters each month and receive 30-minute visits each week. Since the remoteness of the institutions makes the trip very difficult, one visit each month can consist of a conjugal visit with a male prisoner. During the 24-hour period the couple is furnished with a simple room. Women prisoners, in contrast, can have 24-hour visits, but not with their male partner.

Most of the prison staff is recruited from the ranks of the police. Because of this they are referred to as police officers, and they even wear police-style uniforms. Job training is minimal, with most receiving jobs through personal selection by senior officials or by interviews. Living and working conditions are said to be poor. Recent efforts have been made toward a rehabilitation regimen by introducing social workers, educators, and even specialists such as psychologists. As the totalitarian past continues to fade with time, the prison regime continues to improve, albert very slowly. There is still a long way to go toward achieving the standards of management and treatment prevalent in western European countries.

Since the 1990s information on prison conditions has been more difficult to come by. Human rights groups such as Amnesty International collect most if any new information. In its 2003 report the group reported that prison conditions were often austere, plagued by overcrowding, poor sanitation, and mistreatment by staff. Conditions for detainees were even worse in police detention facilities, where minors are often detained with adults. At the Vlora police station cells were at double capacity, without beds, mattresses, and running water and with little ventilation. Few of the detainees had been convicted, but all detainees faced the same draconian regime, including prohibition of reading and writing materials, as well as of radio and television. Conditions were so poor at other police stations that hunger strikes occurred.

In 2000 and 2001 respectively, the General Regulations of Prisons and the Regulation of Prison Police were adopted. By the end of 2001, Albanian prisons held 1,722 prisoners, and another 1,331 were housed in police pre-trial detention units. The total of 3,053 prisoners represents a rate of 90 per 100,000 of the national population. The rate of imprisonment is considered lower than that of most other central and eastern European countries, but overcrowding persists as a continuing problem. As of late 2001 the prison staff to prisoner ration was 1 to 1.2. Among the most important changes has been the implementation of four-month prison training, where security staff members study human rights, European prison rules, law, sociology, and health care service and receive technical-professional training. In 2001 a new staff-training center was opened at Vaqar. Albania has made advances on a number of levels of prison reform over the past few years. Prisoners are now enjoying increased exercise time greater availability of telephones, private intimate visits once a month, more opportunities for early release, and an increase in the number of vocational and educational programs.

As of late 2003 Albania's General Directorate of Prisons operated under the Ministry of Justice. However, as Roy Walmsley has most recently noted, the Ministry of Public Order is responsible for all pre-trial detainees and remand prisoners, as well as for some of the sentenced prisoners. Albania now reports having 10 prisons and lock-ups at 26 police stations. Police stations are almost twice capacity, holding 783 prisoners. Regular institutions hold 2,389 prisoners and are at 119 percent of capacity. The total number of prisoners is 3,778, or 105 per 100,000 of the national population. Almost 45 percent are pre-trial detainees or remands.

Sources: Walmsley, *Prison Systems in Central and Eastern Europe*, 1996; *Amnesty International Report*, 2003; International Centre for Prison Studies (henceforth ICPS), Albania, 2003; Walmsley, *Further Developments in the Prison Systems of Central and Eastern Europe*, 2003.

ALCATRAZ. The site of one of America's most storied prisons, Alcatraz Island was originally home to America's first U.S. fortification on the Pacific Coast in the 1850s. The island received its name from Spanish explorers in the 1770s when the island's only inhabitants were pelicans, hence its name Isla de Alcatraces, or Island of Pelicans. Alcatraz would never see any military actions, but it came in handy for an assortment of purposes, including imprisoning Confederate soldiers, hostile Indians, conscientious objectors, German civilian internees, and others. Following the Spanish American War, it even served as a convalescent facility for returning soldiers. Never sufficiently utilized, in the 1930s the U.S. Army turned the site over to the Department of Justice during the heyday of the federal public enemy crusade. It was initially envisioned as an ultra-secure facility for housing escape-prone convicts. The Justice Department also foresaw "the Rock" as a place to punish the worst denizens of America's prison system. Alcatraz has been give a number of monikers over the years, including "Uncle Sam's **Devil's Island**," and "Hellcatraz."

Alcatraz opened as a maximum-security prison on June 30,1934. Until 1963 the Rock would hold gangsters, kidnappers, and killers. During its short history as a federal maximum-security institution it gained a reputation as "America's Devil's Island." Despite the prison's security and physical isolation, there were a number of unsuccessful and controversial prison escape attempts during its almost-30-year history as a federal prison. What could have been the most successful prison attempt was barely suppressed during a 1946 rebellion that resulted in the calling in of the U.S. Marines. Cost overruns and the increasingly spurious claim of being escape-proof brough Alcatraz's days as a federal prison to an end in 1963.

Prisoners were given twenty minutes to eat each meal before being marched back to their cells from the dining hall along the corridor known as Broadway. The prison consisted of four three-tiered cellblocks based on the **Auburn system**. Although there were 336 cells, they were never fully utilized. The average inmate population was never more than 275 prisoners. Of the four cellblocks, most prisoners were housed in B and C cellblocks, on either side of "Broadway." The segregation unit, or "treatment unit," was located in D Block. Here were the six cells that comprised "the Hole," where inmates could spend as much as 19 days in solitary confinement in total darkness.

Under the command of the island's first warden, **James A. Johnston**, prisoners were counted 12 times each day. For every three prisoners, he hired one guard. Contrary to popular belief no one was sentenced to Alcatraz; all earned their way through disruptive behavior at other federal prisons. Among Johnston's strategies for controlling the prison were techniques aimed, according to Laura Davis, to "disrupt prison gangs" and "deflate big shots."

Among the most famous denizens of the Rock was a virtual who's who of crime, including Al Capone, George "Machine Gun" Kelly, atomic spy Martin Sobell, and **Robert "Birdman" Stroud**. The next time the prison was in the news following its closure in 1963 was in 1969 when a group American Indian activists took over the island, hoping to turn it into a Native American cultural and educational center. This would not come to pass. Over the next year Alcatraz was beset with drugs, alcohol, and violence as the occupants splintered into factions. On June 11, 1971, U.S. Marshals removed the protestors from the island. By then a number of the island's prison buildings had been destroyed by fire. In 1972 Alcatraz Island became part of the National Park Service.

Sources: John Godwin, *Alcatraz, 1868–1963* (New York: Doubleday, 1963); Laura Davis, "Alcatraz Federal Penitentiary," in *Encyclopedia of American Prisons*, eds. McShane and Williams III, 1996, pp. 21–23.

ALGERIA. The Algerian prison system is governed as a separate function of the Ministry of Justice. A number of the facilities predate Algerian independence going back to French rule. Each province, or *wilaya*, has at least one jail. Individuals convicted of minor crimes are housed in provincial civil prisons. More serious offenders are housed in the three main penitentiaries. Large central prisons are located in Algiers, Medea, Berrouaghia, Oran, Tlemcen, and Constantine. El Harrach, the main prison in Algiers, in particular stands out for its overcrowding and poor sanitary conditions. Attempts are made at most prisons to segregate inmates by length of sentence and serious of crimes.

According to investigations conducted by human rights groups, sanitary conditions in the larger institutions pale in comparison with the civil prisons. Prisoners in civil prisons are allowed once-a-week visits from family members. Conjugal visits can be facilitated at the discretion of the authorities, although most evidence suggests it is rather difficult to visit prisoners in the penitentiaries. Since the prison diet tends toward starch and blandness, families are allowed to contribute more substantial fare to augment the prison diet. Although medical care is rudimentary, prisons typically have contracts with local doctors to treat prisoners, with the more seriously ill being taken care of in hospitals.

A number of individuals are detained in Saharan security camps, which are marked by extreme heat, poor food, overcrowding, and inadequate sleeping conditions. Because these camps are geared toward security-related actions, relatives often are not notified about prisoners in detention. To make matters worse, detainees are often released near the camps without any conveyance to their homes. At the beginning of 2002, Algerian prisons contained 34,243 prisoners, a rate of 110 per 100,000 of the national population.

Sources: Library of Congress Country Studies (henceforth LCCS), "Algeria," December 1993; Roy Walmsley, *World Prison Population List* (henceforth *WPPL*), 4th ed. (London: Home Office, 2003); ICPS, Algeria, 2003.

ALSTORPHIUS GREVELINK, P. W. (1808–1896). In Dutch penal circles Alstorphius is credited with documenting prison conditions throughout the Netherlands during a prison tour in 1857. His findings are virtually the only statistics to survive from this era. A former lawyer, he was appointed prison inspector in 1854. His prison tour in 1857 included extensive interviews with prison warders, governors, doctors, and educators. He concluded that Dutch prison conditions were inhumane, specifically targeting the regime of cellular confinement. Alstorphius was allowed to speak to prisoners as well, with many reporting they were satisfied with their confinement because they could be "their own boss," avoiding the violence and conflict that predominated in congregate prisons. Following his travels he wrote a report that recommended a combination of solitary confinement at a maximum of three years, with communal confinement. However, supporters of solitary confinement ruled the day and responded with a barrage of criticism. In 1872 Alstorphius was honorably discharged from his position as prison inspector.

Source: Herman Franke, *The Emancipation of Prisoners* (Edinburgh: Edinburgh University Press, 1995).

AMERICAN SAMOA. This island's Corrections Agency is the responsibility of the Department of Public Safety. As of the end of 2002 the only prison was the Tafuna Correctional Facility, which held 169 prisoners. This would represent 169 per 100,000 of the national population.

Source: ICPS, American Samoa, 2003.

AMNESTY INTERNATIONAL. British lawyer Peter Benenson founded Amnesty International in 1961. According to the organization's lore, Benenson had read a newspaper story about two Portuguese students who were sentenced to seven years in prison for raising a toast to freedom. Benenson started a letter-writing campaign to show support for the students. Little could he imagine what the impact of this would be. Less than a year later letter-writing groups were at work in more than a dozen countries. By 1962 Amnesty had letter-writing campaigns on behalf of human rights in more than twenty countries in Africa, South

America, Asia, Europe, and North America. That same year the now familiar Amnesty emblem of a candle and barbed wire was designed by one of these groups.

During its early stages Amnesty International focused on the rights of political prisoners as described in Articles 18 and 19 of United Nations Declaration of Human Rights. Over the next decades this international nongovernmental organization would enlarge its mission to focus on all categories of human rights violations. In 1977 the group was awarded the Nobel Peace Prize for its efforts. Presently close to 7,500 Amnesty International groups with almost 1 million members operate in 162 countries and territories. During its more than 40-year history the group is estimated to have defended more than 44,000 prisoners around the world.

Sources: Sifakis, *The Encyclopedia of American Prisons*, 2003; http://www.amnesty.org/.

ANDAMAN ISLANDS. Port Blair in the Andaman Islands was used as early as the 1850s as a transportation destiny for British prisoners following the Indian Mutiny. Beginning in 1867 British authorities began sending Indian convicts and common criminals to the penal colony on the Andaman Islands; most of these individuals had been arrested for either murder or armed robbery. Convicts were housed in a number of barracks and villages around the harbor of Port Blair or on several islands adjacent to it. There were 11,000 convicts here by 1910. The settlement was consistently plagued by epidemic disease and inadequate medical support, leading to recommendations to close it beginning in 1924. In the twentieth century the penal colony became synonymous with political prisoners. The first Indian nationalist prisoners were transported to the Andamans in 1905 following the first partition of Bengal. British authorities continued to send Indian nationalists to the penal colony until Japanese forces captured the islands during World War II. Following the war, it was returned to British hands and the penal colony was abolished. Today the Andamans remain a tourist destination.

Source: Satadru Sen, *Disciplining Punishment: Colonialism and Convict Society in the Andaman Islands* (New York: Oxford University Press, 2000).

ANDORRA. The Andorran prison system, or *Centre Penitentiare*, is operated under the Ministry of Interior Justice. In late 2003 the tiny nation's two prison facilities housed 61 prisoners, more than three quarters of whom were either untried or unsentenced. The rate of imprisonment is 90 per 100,000 of the national population.

Source: ICPS, Andorra, Europe, 2003.

ANGOLA. Imprisonment was first introduced to Angola by the Portuguese colonizers in the 1570s. Those incarcerated included criminals, slaves, and those banished from Portugal and Brazil. The Portuguese continued to banish criminals to Angola into the 1930s in part as an alternative to execution. Angola's first major prison was the construction of the fortress São Miguel, with its accompanying prison in 1576. Although several similar detention facilities were built, São Miguel remained the main place of confinement up to the nineteenth century, when the dungeons of the Penedo fortress became more prominent. Initially most of the prison population was white, but over time the fortress held black prisoners as well.

Before 1624 Portugal had not created a separate prison administration or even a budget for the prisons. Prisons were meant to prevent individuals from fleeing to freedom. Not until 1742 was the first definite term of sentence imposed. In 1869 and 1876 Lisbon proposed the creation of penal farms, but it would take until 1883 for these establishments to open. The more modern concept of central prisons took until the twentieth century to take hold. But as late as 1961, the main correctional tool in Angola remained forced labor on prison farms.

With the end of the civil war in 1978, the MPLA (Popular Movement for the Liberation of Angola) Labor Party took over the colonial prison system. A number of students from the National School of Penal Technology, inaugurated in 1976, have been trained in penology in **Cuba**. The Ministry of Justice supervises the penal system. The system is divided into maximum- and minimum-security prisons. In addition, there are "production camps," which supposedly rehabilitate prisoners through work and re-education programs. Although mistreatment of prisoners has been widely reported, protocol suggests that the treatment of prisoners is determined by behavior and extent of rehabilitation.

The main prisons include a maximum-security institution opened at Luanda in 1981 and several provincial and local prisons. Most political detainees are held at the Estrada de Catete prison in Luanda and the Bentiaba detention camp located in Namibe Province. The most important detention center in the rural districts is located at Tari in Cuanza Sul Province. Here prisoners are held on a labor farm, living in barracks or huts and working at forced labor. In the early 1980s prisoners at Tari included those already sentenced, awaiting trial, or detained without trial as security threats.

In 1984 Angola was cited by the International Labor Organization for violation of ILO Convention 105, which prohibits the utilization of forced prison labor. Despite this citation, reports continue to flourish concerning the mistreatment of political prisoners through force, solitary confinement, and public humiliation. Although such alternatives as political re-education once flourished, their practice seems to have been discontinued. During the Cold War years, East Germans reportedly operated a political re-education camp, and Cuban and East German foreign advisors helped operate detention centers and train Angolan state security personnel. As of the middle of 2002, the prison population was 4,975, or 37 per 100,000 of the national population.

Sources: Kurian, *WEPP*, 1989; LCCS, Angola, February 1989; Jan Vansina, "Confinement in Angola's Past," in *A History of Prison and Confinement in Africa*, ed. Bernault, 2003, pp. 55–68; Walmsley, *WPPL*, 2003.

ANGOLA PENITENTIARY (USA). Louisiana's first penitentiary was opened in 1834 and was modeled after the **Auburn** prison. Situated 60 miles north of Baton Rouge, it has grown into one of America's largest medium-maximum security prisons. More prison farm than traditional prison, Angola lies on 28 square miles on a floodplain on the eastern bank of the Mississippi River. Today, known as both Angola and Louisiana State Penitentiary, it is home to just under 2,000 inmates, two thirds of them serving life sentences. The prison's news magazine, *The Angolite*, has won national awards for journalism under the supervision of inmate editor Wilbert

Rideau. Rideau is one in a long line of penal luminaries to have passed through Angola, including musicians Freddy Fender and Huddy "Leadbelly" Ledbetter.

At Angola's founding its prison routine reflected its Auburn roots, with prisoners working in congregate settings by day, producing various leather, cotton, and woven products. Nights were spent in solitary confinement. In the years leading up to the American Civil War prisoners were leased out to private businesses, with little concern for rehabilitation. It has been estimated that perhaps 3,000 inmates perished under brutal conditions on the plantations and farms to which prisoners were leased. Except for a short respite during the Civil War, the lease system continued in the postwar years. With a labor shortage caused by the war and the abolition of slavery, the 222 prisoners in Angola were used as a stopgap measure on private farms, as well as much-needed laborers on public works projects.

In 1901 the land of the present prison was purchased from the inmate-leasing family. These lands included a cotton plantation and several smaller sugarcane plantations. To this day farming has been considered the main industry of the prison. One of the early general managers introduced a system that allowed selected convicts to supervise the inmate population. During the past century Angola gained a reputation for brutal physical punishment and abusive work conditions. These abuses came to public attention in 1951 when 37 inmates cut the heel tendons on their left legs to protest the prison regime. Following this episode a new regime was adopted to improve conditions. Today the prison is made up of a primary prison and six "outcamps." Prisoners now have access a number of law libraries and to increased recreational and work choices. Its annual prison rodeo is prominent, with thousands of visitors watching 200 inmates compete in rodeo competition. The prison was recently profiled in the book *God of the Rodeo*. Angola's prison factories include facilities for making license plates, mattresses, brooms and mops, and even silk screening. As late as the mid-1990s Angolan inmates were operating the only prison radio station, KLSP, licensed by the Federal Communications Commission. The station is supported by fund earned by prisoners through blood donations.

Sources: Mark T. Carleton, *Politics and Punishment: The History of the Louisiana State Penal System* (Baton Rouge: Louisiana State University Press, 1971); A. Butler and C.M. Henderson, *Angola: Louisiana State Penitentiary: A Half Century of Rage and Reform* (Lafayette: Center for Louisiana Studies, 1990); Daniel Bergner, *God of the Rodeo: The Search for Hope, Faith, and a Six-Second Ride in Louisiana's Angola Prison* (New York: Crown, 1998).

ANTIGUA AND BARBUDA. The prisons are administered by Her Majesty's Prison Service, under the Ministry of Justice and Legal Affairs. In 1998 the island reported one prison facility holding 186 prisoners, or 278 per 100,000 of the national population. The prisons are the security responsibility of the police force.

Sources: Kurian, *WEPP*, 1989; ICPS, Antigua and Barbuda, Caribbean, 2003.

ARGENTINA. The first penal institutions built in Argentina were **houses of correction.** Beginning in 1816 several of these institutions were in operation in Mendoza and General San Martin. But as late as the 1870s, little progress in prison reform could be observed in Argentinean prisons. In 1877 the country's first penitentiary was opened in Buenos Aires. Based on a combination of **Pentonville** construction and **Auburn** discipline, prisoners worked in congregate settings during the day and were confined to solitary cells at night. Ernesto Bunge designed the Buenos Aires prison. In 1880 what was once a provincial prison made the transition to federalization.

During the 1880s the influence of Italian positivism and the studies of **Cesare Lombroso** persuaded the Association for Juridicial Anthropology to embark on a drive to collect criminal statistics. The groundbreaking work by Argentina's premier criminologist and progressive reformer, **Jose Ingenieros**, made the Buenos Aires penitentiary a must-see attraction for foreign visitors.

The province of Buenos Aires opened a correctional institution at Sierra Chica in 1882. This was followed in 1890 with the inauguration of Cordoba Prison, Ushiaia (1902), and Olmos Prison (1935).

In 1904 substantial progress toward modernization occurred when the Buenos Aires Penitentiary adopted a model regime instituted by the penologist Antonio Ballve. By then the prison was similar to **John Haviland**'s model, with 5 radiating wings containing all 704 cells on two tiers.

A number of penologists consider Argentina to have one of the leading prison systems in Latin America. The prison system has 15 federal and 60 provincial prisons. The federal system is considered the best run of the two, with the best prisons located in Santa Fe and Buenos Aires.

The General Directorate of Penal Institutions and the Ministry of the Interior, under the direction of a director general, control the federal prisons. Under the director general is a council made up of a professor of penal law, the director of the Released Convicts Welfare Agency, and the chief of the National Prison and Criminal Registry. The provincial prisons have similar organizations.

By the 1990s prisoners were evenly distributed between the federal and provincial institutions. According to Argentina's Penal Code, provincial prisoners are housed in federal institutions if their sentences are over five years and if provincial facilities are at full capacity. Prisoners often are allowed to work and earn wages under confinement.

Besides traditional facilities, the federal system offers prison farms and "open-door" minimum-security institutions. Rounding out the Argentina penal system is a number of special "homes" for women and juveniles designed to offer training in various trades and agriculture. More than 100 institutions cater to juveniles alone. Although the institutions are hampered by overcrowding, Argentina uses a grade system to determine release based on good behavior and attempts at rehabilitation.

During the military dictatorship that reigned between 1976 and 1983, 340 facilities were opened as detention centers. The largest and most feared of these was the Naval Mechanics' School (ESMA) in Buenos Aires. Some estimates suggest that 30,000 individuals, including armed insurgents and critics of the government, were tortured and killed in these centers. Close to 5,000 prisoners were handled at the ESMA location. According to one report less than 200 survived. The facility even housed a maternity center for pregnant prisoners. After birth most babies were given away to military households.

Despite being overcrowded, Argentinean prisons are generally considered sanitary. Although the Penal Code guarantees prisoners single cells, overcrowding has forced authorities to double and sometimes triple house inmates. In 1983 Argentina made the transition back to democracy, but protests, hunger strikes, and riots have nonetheless sporadically plagued the prison system. Riots in 1985 were reportedly sparked by disrespect toward family members and the brutal handling of prisoners during cellblock searches. Recent additions to the prison system have either been penal colonies or prisons that follow the **telephone pole design**, a good example of which is Santa Rosa Prison (1940). Other jails have opened more recently at Resistencia, General Pico, and Barilo. By mid-1999 Argentinean prisons held 38,604 prisoners, representing 107 per 100,000 of the national population.

Sources: Rupert Croft-Cooke, "Prison Reform in Argentina," *Pan American Bulletin* (1937), 71:695–697; Kurian, *WEPP*, 1989; Salvatore and Aguirre, eds. *The Birth of the Penitentiary in Latin America*, 1996; Johnston, *Forms of Constraint*, 2000; Walmsley, *WPPL*, 2003. Larry Rohter, "A Struggle with Memories of Torture Down the Street," *New York Times*, March 8, 2005, A4.

ARMAGH PRISON. One of Northern Ireland's oldest prisons, it first opened its doors in 1782. Designed by architect Francis Johnston, behind its benign decorative façade was a punitive prison regime that until the 1850s disciplined prisoners with the notorious **treadmill**. Prisoners sentenced to it were expected to maintain a pace of 48 steps per minute for 10 minutes before getting a 5-minute break. The prison initially consisted of eighteen cells and six debtors rooms. There was no chapel, infirmary, or separation of inmates by gender. Single cells were crammed with four or five inmates per cell at times. By the 1830s condition seemed to improve with the addition of a hospital in 1837. Following the Irish partition in 1824 the prison was used only for females. In 1969 a number of short-term prisoners were moved to Armagh, which at that time contained mostly women prisoners and 60 young male offenders. The prison was closed down in March 1986 following the opening of the new women's facility at Maghaberry.

Source: Ryder, *Inside the Maze*, 2000.

ARMENIA. Major prisons are in operation in Sovetashen, Artik, and Kosh. Jails are the mainstay at the local level. The entire prison system was under the direction of the Ministry of Internal Affairs until 2001. Despite the breakup of the Soviet Union, the former Soviet prison system still heavily influences Armenian prisons. Prisoners are divided into two major categories: labor colonies reminiscent of the earlier era, and prison communities influenced by Western prison reform. Among the more recent reforms are efforts to create separate general and high-security facilities for teenagers and for women. Adult males are imprisoned in four categories ranging from minimum to maximum security. Despite some steps toward reform, the Armenian prison system reflects the poverty and weak government that predominates in a poor nation beset by organized crime, corruption, and powerful family and regional clans. **Human Rights Watch** has recently expressed concerns about the lack of a juvenile justice system. In addition, it has targeted the length and conditions of pre-trial conditions, limited access to visitors for children detained before trial, the frequent detention of juveniles with adults, the absence of facilities for physical and psychological rehabilitation, and the disproportionate length of sentences in relation to seriousness of offenses.

In 2002 important legislation was adopted that expanded the rights of pre-trial detainees. Among these concessions was the right of detainees to visit with relatives and to have more access to information regarding their judicial status. In 2001 the prison system, now known as the Criminal Executive Department, was placed under the Ministry of Justice. In the new reorganization three new divisions were added dedicated to legal affairs and international relations, psychosocial rehabilitation, and medical services. As of 2001 Armenia operated fourteen penal institutions, including four pre-trial detention facilities for male adults, one combined (both open and closed) pre-trial detention center, five adult correctional colonies, one combined correctional colony, two open colony settlements, a national hospital catering to prisoners, and a separate pre-trial detention center for minors and women. During the prior administration only number recognized these institutions. Today their names reflect their various locations.

By the end of 2001 the prison system had the capacity to hold 7,020, with an average of 500 inmates per facility. The largest facilities included the pre-trial prison at Nubarashen, which could hold 1,250, and the prison colony of Kosh with 1,130. At last count the prison population stood at 2,866. Most recently the prison population has been reduced to decrease the prison population and save money. To accomplish this more than 3,000 prisoners have been released in an amnesty. With 92 prisoners per 100,000 in 2004, Armenia now has, except for the Balkan countries and **Albania**, the lowest prison population in central and eastern Europe.

Sources: LCCS, March 1994; *Human Rights Watch World Report*, 2001; Walmsley, *Further Developments in the Prison Systems of Central and Eastern Europe*, 2003; ICPS, Armenia, 2004.

ARTHUR, SIR GEORGE (1784–1854). The British penal administrator Lieutenant-Governor Sir George Arthur, according to writer Robert Hughes, was "one of the most controversial figures in early Australian history." Arthur had formerly been in the military, having seen action in the Napoleonic Wars. In 1815 he was appointed superintendent of British Honduras, where he ruled over a "slave state." Many observers consider his eight years in Honduras as being a major influence in the type of punitive regime he would establish in the Australian penal colonies.

Arthur arrived at **Van Diemen's Land** in Australia in 1824 with the intention of turning it into what Hughes described as an "ideal police state where surveillance was constant and total." His strategy required dividing Van Diemen's Land into nine police districts, each with a separate police magistrate who commanded a unit of constables and "field police." Each in turn was answerable to Arthur himself. Arthur maintained files on all the colony's inhabitants—convict or freeman. When a convict reached the colony through the **transportation** process, an interrogator was expected to compile a life history of the convict.

Under Arthur's leadership, the penal colony had seven levels of punishment. In ascending order of severity they included individuals holding a **ticket-of-leave**, those assigned to work for free settlers, forced labor on public works projects, labor on roads near established communities, forced labor on **chain gangs**, banishment to isolated prison communities, and penal settlement labor in chains. Individuals could improve their conditions through good work and behavior. Despite his penchant for hard labor, his intentions were more reformative than vindictive in nature.

Arthur came to prominence with the establishment of the penal settlement of **Port Arthur** in 1830, which he created as a site for additional punishment. It was located on the Tasman Peninsula, connected only by a narrow strip of land guarded by ferocious dogs and natural barriers consisting of towering cliffs, making the site "a natural penitentiary." In 1833 Arthur's penal philosophy was made available to the public in his book *Observations on Secondary Punishments*. Arthur returned to England in 1836.

Sources: Shaw, *Convicts and the Colonies*, 1966; Hughes, *The Fatal Shore*, 1987.

ARUBA. Operated by the Dutch national prison administration, as of 1998 the island had a prison population of 223, or 237 per 100,000 of the national population.

Source: ICPS, Aruba (Netherlands), Caribbean, 2003.

ATTICA PRISON. New York's maximum-security prison at Attica was opened in 1931. When it opened, officials regarded the more than nine-million-dollar prison to be the most secure prison in the world. Architecturally, the institution consists of four cellblocks forming a square and surrounded by a larger walled enclosure. The walled enclosure contains industrial shops, mess hall, and a number of other services, all connected by covered corridors. By 1954 security was maintained with the help of centrally operated sliding grilled doors. In 1966 a fifth cellblock was added.

The prison is best known as the scene of America's bloodiest prison riot, in which 43 inmates and hostages were killed in 1971, "one of the bloodiest one-day encounters between Americans since the Civil War," according to the 1972 New York Special Commission on Attica. By the 1970s Attica was an aging reminder of the Gothic Auburn-oriented prisons of the 1930s. Housing mostly poor minority offenders from urban areas, Attica was only one of many prisons in the 1970s that were overcrowded and plagued by poor food and medical care. However, other social factors had emerged during this era that made prisons smoldering tinderboxes rife with racial tensions exacerbated by a system that saw a virtually all-white prison staff in control of a predominantly minority inmate population.

Attica was home to Black Panthers, Puerto Rican Young Lords, and Black Muslims. During summer 1971 these groups participated in an inmate-taught sociology class that allowed them to temporarily surmount their differences in order to collaborate in a protest for better conditions. When peaceful protests began, the leaders, whom officials regarded as "troublemakers," were transferred to other facilities. The prisoners attempted to get the attention of New York corrections commissioner, sending him a manifesto for prison reform. Communication between the two parties was one-sided with little response from the prison administration. Offered suggestions to move the five signers of the manifesto, who were members of the Attica Liberation Faction, to another prison, Oswald balked, setting into motion a series of events that would culminate in the infamous riot.

News of the death of Black Panther George Jackson at San Quentin Prison on August 21, 1971, following an aborted prison break reached Attica the next day. Tensions between inmates and guards rose over the next two weeks. The guards resented several recent concessions to the prisoners, leading to a more punitive regime on the part of the officers. A confrontation resulting from a misunderstanding between several inmates and guards on September 8 provided the spark for the conflagration that would begin the following day.

Over one half of the prison's more than 2,2000 prisoners took part in the seizure of the prison. It took less than a half hour to seize several dozen hostages and take control of the four main cellblocks and their corridors. Inmates delivered a statement with a number of demands to prison officials, including higher wages and more political and religious freedom. The inmates also demanded total amnesty and protection from reprisals. Negotiations between prison inmate leaders and officials included two dozen observers, including civil liberties lawyer William Kuntsler. However, when one of the hostages succumbed from injuries in the initial confrontation, the prison administration refused to offer prisoners amnesty. Despite intense negotiations that were considered innovative for the era, negotiations were abruptly ended on September 13 as 1,500 armed sheriff's deputies, New York State troopers, and prison guards began their controversial assault on the rioters. When the smoke cleared from the excessive shooting by the rescue team, 28 prisoners and nine hostages were dead, and dozens were wounded. One more hostage would die later. Subsequently, prison officials reported that all the hostages had their throats slit by the prisoners. This irresponsible claim would later haunt officials when autopsies proved that all were killed by gunshots from the rescuers. After years of litigation between the state of New York and prisoners, the state awarded survivors an $8 million settlement. By the time the case was settled in 2000, more than 400 of the prisoners had died. However, those that survived shared the settlement. *New York Times* reporter Tom Wicker, who served as an observer during negotiations, wrote the best firsthand account of the Attica riot. His book *A Time to Die* was published in 1975.

Sources: Wicker, *A Time to Die*, 1975; McKelvey, *American Prisons*, 1977; Vergil L. Williams, *Dictionary of American Penology* (Westport, CT: Greenwood Press, 1979); Sifakis, *Encyclopedia of American Prisons*, 2003.

AUBURN PENITENTIARY. New York's Auburn Prison was constructed between 1816 and 1825 and is considered central to the development of the **Auburn system** that dominated American prison construction in the nineteenth and early twentieth centuries. In order to relieve the overcrowding at New York City's **Newgate Prison**, the state authorized the construction of a new penitentiary in Auburn, New York, in 1816. Construction under the watchful eye of local carpenter and subsequently the prison's first warden William Brittin began the same year. In response to the failure of the congregate prisons that housed a number of prisoners in large rooms in prisons such as Walnut Street and Newgate Prison, New York officials followed the urgings of **Jeremy Bentham** and **John Howard** and included cellular confinement in the initial construction of the south wing. This wing was designed by Jonathan Daniels and comprised 28 rooms that could hold between 8 and 12 prisoners, as well as 61 cells that could hold two inmates each. A spate of disorder after receiving the first prisoners in 1817 made it necessary to reconstruct this wing by adding a number of individual cells. Although a number of reformers have been mentioned as the inventor of the Auburn system, there is no consensus as to who should be awarded this accolade. What is clear, according to prison expert Norman Johnston, is that a number of individuals made contributions, including

Elam Lynds, William Brittin, John Cray, Thomas Eddy, and Gershom Powers. Regardless, the design was distinctive and innovative, and the "grouping of cells to form a freestanding unit, or island, separated from exterior walls and hence secure from escape attempts" was a significant departure in prison design and would dominate the field over the next century.

With the help of inmate labor the north wing was opened in 1825. Its design was inspired by the oversight provided by William Brittin, architect John Cray, and **Louis Dwight.** The north wing contained 550 single cells measuring seven and one-half feet by three feet eight inches, and seven feet in height (smaller than the Pennsylvania model). Cells were arranged back to back on five tiers surrounded by a long building. Cells faced corridors lined with high windows that allowed in indirect light. Cell doors were made of oak with iron grating in the upper portion in order to allow light and heat. Despite attempts to prohibit inmates from communicating, the existence of ventilation ducts allowed inmates to communicate with each other clandestinely. Since cells wall were so thick, guards could not hear them.

The New York legislature recommended dividing prisoners into three classes, with the most volatile inmates kept in solitary confinement in the north wing. The less dangerous inmates would be kept in solitary confinement three days a week but were allowed to work in a congregate setting the rest of the week. The least threatening inmates were allowed to work in a congregate setting six days a week before returning to solitary confinement at night. Auburn Prison in its earliest stages represented the confluence of two prison models. Incarceration for the most hardened offenders reflected the **Pennsylvania system** introduced by Quaker reformers in Philadelphia. Auburn initially housed up to eighty prisoners in solitary confinement and prohibited from working. Forced to lay supine by day until the completion of their sentences a number of prisoners in this class unsurprisingly fell victim to physical and psychological maladies. By 1825 this part of the experiment was abandoned and the more recognizable Auburn system emerged.

Almost from the very building Auburn Prison was plagued by poor lighting, ventilation, and heating. Although stoves were situated in the corners of the prison for heating purposes, they were wholly inadequate. Despite attempts to use steam heat in 1839, conditions remained the same in the cold New York winters. Although Bibles were proffered to aid in prisoner reformation, light was too deficient to read. Poor conditions were compounded by the stench of the toilet buckets in each cell.

Auburn introduced a number of features that became common in American prisons into at least the 1930s. A form of military discipline was utilized that expected prisoners to walk silently in a "lockstep" march, single file, standing erect, with faces always facing guards who monitored for conversation. Auburn also introduced black-and-white-striped uniforms as well as shaved heads. All visits and mail were prohibited. The public was allowed to observe prisoners at work through a small window after paying a fee of twenty-five cents.

During its early history Warden **Elam Lynds** became the embodiment of the rigid system. By the 1830s Auburn became the most popular model in the United States. With convicts working in a congregate setting by day, the prison industries exceeded the profits of the competing solitary Pennsylvania system, in which prisoners worked on piecework alone in their cells. But by the mid-nineteenth century the deficiencies of this system became readily apparent to reformers, who successfully lobbied to gradually eliminate lockstep marching, shaved heads, and striped uniforms.

Punitive features such as flogging and contract labor soon became history as well, as public support became more favorable toward a more rehabilitative regime.

Sources: McKelvey, *American Prisons*, 1977; Christianson, *With Liberty for Some*, 1998; Johnston, *Forms of Constraint*, 2000.

AUBURN SYSTEM. The Auburn system influenced the construction of prisons in most of the United States in the 1820s and 1830s. Following the opening of **Auburn Prison** by the 1820s, most prison systems adopted this construction because it was cheaper than the competing **Pennsylvania system** design and its use of congregate labor made it more financially productive. While there was little argument that the Pennsylvania system offered spacious accommodations, replete with better sanitation and heating, observers weighed the physical and psychological impact of solitary confinement on Pennsylvania prisoners with the opportunities for profit in the Auburn model, and the Auburn system won out. Subsequently, prisons were constructed with between three and five tiers of cells, containing between 150 and 250 cells, in Connecticut, Massachusetts, Maryland, Vermont, Tennessee, New Hampshire, Georgia, the District of Columbia, and Ohio between 1827 and 1834. Eventually all American prisons in the nineteenth century except for Pennsylvania, and New Jersey's Trenton Prison between 1833 and 1837, would adopt the Auburn model.

Sources: Paul F. Cromwell, "Auburn: The World's Second Great Prison System," in *Penology: The Evolution of Corrections in America*, ed. George G. Killinger and Paul F. Cromwell (St. Paul, MN: West Publishing, 1973) pp. 6–73; Johnston, *Forms of Constraint*, 2000.

AUSTRALIA. Australia served as Britain's penal colony from 1787 until 1852. When gold was discovered in New South Wales and Victoria in 1851, the notion of sending convicts to this prospective El Dorado seemed self-defeating. At the same time it had become less cost effective for England to ship its prison population to Australia. The first convict ships unloaded their cargo of 750 convicts at Botany Bay on January 26, 1788. The number of convicts transported to Australia has been estimated at 187,000, most after 1815 and the end of the Napoleonic Wars. During the era of transportation only South Australia and Western Australia were settled without the stimulus of convict settlers. According to John Hirst the Australian **transportation** era had a significant impact on the post-1852 developments in British corrections by introducing a number of innovations that developed in Australia to the British penal system, including the ticket-of-leave system, the practice of parole, and parole supervision. In his magisterial work *The Fatal* Shore, Robert Hughes went a step further, proclaiming Australian transportation "the most successful form of penal rehabilitation that has ever been tried in English, American or European history."

Although Australia was created as a virtual prison populated by both free and convict settlers, it was necessary to create penal institutions for convicts who could not be controlled under the existing system. In response early Australian officials devised a homegrown system of transportation by which these offenders were removed to remote communities such as **Van Diemen's Land** and **Norfolk Island**.

By the 1990s the majority of Australia's maximum-security facilities were more than a century old. Little expenditures were devoted to improving or updating Australian prisons until the 1960s and 1970s, when the prison populations began to increase. As crime rose and overcrowding overtook many prison populations, an era of economic prosperity made funding available, resulting in the implementation of new rehabilitation and reformation regimes. The state of Victoria, for example combined its prison system with its other correctional services within its Ministry of Social Welfare. Over the following years new alternatives to traditional incarceration have gained increased support.

Australia's correctional system varies from state to state, with no unified or federal system. Composed of six states and two territories, each having its own laws and procedures, Australia is unique in its lack of correctional conformity. For example as of the 1990s, Queensland was the only state that specifically provides the suspended sentence to first-time offenders. In the Australian Capital Territory and Tasmania the split sentence is utilized as a form of parole. The split sentence itself is a combination sentence that includes a term of incarceration with the possibility of release on recognizance. The other states offer only straight parole. New South Wales has experimented with "out-residents," by which prisoners are allowed to live at home but work in prison industries.

Today Australia has more than 8 state prisons. New South Wales, with 21, has the largest number of prisons, and the least number are in Tasmania, with just 3. According to Philip Reichel, most states house half their inmates in a large prison institution, with the rest scattered throughout a number of smaller facilities. Reflecting the variation in prison rates, Western Australia typically leads the states in the number of prison sentences handed down, with an enormous number of Aboriginals imprisoned. In 1993, according to at least one source, the Australian Aboriginal population was "the most imprisoned ethnic group in the world." During this period Aboriginals represented almost 20 percent of the prison population, but only 2 percent of the total Australian population. One 1996 study found that Aboriginals were imprisoned at a rate of 1756 per 100,000 Aboriginal adults, compared to a rate of 117 per 100,000 adult Australians. This disparity varied statewide from 18 to 1 in South Australia and Western Australia to 2 to 1 in Tasmania.

In March 1999 the average prison rate was 14 per 100,000 of the adult population. This would break down to 476 per 100,000 in the Northern Territory, 209 in Western Australia, 197 in Queensland, 144 in New South Wales, 122 in South Australia, 89 in Tasmania, 70 in Victoria, and 52 in the Australian Capitol Territory.

As of mid-2001 the prison population stood at 22,458, or 116 per 100,000 of the national population. These figures include pre-trial detainees and prisoners in penal institutions. Ascertaining the actual number of prisoners in Australia today is difficult, since the only statistics the government releases are rates based on the total number of the adult population. As in the United States, prison rates vary from state to state. Similar to the United States, both countries employed community-based supervision for close to 30 percent of the prisoner population. In the 1980s Australia moved in the direction of making prison the sentence of last resort, whereas the United States has resorted to the imprisonment of individuals in greater numbers and for longer periods of time. The most common forms of community-based corrections used in Australia are probation, or "supervised recognizance," community service and work orders, and parole.

The most recent report from mid-2003 indicates Australia holds 22,781 prisoners in 123 penal establishments. These include 80 government-operated prisons, 7 privately operated prisons, 15 court cell complexes, and 12 Periodic Detention Centres. The country has a prison population rate of 114 per 100,000 of the national population.

Sources: Shaw, *Convicts and the Colonies*, 1966; William Clifford, "Innovations in Australasia," in *Innovations in Criminal Justice: In Asia and the Pacific*, ed., Clifford, 1979, pp. 267–291; Hughes, *The Fatal Shore*, 1987; John Hirst, "The Australian Experience: The Convict Colony," in *Oxford History of the Prison*, eds. Morris and Rothman, 1995, pp. 235–265; Arie Feiberg, "Sentencing and Punishment in Australia in the 1990s," "Prison Populations Up, Sentencing Policy Harsher in Australia," and "Understanding Rising Prison Populations in Australia," in *Penal Reform in Overcrowded Times*, ed. Tonry, 2001, pp. 207–221; Reichel, *Comparative Criminal Justice Systems*, 2002; Walmsley, *WPPL*, 2003; ICPS, Australia, 2004.

AUSTRIA. One of the country's earliest prison codes dates back to 1785, obligating prisons to incarcerate prisoners with sufficient light, bread, and water. The current penal code is based on the Josefine Code of 1787 and subsequent revisions in 1803 and 1857. Until the nineteenth century most prisons were located in castles, forts, and former church buildings. By the 1850s the practice of incarcerating inmates in chains and using corporal punishment were abolished. The Roman Catholic Church directed the Austrian prison system until 1865. In 1932 workhouses were established for petty offenders disinclined to work, with sentences limited to three years, except in cases of recidivism. By the late 1980s prisoners were required to perform constructive work in Austrian prisons. Accordingly, if the money earned on the prisoner's labor exceeds the state's expenses, the prisoner is due a wage. Part of this money is saved for the prisoner's release.

Since the 1960s new penal code revisions have stressed rehabilitation, work, prison wages, and education. Today all custodial institutions, from the county jail to the maximum-security institute, are under the direction of the Ministry of the Interior. However, program implementation is often limited by budget constraints.

Austria's current penal system consists of 29 institutions, among them penitentiaries located at Garsten, Graz, Hertenberg, Schwarzau, Stein, Suben, and Vienna, and Simmering. Despite a spike in crime rates in the late 1980s, the prison population dropped from 7,795 in 1987 to 5,975 at the beginning of 1990. Austria's current rate of incarceration is 100 per 100,000 of the national population, the highest rate in more than a decade.

Sources: LCCS, "Austria," December 1993; Johnston, *Forms of Constraint*, 2000; Walmsley, *WPPL*, 2003; ICPS, Austria, 2004.

AVERLINO, ANTONIO (c. 1400–1469). Florentine architect Antonio Averlino, better known as Filarete, wrote *Treatise on Architecture* in the 1460s. In this book he described several prison designs. Perspicacious for his time, Averlino visualized a large prison that would be ideally located among the city's government buildings. Foreshadowing future penal innovations, the architect devised a system in which prisoners could essentially move from inadequate quarters to better housing through proper deportment. He also suggested that prisoners wear uniforms reflecting the nature of their offenses.

Source: Johnston, *Forms of Constraint*, 2000.

AZERBAIJAN. The prison system is titled the Chief Department for the Execution of Court Decisions. It operates under the Ministry of Justice. It has control of corrective labor colonies, parole centers, and open prisons. As of 2003 Azerbaijan had 52 penal institutions, including 3 pre-trial institutions, 1 closed prison for those serving long sentences, 19 colonies, 15 agricultural colonies, and 14 urban special facilities that holds prisoners sentenced to "restraint of liberty." The 19 prison colonies are devoted to specific prison classes. One is for juveniles, another for women, yet another houses former police officers, army staff, and other members of the civil service. Other colonies are dedicated to the central prison hospital, and facilities for in-patient tuberculosis treatment, and another for the aftercare of tuberculosis patients.

Following the breakup of the Soviet Union, Azerbaijan was the first former Soviet state to transfer its prison system from the Ministry of Internal affairs to the jurisdiction of the Ministry of Justice. The reorganization of the prison system was an attempt to humanize it by improving judicial decisions and making the entire correctional process more humane.

At the time of the breakup, Azerbaijan had 16 labor colonies housing 5,053 inmates, a ratio of 80 per 100,000 inhabitants. Of these colonies, 2 were minimum security, 4 medium security, 3 medium-to-maximum, and 1 women's colony (housing 60 inmates). Azerbaijan labor colonies were governed by procedures similar to those used by other Russian federation states. However, limits on visits and packages have been abolished for all inmates except those serving in prisons (as opposed to labor colony sentences). Inmates are not allowed to make phone calls.

The most recent prison population statistics indicate that despite a capacity for 24,670 inmates, Azerbaijan prisons held only 16,345 prisoners, even though three new colonies were added in 2001. Despite a slight decrease in prison population, the incarceration rate of 198 per 100,000 was considered higher than that of its western neighbors **Armenia** and **Georgia**, but still lower than Russian Federation countries on its northern borders. Explanations for any decline in prisoners in this period take into account a number of amnesties between 1996 and 2001.

As of 2001 there were no reports of overcrowding. Like most central and eastern European countries Azerbaijan does not maintain single cells. The largest number of individuals held in a congregate cell was 120 in the prison colony No. 1 in Baku's Nizami District. The prison system can point to a number of achievements over the past decade, including the introduction of information technology to better manage prisons, improved training of staff, better staff morale and working conditions, and a vast improvement in prison facilities. In 2002, Roy Walmsley noted, the Council of Europe reported "remarkable changes in the field of prison reform in Azerbaijan" between 1999 and 2001.

Despite these positive pronouncements there was still a lack of work for prisoners, a dearth in staff training, and a shortage of meaningful activities for prisoners. In addition, tuberculosis continues to plague the system. As of 2001 only 15 percent of prisoners were employed, with the majority involved in domestic and cleaning work, catering, carpet and furniture manufacturing, building maintenance, and agricultural activities.

The improvement of the prison staff has been hamstrung by a lack of financial resources. Most recent reports indicate a total staff of 5,547, of whom 10 percent were women. Basic staff training lasts three months. A breakdown of the classification of employees lists almost one quarter as university-trained officers, almost 50 percent as guards, and the rest as civilian workers.

Sources: Human Rights Watch, *Global Report on Prisons*, 1993; ICPS, Azerbaijan, Europe, 2003; Walmsley, *Further Developments in the Prison Systems of Central and Eastern Europe*, 2003.

B

BAGNE. The term *bagne* or *bagno* has been used in southern European countries such as France, Spain, and Italy in reference to penal colonies and regimes that featured hard labor, usually on public works projects such as fortresses, harbors, and roads. Popularized in France in the nineteenth century, bagnes were formerly land detention cells for **galley** slaves in an earlier era. These were converted to hold serious offenders sentenced to anywhere from a death sentence to ten years of incarceration. Prominent French bagnes were located in proximity to military ports, including Toulon, Brest, and Rochefort. Here prisoners were chained together in a barracks-like prison. The French eventually replaced the local bagnes with penal colonies in Algeria, New Caledonia, and Guiana, which featured the notorious **Devil's Island**. According to prison architectural historian Norman Johnston, bagnes resembled mammoth dormitories, citing one in Rochefort that held 2,000 convicts in four large rooms.

Source: Johnston, *Forms of Constraint*, 2000.

BAHAMAS. The Bahamas Prison Service is the responsibility of the Ministry of National Security. As of 2002 the Bahamas had one prison facility holding 1,280 prisoners. According to 1998 population figures this would be a rate of 410 per 100,000 of the national population.

Source: ICPS, Bahamas, Caribbean, 2004.

BAHRAIN. As of 1992 there were between 220 and 270 individuals held in Bahraini jails. Less than half were serving sentences for security-related offenses. Under the State Security Act of 1974 citizens can be detained for up to three years, with the right to appeal after three months and thereafter every six months. Reports indicate that individuals sentenced in ordinary criminal courts are given the usual guarantees, including the right to counsel and, if necessary, to legal aid. However, individuals charged with security-related offenses are tried in a higher court and in secret, and they are not provided with the same procedural guarantees. Human rights groups have reported the torture and physical abuse of prisoners by members of the Security and Intelligence Service (SIS). The most recent statistics for the prison population indicate 911 prisoners in late 1997, or 155 per 100,000 of the national population, including pre-trial detainees.

Sources: LCCS, "United Arab Emirates: Internal Security," January 1993; Walmsley, *WPPL*, 2003.

BANGLADESH. Under the direction of the British East India Company in the late eighteenth century were more than 75,000 prisoners held in 300 different jails. In most cases prisoners were handled in similar fashion to slave laborers as they worked on roads and highways. The colonists wasted very little contemplation on the conditions of the jails, where disease and unsanitary conditions resulted in high mortality rates.

The first stab at prison reform occurred in 1836, when the Jail Inquiry Commission was convened to improve jail conditions, the commission subsequently recommended more floor space, better sanitation and diet, and medical care for prisoners. Most of their suggestions fell on deaf ears, however, and conditions continued to deteriorate. Three more attempts at reform took place in 1877, 1889, and 1892, leading to the Prison Act of 1894 and the implementation of a reform regime. Twenty-five years later the Jail Commission of 1919 introduced later parole and probation.

Today the Penal Code of 1860, the Prisons Act of 1894, and the Prisoners Act of 1900, all heavily influenced by the British colonial experience, regulate the Bangladeshi penal system. Prisons or jails, used interchangeably, house pre-trial detainees, those on trial, the convicted, and individuals under protective custody. Although there are no separate institutions for men and women, they are confined in separate areas of the prisons. In addition, several juvenile facilities have been established. Because of a paucity of resources the prison system is plagued by overcrowding and poor sanitation. Although probation is used sporadically, parole and community corrections are virtually nonexistent.

Incarceration is viewed as retributive punishment, with little inclination toward reform or rehabilitation. Currently there are eighty jails, varying in size and purpose. They are divided into three categories, central, district, and *thana*. Central jails have been established in the regional headquarters for long-term prisoners with a history of recidivism and violence. Housing between 1,000 and 2,000 inmates they are comparable to maximum-security facilities in the United States. An industrial regime and agricultural farms that produce crops for inmate consumption characterize these institutions. While only a fifth-grade education is available for prisoners, central jails also offer hospitals. District facilities hold long- and short-term inmates, with capacities for 300 to 1,300 inmates. Prisons are generally supervised by a director of prisons at the police range or division level, and jail superintendents at the district level. Beginning in 1987 lower levels of incarceration can be found at *thanas* (station house for rural-based administrative unit) and village police backups. Prison police staffs all prison facilities.

Bangladeshi imprisonment is divided into rigorous and simple types. For those sentenced to rigorous incarceration, labor is mandatory. Under the simple sentence, which is rarely more than one month, work is optional.

Unlike inmates in many Western nations, Bangladesh prisoners are not classified with any scientific intent; instead they fall under a colonial classification system divided into three categories. The Bengali Jail Code defines Division I and II inmates as those who "by social status, education, and habit of life have been accustomed to superior living standards." Prisoners who do not fit into the first two categories are placed in Division III and are further divided into "star class," or first-time offenders, and "ordinary class."

Prison visits are severely restricted, and conjugal and family visits are prohibited. Inmates are also prohibited from using telephones and law libraries. Counseling and therapy sessions are not provided nor are day rooms, exercise areas, and dining facilities. In 2004 the prison population was 74,170, which represents a rate of 50 per 100,000 of the national population. In 2004 the prison system was composed of 11 central prisons and 55 district prisons, with the combined capacity to hold 25,712. However, as recently as May 2004 the prisons were at 285.5 percent of official capacity.

Sources: Singh, *Indian Prison*, 1979; Mohammed Bin Kashem, "Corrections in Bangladesh," in *International Criminal Justice*, ed. Rounds, 2000, pp. 137–149; Mohammed Bin Kashem, "Jails in Bangladesh," *International Journal of Comparative and Applied Criminal Justice* no. 1 (1996) 20:31–40; Walmsley, *WPPL*, 2003; ICPS, Bangladesh, 2004.

BANK-KWANG PRISON (THAILAND). One of Asia's best-known prisons, it has earned the monikers "Big Tiger" and "Bangkok Hilton" through its prominence as one the most notorious prisons in the world. Construction on Bang-Kwang Central Prison began in 1902 but was not completed until 1931. It is surrounded by almost 8,000 feet of twenty-foot walls. Built to hold 4,000 inmates, it was at double capacity as recently as 2004. The prison's most recognizable features include a 5-story-high watchtower, 25 workshops, a hospital, 11 dormitories, and 11 dining halls. The perimeter of the prison is surrounded by a three-foot-deep system of high-voltage electrification. Its prisoner-to-staff ratio of 25 to 1 is considered the highest in Asia. To supplement the lack of guards, the prison uses trusties, referred to as "blue boys," for their blue uniforms. They are usually armed with batons. With the majority of prisoners incarcerated for drug offenses, it should not be surprising that the drug trade flourishes behind prison walls. In order to combat this problem, officials apparently look the other way, condoning the murder of anyone involved in the drug trade. In one year alone an estimated 2,500 prisoners were murdered.

By all accounts food, sanitation, and medical care are substandard. Prisoners typically share cells with 18 to 23 others. Each cell is provided a hole in the floor for a toilet. The lucky prisoner is one who has been provided a mattress. Most basic necessities are considered luxuries that one has to pay for. Little attempt is made to separate inmates with communicable diseases such as tuberculosis and HIV from the healthy. Some prisoners have asserted that it is easier to find heroin than decent food. The dreadful conditions of the Central Women's Correctional Institution on the other side of town, better known as the Bangkok Hilton, have been dramatized in an Australian TV series of the same name starring Nicole Kidman in 1989 and have been featured in the film *Brokedown Palace*.

Source: Scott Christianson, *Notorious Prisons*, 2004.

BARBADOS. Barbados has one prison holding 992 prisoners as of late 2003. Almost 25 percent are either pre-trial detainees or on remand. The prisons are considered at 30.4 percent of capacity, with a national prison population rate of 367 per 100,000 of the national population.

Source: ICPS, Barbados, 2003.

BARKER, LILLIAN CHARLOTTE (1874–1955). Born in Islington, Lillian Barker rose from humble public school teacher to England's first female assistant prison commissioner and is considered a pioneer in the development of women's prisons. She took an early interest in delinquent behavior and in 1913 was appointed principal of the London County Council's Women's Institute, an early women's correctional facility. Following World War I she was appointed governor of the **Borstal** Institution for Girls at Ayelsbury in 1923. Here, she was credited with transforming the facility from a conventional prison to a model of progressive reform, with its emphasis on education, guidance, and rehabilitation. In 1935 Barker's visionary approach was rewarded when she was the first woman appointed assistant commissioner in England. Her responsibilities included women's prisons in England, Wales, and Scotland, in the process transforming these institutions into modern penal regimes.

Sources: Phillips and Axelrod, *Cops, Crooks, and Criminologists*, 1996.

BASTILLE. Prior to the outbreak of the French Revolution, French prisoners were housed in a number of infamous prisons. However, by the end of the eighteenth century none was more notorious than the Bastille, which by that time had become the symbol for the feudal past. This Parisian prison became synonymous with political imprisonment during the eighteenth century.

Its origins can be traced back almost as far as the **Tower of London**. Some legends suggest that its first prisoner was its very own architect. Its construction began in 1369 under Charles V. It was originally designed to guard the entrance into Paris, but by the end of the 1600s its military value diminished and the structure was generally used to house individuals of influence. The institution housed a variety of prisoners, including many common criminals. Although it was widely viewed as a symbol of political oppression, when it was stormed in 1789, of the seven inmates freed, none were political prisoners. The word *bastille* comes from the word *bastide*, which in medieval times signified a fortress.

The Bastille was essentially of rectangular construction and featured eight round towers. The edifice was joined together by 100-foot walls. Each of the eight towers had a name. For correctional purposes the most interesting was the Tour de la Liberte, so named because it contained prisoners who were free to walk the prison courtyards. Although the Bastille was surrounded by a moat, in 1789 the moat was bone dry.

The Bastille attained prominence as a prison when Richelieu turned it into a state prison to confine individuals who had committed crimes or were arrested under arbitrary orders of the monarchy. Home to a number of famous prisoners, none can match the legend of the "man in the iron mask." Confined in the prison from 1698 until 1703, this individual, according to recent scholarship, was an agent of the Duke of Mantua named Mattoli. As far as the legend, the mask was actually a velvet one to conceal his identity as a double agent. As many as 55 prisoners were housed here during Richelieu's day. Included in their ranks were several "extravagant" monks and priests, political plotters, three forgers, some foreigners, prisoners of war, and suspected spies. When Louis XIV took the throne, these prisoners were joined by journalists and gazetteers who criticized the king; others included scandalous witches and forgers. By the late 1680s orders were issued to keep private the names of prisoners, ushering in an era of mystery and sinister secrecy that would not end until the storming of the fortress in 1789.

Despite its reputation as a medieval hell, the prison was actually considered easier than other French jails and prisoners were fairly well treated. Initially, it was customary for prisoners to bring their own furniture and servants and even to supply their own meals. But in the 1700s the Bastille's administration was brought into conformity with other prisons. Still, reports indicate that food was more than adequate and prisoners were allowed freedom to decorate. Toward the end of the eighteenth century a number of rooms made the transition to prison cells replete with bars over windows and locks on doors. By November 1789 the prison was completely demolished. Standing in its location today is the *Place de la Bastille*, where tourists can detect some of the remains, albeit not in their original positions.

Sources: Jacques Godechot, *The Taking of the Bastille, July 14th, 1789* (New York: Charles Scribner's Sons, 1970); Morris and Rothman, eds., *Oxford History of the Prison*, 1998.

BATES, SANFORD (1884–1972).

BATES, SANFORD (1884–1972). Bates was the first head of the **Federal Bureau of Prisons**. Born in Boston and educated at the Northeastern University law school, Bates served stints in the Massachusetts House of Representatives as well as the state senate before his accepting an appointment as the commissioner of Boston's penal facilities in 1918. Bates was a hardy advocate for rehabilitation from the start and early on introduced school programs to the city prisons. He went on to serve a decade as Massachusetts state commissioner of the Corrections Department. During his tenure in this position he made his reputation as a prison reformer by reorganizing the **parole** system, introducing new prison industries and opportunities for inmates to earn a wage, and making available university extension courses.

Bates was elected president of the American Prison Association in 1926 and three years later was selected as superintendent of America's five federal prisons. The following year in 1930 the attorney general nominated Bates as director of the newly created Federal Bureau of Prisons. From the start he railed against the tradition of political patronage and insisted on hiring wardens according to their merit. His actions led the Federal Bureau of Prisons to hire wardens by civil service selection and appointment. During his 7 years at this position he oversaw the addition of 15 more federal facilities, including **Alcatraz**. In 1936 his seminal work *Prisons and Beyond* was published and for many years was the standard reference in corrections. In 1937 Bates resigned to take the position as executive director of the Boys' Clubs of America. But despite his hopes of improving the lives of young people, he found the job unrewarding and quit within a month. He went on to serve terms as New York State parole commissioner and director of New Jersey's state corrections system. Between 1940 and 1943 Bates served as president of the American Parole Association. Although he retired from public service in 1954, he continued his campaign for better prisons and rehabilitation and served on the board of the Federal Prison Industries until his death in 1972.

Sources: Keve, *Prisons and the American Conscience*, 1991; Rodney Heningson, "Sanford Bates," in *Encyclopedia of American Prisons*, eds. McShane and Williams, 1996, pp. 51–53.

BEAUMONT, GUSTAVE DE. *See* TOCQUEVILLE, ALEXIS DE

BECCARIA, MARCHESE CESARE (1738–1794). Most scholars consider Beccaria the most influential Enlightenment thinker on penal reform and an early critic of the criminal justice system and capital punishment. Born into the Milanese nobility, Beccaria cut short his Jesuit training to study law at the University of Pavia. After receiving his degree in 1758 he returned to Milan, where he dedicated himself to supporting the social change accompanying the Enlightenment sweeping Europe. In his treatise *On Crimes and Punishments* (1764) he challenged many of the accepted notions about crime and punishment. Although his essay was not yet published in English, American patriot John Adams famously quoted from it in his successful defense of British soldiers during the Boston Massacre Trial in 1770. Like many thinkers of his day he believed the purpose of criminal justice was to punish not harsher but better; let the punishment fit the crime. Beccaria argued that deterrence can be achieved more readily through the certainty of punishment rather than the severity of it. He asserted that punishment should be dictated by the severity of the offense, creating a graduated series of punishments. His writings would later influence reformers such as **John Howard** and Thomas Jefferson, as well as Quaker reformers in Pennsylvania, and became a driving force behind penal reform in the United States. The eclectic Beccaria is also credited with anticipating the economic notions of Thomas Malthus and Adam Smith and creating one of the world's first veterinary schools; he was also an early proponent of a decimal system of weights and measures.

Sources: Coleman Phillipson, *Three Criminal Law Reformers: Beccaria, Bentham, Romilly* (London: J. M. Dent and Sons, 1923); George Sarton, "Beccaria (1738–1794)," in *Bulletin of the History of Medicine*, supplement no. 3 (Baltimore: Johns Hopkins University Press, 1944); Maestro, *Cesare Beccaria and the Origins of Penal Reform*, 1973.

BEDFORD PRISON, COUNTY GAOL. Bedford County Gaol has become most identified with the penal career of **John Howard** of Bedfordshire. But Howard was not the first luminary identified with the prison. From 1660 to 1672 and then again in 1677, John Bunyan was an inmate in the prison. Imprisoned for refusing to worship in the Church of England following the Restoration of the Monarchy, Bunyan immortalized his stay there in his *Pilgrim's Progress*.

Howard's association with Bedford County Gaol began when he became the High Sheriff of Bedfordshire in 1773. According to Eric Stockdale, there has been a prison in Bedford since the twelfth century. When Howard became sheriff he also became responsible for the county prison and making sure that sentences by the county courts were carried out. Immediately upon assuming his duties Howard found the list of printed fees charged to prisoners. Jailers made a decent living charging their charges for room and board, as well as a host of other charges. All indications suggest that Howard's experiences as sheriff of Bedford County stimulated his concern for prison reform that would later lead to historic surveys of European prisons and the publication of his book the *State of the Prisons*.

Source: Stockdale, *A Study of Bedford Prison, 1660–1877*, 1977.

BELARUS. Since the fall of the Soviet Union, Belarus has made sporadic strides toward bridging the gap between Soviet penal practices and more democratic conditions. Human rights abuses are still reported, especially beatings in Hrodna Prison.

The prison system falls under the direction of the Ministry of Internal Affairs, managed by the head of the Committee for the Execution of Punishment (the prison administration). As of the mid-1990s Belarus had 35 penal institutions. Of these, 8 are pre-trial detention centers with capacities to hold from 160 to 2,040 detainees. Two are prisons known as *tyroomi*, 18 are a variety of colony-settlements, and 3 are education colonies for juveniles. Combined, these institutions had the capacity to hold more than 40,000 inmates, with an average population of more than 1,150, higher than the average penal system of central and eastern Europe. As of late 1994 these institutions held more than 45,000 prisoners, a ratio of 445 per 100,000 of the general population. This proportion was exceeded in the region only by **Russia**.

From what is known, prison overcrowding is rampant. Single cells are virtually unheard of, with the norm closer to seventy prisoners in a room. Despite these factors, sanitation, hygiene, and sleeping conditions are reportedly adequate, with each prisoner provided a separate bed. Food and medical services are adequate, and prisoners are allowed to wear their own clothing if it is deemed clean and proper. There are apparently no limits on writing correspondence, but visits are allowed only once every three months.

Other than pre-trial detainees, all prisoners if able are required to work. There are opportunities for remedial education, and the facilities have decent enough libraries. Increased emphasis has been placed on preparing inmates for freedom. Only pre-trial detainees can have radios or television. With a staff of more than 4,500, new training facilities have been established, but there is still a low staff-to-prisoner ratio, sometimes as low as one staff per 100 prisoners. Information on the prison system remains sketchy because of routine denial of access to groups such as **Amnesty International**.

Recent figures suggest that in 2001 Belarus maintained forty penal facilities. One quarter of these were devoted to pre-trial detainees. Prison capacities ranged from 150 to 2,800 prisoners. Although the prison population has fallen in recent years, its rate of 554 per 100,000 is considered the second-highest in Europe, only exceeded by the Russian Federation. Overcrowding and low staff-to-prisoner ratios still plague the prison system. At the end of 2001 the prison population stood at 135.7 percent of its 43,400-prisoner capacity. Despite this problem the prison system can point to a handful of achievements, including longer family visits, better education programs, and one of the highest employment rates for sentenced prisoners in central and eastern Europe.

Sources: LCCS, "Belarus," June 1995; Walmsley, *Prison Systems in Central and Eastern Europe*, 1996; Walmsley, *Further Developments in the Prison Systems of Central and Eastern Europe*, 2003; ICPS, Belarus, 2004.

BELFAST PRISON. *See* CRUMLIN ROAD PRISON

BELGIUM. By the end of the eighteenth century the penal regimes in force at Ghent and Vilvorde prisons were well known to penal reformers thanks to the surveys and writings of **John Howard**. Vilvorde was constructed between 1772 and 1776, and the Ghent House of Correction between 1772 and 1775. However, as a result of the exigencies of the Napoleonic Wars and pressure from workers to end the unfair competition offered by prison labor, both institutions declined in importance by 1810. Belgium adopted the **Pennsylvania system** of separate confinement in 1838 after Belgian prison reformer **Edouard Ducpetiaux** toured American prisons. The first prison to be built on this model was Tongres Prison in 1844. Between 1844 and 1919 Belgium built a number of prisons mostly based on some variation of the **radial model**. **John Haviland**'s Western Penitentiary (Pennsylvania) influenced the construction of Verviers Prison in 1853. According to Norman Johnston, the prisons at Louvain (1860) and St. Gilles (1885) were the best exemplars of the Pennsylvania system. Between 1844 and 1885 Belgium built twenty-five prisons with a total capacity of 4,775 cells.

Although steps were taken toward a reformative regime, facemasks were not phased out until 1920. That year saw a number of advances in the realm of "scientific" penology. In 1920 laboratories of criminal anthropology were established in ten Belgian prisons. Although this pseudo-science has been mostly repudiated, it created the groundwork, at least in Belgium, for more intensive examinations of inmates using medical, neurological, and psychological tests. In addition, social assistants were brought into the picture to make a thorough investigation of each inmate's social case history, which took into account the inmate's family situation, educational status, medical treatment, vocational training, and prison labor. This examination would serve as the basis for classification and proper institution for confinement.

By the 1940s most of the country's newest prisons had been built in the countryside. The most famous of these penal colonies was at Merxplas, founded in 1870. Almost 30 miles from Antwerp, this 2,8000-acre colony featured a several specialized institutions and hospitals. Larger prisons were located in Brussels, Louvain, Gand, Anvers, Liege, Mons, Bruges, Namur, and Charleroi. Penologists were most taken with experimental reforms involving young offenders. According to John Gillin, juvenile offenders were classified according to whether they should be trained in the trades or in agricultural work. Most youth facilities used a **mark system** to determine inmate release and emphasized adult guidance as significant in any youthful offender's reclamation program.

In 1888 Belgium became the first European country to introduce the suspended sentence as a way of reducing prison populations (France followed in 1891). Like many western European nations, the Belgian penal system emphasizes conditional sentencing. More than half of all prison terms involve prisoners serving detention only on weekends after they pay judicial fines and penalties. Similarly, Belgian prisons have a reputation for efficiency, sanitation, and successful rehabilitation programs. However, prospects for more punitive sentences loom on the horizon because of a high degree of recidivism in the late 1980s. At the end of 2003 the prison population stood at 9,147, or 88 per 100,000 of the national population. Almost 40 percent of the prisoners were untried.

Sources: A. Delierneux, Jr., "Evolution of the Prison System in Belgium," *Annals of the American Academy of Political and Social Science*, September 1931, pp. 181–182; Gillin, *Taming the Criminal*, 1931; Patricia O'Brien, "The Prison on the Continent: Europe, 1865–1965," in *Oxford History of the Prison*, eds. Morris and Rothman, 1998, pp. 203–231; Johnston, *Forms of Constraint*, 2000; Walmsley, *WPPL*, 2003.

BELIZE. The Belize Department of Corrections falls under the Ministry of the National Security. As of 1998 the country had two prison facilities holding 1,097 in a system designed for 500. The prison rate is 459 per 100,000 of the national population. The prison population has almost doubled since 1992.

Source: ICPS, Belize, Central America, 2003.

BENIN. The Benin Penitentiary Administration is governed by the Ministry of Justice, Legislation, and Human Rights. As of 2000, this African country reports a prison population of 4,961. According to the official capacity of the prison system of 1,950 in 2000, this would indicate sever overcrowding and a prison population rate of 81 per 100,000 of the national population.

Source: ICPS, Benin, 2003.

BENNETT, JAMES VAN BENSCHOTTEN (1894–1978). Born in Silver Creek, New York, and educated at Brown University, Bennett became affiliated with prisons in 1926 when he was designated to help a congressional committee investigate the federal corrections system. His investigations revealed systematic abuse and prison conditions marked by violence and poorly paid and trained correctional officers. Most authorities credit Bennett's revelations with spurring Congress to create the U.S. Justice Department's Bureau of Prisons in 1930.

After serving as assistant director under **Sanford Bates**, he was selected to replace him following his resignation in 1937. Like his predecessor, Bennett earned a reputation for fairness and treating prisoners with dignity and maintaining a policy of rehabilitation. By preserving the continuity of the agency's general philosophy, he remained friends with Bates for the rest of his life. Although it is unknown whether Bates or Bennett was the provocateur, sometime in the late 1930s guards were relieved of their billy clubs. Despite their fears about personal safety, all indications suggest that the relationship between staff and inmates improved.

During his tenure the federal prison system introduced programs of psychiatric counseling and medical care, and he set up institutions catering to short-termers as well as youth reformatories as alternatives to hard time. He also is credited with introducing the nation's first halfway house program and establishing Federal Prison Industries to supervise vocational training and industrial projects for federal prisoners.

Before retiring as director in 1964, he played a crucial role in creating the Juvenile Delinquency Act of 1938 and in passing legislation in 1948 that provided psychiatric services for mentally ill offenders. During the 1950s he campaigned for the passage of the Federal Youth Correction Act and a number of diagnostic sentencing laws.

Sources: Keve, *Prisons and the American Conscience*, 1991; Phillips and Axelrod, *Cops, Crooks, and Criminologists*, 1996.

BENTHAM, JEREMY (1748–1832). Considered a child prodigy, Bentham was educated at Westminster and Oxford, earning a law degree in the process. An admirer of **John Howard**, Bentham was called to the bar in 1772, subsequently coming to prominence for his writings on law and political economy. Bentham became disillusioned with the current state of the legal system in England and began a transition to social and legal reformer. He became associated with the philosophical radicals known as the Utilitarian, best known for their support of criminal justice reform that would offer the "greatest good of the greatest number" of people.

Bentham's association with prisons stems from his blueprint for the **Panopticon**, his vision of the perfect prison. What is clear is that his Panopticon was little more than "a simple idea in architecture" and was never fully realized. There is still a lack of consensus on which building influenced the panopticon design. However, there is evidence to suggest that he got the idea after visiting the Royal Military School in Paris. Another potential model included a rotunda built in the Chelsea Ranelagh Gardens. The accepted version, however, has Bentham joining his brother, naval architect Samuel Bentham, in 1787 in St. Petersburg, where he found his brother designing a circular two-story factory. By the building's circular structure meant workers could be observed by one or two supervisors from a central vantage point. From this Jeremy deduced the value of such a design for poorhouses, hospitals, and even prisons. Bentham's vision called for a large structure covered by a glass roof. Beneath it was a central cupola from which guards could constantly observe prisoners in their cells, which were arranged like spokes from a wheel. Bentham described his plan in great detail in his two *Panopticon Postscripts*, published in 1790 and 1791. But according to Miran Bozovic, neither work found its way into English bookstores. Although England never built a prison to this exact design, several American prisons, including Stateville Prison in Illinois, were influenced by the Panopticon. Bentham died before he could see his blueprint become a reality in countries as diverse as Spain, Holland, and Cuba, which built modified versions of the circular prison.

Initially Bentham advocated solitary confinement, but later he became a supporter of double and triple celling. Bentham was a resolute opponent of torture and harsh corporal punishment. He believed that inmates should be allowed seven and a half hours' sleep (eleven on Sunday). In addition he proposed prohibitions on smoking and drinking. He reportedly placed the prison governor's toilets in a location where the prison governor could look into the prison with some "regularity."

Sources: Janet Semple, *Bentham's Prison: A Study of the Panopticon Penitentiary* (Oxford: Clarendon Press, 1993); Jeremy Bentham, *The Panopticon Writings*, 1995; Johnston, *Forms of Constraint*, 2000.

BERMUDA (UK). The Bermuda Department of Corrections reported a prison population rate of 343 in late 2003. The island's 3 prisons were at 93 percent of capacity. The prison population rate is 532 per 100,000 of the national population.

Source: ICPS, Bermuda (UK), 2003.

BETO, GEORGE J. (1916–1991). As the prison director for the Texas Department of Corrections, George Beto became one of America's best-known prison administrators of the second half of the twentieth century. Born in Hysham, Montana, to a Lutheran minister and educated at Valparaiso University and Concordia Lutheran College, he went on to earn his doctorate in education from the University of Texas at Austin. Beto would become an ordained minister himself in 1939. His affiliation with the Texas prison system began in 1953 when then-governor Allen Shivers appointed him to the Texas Prison Board. During his tenure on the board he was able to observe the transformation of the Texas prison system under the direction of Director Oscar Byron "O.B." Ellis. While on the board Beto would play an important role in improving the educational and religious opportunities afforded the state's prisoners, and he would be credited with introducing a General Education Development (GED) program to the Texas prison system.

At the end of the 1950s Beto was appointed president of Concordia Theological Seminary in Springfield, Illinois. His move to Illinois was a pivotal moment in his career because it gave him the opportunity to meet Warden **Joseph E. Ragen**, the influential director of the Illinois State Penitentiary, better known as **Stateville Prison**. Ragen was regarded as one of the toughest and most efficient prison directors in the country. Ragen encouraged the Illinois governor to appoint Beto to the state parole board, enabling Beto to gain firsthand knowledge in dealing with prisoners on an individual basis.

Within hours of the sudden death of O.B. Ellis in 1961, Beto was summoned by Texas officials to take over as prison director. After an initial refusal, he relented after he was assured he could also serve as chief chaplain. During his 10-year stint as prison director, Beto adopted some of his mentor's strategies from Stateville. In the process Beto is credited with running an efficient prison system, cutting down on escapes, and increasing the productivity of the state's prison farms.

In his tenure as director, Beto earned the moniker "Walking George" for his proclivity of walking through various prisons, often abruptly showing up when employees and prisoners least expected him. Beto would also play an important role in developing the criminal justice program at Sam Houston State University. After stepping down as director in 1972, Beto devoted the rest of his life to the field of corrections as a professor of criminology and corrections and as a consultant to prison systems throughout the world.

Sources: Charles Jeffords and Jan Lindsey, "George J. Beto," in *Encyclopedia of American Prisons*, eds. McShane and Williams, 1996, pp. 58–61; Jones, *Criminal Justice Pioneers in U.S. History*, 2005; Paul M. Lucko, "Beto, George John," *The Handbook of Texas Online*, www.tsha.utexas.edu, January 13, 2005.

BHUTAN. Not much is known about this small Asian nation's prison system. The main prison is Thimphu Central Prison, located in the capital city of Thimphu. There is another prison at Chemgang, some eight kilometers to the east.

Source: ICPS, Bhutan, Asia, 2003.

BICETRE, THE. Paris's Bicetre Prison started out as a lunatic asylum before it was transformed into a prison for **galley** slaves chained "twenty-six at a time." The large complex of buildings that made up the Bicetre had a bleak reputation from the beginning, with one eighteenth-century observer painting it as "a hospital for infecting the sick and a prison for breeding crimes." In the early 1790s **Jeremy Bentham** suggested making the hospital into a **panopticon**. According to architectural historian Robin Evans, in 1788 a section of the Bicetre was demolished and replaced with 18 **dungeons**. The Cabanons de Surete of Bicetre, as the dungeons became known, held prisoners chained to walls. Prisoners were fed their meals and received air and light only through small grills at the top of each "subterranean pit." Evans claims this purpose-built dungeon was a rare construction.

Sources: DeFord, *Stone Walls*, 1962; Evans, *The Fabrication of Virtue*, 1982.

BIG HOUSE. The result of so-called progressive prison reforms, the "big house" movement was underway in the United States by the 1930s. But according Edgardo Rotman, "The Big House exemplifies the superficiality of Progressive reforms" in a number of areas. In these huge facilities professional correctional staff were expected to supplant the tradition of short-term political appointees. The big houses were just that, huge prisons that on average held at least 2,500 men. Some of the best-known institutions included California's **San Quentin Prison**, New York's **Sing Sing Prison**, and **Stateville Prison** in Illinois. At the end of the 1920s there were already 2 American prisons housing more than 4,000 inmates. Four others were overflowing with more than 3,000 each, 6 held more than 2,000, and 18 averaged 1,000 inmates. By most accounts the big house movement was a failure. Fraught with isolation, overwhelming noise, and poor conditions, these facilities evidenced that little thought went toward any meaningful regime of rehabilitation. An early motion picture entitled *The Big House* was released in 1930 and in many respects captured the deficiencies of this new model penitentiary, particularly when the warden laments, "It's 3,000 idle men with nothing to do but brood and plot. You can't put them all in solitary."

In the 1930s sociologist Donald Clemmer conducted one of the first examinations of these institutions while serving as a correctional officer at the maximum-security prison at Menard, Illinois. Here he focused on the relationships and hierarchies of the inmate population. His resulting study, *The Prison Community*, saw publication in 1940 and was widely heralded as the seminal work on the examination of prison as "a microcosm of society."

Sources: Jacobs, *Stateville*, 1977; Parish, *Prison Pictures from Hollywood*, 1991; Edgardo Rotman, "The Failure of Reform: United States, 1865–1965," in *The Oxford History of the Prison*, eds. Morris and Rothman, 1995, pp. 151–177.

BIT KILI. *Bit Kili*, the Babylonian term for "prison," according to Edward M. Peters, refers to "any location used to confine criminals, hostages, rebels or those detained for another reason."

Source: Edward M. Peters, "Prison before the Prison," in *Oxford History of the Prison*, eds. Morris and Rothman, 1995, pp. 3–43.

BLACKBURN, WILLIAM (1750–1790). Born into a working-class family in Southwark, Blackburn is considered the first architect to specialize in prison planning and design. Prison architectural historian Robin Evans proclaimed Blackburn "the most significant of all prison architects." Influenced by his friend **John**

Howard, he designed one of his earliest institutions for the Commissioners for Penitentiary Houses under the act of 1779. Although this prison was never built, his name soon was mentioned with the likes of London's best-known architects, leading to his demand as a prison designer. Much of the information on Blackburn's early life is sketchy. In his late teens he was apparently apprenticed to a surveyor, a trade he would fall back on at the end of his life while serving as Surrey County surveyor.

Blackburn designed one of England's first semicircular institutions. Completed in 1791, the Gloucester house of correction at Northleach consisted of five buildings arrayed in a semicircle facing a two-story building housing the governor's residence and a chapel. The main cell building faced the back of the governor's residence. On the second floor there were additional balconies that allowed easy inspection of the prison yards below. Partly inspired by **Jeremy Bentham**'s **panopticon** design, the Northleach design would not be repeated for more than twenty years. Prison scholar Norman Johnston asserted that if anyone should be accorded the moniker of "father of the **radial** plan for prisons, it must be the nearly forgotten London architect" William Blackburn. During the last decade of his life Blackburn influenced the construction of more than a dozen prison facilities in England.

Sources: Evans, *The Fabrication of Virtue*, 1982; Johnston, *Forms of Constraint*, 2000.

BLACK HOLE OF CALCUTTA. On June 20, 1756, East India Company colonists were besieged at Fort William at Calcutta by forces of the nawab of Bengal. The fort was quickly taken, and the surviving 146 colonists were crowded into the fort's small **dungeon** that usually held less than a handful of prisoners-of-war. The subsequent horrors of this confinement were chronicled by survivor John Zephaniah Holwell's *A Genuine Narrative of the Deplorable Deaths of the English Gentlemen and Others who were Suffocated in the Black Hole*, published in 1758. While recent research suggests that much of this account is exaggerated, this experience entered the lore of prison atrocities because only 23 men survived the cramped quarters. The dungeon had only two windows and was crammed so tightly with the standing prisoners that the door could hardly close. In later years a 50-foot-high obelisk was constructed in memory of the dead.

Source: Noel Barber, *The Black Hole of Calcutta* (New York: Fromm International, 1990).

BLOUET, GUILLAUME ABEL (1795–1853). The French architect accompanied **Frederic-Auguste Demetz** on his examination of American prisons for the French government in the 1830s, resulting in their joint report, *Rapports sur les pénitentiers des Etats-Unis*, published in 1837. However, his legacy may seem somewhat tarnished because he turned in architectural blueprints for **Auburn-** and **Pennsylvania**-style prisons without attributing them to **John Haviland**'s Trenton Prison design or Canada's **Kingston Penitentiary**. According to recent research by Norman Johnston, it appears that Blouet later sent Haviland a copy of his report and admitted using Haviland's prison models. On an interesting side note, while conducting research in the Haviland papers at the University of Pennsylvania,

Johnston found "an irritable note concerning Blouet's use, without credit, of Haviland's plans."

As inspector general of French prisons, Blouet along with Demetz and others played a crucial role in the creation of the agricultural prison colony for juveniles at **Mettray**. Based on Blouet's architectural design, Johnston suggests that Mettray may have influenced the development of the **telephone pole**–style prison.

Source: Johnston, *Forms of Constraint*, 2000.

BOLIVIA. Prison reform took a back seat to other social and economic problems for much of Bolivia's history. There were few modifications of the nation's penal code between 1834 and the end of World War II. In 1898 legislation created a national penitentiary system. Although there were requirements for the separation of adults from children, and the sentenced from those awaiting trial, none of these reforms were enacted.

The San Pedro national penitentiary is located in La Paz. Influenced by the **Panopticon**, it opened its doors in 1883 and for many years served as the only prison institution for men. As late as 1953 this prison was targeted by the United Nations for its terrible conditions. There is at least one national penitentiary in the nine political departments, and most provinces have their own jails. In the 1950s a radial-style prison was constructed near Cochebamba. There are a variety of other facilities, including a correctional farm at Caranavi, a reformatory for women in La Paz, and a handful of juvenile institutions. Except for the juvenile facilities, all the others come under the direction of the Ministry of the Interior. The Caranavi Correctional Farm is considered unique for its strict rules, enforced silence at night, and closely monitored behavior. Here inmates work in a congregate setting during the day doing agricultural work and are held in solitary silence at night. Except for the Women's Reformatory at La Paz, run by a Roman Catholic order of nuns, most institutions have been marked by corruption, poor sanitation, and overall unsavory conditions. In its 2003 report **Amnesty International** labeled the country's prison conditions as "very poor," targeting the rampant overcrowding, unsanitary conditions, and inadequate medical care. In mid-1999 the prison population of 8,315 represented 102 per 100,000 of the national population.

Sources: LCCS, "Bolivia: The Penal System," December 1989; *Kurian, WEPP*, 1989; Johnston, *Forms of Constraint*, 2000; *Amnesty International Report*, 2003; Walmsley, *WPPL*, 2003.

BONNEVILLE, ARNOULD DE MARSANGY (1802–1894). Credited as the "European father of parole," Bonnevile was trained as a jurist before making the leap to the prison reformer who established the Ecole Penitentiare in the mid-nineteenth century. Prior to his involvement in prison reform, Bonneville served in a number of positions in the French criminal justice system. He is remembered for several important works on reform, including *Essay on the Institutions Complementary to the Penitentiary System* (1847) and the two-volume *Of the Amelioration of the Criminal Law*, published in 1855 and 1864. In these works Bonneville initiated the progressive prison alternatives of parole, criminal reparation, pardoning power, and rehabilitation. Besides his contributions to reform principles and theories Bonneville founded the Ecole Penitentiare, an innovative institution created for the study of penology.

Sources: Andre Normandeau, "Arnould Bonneville de Marsangy," *Journal of Criminal Law, Criminology, and Police Science* no. 1 (March 1969), 60:28–32; Phillips and Axelrod, *Cops, Crooks, and Criminologists*, 1996.

BOOT CAMPS. In the 1980s and 1990s boot camps became one of the most publicized prison initiatives. Also referred to as shock incarceration centers and intensive confinement centers, boot camps were established in a number of jurisdictions in the United States to subject offenders to comparatively short, military-style training regimens in lieu of longer sentences in traditional correctional institutions. The earliest boot camps opened in New York State prisons in 1979, followed by camps in Oklahoma and Georgia four years later. The Federal Bureau of Prisons soon adopted this strategy as well.

With nearly 36 state and county prison systems establishing boot camps by the mid-1990s, programs and requirements varied by jurisdiction. However, boot camps were usually aimed at younger, nonviolent, first-time offenders. It was hoped that by shocking individuals at such an early stage, they could be derailed from criminal careers. Incarceration varies from three to six months, followed by a period of supervised release in the offender's community. Boot camp regimen was heavily influenced by military and physical training and in some respects harkens back to **Zebulon Brockway**'s support for programs that combined education, athletics, and military discipline. Some camps implemented strenuous labor routines; others were involved in community service projects such as forest preservation, painting churches, maintaining public parks, or repairing public buildings. Boot camps vary as to whether they offer substance abuse treatment, academic classes, life skills training, and vocational training. But virtually all camps emphasize grueling, well-organized 16-hour days with little time for leisure activities.

Boot camps were accepted as alternatives to prison during the "get tough" 1980s and 1990s because the public seemed to view them as being tough on crime and criminals. Others saw the camps as relieving prison overcrowding and cutting costs in contrast with bed space in a traditional prison. There is little evidence that the boot camps have had much impact on recidivism, with Arizona even abandoning the experiment, noting that the recidivism rate for boot camp graduates was higher than for inmates released from traditional facilities. A number of states have witnessed scandals involving brutal boot camp supervisors and guards that have brought into question the value of shock incarceration. Following an investigation in Georgia in the 1990s, the Justice Department described the boot camps as "not only ineffective, but harmful." While there is little consensus concerning the future of this concept, New York's shock incarceration network, Oregon's SUMMIT program, and the Vermont program, which emphasized community service over military discipline, are considered successful.

Sources: Doris Layton MacKenzie, "Boot Camps," in *Encyclopedia of American Prisons*, eds. McShane and Williams, 1996, pp. 61–65; Roberts, *Reform and Retribution*, 1997; Sifakis, *Encyclopedia of American Prisons*, 2003.

BORSTAL SYSTEM. First established in England in 1908 through the Prevention of Crime Act, Borstals were detention facilities used to confine youthful offenders generally between the ages of 16 and 21. Borstals were named after the village of Borstal in Kent, England, the site of the first of these facilities. Prior to 1908 these same offenders would have been held in prisons that had a Borstal system in operation. As early as 1904 **Wormwood Scrubs** incorporated a block of the prison for young inmates.

Borstal sentences ranged from not less than one year to three years in lieu of traditional imprisonment in an adult facility. Evidence suggests that a Borstal sentence was typically longer than the equivalent prison sentence primarily because prison commissioners deemed a six-month Borstal sentence ineffective. Most Borstals attempted to create a regime out of an amalgamation of vocational training, education, and counseling. Youths sentenced to Borstals were usually optimistically regarded as having greater chance for rehabilitation. Borstals placed emphasis on job training and education to help inmates gain a measure of self-respect and discipline. Inmates were incarcerated in a "house system," in which several offenders were assigned to live in a small house with a "head master." Through a **mark system** of graduated rewards, once an offender reaches the pinnacle of the reward system can win release.

Despite all good intentions, Borstals resembled adult prisons with their collaborative treatment regimen. The Borstal system has fallen out of favor in recent times, especially as Borstals exhibit many of the problems that have befallen the adult prisons, including overcrowding and poor conditions. Since Borstal offenders had such high recidivism rates, most critics suggest they did not work. Today there is an increasing effort to divert juveniles to noncustodial adjudication.

Sources: Morris, *Prisons*, 1976; Terrill, *World Criminal Justice Systems*, 1999; Herber, *Criminal London*, 2002.

BOSNIA AND HERZEGOVINA: FEDERATION. In 1998 Bosnia and Herzegovina adopted the new penal procedures that conformed to European Prison Rules. These new penal procedures included a minimum-space allowance per prisoner, the introduction of eligibility for certain benefits after the serving of one fifth of the sentence, the availability of water 24 hours a day, and a reduction of the maximum term of isolation from 30 to 20 days. The prison system of the Federation of Bosnia and Herzegovina is called the Division for the Execution of Criminal Sanctions and has been under the Ministry of Justice since 1968. In 2001 the federation maintained 9 penal facilities capable of holding a total of 1,061 prisoners. The largest institution was Zenica Prison, which could hold 349. Other prisons in descending order of total capacity included Sarajevo, with 223; Tuzla, with 200; and Mostar West, with 142. None of the other facilities could hold more than 63 prisoners. In 2001 the Bosnian prison population of Mostar East Prison was combined with the Croatian Mostar West Prison. By doing this, the number of prisons was reduced to eight.

Zenica Prison is considered the Federation's central prison. Following new construction in 2001 the capacity of the prison was increased to 464. Zenica was the largest prison in the former Yugoslavia and first opened in 1888. The only prison housing inmates serving sentences exceeding one year, it has extended its operations to serve juveniles and offer psychiatric treatment for the mentally ill. A number of other prisons originated during the late nineteenth century apogee of the Austro-Hungarian Empire.

During the Yugoslavian civil war of 1992–1995 the prison population dropped, as it does in most countries during wartime. By the end of 2001 it stood at 54 per 100,000, in line with neighboring **Slovenia, Croatia**, and **Serbia**, but much lower than **Austria** and **Hungary**. Scholars suggest that the low rate corresponds to the low rates that were traditional in the former Yugoslavia.

Among the prison system's most prominent problems has been an increase of overcrowding, a dearth of staff at all levels, and a low annual budget. But these complaints are more than compensated for by the achievements of recent years. Unlike prisoners in the United States, here prisoners do not face voting limitations upon leaving prison. Prison staff report a number of policies that have made the job more rewarding. The adoption and implementation of Council of Europe recommendations by 1999, better work opportunities for prisoners, social assistance for released inmates, and a more treatment-oriented regime bode well for the future of the Bosnia-Herzegovina Federation Prison System.

Since 2001 the prison population rate has been relatively stable. In 2004 the country indicated it had eight prisons holding 1,338 prisoners, a rate of 51 per 100,000 of the national population. These figures do not include 54 individuals undergoing mandatory psychiatric treatment in Zenica Prison.

Sources: Walmsley, *Further Developments in the Prison Systems of Central and Eastern Europe*, 2003; ICPS, Bosnia and Herzegovina: Federation, 2004.

BOSNIA AND HERZEGOVINA: REPUBLIKA SRPSKA. The prison system is in the Division for the Execution of Criminal Sanctions, operating under the Ministry of Justice. In 2004 its six penal institutions were home to 933 inmates. More than 20 percent are pre-trial detainees or remand prisoners. The prisons are considered at 97 percent of capacity. The national prison rate is 67 per 100,000 of the national population.

Source: ICPS, Bosnia and Herzegovina: Republika Srpska, 2004.

BOSTON PRISON DISCIPLINE SOCIETY. Prison reformer **Louis Dwight** founded this organization in 1826. According to prison historian Larry E. Sullivan, its membership was mainly "Congregational and Baptist ministers." During the organization's first decade, Dwight favored he **Auburn system**, which revolved around the silent regime, over the **Pennsylvania system**. The Society supported the utilization of convict labor as a means of teaching prisoners to be "productive" and "how to support themselves after they leave prison." The influence of the Society led states to build prisons based on the Auburn system, including Connecticut's Wethersfield Prison.

It was hoped that together with strict discipline and religious study inmates could be rehabilitated. Dwight exposed the darker side of American prisons in the annual *Reports of the Prison Discipline Society of Boston*. These reports were widely circulated and drew many reform advocates to visit American prisons from overseas. Visitors such as **Alexis de Tocqueville** and Gustave de Beaumont were probably inspired to tour American prisons after reading the Society's reports. Much of the Society's criticism was directed at conditions at the **Walnut Street Jail** and the Pennsylvania system. As late as 1850 the organization was alleging that solitary systems resulted in elevated rates of insanity among inmates.

Sources: Sullivan, *The Prison Reform Movement*, 1990; Christianson, *With Liberty for Some*, 1998.

BOTSWANA. By the end of the 1980s the Botswana Prison Department was operating 17 prisons able to accommodate more than 1,000 inmates. The number of incarcerated inmates has increased substantially since the early 1970s, when sentences were increased for stealing livestock and an increasing number of immigrants were imprisoned prior to deportation. In late 2003 the prison population stood at 5,890, or 327 per 100,000 of the national population. Almost 50 percent of the prisoners are foreigners. In 2003 there were 22 prisons and one Centre for Illegal Immigrants holding 504 of the country's 3,786 prisoners.

Sources: Kurian, *WEPP*, 1989; ICPS, Botswana, 2003; Walmsley, *WPPL*, 2003.

BRANDENBURG-GORDEN PRISON. Referred to by some prisoners as the "German **Sing Sing**," this facility to the west of Berlin received its first prisoners in 1931. When construction was completed four years later, it could hold 1,800 prisoners, which would, according to Nikolaus Wachsmann, make it "the largest German penal institution at this time." In its heyday it was considered on the cutting edge of penal architecture with a glass roof providing above-average ventilation and light. In addition, all cells were fitted with toilets and electric lamps. But the prison's most striking characteristic was its preparations for maximum security, which included floodlighting for roofs and courtyards, towers with searchlights and armed guards, and an electric alarm system on the inside. During the 1930s and 1940s it housed only male prisoners, including a large number of Communist activists and political prisoners. One wing was specifically designated to hold dangerous recidivists. In 1942 the only film shot inside a Nazi prison was made here. *Work and Imprisonment in the Brandenburg-Gorden Penitentiary* was intended to be used for training and recruitment. In April 1945 Soviet Red Army forces liberated the prison, but one last mass execution of 33 inmates was conducted on Hitler's birthday of April 20. In years past, executions had been prohibited at prisons on the Fuhrer's birthday.

Source: Wachsmann, *Hitler's Prisons*, 2004.

BRAZIL. Brazil was one of the first Latin American nations to adopt the penitentiary. Beginning in the 1830s prison reformers borrowed **Jeremy Bentham**'s **panopticon** design as a model for correctional development. The government initially built the *Casa de Correcão*, or House of Correction, in Rio de Janeiro (1834–1850) as other Brazilian states constructed correctional facilities at Bahia, Goias, and Minas Gerais.

Following this burst of enthusiasm prison reform lost momentum and support as states used corrections for other purposes such as "correcting" the behavior of disobedient slaves. Nowhere was this more apparent than at the Casa de Correcao, which reverted from its promise as a reformatory facility to "a house of disease and death."

It was not until 1853 that the American influence had any impact on prison construction. That year Brazil sent a commissioner to survey American prison design and regulations. After visiting facilities in Philadelphia, Trenton, Baltimore, and elsewhere the inspector endorsed the **Pennsylvania system**, which allowed visual inspection by using a radial plan. These changes were incorporated into the Rio de Janeiro prison.

Meanwhile other Brazilian states were influenced by a variety of designs. Some, such as Para, still used old convents; other used military structures. In 1859 Fernando de Noronha Prison was built for long-term convicts on an island off the east coast of the state of Natal. Seventy years later the government would confine political prisoners there. In the mid-1850s the state of Parahyba opened a new facility that was built in the form of a "hollow square." Recife Prison, built in the state of Pernambuco in 1855, and following European models, was regarded as one of the country's most impressive prison structures.

By 1890 the Brazilian prison system was universally regarded as primitive and unreformed. By the twentieth century some improvements were made in the prisons of Fernando de Noronha, Rio de Janeiro, Bahia, and Recife, but juvenile reform still languished far behind.

During the 1890s Brazil implemented **Walter Crofton**'s "Irish progressive system" of classification, and progress was made toward more therapeutic treatment of inmates.

The penologist **Enoch Wines** described the Brazilian penal system in 1879 in his *State of Prisons*, noting that the country was composed of 20 provinces, which included 480 jurisdictions. The construction of prisons was borne by each province. At this time Brazil had one central prison at Fernando de Noronha, an island almost 300 miles northeast of Recife, capital of the province of Pernambuco. Prisons at this institution were kept busy with hard labor and a heady dose of moral and religious instruction.

In the 1870s other prisoners were held in provincial prisons, including those at Rio de Janeiro and São Paulo, a workhouse at Bahia, and a detention facility in Recife. All inmates served their sentences under the **Auburn** model, with strict silence and separation at night and a congregate work setting during the day.

Brazil abolished the death penalty in 1891 but brought it back in 1938. During the 1870s minors under the age of fourteen often served time in privately operated correctional institutions until they were eighteen. Juveniles were taught vocational trades and given moral instruction at institutions such as Villa Izabel in Rio de Janeiro and the Colony Izabel in Pernambuco. An asylum for young girls was set up in São Paulo at Dona Anna Rosa and at Petropolis.

When Brazil built Rio de Janeiro's **Carandiru Prison** between 1911 and 1920, it became the first Latin American nation to incorporate the **telephone pole** design. It was designed with a capacity for 1,300. In 1942 the 1,650-cell Cidade Penitentiary was built in Rio de Janeiro.

Brazil's modern penal system is based on the Penal Code of 1940. According to decree number 898, life sentences are limited to a maximum of 30 years. In the early 1990s the prison population stood at 110,000, a prisoner-to-population incarceration rate of 82 per 100,000. Today there are close to 5,000 penal institutions, broken down into 51 correctional institutions, 27 penitentiaries, 6 houses of custody and treatment, 12 agricultural colonies, and 6 houses of correction. These are complemented by 12 military prisons, 1,580 *cadeias* (regular adult prisons), 2,803 *xadrezes* (jails), and 5 juvenile institutions. Overcrowding leading to waves of unrest, riots, and a major prison-building program has marked Brazilian prisons. Many cells rely on primitive sanitation, as spartan as a pan on the floor in place of a toilet. In many institutions one meal a day, bare concrete floors without beds, and lack of exercise are de rigueur. Prison industries are minimal with emphasis on the manufacture of clothing and straw mattresses, carpentry, and welding.

Human rights organizations have criticized Brazil for housing first-time offenders with more serious offenders, often leading to homosexual rape of younger inmates. According to a 1989 report by Americas Watch, guards take part in selling young prisoners to predatory inmates. In other cases murder by lottery systems have been reported in which inmates kill others in an attempt to relieve overcrowding. According to some reports a "death lottery" at the Belo Horizonte prison led to the murder of 17 inmates in one 2-month period. Prison riots have been even bloodier, including a 1992 episode at the São Paulo prison, which claimed the lives of 111 inmates, the majority of whom were pre-trial detainees who were housed with prisoners serving up to 30-year sentences.

There are more than 8,500 women incarcerated in Brazil's prisons, jails, and police lockups. At 4 percent of the inmate population this gender distribution is similar to that in other Latin American countries. Many female inmates are housed in facilities run by various religious orders and are not always referred to as prisons. Here, conjugal visits are permitted, and young children are sheltered with their mothers. The São Paulo Women's Penitentiary is the largest women's prison in the country. Its four main cellblocks were built for a capacity of 256, but they often held up to 400.

Today Brazil incarcerates more people than any other Latin American country. It also leads much of the world in its ratio of prison staff to prisoners and number of escapes. Brazil is also home to South America's largest prison. In June 2004 police in Rio de Janeiro's Beneficia Detention Center found 38 dead inmates after a 3-day rebellion. This followed a similar riot just five weeks earlier that resulted in the deaths of 14 inmates. It is estimated that Brazil's prisons hold 285,000 prisoners in a system meant to hold 180,000. While conditions vary from state to state and between institutions, overcrowding, poor sanitation and ventilation, and a relative lack of public empathy for the plight of inmates most often mark them. Most observers suggest this can be explained by Brazil's high rate of violent crime.

Sources: *WEPP*, 1989; Zelma W. Henriques, "Treatment of Offenders in Denmark and Brazil," in *Comparative and International Criminal Justice Systems*, ed. Ebbe, 1996; Salvatore and Aguire, eds., *The Birth of the Penitentiary in Latin America*, 1996; Human Rights Watch, *Behind Bars in Brazil*, 1998; Johnston, *Forms of Constraint*, 2000; Harold Olmos, "Prison Scene Sparks Outcry," *Houston Chronicle*, June 2, 2004, 11A.

BRIDEWELLS. Henry VIII's palace at Bridewell was completed in 1520. Over the years its use changed. The indigent and the sick had relied on monasteries for alms over the centuries. With the dissolution of the monasteries after 1536, the poor had few alternatives for subsistence. Some turned to petty theft and other to crime as the dissolute swarmed into London. In 1553 Edward VI donated the use of Bridewell Palace as a "hospital for moral, not physical deformities," leading to its function as a **house of correction** and house of occupation. During the following years Roman Catholics, nonconformists, and petty offenders were housed in Bridewell. By the 1630s it was common to administer whippings to vagrants and prostitutes on their first arrival. Adults were given twelve lashes, and children half that. Large crowds witnessed public floggings, with few alternatives for entertainment.

Subsequently, Parliament ruled that every county should open a "Bridewell." Every day local officials called beadles made their rounds in their respective wards and collected vagrant and idle people to Bridewell. Here the governors decided whether to incarcerate their prospective charges. Petty criminals, vagrants, and the indigent were incarcerated at these facilities and were required to work at a number of tasks, including manufacturing products for sale, baking, and milling. The work regimen was intended to make the institution almost self-supporting. Typically the more dissolute women were consigned to the spinning room, while the more skilled would be requisitioned to the nail house, and the worst vagabonds to the bake house and mill. Prisoners were paid for their labor, and in turn they were charged for meals. Over time the range of occupational instruction increased, with women mending and men learning to make mortar. By 1563 a system of apprenticeship had been inaugurated for the children of poor freemen as well as young street children. Within sixteen years Bridewells offered 25 different occupations, including making pins, silk, lace, gloves, felts, and tennis balls. Along with the work discipline was the ever-present threats of whipping, torture, and restricted diets for those who did not take full advantage of the workhouse. Over the next several decades other English communities founded similar institutions, mostly in response to the alarming increase in vagrancy.

The original Bridewell was consumed by the Great Fire of 1666 and then rebuilt. In 1791 it abandoned the whipping of women and was finally closed in 1855. In 1863 it was demolished.

Sources: Austin van der Slice, "Elizabethan Houses of Correction," *Journal of Criminal Law and Criminology* (1937), 27:45–57, 63–67; Howard, *John Howard*, 1963; Joanna Innes, "Prisons for the Poor: English Bridewells, 1550–1800," in *Labour, Law, and Crime: An Historical Perspective*, ed. Francis Snyder and Douglas Hay (London: Tavistock Publications, 1987), pp. 42–122.

BRINKERHOFF, ROELIFF (1828–1911). Born in Owasco, New York, he studied law and passed the Ohio bar in 1852. He served stints as a lawyer and a newspaper publisher, and during the Civil War he served as a quartermaster. His affiliation with the American prison system began when he became a member of the Ohio State Board of Charities in 1878. In 1882 he was selected president of the National Conference of Charities and Corrections. The following year he enlisted in the National Prison Association. By 1893 he was president of the organization, a post he would hold for four years.

Brinkerhoff earned a reputation as a prison reformer and an opponent of the political patronage system. During his stint as director he crusaded for professional standards in correctional work and became a stalwart supporter of **parole**. In part because of his support, Ohio became the first state to pass a parole law in 1885. During the 1890s he lobbied for the creation of a federal prison bureau.

BRITTIN, WILLIAM (d. 1821). A veteran of the War of 1812, Brittin worked as a master carpenter and general contractor during the construction of the **Auburn**

Penitentiary beginning in 1816. Historian Blake McKelvey suggested that Brittin was probably conversant with the building plans of the **Ghent Maison de Force**, built in 1773, which was published in **John Howard's** *State of Prisons*. Brittin became the prison's first warden the following year when the first group of 58 prisoners arrived to help complete the building. He continued to oversee the project until his death in 1821. He was followed by the more prominent warden **Elam Lynds**.

Sources: McKelvey, *American Prisons*, 1977; Phillips and Axelrod, *Cops, Crooks, and Criminologists*, 1996.

BRIXTON PRISON. Originally built as a **house of correction** in 1820, today Brixton Prison is considered the oldest prison in London still receiving prisoners. Intended for a capacity of 175, it usually exceeded its quota by more than 200. Its small cells and poor living conditions earned it a reputation as the one of the most insalubrious prisons in London. In 1821 it became the first prison in England to introduce the **treadmill**. The facility was later expanded to hold up to 800 prisoners. When a woman was received, she underwent a four-month probationary period served in solitary confinement before advancing into a condition of silent association. Over time female inmates could earn privileges, including limited conversation, payment for labor, and more letters and visits. Women who became pregnant at **Millbank** were transferred to Brixton.

In 1853 the government turned Brixton into a facility for women who preferred prison in England to transportation to Australia. Brixton is considered the first institution exclusively for women in England. It provided a convict nursery where children could stay with their mothers until they were four years old. This was later limited to children under one year. However, by 1860 women could keep their children until the end of their sentences. Between 1882 and 1898 Brixton served as a military prison. Since then it has served as a trial-and-remand prison for London and the Home Counties.

Sources: Babington, *The English Bastille*, 1971; Herber, *Criminal London*, 2002.

BROCKWAY, ZEBULON (1827–1920). Brockway belongs in the pantheon of prison reformers who came to prominence in mid- to late-nineteenth-century America. His first affiliation with corrections was as a clerk in Connecticut's Wethersfield Prison in 1848. Four years later he was appointed superintendent of the Albany, New York, Municipal and County Almshouse, where he was credited with establishing the first county facility for the treatment of the insane. At the age of 27 Brockway began to put some of his penal reform theories into practice when he was selected as superintendent of the Monroe County Penitentiary in Rochester, New York. When he took over the Michigan House of Correction in Detroit in 1861, Brockway reportedly claimed to inaugurate his famous strategy of inmate self-government that would later become prominent during his tenure as superintendent of the **Elmira Reformatory**.

A staunch supporter of the indeterminate sentence, Brockway quit his job in Detroit when he could not get legislative support for an indeterminate sentence bill. He soon became involved in the formation of the **National Prison Congress**. At its first convention in Cincinnati in 1870, Brockway presented his paper, "The Ideal for a True Prison System for a State," which offered his vision of prison as a place for the "protection of society by the prevention of crime and the reformation of criminals."

Brockway became a prominent figure in prison reform following his appointment as superintendent of the Elmira State Reformatory in 1876. Here he was credited with introducing a new type of penal regime. Brockway transformed a former prison for adults into an institution for young first-time offenders between the ages of 16 and 31. Stymied in his attempts to apply his rehabilitation theories in a traditional prison setting, he was now afforded the opportunity to apply them to a different class of prisoners.

At Elmira Brockway was determined to apply the National Prison Association's Declaration of Principles (see Appendix I) and eschew many of the practices popularized in the **Auburn system**, including corporal punishment, prison stripes, the silent system, and any other endeavors to degrade inmates. Although he became associated with a less punitive brand of prison supervision, behind prison walls, where prisoners referred him to as "Paddler Brockway," it was another matter. Despite his reputation as a benign ruler, Elmira was governed under a repressive regime that included punishments that sometimes included whippings, swattings with paddles studded with nails, and stints in chains in solitary confinement. During his quarter century at Elmira and despite his public pronouncements about rehabilitation, prisoners were often discharged to freedom with shaved heads and broken health.

Brockway's legacy as a prison reformer parallels his efforts at adopting the indeterminate sentence. Railing against the self-defeating practice of the fixed sentence, Brockway followed in the footsteps of **Walter Crofton** and **Alexander Maconochie**, by implementing a parole system and a grading system that allowed inmates to earn privileges and incentives ultimately leading to early release for good behavior. His strategy attracted great attention in the penal community, and observers from around the world visited Elmira to gain insights in prison reform. The Elmira model eventually comprised three grades. When inmates entered the prison, they were placed in the second grade. In order to move up to the first grade in preparation for parole, each prisoner had to earn nine marks monthly for six successive months. After six months in the first grade the inmate could earn early release. Points were rewarded by finishing school assignments, attending religious and vocational programs, and showing appropriate deportment. Inmates who did not adhere to these requirements were demoted from the second to the third grade. To begin the ascent toward release the inmate than had to complete three months of good behavior before entering the second grade and repeating the steps toward parole.

While Brockway's program would influence the development of America's first formal parole system, his interpretation was closer to conditional release, since each inmate was required to regularly check in with volunteer so-called guardians. Between 1876 and 1913 17 states built adult reformatories based on the Elmira model. However, the warden's legacy has been tainted by charges that he employed brutal corporal punishment for numerous infractions. According to John W. Roberts, "There was compelling evidence of mismanagement" during Brockway's tenure at Elmira. Brockway retired in 1900 but continued his public service until his death. He chronicled his career in his 1912 book *Fifty Years of Prison Service*.

Sources: Patrick R. Anderson, "Zebulon Brockway," in *Encyclopedia of American Prisons*, eds. McShane and Williams, 1996, pp. 65–66; Roberts, *Reform and Retribution*, 1997; Christianson, *With Liberty for Some*, 1998.

BRUNEI DARUSSALAM. The Brunei Prisons Department is the responsibility of the Ministry of Home Affairs. In 2003 the country has two prisons holding 473 inmates, for a prison population rate of 473 per 100,000 of the national population.

Source: ICPS, Brunei Darussalam, Asia, 2004.

BULGARIA. Until the end of the 1980s, the Bulgarian prison system was governed under the authority of the Ministry of Internal Affairs through the Central Prison Institutions Department and Its Prison Service. In 1990 it was placed under the administration of the Ministry of Justice. The Prison Service was responsible for training and managing prison guards. By 1990 the Bulgarian prison system included 13 prisons and 26 minimum-security institutions containing 6,600 prisoners. The most important facilities are located in Bobov Dol, Pazardzhik, Plovdiv, Sofia, Stara Zagora, Varna, and Vratsa. Following the end of the Soviet era, the total prison population declined by 10,000, as a result of a number of amnesties granted to political prisoners.

During the Soviet era all prisoners were expected to perform useful work, undergo political indoctrination, and receive general and vocational education. During this era incarceration facilities consisted of prisons, labor-correctional institutions, and correctional homes for minors. Prisoners were segregated by age, sex, and disciplinary regime. All prisoners were required to perform some type of work within a week of arrival and were paid wages (80 percent paid to the prisoner's family). All conversation had to be in Bulgarian unless a translator was on hand.

During the Soviet era, prisoners could earn more privileges and transfer to a less punitive prison through good behavior. According to the legal code, prisoners had a number of rights, including exercise and outdoor recreation time, visitation by family and friends, gifts such as food parcels, personal effects, and the right to correspond with prosecutors and court officials. Conversely, bad behavior could result in the reduction of privileges and confinement in a stricter environment.

Pazardzhik Prison housed close to 560 inmates in the early 1990s, including 50 incarcerated for murder, 60 for rape, 140 for crimes against persons, and the remainder for property crimes. Less serious offenders were imprisoned in a variety of minimum-security facilities including open and semi-open labor camps. During the first part of 1990, a number of strikes and demonstrations broke out over the ouster of Zhivkov. The strikes became considerably more violent following the release of large numbers of political prisoners, massive strikes on the outside, and a less stable sociopolitical environment. There were several reports of prisoners immolating themselves to protest prison conditions. Conditions were so serious it was necessary to call in the Red Berets to augment the force of prison guards. Subsequently, Bulgaria has taken a number of steps to improve prison conditions and the country's international human rights image.

The Bulgarian prison system has cited a number of recent achievements, including the 1997 creation of transitional hotels, where prisoners can serve the end of their sentences in semi-open facilities. In addition, a number of education and vocational programs have been introduced as well as more focus on preparing prisoners for release. However, the system is still plagued with a lack of financial support, poor morale and attitudes among prison staff, and a lack of community-based punishment alternatives.

As of 2002 Bulgaria's 14 penal facilities included 12 prisons and 2 juvenile correctional facilities. In early 2003 the prison population stood at 9,918, or 127 per 100,000 of the national population. These figures are considered lower than those in most central and eastern European countries, but they conform to the ratios of the nearby Balkan countries of Albania and the former Yugoslavian republics. Although there is overcrowding in some prisons, the entire system as of 2002 was operating at 91 percent of its official capacity.

Sources: Kurian, *WEPP*, 1989; LCCS, "Albania," June 1992; Walmsley, *Prison Systems in Central and Eastern Europe*, 1996; Walmsley, *Further Developments in the Prison Systems of Central and Eastern Europe*, 2003; ICPS, Bulgaria, 2004.

BURKINA FASO. In 1920 French colonizers passed the first decree that established penitentiaries in the former Upper Volta. However, it did not take effect until 12 years later, when the colony was divided into French Sudan, which became Mali, the Ivory Coast, and Niger. Three different regimes would direct Upper Voltan prisons until 1950, when regulations were standardized for the entire colony.

Although there was no official segregation of African and European prisoners until 1928, the separation of prisoners was applied throughout the colonial period. When the number of European prisoners increased following World War II a problem resulted for administrators when African prisoners complained that the Europeans received deferential treatment and better living standards. By 1950 even stricter segregation rules were implemented. Nowhere was this more obvious than in culinary standards—Europeans received their food from the noncommissioned officers' mess hall rather than the prison kitchen. Racial segregation was reportedly most glaring at the Bobo-Dioulasso Prison. As a measure of the discrepancy in standards, it cost 6.5 times more francs to feed a European prisoner than his African counterpart.

Prison labor was used on public works projects prior to the World War I. In 1946 legislation was passed prohibiting all types of forced labor. However, the so-called Houphouet-Boigny law had little impact on the use of mandatory labor until the 1950s. Prisoners were not remunerated for their labor until 1960, more than 130 years after the practice began in French prisons. Despite this advance, Upper Voltan prison conditions were in poor condition by 1960.

During the colonial period most prison managers came from the ranks of the Gendarmie, or police. African guards were given some clout in the smaller rural facilities. The central prison was located at Ouagadougou, the colonial capital. While statistical evidence is hard to come by for any era, it appears that there was a number of escape attempts, as high as 10 percent of the detainees tried in the 1920s. Most evidence suggests that African leaders adopted the colonial model of the prison established by the French in the 1950s. After independence in 1960 Upper Volta was renamed Burkina Faso, but prisons did not take many strides toward improvement. As of late 2002 the prison population consisted of 2,800 prisoners and detainees, or 24 per 100,000 of the national population.

Sources: Laurent Fourchard, "Between Conservatism and Transgression: Everyday Life in the Prisons of Upper Volta, 1920–1960," in *A History of Prison and Confinement in Africa*, ed. Florence Bernault, 2003, pp. 135–153; Walmsley, *WPPL*, 2003.

BURMA. *See* MYANMAR

BURNS, ROBERT ELLIOTT (1890–1965). A successful accountant before World War I, when he returned home after front-line combat and a case of shellshock, his life quickly unraveled. After "being forced" by another man to participate in a store robbery that netted less than six dollars, Burns was captured, tried, and sentenced to six to ten years on a Georgia **chain gang**. In 1922 he escaped the chain gang and fled to Chicago, where within seven years he became a successful newspaper editor and businessman. After Georgia authorities were alerted to his whereabouts, they filed a successful request for return. Burns voluntarily returned on a promise that he would be treated leniently and quickly pardoned. The state had no intention fulfilling its side of the bargain, however, and he was sent back to a chain gang. Out of the state's 140 chain gang camps, Burns ended up in Georgia's harshest one at La Grange.

Burns escaped once more, but this time he fled to New Jersey, where he wrote a series of magazine articles telling his story and exposing the horrific Georgia chain gang system. His collected articles formed the basis for his famous indictment of southern corrections published in 1932, *I Am a Fugitive from a Georgia Chain Gang!* Warner Brothers bought the movie rights to the book and quickly released the movie titled *I Am a Fugitive from a Chain Gang* in 1932 as well. Faithful to the book's narrative, the film starred actor Paul Muni as James Allen, a thinly veiled version of Robert Burns. Although the film was a hit, it did not fare as well with embarrassed Georgia officials, who once more lobbied for Burns's extradition. A number of states came to the defense of Burns, and it would take almost 13 years for his sentence to be commuted to time already served by Georgia governor Ellis Arnall in 1945, the same year that the chain gang was officially abolished. By all accounts the plight of Robert Burns and his subsequent chronicling of his experiences diminished some aspects of the chain gang, but they were still used in Georgia and across the South for years to come. Burns devoted the rest of his life to prison reform.

Sources: Crowther, *Captured on Film*, 1989; Franklin, *Prison Literature in America*, 1989.

BURUNDI. Burundi's prison system operates 11 facilities under the Ministry of Justice. Burundi's prison system has been influenced by the colonial regimes under German and Belgian direction. Accordingly, each province contained a central prison and a work camp designed for prisoners serving long sentences. The best-known prisons are at Rumonga, Gitega, and Muhinga. Like many prisons in economically challenged nations, Burundi facilities are overcrowded and lack the requisite medical care and sanitation. Prisoners are housed according to their criminal records and can receive periodic visits from family members. The nation's prison system offers constructive rehabilitation programs, many revolving around agricultural work. Prisoners fortunate to have the support of family members nearby are encouraged to ask them for food and personal items to supplement prison rations, which have at times been so insubstantial that several prisoners have reportedly died from malnutrition. As of late 2002 the prison population was 8,647, representing 133 per 100,000 of the national population.

Sources: Kurian, *WEPP*, 1989; Walmsley, *WPPL*, 2003; ICPS, Burundi, 2004.

BUTYRKA PRISON. The oldest of Moscow's three main prisons, Butyrka prison started out as a fortress palace in the eighteenth century. It typically held prisoners either waiting for **transportation** to the Soviet **Gulag** or those who had undergone interrogation. A number of Russian luminaries have been guests here, including the Revolutionary poet Vladimir Mayakovsky, KGB founder Felix Dzerzhinsky, and writer **Alexander Solzhenitsyn**. Solzhenitsyn's secretary A. M. Garaseva remembered the prison's excellent library and more relaxed regime. Dzherzhinsky was one of the few prisoners to successfully escape the prison. Russian author Isaak Babel was executed there in 1940, as were a number of other high-profile prisoners. Demolition of the prison began in the early 1960s.

Sources: Asinah.NET Encyclopedia; Applebaum, *Gulag*, 2003.

C

CAMBODIA. The Cambodian penal system has about 200 prisons at its disposal. These institutions are supervised by the Prison Directorate of the Ministry of the Interior and by the People's Security Service. Prisons range from those at the national level to facilities at the local level. The main national prison is T-3, located in Phnom Penh. Built in the early twentieth century, in 1979 T-3 was expanded to hold 1,000 prisoners. This central institution is supplanted at the national level by penal institutions referred to as T-4 and T-5. These two, however, are more labor camps than maximum-security prisons. T-4 is located on the periphery of Phnom Penh; T-5 is situated in Kampong Cham.

Phnom Penh is comprised of 20 precincts, each with its own short-term facility. By law, precinct prisons must transfer prisoners after three days to the central headquarters for confinement at T-3.

Outside the capital city, independent municipalities, provinces, and districts have their own jails and prisons. At the provincial level facilities are administered by the People's Security Service. One of the more prominent examples of this type of facility is TK-1, located in Batdambang City. However, it has been plagued by overcrowding and related problems because it is situated in a region of heavy resistance activity, leading the government to rely on it for detaining captured guerillas, smugglers, illegal border crossers, and insurgent supporters.

By most accounts facilities at the provincial level receive scant support from the government and are often hampered by poor sanitation and egregious conditions.

Prisoners receive a signed release from either the People's Security Service or the Ministry of interior at the conclusion of their sentences and are allowed to return to their home of origin. Because of the nature of Cambodian criminal justice, former prisoners are warned to keep their release papers with them to protect against re-arrest. In 2003 Cambodia had 3 national prisons and 22 provincial and municipal facilities. As of the middle of 2003 the prison population stood at 6,346, or 45 per 100,000 of the national population. Almost one third of the prisoners are either pre-trial or remand prisoners. *See also* S-21

Sources: LCCS, "Cambodia," December 1987; Walmsley, *WPPL*, 2003; ICPS, Cambodia, 2004.

CAMEROON. Historically, Cameroon has been home to a diverse number of ethnic and sociopolitical entities. Evidence suggests that prior to colonialization punishments ranged from fines and shaming to corporal punishment and imprisonment. The Mandara Kingdom, which reached its apogee in the nineteenth century, had a "classical penitentiary system," according to Thierno Bah. The titles of various functionaries from this era indicate the organization behind the prison. The palace prison, or *gulfunye*, housed condemned prisoners. This prison was under the control of the *Tlavunge*. Further divisions of personnel indicate a complex penitentiary system that utilized measures such as solitary confinement, starvation, and physical brutality. There is also evidence that in the early 1800s the Fulani emirate in northern Cameroon was using imprisonment and forced labor. For the local population, these prisons apparently were synonymous with terror. Prison cells were apparently little more than thatched huts. Prisoners were held to the floor with ropes, primitive handcuffs, or iron chains attached to stakes in the floor.

Influenced by French and British colonial precedents, the Cameroonian penal code makes a distinction between imprisonment and detention. The minister of justice directs the prison system. Under his supervision detainees are prohibited from working to earn money to help support their families, whereas prisoners are allowed to do so. Overcrowding, poor food and sanitation, and lackluster medical care plague Cameroonian correctional facilities. During the mid-1980s Amnesty International cited several instances of death from malnutrition. This report spurred the government to improve conditions and begin renovations. Best estimates place the prison population at 20,000, or 129 per 100,000 of the national population. Almost one half of the prisoners are remand or pre-trial detainees. As of mid-2002 the prisons were severely overcrowded at 296.3 percent of capacity.

Sources: Kurian, *WEPP*, 1989; Thierno Bah, "Captivity and Incarceration in Nineteenth-century West Africa," in *A History of Prison and Confinement in Africa*, ed. Florence Bernault, 2003, pp. 69–77; Walmsley, *WPPL*, 2003; ICPS, Cameroon, 2004.

CANADA. Canada's prison system was established when the government of the Dominion of Canada was established in 1867, thereby taking over a number of the former provincial prisons. The most prominent of these institutions was the Kingston Penitentiary in Ontario, constructed in 1835. Other early provincial prisons were built at Halifax, Nova Scotia, and Saint John in New Brunswick. Halifax Prison was formerly known as Rockhead Prison and originated as a city jail in 1854. By 1867 Halifax Penitentiary had installed enough equipment to supply up to 80 convicts with machinery to make brooms, tubs, and clothespins. Overcrowding at Kingston Penitentiary led the government to establish a new facility in Quebec in 1870. Rather than construct a brand new institution an existing juvenile reformatory at St. Vincent de Paul, near Montreal, was converted into an adult prison. In 1911 a new penitentiary was added at Prince Albert, Saskatchewan, and the following year saw Montreal open a provincial jail for Quebec. Throughout most of the twentieth century Canada's nine provinces have operated their own county and municipal jails, as well as several reformatories and industrial farms.

Several important attempts at prison reform were made in the first half of the 1900s. A number of recommendations were set forth in 1919, many embracing new concepts in penology. Among those set forth were the abolition of the stone pile, the availability of well-trained medical staff and teachers, work for prisoners under the state use plan, better food, employment availability for prisoners prior to release, wages for prison labor, the separate confinement for the insane, and better training of prison officers.

Geographical barriers in such a large, sparsely populated country hindered reform efforts, and consequently it took many years to arrive at an adequate classification system. By the 1930s the Kingston, Ontario, penitentiary had a special cellblock to house "star class" prisoners, who were kept separate from other prisoners and given special privileges. During that decade new facilities were constructed at St. Vincent de Paul, near Montreal, and Collins Bay, Ontario, dedicated to prisoners demonstrating the greatest potential for reform. The silent system stayed in force until 1933, the same year that compulsory education was introduced for illiterate prisoners. Not until 1935 was a law passed that made prisoners responsible for buying their own cigarettes, formerly paid for by taxpayers.

Overcrowding in the prisons and a rising crime rate on the outside led the Canadian government to convene a committee under Joseph Archambault to examine the penal system. The subsequent Archambault Report was released in 1938. Among its most important suggestions was the need for a more rehabilitative approach, a suggestion that would resonate into the 1960s.

By 1943 Canada's prison population had reached 75,000. Several methods of conditional release were in operation, including the better-known release for "good-time" served and parole or ticket of leave. However, in Ontario Canada also offered a rather novel alternative that allows the inmate to go through what was called a process of regeneration, whereby the inmate is allowed to work outside in order to support his family. Under this plan the prisoner can sleep either at his home or in the city jail but must be off the streets by eight o'clock each night.

Canadian correctional policy is based on rehabilitation rather than retribution, and imprisonment is considered the punishment of last resort. Penal facilities are managed by the federal government (penitentiaries) and provincial governments (provincial jails, reformatories, training schools). Offenders who are sentenced to two or more years' incarceration are held in federal penitentiaries. These inmates are classified according to their behavior. Dangerous offenders are held in maximum-security facilities, and the rest in medium security. Those with shorter sentences under two years serve time in provincial institutions. Here inmates can work in farm or industrial annexes under moderate direction. A commissioner under the solicitor general of Canada governs federal penitentiaries; provincial jails are under the direction of the corrections branch of the provincial Department of Health and Welfare or the Department of Social Services.

Both systems also maintain separate facilities for women and juveniles. The passage of the Juvenile Delinquency Act of 1970 ensures that juveniles will be confined safely away from adult offenders, whether in a penitentiary, jail, or police station. Most juveniles are incarcerated in detention homes, training schools, or foster homes.

One of the bitterest struggles in Canadian correctional history took place in 1976 when almost 400 inmates of the Archambault maximum-security prison went on a 110-day work strike to protest living conditions. In 1982 three guards and two prisoners were killed during a bloody riot at the same facility.

At present Canada's prison system is administered by the Correctional Service of Canada (CSC), with its headquarters in Ottawa. The system consists of a three-level hierarchy with the commissioner in Ottawa at the top. The next level is the regional level, with five regional headquarters located in Moncton, Laval, Kingston, Saskatoon, and Abbotsford. The third level is the local or institutional level. At this level a classification system operates to determine the type of security level accorded each prison. Of the country's 221 prison facilities 68 are federal prisons and 153 are provincial institutions. These prisons include 18 maximum-security, 17 medium-security, and 13 minimum-security facilities. In addition there are 151 community correctional centers, or halfway houses. In mid-2001 the country's prison system contained 36,024 prisoners, representing 116 per 100,000 of the national population.

Sources: Topping, *Canadian Penal Institutions*, 1930; Colin Goff, *Corrections in Canada* (Cincinnati: Anderson, 1999); Gosselin, *Prisons in Canada*, 1982; Terrill, *World Criminal Justice Systems*, 1999; Walmsley, *WPPL*, 2003; ICPS, Canada, 2004.

CAPE VERDE. The prison system falls under the direction of the Ministry of Justice. In 2003 the country had 2 central prisons, 4 regional facilities, and 5 subregional prisons. As of 2000 these 11 institutions held 755 prisoners, a rate of 178 per 100,000 of the national population. More than one third were pre-trial detainees or remand prisoners.

Source: ICPS, Cape Verde, Africa, 2004.

CARANDIRU PRISON. Brazil's Carandiru Prison has recently been demolished, but in the early 1990s it was Latin America's largest prison, holding 7,400 prisoners in conditions too squalid to contemplate. It came to prominence in 1992 after the prisoners seized control of the facility. Police took back the prison, killing 111 prisoners in the process. Brazilian director Hector Babenco filmed a cinematic portrait of this incident, using the soon demolished prison as his actual set. The movie *Carandiru* was released in 2003 to critical acclaim. It was also based on the 1999 book *Carandiru Station*, which was a national bestseller and brought the debate over the Brazilian prison system into the public forum.

Sources: Larry Rohter, "A Prison Story That Carries a Personal Meaning," *New York Times*, August 4, 2002, p.13; Drauzio Varella, *Estação Carandiru* (Rio de Janeiro: Companhia de Bolsa, 2005).

CARCERES. By the sixth century the Latin term *carcer* was used to refer to penitential confinement. In the Middle Ages monasteries devoted a room for "delinquent clergy" known as the *carceres* or *decaneta*.

Sources: Edward M. Peters, "Prison before the Prison," in *Oxford History of the Prison*, ed. Morris and Rothman, 1998, pp.4–43; Johnston, *Forms of Constraint*, 2000.

CARCER PRIVATUS. Greece and Rome sporadically employed a private prison, or *carcer privatus*, to hold debtors. If debtors failed to pay their debt, they could potentially be used as slave labor. Detention in these private prisons was more often dedicated to holding individuals prior to trial or execution. There is a lack of consensus whether the Romans regularly recognized imprisonment as a penal sanction. Norman Johnston suggests that it was "rarely officially used."

Source: Johnston, *Forms of Constraint*, 2000.

CASA DE CORRECÃO. One of South America's most storied penitentiaries, Casa de Correcão was built in Rio de Janeiro, **Brazil**, between 1834 and 1856. The blueprint for the prison was the work of engineer Manoel de Oliveira, who was reportedly influenced by prison plans from England, Germany, and France. According to Latin American historians Ricardo Salvatore and Carlos Aguirre, this prison should be considered "the first institution of confinement in Latin America to be built following the penitentiary principles." Norman Johnston believes that it was "undoubtedly the last [prison] ever constructed" influenced by early English architectural models. Despite numerous attempts to improve the prison in the late nineteenth century by abolishing corporal punishment, introducing prisoner classification, and better medical treatment, Casa de Correcão was usually plagued by disease, poor sanitation, and overcrowding. According to prison statistics, of the 1,099 prisoners who entered the facility between 1850 and 1869, 245 died before finishing their sentences. Reports indicate that by the 1890s, however, there were only one or two deaths per year.

Sources: Marcos Luiz Bretas, "What the Eyes Can't See: Stories from Rio de Janiero's Prisons," in *The Birth of the Penitentiary in Latin America*, eds. Salvatore and Aguirre, 1996, pp. 101–122; Johnston, *Forms of Constraint*, 2000.

CAYMAN ISLANDS. The Cayman Islands Prison Service operates under the Portfolio of Internal and External Affairs. At the end of 2003 there were two prisons, one for males at Northward, and one for women at Fairbanks. As of mid-2003 they held 210 inmates and were at 84 percent of capacity. Almost one third of the prisoners were foreigners from Jamaica and the United Kingdom. The prison population rate is 501 per 100,000 of the national population.

Source: ICPS, Cayman Islands, Caribbean, 2004.

CENTRAL AFRICAN REPUBLIC. The Prison Administration falls under the supervision of the Ministry of the Interior. In 2002 the country reported 56 prisons with a capacity for close to 6,000 inmates. In 2001 the prisons held 4,168 prisoners, or 110 per 100,000 of the national population.

Source: ICPS, Central African Republic, 2004.

CEYLON. *See* SRI LANKA

CHAD. The Chadian criminal justice system is based on the French system. Amnesty International has reported the detention of political prisoners and an ongoing failure of the government to account for a number of detainees who have disappeared. Although it is difficult to gain information on Chadian prisons, reports from the Department of State describe prison conditions as bordering on primitive. However, this in part is a reflection of a poverty-stricken nation rather than deliberate policy. Given the lack of prison rations, prisoners need access to food from outside sources to survive. Most prison guards are employed without training. Government detention centers for political prisoners, closed to outside inspections, are reportedly worse than the regular prisons. The best information available on the nation's 46 prison establishments is on the main prison in N'Djamena, which is capable of holding 349 inmates but at last count was 249 percent of capacity. During the late 1980s Chad refused the Red Cross access to several thousand Libyans captured in war the previous year. Explanations centered on Libyan refusals to grant similar access to Chadian prisoners. In mid-2002 the prison population reached 3,883, or 46 per 100,000 of the national population.

Sources: LCCS, "Chad: Criminal Justice System," December 1988; Walmsley, *WPPL*, 2003; ICPS, Chad, 2004.

CHAIN GANGS. Immortalized in film and popular culture through such stories as *Cool Hand Luke* (1967) and ***I Am a Fugitive from a Georgia Chain Gang!*** (1932), chain gangs have been sporadically used by various American states during the late nineteenth and early twentieth centuries as an alternative to the physical prison. More a cost-saving venture for poor states with inadequate infrastructure than any type of benevolent alternative, the chain gang was a staple of southern penology in the years following the Civil War.

As early as the late eighteenth century Pennsylvania prisons employed prison labor outside the walls. Clothed in gaudily colored uniforms and chained together, prisoners were the subjects of humiliation, something the Quaker humanitarian groups objected to. At least one observer reported that the convicts were so embarrassed they would have preferred execution. Other states would pass statutes requiring convicts to work at hard labor before the era of the penitentiary. In 1825 Kentucky became the first state to lease out convicted prisoners to private employers. Michigan, Missouri, Alabama, Indiana, Illinois, California, Nebraska, Montana, Wyoming, Oregon, Texas, and Louisiana soon began leasing out inmates as well.

Following the American Civil War a number of Southern states reverted to leasing out inmates to private employers to save money. Because of the exigencies of losing the war, a number of states either could not afford to run a prison or had not even built a penitentiary because the institution of slavery held the most marginalized members of society in lieu of traditional prisons.

According to one early study, by 1923 every state except for Rhode Island had experimented with using chain gangs to improve and build roads. But chain gangs never became an integral part of the penal system of any region outside the South. Throughout much of the early twentieth century chain gangs of stripe-uniformed prisoners alongside armed guards were a common sight in many southern states. The 1920s saw an increased emphasis on chain gang labor to build roads as the automobile rose in popularity, necessitating new and better roads.

By 1886 a study of convict labor by the federal commissioner of labor reported that outside the South, 18 states and territories had provided by law for the working of prisoners sentenced to jail on streets and or public roads. The states of Alabama, Arkansas, Florida, Georgia, Mississippi, North Carolina, Tennessee, and

Texas had passed resolutions that allowed county convict labor to work on public roads. However, in Alabama, Florida, Georgia, Mississippi, and Tennessee authorities had the alternative of hiring or leasing prisoners instead of working them on roads. In 1886 chain gangs were also authorized in California, Colorado, Dakota, Delaware, Illinois, Indiana, Iowa, Kansas, Michigan, Missouri, Montana, Nebraska, Nevada, New Jersey, New Mexico, New York, Utah, and Washington. Most states had provisions for securing chain gang members in chains or a ball and chain. The best explanation why the chain gang was more widely adopted and longer used in the South was the temperate weather in winter and fall.

By 1912 the National Committee on Prison Labor vilified chain gangs as "the last surviving vestige of the slave system," referring to the overwhelmingly black chain gangs. There are no firm statistics, but according to most estimates hundreds if not thousands of chain gang members died from malnutrition, physical abuse, or being shot while trying to escape.

Rules governing chain gangs varied from state to state. For example, a Texas prisoner could avoid labor by paying one dollar per day. Alabama prisoners were expected by law to be chained or shackled and guarded while on work details. Inmates served anywhere from several weeks to a decade on chain gangs. Sleeping arrangements were as fraught with danger as working conditions. In many inmate camps chain gang members were confined in caged wagons, with only a night bucket, a container of water, and a stove to accommodate their needs. In some cases up to 18 prisoners were shackled together in cages measuring 8 feet by 18 feet. Despite several campaigns to provide oversight of the chain gangs and a number of high-profile abuse cases, little if any legislation was endorsed to protect chain gang members. It was only following the furor of **Robert Burns**'s escape from a Georgia chain gang, chronicled in the book *I Am a Fugitive from a Georgia Chain Gang!* and then film in 1932 that any meaningful support for the abolition of chain gangs was garnered. Georgia became the last state to abandon the chain gang in the 1940s. There is little consensus as to how economic chain gangs actually were. Some studies suggest that states saved millions of dollars; others argue that it cost more to maintain chain gangs than prisoners in jails. Clearly by the time chain gangs were disbanded, new automated road-building machinery made the chain gangs counterproductive, except as a form of punishment.

During the "get-tough" 1990s a number of prisons revived the chain gangs. Alabama was the first state to bring it back beginning in 1995. Arizona, Florida, and Iowa followed suit, and six other states had prepared legislation for its return. It was not long before **Amnesty International** and other human rights groups called on the federal government to investigate the abuses of this system, claiming that chain gangs violated the United Nations Standard Minimum Rules for the Treatment of Prisoners. Amnesty International cited chain gangs as "a retrograde step in human rights."

Sources: Jesse F. Steiner and Roy M. Brown, *The North Carolina Chain Gang: A Study of County Convict Road Work* (Westport, CT: Negro Universities Press, 1970 reprint of University of North Carolina Press, 1927); Marilyn McShane, "Chain Gangs," in *Encyclopedia of American Prisons*, eds. McShane and Williams, 1996, pp. 71–73; Christianson, *With Liberty for Some*, 1998.

CHARRIERE, HENRI (1906–1973). Born in southern France, at the age of twenty-five Charriere was convicted of murder. A small-time criminal, he always persisted in maintaining his innocence. Two years later he was sentenced to the dreaded penal colony on French Guiana. During a 12-year period he took part in nine escapes. But none gained more exposure than his escape from **Devil's Island** to freedom in Venezuela in 1945. He chronicled his escape in the international bestseller *Papillon* (butterfly), first published in French in 1969, a quarter-century later. The book was made into the movie of the same name starring Dustin Hoffman and Steve Mc-Queen in 1973. Charriere followed this with *Banco: The Further Adventures of Papillon* in 1973, which details his life in Venezuela after his escape.

Sources: Henri Charriere, *Banco: The Further Adventures of Papillon* (New York: William Morrow, 1973); Crowther, *Captured on Film*, 1989.

CHATEAU D'IF. Immortalized as the setting for the 1844 novel *The Count of Monte Cristo*, by Alexander Dumas, this fortress was built between 1524 and 1531 on a small island in the Bay of Marseille. Unlike the fictional Edmond Dantes of the novel, according to records, no one has made a successful escape from the castle. Although originally designed as a defensive fortress, Chateau d'If was never tested. Instead, the structure was converted into a prison for political and religious prisoners. One source referred to it as a "French **Alcatraz**." More than 3,500 French Protestants, or Huguenots, were imprisoned there, and in 1871 Gaston Cremieux, one of the leaders of the Paris Commune, was executed there. As in most prisons in the seventeenth and eighteenth centuries, prisoners lived according to their standards of wealth. With sufficient wealth one could have a private cell on a higher level, replete with windows and a fireplace. Such amenities came at the prisoner's expense, however. By the end of the 1800s the castle was discontinued as a prison. It made the transition into a national monument and tourist destination by the 1890s.

Source: wikipebia.org/wiki/Chateau_d'If.

CHERRY HILL PENITENTIARY. *See* EASTERN STATE PENITENTIARY

CHILE. Chile was the second South American country to build a penitentiary (following **Brazil**). By 1847 Santiago's prison was in operation, although only partially completed. Prison architects initially seemed to favor the Pennsylvania cellular system. In addition, several **presidios** were used to house prisoners.

Before 1930, penal facilities functioned independently of the federal government. However, legislation in 1930 placed the correctional system under the Ministry of Justice. Under the 1930 penal code, the government called for the construction of a new penitentiary at Santiago, a prison sanitarium for tubercular prisoners at Maipo, and a jail at Santiago that could house 1,000 prisoners. The penal code also required the construction of 40 other jails with a variety of annexes, the enlargement of the penitentiary at Antofagasta, and prisons at Los Andes, Rengo, San Fernando, and Chilean—all these to be completed by 1933. According to a number of sources, the penal system was considered progressive, offering prisoners instruction in a variety of disciplines as well as special courses in the arts, physical culture, and music. Work was usually of the vocational variety rather than purposeless, allowing convicts familiarity with electrical and carpentry equipment.

As of the late 1980s there were 140 institutions holding almost 15,000 inmates.

Institutions are classified according to the length of sentences. For example, prisoners are sentenced to certain institutions if their sentences are 60 days or less; 61 days to 5 years; and sentences longer than 5 years.

There are 23 institutions for women governed by a religious order. Other unique facilities also exist. On Santa Maria Island prisoners work in an agricultural environment with minimal supervision. Although there are no special juvenile institutions, youthful offenders can be sentenced to a special rehabilitation center. In provincial Chile juveniles are kept in special sections of adult prisons. The majority of inmates are either under trial or waiting for it.

Chilean prisons utilize a progressive stage system consisting of four segments. Inmates enter the prison in solitary confinement. At this first stage prisoners serve at least one month with maximum restrictions. At the second stage, prisoners leave solitary confinement and are allowed to contact family and friends, attend classes, and receive some payment for work performed. Gradually in the second stage prisoners can communicate with friends outside the family and receive more pay for work. Living conditions continue to improve until an entire year is concluded at the second stage. At the third stage a prisoner is confined in his cell only at night, enjoys the highest work salary and has maximum autonomy. Conditional release occurs at the final stage based on decisions by judges on periodic visits to penal institutions. If a prisoner fails to behave, each phase can be extended and conditional release can be revoked.

All prisoners sentenced for 61 days to 5 years are expected to work, mainly as a way to reimburse the prison for expenses. Prison labor is used in four different settings, including state use (prison-made goods made for public sale) and public works projects as well as contract work (inmates hired to private contractor but perform work within prison). Prisoners are leased in two ways—either outside to work by day and return at night or under control of the lessee for the entire contract.

With a prison system overcrowded with more than 5,000 inmates, Chile has become the first country in South America to turn to the private sector to repair the prison predicament. In July 2003 the Chilean government began handing out contracts to build and operate ten new prisons capable of holding 16,000 inmates. With a recidivism rate of 60 percent, officials hope this will contribute to a more rehabilitative and safer prison system. Few voices were opposed to **private prisons**, since privatization is such a good deal for the government. Although private prisons will cost slightly higher than the nine dollars per day for inmates in the state prisons, the private prisons will provide a number of services as well, such as better food, clothing, and laundry services.

Sources: Kurian, *WEPP*, 1989; LCCS, "Chile: The Penal System," March 1994; Salvatore and Aguirre, eds., *The Birth of the Penitentiary in Latin America*, 1996; "Can Private Money Ease a Jail Problem," Economist.com, September 11, 2004.

CHILLON, CASTLE OF. The earliest references to this castle can be traced back to 1005. During the past ten centuries Chillon has served as fortress and dungeon. The fortress is located on an islet in the Lake of Geneva measuring 100 by 50 yards. There have been scant renovations to the castle since the fourteenth century. Recent excavations indicate that a subterranean prison was used at one time, with prisoners being lowered into it by rope. By the thirteenth century executions and torture were conducted in the **dungeon**. During the bubonic epidemic of the mid-fourteenth century the Jews of Villenueve were imprisoned and tortured here. Others also suffered in the underground chambers, including witches and religious prisoners. The noted poet Lord Byron visited the prison in 1816 and carved his name in stone in the chamber now known as "Bonivard's prison." Francois Bonivard served several stints in the prison during the conflict between Geneva and the Duke of Savoy in the mid-sixteenth century. Taking literary license, Byron was inspired to write *The Prisoner of Chillon*, in which he embellished Bonivard's story with great aplomb. Bonivard would live another 34 years after his imprisonment while Byron achieved immortality.

Sources: G. Barry Gifford, *The Castle of Chillon and Its Prisoner* (Lausanne: La Tramontane, 1968).

CHINA. The earliest mention of Chinese prisons can be traced back to the writings of Confucius, who noted that the Emperor Fuen VIII used imprisonment in 2000 B.C.E. Another example of the ancient tradition of imprisonment in China was the discovery of a stone tablet dating back to 723 C.E. that noted Buddhist temples were expected to be built near prisons, probably to help in the rehabilitation process. Despite this evidence, it is doubtful these "prisons" were anything more than a cage or a **dungeon** in a castle or fortress.

According to prison authority Norman Johnston, "China was the last of the large national states to reform prisons." Despite sending representatives to various international prison congresses beginning in 1846, Chinese corrections languished behind Western prisons until the twentieth century.

The beginnings of modern Chinese penology can be traced back to 1902, when the government first decreed that vocational workshops should be established for all prisoners sentenced to terms of incarceration. The first model prison was constructed in Beijing (then Peking) in 1909 in hopes that it would become the model for subsequent penitentiaries. Although similar prisons were constructed in the provinces of Fengtien, Hupeh, and Anhui, the onset of the revolution ended this stage of prison reform.

Prison construction was most influenced by Japanese interpretations of Western prison reform, most notably the writings of Japanese reformer Ogawa Jijiruo, who published a book on prison reform in 1906. His prison plans influenced early prison construction in the provinces of Yunnan, Hopei, and Hupei. The most ambitious prison construction began with the Peking First Prison in 1909. It opened in 1912. This prison influenced provincial prison construction, and by 1916 most provinces had opened their versions of the model prison. It is estimated that by the outbreak of the World War I fourteen major prisons and forty minor facilities had been constructed. This coincided with a program to improve China's 1,700 smaller prisons.

Prisons featured a hodge-podge of adaptations from the **Auburn** and **Pennsylvania** systems. Special prison wings were added to existing male prisons to house female and juvenile prisoners. By 1918 there were more than 30 modern prisons. In 1922 the Beijing prison introduced a 24-hour solitary cell system for the first time. That same year reformatory schools for juvenile offenders were established. By 1925 there were 74 prisons built, all inspired by European models and all under the Department of Ministry.

By the 1940s there were three large facilities in Peking and at least one in each provincial capital. In addition, there was a small prison in each district where the magistrate had concurrent judicial functions. The total number of prisons stood at close to 1,700 in China by the mid-1940s.

Early on, Chinese prisons adopted prison labor as one of its mainstays of support. Originally, male prisoners were involved in brick making, blanket and straw hat weaving, the making of canned bean sauce, the manufacture of hairnets, and printing. Prisoners were also in agriculture and in public works construction, such as the building of the Ministry of Justice. Female prisoners were kept busy in gender-stereotyped occupations such as sewing, weaving, and braiding. Compensation for prisoners varied by task, but one third went to the family of the prisoner.

Beginning in 1926 prison officials went through an exhaustive training regimen that included courses in jurisprudence, constitutional law, criminal law, the study of penal rules and administration, methods of identification, police systems, social psychology, hygiene, and prison construction.

By the 1940s Chinese prisons offered a system of rewards for good behavior that could include more frequent visitors and letters, use of personal stationary and underwear, permission to read books from outside the prison library, extra food, and extra compensation for work. Although corporal punishments were not listed, ample evidence shows that unruly prisoners served up to one week in a dark cell.

Following the Communist Revolution in 1949 the prison regime emphasized political education and rehabilitation. According to Terrill, between the 1950s and 1970s this typically included studying the works of Mao Zedong and participating in a three-step process that began with admitting one's guilt for a certain offense, then repenting through a process of self-criticism, and finally resulting in obeying all the rules of the correctional institution and submitting to the authority of the Communist regime. During the subsequent Deng Xiaoping regime, more emphasis was placed on vocational training, education, and preparing to contribute to the Chinese economy.

In the early 1980s the prisons were supervised under the watchful eyes of the people's procurators, who were on site to ensure compliance with the legal code. Prisoners were expected to work eight hours a day, six days a week. For two hours each day prisoners were allowed to study politics, law, state policies, and current events and participate in group discussions. However, they were not prohibited from reading anything not provided by the prison system or speaking dialects that guards could not understand. In addition, inmates were barred from keeping cash, jewelry, or other goods that could be used to curry favor with the guards. Each prisoner could enjoy receiving censored mail but was allowed only one visitor per month.

According to former prisoner and human rights activist Harry Wu, only criminals who have been arrested and sentenced are confined to prisons. Little information is available on China's secret prisons. There is not much difference, in any case, between prisons and labor reform disciplinary production camps. In the early 1990s about 13 percent of criminals were incarcerated in prisons and 87 percent were sentenced to camps. More serious offenders are sentenced to prisons because of the tighter security there. Many of these prisoners are significant political prisoners. Prisoners such as Mao's wife, Kiang Qing, and noted author of *Life and Death in Shanghai* Cheng Nina served stints in prison.

By the late 1980s most Chinese prisoners were sentenced to hard labor. There were two categories of hard labor. For a criminal penalty imposed by the court system, the sentence would result in "reform through labor," which could mean any fixed number of years. However, "re-education through labor" was a sentence from outside the court system typically imposed on sentences of three or four years. Most prisoners of either category worked at the same camps and factory prisons. Each Chinese prison has an alternate production unit name. For example, Beijing No. 1 Prison is also referred to as Beijing Plastic Factory; likewise Hunan Province No. 2 Prison is also known as Hunan Heavy Truck Factory. In 1991 it was estimated that China had between 1,000 and 1,500 prisons. Prison populations averaged between 200 and 5,000 inmates. Using 400 to 500 inmates as an average figure, this would translate into a population of between 500,000 and 700,000.

Any discussion of Chinese prisons must take in the 87 percent of prisoners who serve their sentences in Labor Reform Disciplinary Production Camps, or labor reform camps. These are organized along military lines, with prisoners divided into squadrons, companies, battalions, detachments, and general brigades. Squadrons are composed of 10 to 15 prisoners. The Public Security police appoint two prisoners from each squadron to serve as squad leaders. One leader is responsible for "labor production," the other for "thought reform and political education." Companies are considered the basic organizational unit of labor reform camps. Companies are made up of 10 to 15 squadrons. Battalions are composed of 8 to 12 companies, usually totaling more than 1,000 prisoners. Above the battalion is the detachment, which varies in size. Wu suggests that the detachment "corresponds to the county level" of the People's Republic of China (PRC). Each of the previously mentioned levels is governed by a variety of bureaucratic positions manned by prisoners. One estimate in 1991 placed the number of labor reform camps at 600, which would make a total population of 3 to 4 million. However, according to Walmsley, as of 2001 the prison population was about 1.4 million, or 111 per 100,000 of the national population. Given the paucity of information, the difference in these figures probably reflects the confusion over the nomenclature of the various prison regimes.

Prisoners are given opportunities to trim their sentences by demonstrating repentance and performing meritorious service. In order to receive any reduction prisoners have first to serve one half of their sentences or at least ten years of a life sentence.

By the end of 2004 China reported a prison population of 1,549,000. This figure includes only sentenced prisoners. Of the country's 679 penal institutions, China reported that 30 were devoted to juveniles. Currently the Ministry of Justice handles all sentenced prisoners, and the Ministry of Public Security is responsible for pre-trial detainees. According to the United Nations, taking into account only sentenced prisoners, China's most recent prison rate would be 119 per 100,000 of the national population.

Sources: Jerome Alan Cohen, *The Criminal Process in the People's Republic of China, 1949–1963* (Cambridge: Harvard University Press, 1968); Hungdah Chiu Shao-Chuan Leng, *Criminal Justice in Post-Mao China* (Albany: State University of New York Press, 1985); LCCS, "China: The Penal System," July 1987; Hongda Harry Wu, *Laogai—the Chinese Gulag* (Boulder, CO: Westview Press, 1992); Terrill, *World Criminal Justice Systems*, 1999; Johnston, *Forms of Constraint*, 2000; Dikotter, *Crime, Punishment, and the Prison in Modern China*, 2002; Walmsley, *WPPL*, 2003.

CLASSIFICATION. The first steps toward the classification of prisoners took place in the late eighteenth and early nineteenth centuries. However, as early as the thirteenth century LeStinche Prison in Florence, Italy was separating prisoners by age and gender. Other early prisons, Amsterdam and Ghent, also developed classification systems segregating serious offenders from misdemeanants. Classification was given its greatest worldwide push during the Enlightenment of the early eighteenth century when reformers argued that prisons should be more humane, and the best strategy was to punish better rather than harsher. Before the cellular concept became widespread, prisoners were typically housed together in one large disorderly room, regardless of offense, gender, age, and mental state. The only classification between prisoners at this stage was based along class lines since the richer inmates could afford better accommodations.

The adoption of the Declaration of Principles at the 1870 **National Prison Congress** put the progressive classification of prisoners at the forefront of the prison reform agenda. Important strides toward this goal were made at the **Elmira Reformatory** in 1876. This institution was dedicated to first-time offenders between the ages of 16 and 30.

The popularity of **Cesare Lombroso**'s views on hereditary criminality in the 1880s led a number of scholars to perform research at various prisons where they could examine a "captive audience." According to Scott Christianson "the emerging use of prisons as a social laboratory" would have "enormous ramifications for the study of eugenics, psychology, intelligence testing" and the like. Subsequently scientists tested their notions of intelligence, criminality, and heredity in prisons and a number of them would develop systems of criminal classification. A San Quentin prison chaplain, August Drahms, used statistics to support his scheme for a classification system that hinged on three types of inmates. He labeled them either "instinctive criminals," who were "predisposed to crime," "habitual criminals," whose inspiration was drawn from their societal milieu, or "single offenders," whose offenses were typically out of character. A number of prisons followed suit with other classification studies.

During the 1920s and 1930s the National Crime Commission and the National Commission on Law Observance and Enforcement urged the adoption of new classification procedures. A number of observers have compared the new strategy to the earlier reformatory ideas. According to prison historian John W. Roberts, "classification during the Reformatory Era was rudimentary, superficial, and [was] used primarily for maintaining internal discipline." It was not until the 1930s that the classification of prisoners included specialized screening and individualized treatment. Classification was used to determine the security level of each inmate in order to place the individual in the proper environment. A number of prisons created institution classification committees made up of a warden, captain, chief psychologist and medical officer, chaplain, and education director. As a result of the influence of classification new institutions were needed if offenders were to be separated by category. Therefore a new generation of prisons were built including psychiatric hospitals, minimum and medium security institutions, and farms for narcotic addicts. While the age of scientific penology augured for an entirely new prison system, a number of prisons gave classification little credit and maintained the primitive conditions of earlier years.

By the mid-nineteenth century a number of prisons were establishing reception and diagnostic centers where new prisoners were subjected to a battery of tests and examinations in order to classify each inmate. The Medical Model era introduced more complex and sophisticated classification techniques. As Roberts has noted,

Professor Herbert Quay, for example, developed a typology that placed inmates in one of five personality categories, including inadequate-immature, neurotic-conflicted, unsocialized-aggressive, socialized or subcultural, and subcultural-immature.

The popularity of supermax prisons in the 1980s and 1990s represents one of the latest trends in classification. Prisons such as California's Pelican Bay, the federal prison at Marion, Illinois, and a facility in Florence, Colorado have been opened to house America's most dangerous inmates and the growing number of gang members, with security provided by closed-circuit televisions and computerized locking technology. A return to the earlier supermax strategy first attempted at **Alcatraz Prison** has led to a decline in assault rates on guards. Every possibility has been considered in order to prevent physical contact between staff and inmates.

Sources: Deford, *Stone Walls*, 1962; Sullivan, *The Prison Reform Movement*, 1991; Roberts, *Reform and Retribution*, 1997.

CLINK PRISON. London's Clink Prison has the distinction of giving the prison lexicon one of the most famous monikers for prisons, as in "being thrown into the clink." Others suggest the term was derived from the "clinking and clanking" of prisoners held in chains, fetters, and manacles. Some historians date the Clink's origins to 816 Saxon England, when a synod decreed that all ecclesiastical facilities must maintain space to confine disobedient monks. Considered the lord of the manor, the bishop of Winchester had the power to punish malefactors in his domain. By 860 the bishop of Winchester had established a "Colledg of Preestes [*sic*]" for this purpose. Beginning in the twelfth century, the bishop of Winchester operated a prison inside his palace on the Thames riverside in Southwark. Its walls held both prostitutes and anyone who disobeyed his rules for the almost two-dozen brothels that operated along the Bankside. By the sixteenth century the Clink had made the transition to catering mostly to heretics who took positions counter to the bishop's views. In the following centuries it was used exclusively as a debtors' prison. By the 1730s it had become so deteriorated that it held only two prisoners. The prison was burned down during the Gordon riots of 1780 and was never reconstructed.

Sources: E. J. Burford, *A Short History of Clink Prison* (Clink Prison Museum, London: n.d.); E. J. Burford, *In the Clink* (London: New English Library, 1977).

CLINTON PRISON (USA). Better known by its city location of Dannemora than the county location of Clinton, New York, the origins of Clinton Prison can be traced back to the 1840s, when it became New York State's third prison. In order to facilitate a work regimen revolving around iron mining, it was necessary to modify the **Auburn** silent system; however, though the modifications made the job safer for all concerned, the labor proved less than productive financially. Maine's prison soon joined Clinton in the 1850s as two rare examples of silent system prisons that allowed talking at labor "when necessary." Vermont's prison joined the other two in abandoning lockstep marching as well. In the 1890s an investigation revealed that despite legislation prohibiting brutal disciplinary punishments, a wide range of physical punishments at the prison were still in use, including paddling, solitary confinement in dark cells, and being strung up from the floor by one's thumbs. On the brighter side, it was also in the 1890s when Clinton Prison physician J. B. Ransom made the "first permanent contribution to the treatment of tuberculosis in prison." During this era is was estimated that 45 percent of all prison deaths were the result of this disease. While conducting experiments on tubercular patients Ransom found that the higher altitude and better air in the Adirondack Mountains surrounding the prison made it an ideal destination for other patients, and soon other New York prisons were transferring tubercular patients upstate to Dannemora. Once regarded as the "Siberia of New York," Clinton Prison received its greatest notoriety in 1929 following a bloody prison uprising that left three inmates dead and a number of guards and prisoners wounded. The National Guard was called out in order to end the disturbance.

Source: McKelvey, *American Prisons*, 1977.

COLDBATH FIELDS PRISON. The Coldbath Fields **House of Correction** was built in 1794. Situated just north of the **Bridewell**, this prison earned a reputation for its punitive regime. Inmates were punished with a variety of techniques. Some were force to carry cannon balls, other did three-to-four hour shifts on the **treadmill**, which could accommodate up to 340 prisoners at once. Prisoners could receive only one letter per month and one visit every three months. The staff and management were considered corrupt, even for an era in which this behavior was common. By the time Governor Thomas Aris was replaced in 1799, conditions had deteriorated to the point that the facility was referred to as the Steel, in homage to the French **Bastille**.

The institution was expanded to hold 1,500 prisoners under the administration of the second governor, George Chesterton. In 1834 a regime of total silence under threat of leg-irons, solitary confinement, and a bread-and-water diet was adopted. It had become so overcrowded by 1850 that female prisoners were transferred to Tothill Fields Prison. By 1860 there were 10,000 criminals were passing through Coldbath each year. The prison suffered increasing overcrowding in the following decade, with half of the 1,700 prisoners detained for failure to pay small fines and petty offences. The prison was finally closed in 1885 and then completely torn down four years later.

Source: Herber, *Criminal London*, 2002.

COLDITZ PRISON. A fortress has stood on top of a precipice looking over the Mulde River since 1014. It has made the transition over the centuries from fort to castle to hunting lodge. By the nineteenth century it was serving as a poorhouse and then as an asylum. When Adolf Hitler came to power in 1933, he transformed it into a labor camp for Communist opponents. On the face of it Colditz seemed a perfect location for a high-security prison. When Colditz received its first British prisoners of war in 1940, its 12-foot-thick walls and 90-foot buildings seemed escape proof. But it was not long before prisoners found this ancient facility vulnerable from within, with its simple locks and attics that connected buildings. A German contingent of 200 soldiers offered the security of a ratio of almost one to one with the prison population. Before the end of the war Germany's only high-security prison camp became famous for its 174 escape attempts, of which 32 were successful, or in the parlance of the POWs, "homeruns." Between 1946 and 1950

Colditz was transformed once more into a labor camp, except this time by the Soviets to hold non-Communists and other "undesirables."

Sources: Reid, *The Colditz Story*, 1952; Chancellor, *Colditz*, 2001.

COLOMBIA. Colombia is considered along with **Cuba**, one of the last nations in Latin America to embark on any meaningful prison reform. This began in 1934 with the passage of Decree 1405, which established the ideological underpinnings of the new prison system. The decree elucidated a number of purposes, including the use of incarceration as a tool for "moral regeneration," mandatory work as the best medium of correction, and a treatment regime according to the classification of individual inmates.

A Department of Prisons was soon inaugurated to control a prison system that in 1935 consisted of nine penitentiaries, eighteen *carceles* (jails), one for each judicial district, two agricultural colonies, and a number of local jails. By 1940 new penitentiaries were erected at Picota and Palmira. An agricultural colony at Aciacas soon followed. Other facilities were modernized, including Bogota's Penitenciaria Central and Reformatorio de Menores. Much of the credit for the reforms, in Bogota in particular, goes to Dr. Francisco Bruno, the director of prisons in 1936. These reforms included the establishment of industrial workshops, educational facilities, modern kitchens, and a research institution that would become known as the Instituto de Anthropología y Pedagogía Penitenciaria.

By the 1940s Colombia's penitentiaries were divided into three different categories. The Central Prison in Bogota was considered the only institution in the first category. Architecturally it resembled **Eastern State Penitentiary** in Philadelphia with a number of wings radiating from a central hub. Penitentiaries in the second category included Ibague, Pamplona, and Tunja. The third category consisted of prisons at Cartagena, Manizales, Medellín, Pasto, and Popayan. Complementing this facilities were two agricultural penal colonies at Acacias and Araracuara. A number of prisons were equipped with small spinning and weaving mills, iron works, foundries, and carpentry, mechanical and tailoring shops. Work was mandatory in all institutions.

By the 1980s the Colombian penal code had undergone a number of revisions. But overcrowding was still the major concern. With a capacity to hold 12,000 prisoners, in the early 1980s Colombian prisons were faced with almost triple that number as a result of a rising crime rate and backlog in court cases. Some of the reforms adopted in 1985 were designed to remedy the overcrowding, including the release of 3,000 prisoners who were either waiting for trial or serving sentences of less than two years for minor offenses. By the 1990s the largest maximum-security prison was Bogota's La Picota Prison. Lesser institutions were located in Medellín, Plamira, Ibague, Manizales, Pamplona, Pasto, and Barranquilla. Women were confined exclusively at Tunja and Cuenca. The main centers for juvenile confinement for those aged 14 to 18 were situated in Fagua and Bogota. Rounding out the rest of the prison system in the 1990s are the previously mentioned agricultural penal colonies at Acacia and Araracuara and the jails in each judicial district and municipality, which together represented the largest number of inmates in the prison system. As of mid-1999 the prison system contained 57,068 prisoners, or 153 per 100,000 of the national population.

Sources: Teeters, *World Penal Systems*, 1944; LCCS, "Colombia: The Penal System," December 1988; Jorge Penen Deltieure, "Colombia," in Kurian, *WEPP*, 1989, pp. 69–78; Salvatore and Aguirre, "The Birth of the Penitentiary in Latin America," in *The Birth of the Penitentiary in Latin America*, eds. Salvatore and Aguirre, 1996, pp. 1–43; Walmsley, *WPPL*, 2003.

COMOROS. Maldivians follow the Islamic law, or the sharia. With most punishment limited to fines, compensatory payment, house arrest, banishment to a remote island, and imprisonment, there is little need for any organized prison system or large penal facilities.

Source: LCCS, "Comoros: Penal System," August 1994.

COMPTERS. In medieval London, city sheriffs operated **gaols** (jails) known as compters, supposedly derived from "counter," or the counting and keeping of official records. The compters usually housed misdemeanants, such as debtors, drunks, vagrants, and the like. Compters were also used to hold prisoners when London's principal gaol at **Newgate** was full. The compters earned an unsavory reputation for charging prisoners fees for the most basic necessities.

The Poultry Compter, established in the fourteenth century, was the oldest of the city compters. One observer described its prisoners as "ill-looking vermin," living the most malodorous conditions imaginable. By 1776 Poultry Compter contained 52 debtors, their wives and 163 children. It was torn down in 1817 and replaced by the Whitecross Street Prison, which is considered the last of London's debtor prisons (demolished in 1870).

Other well-known compters were located at Wood Street, Bread Street, and Giltspur Street. Bread Street was built sometime in the fifteenth century and in 1555 was replaced with Wood Street Compter. Burned down during the Great Fire and rebuilt, the Wood Street Compter contained five wards, with prisoners placed according to their wealth. The wealthier were housed on the "Master's Side." In descending order the other wards included the "Knight's Ward," the "Two-Penny Ward," the "Common Ward," and the "Hole" for the most destitute. Inmates such as physicians, attorneys, and artisans could practice their trades from inside the facility. On the other end of the spectrum prisoners were stacked side by side like corpses on the floor of the Hole. Wood Street was closed and replaced by Giltspur Street Compter in 1791.

Source: Herber, *Criminal London*, 2002.

CONGO (BRAZZAVILLE). The Prison Administration of the Congo operates under the Ministry of Justice. In 2002 the small African country had one prison. The most recent figures for the prison population report 918 in 1993, or 38 per 100,000 of the national population.

Source: ICPS, Congo (Brazzaville), 2004.

CONVICT HULKS. With the abrupt interruption of **transportation** of criminals to America by the outbreak of the American Revolution and with few alternatives, Britain's overcrowded prisons forced authorities to search for alternate detention facilities, since the prisons were already so packed. Rather than build new prisons, English authorities came up with a temporary measure that could be used "until the Americans were defeated" and transportation continued to America. Lord North was responsible for drawing up legislation that became known as 16 Geo. III, c. 43, or more commonly as the Hulks Act in 1776. This led to incarcerating some prisoners on derelict warships and merchant vessels, referred to as hulks. The first convict hulk was the *Justitia*, anchored near Woolwich in 1776. During its first 18 months 176 out of the original 632 prisoners perished.

When transportation began to **Australia**, hulks were used to confine prisoners until they sailed. In 1841 there were almost a dozen hulks holding more than 3,600 prisoners. The ships were moored in the Thames River, at Plymouth, Portsmouth, Sheerness, Chatham, and even Bermuda and Gibraltar. Although they were originally envisioned as a temporary practice, this expedient would be used into the mid-1800s. During the heyday of their use, almost 5,000 convicts were imprisoned on hulks in bays and rivers throughout England. Some even confined American prisoners of war captured during the American Revolution on the Hudson River. Some convicts were allowed to work on government projects outside the ship by day, but at night they returned to malodorous conditions featuring poor ventilation, disease, and inadequate sanitation. As late as 1834 the British employed a "juvenile hulk" for inmates classified as the "worst of all." The *Success* was a noted convict hulk that later served in the 1890s and early 1900s as a floating museum or testament to the horrific conditions faced by early prisoners. Most recently New York City officials considered using ships to house inmates to accommodate the overcrowded city prisons.

Convict hulks were not unknown to the United States. Following the 1849 California Gold Rush the city of San Francisco revived the practice. Historian James P. Delgado noted that "ships converted into buildings played an important role in Gold Rush San Francisco." The most prominent of these convict hulks was the *Euphemia*, moored in San Francisco Bay. This former two-masted sailing vessel measured 90 feet long and by February 1850 was welcoming its first prisoners on board. Like many prisons of the period the ship would also hold a healthy contingent of "suspicious, insane, or forlorn persons found strolling about the city at night." In 1853 the state of California employed another prison ship, the *Waban*. However, by the end of the 1850s the conditions on these vessels had deteriorated to such an extent that it was necessary to discontinue this practice, and new jails were constructed on land.

Sources: Shaw, *Convicts and the Colonies*, 1966; James P. Delgado, "Gold Rush Jail: The Prison Ship *Euphemia*," *California History*, Summer 1981, pp. 134–141; Hughes, *The Fatal Shore*, 1987.

CONVICT LEASING. The use of forced convict labor can be found in ancient records dating back at least as far as fifth century B.C. Greece. According to one account from this era, state-owned slaves were leased out to private mining operators to work in silver mines. Up to 10,000 prisoners labored under hazardous conditions, probably resulting in tremendous casualties. Convict labor was used during the Roman Empire and into the Middle Ages. Convicts served as galley slaves and worked in shops in **houses of correction** and **rasphouses**, but it was not until the age of the modern penitentiary that the familiar convict lease system found an environment in which it could prosper and proliferate. Nowhere was this truer than in the United States. Although colonial jails often forced inmates to work, it was not until the opening of the **Walnut Street Jail** in 1790 that prisoner labor was placed at the disposal of outside contractors, who earned their profits from "piece-price labor" accomplished behind prison walls. According to the piece-price arrangement, a private contractor pays the prison an agreed-on price for each completed piece. While the contractor pays for raw materials, inmates work inside the prison and work under the watchful eyes of prison staff. The contract system works a bit differently, although the intent is the same, for both the contractor and the prison to save money and make profits off prisoner labor. According to this system, the contractor still pays for materials but is also responsible for supervising prisoners at work inside prison walls. In return the labor contractors must pay a daily rate for the labor of each convict, which on average is substantially less than they would pay for free labor.

The convict-leasing system diverges from both the piece-price and contract labor agreements on several counts. One of the biggest differences is that in this system prisoners can be taken care of privately inside or outside the prison by contractors. In this system the employer is responsible for clothing, housing, shelter, food, and discipline. The determination of the contractor's fees is based on the number of convicts employed and on the length of their services. According to Alexis Durham III, "The first American leasing arrangement" was signed in Kentucky in 1825.

Although most taxpayers wanted prisons, they did not want to pay for feeding and housing a rapidly growing prison population. When prison officials could not meet the financial obligations necessary for running institutions, they turned to other ideas in order to make prisons self-sufficient. Criminologist Thorsten Sellin suggested that one way to make a profit was to turn "prisoners into penal slaves." Nowhere was this truer than in the post–Civil War Southern states. According to Blake McKelvey, "By 1880 all the former Confederate states and Kentucky as well had surrendered a major part of their criminal populations into the hands of lessees." The widespread adoption of convict leasing in the South was the result of several phenomena. On the one hand, the South had a long tradition of forced labor and slavery, which facilitated the adoption of convict leasing both psychologically and organizationally. In addition, the Civil War had virtually shattered the Southern economy, and even in the war's aftermath there was little financial or public support for a prison-building program. The convict-leasing system represented a marriage of ideas that could work as a stopgap measure in social control until the economy improved.

Life in convict-leasing camps barely came up to standards of simple subsistence. Inmates were confined in portable cages and wooden huts in every imaginable configuration. Water, food, and sanitation were often inadequate. The main overriding concern of lessees was the fear of escapes, which became the main "controlling factor in discipline." Inmates were chained, shackled, and bound with iron balls and chains. Most prisoners left these arrangements only by death or escape. Escape attempts, despite their risks, were a frequent occurrence. According to an 1882 survey, 1,100 prisoners successfully escaped leasing camps in the South over the prior two years. Unfortunately, death was also a frequent visitor as well. The horrible conditions of Southern leasing can be demonstrated by comparing mortality rates with those in Northern prisons. According to McKelvey, the average death rate in 28 Northern prisons was 14.9 per 1,000, compared to 41.3 per 1,000 in the South.

Scandals and public opinion soon took a toll on the existence of convict-leasing systems. When an investigation revealed a 50 percent mortality rate in South Carolina, leasing was abolished in 1885. Similar investigations led to the abandonment of the system in most states, although Alabama and Georgia persisted in its use into the twentieth century. In addition to humanitarian concerns, the growing clout of labor unions contributed to the demise of this practice, challenging the system's unfair competition with the world of free labor.

Sources: Thorsten Sellin, *Slavery and the Penal System* (New York: Elsevier, 1976). McKelvey, *American Prisons*, 1977; Alexis M. Durham III, "Lease System," in *Encyclopedia of American Prisons*, eds. McShane and Williams, 1996, pp. 277–281.

COOK ISLANDS (NEW ZEALAND). The Cook Islands is a self-governing territory protected by the country of New Zealand. The Cook Islands Prison Service operates under the Ministry of Justice. Its only prison is Arorangi Prison, located in Rarotonga. In mid-2003 it held 19 prisoners, or 90 per 100,000 of the national population.

Sources: Kurian, *WEPP*, 1989; ICPS, Cook Islands (New Zealand), 2003.

COSTA RICA. In the 1870s Costa Rica opened two penal colonies for serious offenders on the islands of San Lucas and Coco, off the country's Pacific coast. Other offenders could be exiled or confined to squalid frontier villages. Some observers have likened this early policy to **transportation**. The first steps toward penal reform began with the promulgation of a new penal code in 1880. Based on the **Chilean** code of 1875, despite eliminating **chain gangs** and the death penalty, it never quite lived up to the expectation of penal reformers. In 1885 attempts were made to fund the building of a model penitentiary, and in 1890 an architect visited Europe to study prison construction. Upon his return, plans were approved to build a **panopticon**-style institution near the Palace of Justice, signaling the transition to a prison system with a more urban focus. Both experiments on penal colonies on the islands failed, giving the construction of the new penitentiary even more impetus.

In 1909 the prison received its first inmates, although it was still not completed—the new prisoners would labor to complete it. The Ministry of Government and Police provided prison staff. In 1915 a set of prison regulations was adopted that included classification of prisoners, the production of items for sale, employment of prisoners according to expertise, better sanitary conditions, and visits of physicians and clerics to prisoners. In 1924 this code would be appended. However, politicians lobbied for a stricter regime and once again sent a lawyer to Europe to survey the state of penology. Little resulted from these efforts. By the 1930s minors were hypothetically separated from adults, but they still faced the same insalubrious conditions and overcrowding that plagued the prison. In 1925 a prison was built for women, where they could receive religious and medical counseling. The prison of the Sisters of Good Shephard was considered one of the few shining examples of early penal reform.

In late 2002 there were 26 penal establishments capable of holding 6,032. The most recent reports from 1999 indicate a prison population of 8,526, almost 40 percent of whom were either pre-trial detainees or remand prisoners. This would equal 229 per 100,000 of the national population that year. Among the more prominent facilities are four penal institutions located in the country's central plateau.

There is at least one jail in San Jose and in each of Costa Rica's seven provinces, most operated by the Civil Guard. There are separate maximum-security facilities for men and women, a juvenile facility for males, and another facility for both genders. Prisons include the Central Prison in San Jose, which is dedicated to detainees awaiting trial and to maximum-security prisoners, and the minimum security San Lucas Penitentiary, located on an island in the Gulf of Nicoya. The prison system falls under the direction of the Ministry of Justice and is managed by the Department of Social Adaptation, which is also tasked with hiring guards. The guard-to-prisoner ratio is about 1 to 20. Most training for guards is completed on the job.

Prisoners are not required to work, but they can earn good time and shorten their sentences by entering training programs. Programs such as group therapy, vocational training, and general education are available. Although there are few recreational opportunities, family visits and conjugal privileges are permitted. Radios and other personal property are also allowed. Food and medical care are considered more than adequate.

Source: Henry Giralt, "Costa Rica," in *World Factbook* online; Steven Palmer, "Confinement, Policing, and the Emergence of Social Policy in Costa Rica, 1880–1935," in *The Birth of the Penitentiary in Latin America*, eds. Salvatore and Aguirre, 1996, pp. 224–253, ICPS, Costa Rica, 2003.

CRANK. In the punitive regime that reigned in Victorian prisons, a number of ingenious methods of hard labor were imposed. The most common were probably the **treadmill** and the crank, which was basically a box filled with sand and operated with a handle. The prisoner was expected to turn the handle, which scooped up sand inside the box and then dropped it and then repeated. Cranks were meant to wear out inmates, who were monitored by a ingenious counting device that recorded the number of turns. One prisoner was reputedly sentenced to 10,000 turns per day. In 1898 cranks were outlawed along with the treadmill by act of Parliament.

Sources: Babington, *The English Bastille*, 1972; Herber, *Criminal London*, 2002.

CRAWFORD, WILLIAM (1788–1847). In 1831, Crawford was appointed secretary of the Prison Discipline Society of London. His main charge was to examine prison architecture and prison management systems in America. The reform-oriented secretary had been a stalwart proponent of slavery abolition and penal reform when he toured Philadelphia's **Walnut Street Jail** and **Eastern State Penitentiary** in 1835. Crawford ultimately visited 14 penitentiaries and many local jails. According to Norman Johnston, he was able to clandestinely speak to inmates, enabling him to collect valuable data on discipline, labor practices, medical care, prison construction, and even recidivism. Despite many misgivings, Crawford returned to England most favorable to the solitary regime of the **Pennsylvania system**. However, in his final reports to the Home Secretary he admitted that this system would be too expensive to adopt throughout the country. Crawford found the cruel physical punishments at **Auburn** and **Sing Sing** offensive and the malodorous conditions in Richmond, Virginia's **Panopticon** loathsome.

His support of the Pennsylvania system led England to pass legislation in 1836 that created a five-member board of inspectors to "bring about a uniformity in practice and theory." Two years later the plans were in the works for the construction of a "model prison," which would result in the opening of **Pentonville Prison** in 1842. Crawford rose to prominence with the 1835 publication of *Report on the Penitentiaries of the United States*.

Sources: Christianson, *With Liberty for Some*, 1998; Johnston, *Forms of Constraint*, 2000.

CRAY, JOHN D. (ACTIVE 1820s). Cray was a former Canadian army officer and is credited with introducing lockstep marching and taking part in the formulation of the silent system at **Auburn Prison**. According to W. David Lewis, deputy keeper Cray "devised most of the elaborate techniques which were necessary to maintain the silent system" including the lockstep, downcast eyes, seating arrangements, and the labor regime. Cray ultimately resigned after a clash with warden **Elam Lynds** in 1823 over Cray's attempts to open a school for illiterate inmates and Lynds's propensity for corporal punishment.

Sources: Lewis, *From Newgate to Dannemora, the Rise and Fall of the Penitentiary: 1796–1848*, 1965; McKelvey, *American Prisons*, 1977.

CROATIA. Following Croatia's independence in 1991, efforts were made to improve the prison system. The prison system, or Administration for the Execution of Sentences, falls under the control of the Ministry of Justice. Croatia has 23 penal institutions. There are fourteen district prisons, or county prisons, housing pre-trial and short-sentence detainees, including the facilities at Bjelovar, Dubrovnik, Gospic, Karlovac, Osijek, Pozega, Pula, Rijeka, Sisak, Split, Sibenik, Varazdin, Zadar, and Zagreb. They range in capacity from the 37 at Dubrovnik to 400 at Zagreb. There are six state prisons for those serving sentences of more than six months, including Lepoglava, Pozega, Pozega (females), Turopolje, Lipovica, and Valtura. Lepoglava is the largest with room for almost 900, whereas while the female prison at Pozega can hold less than 50 prisoners. Other institutions include the prison hospital at Lisene Slobode and prisons for juveniles at Pozega and Turopolje. As of mid-1994 the combined population was 3,068. With a prison population of 60 per 100,000 of the general population, during the previous decade it had one of the lowest proportions of prisoners in eastern and central Europe.

As late as 1994 there were no reports of overcrowding, even though the custom of single cells did not pertain here. The largest number in a room or cell was eight. During a prisoner's reception two weeks are taken to classify and place the individual in the appropriate setting. Sanitation, food and medical services are considered adequate, and no limits are placed on writing correspondence. Inmates are permitted up to four visits per month. One feature that is quite exceptional is the practice of allowing inmates to take vacations once a year outside the prison.

The prison staff numbers more than 2,100. Positions are reportedly earned through the training and selection process. Because of the relatively important role played by staff, there are few reports of tensions and conflict behind prison walls. In 1999 a new staff-training center was opened at Lipovica. The greatest obstacle to prison modernization has been the lack of budgetary resources.

Great strides have been made in improving staff and prisoner relations as well as inculcating a sense of humanity. Prisoners are given the opportunity to work beside free residents in factories in Lepoglava, Lipovica, and Pozega. Prisoners staff one public restaurant outside the prison walls of Lepoglava. Inmates are allowed to watch television and are given a number of opportunities to prepare for life on the outside, including "home leaves." There have been few reports of abuses, and human rights groups and organizations are allowed to visit prisoners and prisons. One area of improvement that needs addressing is the lack of maximum-security facilities.

Between 1994 and 2001 the prison population rose from 2,301, or 48 per 100,000 of the national population, to 2,623, or 60 per 100,000. Although it appears crime rates have not increased significantly, public opinion supports a more punitive penal system. The end of the 1990s considered the prison system in full accordance with European prison standards. Most recently the country reported 23 prisons holding 2,852 prisoners, or 64 per 100,000 of the national population. More than one third were pre-trial detainees or remand prisoners.

Sources: Walmsley, *Prison Systems in Central and Eastern Europe*, 1996; Walmsley, *Further Developments in the Prison Systems of Central and Eastern Europe*, 2003; ICPS, Croatia, 2004.

CROFTON, WALTER FREDERICK (1815–1897). Crofton was a visionary penal reformer, parole advocate, and promoter of indeterminate sentencing. He served as commissioner of Irish prisons from 1853 to 1854 and then again in 1869. Constantly searching for better alternatives to traditional imprisonment, Crofton built on a number of **Alexander Maconochie**'s experiments in the Australian penal colonies—most notably introducing the concept of strict supervision of prisoners who had earned tickets-of-leave. This was accomplished by requiring prisoners to submit monthly reports and to avoid any association with known criminals. The police and variors prisoner aid societies were expected to provide surveillance.

Crofton is credited with improving on the **mark system** and developing the so-called **Irish system** of indeterminate sentencing. The Irish system was considered advanced in its day because of its innovative amalgamation of religious, educational, and vocational programs. Inmates who matriculated through the Irish system were expected to proceed through a sequence of stages taking the prisoner through a process of repentance and rehabilitation. Prisoners entered custody in strict solitary confinement before earning enough marks to enter the indeterminate stage that allowed group associations and release under supervision. Foremost among Crofton's strategies, like Maconochie's, was abolishing the flat or fixed sentence, which offered no hope of early release, and replacing it with an indeterminate sentence in which inmates could attain early release through better behavior and self-reform. Although Crofton's ideas were widely heralded, they first found acceptance in the United States before finding wider support in Europe later on. **Zebulon Brockway** would later find inspiration in Crofton's system when he was organizing the **Elmira Reformatory** in the 1880s.

Sources: Phillips and Axelrod, *Cops, Crooks, and Criminologists*, 1996; Roberts, *Reform and Retribution*, 1997.

CRUCIFORM PRISONS. According to prison architectural historian Norman Johnston, cruciform, or cross-shaped, prisons were popular in much of Europe but, except for Canada's **Kingston Penitentiary**, found little support in North America. Built in the 1830s, Kingston Penitentiary was constructed in the shape of a Greek cross, "with three wings devoted to cells and the front wing given over to administration and services." Later on a domed rotunda was added. The cruciform design was a variation of the better-known **radial** design.

Johnston notes that many prisons built after **Pentonville** in 1842 incorporated the cruciform design, featuring "either three or four wings projecting at right angles from a center hall." The first prominent example was England's **Reading County Gaol**, completed in 1844. Countries as varied as China, Colombia, Holland, Hungary, Italy, Japan, Russia, Spain, and Sweden would complete cruciform prisons over the next century. As late as the 1980s England employed the cruciform plan in building new prisons at Hughdown, Sutton, and Swaleside in an effort to facilitate better surveillance of prisoners.

Source: Johnston, *Forms of Constraint*, 2000.

CRUMLIN ROAD PRISON. Originally known as Belfast Prison, Crumlin Road Prison is located on the outskirts of the city center on Crumlin Road. For a number of years its 586 cells made it Northern Ireland's largest prison. Architecturally, its radial design was modeled after **Pentonville Prison**. Crumlin Road Prison received its first prisoners in 1845. Since the Irish troubles began in the first decades of the twentieth century, the prison has held a number of political prisoners and terrorists. In the process it has earned a reputation for escape attempts, riots, and physical violence that has left a number of prisoners and staff dead or badly injured.

Sources: Ryder, *Inside the Maze*, 2000; Louise Purbrick, "The Architecture of Containment," in *The Maze*, ed. Wylie, 2004, pp. 91–110.

CUBA. According to recent reports, Cuba has one of the largest per capita prison systems in the world, with almost 100,000 prisoners housed in 200 prisons and labor camps spread around the island. According to letters smuggled out by imprisoned dissidents, conditions are marked by inadequate health care, physical and mental abuse, and barely edible food. If the 2003 report by the Cuban Commission on Human Rights and National Reconciliation is accurate, there are 100,000 prisoners on an island with 11.3 million people, a ratio of 888 inmates per 100,000 people.

First steps toward modernizing Cuban corrections were taken in 1938 when a new penal and penitentiary system was inaugurated. Under the new legislation a number of new preventive and detention institutions were established, including agricultural colonies, workshops, hospitals, and asylums. By the mid-1940s Cuba had 6 prisons, each located in a provincial capital; 13 jails; and 2 national penitentiaries, 1 for men on the Isle of Pines, and 1 for women at Guanabaccoa. The Guines prison, the provincial prison in Havana, could house 2,000 inmates, whereas the national penitentiary on the Isle of Pines could accommodate twice that number.

All the early institutions called for individual treatment, with congregate work regimen by day and solitary cells by night. In addition, a **mark system** was implemented, leading in some cases to parole. Labor was obligatory, allowing inmates to earn wages to pay for their maintenance to earn a stake that would be given them upon release. By the 1940s Cuba averaged four thousand prisoners annually, or 1 per 1,000 of the population.

According to Human Rights Watch and most other authorities, little information on current conditions is available. Most information is obtained from current and former prisoners, prisoners' relatives, and human rights groups. In 1988 almost 35,000 inmates were housed in Cuban prisons, not including military prisons.

Most evidence suggests that Cuban prison conditions became progressively worse after Fidel Castro came to power in 1959. Conditions would not improve for another 25 years. Prison conditions remain grim, with the paucity of food, medical care, and sanitation in part reflecting the extreme shortages and economic deterioration that have plagued the country following the downfall of the Soviet Union. Estimates of the number of political prisoners range from 500 to 2,000 individuals. They are often housed with common criminals, leading to violence against political prisoners egged on by guards.

According to Jesus Hernandez Cuellas, sociologist Juan Clark noted that Cuba's largest number of political prisoners, 60,000, was achieved in the 1960s. But by the mid-1970s, **Amnesty International** estimates, perhaps one third had been freed. Prior to the Castro regime the highest number of political prisoners was the 5,000 prisoners arrested between 1929 and 1933 during the crackdown by dictator Gerardo Machado. By comparison, dictator Fulgencio Batista held about 500 political prisoners between 1952 and 1958.

Information on the Cuban prison system has been difficult to come by since the Cuban revolution. However, a 1988 delegation from the Institute for Policy Studies was given unprecedented access, of course under the inevitable restrictions. The committee was allowed to visit six prisons and a work camp. Among the group's findings was that the main purpose of the penal system was to reintegrate prisoners into civilian life. While incarcerated, prisoners were remunerated for and involved in productive labor, where it was hoped they would gain technical skills necessary for the post-release world. Political education and discipline were inculcated as well. According to the visitors, prison officials shared a strong faith in their mission.

Among the most negative finds were complaints of solitary and unsanitary confinement, beatings with rubber hoses and sticks, infrequent visits and mail privileges, and lack of ventilation. Praise was reserved for remuneration for working, the availability of jobs (up to 85 percent), the practice of conjugal visits, educational instruction, little prisoner-on-prisoner violence, and the availability of medical care, physical therapy, and outpatient services.

According to the team, the most exceptional prison visited was the Western Provinces Women's Prison in Havana, which they described as a "model prison." Here they found 600 prisoners incarcerated under humane and hygienic conditions. Although anecdotal evidence suggests Cuba has a low crime rate (no statistics are available), the number of prisoners remains very high; most evidence suggests that prisoners serve "extraordinarily long sentences," which in the worst of cases means years in poorly lit and ventilated cells under overcrowded conditions and with infrequent visitors and little access to the outdoors.

In March 2004 Cuba granted the first international media access to Cuban prisons in 15 years. However, this was seen as a ploy to discredit criticism about prison conditions shortly before the United Nations human rights body was to vote on Cuba's rights records. Reporters on this occasion were given limited freedom to examine the freshly painted halls in the hospital wards of the Combinado del Este prison for men and the Manto Negro Western Women's Prison, both in Havana.

The most recent estimates of Cuba's prison population date to 2003. According to criminologist Nils Christie of Oslo University, there were as many as 55,000 prisoners, which would represent 487 per 100,000 of the national population. This represents a significant increase from the estimates of 33,000 in 1997, at 297 per 100,000.

Sources: Israel Castellanos, "The Evolution of Criminology in Cuba," *Journal of Criminal Law and Criminology*, May–June 1933, pp. 218–229; Institute for Policy Studies, "Cuban Prisons: A Preliminary Report," in *Prisons around the World*, eds. Carlie and Minor, 1992, pp. 31–37; Jesus Hernandez Cuellas, "Chronicle of an Unforgettable Agony: Cuba's Political Prisons," *Contacto* Magazine, September 1996, pp. 1–5, www.fiu/edu~fcf/estoria.presidio; Nancy San Martin, "Cuba's Many Prisons May Hold 100,000," *Miami Herald.com*, posted September 22, 2003; Walmsley, *WPPL*, 2003; ICPS, Cuba, 2004; Anita Snow, "Cuba Gives a Rare Look inside Walls of 2 Prisons," *Houston Chronicle*, April 2, 2004, 27A.

CYPRUS. Cyprus is fortunate to have one of the lowest crime rates in Europe, with most punishments for criminal convictions taking the form of fines. The majority of prisoners are incarcerated in the Nicosia Central Prison. The prison population is low, typically under 300. In 1990, for example, the Republic of Cyprus recorded 260 inmates, one quarter of whom were aliens (while they comprised only 1 percent of the population). Many were involved in the Middle Eastern drug trade. By most accounts, Cypriot prisons are relatively humane and offer adequate nutrition and health care. Family members are accorded monthly visits, and legal representatives are not limited in the number of visits. As of 2003 the prison population was 355, excluding the unrecognized Turkish Republic of Northern Cyprus—a ratio of 50 per 100,000 of the national population. Prison numbers have declined since 2001, but they have more than doubled from figures a decade ago.

Sources: Kurian, *WEPP*, 1989; LCCS, "Cyprus: The Criminal Justice System," January 1991; Walmsley, *WPPL*, 2003; ICPS, Cyprus, 2004.

CZECHOSLOVAKIA. *See* CZECH REPUBLIC

CZECH REPUBLIC. Prior to World War II, Czechoslovakia had established a relatively progressive prison system. The prison and its progressive regime had already existed under Hungarian administration, and after the creation of Czechoslovakia from the ruins of the Austro-Hungarian Empire at the Treaty of Versailles in 1919, the old system was adopted by the new government.

During the early twentieth century the prison system saw the development of a rudimentary classification system and employees selected through a civil service process that inculcated a modicum of training prior to service in the prisons. Staff members served a one-year probationary period. A system of tenure and promotions was based on employees taking advantage of continuous in-service training programs. All prisoners, except for political prisoners, were expected to work daily, allowing them to earn a wage according to their skills and accomplishments. A percentage of the wage went to the state for the prisoner's expenses, while the remainder was set aside for release. Any goods manufactured by the prison were handled by the **state-use system.**

As late as the 1940s the prison system still used the Leopoldov structure, originally built in 1669 to defend against the Turkish invaders but used as a prison for more than a century. Despite this outdated facility, most officials cite Czechoslovakian facilities prior to the war as some of the better prisons in Europe. At the time of the Nazi invasion, the penal system was composed of six prisons for offenders serving sentences of one year to life. Two were for first-time offenders at Plzen and Leopoldov. Two were used for incorrigibles and were located at Kartouzy and Ilava. A separate prison for offenders who were chronically ill or invalid was located in Mirov. There was a separate institution for women at Repy, outside Prague. There were also two were two reformatories for boys. One of these was the Reformatory and Penal Institute at Mikulov for boys under the age of 21 and serving sentences under 6 months; more serious youthful offenders were housed at the Komesky Institute at Kosice, which was considered a state reformatory for criminal miscreants.

In addition to the 6 major prisons were 37 prisons attached to the courts of the counties for prisoners under detention and for individuals serving sentences under 1 year. The largest of these was that of the Prague Criminal Court, which could hold more than 800 inmates. There were also 379 prisons connected to the District Police Courts for prisoners under remand or those serving sentences from 12 hours to 1 month.

In the aftermath of the havoc and disruption caused by the war, prison conditions deteriorated, particularly those in the remand, or detention, facilities, where conditions were primitive and medical care haphazard at best. In stark contrast to an earlier era, prisoners as late as 1979 were being charged a daily rate for maintenance—this to be paid after release. Most of the sixteen remand prisons had been built before World War II and some even before World War I. During the Cold War, conditions in many of the prisons worsened after the political turmoil of 1968. Educational programs were slashed, and prisoners were limited to one library book and one newspaper per week. In most cases the library books were collections of speeches by Communist Party officials. The abuse of political prisoners was common. Shortly before the end of the Cold War, the penal institutions, still referred to as corrective educational facilities, were not well known. However, the most publicized were located at Prague-Pankrac, Bory-Plzen, Litomerice in Bohemia, Mirov and Ostrava in Moravia, and Leopdoldov in Slovakia. As late as 1987 the prison system was administered by the governments of the Czech and Slovak socialist republics through the ministries of justice.

In 2004 the Czech Republic reported 35 penal institutions, with a capacity to hold more than 15,000 prisoners. Since the end of the socialist regime a number of offenses, such as leaving the country, were decriminalized. Attempts have been made to remove the former influence of ideology from the legal and penal systems and to introduce a number of measures to protect human rights.

Of the 35 institutions, 9 are mainly for pre-trial detainees and 13 for sentenced prisoners. The remaining 7 facilities are devoted to various categories of female and juvenile offenders. According to Roy Walmsley, Czech incarceration numbers are proportionately higher than incarceration rates in neighboring countries such as **Hungary, Poland,** and **Slovakia.** Overcrowding is more comparable to the figures of **Belarus** and **Romania.**

As in other central and eastern European prisons, most individuals are forced to share cells, with individual confinement reserved for segregation and punishment. Most common are cells housing four to eight prisoners. Some dated facilities, however, confine up to 20 inmates in one cell. This is a consequence of the reliance on older structures such as Valdice, constructed originally as a monastery in 1627, before making the transition to a prison in the 1850s. Other outmoded facilities include Litomerice (1700s) and Mirov (1852).

Over the past decade sanitation, food, and prisoner accommodations have been upgraded, but the prisons are still plagued by insufficient staff. Kitchen facilities vary widely. One facility in Prague offers eleven different types of food each day; in other prisons no special diets are available. Every institution has its own medical center, with access to at least one doctor and three nurses for every 500 prisoners.

In 2001 the Czech Republic was operating 35 prisons; of these one third were dedicated to pre-trial detainees and 21 for mostly sentenced prisoners. Between 1994 and 2001 six new prisons were added to the system. Since 1994 there has been a remarkable drop in the number of pre-trial detainees. At the end of 2004 the prison population stood at 18,442, or 181 per 100,000 of the national population. In the 1990s a number of riots and disturbances occurred as a result of overcrowding. In recent years a slight reduction in the number of prisoners has reflected the increased emphasis on conditional sentences. The largest prisons in the system, holding more than 1,000 inmates, include Plzen, Valdice, Prague-Pankrac, and Vinarice.

Sources: Georges de Fiedorowicz, "The Prison System in the Czechoslovak Republic," Prague: Ministry of Justice, 1930; Georges de Fiedorowicz, "The Educational Aspects of the Prison System in Czecholslovakia," in *School and Society* 47 (April 1938), pp. 513–514; LCCS, "Czechoslovakia: Penal System," August 1987; Walmsley, *Prison Systems in Central and Eastern Europe*, 1996; Walmsley, *Further Developments in the Prison Systems of Central and Eastern Europe*, 2003; Walmsley, *WPPL*, 2003; ICPS, Czech Republic, 2004.

D

DANCE, GEORGE THE YOUNGER (1740–1825). Better known as George Dance the Younger to distinguish him from his equally esteemed father George Dance the Elder, both were eighteenth-century English architects. Dance the Elder had been surveyor to **Newgate Prison** until resigning because of poor health in 1768. The Younger had been assistant surveyor and was immediately tabbed to replace his father. During his tenure as prison surveyor he completely redesigned the infamous prison in 1769. In the renovation ventilated privies were added, but the complete cellularization of the felons' ward was retained. Dance reconfigured Newgate so that there was more complete division between men and women.

Following the Gordon anti-Catholic riots of 1780 a number of prisons and rioters demolished **compters**. Dance was selected to reconstruct the Southwark Compter, which he would do in 1785, adding individual privies to the felons' cells in the process. He would later also provide designs for the Giltspur Street Compter (1787) and the Whitecross Street Debtors' Prison.

Source: Evans, *Fabrication of Virtue*, 1982.

DANNEMORA PRISON. *See* CLINTON PRISON (USA)

DARTMOOR PRISON (UK). During its almost 200 years Dartmoor has earned a reputation that has been compared to **Alcatraz** and **Devil's Island**. It has been home to a diverse lot, including murderers and other malefactors, as well as political prisoners such as Sinn Fein leader and later Irish president Eamon de Valera. The construction of Dartmoor Prison began in 1806. Supervised by architect Daniel Alexander during its construction between 1806 and 1809, it was initially known as Dartmoor Depot. Since timber resources were scarce on the moors, the prison was built with moorstone and granite. It was initially designed to incarcerate French soldiers captured during the Napoleonic Wars. The institution was capable of holding 10,500 prisoners under the watchful eyes of almost 2,000 guards. Eighteen-foot granite walls protected the one-mile-square circumference of the facility. Two more walls were constructed inside the larger walls, enclosing seven two-story prison buildings. Following the War of 1812, one building housed black American inmate captives, and the whites were crammed into four other buildings.

In the late 1850s Dartmoor housed more than 1,100 inmates. Civilians, many of whom were ex-military pensioners, soon replaced military guards. Officials favored the **silent system** combined with solitary confinement at night. Welsh prisoner David Davies was one of the more curious inmates of this period. His compulsion to rob church offertory boxes led him to a number of stints in the prison, where it was said he was so familiar with sheep that he recognized individual sheep by name. Under the administration of English prison chairman **Joshua Jebb**, attempts were made at rehabilitation with a combination of kindness and cruelty. For good behavior prisoners could grow their hair and beards and write more letters. Food was reportedly so plentiful that the inmate's children came daily to bring home leftovers to the family. When **Edmund du Cane** took over the nation's prison system from Jebb, discipline became much more brutal, using methods such as bread-and-water diets and corporal punishment with the "cat-o'-nine-tails" and birch rod.

During World War I the prison was virtually emptied of prisoners so they could serve as fodder for the British Army. By the end of the war over 1,000 conscientious objectors had taken their places. In subsequent years conditions improved, but convicts still had to spend four years on good behavior before they could receive newspapers and smoking privileges. The prison suffered several serious riots. In 1932 nearly 200 prisoners went on the rampage and burned down the Governor's Office before police and army units were able to quell the violence.

At the start of English participation in World War II in 1939, Dartmoor contained 300 prisoners, a number of whom were members of the Irish Republican Army. A number of inmates were allowed to enlist in the services during the war, with one receiving the Victorian Cross for bravery. Military prisoners joined those who stayed behind, but the administration was run by an ex-military officer ready to govern with an iron hand. To suppress the growing number of assaults on correctional staff, corporal punishment by means of the cat-o'-nine-tails was implemented. In 1945 Dartmoor admitted its first **Borstal** boys, young men between the ages of 16 and 21.

As Dartmoor moves into the twenty-first century, it has undergone a transformation, which has included more showers for inmates, with no restrictions on use, and provision of a toilet, hand basin, and central heating in each cell. Roughly 140 officers, including more than a dozen women, patrol the units. Today it is used as a Category B and C Training Prison. The lower-grade C inmates are allowed to work outside the prison, where they can earn a wage to pay for luxuries in the prison canteen. Since the prisoners are not allowed to handle money, however, the wages are kept on the books. Trades training in bricklaying, plastering, computers, and electronics are available, and prisoners are encouraged to pursue hobbies ranging from making models to caring for caged birds.

Sources: Justin Athol, *Prison on the Moor* (London: John Long Limited, 1953); James, *A Glimpse of Dartmoor Prison*, 1995.

DAVIS, KATHERINE BEMENT (1860–1935). The daughter of a well-known educator, Davis became a penologist and later the first woman to fill a cabinet post in New York City government. An early and active promoter of educational advancement for women, after attending Vassar College and receiving her Ph.D. in 1900 from the University of Chicago, she returned to New York. The following year she was appointed the first superintendent of the Reformatory for Women at Bedford Hills. Davis went on to make her mark as an innovator in women's penology by introducing a number of new penological concepts, such as the psychiatric assessment of inmates, which she pursued at the Bedford Hills facility. Anticipating the "medical model" that would emerge decades later, Davis established a diagnostic laboratory, which allowed sociologists, psychologists, and psychiatrists to study prisoners in an academic setting. Davis was an active reformer during the Progressive era, leading to her appointment as commissioner of corrections for the city of New York City, the first woman to hold the position at the municipal level. She led the campaign to reform the prison system, attacking the problem of drug trafficking, separating prisoners by gender, improving sanitation, food, and medical care, and opening up resources for prisoner educational advancement. Despite resistance from prison hardliners, her endeavors to gain more consistent management of prisoners resulted in New York's state legislature putting its stamp of approval on the creation of the New York City Parole Commission in 1915. As the Progressive era reached its apogee of reform in 1918, Davis was ushered out of office but continued to promote social reform until she died twelve years later.

Sources: Sullivan, *The Prison Reform Movement*, 1990; Marilyn D. McShane, "Katherine Bement Davis," in *Encyclopedia of American Prisons*, eds. McShane and Williams, 1996, pp. 141–142.

DEMETZ, FREDERIC-AUGUSTE (1796–1873). Demetz was a French magistrate and penal reformer. Several years after **Alexis de Tocqueville** and Gustave de Beaumont visited American prisons, Demetz along with the architect **Guilluame Abel Blouet** were sent to America by the French government to verify the findings of the earlier visitors. They published their findings in an 1837 report, *Rapports sur les pénitentiers des Etats-Unis*. In this joint effort the authors came out in favor of the **Pennsylvania system** and its separate regime. According to Norman Johnston, the authors delivered model blueprints for an **Auburn**-style prison (based on Canada's **Kingston Penitentiary**) and one for the Pennsylvania system (**John Haviland**'s Trenton Penitentiary), both without attribution.

In later years Demetz was drawn to the problems inherent in confining youthful offenders, many of whom were confined with adult felons. Demetz, along with the aforementioned Blouet, de Tocqueville, and de Beaumont were instrumental in establishing the **Mettray Colony** (it closed in 1939) for children. Johnston suggests that Mettray may have influenced the development of the **telephone pole design**.

Source: Johnston, *Forms of Constraint*, 2000.

DEMOCRATIC REPUBLIC OF THE CONGO. Formerly known as Zaire, The Congo's Prison Services are under the Ministry of Justice. In 2004 there were 198 prison institutions holding an estimated 30,000 prisoners. The main prison is located in Kinshasa. According to recent figures, its 2,598 prisoners made the prison 173.2 percent of its official capacity of 1,500.

Sources: Kurian, "Zaire," *WEPP*, 1989; ICPS, Democratic Republic of the Congo, 2004.

DENMARK. The Danish penal system has evolved following the reform implemented by the First Danish Criminal Code of 1866. The modern penal code can be traced back to 1930, when corporal and capital punishment were abolished, as was imprisonment at hard labor. In addition, prisons for juveniles, influenced by the English **Borstal system,** were introduced.

Currently the Danish Department of Prisons and Probation (Direktoratet for Kriminalforsorgen) is organized under the Ministry of Justice and is responsible for the enforcement of all criminal sanctions in Denmark. Under its direction are 14 prisons and 36 local jails. Of the 14 prisons five operate as maximum-security prisons and the remainder are open, minimum-security prisons. With a low incarceration rate there is little need for large prisons; as a result, the largest facility houses 230 inmates. On average each prison accommodates less than 100 inmates.

As prison populations increased in the 1980s and 1990s, Denmark handled the problem by establishing "prison queues," in which convicted and sentenced prisoners would be notified that they would be informed when there was sufficient room to begin the sentence. Determinations were based on the seriousness of the offense, which required some criminals to be immediately incarcerated because they posed an immediate threat to their community.

As of 1993 the total prison rate represented 68 inmates per 100,000, with an average sentence of 6.2 months of imprisonment. Typical incarceration sanctions include the deprivation of liberty (imprisonment) as well as more lenient alternatives. While prison sentences run the gamut of one month to life, most convicts serve rather short sentences, with only 2 percent consisting of two years or longer. Most recently Denmark has joined several other northern European countries, with rare exceptions, in limiting prison sentences to no more than fifteen years. Most recent reports indicate that Denmark has 56 prisons housing 3,908 prisoners. Over the past decade prison numbers have been relatively stable ranging from 66 per 100,000 in 1992 to 72 per 100,000 in late 2003.

Sources: Kurian, *WEPP*, 1989; Zelma W. Henriques, "Treatment of Offenders in Denmark and Brazil," in *Comparative and International Criminal Justice Systems*, ed. Obi Ebbe, 2003, pp. 57–62; Tonry and Frase, eds., *Sentencing and Sanctioning in Western Countries*, 2001; ICPS, Denmark, 2003; Walmsley, WPPL, 2003.

DESMOTERION. In his play *Prometheus Bound*, Aeschylus describes the epic confinement of Prometheus. The title of the Greek play, *Prometheus desmotes,* translates to "Prometheus chained." In fact, Athens had a prison called the *desmoterion,* or "the place of chains." Prisoners in this primitive facility were given some freedom of movement, but they were probably more often chained, fettered, or held in stocks, neck braces, or other devices that restricted movement.

Sources: Edward M. Peters, "Prison before the Prison: The Ancient and Medieval Worlds," in *Oxford History of the Prison*, eds. Morris and Rothman, 1995, pp. 3–43.

DEVIL'S ISLAND. The world's most infamous penal colony in French Guiana has been immortalized in literature and film. Devil's Island is a small rocky islet off the coast of French Guiana. There is also a prison on the mainland at Kourou, and over time it along with Devil's Island became collectively known as Devil's Island. During its storied history, *Ile du Diable* has passed through the colonial control of several European powers before coming under the domination of France first in

1663. Between 1852 and 1946 more than 80,000 prisoners served time in the tropical, fetid conditions of this French penal colony. Surrounded by sea and dense jungle, few convicts escaped the island.

By 1791 the French penal system required that all men convicted of a second felony be transported for life. At this time Madagascar was to be the destination. With the outbreak of the Napoleonic Wars, however, transportation was not revived in France until 1851.

In the early 1850s, at the same time that Great Britain was abandoning penal **transportation**, France began sending convicts to Guiana and the less well-known New Caledonia in 1865. The penal colony at French Guiana consisted of a mainland prison and three offshore islands. Ironically known as the Safety Islands, the islands of Royal, St. Joseph, and of course *Ile du Diable* completed the penal regime. Debate had raged over transportation for years. However, what turned the tide in its favor was Emperor Louis Napoleon's conviction that since British transportation had led to prosperous colonies in Australia, this form of forced colonization could have similar results for the French. This might have been true for the rest of the colony, but throughout its early history the island of St. Laurent, or "Devil's Island," failed to duplicate the British success in either Guiana or New Caledonia.

Opposition to the penal colony began from the outset beginning in 1852. Despite a healthy opposition, for almost ninety years proponents of the penal regime sent twice yearly convoys of prisoners to Guiana. Devil's Island came to international prominence during the Dreyfus Affair in the 1890s. The scandal had little impact on the island, however, partly because of Dreyfus's silence on the issue once he was returned to France in 1899. Convict convoys were halted during World War I but were resumed in 1921. An early campaign to close the penal colony was begun by French journalists in 1923, but it had little impact. The following year an investigation led to recommendations for improvements, although many considered conditions better in some respects than in French prisons.

A number of books have been instrumental in bringing the horrors of Devil's Island to public attention, including prisoner Rene Belbenoit's 1938 autobiographical *Dry Guillotine*. That same year French authorities stopped sending prisoners. The island facility was shut down completely in 1946, though a number of prisoners decided to remain behind. Today the European Space Agency uses the island as a launch base for satellites. The island has been a fertile inspiration for both motion pictures and literature. The story of prisoner **Henri Charriere** is told in his best-selling books *Papillon* (1969) and *Banco* (1973). In 1973 the former was made into an epic film starring Steve McQueen and Dustin Hoffman.

Sources: William E. Allison-Booth, *Devil's Island: Revelations of the French Penal Settlements in Guiana* (New York: Putnam, 1931); David L. Lewis, *Prisoners of Honor: The Dreyfus Affair* (New York: William Morrow, 1973); Miles, *Devil's Island*, 1988; Crowther, *Captured on Film*, 1989.

DIX, DOROTHEA LYNDE (1802–1887). Born in Hampden, Maine, the self-educated Dix worked as a schoolteacher in Boston from 1821 to 1836. In 1841 she made the transition to social reformer and champion of rights for the mentally ill after conducting a Sunday Bible class to women prisoners at the Cambridge jail.

Over the next two years she reportedly visited every jail and detention facility in Massachusetts. Between 1843 and 1847 Dix traveled nearly 30,000 miles while visiting prisons and poorhouses from coast to coast and from Canada to the Gulf of Mexico.

In a time when little distinction was made between mentally competent prisoners and insane ones, Dix led a crusade for reform for victims of mental illness. Much of her concern for their plight was the result of her visit to a dilapidated jail in Massachusetts, where she saw firsthand the inhuman treatment of all prisoners, particularly those suffering from mental illness. In 1843 her "Memorial to the Legislature of Massachusetts" led to the expansion of the Worcester insane asylum. Her humanitarian crusade received worldwide attention, resulting in the modernization and expansion of a number of institutions in Canada and more than 10 U.S. states. She chronicled her four years visiting American prisons in her 1845 book *Remarks on Prisons and Prison Discipline in the United States.*

Dix lobbied the government for the funding of insane asylums in 1848, but to no avail. Despite President Franklin Pierce's veto of a measure to raise taxes for the insane in 1854 and her being labeled "The American Invader" on her visit to Europe, she was successful in convincing a handful of European countries to adopt her reform ideas. After her return to the United States and a stint as superintendent of women nurses for the Union during the American Civil War, Dix continued her crusade for better conditions in prisons and insane asylums. Between 1856 and 1861 she raised more money for prison reform than had any of her predecessors.

Sources: H. E. Marshall, *Dorothea Dix: Forgotten Samaritan* (Chapel Hill: University of North Carolina Press, 1937); D. C. Wilson, *Stranger and Traveler: The Story of Dorothea Dix, American Reformer* (Boston: Little, Brown, 1975).

DJIBOUTI. The Djibouti Prison Administration is governed under the Ministry of Justice. At the end of 1999 this former French colony held 384 prisoners in four facilities. Over 57 percent were pre-trial detainees and remand prisoners. The national prison population rate was 61 per 100,000 of the national population.

Sources: Kurian, *WEPP*, 1989; ICPS, Djibouti, Africa, 2004.

DOMINICA. The Dominica Prison Service is the responsibility of the Prime Minister's Office. In 2000 there was one prison holding 298 inmates in a facility designed for 175. The prison population rate was 420 per 100,000 of the national population.

Source: ICPS, Dominica, Caribbean, 2000.

DOMINICAN REPUBLIC. Following independence the Dominican Republic adopted the French Criminal Code in 1845. The more modern code was first put into effect in 1884, and in 1924 capital punishment was abolished and replaced by a maximum penalty of 30 years imprisonment at hard labor (for homicide and arson). In 1970 the Dominican Congress passed legislation prohibiting bail in criminal cases.

There are 35 prisons in the country, with the national penitentiary located at La Victoria in Santo Domingo. Other notable institutions are located in Santiago, La

Vega, Puerto Plata, San Francisco de Macoris, Moca, San Juan, Moca, San Cristobal, and Barahona. Law to maintain one prison for those tried and convicted and a separate one for those unsentenced and waiting for trial mandates every judicial district or province. These facilities are the responsibility of the provincial governors. The national penitentiary at La Victoria houses all prisoners serving more than two years' detention. Emphasis is placed on job training at the penitentiary level, with opportunities to learn trades including shoemaking, carpentry, tailoring, and barbering. Those who pursue this training can earn wages for their work—with 30 percent of their earnings going back to families, 25 percent to the prison workshops, 25 percent to the prisoner's pension fund, and 20 percent directly to the prisoner.

Most of the nation's prisons are commanded by police officers. As late as 1990 a police brigadier general supervised La Victoria Penitentiary. By most accounts the Dominican Republic's correctional system is underfunded and suffers from overcrowding and poor sanitation. Following a bloody prison riot in 1988, steps were taken toward improving conditions. As the country became more stable in the late 1980s, the potential for conflict still threatened the prison system, which faced national trends of food shortages, inflation, and deflation. Besides bordering notoriously unstable Haiti, the Dominican Republic also faced the prospect that any localized or generalized disturbance had the potential to spread from the outside into the dark confines of the nation's prisons. As of 2004 the country had 13,836 prisoners, representing 157 per 100,000 of the national population. This is the country's lowest prison rate since 1992.

A fight between rival gangs in Higuey Prison, 90 miles east of Santo Domingo led to a tragic fire that engulfed a crowded cellblock killing 133 prisoners and injuring many others. Among the victims were four Americans who had been convicted of drug trafficking. Prison officials ordered an investigation following the fire and gang fight, which involved guns and machetes. This incident highlighted the problems of the nation's prisons, which have long been overcrowded. Higuey was built to hold 80 inmates in 1960. At the time of the fire it held more than five times that number of inmates.

The nation's 35 prisons were intended to house 9,000, but in 2004 they held more than 13,500 inmates. La Victoria is the nation's largest prison, holding 3,500 inmates in a facility designed for 1,000. Human rights have not only targeted the appalling conditions of the prisons, but also extensive drug and weapons smuggling and sexual abuse. The country has been plagued by poor economic conditions, which have led to a rising crime rate. A number of young prisoners belong to gangs or "naciones," which exist inside and outside of prison.

Sources: LCCS, "Dominican Republic: The Prison System," December 1989; Walmsley, *WPPL*, 2003; ICPS, Dominican Republic, 2004; Jean-Michel Caroit, "Gang Fight and Fire in Overcrowded Prison in Dominican Republic Kill 133 Inmates," *New York Times*, March 8, 2005, A10; Peter Prengman, "At Least 134 Die in Dominican Jailhouse Blaze," *Houston Chronicle*, March 8, 2005, A10.

DOSTOYEVSKY, FYODOR (1821–1881). Born in Moscow, Dostoyevsky resigned from the army to devote his life to literature in 1844. Four years later he was arrested for his affiliation with a socialist group. He was subsequently tried and sentenced to death. His life was spared at the last moment and his sentence was commuted to life in a Siberian prison beginning in 1849. He would spend the next four years at the penal settlement of **Omsk Prison**. He was released when he agreed to return to the army. He received a complete amnesty in 1859. He chronicled his four years in a Siberian labor camp in his haunting classic, *The House of the Dead*, in 1862. Dostoyevsky tells his story in the form of a memoir written by a man serving 10 years of penal servitude for killing his wife.

Source: Fyodor Dostoyevsky, *The House of the Dead*, with introduction by Ernest J. Simmons (New York: Dell, 1959).

DRAPCHI PRISON (TIBET). Formerly a Tibetan military garrison, Drapchi Prison was transformed into the country's largest prison in 1959 following China's invasion of the country. Today it is known by the rather neutral name of Tibet Autonomous Regional Prison No. 1. Most of its inmates were monks, government officials, and soldiers. Currently the prison holds several hundred political and religious prisoners of both genders. The prison regime emphasizes "re-education through labor" and intense ideological studies, all enforced with the brutal use of torture and other physical punishments. Medical care, food, and sanitation are below standard, leading to a high mortality rate among the prisoners. Human Rights Watch has most recently cited Drapchi Prison for its repressive measures and poor treatment of prisoners.

Source: Christianson, *Notorious Prisons*, 2004.

DU CANE, EDMUND FREDERICK (1830–1903). Du Cane is credited with reforming the British prison system in the nineteenth century. Born in Colchester, England, he graduated from military school and was commissioned as second lieutenant in the Royal Engineers. His military service would take him to the penal colonies in Australia, where he organized convict labor on public works projects between 1851 and 1856. Seven years later he was appointed director of convict prisons and inspector of military prisons. Before the 1860s ended he would rise to become chairman of the board of directors of convict prisons.

Du Cane rose to prominence as the architect of **Wormwood Scrubs Prison**, built between 1874 and 1891 on the outskirts of London. This was one of the few prisons in England that did not follow the radial and cruciform design of **Pentonville Prison**. According to Norman Johnston, Wormwood Scrubs "must be considered the first prison constructed on the so-called **telephone pole** plan."

In 1873 du Cane lobbied for a plan that would place all local prisons under government control. Four years later his efforts were approved, and du Cane was selected to preside over the entire English prison system. Besides reducing the mammoth size of the prison system, he also implemented uniform rules of discipline and inaugurated a system of useful employment for prisoners, many of whom were given assistance in assimilating to the free world upon release. However, du Cane was just as capable of implementing a rigid regime based on the precepts of separate confinement and silence. His progressive state system subjected prisoners of all classifications to a regime of "hard bed, hard fare, hard labour." The system consisted of four stages. If the prisoner managed to progress through the stages, at each level he would enjoy better jail conditions. Du Cane introduced a mark system that required each prisoner to earn 224 marks to complete each stage. Marks were earned through good behavior and hard work.

In 1877 du Cane composed England's first "Black Book," which compiled the aliases and descriptions of 12,000 known criminals. The list was supplemented with a more complete system of physical descriptions and later with fingerprints. He retired in 1894.

Sources: Babington, *The English Bastille*, 1971; Phillips and Axelrod, *Cops, Crooks, and Criminologists*, 1996; Johnston, *Forms of Constraint*, 2000.

DUCPETIAUX, EDOUARD (1804–1868). After graduating from the University of Ghent with a degree in Roman and modern law, Edouard Ducpetiaux was appointed **Belgium**'s inspector general of prisons. His interest in prisons had been piqued years earlier when he had been incarcerated for a year after siding publicly with two French journalists in an unpopular cause celebre. While serving in a war between the Dutch and Belgians, he had been captured and sentenced to be executed but was freed by a new Dutch leader. So he was not a dispassionate observer when he filled his new position in 1830. One of his first acts was to diminish the dependence on a production-oriented labor policy at **Ghent** and **Vilvorde** prisons. He also separated prisoners by gender and by age. However, as the new prison inspector he realized that for any meaningful reforms to take place new prisons needed to be constructed. Influenced by visits to England's **Pentonville Prison** and a **Bridewell** in Glasgow, he favored the implementation of the **Pennsylvania system**. So rather than focusing on the congregate work regime, Ducpetiaux leaned toward moral instruction as the best path toward prisoner rehabilitation. His ideas led the government to officially install the separate regime in all the men's prisons in 1844. In 1838 Ducpetiaux had published a three-volume work on prison reform entitled *Des Progres et d'etat actuel de la reforme penitentiare et des institutions preventives aux Etats-Unis, en France, en Suisee, en Angleterre et en Belgique*; one complete chapter is dedicated to prison architecture. In his subsequent prison-building campaign, beginning with the Tongres Prison in 1844, all single-cell prison facilities would replace the congregate plan. Virtually all of Belgium's prisons built between 1844 and 1919 were built on some incarnation of the radial design.

Sources: A. Delierneux Jr., "Evolution of the Prison System in Belgium," *Annals of the American Academy of Political and Social Sciences*, September 1930, pp. 180–196; Johnston, *Forms of Constraint*, 2000.

DUFFY, CLINTON (1898–1982). Born in San Quentin, California, it is no coincidence that he would attain national prominence as warden of **San Quentin Prison** from 1940 until 1952. Duffy's father worked as a prison guard at the noted prison for 35 years. While growing up in the village surrounding the prison, Duffy played "guards and prisoners" with other prison guards' children. However, rather than following in his father's footsteps right out of high school, Duffy joined the U.S. Marines and served in World War I.

Duffy returned to California and found employment in construction and railroad work before taking a job as secretary assistant to San Quentin's warden in 1929, a position he would hold for the next seven years. These years brought him close to the hidden life behind San Quentin's walls, where corporal punishment and the death penalty were part and parcel of the brutal penal system, proving formative in his adoption of a stance against corporal and capital punishment. Following several scandals a new warden was brought in and Duffy was reassigned to other tasks. In 1940 Duffy was appointed a temporary warden while a search was conducted for a full-time replacement. But almost immediately Duffy was able to put his beliefs into practice by abolishing a number of brutal physical punishments that had a long legacy at the prison. He improved prisoner chow and ended the practice of making prisoners wear numbers on their backs, which Duffy regarded as degrading. His efforts during his short turn as interim warden were so successful that he was given a four-year contract as warden.

Unable to get rid of the death penalty, Duffy at least looked for a less brutal form of capital punishment and made the transition from the gallows to the gas chamber. Duffy realized that there were certain parts of the penal system that were beyond his control. However, he would remain a stalwart supporter of rehabilitation. During his 12 years as warden Duffy introduced substance abuse programs and literacy classes, inaugurated a prison newspaper, and lobbied for the use of parole and other alternatives to imprisonment. Before he retired, Clinton Duffy became a nationally recognized personality and collaborated on a book about his life with Dean Jennings, *The San Quentin Story*, published in 1950. Television and the silver screen would also chronicle his life in the 1950s. Following his retirement, his wife Gladys chronicled her life at San Quentin in the *Warden's Wife*, published in 1959. His legacy, according to criminal justice historian Mark Jones, is his reputation as "competent and no-nonsense prison manager" who worked for penal reform.

Sources: Duffy, *The San Quentin Story*, 1950; Sifakis, *Encyclopedia of American Prisons*, 2003; Jones, *Criminal Justice Pioneers in U.S. History*, 2005.

DUNGEONS. No word conjures up the worst conditions of imprisonment more than the word *dungeon*. The word's origins come from the Latin term *domgio*, referring to a precipice where a castle or fortress is built. According to Johnston, it gave rise to the French word *donjon* and the more familiar English version, *dungeon*. Over time this term referred to any tower or keep built on a high natural precipice. When the basements and inner sanctums of these buildings were transformed into places of confinement, *dungeon* became synonymous with its modern meaning.

When **John Howard** conducted his survey of European prisons he referred to places of confinement that lodged prisoners in "semi-basements" and cellars as dungeons, but he found neither the brutality nor the inhumanity of the popular conception of dungeon. According to architectural historian Robin Evans, the utilization of the purposely built dungeon can be traced back to the medieval abbot Mathieu Prieur, who reportedly "dug a subterranean sepulcher into which he threw a monk whom he considered incorrigible." Whatever the case, dungeons have been used since at least the early Middle Ages, but probably as far back as ancient Rome.

Sources: Evans, *The Fabrication of Virtue*, 1982; Johnston, *Forms of Constraint*, 2000.

DWIGHT, LOUIS (1793–1854). Born in New England, Louis Dwight attended Yale College in 1813 intending to enter the ministry. However, a chemical experiment went awry, injuring Dwight's lungs so badly he was permanently unable to lecture from the pulpit. Although his attempts to enter the ministry in traditional fashion failed, in 1824 he decided to distribute the Bible to prisoners. Following a visit to the **Auburn Penitentiary** in 1826, the Boston clergyman described the place as a "noble institution" and a "model worthy of the world's imitation." However, visits to other American penitentiaries earlier that same year left Dwight with a less favorable impression of contemporary prisons, leading him to establish the **Boston Prison Discipline Society** in 1826, leading a membership composed mainly of Congregational and Baptist clergy.

Dwight would be a lifelong advocate for the **Auburn system**, as well as an opponent of the **Pennsylvania system**. If Dwight had a weakness, it was inflexibility when it came to incorporating any competing prison strategies. Nevertheless, Dwight is credited as one of America's first nationally known prison reformer. Dwight oversaw the establishment of a model prison at Wethersfield, Connecticut, and before the first decade of the prison society had ended, he influenced the creation of Auburn-style cellblocks in Massachusetts, New Hampshire, Vermont, Maryland, Kentucky, Ohio, Tennessee, and the nation's capital city. The Boston Prison Discipline Society would eventually distribute thousands of Bibles and religious tracts, which according to Blake McKelvey "formed the nucleus of prison libraries." Dwight's crusade in favor of prison industries came at a time when most Americans were against paying taxes to support prisons. His stance placed his organization in good stead with the American public, particularly after it became known that it had led to a reduction of the tax burden in some states as several prisons became self-supporting. Following Dwight's death in 1854, his society ceased operation as well. By then others were waiting to follow in Dwight's pioneering footsteps.

Sources: Lewis, *The Development of American Prisons and Prison Customs, 1776–1845*; McKelvey, *American Prisons*, 1977; Sullivan, *The Prison Reform Movement*, 1990; Christianson, *With Liberty for Some*, 1998.

E

EASTERN STATE PENITENTIARY. Eastern State Penitentiary, sometimes referred to as Cherry Hill due to its proximity to a cherry orchard, was built between 1822 and 1829 in Philadelphia. Costing more than $750,000, it was the nation's most expensive building to date. According to one architectural historian, it was "America's first building to have a real influence abroad." With 12-foot thick granite walls extending 30 feet high, the 11-acre prison was probably the country's first building with indoor plumbing. The noted British architect, John Haviland, designed Eastern State. Influenced by the **Quaker** impulses of reform and penitence, each prison cell was built for one prisoner to be kept in solitary confinement for the entire sentence. This conception of punishment was inspired by enlightenment attempts to replace brutal punishments, such as flogging and torture. Although the **Auburn System** would predominate in the United States, more than 300 prisons would be built worldwide based on the so-called **Pennsylvania System**.

The prison replaced **Walnut Street Jail**, which had become overcrowded. Architecturally, the edifice resembled a medieval castle with its high walls surrounding seven cellblocks that extended out from a central rotunda like the spokes of a wheel. A number of authorities have suggested that Haviland's prison borrowed from Jeremy Bentham's **Panopticon** model, which was designed so that inmates could be monitored from a single point of observation. Prisoners were housed in extra-large cells, each with walled garden-exercise yards, running water, and heat. Prisoners were expected to work in their cells at productive trades such as shoe making, weaving, and candle-making. The only reading material made available to them was the Bible. With little else to do it was hoped that prisoners would spend their lonely hours reflecting on their sins. Despite the noble goals of the system's creators, many prisoners were driven insane by the oppressive solitary system. One of its most vocal critics was writer Charles Dickens, who visited the prison in 1842. When he came to the United States he was asked what he looked forward to seeing. He replied, "Niagara Falls and Eastern State Penitentiary." From his writings on the subject it would appear that Dickens might as well have avoided the prison. In his book

American Notes: A Journey, he criticized the system as "rigid, strict, and hopeless solitary confinement." He believed "the system to be "cruel and wrong" and that the "slow and daily tampering with the mysteries of the brain" was "immeasurably worse than any torture to the body."

In the early twentieth century the prison abandoned the concept of solitary confinement and it was turned into a congregate institution, where inmates were allowed to work, exercise, and eat together. Eastern State has housed the whole spectrum of criminality from the unknown to celebrities such as Al Capone and bankrobber Willie Sutton. Although the prison was designated a National Historic Landmark in 1965, it held prisoners until 1971.

Sources: Teeters and Shearer, *The Prison at Philadelphia, Cherry Hill: The Separate System of Penal, 1829–1913*, 1957; Charles Dickens, *American Notes: A Journey* (New York: Fromm International Publishing, 1985); Johnston, *Eastern State Penitentiary: Crucible of Good Intentions*, 1994.

ECUADOR. The main penitentiary, based on the **panopticon** model, was the facility Penal Garcia Moreno, named after the president who oversaw its erection beginning in 1870. This Quito prison has also been compared architecturally to **Eastern State Penitentiary** Upon its completion in 1874 it was regarded as one of the largest prisons in the Americas. However, combining the sinister elements of modern architecture with the terror-inducing features of the past, it was far from benign. It was purposely painted black, forcing inmates to live in the specter of shadows and the draconian rules of the **silent system**. Little thought was given to constructive work opportunities, with preference given to drone-like labor not far removed from the **treadmill**.

In the 1890s Ecuador adopted a **progressive system** based on **Crofton's Irish system**. However, the main penitentiary was far removed from any type of classification regime, as the prison continued to house recidivist delinquents alongside troublesome minors sent to detention by parents and masters, much as modern parents resort to military schools. Despite the inauguration of a more liberal regime between 1895 and 1910, prison conditions remained the same.

In 1906 penal code reform introduced deportation as a punishment and inaugurated the establishment of agricultural colonies in the Colon archipelago, which came to fruition by the 1920s. In 1936 a penal colony was organized at Colonia Penal de Mera, on the banks of the Pasraza River. This agricultural unit confines mostly laborers from the rural areas, individuals who are familiar with this regimen. This institution replaced a less successful one in the Galapagos Islands and the archipelago of Colon.

Initially, Ecuador separated offenders by class—the well-to-do in jails with modern conveniences; the poor in unsanitary cells. Following the reorganization of the penal code in 1938, a number of changes were implemented. Penitentiaries were divided into several classes, each housing criminals according to seriousness of offense. The most austere facility, called *reclusion mayor*, requires forced labor and cellular confinement for terms of 4 to 8 years, for up to 16 years in more extraordinary circumstances. The next stage, considered less severe, or *reclusion menor*, ranges from 3 to 6 years, or up to 12 years in more serious offenses. These sentences carry forced labor either in communal factories or outside the walls in agricultural colonies. A correctional prison handles sentences lasting from eight days to five years, as well as misdemeanants serving short sentences. Prisoners are paid small wages, with one third retained as credit and given to prisoner upon release; one third goes toward the maintenance of the institution; and the final third goes to court to cover civil obligations related to the crime committed.

During the 1950s a prison was built in Guayaquil based on the **telephone pole model**. Today the National Directorate of Social Rehabilitation, under the Ministry of Government and Justice, runs the penal system. The older Garcia Moreno Prison in Quito and the Coastal Prison in Guayaquil are the largest facilities in Ecuador. Quito and the capital cities of the Costa and Sierra provinces provide municipal jails.

Despite legislation requiring rehabilitation programs, few such programs exist because of a dearth in space, staffing, and equipment necessary for supporting any meaningful training or education regime. One institution where theory has been put into practice is the women's prison in Quito, where academic and vocational programs flourish. As in a number of Latin American prison systems, prisoners are expected to work and can earn minimum remuneration. Prisoners accrue one third of their wages to be given to them on release. The other two thirds go toward upkeep expenses and trial costs. In the 1980s several private factories had entered into prison work contracts. In addition, two halfway houses established in Quito allowed prisoners to work outside at jobs and visit their families on occasion.

As the 1990s began, most Ecuadorian prisons were characterized by overcrowding and plagued by budgetary restrictions, which diminished prison building and staffing. As late as 1986 the prison system built for 2,600 inmates housed more than 6,000. Historic Garcia Moreno Prison built in the 1870s for 300 inmates, and later remodeled to hold twice that number, held 1,800 by the mid-1980s, with access to only twenty toilets. As the twentieth century drew to a close, human rights groups targeted Ecuador's prisons for their unhygienic conditions, lack of medical facilities, and brutal, underpaid guards ever susceptible to bribes. As of late 1999 the prison system contained 8,520 inmates, a ratio of 69 per 100,000 of the national population.

Sources: Emilio Uzcategui, "Brief Notes on the Ecuadorian Penal System," in *World Penal Systems*, ed. Negley Teeters, 1944, pp. 163–167; LCCS, "Ecuador: Penal System," 1989; Salvatore and Aguirre, "The Birth of the Penitentiary in Latin America," in *The Birth of the Penitentiary in Latin America*, eds. Salvatore and Aguirre, 1996, pp. 1–43; Walmsley, *WPPL*, 2003.

EDDY, THOMAS (1758–1827). An early visitor to Philadelphia's **Walnut Street Jail**, Thomas Eddy, who was a Quaker, would become a pioneer in the early development of American corrections, earning the sobriquet "America's **John Howard.**" Born in Philadelphia to Irish immigrants, Eddy lived a rather peripatetic existence before putting down roots in New York City in 1790 and pursuing a successful career as an insurance broker. As his career blossomed, Eddy was drawn to public service, leading to his first association with the prison system. Eddy had experienced firsthand the worst aspects of incarceration when he was briefly imprisoned for his Tory sympathies in 1780.

In 1796 Eddy inspected the Walnut Street Jail and visited with his old friend Caleb Lownes, who was now its inspector. When he returned to New York, Eddy influenced the passage of legislation that would replace most corporal and capital punishments with imprisonment. Eddy was tasked with supervising the construction of New York's first penitentiary at Newgate in the Greenwich Village. Borrowing from what he saw at Walnut Street, Eddy placed the most emphasis on building congregate rooms and workshops; he dedicated only 14 cells to solitary confinement. During its early years the Newgate Jail seemed destined for success. However, in 1802 it was necessary to call in the militia to suppress a bloody riot and mass escape attempt. Eddy was convinced that a new prison design was necessary—one more like Howard's plan, which included single cells for separate confinement at night and congregate workshops where prisoners worked together in enforced silence on weekdays. Eddy's vision came to fruition with the building of **Auburn Prison**, which received its first prisoners in 1817. However, draconian legislation was passed that would nullify much of Eddy's humane penal code. Under the administration of **Elam Lynds**, Auburn prison earned a reputation for harsh, military-style discipline. But this regime seemed to have the desired effect. One British visitor astounded by the institution's dining hall reported that he could never have imagined that it was "morally possible" for 635 prisoners, including 22 women, to congregate with such silence and order. During the remainder of his life Thomas Eddy continued to crusade in support of a variety of reform issues and until his dying day viewed the Auburn Prison as the best institution of its kind. A product of the Enlightenment, Eddy was familiar with the works of **Cesare Beccaria** and **William Penn**, and in 1801 he published *An Account of the State Prison or Penitentiary House in the City of New York.*

Sources: Lewis, *From Newgate to Dannemora: The Rise of the Penitentiary in New York, 1796–1848*, 1965; McKelvey, *American Prisons*, 1977; Christianson, *With Liberty for Some*, 1998.

EGYPT. As of 2002 Egypt had 42 prisons. With Egypt's population at 67 million in 1998, this amounted to an incarceration rate of 121 per 100,000. According to one report, during the previous decade these prisons had the capacity to hold less than 20,000 but contained 10,000 more.

There has reportedly been little change in the Egyptian prison system in the almost six decades since Anwar Sadat served an 18-month prison term beginning in 1946. In fact, when Sadat came to power in 1975, one of his first acts was to take a pickaxe to the brick wall at Turah Prison, heralding its impending demolition. In his autobiography Sadat reported that his cell contained "no bed, no small table, no chair, and no lamp. . . . You simply can't imagine how filthy" it was, recounting that in the winter "water oozed from the cell walls day and night, and in the summer huge armies of bugs marched up and down."

In the aftermath of the 1952 revolution, Egypt initiated several prison reforms, including building hospitals in major prisons and providing separate institutions for women. The first strides toward a rehabilitative regime were also attempted but were stopped short of any meaningful progress.

More than one third of Egypt's prisons are located in the greater Cairo metropolitan area. Southeast of Cairo is the town of Tora, home to a complex of six prisons. Three more prisons are located northeast of Cairo, at Abu Za'bal. In Qanater, to the northwest, is a facility housing both men and women. This is the country's largest women's prison. This institution covers about 2 acres, part of a larger 32-acre complex for men. It was designed and constructed by the British more than a century ago. Thirty-six male and 2 female officers, 300 soldiers and guards, and

16 civilian employees staff Qanater. About 8 women guards who serve as escorts in all cases staff the women's facility. A smaller jail for women is housed at the Tanta General Prison.

Egyptian correctional institutions include general and central prisons serving certain geographical areas, special-purpose prisons, such as one reserved exclusively for draft evaders, and light-security to medium-security facilities. General prisons may serve one or several provinces (governorates). For example, Tanta General Prison serves the governorates of Kufr al-Shaykh and al-Gharbiyah. Prisoners in these institutions are serving prison sentences of 3 to 15 years. Some serve terms at hard labor; others are sentenced to jail terms of more than three months. Under Penal Law 18, a "jail term" is defined as not less than 24 hours or more than three years.

Light-security prisons include agricultural institutions such as Tora Mazraa, built by the British in 1908. According to recent reports by Middle East Watch, this facility was the least overcrowded and in the best condition of all the facilities that were inspected.

Egypt has three maximum-security prisons, or *liman* in Arabic: Abu Za'bal Liman, Tora Liman, and Wadi Natroun Liman. Prisoners at these institutions are serving terms at "hard labor" for serious crimes. Prior to 1960 hard labor was more akin to torture as prisoners worked in stone quarries shackled by leg irons. This was outlawed in 1960 and replaced by work in factories in maximum-security liman. For the most part then hard labor has little meaning. The only differentiation is that most sentenced prisoners receive family visits every twenty-one days, whereas those at hard labor have to wait one month between visits. In contrast is the Tora prison complex, home to six prisons. Since it houses Egypt's most important political prisoners, this site is considered the nation's most secure and heavily guarded facility. Tora Istikbal, meaning "reception" in Arabic, was designed as a reception prison and today functions as a major holding center for suspected Islamist security detainees. Some are held for short terms of several months duration; others serve longer terms of several years. According to Article 16 of the Egyptian penal code, a "prison term" is defined as a sentence of not less than three years or more than 15 except in special conditions specified by law.

The Prisons Foundation under the Ministry of the Interior administers the Egyptian penal system. Officials and employees in the Ministry of Interior hold military-style ranks but are operatively separate from the military. A Prisons Administration officer commands each prison. In the case of multiprison facilities such as at Tora, individual prisons are under the directorate of separate administrators, but an overall commander has responsibility for the entire complex. Complementing the official personnel and guards are civilian employees, referred to as "government workers," who perform clerical work and other tasks.

Egyptian prisons house a diverse population, including sentenced prisoners, prisoners currently under investigation, prisoners already charged and awaiting trial, and detainees held without charge under Egypt's Emergency Law, first imposed in 1967. Except for one year in the early 1980s the Emergency Law has continually been in force. Under this law individuals can be detained who fall under a broadly described umbrella of offenses related to suspicion of endangering public order or security.

According to most sources, prisoners are strictly segregated by categories. These include prisoners serving sentences for criminal and security offenses; these individuals are housed in separate sections of a facility and prevented from mixing with unsentenced prisoners. Prisoners detained without trial or charge are rigidly segregated from other prisoners. In addition, those already sentenced for criminal offenses are separated from others serving time for security offenses. Those convicted for similar offenses, such as drug trafficking or murder, are typically held together.

Under the Egyptian penal code a number of prisoners' rights are enumerated. According to Article 42, "Every prisoner arrested, incarcerated, or having his freedom limited in any way must be treated in a way that maintains his human dignity and should not be harmed physically or mentally." Prisoners have the right under Egyptian law to complain to prison administrators. Complaints should then be recorded in the prison register and transmitted to the *niyaba al-'amma* (a place where incidents are investigated) within the Ministry of Justice. The niyaba is responsible for the external oversight of the prison. Attorneys representing this office are required to make monthly, unannounced inspections to monitor prisoners' treatment. However, human rights inspectors have noted in the 1990s that prisoners were often denied access to niyaba inspectors.

Inmates are allowed out of their cells for at least one hour per day, with many inmates reporting outside activity numbering several hours. Not all prisoners were given access to fresh air, however; they simply had their cells opened, allowing them to walk the corridors and atriums. On the other extreme, women prisoners reported that they were rarely allowed out of their cells.

According to official policy, prisoners are informed of disciplinary rules upon admission. Each prison apparently has written rules and procedures, and guards are given brief instruction on how to work in prisons. Although international law prohibits corporal punishment for disciplinary offenses, Egyptian law allows the beating of juvenile prisoners and the whipping of adults as part of the discipline process. Prisoners can also be placed in solitary confinement up to 15 days for each offenses. Prisoners are allowed to receive only three newspapers, all considered part of the governments "semi-official press." Opposition papers are prohibited. Although families can bring books, the substance is tightly controlled.

The computerization of prisoner records began in 1989. Typically a prisoner's file includes accusation, action taken, where action was taken (which police station), length of sentence, home address, date of birth, health status, previous arrests, release code, sex and marital status, behavior, and expected release date.

Living conditions vary widely in the prisons. Officials at Tanta General Prison claim that prisoners receive three meals daily. These meals include some combination of cheese, fowl, lentils, rice, jam, meat, dates, and fried ground chickpeas. However, prisoners from other African countries are often dependent on begging for food from fellow inmates. Several prisoners at Abu Za'bal claimed they were fed only twice a day and were forced to supplement their diet with food donated from relatives and cooked on makeshift stoves. This way, one inmate added, "we can eat when we decide we are hungry."

According to Amnesty International, at the end of 2002 thousands of suspected supporters of banned Muslim organizations and dozens of prisoners of conscience were held in detention without charges or trial.

Sources: Anwar el-Sadat, *In Search of Identity: An Autobiography* (New York: Harper and Row, 1977); LCCS, "Egypt: The Penal System," December 1990; Middle East Watch, *Prison Conditions in Egypt* (New York: Human Rights Watch, 1993); *Amnesty International Report*, 2003.

ELMIRA REFORMATORY. Elmira gained a certain amount of notoriety during the American Civil War, when it served as a Union prisoner-of-war site where thousands of Confederate prisoners perished during the 1860s. Several years after the war's conclusion the New York state legislature selected this site for the construction of a model reformatory. By the time the facility received its first prisoners in July 1876, **Zebulon Brockway** had been selected as its first superintendent. The initial prisoners were transferred from **Auburn Prison**. A number of scholars consider the new prison's regime as one of the earliest attempts to put into practice the Declaration of Principles (see Appendix I).

The Elmira Reformatory was designed for first time offenders between the ages of 16 and 30 years old. Inmates were sentenced to the institution for indeterminate periods. Built as an alternative to the **Auburn** and **Pennsylvania** systems, it kept the familiar Auburn architectural design but eschewed most other aspects, including corporal punishment, striped uniforms, lockstep marching, the silent system, and other humiliating attempts to control prisoners.

Elmira implemented several new programs, including education classes in religion and ethics, vocational training in a variety of trades, and still other programs devoted to creating a prison band, a prison newspaper, and various athletic leagues. When prisoners were not working, they followed a regimen familiar to any military school graduate. Decked out in military garb, inmates were equipped with toy rifles and swords and were drilled to the tune of a fife and bugle band.

Alexander Maconochie's Australian penal experiments and **Walter Crofton**'s **Irish system** most markedly inspired the institution. Under Brockway, Elmira classified inmates into three classifications, or grades. Inmates with behavioral problems and those averse to rehabilitation were placed in the third grade, at the lowest level. New prisoners were placed in the second grade for their first six months. If they responded favorably to the regimen, they could advance to the intermediate or first grade. At this point they could earn more privileges, or "marks," which were equivalent to credits. Prisoners who did not perform well at the second stage would be demoted. In this way prisoners could earn a reduction of their sentences by matriculating successfully through the various grades toward parole.

The Elmira system ultimately failed as inmates figured out ways to beat the system. Since inmates had no idea how long they would serve, tension was always present. Reports later filtered out beyond the walls that indicated that Brockway did not always practice what he preached. His predilection for corporal punishment earned home the moniker "Paddler Brockway." A number of prisoners were broken down by the system, leading Brockway to transfer them to institutions for the insane. Despite mixed results, Elmira was a step forward in the establishing a method for the classification of inmates.

Elmira influenced the construction of reformatories in at least twelve states over the next 25 years, peaking in 1910. The education programs introduced by Brockway were among the first in the country to include all prison inmates in some meaningful reform program. Unfortunately, the majority of the personnel selected to direct these programs were inadequate for the job, and the complicated grading system became too onerous to maintain. In a majority of cases it was easier to place all well-behaved inmates in the first grade, a handful in second grade, and those being punished in the third grade. Ultimately, Brockway's successor would return to a regimen of custody and treatment. Today the Elmira Reformatory is now the

Elmira Correctional and Reception Center, a maximum-security facility. Historian Beverly Smith suggested, "In truth, it always was."

Sources: R. G. Waite, "From Penitentiary to Reformatory: Alexander Maconochie, Walter Crofton, Zebulon Brockway, and the Road to Prison Reform—New South Wales, Ireland, and Elmira, New York, 1840–1970," in *Criminal Justice History: An International Annual*, ed. L. A. Knafla (Westport, CT: Greenwood Press, 1993); Beverly Smith, "Elmira Reformatory," in *Encyclopedia of America Prisons*, eds. McShane and Williams, 1996, pp. 194–197; Christianson, *With Liberty for Some*, 1998.

EL SALVADOR. According to the 1983 constitution El Salvadoran prisons were supposed to emphasize rehabilitation over a punitive regime. Administration of the prison system falls under the aegis of the director general of penal and rehabilitation centers, who serves under the minister of justice. By the end of the 1980s the prison system comprised three national penitentiaries and more than thirty jails and preventive detention centers scattered throughout the small country. Federal penitentiaries were located in Ahuachapan, Santa Ana, and San Vicente. These institutions are considered the main confinement institutions and house close to half the nation's inmates. Outside the federal system, other facilities receive little direction or oversight.

There are two women's prisons at Ilopango and Santa Ana, which detain mostly prostitutes serving six-month sentences. The country's prisons run the entire gamut from simple frame structures with little security to professionally designed buildings with adequate security and facilities.

The nation's security was threatened during the bloody war with FMLN (Farabundo Marti National Liberation) guerillas in the late 1980s, when insurgents targeted jails as well as military installations, resulting in the release of a number of prisoners. Recent information on the prison system is difficult to come by; however, it was estimated to approach 5,000 inmates annually nationwide in the 1980s. By the beginning of 2000 the prison population had reached 6,914, or 109 per 100,000 of the national population. By late 2002 El Salvador was reporting 10,278 prisoners in a prison system designed for 6,137, a capacity rate of 167.5 percent. The national rate of 158 per 100,000 represents a significant increase since the 99 per 100,000 of 1992.

Sources: LCCS, "El Salvador: The Penal System," 1988; Kurian, *WEPP*, 1989; Walmsley, *WPPL*, 2003; ICPS, El Salvador, 2004.

ENGLAND AND WALES (UK). Before the dim outline of the English prison system could be discerned, individuals were incarcerated in small gaols (jails) and houses of correction. Long before there was a professional prison staff, gaolers (jailers) made a living by charging inmates for food and lodging. Without a classification system no distinction was made between debtors, felons, and those awaiting trial, with many already destined for **transportation** to America. Following his whirlwind survey of prison conditions the prison reformer **John Howard** published his survey of the "State of the Prisons" in 1777, singling out English detention facilities as "filthy, corrupt-ridden and unhealthy."

When the transportation of criminals to America was interrupted by the American Revolution, British authorities substituted broken-down vessels as **convict**

hulks as a "temporary expedient." Not until transportation was shifted to Australia in 1787 did use of the convict hulks diminish, although they were not discontinued until 1859. During the Napoleonic Wars that ended in 1815 hulks were estimated to hold 70,000 prisoners, many of whom were prisoners-of-war.

A new era dawned in 1816 with the opening of England's first penitentiary at **Millbank** under the direction of the Home Office. The passage of the Gaol Act of 1823 was the earliest such legislation directed at standardizing the running of the nation's prisons. Other acts followed, including the Prisons Act of 1835, which organized the protocol for appointing the five inspectors of prisons, and the Act of 1844, which authorized the appointment of a surveyor general of prisons and inaugurated a scheme for controlling the construction of prisons. Subsequently, an institution for minors was opened at Parkhurst in 1839, and the model institution at **Pentonville** received its first inmates in 1842. Between 1842 and 1848 54 prisons were erected containing a total of 11,000 separate cells, most following the separate cell design of Pentonville.

Despite the intentions of penal reformers to improve prison conditions, prisons remained unsanitary and inadequate. In 1877 legislation was passed that would transfer the responsibilities of local justices to the home secretary, who in turn would also take over the cost of running the prison system. The administration of the system was placed in the hands of a newly created five-member Prison Commission. **Edmund du Cane** was selected as the chairman of the Prison Commission in 1878. Among his first efforts was the closing of 38 out of the country's 113 local jails. Over the following decade another 15 would be discontinued. Du Cane was an avid supporter of separate confinement in order to avoid the contagion of other criminal minds and to allow the inmate time to contemplate his ways. Initial protocol in local jails expected the prisoner to serve the first month sleeping on a wooden plank with piecework to be accomplished alone—typically tedious jobs such as picking oakum. After the first month inmates might be forced to work together on either the **crank** or **treadmill**, always in silence. During the first three months visitors and mail were prohibited, and after this period both were allowed but only in three-month intervals. In comparison individuals sent to convict prisons spent their first nine months in solitary confinement. Whenever a convict came upon a visitor, he was expected to turn and face the wall. Outfitted in a demeaning prison wardrobe, prisoners were given scant opportunities for personal hygiene.

The issuance of the Gladstone Report in 1895 reflected a changing attitude toward prisoners by emphasizing the reformative purpose of prison. Among its most important recommendations was the abolition of the crank and treadmill and any other form of unproductive labor. It also recommended making more efforts at classifying prisoners, increasing educational opportunities, establishing a juvenile reformatory for offenders up to 23 years of age, and more aftercare programs for prisoners. The 1895 Gladstone Report is considered the definitive statement of England's penal policy for the next half-century. However, implementing these goals had to wait until the twentieth century, when a number of these suggestions were put into practice, including the creation of separate facilities for offenders between the ages of 16 and 23, the establishment of a pre-release prison, and the segregation of career criminals under special conditions.

At the turn of the century the United States had just witnessed the world's first juvenile court, when in 1899 Chicago's Cook County introduced this new court. At the same time movement was afoot in England to develop an institution for young offenders. In 1902 a wing of a convict prison at Borstal was transformed into prison for young offenders, establishing a number of the basics that became part of the **Borstal system**. The passage of the Prevention of Crime Act in 1908 gave the Borstal experiment legal sanction. Now the courts could sentence 16-to-20-year-olds "to detention under penal discipline in a Borstal Institution for a term of not less than one year nor more than three years of imprisonment."

Conditions generally improved in English prisons in the early twentieth century. Prison diet improved, and exercise became more common for inmates. Following World War I, attention returned to prison reform. In 1922 **Alexander Paterson** began a two-decade stint as prison commissioner. He abolished a number degrading punishments, increased privileges, improved vocational training, and even created wage-earning opportunities for prisoners. But Paterson's greatest legacy was his improvement of the Borstal system.

With the outbreak of World War II a virtual avalanche of prisoners and Borstal trainees was released to contribute to the war effort while some prison facilities were converted for other uses. However, by the end of 1940 the prisons were once more faced with overcrowding. By 1945 the average daily prison population was 14,708, compared with 10,326 five years earlier. The passage of the Criminal Justice Act of 1948 abolished hard labor and penal servitude but replaced it with longer prison sentences deemed necessary for rehabilitation programs.

Overcrowding continued to plague British corrections into the 1950s. In response the government opened 17 open- and medium-security prisons and Borstals. In 1952 the average prison population had risen to 23,670. The steady increase in population and the changing environment and values of the 1950s led to the release of the "White Paper Penal Practice in a Changing in a Changing Society," published in 1959. The aim of the white paper was to prevent recidivism and to use alternatives to imprisoning young offenders.

Andrew Ashworth noted in 1992 that beginning in the mid-1970s prison "overcrowding became the dominant feature of the English criminal justice system." Despite strategies to reduce the population, conditions have only gotten worse. The 1970s were marked by a number of prisoner riots and demonstrations. New problems created more challenges, particularly the growing number of terrorists and prisoners serving life sentences. One of the main reasons for the overcrowding has been the get-tough approach favored by both the Conservative and Labour parties, both trying to "out tough" each other with strict mandatory sentences. A rising crime problem has also thrown public support behind a number of get-tough initiatives. By the late 1990s, according to Rod Morgan, England was facing its "biggest surge in the prison population in English penal history."

In 1997 England purchased a five-deck U.S. prison barge, dubbed the "floating Alcatraz" and the "Alcatraz of Britain." Formerly known as the *Resolution,* it was renamed Her Majesty's Prison Ship *Weare.* Critics, however, called the ship a "nightmare" for inmates. New York's Department of Corrections was thrilled to get rid of what had once been a drug rehabilitation center for 6.4 million dollars. British officials responded to criticism by noting the nation's current jail shortage. One member of the **Howard Association**, perhaps said it best, noting, "We are always taking the ideas America has rejected, like the boot camps and prison ships, rather than their best practices."

Virtually all statistics on England's prisons include those for Wales as well. In late 2004 England and Wales had 138 prisons holding 74,770 inmates. Prison institutions include local prisons, remand centers, training prisons, young offender institutes, and open prisons. The prisons were considered at 109 percent of capacity and the prison population rate stood at 141 per 100,000 of the national population. This represents a significant rise in the prison population over the past 15 years. In 1992 the ratio stood at 90 per 100,000 with 45,817 prisoners and has grown each year since then. The Home Office estimates that by 2008 the prison population will increase to 84,000. Nineteen of England's prisons have been built since 1995. Seven of these were designed, constructed, managed, and financed under the Private Finance Initiative. These facilities will revert back to the United Kingdom in 25 years.

Sources: wikipedia.org/wiki/United_Kingdom_prison-population; Ian Waldie, "Critics Fear Prison Ship to Be 'Alcatraz of Britain," *Houston Chronicle*, March 14, 1997, 25A; Rod Morgan, "Imprisonment in England and Wales: Flood Tide, but on the Turn?" pp. 253–256, and Andrew Ashworth, "New Sentencing Laws Take Effect in England," pp. 239–242, both in *Penal Reform in Overcrowded Times*, ed. Tonry, 2001; ICPS, United Kingdom: England and Wales, 2004.

ERGASTULUM. Early references to the *ergastalum* as a place of forced detention can be found in the Roman Twelve Tables. In 817 Benedictine priors met in Aix-la-Chapelle to set standards of punishment in monastic prisons. Among the agreed-upon standards of correction was the establishment of a separate facility, known as the *ergastalum*, which would be dedicated to prisoners considered escape risks or those who had committed serious crimes. However, according to most sources, despite their good intentions, conditions were usually primitive and brutal in monastic prison rooms.

Sources: Edward M. Peters, "The Prison before the Prison," in *Oxford History of the Prison*, eds. Morris and Rothman, 1998, pp. 3–43; Johnston, *Forms of Constraint*, 2000.

ESTONIA. Following the breakup of the Soviet Union crime rose precipitously in Estonia. Cases of street crime, murder, and theft rose dramatically. After Estonia attained independence in 1991, the new administration attempted to implement a number of modern prison practices. The Department of Prisons is administered under the Ministry of Justice. By August of 1993 there were 4,500 prisoners incarcerated in the country's 10 prisons. The main penal institutions are located in Tallinn (Central), Maardu, Harku, Murru, Rummu, Amari, Tallinn, Parnu, Sooniste, and Vijandi. Harku is the only prison designated specifically for females. By the end of 2002 a new prison was expected to open in Tartu. This institution was to be capable of holding 1,000 prisoners, the majority of whom were expected to be pre-trial detainees. At the same time the Central Prison was supposed to be shut down, with its hospital facilities moving to Vijandi.

Thirty-seven percent of those incarcerated, in 1994 were pre-trial detainees. Estonia's imprisonment rate is considered lower than the rate of other European republics that were formerly part of the Soviet Union, but it is higher than those of eastern and central European countries that were not. Estonian officials are endeavoring to align the prison population with those in neighboring Scandinavian countries in order to bring it down from 270 per 100,000 of the general population to 65 per 100,000. However, the most recent figures from 2004 place the prison population at 4,571, which would be 339 per 100,000 of the national population.

Although the prison capacity is estimated at more than 6,000, the institutions have been running under 100 percent capacity since 1994. Steps have been taken to adopt single-cell accommodations. Most facilities date to the Soviet period and are in dire need of repairs. The criminal code introduced in 1991 classifies prisons as minimum, medium, and maximum security as well as pre-trial detention centers. However, the new code continued the Soviet preference for a three-step **mark system,** in which prisoners begin their sentences in quarantine, considered the strictest level of confinement. The maximum amount of time is six months in medium-secure prisons and twelve months in maximum security. During quarantine a prisoner works and lives in a single cell under constant surveillance. Number of restrictions apply at this level. Prisoners are transferred to another level at the discretion of the prison director. The second two stages are general and preferential, each coming with less restrictions as the prisoner navigates toward a less punitive regime.

Sanitary conditions and food are considered at best adequate. Disciplinary measures remain rather punitive. According to Article 147 of the penal code prisoners can be placed in a single locked cell up to six months in maximum-security prisons and up to one month in minimum security. Other punishments include the denial of visits and solitary confinement, or *carcers*, up to fifteen days in poorly lighted spaces with little heating. Visitors are allowed short visits of not more than three hours for friends and extended family as well as long visits of up to three days for immediate family. Prison officials have increasingly recognized that allowing prisoners to serve sentences closer to home leads to more contacts with family and helps accelerate the prisoner's assimilation back into the community when the sentence is completed.

The prison staff has more than 2,200 officers, creating a staff-to-prisoner ratio of 1 to 1.9. Attempts are being made to help a number of staff members make the transition to social workers with more professional skills through better training and education. Despite the number of staff members, some prisons still experience poor morale and control problems. Almost 60 percent of prisoners and 70 percent of staff are ethnic Russians, and this has led to a number of human rights abuses directed at ethnic Estonians. Because of poor economic conditions only a minority of prisoners have found employment in prison workshops. In Tallinn Prison, for example, only 50 out of the 450 prisoners worked. Improved relations with its Scandinavian and Baltic counterparts may facilitate the modernization of Estonian prisons to alleviate these conditions.

During the late 1990s the European Committee for the Prevention of Torture published a report targeting the conditions of police detention and punishment. The report described police detention facilities as "extremely poor." Despite subsequent follow-up visits, prison conditions had not improved. The committee also characterized the main prisons as having unacceptable conditions, including the Central Prison at Tallinn, which was described as having "intolerable" conditions for remand prisoners. The facility was scheduled for closure at the end of 2002.

Sources: LCCS, "Estonia: Crime and Law Enforcement," January 1995; Walmsley, *Prison Systems in Central and Eastern Europe,* 1996; *Amnesty International Report,* 2003; Walmsley, *Further Developments in the Prison Systems of Central and Eastern Europe,* 2003; Walmsley, *WPPL,* 2003.

ETHIOPIA. Only sketchy information on Ethiopian prisons is available. The administrator of prisons is responsible for the direction of the national penal system.

Each of the country's administrative units has at least one correctional facility. These include the regional unit or *kifle hager*, the subregion, or *awraja*, and the *wereda*, or district level. The most modern facility is Addis Ababa's Akaki (central) Prison, constructed in 1974. This institution has separate units for female political prisoners. Akaki housed the largest number of political prisoners overall, with almost 1,500 in 1989. Political prisoners can be found in most Ethiopian prisons. In Addis Ababa a number of dissidents are confined in various locations, including the Fourth Division headquarters, the national police headquarters and interrogation center at the Third Police Station, and the Menelik's Grand Palace. Because of the current political climate a number of political prisoners are incarcerated in three facilities in Asmera.

Other penal facilities can be found at most police stations and army garrisons. In addition, every peasant association operates its own jail. There is also a prison farm at Robi in Arsi, which can accommodate more than 800 prisoners. In the late 1970s the Ethiopian government came up with a plan for using inmates convicted of minor offenses for agricultural labor on minimum-security state farms. By 1980 there was only one institution devoted to the rehabilitation of juveniles. This housed only males, since female juveniles were placed in the custody of family members or guardians.

Little progress was made in terms of human rights and rehabilitation strategies prior to the 1990s. Following the emergence of the Marxist regime in the 1970s, a number of youthful political detainees were held with adults until the end of their "political rehabilitation." In the late 1970s the Cuban government helped construct several new prisons that had cells for solitary confinement. During Ethiopia's flirtation with Cuba's Marxists regime prison authorities borrowed several features of the Cuban prison regime. Political prisoners faced a regime of brutal beatings, exhausting work, and political indoctrination. One sign of rehabilitation was a prisoner's willingness to torture a fellow prisoner.

Amnesty International has targeted Ethiopian prisons on a number of occasions. In 1978 it reported that prisons failed to live up to the standards set by the United Nations regulations for the treatment of prisoners. Overcrowding was rampant, with up to 50 prisoners sometimes sharing cells that measured four meters by four meters. Additional violations included the lack of the most basic sanitary facilities, poor ventilation, and even poorer medical treatment. Prisoners were usually able to survive thanks to contributions from friends and family members on the outside. When a prisoner had died, the family was notified that "food is no longer necessary" for their relatives.

In the late 1980s conditions had improved somewhat in Addis Adaba's Central Prison, but they were still below the minimum United Nations requirements. At the turn of the 1990s the more than 4,500 inmates at this nineteenth-century prison were allowed a number of privileges, including regular visits from family members, who were allowed to bring so-called comfort items such as food, books, medicine, and clean laundry. Even though basic medical treatment was available at the Central Prison, prisoners still had the option to visit an independent physician or local hospital. Prisoners were allowed to freely associate by day and could take advantage of secondary schooling opportunities. Despite small steps toward reform, by the 1990s Ethiopia's best prison was considered substandard. Outside the capital city conditions were even worse at facilities in Asmera, Mekele, and Harrar.

The larger institutions placed more emphasis on prison labor, in part because of the higher operational costs. Production was viewed as more important than vocational training. The most common prison industry was weaving, using outdated looms. Prison weavers produced the cotton used to make clothes and rugs. Other prison industries included carpentry, blacksmithing, metalworking, flour milling and baking, and jewelry making. Prisoners were compensated with about 10 percent of the proceeds, with the remaining 90 percent going toward the operation of the prisons. Most information indicates that prison guards were drawn from the ranks of military applicants, who were in turn paid with small plots of land that could be used by the guards during their tenure. No information on the number of prisoners is available.

In 2003 the Federal Prison Administration as well as nine State Prison Administrations operated under the Ministry of Federal Affairs. In 2003 it was estimated that the country had 2 federal prisons and 112 state prisons holding close to 65,000 if one exclude police facilities. The prison rate would be 92 per 100,000 of the national population.

Sources: LCCS, "Ethiopia: Prisons," 1991; ICPS, Ethiopia, 2004.

F

FAEROE ISLANDS. The Department of Prisons and Probation operates under Denmark's Ministry of Justice. Not exactly a hotbed of crime, most recent reports from 2003 indicate 28 prisoners in one facility, or 86.7 per 100,000 of the national population.

Source: ICPS, Faeroe Islands (Denmark), 2004.

FARNHAM, ELIZABETH (1815–1864). Elizabeth Farnham was an avid supporter of reformer **Elizabeth Gurney Fry**. Appointed head matron of **Mount Pleasant Prison**, the women's section of **Sing Sing Prison**, in 1844, Farnham embarked on a regimen that allowed female inmates to decorate their cells as they saw fit in the hopes of establishing a nourishing if not domestic environment. She is best remembered for instituting a brief period of radical experimentation in the women's prison, eliminating such **Auburn** mainstays as the rule of silence. However, she soon ran afoul of the male-dominated bureaucracy after inaugurating a prison education for the women. Other sources suggest that her mild regime at Farnham led to jealousy and disruption among the male inmate population, necessitating her removal and the implementation of a more punitive regime. While at Sing Sing Prison she applied the "latest" phrenological advances to the study and treatment of criminals. By 1846 she had been replaced after only a two-year stint.

Sources: McKelvey, *American Prisons*, 1977; Lucia Zedner, "Wayward Sisters: The Prison for Women," in *The Oxford History of the Prison*, eds. Morris and Rothman, 1998, pp. 295–324.

FEDERAL BUREAU OF PRISONS (USA). *See* UNITED STATES FEDERAL BUREAU OF PRISONS

FIJI. The Fiji Prisons Service falls under the direction of the Ministry of Justice. In 2003 the island held 982 prisoners in eight receiving centers and six traditional prisons, a rate of 117 per 100,000 of the national population. The largest prison is located in Suva. Three prison facilities are located on Viti Levu. Other facilities are located at Vanua Levu, Taveuni, and Rotuma. There is a prison farm near Uva at Maboro. In the late 1980s the emphasis of the prison regimen was directed at rehabilitation, education, and vocational training.

Sources: Kurian, *WEPP*, 1989; ICPS, Fiji, 2003.

FILARETE. *See* AVERLINO, ANTONIO

FINLAND. In 1931 Finland adopted indeterminate sentencing, a number of years after its Scandinavian neighbors Denmark and Norway. Finland experimented with a "treatment ideology" in the 1940s and 1950s by replacing prisons with treatment institutions. However, by the end of the 1950s this approach had fallen out of favor. Finnish prison sentences are broken down into three categories. The least severe consists of fixed terms of fourteen days to three months, followed by fixed terms of between three months and twelve years, but with the possibility of parole. The most serious term is life imprisonment (for murder), with only a presidential pardon for salvation.

Today few citizens face imprisonment in Finland. Of the almost 300,000 individuals sentenced for crime in 1986, less than 9 percent went to prison. Beginning in the 1970s the Finnish prison population saw a steady decrease, from 5,600 in 1976 to 4,200 10 years later. However, the prisoner rate of 86 per 100,000 is considered high compared to most Nordic countries. By 2001 the number of prisoners had decreased to 3,040, or 59 per 100,000 of the national population, more in line with other Scandinavian countries.

Two types of prisons predominate, closed and open institutions. Open prisons can be either located at a permanent site or like a labor colony, function during a limited time long enough to complete a specific work regime. Individuals selected for open facilities are typically confined for nonpayment of fines or are serving less than two years, physically able to work, and do not represent an escape risk. In recent years the Finnish prison system has moved toward a regime of more lenient sanctions and a reduction in the use of prison sentences. Currently, the Department of Prison Administration operates under the Ministry of Justice. As of 2004 Finland had 37 penal institutions, including 16 closed prisons, 5 open prisons, 14 open prison units including 4 labor colonies, and 2 prison hospitals. In mid-2004 there were 3,719 prisoners, representing 71 per 100,000 of the national population.

Sources: Inkeri Antilla, "Corrections in Finland," in *International Corrections*, eds. Wicks and Cooper, 1979, pp. 103–122; LCCS, "Finland: Sentencing and Punishment," December 1988; Tapio Lappi-Seppala, "Sentencing and Punishment in Finland: The Decline of the Repressive Ideal," in *Sentencing and Sanctions in Western Countries*, eds. Tonry and Frase, 2001, pp. 92–150; ICPS, Finland, 2004.

FLEET PRISON. Built in the twelfth century, Fleet Prison became London's most famous debtors' prison and was the first building in London constructed for the specific purpose of being a **gaol** (jail). It was rebuilt numerous times and by the fourteenth century was holding debtors, individuals convicted in the Court of Star Chamber, and those charged with contempt of the Royal Courts. Among its most distinguished prisoners was the poet John Donne, who spent a stint in Fleet Street in 1601, and later **William Penn**. It was demolished by the Great Fire of 1666 and then rebuilt. Partly because of its prominence as a jail for debtors and bankrupts, it was burned down once more during the 1780 Gordon Riots.

The Fleet Prison had a well-earned reputation for cruelty and corruption. The office of warden, or **keeper**, was considered a hereditary position. The position of keeper was a highly lucrative position with opportunities to earn fees for providing prisoners with food, lodging, and even short-term release. In the eighteenth century an individual purchased the office of the Keeper of the Fleet for 5,000 pounds. When he stepped down, he then sold the position to the deputy warden for the same price. During its heyday prisoners of both sexes mingled freely, leading one observer to describe it as the "largest brothel in England." Here women could improve their conditions by selling their bodies. The prison was usually overcrowded. In 1774 it held 243 debtors along with 475 members of their families who had nowhere else to go. The prison was finally closed in 1842.

Source: Herber, *Criminal London*, 2002.

FOLSOM PRISON (USA). Folsom Prison is one of California's best-known penitentiaries, made famous by country music singer Johnny Cash and his 1956 *Folsom Prison Blues*, a fictionalized account of a prisoner's stay there. Cash later performed a concert there in 1968. Folsom State Prison, or Folsom State at Represa, is one of 333 institutions operated by the California Department of Corrections. It is located in the city of Folsom almost twenty miles from Sacramento, the state's capital.

When it was completed in 1880, Folsom was next to **San Quentin Prison**, the state's second-oldest prison. Construction began on the unit designed for 100 inmates in 1878. Built on the same location of a gold mining camp along the American River, the first guards would spend their free time sifting sand for gold flakes. In the late nineteenth century the Enlightenment-driven prison reform movement had not yet reached California. When prisoners were not busy at hard labor, they spent most of their time in four-foot-by-eight-foot cells, with only candles or oil lamps for light and heat. Ventilation consisted of six-inch air slots in solid iron doors. In the 1940s air holes were finally drilled into the same doors in use today.

During its first half century the prison earned a reputation for brutality that it carried into the twentieth century. In 1884 Folsom introduced a canvas and leather straitjacket that was still in use in the early 1900s, as was the "iron claw," a restraining device that strung up troublesome inmates by their thumbs. In the 1940s most prisoners worked in the same rock quarries that were used to build the prison's original walls.

By the 1960s Folsom was still struggling to catch up with the penological strides of the twentieth century. With a capacity in 1960 for 2,350, it held close to 3,000. Much had changed, but it was still crowded with 4,000 recidivist inmates. Several renovation projects led to the creation of two separately run prisons in 1993. Once one of America's first maximum-security prisons, in 1992 it made the transition to housing medium-security inmates. The newer of the two sections was built in 1986 and now holds about 3,400 maximum-security prisoners; the "Old Folsom" is dedicated to 3,700 medium security prisoners. As of 2000, Folsom held 7,246 prisoners in the two lowest levels of security.

Sources: wikipedia.org/wiki/Folsom_State_Prison; Deford, *Stone Walls*, 1962.

FOX, LIONEL WRAY (1895–1960). Lionel Wray Fox was one of England's leading prison reformers of the twentieth century. Born in Halifax and educated at Hertford College, Oxford, Fox earned distinction for his service in World War I. Following hostilities, Fox served in the Home Office from 1919 to 1925, when he began a nine-year stint as secretary to the Prison Commission. Fox came to prominence in 1934 with the publication of *The Modern English Prison*, considered a pioneering work on penal reform. In 1941 he was appointed chairman of the Prison Commission. In 1952 Fox published *The English Prison and Borstal Systems*, which is still considered a classic work in penology. In this book Fox outlined a variety of alternatives to traditional imprisonment, including the "open-prison" system. In 1959 he was one of the authors of the white paper "Penal Practice in a Changing Society," which stimulated one of Great Britain's largest prison-building programs.

Sources: Fox, *The English Prison and Borstal Systems*, 1952; Phillips and Axelrod, *Cops, Crooks, and Criminologists*, 1996.

FRANCE. French prisons have been celebrated and reviled during their more than 600 year history. When this subject is broached fortress prisons such as the **Bastille** and penal colonies in the tradition of **Devil's Island** come to mind. The Bastille saw early use as one of Paris's city gates before making the transition to a prison in 1417. The Conciergerie was another prominent prison. Connected to the Palace of Paris, its name was derived from the French *Concierge,* or the habitat of the royal door keeper. During its history it housed a number of luminaries, including Marie Antoinette and Robespierre. Less well known, but just as storied were the Temple Prison, which was considered Paris's strongest facility but was demolished in 1811, the For-l'Eveque, or *forum episcopi,* built for ecclesiastical prisoners in 1611 and in use until 1780, and **Bicetre**, which was once infamous as an insane asylum but has seen service as a hospital, almshouse, and prison through the years. As late as 1835 galley slaves waited for their assignment in the Bicetre. Since its inauguration in 1851, Devil's Island has been a "hell on earth" and "dry guillotine" for hundreds of thousands of French offenders.

France sent several delegations to America in the nineteenth century to determine which direction the French prison system should take. The first commissioners included Gustave de Beaumont and **Alexis de Tocqueville**, neither of whom was favorable to the separate system. However, the next commission made up of architect **Guillaume Blouet** and judge Frederic Auguste Demetz lent their endorsement to this model. But because of the high cost of making the transition from the old congregate system, it would not come into fruition until 1875, and even then it would lack several features of the **Pennsylvania** model.

In June 1875 legislation was passed that officially replaced the older congregate methods with the separate system. Six years later an additional act was passed that prohibited all communication between prisoners during their entire term of incarceration. Prisoners were also required to wear a facemask any time they walked through the prison halls.

Central houses of hard labor have had a long history in France beginning with a decree passed in 1808 that divided these institutions into two groups. Central houses of labor strictly separated all inmates. However, in the **houses of correction** sentences of one to ten years are served in a congregate setting. Central houses were originally located in Poissy, Melun, Beaulieu, Gaillon, Fontevrault, Rion, Nimes, Thouars, Loos, and Clairvaux. Central houses for women were at Clairmont, Rennes, and Montpelier. Labor is compulsory and for state use (not open market). Since most of the work is handicraft oriented, prisoners can work in their cells. In 1885 legislation was implemented facilitating the **transportation** or relegation of convicts to penal colonies.

In 1568 early attempts were made to treat juvenile offenders differently from their adult counterparts. Reform did not begin on a high note, however, with most measures directed at whipping children, as young as 12 years of age, who could not be controlled by parents, in asylum prisons such as Bicetre and Saltpetriere. In 1791 more humane treatment superseded the whip, and minors under 21 were sent to houses of correction. But these facilities merely replaced corporal punishment with the deleterious conditions of the contemporary prison—unsanitary and unfit places for children. In 1827 steps were taken to remedy this situation with the opening of the Abbe Ausoux in Paris. Over the next 12 years several juvenile houses of correction were founded, inspired by the Houses of Refuge in vogue in America. Over the course of the next 40 years a variety of initiatives were passed improving the conditions of juvenile confinement.

Prior to World War II, French prisons were administered under the outdated administration by the Ministry of the Interior. Following liberation in 1945, the Penal Service was more effectively placed under the aegis of the Ministry of Justice. After this transfer the environment was ripe for reform measures. Reflecting reforms of a previous era, one of the most important developments in French corrections following the war was the introduction of a five-phase progressive regime. In the first phase a prisoner is kept in maximum-security isolation for nine months. Then he is interviewed and evaluated. At this time the prisoner either advances to the second phase or is kept in the first phase for further study. At the second phase prisoners eat and sleep in isolation but also take part in a work regime; this step lasts from six to twelve months. The third phase lasts one year. At this point they sleep in isolation at night but participate in-group activities by day. In the fourth stage prisoners have the opportunity to work outside the walls by day, returning to the prison at night. The final phase consisted of conditional release, where the prisoner works unsupervised and is placed on parole for three years. The progressive regime would predominate until its abolition in 1975.

In 1975 the French penal system underwent an important reorganization that included most importantly the abandonment of the progressive regime. By the late 1970s France had a prison population of 31,563, more than one third of whom were either awaiting trial or appealing their convictions. At that time the Prison Service employed a staff of almost 11,000, indicating a staff-to-prisoner ratio of more than 3 to 1. Modern French prisons fall under a number of categories. Local prisons, or jails, hold pre-trial prisoners and convicted offenders whose sentences do not exceed one year. These prisons run the gamut from the smallest, holding 20, to larger facilities such as Paris-Fleury-Merogis, which accommodates twice that. These institutions are typically plagued by overcrowding and poor medical services.

France employs special units for special cases. For example, here are prison hospitals at Paris-**Fresnes Prison** and Marseilles-Baumettes. There are also separate facilities for the elderly, the physically handicapped, and the chronically ill. Those who suffer from behavioral and mental disorders are housed at centers located at Chateau-Thierry and Haguenau.

Over the past decades several facilities have been organized specifically for women, such as the long-term institution at Rennes. Establishments created for the most serious male offenders include detention centers and *maisons centrales*. The latter is based on the **Auburn system**, where congregate work is the dominant feature. These are considered high-security facilities meant to hold between 250 and 550 prisoners. However, there has also been much progress in integrating rehabilitation programs to prepare for the reintegration of prisoners into society. The detention centers are either open or closed facilities, both geared to resocialization.

Of the country's 185 prisons, more than 100 were built more than 80 years ago. In 1999, 124 prisoners committed suicide in French jails, one of the highest rates in Europe. Today the French Prison Service falls under the direction of the Ministry of Justice. In early 2004 there were 56,957 held in 185 prisons. This was 124.7 percent of capacity, or 95 per 100,000 of the national population. These numbers indicate a slight increase over the past twelve years, from a low of 78 per 100,000 in 2001. The prison figures only include prisoners held by the national prison administration in metropolitan France.

Sources: Teeters, *World Penal Systems*, 1944; Yvonne Marx and Xavier Nicot, "The French Penal System," in *International Corrections*, 1979, pp. 57–69; Patricia O'Brien, *The Promise of Punishment: Prisons in Nineteenth Century France* (Princeton, NJ: Princeton University Press, 1982); Kurian, *WEPP*, 1989; ICPS, France, 2004.

FRANCI, FILIPPO (ACTIVE 1670s). One of the earliest examples of the use of cellular confinement was at the hospice of San Filippo Neri, operated in Florence in 1677. It was opened by the priest Filippo Franci in an a former palace as a sanctuary for homeless and delinquent boys, the equivalent of today's street children. In the transformation of the building from palace to hospice, small cells were built and 33 priests and "lay protectors" were anointed as supervisors. Norman Johnston compares their duties as vocational instructors as similar to the now familiar parole officer.

Franci's regime included constructive daytime activities, followed by nighttime solitary confinement with visits by two "protectors." Inmates were never given the opportunity to see each other, since every time they left their cells their faces were concealed. For more than a century the hospice directed its regime of rehabilitation in a manner prescient for its time. Criminologist Thorsten Sellin proclaimed that this was the "first practical attempt to use this mode of treatment [24-hour segregation] for the avowed purpose of correction and reformation."

Sources: Thorsten Sellin, "Filippo Franci—a Precursor of Modern Penology," *Journal of the American Institute of Criminal Law and Criminology* 17 (May 1926), pp. 104–112; Johnston, *Forms of Constraint*, 2000.

FRENCH GUIANA. Best known as the site of France's notorious penal colony and **Devil's Island**, today there is one prison holding 590 inmates. The prison rate is

324 per 100,000 of the national population. This prison is directed by the French Ministry of Justice.

Source: ICPS, French Guiana/Guyane, South America, 2004.

FRENCH POLYNESIA. Like **French Guiana**, this territory's prison system is also operated under the French Ministry of Justice. In 2003 the islands three prisons held 291 prisoners in space designated for 149. The prison rate is 120 per 100,000 of the national population.

Source: ICPS, French Polynesia (France), Oceania, 2003.

FRESNES PRISON. The largest prison in **France**, it was constructed between 1895 and 1898, it was modeled on what later became known as the **telephone pole design**, which was considered a radical departure from traditional prison layouts. It would become a popular prison model in the United States in the twentieth century. Fresnes Prison, located in the town of Fresnes near Paris, is considered the first penal institution where cell houses extended crosswise from a central corridor, in the process bisecting the housing units at right angles while connecting all the cell houses and other facilities. Poussin favored this design because he felt it would provide better light and ventilation. Fresnes consisted of three long cellblocks, each with 506 cells. It was capable of holding more than 1,500 prisoners in single-cell confinement. Originally inmates were limited to one-year sentences in these conditions. Each individual cell was equipped with its own toilet, water tap, bed, chair, folding table, and wall shelves.

Under Nazi occupation during World War II, the prison was devoted to holding captured British agents and members of the French Resistance. Many were tortured and executed here. As the Allied forces made their way from Normandy to Paris in 1944, the Gestapo killed most of the prisoners who were still alive only weeks before the liberation of Paris.

Source: Johnston, *Forms of Constraint*, 2000.

FRY, ELIZABETH GURNEY (1780–1845). Born into a wealthy Quaker family, Elizabeth Fry rose to prominence as a prison reformer in her native England. She was drawn to her life's work following a visit in 1813 to London's **Newgate Prison**. Fry was particularly shocked by the conditions under which women were held. In one room alone she found 120 female prisoners, drinking alcohol and with only the bare floor for sleeping arrangements. Although she did not return to Newgate for four years, during which time she gave birth to her ninth and tenth children, she never forgot the odious conditions at Newgate. In 1817 she formed a group of 12 mostly Quaker women, a reform group called the Association for the Improvement of Female Prisoners in Newgate, and was successful in improving the conditions for women prisoners. She was credited with improving the food, bedding, and clothing, and replacing male jailers in the women's wing of Newgate with female matrons and officers. However, their efforts would not have been successful had they not received support from the Newgate keeper and several sheriffs. Together, the officials and Fry's reformers came up with a set of rules that were accepted by the women prisoners. The women prisoners were encouraged to hold up their part of the bargain by taking efforts to reform themselves by abstaining from begging, swearing, gaming, and immoral conversations. At the same time they agreed to keep busy learning marketable skills such as needlework and knitting. They also agreed to attend Bible study each morning and evening. In 1818 Mrs. Fry was recognized for her efforts when she was invited to give evidence before a House of Commons Committee on Prisons. During the last decades of her life Fry never wavered from her crusade, and in time her reform efforts were borrowed by other institutions, improving conditions for women prisoners as they awaited release or **transportation** to Australia.

Sources: Ann D. Smith, *Women in Prison* (London: Stevens and Sons, 1962); Babington, *The English Bastille*, 1971.

FURTTENBACH, JOSEPH (1591–1667). This German architect published plans and descriptions of several prisons in his 1653 book *Architectura Universalis*. What strikes the reader is Furttenbach's belief in the reformative value of single-cell confinement in such an early era. The book also included plans for arsenals, schools, and **lazarettos** based on the **cruciform** design.

Source: Johnston, *Forms of Constraint*, 2000.

G

GALLEY SLAVERY. Long before the advent of the penitentiary, the ancient Romans used galley servitude as a form of punitive bondage. According to historian Pieter Spierenburg, the French "pioneered" the use of galleys in Europe by the fifteenth century. Spierenburg suggests that galley use in Europe started out not as a "criminal punishment" but as "disciplinary institutions meant to deal with problems of poverty and marginality." By the sixteenth century galleys became more common in southern Europe, including Spain and the Italian states. The popularity of manpowered ships in the more southerly climes of the Mediterranean region was often necessitated by insufficient winds for sailing. Among the denizens forced to man the oars of the large, low ships were vagrants, transients, beggars, and delinquents. Later, galley servitude was sometimes used as an alternative to the death penalty in some countries. In 1748 France eliminated galley servitude, and by the end of the century this form of punishment was abolished. A number of the southern European countries made the transition to **bagnes**, or penal colonies.

Sources: Pieter Spierenburg, "The Body and The State: Early Modern Europe," in *Oxford History of the Prison*, eds. Morris and Rothman, 1995, pp. 44–70; Johnston, *Forms of Constraint*, 2000.

GAMBIA. The Gambian Prison Service is the responsibility of the Ministry of the Interior. In 1999 the prison system had a capacity to hold 780 inmates. In 2002 the country's three prisons were below capacity with 450 prisoners, or 32 per 100,000 of the national population.

Sources: Walmsley, *WPPL*, 2003; ICPS, Gambia, Africa, 2004.

GAOLER. The gaoler, or jailer, was a combination of prison guard and officer. This position came to prominence in Great Britain sometime between the seventeenth and eighteenth centuries. Early documentary evidence is rather sketchy. What is clear is that by the early eighteenth century the most recent sheriff or county law enforcement officer made the appointment of gaoler. Anyone considered for this position was expected to meet certain qualifications and be a respected member of the community. There is a remarkable story involving the sinecure-like position of the Richardson-Howard family. Between 1711 and 1814 six members of this family held the post of gaoler for a combined total of 70 years. Most extraordinary is that the position of high sheriff changed annually, so appointments were for only one year at a time—meaning that representatives of this family were appointed 70 times. Although men predominated at this position, women gaolers also were employed—but these were typically the wives of gaolers who helped run their husbands' gaols, even taking charge under certain conditions.

Since gaolers were not paid a salary prior to **John Howard**'s campaign for reform, many gaolers earned their livings by selling food and drink to prisoners or charging fees for basic living provisions. Justices of the peace fixed these fees. According to one fee sheet from 1753, prisoners were charged an entrance fee, a fee for lodging, and a fee for use of sheets and bedding each week, as well as a discharge fee.

Sources: Eric Stockdale, "John Howard and Bedford Prison," in *Prisons Past and Future*, ed. Freeman, 1978, pp. 15–24; Evans, *The Fabrication of Virtue*, 1982.

GAOL FEVER. Also known as jail fever, this disease, a form of typhus, decimated prisoners in the eighteenth century, taking more lives than the gallows. Gaol fever took the lives not only of prisoners but also of judges, lawyers, jury members, jail keepers, and most notably the reformer **John Howard**. The incidence of gaol fever is considered a stimulus for prison reform after the 1770s. According to Robin Evans, England experienced a "wholesale building program." Between 1775 and 1795 more than 40 were erected. Evans suggests that this massive rebuilding program was the result of "the American War of Independence and an unexpected outbreak of gaol fever." In an era before the discovery of the germ theory (1883), reformers reasoned that new prisons should be designed with better ventilation, clean water supply, and proper nutrition in mind. In his seminal work *The State of the Prisons*, Howard describes the almost complete lack of medical attention and poor sanitary conditions of British prisons in 1777.

Sources: Howard, *John Howard: Prison Reformer*, 1963; Evans, *Fabrication of Virtue*, 1982; Herber, *Criminal London*, 2002.

"GARNISH." During the seventeenth and eighteenth centuries the only British subjects in prisons were either debtors, convicted individuals awaiting **transportation**, or those awaiting trial. As soon as most of these unfortunates were thrust behind bars, they were expected to pay the other prisoners a "garnish" tax or face having their clothes stripped off by the other inmates. When **John Howard** began work at **Bedford Prison**, a large sign at the front gate read, "All persons that come to this place, either by warrant, commitment, or verbally, must pay before discharged, fifteen shillings and four pence to the gaoler, and two shillings to the **turnkey**." Sights like these led Howard to campaign for more equitable and professional correctional practices and spurred him on to visit prisons throughout Europe during the last two decades of his life.

Source: Howard, *John Howard*, 1963.

GATEHOUSE PRISONS. No gatehouse prison was as famous as London's **Newgate Prison**. A gatehouse had been positioned at this site since the Roman period. Prior to the advent of the prison, castle and city gatehouses were used to confine prisoners, usually just temporarily. The most common explanation for the origin of this practice was a Norman edict in 1166 that required sheriffs to use the king's castles as local prisons. Over the subsequent decades a series of laws against vagrants and transients pushed the prisons to the outskirts of the city, near the city gates, since this is where most of the "strangers" or vagrants were arrested.

According to Norman Johnston, more attention was paid to strengthening the outer walls of castles by the thirteenth century. As a result, more attention was also paid to improving the various parts of the walls, including the gatehouse and castle prison quarters. The gatehouse became a more important position, since it controlled access to the castle grounds. As a result, the gatehouse was enlarged to create rooms for guards. The gatehouse prison was typically a small cell next to the guard's quarters and on the same level as the passageway. This enabled a guard to watch prisoners and act as gatekeeper simultaneously. As other walls were built to surround the towns that grew outside of the castle, more gatehouses were required and in the process more gatehouse cells were built.

Sources: Pugh, *Imprisonment in Medieval England*, 1970; Evans, *The Fabrication of Virtue*, 1982; Johnston, *Forms of Constraint*, 2000.

GEORGIA. The Georgia Department of Punishment Execution falls under the Ministry of Justice. In late 2004 17 prison establishments held 7,091 prisoners. Slightly more than 50 percent of the prisoners are either pre-trial detainees or remand prisoners. Currently the prison rate is 165 per 100,000 of the national population, compared to 202 per 100,000 in 2001, and 248 per 100,000 in 1998.

Source: ICBS, Georgia, Europe, 2004.

GERMANY. Prior to unification, the German states used a variety of penal procedures. **Workhouses** were established long before the reforms of **John Howard**. Following the examples set by London's **Bridewells** and Amsterdam's **rasphouses**, Bremen inaugurated its first one in 1609, Lubeck in 1613, and Hamburg in 1622. The era of John Howard inspired even more reliance on workhouses for the vagrant and indigent population. Various cities put felons to work on streets or in quarries, while prisoners at Bayreuth polished marble and those in Nuremberg likewise polished lenses.

On his visit to the German states John Howard reported the thriving workhouses in Bremen, Lubeck, and Hamburg, but apparently he had nothing positive to report on the state of prisons.

Prussia and several other German states adopted the **Pennsylvania system** of separate confinement after 1834, following the return of Dr. **Nicolaus Heinrich Julius** from studying penal philosophy in America. While a number of modifications were initiated, the separate system remained popular into the Nazi era. International penology helped shape early German prison reform. King Frederick William IV was particularly taken by the construction he observed at **Pentonville Prison**. In 1846 Frankfurt hosted the first international prison congress, albeit an official meeting. In the mid-nineteenth century some of the German states began to move away from the separate system, in part because of the system's high costs.

German prisons of the nineteenth century came in a variety of styles. Some prisons were buildings modified from other purposes, and many were based on a **radial** design. Two of the most prominent prisons of this era were Berlin's **Moabit Prison** and Ratibor Prison built in what is now Poland. Few prisons in Germany during the nineteenth century followed nonradial design. According to prison authority Norman Johnston, the German states "did more to replace its old congregate prisons with new cellular construction" in the nineteenth century than any European country except for England and Belgium.

Before World War II, Germany offered several types of prisons for convicted offenders. In the *Zuchthaus*, prisoners serve minimum sentences of one year and maximum of life. Similar to the American **reformatory**, the *Gefaengis* housed offenders serving a minimum of one day and maximum of five years. Serving a sentence in the latter institution was considered less stigmatizing, since those in the former could face permanent or temporary prohibition to work at certain professions or to enjoy certain civil rights.

Before the Nazis took over, Germany prisoners were classified according to recidivism patterns. A **mark system** was established that allowed prisoners to gain more privileges through good work and behavior, resulting in more mail, reading material, extra visits, and the like. When the Nazis took power in the 1930s, reformatories and correctional institutions aimed at the young offender became progressively harsh and repressive. In the *Jugend-Gefangnisse,* there was little if any opportunity for young offenders to listen to radio, play tournaments, engage in sports, or partake of various hobbies. According to the penal regulations of the day, "The young offender must be kept under strict discipline."

In the 1930s and 1940s most prison sentences were fixed, with little regard paid to indeterminate sentencing. Cells were especially spartan, food and clothing simple, and labor or handicraft work stressed. Not surprising, German prisons in the early Nazi era favored repression and deterrence over rehabilitation and reformation.

Between 1963 and 1994 the prison population fell from 56,870 to 34,398. According to Hans-Jorg Albrecht, sentencing policies and practices in Germany "changed substantially since 1970 as a result of a substantial shift from imprisonment to fines, probation, and various diversionary programs." By the mid-1970s there were 168 prisons facilities holding 34,608 prisoners. The system had the capacity to hold 58,000. A number of prisons were still housed in original nineteenth-century prisons modeled after the Pennsylvania system. However, from the 1950s through the 1970s West Germany witnessed a significant prison construction campaign in an attempt to move away from the isolation and surveillance regimes of the earlier century. Among the more prominent new prisons was Lingen-Ost Penitentiary, which features "a system of decentralized bungalows." However, others have followed in the footsteps of the sterile fortresses from the punitive era, such as Hanover Prison, built in the 1960s. Still others, such as Stuttgart-Stammheim Prison, look to the future with an architectural design featuring electronic surveillance technology and a sterile environment. In the 1960s and 1970s a number of prisons were built on the **telephone pole model**, including Brockwede I and II, Iserholm, and Pont, all located in Nordrhein-Westfalen.

Following reunification in 1990, East Germany's prison population fell from 24,000 to 5,000 as a result of the diminution in political crimes and the adoption of West Germany's criminal code. In the early 1990s fines were the most common penal sanction. For example, of 600,000 sentenced for criminal acts that year only 100,000 were sentenced to prison.

Currently Germany's Prison and Probation Service operates under the Ministry of Justice. As of the end of 2003 Germany's 222 penal institutions were at 100.5 percent of capacity, holding 79,153 prisoners, or 96 per 100,000 of the national population. Almost one third of the nation's prisoners are foreigners.

Sources: Wines, *Punishment and Reformation*, 1895; Hans von Hentig, "Germany's Prison System," *Annals of the American Academy of Political and Social Science*, September 1931, pp. 174–179; Marie Munk, "The Philosophy of Criminal Justice in the United States and in Germany," *Prison Journal*, July 1937, pp. 349–357; Robert Gellately, "The Prerogatives of Confinement in Germany, 1933–1945: Protective Custody and Other Police Strategies," in *Institutions of Confinement*, 1996, pp. 191–211; Christina Vanja, "Madhouses, Children's Wards, and Clinics: The Development of Insane Asylums in Germany," in *Institutions of Confinement*, 1996, pp. 117–132; Karl Tilman Winkler, " 'Comparing Apples and Oranges?': The History of Early Prisons in Germany and the United States," in *Institutions of Confinement*, eds. Finzch and Jutte, 1996, pp. 213–234; Hans-Jorg Albrecht, "Sentencing and Punishment in Germany," in *Penal Reform in Overcrowded Times*, ed. Tonry, 2000, pp. 139–145; Johnston, *Forms of Constraint*, 2000; Wachsmann, *Hitler's Prisons*, 2004.

GHANA. Prisons did not exist in traditional Ghana. However, British merchants established prisons in Ghana by the mid-nineteenth century, including the infamous Cape Coast Castle. As early as 1850 the British had set up three more prisons capable of holding more than 120 prisoners. Most inmates were put to work on road gangs. It was not until 1860 that the British colony established a Prisons Ordinance regulating the care of inmates. The colony favored a **separate system** approach of solitary confinement, penal labor, and meager diet. At the turn of the century colonial officials from Great Britain supervised the country's prison system under the watchful eyes of European prison guards. The British built early prisons at the Ussher Fort and at Nsawan. According to John A. Arthur, both prisons exemplified the penal philosophy of the nineteenth century and were constructed following the **Bridewell** workhouse and **house of correction** models of the late-sixteenth century. However, there was no attempt to separate prisoners according to gender and classification.

Few facilities were built following World War II, but native Ghanaians did take over many of the British posts and by 1962 staffed all prison positions. During the administration of Nkrumah little attention was paid to penal conditions, but following his overthrow a commission was formed to investigate prison conditions in 1968. Among its findings was that out of the nation's 29 prison facilities, 9 were unfit for habitation, 2 could be utilized only as temporary police lockups, and 13 were suitable for short-term detention. But political infighting and corruption caused the commission's recommendations to be cast aside as prison conditions continued to deteriorate.

Since Ghana attained independence, ministerial responsibility for the prison system has been assigned and reassigned until being fixed by statute, with separate requirements for adults and juveniles. Currently adult prisoners are handled under the Prison Ordinance, which established guidelines for prison operation and maintenance. In 1969 the new constitution created a Prison Service, headed by a director chosen by the nation's chief executive. Juvenile offenders are governed under the Criminal Procedure Code.

In 1992 the prison system consisted of 27 institutions, including 6 central prisons located Sekondi, Kumasi, Tamale, and Nsawan, with two facilities, Ussher Fort and James Fort, in Accra. There is little distinction in the prisons between petty offenders and career criminals, resulting in their incarceration in the same facilities. Women are confined at two central prisons at Ekuasi and Sekondi. Local prisoners facing short-term confinement or under remand are housed in 15 smaller prisons, 6 of which have separate lodging for women. Prisoners categorized as well behaved can serve time in several open prison camps located at James Camp near Accra and Ankaful near the Cape Coast. These camps are the only facilities not burdened by overcrowding. This form of confinement is highly sought after, since the camps offer opportunities to work in industrial workshops and farms, adequate medical care, and other amenities. The previously mentioned correctional facilities are supplemented by a number of remand homes, probation houses, and industrial schools directed by the Ministry of Labor and Social Welfare.

The Prisons Service Board promulgates prison policies and regulations. The board is made up of a member-chairperson from the Public Services Commission, the Prison Services director, a representative of the attorney general, the principal secretary of the Ministry of Employment and Social Welfare, a medical officer of the Ghana Medical Association, and three other members, one of whom must be female, and the other two representing religious organizations.

As in other developing nations, understaffing plagues Ghana's prison system; however, the quality of the staff has noticeably improved in recent years. The staff shortage is partly a consequence of the requirement that there be one staff member for every three prisoners, although it is exacerbated by the exigencies of budgeting, which have increased the ratio to 1 to 5 in many facilities. A number of Ghanaians consider a career in corrections. Guards, or warders, have improved, and now women officers number among the ranks. The majority are recruited from the most literate ethnic groups—the Ewe and Ga. A six-month training regimen is conducted at a school in Maamobi, outside Accra. Today's Ghana Prisons Service operates under the Ministry of the Interior. There are now 43 penal institutions, including 18 local prisons, 9 central prisons, 7 women's prisons, and 9 settlement camps. As of late 2003 Ghana held 11,379 prisoners, representing 54 per 100,000 of the national population.

Sources: Kurian, *WEPP*, 1989; LCCS, "Ghana: Prison System," November 1994; John A. Arthur, "Development of Penal Policy in Former British West Africa: Exploring the Colonial Dimension," in *Comparative and International Criminal Justice Systems*, ed. Ebbe, 1996, pp. 67–81; Bernault, ed., *A History of Prison and Confinement in Africa*, 2003; Walmsley, *WPPL*, 2003; ICPS, Ghana, 2004.

GHENT MAISON DE FORCE (PRISON). A house of correction was founded in 1627 when Ghent was an Austrian province of Flanders. It held both adult and juvenile prisoners. By the 1770s it was decided to rebuild the original house of correction in Ghent as a *Maison de Force* to hold offenders in separate cells, a major step in prison innovation. Adopting the regime made famous at **San Michele Hospice** and later by the **Auburn system,** the reconstructed prison featured separate cells arranged in eight trapezoidal clusters, each devoted to a different classification of prisoners. Prisoners worked in a congregate setting by day and slept in separate cells at night.

By 1771 Austrian Flanders was plagued by rising crime and public disorder. Count **Jean Jacques Philippe Vilain** was selected to reform the penal system. He based much of his plan on the workhouses of Amsterdam, which included a regimen of communal day work and nighttime isolation. In his memoirs Vilain noted his opposition to corporal punishment and his support for forced labor combined with forced detention. The major distinction here was that the work should be remunerated and constructive beyond financially supporting the institution. Prison historian Norman Johnston suggests that the Ghent House of Correction was the first institution to apply the principles of night isolation and separation by gender, age, length of sentence, and degree of criminality at the same time.

Construction took place between 1772 and 1775, although the institution received its first prisoners in 1773 following the completion of four units. The prison was initially regarded as a model institution. Over the next decades overcrowding required more than one prisoner to a cell. A decline in prison industry led to less emphasis on training. Under French control the prison fell further into disrepute. Between 1824 and 1827 the prison underwent new construction, and by the 1830s the original vision of the prison had become a reality, with the capacity to hold 2,600 inmates. Used for prisoners for the next century, it was partially destroyed during World War II.

Sources: Teeters, *World Penal Systems*, 1944; Johnston, *Forms of Constraint*, 2000.

GIBRALTAR (UK). Gibraltar is considered a British dependent territory. The Gibraltar Prison Service is directed by the Department of Social Service. In 2003 there was one prison holding 31 prisoners, a rate of 31 per 100,000 of the national population. Nearly half the prisoners are either remand or pre-trial detainees.

Source: ICPS, Gibraltar (United Kingdom), 2004.

GORING, CHARLES BUCKMAN (1870–1919). An English psychiatrist and philosopher, Charles Goring came to prominence with the 1913 publication of *The English Convict*. A lifelong affiliation with the English prison system as a medical officer allowed him to study 3,000 inmates. As a result of his extensive research, he supported education and rehabilitation in the prison regimen. His support eventually repudiated **Lombroso's** influential thesis on hereditary criminality. Although Lombroso is most remembered as the first social scientist to advocate education as a deterrent to crime, Goring has left a more indelible imprint on modern prison reform.

Sources: Edwin D. Driver, "Charles Buckman Goring," *Journal of Criminal Law, Criminology, and Police Science* 47, no. 5 (January–February 1957) pp. 515–525; Phillips and Axelrod, *Cops, Crooks, and Criminologists*, 1996.

GREAT PRISON, THE. In the Book of Genesis there is a description of an early Egyptian prison. The Great Prison, or *hnrt wr*, at Thebes (present Luxor) was the pharaoh's prison. In Egyptian the word *hnr* is derived from the verb "to restrain." The prison was reportedly located in a former granary and housed foreign offenders. Prisoners were expected to work during their confinement.

Sources: Edward M. Peters, "Prison before Prison: The Ancient and Medieval Worlds," in *The Oxford History of the Prison*, eds. Morris and Rothman, 1998, pp. 3–43.

GREECE. The use of imprisonment in Greece can be traced back to ancient Athens, which according to Norman Johnston prescribed it "only for crimes of high treason or debt to the government." Plato even proposed several types of state prisons in his classical work remembered as *Plato's Laws*, dating back to the tenth century B.C. Historian Edward M. Peters suggests that "short or long terms in prison" were used for other offenses as well.

There was little prison reform in Greece before the twentieth century partly because of scant financial resources. What prisons Greece did construct tended to be rather small and rectangular-shaped, and they were typically overcrowded. Most had originally begun life as other dwellings, before their ultimate transformation into prisons when needed. Most did not have cells. Prominent examples were located at Nauplia, Kalamion, and Salonica. Two purpose-built prisons, include Sygrou Prison, built in 1887 and destroyed during World War II, and a circular prison built at Samos. In 1911 Greece adopted the suspended sentence as an alternative to imprisonment.

Today the Greek prison system is the responsibility of the Ministry of Justice. In late 2003 there were 25 penal institutions holding 8,841 prisoners, almost one third of whom were pre-trial detainees or on remand. The prison rate is 83 per 100,000 of the national population.

Sources: Edward M. Peters, "Prison before the Prison: The Ancient and Medieval Worlds," in *Oxford History of the Prisons*, eds. Morris and Rothman, 1998, pp. 3–43; Johnston, *Forms of Constraint*, 2000; Saunders, *Plato's Penal Code: Controversy and Reform in Greek Penology*, 1991; ICPS, Greece, 2004.

GREENLAND. Greenland's Department of Prisons and Probation is the responsibility of the Danish Ministry of Justice. In late 2003 Greenland maintained 5 institutions, including 4 prisons and 1 open unit or hostel devoted to juvenile offenders. Of the island's 100 prisoners, 10 are in the hostel. The prison rate is 177 per 100,000 of the national population.

Source: ICPS, Greenland (Denmark), 2004.

GRELLET, STEPHEN (ACTIVE 1810s). Stephen Grellet, or Etienne de Grellet de Mobillier, was the son of a French-American Quaker who had served as the controller of the French Mint. Grellet was drawn to the cause of prison reform sometime in the early 1810s, resulting on his visit to England to survey prison conditions. Despite war between the two countries, Grellet traveled from France to England and in early 1813 met up with noted Quaker prison reformer **Elizabeth Fry**. While in London he won permission to visit **Newgate Prison** and was appalled at the conditions he found in the newly rebuilt facility. He soon enlisted Fry in his crusade to improve conditions at Newgate and to distribute clothing to the poorly clothed men and women (babies were often naked). Over the next three decades Fry became known as the Angel of Newgate.

Source: DeFord, *Stone Walls*, 1962.

GRENADA. Her Majesty's Prison in Grenada is under the Prime Minister's Office. The island's one prison was built to hold 115 prisoners, but as of mid-2002 it held 333 inmates, a rate of 297 per 100,000 of the national population.

Source: ICPS, Grenada, 2003.

GUADELOUPE (FRANCE). This French territory has two penal institutions, both under the direction of the French Ministry of Justice. The island reports a prison population of 695, or 159 per 100,000 of the national population.

Source: ICPS, Guadeloupe (France), Caribbean, 2003.

GUAM (USA). Guam's Department of Corrections reports a prison population of 542, or 334 per 100,000 of the national population.

Source: ICPS, Guam (USA), Oceania, 2003.

GUANTANAMO BAY. Better known by its abbreviations GTMO and "Gitmo," the Guantanamo military base was established on the island of Cuba in 1898 during negotiations after the Spanish-American War. According to agreements signed with the Cuban government in 1902 and 1903 and a treaty in 1934, the United States was allowed to keep a lifetime lease for the base at the equivalent of 4,000 dollars per year in rent. Reports indicate that since Castro came to power in 1959, he has cashed only one of these checks. The American occupation of the southeastern tip of the island remains a controversial topic on a number of fronts. GTMO is prominent today as a detention facility. Beginning in the 1970s it was used to detain Cuban and Haitian refugees who had been picked up on the high seas. However, following the terrorist attacks on September 11, 2001, preparations were made to house suspected al-Qaeda and Taliban members beginning in 2002. A number of these Afghanistani prisoners are housed at Camp X-ray, Camp Delta, and Camp Echo. Hundreds of prisoners are now held on the base from the conflict in Afghanistan, many without being charged. The location of the base outside the United States for the detention of prisoners places it under the sovereignty of Cuban law, therefore circumventing the constitutional rights that govern American criminal justice. The continued use of the base for prisoners from the Afghanistan conflict has been the target of human rights groups such as the International Committee of the Red Cross. Despite American claims that the detention facilities are "being operated at very high standards," accounts by former prisoners indicate that prisoners have been tortured and confronted with religious persecution and forced druggings.

Sources: www.guantanamo.com;nytimes.com/2004/11/30/politics/30gitmo; Wikipedia.org/wiki/Guantanamo_Bay.

GUATEMALA. The Guatemala Prison System is operated under the Ministry of Government, whereas local jails are considered the jurisdiction of local police and officials. There are an additional 19 prisons for men and about the same for women in other departments across the country. The main penitentiaries for men are located near Guatemala City, Quezaltenango and Escuintla. Recent reports indicate that the prison system houses 8,307 prisoners in a system with the official capacity to hold 7,233 inmates. Overcrowding and poor conditions predominate, as does inadequate security and medical facilities. In 2003 58 percent of the inmates were remand or pre-trial detainees. The prison rate is 68 per 100,000 of the national population.

The Zacapa prison, which was designed for 140 prisoners, holds 325 inmates and conditions are grim by all accounts. Pavon Prison and Preventivo Prison in Guatemala City hold 3,525 prisoners in space designed for 2,482. More than half the nation's prisoners are being held in pre-trial status. Although pre-trial detention is limited by law to three months, longer terms are routine. Prisons are plagued by drug-related corruption and sporadic escape attempts. A number of prisons are aided by the military in guarding the prison perimeters.

In 2001 more than seventy-five prisoners escaped from the Escuintla maximum-security prisons. Following an investigation, it was determined that prison officials collaborated with prisoners. As a result the prison director was sentenced to 16 years in prison; a number of other officials received lesser sentences.

Separate facilities for the 452 women prisoners are available but suffer from the same problems as the men's facilities. The main women's prison is Saint Teresa. There are several facilities specifically for minors, one for girls and two for boys.

Sources: www.state.gov/g/drl/rls/hrrpt/2003/27900; Kurian, *WEPP*, 1989; ICPS, Guatemala, 2004.

GUERNSEY (UK). The Guernsey State Prison is the responsibility of the State of Guernsey Home Affairs Committee. As of 2003 the island's one prison held 83 inmates, a ratio of 128 per 100,000 of the national population.

Source: ICPS, Guernsey (United Kingdom), 2004.

GULAG. "Gulag" is actually an acronym for *Glavnoe Upravlenie Lagerie*, which translated from Russian means "Main Camp Administration." The administration of the camps was primarily the responsibility of the Soviet internal police and security service that operated the penal system of force labor camps. D. M. Thomas, the biographer of noted political prisoner **Alexander Solzhenitsyn**, suggests that "it appears Solzhenitsyn was the first to use the word [*gulag*] as an independent noun." The publication of the English and French translations of Solzhenitsyn's first volume of *The Gulag Archipelago* in 1974 introduced the world to some of history's worst atrocities.

By the early 1720s Peter the Great was utilizing prisoners on forced public works projects building roads and fortresses and even in ships in his namesake capital St. Petersburg. In 1722 he began to specifically banish criminals with their entire families to exile in the wilds of eastern Siberia, where they were expected to work in the silver mines. With the abolition of the death penalty in 1753, czarist Russia began to transport all the formerly condemned to labor camps, or *katorgas*, in Siberia for life. "Katorga" is derived from the Greek word *kateirgon*, which means "to force." Other early work camps were located on the island of Sakhalin in the

North Pacific and on the Solovetski Islands in the Arctic Ocean. For most of these prisoners forced labor was a death sentence without a writ of execution. Although hundreds of thousands perished in forced labor projects under the czars, the phenomenon left behind a legacy that suggested Peter's forced labor regime was economically profitable.

By the time of the Russian Revolution, the katorga was considered a rare type of punishment. The total population of convicts in the work camps was estimated at 28,600. Following the Bolshevik Revolution the more familiar Gulag system was fine-tuned under first Vladimir Lenin and then Josef Stalin. In 1917 Lenin announced that "class enemies" should be treated as criminals, whether there was evidence or not. It was not long before the katorgas were overflowing with class enemies ranging from former nobles, businesspeople, and large landowners to government officials who had been accused of sabotage and corruption. Lenin not only would absorb the tsarist security apparatus but would reorganize it into a vast killing machine.

The Gulag was formerly inaugurated as the "Ulag" on April 25, 1930, but renamed the "Gulag" in November. Stalin's totalitarian rule led to one economic catastrophe after another with failed harvests and poor production routine. Rather than accept blame for poor planning and leadership, he found it easier to blame failure on corruption and sabotage. At the same time Russia's burgeoning industrialization program was badly in need of cheap labor to help provide natural resources to fuel the program. In order to solve both problems it soon became customary to use the secret police apparatus to arrest and denounce citizens for sabotage, corruption, and all manners of clandestine activities. As Stalin's control over the secret police expanded in the 1930s, the Gulag population would swell from 200,000 prisoners in 1932 to one million in 1935, if one included the other penal colonies as well. After the Great Purge in 1937 this number was doubled. Only with the outbreak of World War II was their any decline in the laborer population. Hundreds of thousands of prisoners were released so that they could be conscripted into the army and sent directly into action against the Germans.

Following the end of hostilities the prison camp population was replenished with criminals, deserters, repatriated Russian prisoners of war, large numbers of civilians, and even Nazi death camp survivors. By the early 1950s the camps were crowded with at least 2.5 million prisoners. Following the death of Stalin in 1953, a number of amnesties led to the release of thousands of political prisoners and common criminals. In January 1960 the Gulag was officially eliminated. More than a million Gulag deaths have been documented for the years 1934 to 1953. Despite proclamations to the contrary, Anne Applebaum documented the release of political prisoners from the Gulag as late as 1987. After the Soviet archives were opened, Applebaum and other scholars conducted painstaking examinations of the records to determine the number of individuals in the forced labor camps. In her magisterial study *The Gulag*, published to wide acclaim in 2003, Applebaum came up with a figure of 28.7 million between 1929 and 1953. Of these she estimated that 2,749,163 died in the camps.

During the Gulag era once prisoners were freed from a camp or prison they were restricted from working in a number of occupations; some were even restricted from living in larger cities. While incarcerated most prisoners were engaged in labor related to logging or mining. Failure of a prisoner to fill a productivity quota resulted in a diminution in rations that often led to death. Despite living under the harshest weather conditions inmates were never adequately clothed or fed, and they seldom had access to medical care. Most of the Gulag camps were located in the most remote regions of Siberia, in areas without roads or food sources but rich in natural resources. Labor camps could be found virtually throughout the entire Soviet Union, including Russia, Belarus, Ukraine, and Mongolia. Some camps were fortified; others were recognizable only by posts. Escapes were rare because of weather conditions and the proximity to native tribes motivated by rewards to capture escapees. Camp guards had more than enough motivation to prevent escapes, since if an inmate escaped during a guard's watch, the guard could be stripped of his position and become an inmate in the Gulag himself.

Sources: Thomas, *Alexander Solzhenitsyn*, 1998; Applebaum, *Gulag*, 2003.

GUYANA. Guyanese prisons fall under the direction of the Minister of Home Affairs. The main prisons at Georgetown, Mazaruni, and New Amsterdam are under the command of one director. Typically, first time offenders are sentenced to New Amsterdam, with longer sentences characterizing detention at Sibley Hall, Mazaruni. Recidivists serving sentences longer than three months are jailed at either Georgetown or Mazaruni.

Prisoner care is the main responsibility of a chief probation officer, who is also charged with the administration of juvenile facilities at the Essequibo Boys' School and the Belfield Girls' School. In the 1970s and 1980s there was a growing emphasis on rehabilitation and training, but these seem to have diminished in the wake of a growing drug trade by the 1990s.

In 1991 the Guyana Human Rights Association reported that the country's three main prisons, located at Georgetown, Mazurani, and New Amsterdam, were overcrowded and plagued by deterioration. The reliance on mandatory sentences for narcotic offenses has been blamed for the increase in the inmate population. Without the expansion of facilities, malnutrition and AIDS have become widespread in Guyanese prisons. According to reports from late 2001 the prison system housed 1,507 inmates, representing 157 per 100,000 of the national population, an occupancy rate of almost 121 percent.

Sources: Kurian, *WEPP*, 1989; LCCS, "Guyana: The Courts and the Penal System," January 1992; Walmsley, *WPPL*, 2003.

H

HAITI. Information on Haiti's penal system is difficult to come by. Haiti has long been noted for its human rights abuses, and as early as 1934 a member of the United States Marine Corps noted that the prisons were "a disgrace to humanity." Haiti's penal system can be traced back to its first penal code in 1835. Since then it has been amended numerous times. The two main penal facilities are located at Fort Dimanche and the National Penitentiary, both in the capital city of Port-au-Prince. Other municipal prisons are in Les Cayes, Hinche, Gonaives, Cap-Haitien, and Port-de-Prix. Most institutions use prison labor only for goods available to public agencies for state use. While prisoners are allowed to receive visitors, food, and medical attention, poor conditions predominate, particularly at the military prison, Casernes Dessalies. Reports have filtered out from here reporting widespread abuse, including lack of windows and light, and only a bucket for a toilet. The latest prison statistics from 1999 indicate a prison population of 4,152, representing 53 per 100,000 of the national population.

In 2004 the Port-au-Prince prison was the scene of a bloody riot that left seven prisoners dead and four police officers injured. It was reportedly touched off when a group of prisoners broke out of their cells and attacked guards, forcing them to fire into the prisoners. This incident led to the release of information indicating that the prison held 1,070 inmates, hundreds more than it was designed to accommodate.

Sources: Kurian, *WEPP*, 1989; LCCS, "Haiti: The Judicial System and Public Order," December 1989; Walmsley, *WPPL*, 2003; "Guards Kill Seven Prisoners in Riot," *Houston Chronicle*, December 2, 2004, A21.

HANOI HILTON. *See* HOA LO PRISON

HAVILAND, JOHN (1792–1852). Best known as the architect of **Eastern State Penitentiary**, Haviland was born in Somerset, England, and served an apprenticeship under London architect James Elmes, who had designed several prisons. Haviland made his way to the United States, arriving in Philadelphia by 1816. A scarcity in skilled architects enabled Haviland to secure his place in the architectural hierarchy of the young country quickly. Haviland oversaw the completion of Eastern State Penitentiary in the mid-1820s. Visitors from around the world visited Philadelphia to see the country's largest public building at that time and to observe the **Pennsylvania system** in action, a system in which all inmates lived and worked in solitary confinement. His blueprint for Eastern State Penitentiary included the nation's first flushing toilet in a public building. His success led to more projects, including the designing of Pennsylvania's Western State Penitentiary in Pittsburgh. He later designed prisons for the states of Rhode Island, New Jersey, Missouri, and Arkansas, as well as New York City's **Tombs Prison**.

Although the Pennsylvania system found more support outside the United States, Haviland was in demand as an architect throughout the 1830s and 1840s. Haviland's name is secure in the pantheon prison design, having developed the **radial** prototype for the Pennsylvania system. Haviland's notions were not that original, but his modifications of existing designs at **San Michele** in Rome and the **Ghent Maison de Force** were.

Sources: Herman Mannheim, "John Haviland," *Journal of Criminal Law, Criminology, and Police Science* 45, no. 5 (February 1955), pp. 509–519; Norman Johnston, *Eastern State Penitentiary: Crucible of Good Intentions* (Philadelphia: Philadelphia Museum of Art, 1994).

HAYES, RUTHERFORD B. (1822–1893). Best remembered, or forgotten, as the nineteenth president of the United States, Rutherford B. Hayes stands alone as the only president to play an important role in prison reform. Born in Ohio and educated at Harvard Law School, Hayes was a staunch abolitionist before fighting for the Union in the American Civil War. He used his heroic service in the war, and his six battle wounds, as a stepping-stone to the United States House of Representatives before the war had even ended. It was while serving as Ohio governor in the late 1860s that he was drawn to prison reform. In 1870 Cincinnati, Ohio hosted the **National Congress of Penitentiary and Reformatory Discipline**. As governor he played a crucial role in the logistics of the convention. Hayes was elected as the first president of the **National Prison Association** at the convention. Following his term as president between 1877 and 1880, he returned to the campaign for prison reform. In 1882 he was re-elected president of the National Prison Association, a position he would win each year until his death in 1893.

Hayes's penal philosophy favored rehabilitation and the reintegration of prisoners into society. As U.S. president and in other positions in public life Hayes was a strong supporter of civil service reform. He saw political patronage as one of the biggest obstacles to prison reform, noting that reform was reliant on honest administration and management. Hayes vehemently opposed the southern convict-leasing system, which he saw as de facto slave labor. He was also an early opponent of the emerging pseudo-sciences advocated by **Cesare Lombroso** and others. To the end of his life Hayes believed that environmental factors could determine one's path in life.

Sources: McKelvey, *American Prisons*, 1977; Jones, *Criminal Justice Pioneers in U.S. History*, 2005.

HELDERSTROOM PRISON. This South African prison farm, established in 1971, is located 120 kilometers from Cape Town. Situated on prime agricultural land, it contains two almost identical prisons, Helderstroom Maximum-Security Prison and Helderstroom Medium-Security Prison. The majority of the more than 330 members of the Prisons Service staff maintain permanent residence on the prison farm. In 1989 the combined prison population was 2,397 prisoners, with a staff-prisoner ratio of 1 to 7.2. All prisoners were serving sentences not to exceed two years, typically for common crimes.

Source: Dirk Van Zyl Smit, "Helderstroom Prison, South Africa," in *The State of the Prisons—200 Years On*, ed. Dick Whitefield, 1991, pp. 69–87.

HER MAJESTY'S PRISON SERVICE. Her Majesty's Prison Service is the executive agency charged with managing the prisons of the United Kingdom. It answers to the Home Office. In 2004 plans were announced to integrate the Prison Service into the new National Offender Management Service by June 2004. According to Home Secretary David Blunkett, the department will be "a new body to provide end-to-end management of all offenders." The head of the new administration will have the same title as the former head of the prisons service—director general.

In 2004 the Prison Service, with its staff of 44,000, was responsible for 72,000 prisoners held in 138 prisons. However, the Prison Service does not manage all prisons in the United Kingdom. As of early 2004 seven prisons had already been designed, constructed, managed, and financed privately, with several more on the drawing board. Ultimately, the Prison Service has oversight of these facilities.

According to its official statement of purpose, "Her Majesty's Prison Service serves the public by keeping in custody those committed by the courts. Our duty is to look after them with humanity and help them lead law-abiding and useful lives in custody and after release." Each week the Prison Service releases population statistics.

Sources: wikipedia.org/wiki/Her_Majesty's_Prison_Service; www.hmprisonservice.gov.uk.

HOA LO PRISON. Hoa Lo (the Oven) Prison was Indochina's second central prison. Built on the periphery of Hanoi's French Quarter, it received its first inmates in 1898. It was built for a capacity of 460 inmates. In 1913 renovations to relieve overcrowding led to an expansion to hold 600 prisoners. However, overcrowding continued to plague the facility. In 1916 the average daily capacity had risen to 730. Six years later Hoa Lo was handling almost 900 prisoners, and by 1933 the inmate population averaged 1,430. During the Vietnam War in the 1960s and 1970s Hoa Lo became infamous as the prisoner-of-war facility referred to by American prisoners as the Hanoi Hilton.

Source: Zinoman, *The Colonial Bastille*, 2001.

HOLLOWAY PRISON. Holloway Prison was built in close proximity to **Pentonville Prison**. It received its first prisoners in 1852 (recent evidence suggests 1849) when it was known as the **house of correction** for the City of London, Holloway. It was initially conceived as a way of relieving the overcrowding at **Newgate Prison**. Holloway, like a number of prisons built during this period, was rather ornate, perhaps to hide its actual purpose. It held 352 prisoners in what many people called Holloway Castle because of its signal tower and battlements. In its early years education was available, but silence was strictly enforced. There was also a **treadmill** capable of raising water for the prison. When Newgate's women's wing was demolished in 1861, the prisoners were sent temporarily to Holloway until reconstruction was completed. In 1877 the facility became part of the state prison system. For a short time in the 1890s it held only male prisoners. In 1902 it was turned into the now familiar women's prison and work was undertaken to enlarge its capacity to almost 1,000 inmates. In the early 1900s a number of suffragettes were ensconced here. For a short time during World War II the women were removed to Aylesbury Prison, and Holloway was dedicated to holding mostly political prisoners, aliens, or war opponents such as Sir Oswald Mosley. In 1955 Holloway was the scene of the hanging of Ruth Ellis, the last woman executed in England. It still operates as a women's prison.

Sources: Babington, *The English Bastille*, 1972; Herber, *Criminal London*, 2002; Johnston, *Forms of Constraint*, 2002.

HONDURAS. The Honduran penal system is composed of separate penal systems for men and women. The *Direccion Nacional de Establecimientos Penales*, or National Directorate of Penal Establishments, is under the administration of the Ministry of Government and Justice and is responsible for the national penitentiary and other facilities dedicated to male inmates. Female inmates fall under the domain of the National Board of Social Welfare, which has jurisdiction over the Female Center of Social Adaptation. Both of these come under the direction of the Ministry of Work.

In most cases inmates sentenced to three years' or more incarceration are housed in the national penitentiary in Tegucigalpa. Those serving between 90 days and 3 years are consigned to a department jail. Sentences of less than 90 days are served in local jails.

In 1986 Honduran prisons housed 3,635 prisoners, all males except for 57 female prisoners. All female prisoners, regardless of sentence, are imprisoned in the Cefas penitentiary just outside of Tegucigalpa. Honduras is divided into 18 departments, each with a department jail, except for Francisco, which has none, and El Paraiso, which has 2. By the 1990s Honduran prisons were overcrowded and offered inmates few services. Medical and psychiatric care barely exist, but inmates can buy medicine from the outside if they can afford it. Inmates are also responsible for supplying their own toiletries and clothes. Only Cefas offers the amenities of television, sports, and other recreational facilities. Most prisons allow conjugal visits, and in some facilities inmates have the opportunity to attain basic literacy. Daily prison fare does not go beyond rice, tortillas, and coffee. According to many reports the bribery of guards and administrators for better food and other luxuries is rampant.

Today Honduran prisons are filled far beyond their capacity, increasingly with children who have turned to crime. As late as May 2004 Honduran officials promised to improve the severely overcrowded conditions. This after a cellblock housing gang members erupted into flames killing 103 gang members. Described as "time bombs" by some authorities, Honduran jails hold more than 100,000 gang members representing 500 different gangs. Much of the recent overcrowding is blamed on a crackdown in August 2003 that outlawed gang membership and inaugurated 12-year sentences for gang members. Currently Honduran penitentiaries consist of 27 ramshackle buildings, which house 13,000 prisoners, twice their designed capacity. In mid-2004 the prison population stood at 11,236, or 158 per 100,000 of the national population.

Sources: LCCS, "Honduras: The Penal System and Human Rights," December 1993; Walmsley, *WPPL*, 2003; Kent Gilbert, "Honduras Blaze Kills 103 Inmates," *Houston Chronicle*, May 18, 2004, 12A.

HONG KONG (CHINA). Even before its turnover to **China**, Hong Kong had a prisoner-to-population ratio of 200 to 100,000, an imprisonment rate higher than any found in the United Kingdom, the colonial power that introduced the territory's first prison system. This rate is also considered rather high by Asian standards as well. As of 1997 Hong Kong had 22 penal institutions, all operated by the Hong Kong Correctional Services Department (CSD). The system was designed to hold up to 10,442, but many prisons are overcrowded.

In addition to administering the penal system, the CSD was tasked with managing detention camps for Vietnamese refugees, whose numbers often surpassed the penal population. Hong Kong had a huge prison staff in 1997, almost equal to the prison population. Prison officers are characterized as proto-military wearing military-style uniforms, divided into ranks, and inculcated with military discipline. However, they differ from the military in that they are armed only with wooden truncheons.

Hong Kong prisons adhered to a strict inmate classification regime, separating prisoners by sex, age, security level, and status, whether sentenced or unsentenced. Prisoners are also divided into categories of offense. There are 10 prisons for adult offenders, as well as a psychiatric center and a **remand** facility. Two maximum-security facilities include Stanley Prison, constructed in 1937, and Shel Pik. Stanley is the largest facility. There are four medium-security prisons, with Victoria Prison the most prominent. Likewise Ma Hang is the most prominent minimum-security prison.

In the late 1990s most prisoners were ethnic Chinese, although a number of foreign prisoners were incarcerated from Vietnam, the Philippines, Pakistan, and Thailand. Prior to the turnover to China, Chinese prisoners were immediately deported back to the mainland following their release.

In 2004 the Hong Kong Correctional Services Department was operated under the Administrative Government. In 2004 there were 28 facilities holding 13,226 inmates. The prison ratio is 189 to 100,000 of the national population.

Sources: Human Rights Watch, "Hong Kong: Prison Conditions in 1997," www.hrw.org/res earch/hongkong/hk-ovrv.htm; ICPS, Hong Kong (China), 2004.

HOUSES OF CORRECTION. There is little meaningful difference between the workhouse and the house of correction. The concept behind both is the same—the notion that work and its accompanying work ethic can be forcefully inculcated. What is clear is that in the sixteenth century changing social conditions in England and the Low Countries resulted in an increase in the number of vagrants, prostitutes, and other petty criminals on the loose. Vagabonds and transients had been considered threats to English society since the aftermath of the Black Death in the 1340s. By the 1500s English society faced even more dislocations following the dissolution of the monasteries and a wave of agricultural enclosures. As a result, even more homeless and rootless poor were left to their own devices to survive. The Elizabethan rulers introduced stopgap measures that included creating houses of correction, something between a poorhouse and a jail, which according to prison historian Sean McConville eventually "became rivals of the jails." He cites London's **Bridewell**, which received its first charges in 1556, as the first of these institutions. Over the next two centuries houses of correction would be used to suppress vagrancy and transiency.

Those targeted for discipline at the houses of correction were typically those viewed as not contributing to society and needing a sturdy dose of discipline to "correct" their behavior. In 1576 the English Parliament ordered that each county should have a house of correction, and by the 1770s the concept had spread throughout Europe. Many of the houses of correction were self-supporting through the production and sale of various items. Some were fitted with spinning rooms, nail factories, and carpentry shops; others produced pins, laces, gloves, and even tennis balls. Discipline was ever-present in the case of recalcitrant workers.

Amsterdam contributed its version of the house of correction in the guise of the **rasphouse** in the sixteenth century. One of the more significant houses of correction was **San Michele Hospice** in Rome, established by Pope Clement XI in 1704. The opening of the **Ghent Maison de Force** in 1775 would prove even more influential, both architecturally and philosophically. **John Howard** would make a survey of Europe's houses of correction and prisons in the 1770s. Apparently he was favorably impressed, since when he returned to England he campaigned to have the productive work and penitence scheme of the house of correction integrated into England's prison regime.

Sources: DeFord, *Stone Walls*, 1962; Sean McConville, "The Victorian Prison, England, 1865–1965," in *Oxford History of the Prison*, eds. Morris and Rothman, 1995, pp. 117–150.

HOWARD, JOHN (1726–1790). John Howard was an eighteenth-century pioneer in prison reform, who was described by John Wesley as "one of the greatest men in Europe." Born to wealth, Howard inherited a fortune while in his teens. Leading the peripatetic life of a country squire, he was taken prisoner on the high seas by French privateers in 1757, beginning a lifelong interest in prison conditions.

Howard's early association with criminal justice issues can be traced to his stint as sheriff of Bedfordshire beginning in 1773. Rather than regarding the position as an aristocratic sinecure, Howard embarked on an inspection tour of the jails under his control. Needless to say, he found conditions utterly appalling.

He took his crusade for prison reform to the national level in 1773, beginning a tour of more than 100 British prisons between November 1773 and March 1777. He found conditions just as dreadful. This was partially attributable to the British adoption of **transportation** to the American colonies in 1776.

Following his prison investigation Howard wrote his seminal work *State of Prisons in England and Wales*, published in 1777. Howard noted that between 1773 and 1775 more prisoners died in jails than by execution. His study is considered the most exhaustive examination of English prisons ever conducted. This work is a seminal moment in the history of prison reform and is credited with convincing Parliament to pass the **Penitentiary Act of 1779**. This legislation established England's first penitentiary, created to humanely house inmates under an obligatory set of standards for the treatment of prisoners. Howard continued his campaign for better prisons into 1790. However, his good work was cut short when he contracted **gaol fever**, a form of typhus, while visiting a hospital ward in the Ukraine. He died in 1790 (1791).

Sources: Edgar C. S. Gibson, *John Howard* (London: Methuen and Company, 1901); Howard, *John Howard*, 1958; Christianson, *With Liberty for Some*, 1998.

HOWARD ASSOCIATION. Named for **John Howard**, the Howard Association is a prison reform group first established in 1866. It continues as an advocacy organization promoting humane conditions in places of incarceration. In 1921 it was united with the Penal Reform League and became known as the Howard League for Penal Reform.

One of its best-known secretaries was noted penal reformer **William Tallack**. The original Howard Association published annual reports and records between 1907 and 1920; after its merger its official publication became known as the *Howard Journal*. Among the reforms this journal has been credited with advancing was the prohibition of flogging in Great Britain.

Sources: Teeters, *World Penal Systems*, 1944; Howard, *John Howard*, 1958.

HOWARD LEAGUE FOR PENAL REFORM. *See* HOWARD ASSOCIATION

HOWE, SAMUEL GRIDLEY (1802–1876). An early proponent of **parole**, Samuel Howe was raised in Boston and later earned a medical degree from Harvard Medical School. Following graduation he traveled throughout Europe and met such luminaries as Lord Byron and the Marquis de Lafayette, and he even found time to fight in the Greek war of independence. His affiliation with prison reform began in the 1840s when he campaigned for the better reintegration of prisoners into society. He joined the **Boston Prison Discipline Society**, where he became a minority leader, challenging **Louis Dwight**'s championship of the **Auburn system** over the **Pennsylvania system**. As leader of the society Dwight prohibited any mention of European studies supporting the Pennsylvania system. As a form of protest Howe wrote *An Essay on Separate and Congregate Systems of Prison Discipline* in 1846. According to Scott Christianson, Howe's support for the separate system was predicated on his notion that races should be separated from each other. But Howe was also one of the foremost abolitionists of his era.

In 1865 Howe was selected as chairman of the Massachusetts Board of State Charities, the organization empowered to examine the state's correctional facilities and almshouses. Howe is credited with coining the word *parole*, loosely translated from the Greek "word of honor." He continued to champion various "good behavior" incentives that would lead to a reduced sentence.

Sources: Samuel Gridley Howe, *An Essay on Separate and Congregate Systems of Prison Discipline* (Boston: W. D. Ticknor, 1846); McKelvey, *American Prisons*, 1977; Christianson, *With Liberty for Some*, 1998.

HULKS. *See* CONVICT HULKS

HUMAN RIGHTS WATCH. Like **Amnesty International**, Human Rights Watch is an international nongoverning organization. The organization began as Helsinki Watch in 1978 and was established to monitor human rights violations in the Soviet Union as well as to observe the Helsinki Accords. Similar human rights groups formed around the world, and in 1988 they combined to form the Human Rights Watch. The organization is currently based in New York City.

Source: Human Rights Worldwide, www.hrw.org.

HUNGARY. Between 1949 and 1961 the Hungarian prison system consisted of labor or internment camps and prisons offering three different punishment models. In 1961 the new government abolished labor camps and the old forms of punishment associated with the Communist regime, replacing them with a system of four regimes—three types of penitentiaries and the local jail. The most draconian of these regimes was incarceration in penitentiaries. Local jails were at the other end of the punishment spectrum. In 1975 the government introduced an additional regime for prisoners sentenced for a violent crime for the fourth time (if each sentence is at least one year). By the late 1980s the familiar labor camps of the Communist regime had been discontinued. In 1989 prisoners serving the harshest sentences went on a hunger strike at Vac Prison, outside Budapest, after a prisoner burned himself to death in protest. The government capitulated and abolished this regime, which affected 282 male prisoners and 14 female prisoners.

The Hungarian Prison Service is the responsibility of the Ministry of Justice. In late 2003 the country's 33 penal institutions, which include 2 hospitals, held 16,700 prisoners in a system designed for 11,310. The prison population rate is 165 per 100,000 of the national population.

Sources: Clara D. Rackham, "The Hungarian Prison System," *The Penal Reformer*, January 1938, pp. 10–11; Kurian, *WEPP*, 1989; LCCS, "Hungary: Penal System," September 1989; Walmsley, *Prison Systems in Central and Eastern Europe*, 1996; ICPS, Hungary, 2004.

I

I AM A FUGITIVE FROM A GEORGIA CHAIN GANG! At the height of the Great Depression former Georgia **chain gang** fugitive **Robert Elliott Burns** chronicled his experience in his 1932 book *I Am a Fugitive from a Georgia Chain Gang!* The book describes his plight as an unemployed World War I veteran who is arrested for a six-dollar robbery with two others and is sentenced to a six-to-ten year stint on a chain gang. In 1922 he escapes to Chicago and becomes a prominent publishing executive. When he is promised that if he returned to Georgia he will be pardoned, he accepts the offer in order to put this part of his life behind him. However, when he returns to Georgia in 1930, the state withdraws its promise and puts him back on the chain gang. After escaping once more he begins a crusade against the chain gang system by publishing a series of articles exposing the brutal system. These articles were eventually collected and make up the nucleus of his riveting book. His story found an even larger audience when Warner Brothers immediately bought the story rights in 1932 and released the movie with a similar name starring Paul Muni in the lead role that same year. Robert Burns would serve as technical advisor on the film during the four weeks it took to make the movie. However, Warner was required to make one concession by not referring to the state of Georgia in the film.

Sources: Crowther, *Captured on Film*, 1989; Parrish, *Prison Pictures from Hollywood*, 1991.

ICELAND. As of 2001 Iceland had a total prison population of 110 out of a population of 286,000—a ratio of 38 per 100,000 of the national population. It goes without saying that crime is not a high priority in Iceland.

Source: Walmsley, *WPPL*, 2003.

ILLINOIS STATE PENITENTIARY. *See* STATEVILLE PRISON

INDIA. In 1787, just four years after Britain gained control of India, Indian prisoners were confined to Bencoolen, in southwest Sumatra. The first group of prisoners at Bencoolen was used in jungle clearing and road building. Similar to most other countries, India's earliest prisons were used to temporarily confine offenders awaiting trial, sentence, or execution. By 1836 India had a large number of jails capable of holding more than 70,000 prisoners. That same year a system of classification was developed. Discussion of prison reform began in 1835 when a committee was convened to examine the deterrence value of prisons. Two other committees subsequently examined the problem in 1864 and in 1877. All three of these committees rejected the concept of imprisonment and made few changes in the direction toward professional corrections, despite reforms underway in Great Britain. In 1846 the first Central Prison was constructed in Agra.

By the 1850s India had implemented a number of concepts advocated by **John Howard**. However, while India was a colony of Great Britain, the **treadmill**, floggings, and **transportation** remained part and parcel of a punitive prison environment.

This would all change in 1888, when recommendations for prison reform by the Fourth Jail Commission were accepted and in 1894 the Prisons Act laid the foundation for contemporary prison administration in India. Several reforms resulted, including classification and separation of inmates, health care, discipline, and work schedules. Other committees would contribute to the groundwork of modern corrections. In 1919–1920 the Indian Jails Committee named reformation and rehabilitation of inmates as major objectives. And in 1940 the first Jail Training School for wardens and officers was established.

By the 1940s Indian prisons followed a horizontal pattern in which many prisons spread over hundreds of acres, with plenty of space to cultivate gardens and flowers. Most buildings were one story, with only roughly 20 percent of the inmates confined to cells. A number of reforms were implemented prior to independence. Sanitary measures and physical training were improved, and education and libraries were made available, as were moral and religious instruction. Although no combined religious services or singing was allowed, an exception was made for European wards where Christian services were held. It is no surprise this created tensions between the Hindu and Muslim prisoners, who agitated either for the abolition of the practice or for permission to conduct similar services.

In the 1940s labor became less penal in character, allowing individuals to learn various crafts, such as carpentry, blacksmithing, painting, tinning, masonry, and construction work; others made progress in the arena of agriculture.

Following independence in 1947 increased emphasis was placed on training correctional staff. Between 1957 and 1959 the Eighth Conference of the Inspectors General of Prisons and the India Jail Committee prepared a *Model Prison Manual*. This manual established scientific guidelines for the correctional treatment of various classes of offenders. In addition, a Central Bureau of Correctional Services was established at the national level to coordinate correctional services and sponsor training programs for prison personnel.

By the 1970s more emphasis was placed on finding alternatives to imprisonment. Although the convicted prison population is remarkably small for a country of one billion people, remanded prisoners awaiting trial, referred to as "undertrials or detenus," vastly outnumber convicted prisoners. One of the more disturbing trends in recent Indian corrections is the number of people incarcerated for minor and technical violations, which further contributes to rampant overcrowding. Many of these prisoners are being held under various acts sanctioning preventive detention. By the late 1980s more than half the prison population consisted of individuals awaiting trial. Prison crowding became such a problem by the 1990s that in some prison barracks prisoners were forced to sleep in shifts because of inadequate space. In addition, most prisons house all categories together, including young offenders and adults, along with women and children. Insufficient medical services and almost nonexistent psychiatric care have only added to a prison system in crisis.

Similar to many work programs around the world, antiquated prison industries do little to prepare inmates for the free world, relegating inmates to wasteful and unproductive labor. Despite prison strikes for better conditions and demands for reform, Indian correctional institutions made little progress and as a result were targeted by human rights groups for torture, cruelty, and unsanitary conditions in the 1970s and 1980s. The media helped mobilize public support for reform after publicizing prison conditions in 1980. That year the government appointed an India Committee on Jail Reforms to look into conditions in Indian correctional facilities. As a result, the committee issued a report emphasizing reform measures and making suggestions at improving the coordination of the legislature, police, judiciary, and corrections. Since the 1980s various steps have been taken toward improving the quality of corrections in India. But given competing priorities for the allocation of scant resources, it remains to be seen whether corrections will be sufficiently high on the list to allow modernization in the twenty-first century.

For the most part prison conditions continue to vary state by state, with the more prosperous states offering better facilities and more rehabilitation programs. Although conditions for holding prisoners varies, India apparently still maintains a leftover from the colonial past, in which foreigners, prisoners of high caste, and political prisoners are segregated from lower-class inmates and given better treatment, which may include larger cells, better food, and access to more reading materials.

By the 1980s India had 76 central prisons (with capacity for 79,544), 250 district prisons (63,654), 822 sub-jails (26,057), 20 special jails, and 27 open jails (4626). Only 6 institutions are dedicated to female offenders, with a capacity to hold less than 1,000. In addition, there are 8 juvenile jails (capacity for 1,827) and 11 **Borstal** schools (2,102).

As of mid-2003 India's prison population had increased to 313,635, but the prisoner population ratio remained stable at 29 per 100,000 of the national population. The country reported 1,119 penal facilities, including 98 central prisons, 266 district prisons, 671 sub-prisons, 21 open prisons, 13 women's prisons, 12 Borstal schools, 9 juvenile camps, 25 special prisons, and a handful of other facilities. More than 70 percent of the prison population were pre-trial detainees or remand prisoners.

Sources: F. A. Barker, "Twenty Years of Penal and Prison Reform in India," *Howard Journal*, Autumn 1941, pp. 52–59; B. V. Trivedi, *Prison Administration in India*, 1978; Chadha, *The Indian Jail*, 1983; K. Chockalingham, "The Development of Corrections in India," in *Current International Trends in Corrections*, ed. Biles, 1988, pp. 106–113; Mohanty and Hazary, *Indian Prison System*, 1990; LCCS, "India: Penal System," September 1995; Rani Dhavan Shankardass, ed., *Punishment and the Prison: Indian and International Perspectives* (New Delhi: Sage Publications, 2000); Walsmley, *WPPL*, 2003; ICPS, India, 2004.

INDOCHINA. *See* VIETNAM

INDONESIA. Most of the guidelines for the treatment of offenders can be found in the old Colonial Prison Regulations of 1917. However, the regulations have been greatly modified over the past several decades, with the system striving to become more humanitarian and directed toward the goal of rehabilitation.

Following independence from Dutch colonial rule in 1945, the Penitentiary Service of Indonesia convened several conferences to discuss measures for developing methods of treatment for offenders. In 1963 these meetings resulted in the adoption of the concept of *Pemasyarakatan*, or the idea of resocialization. Several experiments were undertaken by the Directorate General of Penitentiaries prior to formalizing a strategy to put theory into practice. For example, offenders can undergo a progressive stage system in which through good behavior they can earn time for good behavior and entry into a less strict prison regimen. As the prisoner improves, he is given more responsibility, with opportunities to interact with the outside community.

In the late 1960s Indonesia adopted several improvements to better conform to the United Nations Standard Minimum Rules for the Treatment of Offenders. Among the changes was the reconstruction of colonial-era institutions using advances in modern prison architecture. In order to rehabilitate these prisons for a new era it was necessary to bring them up to modern international standards that required running water, electricity, separate cells, recreational areas, a hospital, and a library. Some of the more recent prisons are located at Trenggalek and Tulungagung in East Java.

Today the Directorate General of Corrections under the Department of Justice administers prisons. There are 378 prisons in Indonesia, with the largest located in Java. Of these, 362 are for adults and 16 for juveniles. Each major city has access to at least a prison and several local jails. A large penal colony containing more than 6,000 inmates in nine separate prisons is located in south-central Java on the island of Nusa Kambangan. However, despite the advances of the 1960–1990 period, most prisoners are housed in overcrowded conditions, without electricity or running water. In 2003 Indonesia had 378 penal institutions, 16 of which were for juveniles.

Outside Java few institutions separately house juveniles and women. When this occurs, youth and females are at least segregated from adult male prisoners. Indonesia has a relatively small prison population rate of about 38 per 100,000 (2003). The only Asian-Pacific country with a smaller prison population is India, with 29 per 100,000. By the middle of 2003 there were 84,357 people in prison. However, these figures are based only on government reports, which Indonesia has not been always been forthcoming with when it comes to criminal justice issues. With more than 219 million people, Indonesia's 17,000 islands make up the fourth-largest national population in the world (only one third are actually inhabited). Even if these figures can be accepted at face value, the prisons are still over capacity at 129 percent.

Prison conditions in Indonesia remain a concern for human rights groups. Reports have included violence between inmates, bribery of guards, juveniles mixed with adults, and rape used as a tool by interrogators.

Sources: Oemer Seno Adji, "Innovations in the Criminal Justice System in Indonesia," in *Innovations in Criminal Justice in Asia and the Pacific*, ed. Clifford, 1979, pp. 98–114;

Kurian, *WEPP*, 1989; LCCS, "Indonesia: Penal System," November 1992; Walmsley, *WPPL*, 2003; ICPS, Indonesia, 2004.

INGENIEROS, JOSE (1877–1925). The Argentinean Jose Ingenieros was considered "the leading criminologist" in Latin America during his lifetime. His championing of the Buenos Aires Penitentiary garnered the institution international recognition and attracted "progressive visitors" from abroad. Ingenieros rejected Lombroso's version of positivism in favor of a more complex version. He was a strong proponent of penitentiaries and reformatories based on American models, including the **Elmira Reformatory** and the agenda of the **National Prison Congress** of 1870.

Ingenieros conjured up a three-prong plan for "social defense" that included crime prevention, the rehabilitation of delinquents, and the reentry of ex-convicts into the free world. He explained his ideas in the 1913 work *Criminologia*. By 1910 his efforts led to the international prominence of the National Penitentiary in Buenos Aires. Although it emphasized manufacturing and labor, unlike a typical **Auburn** prison, this facility allowed prisoners to speak with one another during the congregate workday.

Source: Jose Ingenieros, *Criminologia* (Madrid: D. Jorro, 1913); Ricardo D. Salvatore, "Penitentiaries, Visions of Class, and Export Economies: Brazil and Argentina Compared," in *Birth of the Penitentiary in Latin America*, eds. Salvatore and Aguirre, 1996, pp. 194–223.

IRAN. Following his selection as ruler by the Iranian parliament in 1925, one of Shah Reza Pahlavi's first acts was to create a new penal code based on European models. After 1926, prison conditions improved and facilities were modernized. A large penitentiary was erected in Tehran along the lines of its European counterparts, which also included a modern hospital. Recidivist criminals were kept apart from other offenders, and minors between the ages of 15 and 18 were segregated from adults. Emphasis was placed on preparing prisoners for release through a variety of training programs that ranged from teaching handicrafts and mechanical skills to training in art and sculpture.

During the reign of the second Reza Shah Pahlavi in the 1960s and 1970s, attempts were made to further modernize and reform prison conditions. A rehabilitation regime was adopted that allowed prisoners to learn trades, crafts, and farming techniques. In addition, prisoners could earn a wage and take advantage of educational training in an attempt to raise the literacy level. As a result of this program a number of "open prisons" were established that allowed prisoners to work in the free world (conditional liberty) during the day and return to confinement at night. Qezelhesar Detention Center, housing 1,200 inmates outside Tehran, was considered the model for this reform regime.

Following the Iranian Revolution in 1979 the penal code was revised to conform with the Islamic legal code, or Sharia. Executions and physical punishments increased with the reintroduction of stoning and the development of a machine for the surgical amputation of four fingers on the right hand for thieves. Prison conditions have rapidly deteriorated since the 1980s. According to reports that have filtered out of the prisons, facilities are overcrowded with political prisoners, and the former reform regime of the secular government has been replaced with a draconian system of torture, poor food and sanitation, and little regard for human rights. The most infamous of these institutions is Evin Prison in Tehran.

Iran's Prisons Organization operates under the judiciary. As of 2002, Iranian prisons contained 163,526 prisoners, a ratio of 229 per 100,000 of the national population. The prison population has substantially declined since then to 133,658 prisoners in mid-2004, or 194 per 100,000. There are currently 184 institutions—156 adult and 28 juvenile facilities. Prison facilities are still vastly overcrowded, with prisons more than double capacity at 243 percent as of 2001.

Sources: Teeters, *World Penal Systems*, 1944; Kurian, *WEPP*, 1989; Walmsley, *WPPL*, 2003.

IRAQ. Before the American invasion in 2004, the Iraqi penal system was dominated by the now notorious central prison at **Abu Ghraib** near Baghdad. Under the regime of Saddam Hussein thousands of individuals were detained in Abu Ghraib and three smaller prisons located in the governates of Al Basrah, Babylon, and Nineveh. There were additional detention centers located throughout Iraq, with little information available beyond the nation's borders. Human rights groups found it virtually impossible to monitor prison conditions after the Baath Party seized power in 1968, and when Saddam Hussein seized power in 1979 any independent monitoring was out of the question. Until 2004 the Ministry of Social Affairs and Labor administered the penal system. Currently the Iraqi Correctional Service operates under the Ministry of Justice. During the Hussein years prison conditions varied according to the classification of prison. Untried prisoners were kept separate from convicted inmates in Abu Ghraib; females were isolated from males, and felons from less serious offenders. According to recent sources political prisoners were separated from common criminals as well.

In October 2002 the Revolutionary Command Council, Iraq's highest executive body, issued Decree No. 25, which was signed by Hussein authorizing the release of all prisoners. Included in the carefully worded document was permission to release "prisoners, detainees and fugitives jailed for political reasons and all other ordinary reasons, including [those] sentenced to death . . . inside or outside Iraq." What has become readily apparent was that Arabs condemned or accused of spying for Israel and the United States were excluded. According to **Amnesty International**, the majority of those released had been incarcerated for drug smuggling, illegal weapons, collaboration with Iran, corruption, and bribery. Following the amnesty thousands of expatriate Iraqis reportedly flocked home to take advantage of the new policy. It is unknown what fate awaited them or if their names joined the list of the thousands who "disappeared" in the 1980s and in 1991.

In 2003 a U.S.-led coalition invaded Iraq and publicized the draconian conditions in Iraq's prisons under Saddam Hussein. After the Abu Ghraib scandal in January 2004 the U.S. military began to overhaul the Iraqi prison system. Under the new system before any interrogation of a prisoner begins, an interrogator and analyst must submit a plan to a lawyer for approval. A lawyer who considers the interrogation procedures inappropriate can overrule the plan. Most recently Abu Ghraib has been greatly reduced as new facilities are opened. Among the new detention centers are Camp Liberty, Camp Bucca, and Camp Redemption. American and Iraqi officials agreed in July to set up a new system by which six Iraqi and three American military officials would review each prisoner's case. American authorities claim that 60 percent of the interviews lead to releases. In mid-2004 there were 7,000 "actual" criminals in custody plus more than 8,000 prisoners whom the United States considered security threats. If these figures are accurate, taking all prisoners into account would mean a prison population ratio of almost 60 per 100,000 of the national population.

Sources: LCCS, May 1988; *Amnesty International Report*, 2003; ICPS, Iraq, 2004; Norimitsu Onishi, "Transforming a Prison with U.S. Image in Mind," *New York Times*, September 16, 2004, A13.

IRELAND. By the time London's **Pentonville Prison** was completed in 1842, Ireland could boast several prison structures that were, according to Norman Johnston, "relatively new and in good condition." However, Ireland was well behind England in any meaningful prison reform efforts. This was in no small part because of the impoverishment of Irish society in the 1840s. Several counties were able to construct prisons following the traditional **radial** design. Mountjoy Convict Prison (1850) and Mountjoy Female Prison (1855) were built in Dublin following the familiar Pentonville design. Architect Charles Pierce designed the Convict Prison. Later on the female prison was converted to St. Patrick's **Borstal**. As the Irish population emigrated from the country, a number of county prisons were demolished or transitioned to other uses. As late as 1960 the Republic of Ireland maintained three prisons, and Northern Ireland had two.

Despite the paucity of prisons Ireland has been prominent in several areas of penal reform. Foremost was **Walter Crofton**'s contributions to the reform-oriented Irish Penitentiary System of the 1850s and 1860s by incorporating indeterminate sentencing. As the commissioner of Irish prisons between 1853 and 1854, and then again in 1869, Crofton based his "Irish system" on a number of reform experiments conducted by **Alexander Maconochie** in the Australian penal colonies.

As of late 2002 Irish prisons held 3,378 prisoners, or 86 per 100,000 of the national population. Northern Ireland, by contrast, held 1,058 prisoners, a ratio of 62 to 100,000.

Sources: Johnston, *Forms of Constraint*, 2000; Ryder, *Inside the Maze*, 2000; Walmsley, *WPPL*, 2003.

IRISH SYSTEM. Developed in the mid-nineteenth century by **Walter Crofton** and **Joshua Jebb**, the Irish system provided prisoners a reformative regime fusing religious, educational, and work programs with a graduated classification system that allowed an inmate to earn early release. According to this system prisoners began their sentences in solitary confinement, with no work assignments and reduced rations. Through good conduct, inmates could win advancement to the next stage of imprisonment, which was characterized by improved rations and congregate labor. During the final stage of incarceration prisoners could be transferred to a less restrictive prison setting, allowed work assignments in the free community, and finally earn marks toward early release. But before the final stage, prisoners must prove they had been rehabilitated to the satisfaction of administrators. The Irish system received early support in the United States and slowly found an audience in Europe as well.

Sources: DeFord, *Stone Walls*, 1962; Sullivan, *The Prison Reform Movement*, 1990.

ISLE OF MAN (UK). The Isle of Man Prison Service operates under the Department of Home Affairs. At the end of 2003 Her Majesty's Prison Douglas was the island's only prison. It held 68 prisoners, a figure that would represent 92 per 100,000 of the national population.

Source: ICPS, Isle of Man, United Kingdom, 2004.

ISLE OF SAINTE MARGUERITE (ISLE OF LERO). This island near present-day Cannes, France, has been occupied dating back to the Roman Empire. It was formerly known as the Isle of Lero, after a fourteenth-century chapel built by crusaders to pay homage to Saint Margaret of Antioch. The island has served strategic purposes for the French and the Spanish into the seventeenth century, when the island's Fort Royal was transformed into a French prison. After its transformation was completed in 1712, the prison became notable for the incredible thickness of its walls. The fort served as a French state prison into the twentieth century. Among its most famous prisoners was the "Man in the Iron Mask."

Source: www.cannes-on-line.com/Anglais/histmargueriteuk.

ISRAEL. The foundations for the Israeli prison system were laid during the years of the Palestinian Mandate between World War I and the establishment of the State of Israel in 1948. According to Joseph Eaton, prisons played an insignificant role in the Jewish community before independence. At the time of the British withdrawal there was little in the way of prisons. Correctional facilities for the most part consisted of old, deteriorating buildings in the old part of Jerusalem, Jaffa, Haifa, and Acre, which had been built centuries ago. Upon independence the Israeli government closed these decaying dungeons.

Regardless of the animosities of earlier years, British antecedents influenced the Israeli prison system. Many Israeli lawyers were trained in Britain. Israel even adopted a probation code first drafted in England, though ultimately rejected there. The criminal laws in force at independence were continued under the new government. One major change was the abolition of flogging as a legal punishment. Three secretaries administered penal affairs under the British, a system also continued under the new government. According to Joseph Eaton, the continuity between British and Israeli penal policies lends credence to the notion that new institutions do not automatically emerge after a revolution or independence. It seems that in low-priority domains such as prisons, change occurs during transition only if prisons were part of the focus of the struggle for independence.

On January 12, 1949, a converted police citadel at Tel Mond was transformed into a prison. Given low rates of criminality, it was thought that this facility built for 120 prisoners would be sufficient for the next decade. But only eight months after the birth of the state of Israel, there were 87 prisoners. In a matter of weeks a general amnesty reduced the prison population to 29. However, the number of prisoners would soon rise precipitously. As a result, officials were forced to upgrade and reopen prisons from the Mandate at Jaffa and Haifa.

According to Zvi Hermon, the early Israeli prison experiment has some parallels to America's first prison reform at Philadelphia's **Walnut Street Jail**. Following Israeli independence there was a sharp increase in prisoners leading to overcrowding at Tel Mond. This required using space marked for workshops, dining room facilities, and rehabilitation programs as prison cells. Similarly, after American independence, initial enthusiasm for Walnut Street Jail was turned into disappointment as overcrowding led to a downturn in prison conditions.

In the 1950s prisons were overcrowded with more than 800 prisoners, resulting in idleness and little room for exercise or work. One alternative was to build a minimum-security camp surrounded by barbed wire instead of stonewalls near the towns of Lod and Ramleh. Known as Ma'asiahu (named after the only policeman mentioned in the Bible), it could house 144 inmates. Created for nondangerous prisoners, the new facility was to be the beginning of a new era of prison reform in Israel.

In 1953 Israel leased an old Arab farm named Damoun, located on Mount Carmel not far from Haifa. Following its retrofitting Damoun would serve as a medium-security prison capable of holding 250 short-term prisoners. Its success led to the reconditioning of a number of old police buildings and the opening of new prisons in Shatta, Ramleh, and Kefar Yonah.

By 1958 criminal infractions were clearly on the rise. Israel had no long-range plan for handling increasing rates of criminal deviancy. Here a trend emerges that is also common in other developing countries—prisons rank low in priority. By the late 1950s, although there were 487 correctional officers, there were virtually no experienced prison administrators. During the British occupation few Jews were interested in prison service when nation building and independence loomed as a greater priority. It was only toward the end of British rule that several Jews entered prison work at the behest of the underground army known as the Haganah. They were tasked with guarding and protecting the growing number of Jewish political prisoners. In the process, some were illegally able to obtain weapons and supplies held in prison armories.

By 1962 prison employees numbered more than 630. As a number of Arab and North African countries won independence in the late 1950s and early 1960s, many poor Jews entered Israel, some with criminal backgrounds, others mentally ill—an unintended consequence of Israel's immigrant program, which provided little screening and admitted any Jewish person even without a visa.

In 1967 a women's prison was opened near Netanyah. With a capacity for up to 80 inmates, it was the only prison dedicated exclusively to female prisoners well into the 1980s.

Today the penal system in Israel and the occupied territories is administered by the Israel Prison Service, a branch of the Ministry of Interior and headed by the Israel Prison Service commissioner. A number of Israeli prisons date back to the British mandate of the 1930s. Police lockups located in every major town and military detention centers in Israel and the occupied territories complements the Prison Service.

In 1987 the Prison Service managed 13 prisons and detention centers in Israel and 8 penitentiaries in the Gaza Strip and the West Bank. Those Palestinians from the occupied territories serving terms of more than five years were imprisoned in maximum-security prisons in Israel. By the end of the 1980s there were close to 4,000 prisoners in Israel and slightly more than that in the occupied territories. The one facility dedicated to women is now located at Neve Tirza, which held 97 inmates. These numbers do not reflect the large number of Palestinians held in military detention centers. In the late 1980s almost half the detainees were housed at a tent camp in the Negev Desert near Egypt, known as Ketziot. Ketziot was always rife with tensions and conflict. Many of those confined here come from business and professional backgrounds. Given draconian rules such as the prohibition against radios and books, as well as the extreme climatic conditions, overcrowding, and unremitting boredom, it is not surprising that this camp, like others, was often a hotbed of dissent.

Conditions were worst at maximum-security prisons in Ram Allah and the largest prison in Beersheba. During the late 1980s a number of new facilities were built, but cells still lagged behind the growing numbers of prisoners. Human rights groups in the 1980s reported instances of abuse and violence by the staff as well as a dearth in occupational and rehabilitation programs. Attempts were made at improving conditions in the late 1980s, with vocational training available for small numbers of prisoners in carpentry, bookbinding, tailoring, printing, and shoemaking. Others were given the opportunity to complete secondary education programs.

In 1986 almost 40 percent of Israeli prisoners were sentenced for property crimes and another 19 percent for drug offenses. At the same time roughly 40 percent of prisoners in the West Bank and the Gaza Strip were serving sentence related to terrorist activities.

Currently the Israel Prison Service operates under the Ministry of Public Security. In mid-2004 the country's 24 penal institutions held 13,603 prisoners, a rate of 209 per 100,000 of the national population. Since 1997 the overall prison rate has risen from 147 per 100,000.

Sources: Zvi Hermon, "The Israeli Prison Service," in *Treatment of Offenders in the State of Israel* (Tel Aviv: Government Printing Press, 1955), p. 57; Eaton, *Prisons in Israel*, 1964; Israel Drapkin, "Corrections in Israel," in *International Corrections*, ed. Wicks and Cooper, 1979, pp. 123–139; Gad J. Bensinger, "Corrections Israel and the United States: A Comparative Analysis," *International Journal of Comparative and Applied Criminal Justice* 8, no. 1 (Spring 1984), pp. 55–62; Walsmley, *WPPL*, 2003; ICPS, Israel, 2004.

ITALY. Italy's prison system developed during the pre-unification period. At unification in 1861 the system was composed of almost 1,500 custodial prisons and jails and close to 30 penitentiaries. Many of them had been converted from convents, forts, and barracks to what one authority has described as the "Tombs of the Dead." There are a number of early examples of institutions preceding the development of modern corrections in Italy. One of the earliest examples of a prison sentence as part of the penal code in Italy can be traced back to the Constitutions of Melfi in 1231, which prescribed up to one year's imprisonment for anyone who falsely claimed to be a physician. Historians mention Rome's Sastel San Angelo, better known as the Prison of Theoderic, the Ostrogothic king.

Florence introduced an official city prison, known as **Le Stinche**, in 1304, but it was used mainly to hold individuals awaiting trial or execution. It is also recognized as one of the earliest prisons to separate inmates, in this case by age, gender, seriousness of offense, and degree of sanity. It became so well known that later prisons built in Sienna and Pitoia were informally referred to as Le Stinche as well.

Italian penal reform efforts can be traced back to at least 1431, when Pope Eugenius IV ordered officials to visit prisons twice a month to monitor complaints and conditions and to recommend remedies. Penal reformers have long acknowledged the hospice at **San Michele** in Rome as an early exemplar of solitary confinement. In 1778 **John Howard** visited Italian prisons, where he found rather loathsome conditions.

By the early 1860s Italy's new regime had passed legislation for the construction of cellular jails, but lack of funding ended any movement in this direction. In 1866 the island of Sardinia was home to four facilities modeled on the **Auburn system**. By 1870 there were two prisons in Italy based on the **Pennsylvania system**, as well as 52 others representing a combination of schemes. In 1889 the government finally adopted a penal code that opened the door to uniform prison legislation. The new system preferred a combination of the Auburn and Pennsylvania models. But any reforms were soon cut short once more because of a lack of funding and the opposition to prison labor from free market sources. By the outbreak of World War I, few strides had been made toward improving the nation's prisons.

In 1931 a new penal code was adopted that led to a number of innovations. Palermo inaugurated the first Institute for the Aid of Discharged Prisoners that same year. Built with funds raised by private and public subscriptions, similar institutions were soon opened in Rome, Milan, Florence, and Naples. In a poor country such as Italy, it has always been difficult for prisoners to find work. But according to this new program, upon their release from prison former inmates can take advantage of work opportunities at one of these institutions for discharged prisoners and then return home at night. During this process individuals could learn a trade or skill according to their particular aptitudes and receive a wage (less than the prevailing average).

Another interesting feature of the Italian prison system known as "labor in the open," or "*All' Aperto*," was introduced. Workshops in the open included agricultural colonies set up in Sardinia and in the Tuscan archipelago. Five of these colonies covering 10,000 acres were created in Sardinia, and three existed in the Tuscan region. A second type of labor camp included mobile groups of prisoners who leave the institution by day and return at night. But the second type proved cost prohibitive as a result of the additional security required.

In 1971 construction was completed on Rebibbi Prison, a **radial** prison built for 1,400 men in Rome. It uses single- and four-bed cells in similar three-wing radial-cell buildings connected by secure covered passageways. The adoption of a new penal code marked Italy's transition from the old inquisitorial system to a more modern adversarial system. Despite this shift, the new code remains distinct from Anglo-American law because of the obligatory nature of Italian penal action, which takes discretion out of the sentencing process.

The General Direction administers the modern prison system for Prevention and Penalty Institutes, a state agency under the Ministry of Justice. Although most inmates are required to work, prison work is not considered forced labor and prisoners are remunerated. Some are even permitted to work outside the prison under certain conditions. Provisions have been made to allow prisoners to earn university credits and attend classes. They are allowed to receive weekly visitors and can communicate by telegraph, in writing, or telephone. It has been mandated by law that psychological and medical assistance should always be available.

By 1993 Italy maintained 154 district detention facilities for male prisoners awaiting trial, and 6 for women. There are also 27 penitentiaries for men and 2 for women. These are complemented by a number of specialized units, including two for working prisoners, two psychiatric hospitals for offenders, one semicustodial facility for those on day release, a national facility where prisoners under psychological observation take part in re-education programs, and four prisons oriented toward drug addiction.

In January 1997 the total prison population (including detainees) stood at 49,477, or 85 per 100,000. The following years reports indicated a population of

55,136 prisoners, or 95 per 100,000 of the national population. According to an agreement prisoners from San Marino and Vatican City are also held in Italian jails.

Despite Italy's rich tradition of reform, Amnesty International has targeted a number of Italian prisons because of overcrowding and violence. In May 2000 a decree was passed that introduced measures to begin a three-year overhaul of the prison system. The following month new legislation granted prisoners new rights, such as better food, light switches inside cells, and more outdoor visits and phone calls. These reforms were sparked by a scandal involving eighty prison guards arrested for beating prisoners at a Sardinian prison. Despite these efforts, a 2003 report on prison conditions indicated that the prison system was still plagued by overcrowding, inadequate medical assistance, poor sanitation, high levels of self-mutilation, and suicides. Both prisoners and staff have mounted protests in response to these conditions.

Sources: Susan B. Carrafiello, *"The Tombs of the Living": Prisons and Prison Reform in Liberal Italy* (New York: Peter Lang, 1998); Pietro Marongiu and Mario Biddau, *World Factbook of Criminal Justice Systems: Italy*, 2002; www.ojp.usdoj.gov/bjs/pub/ascii/ wfbcjita.text.

IVORY COAST (COTE D'IVOIRE). As in most poor Third World countries harsh penal conditions reflect the lives of those outside the walls as well. In 1966 the prison population stood at 3,754, the majority of whom had already been sentenced. By the 1970s the prison population almost doubled to somewhere between 5,000 and 7,000 inmates. Virtually half the prisoners were housed at the two largest prisons, located at Yopougon on the outskirts of Abidjan, and at Bouake prison. The prison population at Bouake increased from 1,100 in the early 1970s to almost 13,000 in 1985. Most reports indicated that the majority of Ivorian inmates in the 1980s were expatriate from nearby African nations. Compared to most Third World countries, the Ivorian prison population came out more favorably because of the ratio of convicted prisoners to those awaiting sentencing. During the 1970s a number of wholesale amnesties were given to prisoners. To celebrate the twenty-fifth anniversary of Ivory Coast independence in 1985, the president ordered the release of almost 10,000 prisoners who were not incarcerated for violent crimes or robbery. The introduction of so-called **supermaximum prisons** in recent years has, according to Florence Bernault, fed the public imagination, with many citizens fearing the new institutions as "horrific places, where wardens can exert unchecked, sometimes lethal violence on detainees." Figures from late 2002 indicate a prison population of 10,355, or 64 per 100,000 of the national population.

Sources: Bernault, ed., *A History of Prison and Confinement in Africa*, 2003; LCCS, "Ivory Coast: Prison System," November 1988; Walsmley, *WPPL*, 2003.

J

JAIL. *Jail*, or *gaol*, is derived from the Latin word *geola*, which in turn became the English "jail." Jails are usually locally oriented and handle short-term prisoners and are classified as minimum security. In the United States the typical county jail detains individuals awaiting trial or those already convicted of a misdemeanor and serving less than a one-year sentence. In contrast to state prisons, many jails have wings holding both men and women in the same facility.

Sources: wikipedia, wikipedia.org/wiki/County_jail; Roth, *Crime and Punishment*, 2005.

JAMAICA. Jamaica's Department of Correctional Services is the responsibility of the Ministry of National Security and Justice. This department is also charged with operating training schools for guards, who are referred to as wardens. In the mid-1980s prison conditions deteriorated in almost every regard. Critics have targeted overcrowding, poor food and sanitation, and inadequate medical care. The worst culprits were the police station jails and the two maximum-security prisons.

By 1986 Jamaica was operating correctional centers in eight locations, including the General Penitentiary, St. Catherine District Prison, Gun Court Prison, Fort Augusta, Tamarind Farm, New Broughton, and St. Jago Women's Center. These facilities housed a combined 3,452 inmates in space intended for 2,861. The nation's main maximum-security institution is the General Penitentiary in downtown Kingston. Despite a capacity for 800, it typically holds double that. The other maximum-security institute is St. Catherine's, which holds more than 1,000 inmates serving shorter sentences.

Gun Court Prison, better known as South Camp Rehabilitation Centre, located in Kingston and open to the public, is readily recognized for its steel mesh and gun turrets. Fort Augusta Prison was built in 1970 to guard the Kingston Harbor but has been transformed into a minimum-security prison for up to 105 guests. Individuals who display potential for rehabilitation are transferred from the General

Penitentiary to Fort Augusta to finish their sentences. First-time offenders sentenced to long terms are housed at the Richmond Prison Farm, a maximum-security prison with the capacity for more than 100. In 1986 less than 120 prisoners were confined in the St. Jago's Women's Center and New Broughton.

A number of prison construction projects were begun in 1985, with others on the drawing board. In 1985 the Rehabilitation of Offenders Bill and the Corrections Act formally changed the terms *prisoner* to *inmate, prison officer* to *correctional officer*, and *prison* to *adult correctional center*. It has also been credited with creating employment programs for prisoners, providing better pre-release and aftercare preparation for the social integration of inmates, and introducing new standards for governing and inspecting correctional facilities. The detention institutions for juveniles include the maximum-security Hilltop facility, open schools for boys in St. Ann and Rio Cobre in St. Catherine, and similar ones for girls in St. Ann and Lower Esher in St. Mary's. By the mid-1980s 218 boys and 100 girls were serving custodial sentences in these institutions. As of mid-2003 the prison population was 4,744, or 176 per 100,000 of the national population.

Sources: LCCS, "Caribbean Islands: The Penal System," November 1987; Kurian, *WEPP,* 1989; Walmsley, *WPPL,* 2003; ICPS, Jamaica, 2004.

JAPAN. Some scholars trace the earliest use of incarceration in Japan to the eighth century when a penal sanction similar to forced labor was used. Under the domination of China's T'ang Dynasty, offenders sentenced to this punishment were incarcerated from one to three years and forced to labor on public works projects. By the tenth century an era of rival warlords led to more severe punishments and banishment; corporal and capital punishment replaced incarceration. In the 1700s during the Tokugawa Shogunate penal servitude was reintroduced, most notably at the Edo labor camp, in what is now Tokyo. This camp was more like preventive detention facilities than what we now consider a traditional prison. But it was here that vagrants, transients, and those seeming to lack moral tendencies were given free room and board, as well as moral education and vocational training. Upon release inmates were given funds to help set them in the right direction toward rehabilitation. One high-ranking prison official has most recently compared eighteenth-century Japanese prisons favorably to the Amsterdam model of the 1590s.

Modern Japanese corrections can be traced back to the period following the Meiji Restoration of 1868. During the Meiji period Japan adopted a number of modern institutions, including the Penal Code of 1870, which adopted imprisonment and paved the way for the abolition of corporal punishment in 1872. By 1888 a halfway house was opened catering to released prisoners. Institutions like this were important in a culture in which families often ostracized former prisoners because of the shame they had brought on the family. These aftercare facilities, staffed by volunteer staff, helped convicts with nowhere to turn, enabling them to make the transition back to the free world. Between 1880 and 1900 the prison population almost doubled from 86,000 to 160,000, giving impetus to a prison-building campaign based on British red-bricked facilities.

Until 1899 prisons were separately administered under the jurisdiction of prefectural governments. But overcrowding and inadequate and poorly trained staff led to a number of disturbances, including 146 escape attempts in 1898 alone. At the turn of the twentieth century the central government took over prison administration.

The passage of the Prison Law of 1908 played a major role in the evolution of Japanese corrections. Influenced by Anglo-American legal procedures of the day as well as French and German ideas, the law set prison standards for the next 80 years. A number of advances were inaugurated into the 1930s, including uniform treatment programs and better classification procedures. By the 1960s minimum-security facilities became increasingly popular.

Beginning in the late 1940s the prison population saw a sharp decline. In 1950 the prison population was 103,204, 83,492 of whom were sentenced that year. By the mid-1980s fines became the most dominant form of punishment, and in 1984 only 45,035 were imprisoned, increasing the total prison population to 54,508 in a country of 120 million.

Over recent decades Japanese correctional institutions have been characterized by strict discipline. As a result, there is little disorder and few incidents. By 1986 the prison population stood at more than 55,000 prisoners. That same year only 15 incidents were reported in the entire system, including only one assault on staff and three assaults on other inmates.

What strikes foreign visitors and correctional authorities is today's rigid inmate discipline based on military drill and order. At the same time prisoners are ensured that they will be protected from other inmates and fairly treated. It is compulsory for all sentenced prisoners to work. Forced but productive labor reportedly helps maintain discipline and lowers costs.

Another aspect that characterizes Japanese prisons is the close relationship forged between prison officers and inmates. Besides the traditional demands placed on guards, they are expected to play an important role in counseling inmates. As a result, inmates usually address officers as "sensei," denoting teacher, master, or mentor. As of 1987 Japan's staff-inmate ratio of 1 to 3.3 was lower than that of many Western nations. Since there has been a fairly stable prison population, it has been unnecessary to introduce the plethora of non-institutional sentences so popular in overcrowded prisons.

Today the Ministry of Justice administers the Correctional Bureau. It also controls three women's guidance homes designed to rehabilitate prostitutes. Prison staff members receive training in Tokyo and in a number of branch training institutes located in each of the eight regional correctional centers maintained by the Correctional Bureau.

The classification of prisoners takes into account gender, nationality, type of penalty, length of sentence, degree of criminality, and current mental and physical health. The prison regime emphasizes rehabilitation, resocialization, and reform. Prisons offer a number of educational and vocational training programs, supplemented by a heavy dose of social values. Most inmates work for pay and receive a small check when they leave prison. Prisoners also have the opportunity to earn better cells and extra privileges through good behavior incentives.

In 2004 the Japanese prison population had risen appreciably to 73,734, a ratio of 58 per 100,000 of the national population. Japan's 189 penal institutions currently include 67 prisons, 5 branch prisons, 7 detention houses, and 110 branch detention houses. With prison occupancy at 105.8 percent it seems inevitable that overcrowding will be a problem. Since 1992 the prison population has steadily risen, increasing from 45,802 in 1992 to 61,241 in 2001, or 48 per 100,000 of the national population.

Sources: Keisi Miyamoto, "The Future of Prisons—a View from Japan," in *Current International Trends in Corrections*, ed. Biles, 1988, pp. 83–92; LCCS, "Japan: The Penal System," January 1994; Terrill, *World Criminal Justice Systems*, 1999; Fairchild and Dammer, *Comparative Criminal Justice Systems*, 2001; Reichel, *Comparative Criminal Justice Systems*, 2002; Walsmley, *WPPL*, 2003; ICPS, Japan, 2004.

JEBB, JOSHUA (1793–1863). Born in Chesterfield, England, Jebb initially leaned toward a military career, fighting against America during the War of 1812. While still in the army in 1837 Jebb was appointed as England's first surveyor general of prisons, a position that required him to serve as consultant on the construction of English prisons. He collaborated in the designing of a number of county and borough prisons and was instrumental in the creation of the model prison at **Pentonville**. He served as commissioner of this prison beginning in 1841.

Thanks in part to Jebb's efforts the practice of the **transportation** or exiling of prisoners to colonial prisons was abolished. During his tenure at Pentonville, felons served initial periods of strict separation before being transferred to prisons more closely integrated with the community in order that convicts could be put to work on public works projects.

In 1844 Jebb was appointed to a royal commission to investigate the punishment of military crime. The commission's recommendations included creating a prison exclusively for military prisoners. Jebb would be selected as the first inspector general of military prisons and until 1850 would serve as both inspector general of military prisons and Pentonville commissioner. In 1850 England finally created a unified board to govern all English prisons. Jebb was selected as the first chairman of the Directors of Convict Prisons, ushering in an era of increasingly progressive prison reform.

Prison scholar Norman Johnston asserted that of all the prison designers, "Jebb, along with **Blackburn** and **Haviland** had the greatest effect on nineteenth-century prison architecture in Europe and subsequently in Asia and South America." Johnston cites Jebb's opposition to congregate imprisonment and the use of classification as it developed in Great Britain. Jebb was a proponent of the **Pennsylvania system** and introduced a number of the solitary system's attributes in the construction of Pentonville Prison. This prison would become one of the "most copied prisons in the world."

Sources: *Dictionary of National Biography* 29 (1921–22 reprint), pp. 698–699; Johnston, *Forms of Constraint*, 2000.

JERSEY (UK). Her Majesty's Prison La Moye is the responsibility of the States of Jersey Home Affairs Committee. In late 2003 Jersey's only prison held 170 prisoners, a prison population of 188 per 100,000 of the national population. This represents an increase from the previous year's figures of 136 prisoners and a rate of 156 per 100,000.

Sources: Walmsley, *WPPL*, 2003; ICPS, Jersey (United Kingdom), 2004.

JOHNSTON, JAMES A. (1876–1958). Johnston had served as a lawyer, banker, and civic leader before being tabbed as the first warden of the infamous federal prison of **Alcatraz** in 1934. However, Johnston was no stranger to corrections, having taken over as warden of California's **Folsom Prison** 20 years earlier and served in the same capacity at **San Quentin Prison**. At Folsom he earned a reputation as a reformer for abandoning prison stripes and corporal punishment. And at San Quentin he introduced honor camps and used a treatment-oriented approach. No one could have predicted his transformation into one the nation's toughest prison wardens.

Johnston is credited with shaping the regimen of the new maximum-security prison at Alcatraz. According to writer Jay Stiller, "Johnston pushed penology into the realm of mad science." On "the Rock" the former reformer became a paragon of strict and efficient management. From the moment convicts were awaken for breakfast at 6:30 A.M. to their return to their cells at 5:30 P.M., to lights out at 9:30 P.M., the relatively small inmate population of 275 was under the control of Johnston's administration. Johnston devised the prison's security system, everything from the modern full-body metal detectors to the tool-proof steel; and he made stringent rules—20 minutes for each meal, random strip searches and shakedowns, and head counts from twelve to thirty times each day. Whereas the typical prison had a guard to prisoner ratio of 1 to 10, Alcatraz had one guard for every three prisoners. In keeping with the prison's **Auburn** influence, silence was strictly enforced, leading one former inmate to admit, "The no talk rule is the hardest thing in Alcatraz life."

During his 14 years as warden of Alcatraz, Johnston bravely faced down escapes, riots, strikes and sit-downs, and in 1946 he even had to call in the U.S. Marines to quell a prison revolt. He made it a habit to walk into the huge dining hall by himself and even turning his back toward the convicts as they filed out. However, on one occasion in 1937 his bravery was rewarded with a severe beating from an inmate during a prisoner work strike. Johnston retired in 1948. His legacy is mixed, his reforms and good work at San Quentin and Folsom overshadowed by his brutal regime at Alcatraz.

Sources: Laura Davis, "Alcatraz Federal Penitentiary," in *Encyclopedia of America Prisons*, eds. McShane and Williams, 1996, pp. 21–23; Jay Stuller, "There Never Was a Harder Place than 'the Rock,'" *Smithsonian* 46 (1989), pp. 84–88; Sifakis, *The Encyclopedia of American Prisons*, 2003.

JORDAN. Jordan's prison system is administered by the Prisons Department of the Public Security Directorate under the Ministry of Interior. There are between 11 and 25 prison facilities. Amman Central Prison is the most important facility in the system. All other institutions are managed by regional police chiefs and so are often alluded to as "police jails." Important prisons are located at Irbid and Al Jafr. Convicted offenders sentenced to more than one years are usually transferred to Amman, and those serving three months to one year are confined in regional camps. Those serving less than three months are detained in local units.

Penal institutions combine the convicted with those awaiting trial. Separate sections are reserved for women in the larger prisons. In the bigger cities police jails try to do the same. Amman is also home to a juvenile detention center housing those under nineteen convicted of criminal offenses. Upon reaching nineteen, inmates are transferred to larger prisons to finish their sentences.

Most of the provisions by which the prison system is operated can be found under the Prison Law of 1953. Jordan is considered the first Arabic nation to acknowledge the theory of rehabilitation as an alternative to retribution. However, a lack of facilities and trained staff rehabilitation means this acknowledgment remains mostly in the realm of theory rather than practice. Human rights reports have indicated prison overcrowding alleviated by an occasional amnesty. In 1986 Amman opened a new central prison called Juwaidah, which replaced the deteriorating structure at Al Mahatta. By the end of the 1980s both Al Mahattah and the Az Zarqa military prison were cited for human rights violations by **Amnesty International**. In mid-2002 5,448 prisoners were held in space designed for 6,801, a prison population rate of 106 per 100,000 of the national population. More than 40 percent were either remand prisoners or pre-trial detainees.

Sources: LCCS, "Jordan: Prison System," December 1989; ICPS, Jordan, 2004.

JULIUS, NICOLAUS HEINRICK (1783–1862). Sometimes referred to as the "German **John Howard**," Nicolaus Julius was a Prussian physician who was drawn to penology while working on the staff of a poorhouse. Julius surveyed other prisons and became an authority on penology. In 1827 he lectured on behalf of prison aid societies in Berlin. By the 1830s Julius was considered a prominent authority in criminology. His book on prison architecture was published in 1828 in German and translated into French as *Lecon sur les prisons* in 1831.

Julius came to the attention of Crown Prince Frederick William III while giving a lecture on behalf of prisoner aid in 1827. In 1834 the crown prince, a friend and admirer of Quaker reformer **Elizabeth Fry**, appointed him as a commissioner tasked with studying the penitentiary system in the United States. Upon his return the once vehement opponent of the **Pennsylvania system** became an advocate for separate confinement. Julius chronicled this experience in his 1839 book *Nordamerikas sittliche Zustande: Nach eigenen Anschauungen in der Jahren 1834, 1835 and 1836.* Julius served as professor of criminology at the University of Berlin and carried on a correspondence with prison architect **John Haviland**.

Sources: Teeters, *World Penal Systems*, 1944; Johnston, *Forms of Constraint*, 2000.

K

KAZAKHSTAN. What little information is available is gleaned from human rights groups. The popular opinion is that in the early 1990s, despite the strict control of politics by the ruling party, the country enjoyed a surprisingly high rating for human rights standards for prisons. With the concomitant rise in crime with independence prisons became overcrowded, but human rights groups, at least in the 1990s, did not report any accounts of torture or degrading treatment. According to **Human Rights Watch,** as late as 1999 human rights monitors were still allowed to investigate conditions without harassment.

Conditions had clearly worsened after 2000 with reports of torture and mistreatment, and of several detainees dying under suspicious circumstances. Despite motions toward abolishing the death penalty, a number of people were sentenced to death and executed in 2002. Families of the condemned also faced the dilemma of not knowing in advance when a relative would be executed, typically not finding out until several weeks afterward by telegram. In addition, the law mandated the family could not be informed of the burial site for two years. By mid-2001 the prison population stood at 84,000, or 522 per 100,000 of the national population, significantly higher than in most Central Asian countries. Recent reports from 2004 indicate a dramatic decrease in the prison population to 58,300, or 386 per 100,000 of the national population. This is the first time since 1992 that the prison ratio fell under 60 per 100,000. Today there is a dual prison administration. The Committee of the Criminal-Executive System operates under the Ministry of Justice and is only responsible for sentenced prisoners. Pre-trial responsibilities fall on the Department for Places of Detention under the Ministry of Internal Affairs.

Sources: LCCS, "Kazakhstan: Human Rights," March 1996; *Human Rights Watch World Report*, 2001; *Amnesty International Report*, 2003; ICPS, Kazakhstan, 2004.

KEEPERS. The origins of the modern-day correctional officer can be traced back to medieval gaolers and keepers. Early keepers ran their prisons like businesses.

Keepers typically purchased the appointment or were appointed on the condition that they give the jail owner a percentage of the profits. Although keepers received poor wages, there were always applicants waiting for the position. It could become quite lucrative for more enterprising individuals. Since medieval prisoners were expected to pay for all provisions, including food, drink, and clothing, a keeper could make a tidy profit supplying his charges. In addition, keepers traditionally charged a fee when prisoners entered jail and when they were released. Some keepers even maintained their own breweries and bakeries in the jails. In the fourteenth century attempts were made to regulate fees in London to prevent exorbitant charges.

In the eighteenth century prison reformer **John Howard** led a campaign to abolish the fees and profit-making ventures maintained by jailers and to replace these with a fixed salary subject to public authority. By the 1800s jailers and keepers were more commonly referred to as warders. In 1823 Sir Robert Peel's Prison Act put Howard's theories into practice by requiring that jailers become paid employees of the local government, forbidden to charge fees of any kind from prisoners. Despite these noble attempts at reform there was little ability to enforce the legislation. It would therefore only apply to jails in London, county jails, and 17 provincial jails. Debtor's prisons and municipal jails were little affected.

Sources: Howard, *John Howard*, 1963; Morris and Rothman, eds., *Oxford History of the Prison*, 1998.

KENYA. This British colony in East Africa went to great efforts to create a prison system. In 1911 an autonomous Prison Board was selected to administer the various penal institutions. At this time there were about 30 penitentiaries. The prisons were classified according to sentences. Two prisons were devoted to incarcerating individuals with terms of more than three years' imprisonment. Five were dedicated to those with medium sentences ranging from six months to three years. Twenty-three district prisons held short-termers. In the mid-1920s prisoners were relocated according to work production and labor projects. By 1927 there were 22 detention camps where prisoners were worked at hard labor.

By the 1930s Kenya had thirty prisons, 23 of which were district prisons. By 1941 they held 36,000 detainees and just 10 years later, 55,000. In 1933 the government began building prison camps devoted to agricultural and public works projects to accommodate the majority of prisoners sentenced to force labor. During the Mau Mau liberation movement of the 1950s, usually referred to as the Mau Mau insurgency, the British added fifty temporary "emergency camps" capable of holding thousands of Kikuyu prisoners. According to recent research by historian Caroline Elkins, the British built a "vast system of detention camps," which held as many as 80,000 suspected Kikuyu "insurgents." Elkins's investigation revealed that the British had actually detained between 160,000 and 320,000 mostly male Kikuyu in the camps. Women and children were typically held separately in hundreds of enclosed villages surrounded by spiked trenches and barbed wire. Elkins asserted that contrary to the accepted figures, "the British had actually detained 1.5 million people, or nearly the entire Kikuyu population." Elkins suggests that this program of detention was in reality a well-thought-out campaign to decimate the Kikuyu, and in the process it ended the lives of tens of thousands of Kikuyu.

Today the Kenya Prisons Service operates under the Ministry of Home Affairs, Heritage, and Sports. In 2002 the country's 92 penal institutions included 89 prisons, 2 **Borstals**, and 1 Youth Corrective Training Centre. As of mid-2002 Kenya held 35,278 prisoners, or 111 per 100,000 of the national population. Almost 40 percent of the prisoners were either remand prisoners or pre-trial detainees. As of last count in 1996 the prisons were at 228.1 percent of capacity.

Sources: Kurian, *WEPP*, 1989; Bernault, ed., *A History of Prison and Confinement in Africa*, 2003; ICPS, Kenya, 2003; Caroline Elkins, *Imperial Reckoning: The Untold Story of the End of the Empire in Kenya* (New York: Henry Holt, 2005).

KILMAINHAM JAIL. Built in 1796, this Irish jail is located in Kilmainham, Dublin. During its more than 140-year history a number of Ireland's most famous rebel leaders have been imprisoned and executed here. When it was built in the 1780s, it was known as the New Jail to distinguish it from the fetid dungeon nearby. Before it was abandoned as a prison in 1924, Irish leaders of the 1916 Easter Rebellion were held here, including Eamon de Valera and Patrick Pearse. The future president of Northern Ireland, Eamon de Valera was the prison's last prisoner. In more recent times the deserted jail has stood in for other prisons in the films *In the Name of the Father* (1993), *The Italian Job* (1969), and *Michael Collins* (1996). The prison is now restored and open to the public.

Sources: wikipedia.org/wiki/Kilmainham_Jail; Johnston, *Forms of Constraint*, 2000.

KING'S BENCH PRISON. Originally built in Southward, London in the fourteenth century to hold prisoners awaiting trial at the Court of King's Bench, this prison was burned down for the first time in 1381. During subsequent rebuilding it held debtors and religious prisoners into the sixteenth century. As in most prisons of this era, prisoners lived according to their means behind bars. However, after an investigation in the 1750s that found rampant extortion on the part of the jailers, overcrowding, and lascivious behavior among the inmates, a larger facility was built between 1755 and 1758. On its completion it contained 224 rooms. It too was destroyed during the Gordon riots of 1780, and once more rebuilt. Reopening in the early 1800s, rich prisoners continued to enjoy their accommodations. By one count in 1808, the prison held almost 30 gin shops, a butcher's shop, a wine room, and other amenities. According to one historian, the prison was viewed as the "most desirable place of incarceration in England" in the late 1820s.

A variety of different fees could buy a prisoner a leave of absence or permission to live outside the prison. On the other side of the coin were the poor prisoners who barely survived thanks to a "begging box" at the front gate. Upon the ascension of Queen Victoria, the prison was renamed the Queen's Bench Prison. After the abolition of imprisonment for debt in 1869, the prison housed mostly military prisoners before its final demolition in 1880.

Source: Herber, *Criminal London*, 2002.

KINGSTON PENITENTIARY. Completed in 1835, this Canadian maximum-security prison is located in Kingston, Ontario. Originally known as the Provincial Penitentiary of Upper Canada, it is considered one of the oldest prisons in continuous use in the world. Although still uncompleted, it received its first prisoners in 1835. Heavily influenced by American penal reforms, the institution was finished under the supervision of an **Auburn** construction entrepreneur. The Auburn system gained increasing influence on Kingston when a former Auburn administrator was selected as Kingston's first director.

In 1934 a facility was opened for women directly across the road. Built between Front Road and Lake Ontario, it is the only Canadian prison built along the waterfront. Today it is referred to locally as Kingston Pen. Security was substantially increased in 1971 following a riot that resulted in several deaths and the destruction of much of the institution. Today it houses up to 400 inmates in individual cells. There are an additional six prisons in Kingston ranging from low-security facilities to **supermaximum** such as Kingston Pen and Millhaven Penitentiary. In 1999 the first successful escape was made, a feat previously considered impossible. Today the prison houses the country's most dangerous criminals. In close proximity are eight other prisons ranging from low security to maximum security.

Source: Luc, *Prisons in Canada*, 1982.

KIRIBATI. The Kiribati Prison Service operates under the Office of the President. Since 1968 the small Oceanic island has operated four closed prisons for men and one for women. The prison population is 55, with a ratio of 56 per 100,000 of the national population. The five prisons are all located in major population centers. The Central Prison on Tarawa Island holds prisoners sentenced to two months or more. Individuals sentenced to shorter sentences are permitted to serve their sentences at home. In the late 1980s there were no provisions for helping released prisoners, but there was also some stigma attached to imprisonment. Most male prisoners are required to work on public works projects such as road construction and seawall repairs, whereas women are engaged in light handicrafts work.

Sources: Kurian, *WEPP*, 1989; ICPS, Kiribati, Oceania, 2004.

KNUCKLE VOICE COMMUNICATION. According to popular lore, **San Quentin** prisoner Ed Morrell introduced the "knuckle voice" prisoner communication system to American prisons in the late nineteenth century. Morrell had learned the method from a former prisoner of Russia's St. Peter and Paul fortress in St. Petersburg. According to one popular historian the code was based on a pattern called the Siberian Square. The code consisted of a vertical lists of numbers from 1 down to 5, and horizontal numbers 1 to 6. Each number corresponded to the accompanying letters of the alphabet. To communicate a prisoner would use a series of raps to indicate each letter. For example letter *A* consisted of a rap, a pause, and then another rap. The second letter *B* would consist of one rap, pause, and two raps. It took several months for Morrell to learn the system, which he would later teach to other convicts. Eventually the system popped up in most major American prisons.

Source: Sifakis, *The Encyclopedia of American Crime*, 1982.

KOREA, NORTH. The North Korean correctional system is rooted in Confucian moral precepts and Marxist philosophy. According to the penal code adopted in 1950 at the outset of the Korean War, the purpose of punishment was "to suppress class enemies, educate the population in the spirit of socialist patriotism," and rehabilitate individuals who commit crimes based on capitalist influences. The clandestine and shadowy nature of North Korea has hampered any detailed examination of its criminal justice system. In the 1990s several detention camps housed convicted inmates, and political prisoners were held in separate concentration camps by the State Security Department. As of 1991 between 100,000 and 150,000 prisoners were held in the latter facilities. These camps are strategically located in the more remote parts of North Korea in places such as Tongsin and Hich'n in Chagang Province; Onsg, Hoeryng, and Kyngsng in North Hamgyng Province; Tksng, Chongpyng, and Yodk in South Hamgyng Province; Yngbyn and Yongch'n in North P'yngan Province; and Kaech'n and Pukch'ang in the South P'yngan Province. Prisoners selected for these camps are sent with their families and are forbidden from marrying, forced to grow their own food, and are now entirely cut off from the outside world. The detainees are classified as either anti-party factionalists, anti-revolutionary elements, or opponents of the succession of Kim Jong II. Whether these prisoners were ever reintegrated back into society is unknown.

Other prison camps are devoted to more traditional punishments, and most information indicates that they do return to society after finishing their sentences. These facilities include prisons, prison labor centers, travel violation centers, and sanatoriums. As of 1991 there were 17 basic prisons at the city or provincial level. They are supervised under the Ministry of Public Security. Other types of prisons exist, but information is sketchy. What is known, however, is that there are labor prisons at the city or provincial level and that separate institutions house adults and juvenile convicted of penal violations. A number of reports indicate that minor political officials, ideological offenders, or persons with strong religious beliefs are sent to sanitariums where they are treated as if they had mental illness.

Source: LCCS, "North Korea: Punishment and the Penal System," June 1993.

KOREA, REPUBLIC OF SOUTH. The Correction Bureau is the responsibility of the Ministry of Justice. In 2004 South Korea was operating 47 prison facilities. Thirty were correctional institutions, including 1 for women, 2 for juveniles, and 1 open unit. The remaining institutions include 2 social protection houses, 10 detention center houses, and 5 detention center branches. Designed for a capacity of 43,300 prisoners, in mid-2003 the facilities were overcrowded with 59,413 prisoners, a ratio of 125 per 100,000 of the national population. However, these figures represent a decline from the past decade, when the ratio ranged from 152 to 136 per 100,000.

Source: ICPS, Republic of South Korea, 2004.

KOSOVO (KOSOVA). Since 1999 Kosovo has been given "substantial autonomy within the Federal Republic of Yugoslavia." Subsequently Kosovo organized the Penal Management Division or Kosovo Correctional Service. Prior to the Yugoslavian conflict this region had six prisons. By 2001 Kosovo had reorganized a number of institutions, including Istok Penitentiary at Dubrava, its only maximum-security facility. The first prison to open following the civil war was a detention center at Prizren. Other institutions include Lipjan, Mitrovica, Peja (Pec), Pristina, and Gjilani. These seven institutions are supervised by prison directors from the United Nations but are staffed with Kosovars. In mid-2002 the prisons held 521 inmates in space with the capacity for almost double that. Before the end of the year the prison population rose to 965, however. The prison service is in the process of constructing new prisons and renovating old buildings to increase the capacity to 1,600.

Source: Walmsley, *Further Developments in the Prison Systems of Central and Eastern Europe*, 2003.

KREMLIN, THE. Moscow's Kremlin, the symbol of Communist Russia, was once used as a prison facility. Construction on its Trinity Tower began during the reign of Ivan the Great in 1495. While the building was undergoing periodic repairs in the mid-1890s, laborers discovered an underground structure with trap doors that led to **dungeons.**

Sources: Voyce, *The Moscow Kremlin*, 1955; Johnston, *Forms of Constraint*, 2000.

KYRGYZSTAN. Although the Soviet era ended over a decade ago, little is known about the contemporary penal regime. During the Soviet era, Kyrgyzstan was home to at least 12 labor camps and 3 prisons. At least one of the camps was a uranium mine labor camp where prisoners were required to work without any protective equipment. Most authorities presume that this country is suffering from the overcrowding and poor conditions that plague most former Soviet states. In 1995, following a purge in the Ministry of Internal Affairs, a former assistant minister of internal affairs was selected as the new head of the prison system. In 2002 the prison population stood at 19,500, or 390 per 100,000 of the national population. In 1996 the country reportedly had forty penal institutions operating at 112.6 percent of capacity.

Sources: LCCS, "Kyrgyzstan: Internal Security," March 1996; Walmsley, *WPPL*, 2003; ICPS, Kyrgyzstan, 2004.

KUWAIT. Kuwait's prison system operates under the Ministry of the Interior. In the mid-1990s reports indicated Kuwait held 1,735 prisoners in 4 facilities, which included 2 adult prisons and 2 juvenile prisons. The prison rate at this time would have been 102 per 100,000 of the national population.

Source: ICPS, Kuwait, 2004.

L

LAOS. The Laotian prison system, which operates under the Ministry of Justice, has four types of confinement, under the classifications common criminals, political deviants, social deviants, and ideological deviants. The three latter categories are vaguely defined, leading to prison terms that are often arbitrary and indeterminate in length. Seen as less threatening to the regime, common criminals and social deviants are confined in so-called rehabilitation camps. Sometimes political prisoners are also held there, but most sentences at these facilities are between 6 and 12 months. Those accused of ideologically related crimes are held in remolding centers. The more politically dangerous, typically former government officials, are held in re-education centers. The average sentence at these detention facilities is between three and five years, but it can be longer. At most Laotian confinement centers prisoners work under a punitive regime with limited food and medical treatment. According to one 1986 report, despite the political diversification of crimes there is little political indoctrination. Bribery has become a common method of obtaining food and medicine. According to interviews with former prisoners, most inmates had been arrested and sentenced to indeterminate stints in prisons without trial.

There is much conjecture as to the current status of detention centers. As far back as 1984 the capital of Vientiane reported that all re-education centers had been closed. During this era **Amnesty International** estimated that there were as many as 7,000 political prisoners in these centers. In the 1980s the government admitted that some former inmates were still being held in remote areas but were there on their own volition. There is evidence that in the late 1980s the government did close re-education centers and released most of the prisoners. By the end of the 1980s Laos had taken measures to release a number of political prisoners, including many held since 1975. Several hundred high-ranking inmates and officers from the former U.S.-backed Royal Lao Army were released at this time from re-education centers in the province of Houaphan. However, freed prisoners reported that hundreds of prisoners still remained in eight other camps. They also reported a regimen of manual labor featuring road repair, tree cutting, and other public works projects. By most accounts prison conditions were spartan, with prisoners routinely denied visitors and medical assistance.

Sources: MacAlister Brown and Joseph J. Zasloff, *Apprentice Revolutionaries* (Stanford, CA: Hoover Institution Press, 1986); LCCS, "Laos: Detention Centers," July 1994.

LA SANTE PRISON. Built in 1867, Paris's La Sante Prison has earned a reputation as one France's worst prisons. During its history it has housed terrorists, spies, politicians, and poets. Writers such as Paul Verlaine and Guillaume Apollinaire have spent time there, and currently Carlos the Jackal, once the world's most wanted terrorist, is serving his life sentence in what symbolizes to the French the darkest side of incarceration. The prison houses more than 1,200 prisoners, and every year a handful commit suicide. Forty percent of its occupants are just awaiting trial.

Sources: Elaine Ganley, "Book Exposes Horrors in Fabled Paris Prison," *Houston Chronicle*, January 29, 2000, 25A; Veronique Vasseur, *Chief Doctor at La Sante Prison* (Paris: Le Cherche Midi, 2000).

LATROBE, BENJAMIN HENRY (1764–1820). The British-born architect Benjamin Latrobe was hired to design Virginia's Richmond Penitentiary in 1796. Latrobe was familiar with the European prisons of the era, but he wanted to familiarize himself with American exemplars before designing Richmond. Although construction began in 1797, Latrobe decided to visit Philadelphia's **Walnut Street Jail** in 1798 and by all accounts was impressed.

By 1800 Latrobe's vision had been realized in Richmond. The finished version was a modified, semicircular version of the **panopticon** design. The Virginia penitentiary consisted of three floors arranged in a semicircular horseshoe shape. Exposed balconies on the outside permitted access to each cell. However, from almost the very beginning the prison was hampered by poor ventilation, plumbing, and sanitation. Virginia prison historian Paul Keve noted the irony of the state owning "one of the most elegantly designed prisons in the country while at the same time suffering with one of the least utilitarian and least humane of America's prison buildings." Nonetheless, Latrobe is credited with professionalizing American architecture in the years before the Civil War. Latrobe would later help design and construct the U.S. Capitol for President Thomas Jefferson.

Sources: Paul W. Keve, *The History of Corrections in Virginia* (Charlottesville: University of Virginia Press, 1986); Johnston, *Forms of Constraint*, 2000.

LATVIA. In 2000 the Latvian Prison Administration was placed under the control of the Ministry of Justice. As of 2004 Latvia had fifteen prisons. Six were closed prisons; three were semi-closed, including a women's facility; two were open facilities; three held pre-trial detainees; and one was a juvenile correctional institution. Combined, these institutions had a capacity for 9,096 prisoners. The largest institution is the Central Prison, capable of holding 2,101. The women's prison could hold up to 347; other institutions could hold on average between 470 and 970 inmates. The two most recent prisons are the pre-trial facility at Liepajas and the open prison of Olaines.

In the early 1990s the prison population hovered around 8,500 and then peaked at 10,300 in 1996. By early 2001 the population stood at 8,831. By the end of

2002 the number of prisoners had decreased to 8,486, or 361 per 100,000 of the national population, giving it the highest ratio in northern Europe. It is six times higher than that of any Nordic country. However, prisons are still at only 89 percent of their total capacity. The only institutions reporting problems with overcrowding have been the pre-trial institutions. Conforming to most eastern and central European prison systems, Latvia's prisons rarely keep prisoners in single cells. Latvia has adopted European Prison Rules standards, so most living standards have been upgraded, juveniles have been separated from adults, and untried prisoners are held separate from convicted inmates. The main problem that continues to afflict the prison system is tuberculosis, in part a result of a dearth in modern medical equipment at some prisons.

As of 2001 the prisons were operated with a staff of 2,237. Staff training has improved in recent years, and new recruits attend three-month training seminars. Individuals sentenced to prison are not obligated to work, but those who decide to work can earn a salary not less than the minimum wage. Latvian prisons are still confronted with a lack of budgetary resources, numerous pre-trial detainees, and a court system that continues to favor prison sentences over alternatives. Prisoners can vote once they are released from prison. In mid-2004 Latvia's prison population stood at 7,857, or 339 per 100,000 of the national population. The last time the prison rate was this low was in 1992, when it was 314 per 100,000.

Sources: Walmsley, *Further Developments in the Prison Systems of Central and Eastern Europe*, 2003; Walmsley, *WPPL*, 2003; ICPS, Latvia, 2004.

LAWES, LEWIS EDWARD (1883–1947). The son of a correctional officer, Lewis Edward Lawes entered the penal profession as a guard at Clinton Prison in New York in 1905. He is credited with continuing the reform impulse at **Sing Sing Prison** that was first introduced by **Thomas Mott Osborne**. Lawes would rise from chief guard at **Auburn Prison**, to superintendent of the New York City Reformatory at the age of 32, and then to warden of Sing Sing. He would spend more than two decades in this position. Following in the footsteps of Osborne he introduced a **Mutual Welfare League** that enabled inmates to govern themselves in a number of ways. But unlike other systems of inmate governance prisoners, the league held no sway over other prisoners, a situation that Lawes felt added undue tension to the already volatile nature of prison life. Over time he became an opponent of capital punishment. In 1928 Lawes saw the publication of his book *Life and Death in Sing*. He followed this up four years later with *Twenty Thousand Years in Sing Sing*, which he famously dedicated "To those tens of thousands of my former wards who have justified my faith in human nature."

Sources: Lawes, *Twenty Thousand Years at Sing Sing*, 1932; Deford, *Stone Walls*, 1962; Sifakis, *Encyclopedia of American Prisons*; 2003.

LAZARETTO. A lazaretto is hospital meant to quarantine individuals with contagious diseases. Such hospitals were typically located in seaports. Prison architectural historian Norman Johnston suggests that Europe's lazarettos and other early hospital plans provided some of the inspiration for modern "purpose-built" prison designs. Johnston cites as one example the sixteenth-century San Pacrazio lazaretto on the outskirts of Verona, which featured an interior court "divided into four sections, each with a water supply." **John Howard** discussed these type of institutions in his *Account of the Principal Lazarettos in Europe* (1789), which chronicled his peregrinations through Europe. Howard cites plague hospitals in Marseille, Genoa, Messina, and other southern European ports, many of which featured small rooms and iron-barred windows.

Sources: Howard, *An Account of the Principal Lazarettos of Europe*, 1789; Johnston, *Forms of Constraint*, 2000.

LEASING SYSTEM. *See* CONVICT LEASING

LEAVENWORTH PRISON. One of the most storied American prisons, Leavenworth has been home to prisoners such as Robert "The Birdman of Alcatraz" Stroud, who only raised birds at Leavenworth, and the two Will Wests. In 1903 penitentiary officials were dumbfounded to find out that the institution held two black convicts named Will West, and according to photographs and their Bertillon system the two seemed identical. This embarrassment set into motion a series of events that would lead the transition from Bertillon identification to fingerprinting and in 1904 the entire prison population was fingerprinted for the new identification system. By 1907 Leavenworth had one of the largest fingerprint collections in the United States, with 20,000 prints. It eventually became the Identification Center for the United States and in 1924 became the nucleus for the FBI fingerprint system in Washington, D.C.

Leavenworth was designated as America's first federal penitentiary. However, its construction took forever. As a result, the federal penitentiary at Atlanta, which began construction after Leavenworth, opened four years earlier. A military prison formerly sat at this site in Leavenworth, Kansas. Construction for the new federal prison began in 1896, but it did not open until 1906. Amazingly, construction was not totally finished for more than another twenty years. The cellblocks were finished only in 1919, shoe shops in 1926, and a brush and broom factory in 1928. Designed by architects Thomas Young and William Eames to hold 1,200 prisoners, stylistically the prison was of **radial** design, with four cellblocks radiating from a domed structure referred to as the Big Top. The dome was reportedly modeled after the U.S. Capitol Building in Washington, D.C. A fifth spoke housed a school and offices. According to architect Eames, when the prison was completed, it would be "a city within a city," the first penitentiary "in the world to be entirely self contained," citing the existence of its own power plant, water supply, maintenance shop, hospital, and "the first school ever built inside a penitentiary."

According to its census in 1910, by Thanksgiving of 1909 the institution held 887 inmates, 504 of whom were white. Inmates represented almost two-dozen different countries. Although cells were intended to hold single inmates, overcrowding and double bunking soon became the rule. By 1920 the prison population was at almost double capacity.

Sources: Keve, *Prisons and the American Conscience*, 1991; Early, *The Hot House*, 1992; Joe Jackson, *Leavenworth Train* (New York: Carroll and Graf, 2001).

LEBANON. The little information available suggests that the country maintains 23 penal institutions and 8 temporary facilities. The Ministry of the Interior is responsible for running the system, and plans have been in the works to transfer it to the Ministry of Justice eventually. As of mid-2004 there were 5,535 prisoners, a prison rate of 146 per 100,000 of the national population. With a prison system built with the capacity to hold 4,800, this rate shows the prisons were overcrowded at 115.3 percent of capacity. Since 1993 the prison population had more than doubled from its 2,515 population to its current level. Another study from 2002 indicates that prison population could be as high as 8,285 if pre-trail detainees are included. Together this represents a rate of 230 per 100,000 of the national population.

Sources: Walmsley, *WPPL*, 2003; ICPS, Lebanon Brief, 2004.

LEFORTOVO PRISON. Moscow's Lefortovo Prison was initially a nineteenth-century military prison. Never intended to hold a large number of inmates, its cells had a reputation for insalubrity. The building itself is shaped in a K configuration. By the 1930s it had become so overcrowded it was necessary to build a new unit in a monastery outside Moscow. Although it was officially known as "Object 110," prisoners referred to the prison by the original name of the monastery, Sukhanova. Since KGB head Lavrenty Beria had an office in this building, it came as no surprise that the facility garnered a reputation for torture and brutality.

Source: Applebaum, *Gulag*, 2003.

LESOTHO. The Lesotho Prison Service operates under the Ministry of Justice and Human Rights. The country's 14 penal institutions held 3,000 prisoners in 2002, a rate of 143 per 100,000 of the national population, an increase over the rate of 122 reported in 1999. More than one third of the prisoners are pre-trial detainees and remand prisoners.

Source: ICPS, Lesotho, Africa, 2003.

LE STINCHE PRISON. This early European prison was built in Florence, Italy, in the 1290s. It received its first prisoners in 1304, and according to prison historian Norman Johnston was "one of the earliest purpose-built prisons." It is significant for its separation of prisoners by sex, age group, degree of sanity, and seriousness of offense, as well as its emphasis on prisoner re-education. It originally consisted of five large holding rooms; it was not until the 1800s that a cell building was added.

Sources: Marvin E. Wolfgang, "A Florentine Prison: Le Carcere della Stinche," *Studies in the Renaissance*, 7:148–166, 1966; Johnston, *Forms of Constraint*, 2000.

LIBERIA. The Liberian Code of Laws of 1956 specifically states that the goal of imprisonment is rehabilitation. By the end of the 1980s there were at least 20 facilities that could be defined as prisons. Of these, three were in the capital of Monrovia, including the Central Prison, the Municipal Jail, and the Belle Yella Camp. The other 17 facilities include scattered county, district, and magisterial jails. As of

1989 the prison system was plagued by a lack of direction and organization. There is no real continuity in prison administration, with some facilities operated by military personnel or police, and others by the Department of Justice. At this time there was little if any attempt at separating prisoners by classification. As a result, adults and juvenile, men and women, detainees and hardened convicts, often shared the same space. As in most poor countries there is little budget for improving the jails, with some barely more than a mud hut and others are made of concrete. The Central Prison is reportedly only one of two facilities with plumbing; for the most part jails are unsanitary with inadequate light and ventilation. Prisoners are faced with the prospect of using the jail floors for sleeping as well as for toilets. Years of strife and civil unrest have contributed to overcrowding. Jails in the more sparsely populated areas allow prisoners to raise their own food to supplement meager rations. Many others are reliant on handout from friends and family in order to survive. No other current information is available.

Source: Kurian, *WEPP*, 1989.

LIBYA. The Libyan criminal justice system is heavily influenced by the Islamic legal tradition. The General Department of Judicial Police administers the prison system, which is the responsibility of the Secretariat of Justice and Public Security. Information prior to 2003 is available only on three facilities. These include the Central Prison at Tripoli, Kuwayfiyah Prison in Benghazi, and Jdeida Prison on the outskirts of Tripoli. Evidence suggests the presence of a number of smaller jails in various towns and the construction of two new prisons in Tripoli and Darnah prior to normalization of relations with Libya. Efforts by human rights groups to gain access to Libyan penal facilities were routinely denied, however. In 1975 Libya reported to the United Nations that it was reorganizing the prison system by moving from a punishment-oriented regime to one emphasizing education, training, and rehabilitation. According to Law No. 47, the administration was making efforts to integrate some type of indeterminate sentencing by which individuals can move toward early release through good behavior and attitude. Whether substantial change has resulted is unknown because of the barriers to visitors from outside the country. In mid-2004 the national prison administration reported 33 prison facilities holding 11,790 prisoners. This is well over their capacity for 7,000 inmates. More than 56 percent of the prisoners are either pre-trial detainees or remand prisoners. A breakdown of the foreign population that makes up more than one third of the prison population reveals it is 12.8 percent Arab and 21.6 percent African. The current ratio is 207 prisoners per 100,000 of the national population.

Sources: LCCS, "Libya: Criminal Justice System," 1987; Kurian, *WEPP*, 1989; Walmsley, *WPPL*, 2003; ICPS, Libya, 2004.

LIECHTENSTEIN. This diminutive European country of 34,200 inhabitants has 1 prison facility holding 18 prisoners at last count. Of these, 6 are reportedly serving their sentences in neighboring **Austria**. The prison rate represents 53 per 100,000 of the national population.

Source: ICPS, Liechtenstein, 2004.

LIPARI. This small island near Sicily held political prisoners and opponents of fascism during the reign of Italy's Benito Mussolini. It became known as the "fascist Devil's Island" in the 1920s and 1930s.

Source: Francesco Nitti, *Escape* (New York: G. P. Putnam, 1930).

LITHUANIA. Lithuania's Prison Department operates under the Ministry of Justice. As of early 2004 the prison system housed 8,062 prisoners, a rate of 234 per 100,000 of the national population. The prison system operates 15 facilities, including 2 pre-trial prisons, 9 semi-closed correctional labor colonies, an open-style settlement colony, a colony for juveniles, a medical colony dedicated to tuberculosis patients, and a prison hospital. The current system has capacity for 9,578 prisoners. The prison population has peaked and fallen since the 1990s, cresting at 14,400 inmates in 2000. However, amnesties and the diminished use of pre-trial detention have helped reduce the prison population from its 2000 zenith.

The most recent figures for prison staff suggest an overall staff-to-prisoner ratio of 1 to 2.9. But the staff number is double if one included management, security, and treatment staff. Among the prison system's most pressing objectives are the development of more activities, vocational training programs, social rehabilitation programs, and more educational training. Problems include overcrowding, drug use among inmates, longer prison sentences, lack of financial resources to refurbish prisons, and lack of alternatives to incarceration. The largest prisons are the semi-closed labor colonies at Alytus and Maijampole, each with the capacity for 1,316 prisoners. Two other colonies capable of holding more than 1,000 inmates are located at Pravieniskes.

Sources: LCCS, "Lithuania: Penal Code and Prisons," January 1995; Walmsley, *Further Developments in the Prison Systems of Central and Eastern Europe*, 2003; Walmsley, *WPPL*, 2003.

LOMBROSO, CESARE (1836–1909). Considered the father of the Positivist School of Criminology, Lombroso explored the notion of hereditary criminality. Building on research for a B.A., Morel—who wrote a *Treatise on Degeneracy* (1857) and *Formation of Typology in Degeneracy* (1864), and a number of others—the Italian professor of medical jurisprudence and psychiatry theorized that some individuals were born to be criminals and therefore could be regarded as a distinct species, *homo delinquens*. Lombroso's contentions are well known and while criminologist Edwin Sutherland argued in 1962 that "Lombroso's impact had the disastrous effect of leading criminology up a blind alley for forty years," from a penological point of view, his theories challenged the reigning notions that criminals could be rehabilitated and reformed in prison. Lombroso's best-known book was *L'Uomo Delinquente*, or *Criminal Man*, first published in 1876. In this work, Lombroso describes prisons as "criminal universities" and challenges the benefits of cellular confinement, which he argued, "has not attained its object and does not prevent communication between prisoners." His other "findings" suggest that the impact of education on crime "is very slight," and that trades training simply brings the poor and unskilled "into contact with wealth," creating more opportunities for criminal activities. On the other hand, Lombroso recognized that although poverty bred crime, wealth was no barrier to similar behavior since "the possession of wealth is frequently an incentive to crime, because it creates an ever increasing appetite for riches." As far as the effectiveness of imprisonment, he lamented that although prison was more humane than past punishments, it was "illogical" and neither intimidated nor reformed offenders.

Sources: Gina Lombroso-Ferrero, *Criminal Man, According to the Classification of Cesare Lombroso* (Montclair, NJ: Patterson Smith, 1972).

LONG KESH DETENTION CENTRE. Between 1941 and 1971 the British Royal Air Force operated RAF Long Kesh ("long meadow" in Irish) near Lisburn in Northern Ireland. When it was discontinued in 1971, the ramshackle base was transformed into a detention center to hold both republican and nationalist prisoners. Inmates referred to it as the Long Kesh concentration camp. With its barbed wire compounds, corrugated iron huts, floodlights, and guard dogs, even at its closure in 1971 it had the look of a 1940s prisoner-of-war camp. Most prisoner accounts describe a prison that made every type of inclement weather seem worse—colder in winter, sweltering in summer. However, within five years the makeshift structures of Long Kesh were abandoned for the newly built H-Blocks of what would become known as **Maze Prison.**

Long Kesh was initially operated without a formal prison regime. Prisoners could wear their own clothes and were not obligated to work. They could elect their own officers, forming a council to parley with prison officials. Following a number expansion projects the prison had grown to 22 compounds holding up to 2,000 prisoners. Prisoners were separated by factional allegiance at their own request. Exclusive compounds were maintained for even splinter groups. Among the factions were two Irish Republican Army (IRA) groups composed of "Originals" and the newly formed "Provisionals." The Loyalists were divided into the Ulster Defence Association, the Ulster Volunteer Force, Ulster Freedom Fighters, and the Red Hand Commandoes.

Prison security was provided by the British military. Four guards manned each compound. A breakdown of their positions would find one in a sentry box at the compound gate, two patrolling the perimeter fences between the compounds, and a fourth guard on reserve for the unexpected. Over time a number of staff were recruited from the community. In 1972 Long Kesh was rechristened Her Majesty's Prison Maze. One of the best accounts of life inside Long Kesh is *Behind the Wire* by Phil McCullough.

Source: Ryder, *Inside the Maze*, 2000.

LOWNES, CALEB (1754–1828). Lownes was a Quaker iron merchant and leading member of the **Philadelphia Society for the Alleviation of the Miseries of Public Prisons.** Lownes began his affiliation with prison reform shortly after the end of the American Revolution. In the 1780s, Lownes joined Benjamin Franklin, **Benjamin Rush,** and others to lobby for the abolition of the death penalty. Their campaign led to the legislation of 1786, which substituted all capital offenses, except for two, with hard labor on local public works projects.

Lownes along with Benjamin Rush advocated building a cellblock of solitary cells based on the ideas of **John Howard.** In the 1790s Lownes rose to prominence as the warden of the **Walnut Street Jail** and as the co-author with William Bradford of *An Account of the Alteration and Present State of the Penal Laws of Pennsylvania*, published in 1792. Under his supervision the Walnut Street Jail was hailed internationally for its work regimen, which included shoemaking, weaving, tailoring, and more grueling activities such as beating hemp, grinding plaster of Paris, and **oakum picking**. Special attention was focused on the notion of separate cell confinement at night and congregate work by day. However, in 1808 Lownes tendered his resignation lamenting the overcrowding that impinged on the labor program.

Sources: McKelvey, *American Prisons*, 1977; Sullivan, *The Prison Reform Movement*, 1990.

LUBYANKA PRISON. Moscow's Lubayanka Prison was originally the site of insurance company offices. Its parquet floors continue to remind observers of its former use. Prisoners were required to wash these floors every day. In the 1920s an anarchist who later became the secretary for **Alexander Solzhenitsyn** served a short sentence and years later recounted that during her sentence food was delivered by "waitresses wearing uniforms." Following the death of Josef Stalin in 1953, its use as a prison was discontinued. One of Moscow's three main prisons prior to the 1950s, Lubayanka is still utilized as headquarters for the FSB, which replaced the NKVD and KGB, the Soviet Union's security agencies, after the fall of the Soviet state. In its heyday it was used as a reception and interrogation location for important political prisoners. In 1956 the prison contained 118 cells, the majority of which were very cramped but still held from one to four prisoners. This notorious Soviet prison became the inspiration for a number of writers. *Doctor Zhivago* author Boris Pasternak's mistress, and the purported inspiration for his heroine Lara, was held here in 1949. Noted Russian prisoner and gulag survivor Alexander Solzhenitsyn spent a stint here as well in the 1940s. Raoul Wallenberg, the savior of many Bulgarian Jews during World War II, was reportedly executed in Lubyanka in 1947. According to author Anne Applebaum, Lubyanka's last prisoner was U-2 pilot Gary Powers, downed over the Soviet Union in his spy plane in 1960.

Sources: Thomas, *Alexander Solzhenitsyn*, 1998; Applebaum, *Gulag*, 2003.

LUCAS, CHARLES JEAN MARIE (1803–1889). The noted French penal reformer is best remembered for writing one of the first critiques of capital punishment. His three-volume opus, *The Penitentiary System in Europe and the United States*, published in 1828, reportedly influenced the development of what Lucas referred to as "penitentiary science." In 1865 Lucas used his own money to open an institution for juveniles at Val d'Yevre near Bourges. Seven years later it was taken over by the French government.

He had his first opportunity to put his ideas into practice when he was appointed inspector general of French prisons beginning in 1830. Prior to his retirement 35 years later, he wrote the acclaimed *Reform of Prisons; or, Theory of Imprisonment*, in which he argued that more focus should be placed on the prisoner and society rather than on the crime itself, a revolutionary thesis for the first half of the nineteenth-century.

Sources: Teeters, *World Penal Systems*, 1944; Andre Normandeau, "Charles Lucas," *Journal of Criminal Law, Criminology, and Police Science* 61, no. 2 (June 1970).

LUXEMBOURG. The Ministry of Justice directs Luxembourg's prison system. Most recently the country reported that its 2 prison facilities housed 498 inmates in a system capable of handling almost 800 inmates. The prison rate is 111 per 100,000 of the national population. This represents an increase over the past 6 years from 92 per 100,000 in 1998 to 357 per 100,000 in 2001.

Source: ICPS, Luxembourg, 2004.

LYNDS, ELAM (1784–1855). Born in Connecticut, Elam Lynds, an ex-military officer and veteran of the War of 1812, was hired as the chief jailer at **Auburn** prison when it opened for business in 1817. At over six feet tall he cut an imposing figure. Lynds earned an early reputation as a violent disciplinarian. Within several years he had moved the prison away from **Thomas Eddy**'s humane penal code. Under his watch, Lynds placed inmates on bread-and-water diets, put them in stocks and irons, and freely employed flogging for violating prison rules. Following the resignation of the head prison agent in 1821, Lynds was appointed warden. Insisting on tight discipline, he equipped each prison assistant with a cat-o'-nine-tails made of cowhide.

Lynds was an early proponent of solitary cells. With the support of the New York legislature, 80 convicts were held in complete isolation in complete silence day and night. With nothing to occupy their time prisoners were inclined to lie supine throughout the day. However, Lynds prohibited convicts from lying down in bed during the daylight hours, explaining that this prohibition would help prevent muscle atrophy. As a result, a number of prisoners either committed suicide or went insane.

In 1825 the separate cell and silent system was applied to the entire Auburn prison. Despite the resistance of inmates to silence, Warden Lynds quickly won compliance with the lash. By the 1820s Lynds was widely criticized for his use of whipping, but few could argue with the results of his harsh regime. Even Rev. **Louis Dwight** of the Boston Prison Discipline Society regarded Auburn as a testament to order and subordination, and Thomas Eddy described the Auburn prison as the best in America. In 1825 Lynds was ordered to bring 100 inmates to the town of Ossining, New York, and built what would become the notorious **Sing Sing Prison**. At Sing Sing, Lynds introduced the first striped prison uniforms. Three years later he returned to Auburn but was relieved of his duties because of his draconian propensities. He returned to Sing Sing until he was dismissed in 1845, ending a controversial career in corrections. However, he was fired for financial irregularities involving kickbacks and selling prison food for profit, rather than for his predilection for the whip.

Lynds's legacy is mixed: some regarded him as a "borderline sadist"; others credited him with introducing prison discipline and order as well as the Auburn system, in which prisoners worked in a congregate setting by day and slept in solitary confinement by night.

Sources: McKelvey, *American Prisons*, 1977; Christianson, *With Liberty for Some*, 1998.

M

MACAU (CHINA). This country has one prison holding 891 prisoners. This is well under its capacity to hold 1,200 and represents a ratio of 184 per 100,000 of the national population. Macau Prison is administered under the Ministry of the Interior. The prison population has been stable over the past five years but has seen an increase compared to the 1990s.

Source: ICPS, Macau (China), 2004.

MACEDONIA. The Macedonian Directorate of Prison Administration operates under the Ministry of Justice and Adminsitration. As of 2001 the system operated eight prisons, four of which have open sections. The prisons include the closed facility of Idrizovo, an open prison at Struga, and semi-open faculties such as the juvenile facility at Ohrid. The largest prison, with the capacity to hold half the country's prisoners, is Idrizovo Prison, which also offers an open section at Veles. Skopje Prison also operates an open section at Kriva Palanka. Recent reports indicate that the house of correction at Tetovo is temporarily closed because of conflict in that area of Macedonia. The current prison population is 1,598, or 78 per 100,000 of the national population, a figure lower than those of most central and eastern European countries, but not unlike those of the other former republics that once made up Yugoslavia. Recent reports indicate that overcrowding is not a problem. As is customary for this part of Europe, few prisoners are confined to single cells, with the typical accommodation housing five prisoners. Prisoners are separated according to conviction status and by gender and age. Among the most pressing objectives are the improvement of staff training and health care, as well as the renovation of deteriorated prison facilities. Macedonia's prisons have already achieved a number of objectives, bringing the nation's system in line with Europe's Prison Rules standards.

Sources: Walmsley, *Further Developments in the Prison Systems of Central and Eastern Europe*, 2003; ICPS, Macedonia (former Yugoslav Republic of), 2004.

MACCORMICK, AUSTIN H. (1893–1979). Born in Canada and raised in Maine, Austin MacCormick wrote his senior essay at Bowdoin College on noted penologist **Thomas Mott Osborne**. His scholarship led to an appointment as a research assistant to help examine the state's prison system. Taking a page from Osborne's career, MacCormick assumed the disguise of a forger and spent an anonymous week in the state penitentiary. Upon his release he wrote a scathing indictment of the prison regime.

MacCormick completed graduate work at Columbia University in 1916 and then wrangled a position under his idol Thomas Mott Osborne, who was studying a naval prison at Portsmouth, New Hampshire. MacCormick checked in once more under an alias and exposed the terrible conditions in the naval prison. Soon after, Osborne was named its commanding officer and MacCormick his executive officer. Together they were able to make an impact on the prison population, soon restoring the majority of inmates to active naval duty.

In 1933 MacCormick was selected as acting warden at the Chillicothe Reformatory. But he resigned barely six months later when Mayor Fiorello LaGuardia appointed him New York City corrections commissioner. As commissioner he exposed the scandalous conditions at New York City's Welfare Island Prison. During the remainder of his career he became a leading supporter of "individualized treatment." He later served as assistant director of the Federal Bureau of Prisons, where he was placed in charge of academic and vocational training, and then as president of the American Correctional Association.

Sources: Keve, *Prisons and the American Conscience*, 1991; Phillips and Axelrod, *Cops, Crooks, and Criminologists*, 1996.

MACONOCHIE, ALEXANDER (1787–1860). Born in Edinburgh, Scotland, Alexander Maconochie was only nine when his lawyer father died. In 1804 he joined the Royal Navy and served in a variety of capacities until the defeat of Napoleon in 1814. Over the next thirteen years he studied geography and politics while maintaining an interest in Pacific colonization. He would serve stints as professor of geography at University College, London, and then as the first secretary of the newly created Royal Geographical Society. In 1837 he was selected to visit the Pacific Ocean. Before his leaving, friends in the Society for the Improvement of Prison Discipline asked him to complete a questionnaire after visiting the penal colony of **Van Diemen's Land**. He mentioned that upon his visit he was almost immediately struck by the brutality and punitive nature of the penal colony. The eventual publication of Maconochie's scathing rebuke of the colony caused an uproar in the English press. However, socially his report backfired and he soon found his family ostracized for his vilification of the "slave owners" of Van Diemen's Land.

By the 1840s Maconochie had become a firm advocate of what became known as the **mark system**, which offered sentences that were no longer definite and fixed but of indeterminate length. In this system convicts could earn marks for good behavior and hard work, leading to early release. Essentially they would be allowed to buy their way out of prison with a number of marks. For example, a seven-year sentence could be ended by the accumulation of 6,000 marks. Marks could be exchanged for goods as well—food, tobacco, and other luxury items could be purchased with marks. Between 1840 and 1843 Maconochie put his theories into practice at the penal colony on **Norfolk Island**. According to historian Robert

Hughes, his ideas "were a century ahead of their time." But politics and criticism from opponents of his system intervened and led to his release and the end of his noble experiment in 1843. While opinions were mixed concerning his achievements at the time, most indicators suggest that he cut the recidivism rate of inmates and improved behavior and morale among prisoners.

Between 1849 and 1851 he served as governor of Birmingham Borough Prison. However, he could do little to moderate the sadism of the new prison's deputy governor, and in 1851 Maconochie was either fired or resigned. He would die in obscurity.

Maconochie published a number of works on penal issues, including *Thoughts on Convict Management and other Subjects connected with the Australian Penal Colonies* (1838), *General Views Regarding the Social System of Convict Management* (1839), *Principles of the Mark System, now sought to be introduced into Transportation, Imprisonment and other Forms of Secondary Punishment* (c. 1845), *Norfolk Island* (1847), and *The Mark System of Prison Discipline* (1857).

Sources: John Vincent Barry, "Alexander Maconochie," *Journal of Criminal Law, Criminology, and Police Science* 47, no. 2 (July/August 1956) pp. 145–161; Barry, *Alexander Maconochie of Norfolk Island*, 1958; Hughes, *The Fatal Shore*, 1987.

MADAGASCAR. The country's penal code has been most influenced by French penal code procedures. Madagascar has a national prison system, which included a central prison in each province for inmates serving less than five years. At the central locations of various courts there are at least 25 lesser prisons for prisoners serving less than 2-year terms and for those awaiting trial. At the local, or sub-prefecture level, jails are maintained for individuals serving less than six months. Women sentenced to long terms in prison are housed in the Central Prison, or *Maison Centrale,* in Antananarivo. Inmates serving terms exceeding five years are housed on island prisons that have been built on coastal islands such as Nosy Lava and Nosy Be. Most reports indicate that prison conditions are rather severe, with single cells holding up to eight prisoners. Prisoners are reliant on family and friends to supplement their meager daily rations of food. Those without outside support have reportedly gone days between meals. Medical treatment is wholly inadequate, leaving prisoners to languish from malnutrition, infections, malaria, tuberculosis, and other ailments. Other reports indicate that female inmates are engaged in prostitution with help from guards, and children are normally housed with their mothers during their sentences. By late 1999 the country's 97 penal establishments held 20,109 prisoners, or 130 per 100,000 of the national population.

Sources: Kurian, *WEPP*, 1989; LCCS, "Madagascar: Penal System," August 1994; Walmsley, *WPPL*, 2003; ICPS, Madagascar, 2004.

MAIDSTONE PRISON. This English prison served as a county jail for almost 200 years before its conversion to a prison in the 1740s. **John Howard** visited it on several occasions in the eighteenth century and found it to be overcrowded with poor ventilation. In 1811 reconstruction of the prison began under the direction of Daniel Asher Alexander, the architect of **Dartmoor Prison**. It was completed in 1819 at a final cost of 200,000 pounds. The buildings were constructed from locally quarried Kentish Rag Stone on a 14-acre site. The original plan called for individual cells to hold 552 prisoners, including 62 women. The first 141 prisoners arrived in March 1819. Seven years later the courthouse was built in the front of the prison. Embracing some of the suggestions made by John Howard, Maidstone included individual cells for prisoners as well as dayrooms, courtyards, and offices. Strict segregation of prisoners according to offenses was maintained, and a number of improvements were made to the water supply, sanitation, and ventilation.

The only vestiges of the original construction are the large and small roundhouses, the Weald Wing, the Administration Block, the Training Complex, the Visits Building, and the perimeter wall. Today the prison averages 560 inmates in 4 cellblocks. Of these, 140 are serving life sentences; the rest are serving more than 4-year terms. Maidstone will not accept any prisoner who has less than 18 months of a sentence left to serve, has attempted to escape from prison in the last 2 years, or needs in-patient health care.

Today Maidstone is classified as a "closed training prison" housing prisoners who are viewed as a minimum threat to public safety. Over the past century there have been a number changes made to the prison, usually facilitated with the help of prison labor.

Sources: Dick Whitfield, "Maidstone Prison, England," in *The State of the Prisons—200 Years On*, ed. Whitfield, 1991, pp. 13–29; "HMP Maidstone Information Packet," 2002/2003.

MAISON DE FORCE. *See* GHENT MAISON DE FORCE (PRISON)

MALAWI. British law and African customs have influenced Malawi's criminal justice system. There are about 20 small jails scattered across the country. The main prison is in Zomba, with other prominent facilities in Lilongwe, Kanjedza, and Mzuzu. There is also an open prison farm dedicated to first-time offenders, as well as a facility for juveniles. Regardless of the facility, prisoners are expected to work. As of mid-2002 the prison population was 8,769, or 76 per 100,000 of the national population.

Sources: Kurian, *WEPP*, 1989; Walmsley, *WPPL*, 2003.

MALAYSIA. The Malaysian Prison Department operates under the Ministry of Home Affairs. In late 2003 the country's 33 prison establishments held 39,258 prisoners. The facilities include 24 prisons, 3 rehabilitation centers, 5 advanced approved schools, and 1 detention center. Prison overcrowding remains a serious concern. In January 2004 the Malaysian government was asked to improve conditions at the Kajang women's prison, which held 1,450 inmates in a prison with the capacity to hold 450. The introduction of a parole system at the end of 2004 was intended to reduce the overcrowding. It seems that special security prisoners are confined separately.

Prison facilities run the gamut from conventional walled prisons to open farms and detention camps. First-time offenders and better-socialized inmates are sentenced to the Central Training Prison at Taiping. Regional training prisons for recidivists are located at Pinang, Alor Setar, Kuala Lumpur, and Johor Baharu. The reform schools at Telok Mas, Ayer Keroh, and Malacca are for juvenile males; girls are confined to the Batu Gajah. Local prisons for minor offenders are located at

Sungei Petani for male juveniles, Kuantan for adult males; others are located in Kuala Lumpur, Georgetown, Alor Setar, and Pengalan (for women). Detainees awaiting trial are held at Taiping and Muar. Other prisons include central prisons in Sarawak and Sabah, regional facilities at Simannang, Sibu, Miri, Limbang, Sandakan, and Tawau. There is also a minimum-security prison at Keningau and detention camps at Kuching and Kota Kinabalu.

Sources: Kurian, *WEPP*, 1989; ICPS, Malaysia, 2004.

MALDIVE ISLANDS. The Maldive Islands had 1,098 sentenced prisoners in 1996, or 414 per 100,000 of the national population. The prisons operated under the Ministry of Justice.

Source: ICPS, Maldive Islands, Asia, 2004.

MALEFIZHUAS, THE. The Malefizhaus was a two-and-a-half-story prison purpose built in Bamberg, Germany, in 1627 to confine "witches, sorcerers, and sinners." A local bishop ran the prison. Its main purpose was to punish and rehabilitate such malefactors. The second floor held prisoners in single cells facing a broad central corridor. An altar was placed at the end of the hall. The building was heated with stoves lit from the outside, a system that Johnston reports "was common in that part of Europe."

Source: Johnston, *Forms of Constraint*, 2000.

MALI. Mali's prison system is the responsibility of the Ministry of Justice. In 2000 its 58 prisons held 4,040 prisoners, more than two thirds of whom were either pretrial detainees or remand prisoners. The prison rate is 34 per 100,000 of the national population.

Source: ICPS, Mali, Africa, 2004.

MALTA. Malta's Department of Correctional Services is operated under the Ministry of Home Affairs. In 2002 the island had 1 main prison holding 278 prisoners. One third of the prisoners were awaiting trial. More than one third of the prisoners are foreigners. The prison population rate is 72 per 100,000 of the national population.

Source: ICPS, Malta, 2004.

MAMERTINE PRISON. Built in ancient Rome in 64 B.C.E., the Mamertine Prison was a series of dungeons housing offenders in large, caged rooms under the main sewer of Rome. Other scholars have dated one of Mamertine's lower chambers to as far back as the 200s B.C.E. It is possible that a similar chamber used to hold prisoners underground in Syracuse inspired construction of Mamertine. The name Mamertine is medieval and probably was derived from the temple of Mars Ultor constructed in the vicinity.

Sources: Samuel Platner and Thomas Ashby, "Mamertine Prison," *A Topographical Dictionary of Ancient Rome* (London: Oxford University Press, 1929); Johnston, *Forms of Constraint*, 2000.

MANDELA, NELSON (b. 1918). Nelson Mandela was one of the most famous prisoners of the twentieth century. Born in Qunu in the Transkei, as Rolihlahla, he was the first member of his family to attend school. His Methodist schoolteacher gave him his English name, Nelson. Mandela later attended college and law school while also participating in his favorite sports of boxing and running. By the age of twenty he had already taken part in his first political protest. Soon after, he earned his law degree at the University of South Africa in Johannesburg. During his years at law school Mandela was involved in the political opposition to the minority white rule. In the 1950s he joined with Oliver Tambo in operating a law firm providing free and low-cost counsel to poor blacks. He also continued to be active in opposing the apartheid government. Despite his support of nonviolent struggle, he was arrested along with 150 others in 1956 and charged with treason. Following his exoneration and the subsequent shooting of unarmed protestors at Sharpeville, Mandela converted to armed struggle.

Despite a government ban on anti-apartheid organizations, Mandela became leader of the African National Congress's armed wing, the "Spear of the Nation." Mandela organized a sabotage campaign and arranged for support for paramilitary training from other African governments in preparation for civil war. In 1961 he was arrested on a tip from the American CIA and imprisoned for five years. He would end up serving the next 26 years in prison for his admitted role in sabotage operations and for a number of other spurious charges. In 1985 he refused a conditional release on his agreeing to condemn armed resistance, and he remained in prison until 1990. The slogan "Free Mandela" had meanwhile made him a larger-than-life hero around the world. In 1993 he shared the Nobel Peace Prize with state president Frederik Willem de Klerk. Then in 1994 Mandela became South Africa's first black head of state. He retired in 1999 but still remains active in a number of human rights initiatives.

Sources: Nelson Mandela, *Long Walk to Freedom: The Autobiography of Nelson Mandela* (New York: Little, Brown, 1995); Anthony Sampson, *Mandela: The Authorized Biography* (New York: Knopf, 1999).

MARION PENITENTIARY. The federal penitentiary at Marion was built in 1963 as a replacement for the less feasible accommodations on **Alcatraz**. Located in the middle of a wildlife refuge in southern Illinois, Marion is considered one of the nation's most secure prisons. In 1979 a new policy allowed other federal prisons to send their most problematic inmates to Marion. A number of these prisoners were gang members who had attacked officers or killed inmates at other institutions. The spartan single cells contain concrete fixtures and a stainless steel toilet to eliminate the ever-present prison parts made into knife-like shanks. The austerity of the complex is amplified by interior remote-controlled gates and closed-circuit television surveillance.

In the 1980s Marion was plagued by escape attempts, riots, serious encounters between inmates and guards, and nine murders. In one day alone two guards were killed in unrelated attacks. Subsequently a lockdown left prisoners in their cells 23 hours per day and limits were placed on commissary transactions. By the mid-1990s Marion held 335 inmates serving average sentences of 40 years. Special cells are located in the basement dedicated to famous criminals who have threatened national security, including spies John Walker Jr. and Jonathan Pollard. Most recently the prison was home to the late Gambino gang boss John Gotti, who died in 2002.

Other high-profile residents include Westies gang boss Jimmy Coonan and Philadelphia mob boss Nick Scarfo. In the 1990s the Federal Bureau of Prisons opened a new **supermaximum** prison in Florence, Colorado.

Sources: Marilyn McShane, "Marion Penitentiary," in *Encyclopedia of American Prisons*, eds. McShane and Williams, 1996, pp. 318–319; Sifakis, *Encyclopedia of American Prisons*, 2003.

MARK SYSTEM. English prison reformer **Alexander Maconochie** is generally credited with introducing the Mark System of indeterminate sentencing to corrections. In 1840 Maconochie was appointed governor of the penal colony on **Norfolk Island,** some 800 miles off the coast of Australia. Maconochie opposed the traditional fixed prison sentence in favor of an "indefinite" sentence or mark system. According to his strategy, prisoners could earn "marks" or "credits for good behavior and hard work." In this way a prisoner could earn early release from prison with the provision that he will be returned to finish his term if he reoffends. In the initial stage, prisoners entered the system in separate confinement. The next step included "social labor" by day and solitary confinement by night, followed by "social treatment both day and night." Prisoners on the right path could rise from one grade to another before earning the right to become part of a small group of inmates who worked together and were responsible for each other's behavior. Discipline then became more relaxed for the inmates as they prepared to reenter the free world. However, if a prisoner backslid he could lose marks. **Walter Crofton** adapted the mark system for the more widely-used **Irish System,** which involved matriculating through a series of five classes leading to transfer to an open prison.

Sources: Deford, *Stone Walls*, 1962; Hughes, *Fatal Shore*, 1987.

MARSHALL ISLANDS. The Marshall Islands prisons are the responsibility of the chief of police. In the 1990s there was 1 main prison on Majuro Island holding less than 20 prisoners. There are smaller prison facilities on Ebeye Island holding close to a dozen prisoners. The prison rate in mid-1994 was estimated at 44 per 100,000 of the national population.

Source: ICPS, Marshall Islands, Oceania, 2004.

MARTINIQUE, FRENCH. In 2003 Martinique had one prison holding 643 inmates. Designed for 490, it was considered at 131.2 percent of capacity. The prison rate is 164 per 100,000 of the national population.

Source: ICPS, Martinique (France), 2003.

MATAS. Indigenous prison staff employed by colonial Indochinese prisons were referred to as matas. Matas fell into four categories of "surveillants." Matas were always subservient to the European staff. According to Peter Zinoman, the poorest prison guards in Europe were paid five times more salary than the lowly matas, who came from lower-class social origins. In their subservient position, matas were often barred from carrying keys and firearms and were thus left to protect themselves with nightsticks. Their main job was to stand guard at various locations around the prison and observe the inmates whenever they left their cells. In like manner, European guards were expect to keep tabs on their indigenous counter-parts. They also functioned as a type of **trustee** by supervising prisoners at work sites outside prison. Similar to French guards drawn from the ranks of retired mil-itary, the majority of matas were retired or unemployed ex-soldiers. At the end of the nineteenth century matas were expected to have had at least fours years of mil-itary experience. The different ranks of uniform emblems distinguished matas. Like the trustees in American prisons, matas earned a reputation for extorting money from prisoners and for other forms of corruption, such as running illicit gambling and sex rackets in the prisons.

Source: Zinoman, *The Colonial Bastille*, 2001.

MAURITANIA. After the government adopted the Sharia, or the Islamic legal sys-tem, in 1980, the treatment of prisoners in penal institutions became much more punitive. Human rights groups have identified a large number of cases in which tor-ture and detention without charges have been used. Black prisoners have been sin-gled out for the worst treatment. Friends and relatives have also reported harassment and repression by authorities. The prison system consists of 18 facili-ties administered under the Ministry of Justice. In mid-2002 the prison population stood at 1,354, representing 48 per 100,000 of the national population. Although the prisons are near 150 percent of capacity, it is still and improvement over the figures from the past 8 years.

Sources: LCCS, "Mauritania: Law and Crime," 1988; Walmsley, *WPPL*, 2003; ICPS, Mau-ritania, Africa, 2004.

MAURITIUS. The most recent information suggests that the prison system con-sists of a traditional prison, a rehabilitation center, a juvenile facility, and an in-dustrial school. In mid-2002 there were 2,438 prisoners, or 203 per 100,000 of the national population.

Sources: LCCS, "Madagascar: Penal System," August 1994; Walmsley, *WPPL*, 2003.

MAZE PRISON. Her Majesty's Prison Maze is known as the Maze, after a nearby village. The term actually means "plain" in Irish. Located some ten miles from Belfast, the Maze Prison became prominent during the conflict in Northern Ireland in the 1970s. The Maze Prison was opened in 1976, at the height of the so-called troubles in Northern Ireland, and achieved worldwide attention during a 1981 hunger strike that ended after the starvation deaths of ten prisoners. It was built close to the **Long Kesh** internment center as a maximum-security prison for polit-ical prisoners. The prison is situated on 270 acres of boggy low-lying land. During the 30-year sectarian conflict more than 10,000 prisoners have passed through the Maze and Long Kesh facilities. By the early 1980s nearly one third of the prison-ers in Maze were serving life sentences. Despite strict security 38 prisoners broke out in a mass escape in 1983, the largest jailbreak in British history. In the process 1 prison officer was killed and 5 other injured. Half the prisoners escaped recap-ture. The Maze earned a reputation for brutality during its first 20 years. A num-ber of guards from the Northern Ireland Prison Service, as well as Irish Republican Army (IRA) and Loyalist leaders, have been murdered here and at Long Kesh.

Between 1974 and 1993, Loyalist or IRA inmates killed 29 employees of the Northern Ireland Prison Service.

In the 1980s the government introduced a number of reforms. IRA and Loyalist prisoners were detained according to affiliation. Each group organized itself along military lines and maintained such control of their H-block that prisoners could be murdered over political differences.

The design of the Maze Prison is rather unremarkable. It consists of 8 H-blocks surrounded by a 17-foot concrete perimeter wall and is guarded by 12 30-foot watchtowers. The construction of the prison was the same design used in the re-building of Louisiana's **Angola Penitentiary** in 1955.

Prisoners played an important role in the peace process by participating in talks with officials that led to the Good Friday Agreement on April 10, 1998. Over the next 2 years an accelerated program of prisoner release led to the release of 428 prisoners. On September 29, 2000, the last 4 prisoners in The Maze were transferred to other institutions and the prison was closed.

Sources: Jim Challis, *The Northern Ireland Prison Service, 1920–1990: A History* (Belfast: Northern Ireland Prison Service, 1999); Ryder, *Inside the Maze*, 2000; Wylie, *The Maze*, 2004.

McNEIL ISLAND FEDERAL PENITENTIARY. McNeil Island Federal Penitentiary is America's oldest federal prison. In the 1860s the northwestern region of the United States, particularly the Territory of Washington, was rather isolated but still required a federal prison for its increasing population and its concomitant rise in crime. In 1870 a 27-acre site was selected on McNeil Island. Five years later it received its first 10 prisoners. Although Washington became a state in 1889, the prison remained under the control of the U.S. Marshal until 1910. In 1907 McNeil was designated as the prison for all federal prisoners sentenced on the Pacific Coast and the Territory of Alaska. Over the next 30 years more land was purchased to house a larger population. By 1936 McNeil Island Federal Penitentiary consisted of the entire island as well as two nearby islands. One of the prison's early inmates was **Robert Stroud**, who began his sentence in 1909, decades before he would earn the moniker "The Birdman" at **Leavenworth Prison**.

METTRAY COLONY FOR BOYS. The brainchild of French penal reformer **Frederic-Auguste Demetz**, France's Mettray Colony for Boys was an early example of an "open agricultural" colony for juveniles. Norman Johnston asserts that it was established as a way of responding to the neglect and brutality faced by juveniles held in adult facilities. Other notables played a part in the inauguration of the colony, including such well-known reformers as architect **Guillaume Abel Blouet**, who designed it, Gustave de Beaumont, **Alexis de Tocqueville**, and the **Duc de la Rochefoucauld-Liancourt**.

The Mettray Colony for Boys received its first charges in 1840. The concept behind the rural facility, located outside Tours, was to subject juveniles and various young miscreants to a domestic environment deemed "family-like" and "wholesome." Similar to a minimum-security or open facility, the colony was not surrounded by walls, and the windows of the dormitory were not equipped with bars. What distinguished this unit from other forms of confinement was the way the lodgings were dispersed in the colony and its implementation of a "family model of treatment." Johnston has suggested that this colony may have inspired the development of the **telephone pole design**.

Source: Johnston, *Forms of Constraint*, 2000.

MEXICO. Although the Mexican federal constitution of 1857 had authorized the creation of a prison system, little progress toward this end occurred over the next quarter century. Plans for a wheel-like prison big enough to hold 600 inmates were on the drawing board from at least 1848. Mexican prison experts found the **Auburn** model unsuitable for the Mexican climate. A commission was once more examining plans for a national penitentiary in the 1870s, but this plan languished as well.

By the end of the 1870s Mexican prison reformers cited the Belen Prison in Mexico City as everything that was wrong with contemporary prisons. At Belen, prisoners of both genders, young and old, were crowded into the same facility, which was plagued with common halls, little sun, and little ventilation. Critics charged that this prison provided socialization and entertainment rather than a rehabilitative or correctional regime.

In 1900 the first Mexican penitentiary was finally completed. Based on the **Pennsylvania system**, the National Penitentiary (Distrito Federal) in Mexico City was similar to **Eastern State Penitentiary**, except for several modifications. When it was completed, it was described as being in the form of a star with seven corridors radiating from a central cupola. One of the more unusual characteristics of this penitentiary is that it contains two swimming pools and a tennis court. Later on the prison became known as Lecumberri Prison. In subsequent years it housed up to 5,000 prisoners at one time. The Mexican states of Jalisco, Guadalajara, Guanajuato, Durango, and Puebla opened new prisons also based on the **radial** design. In 1906 the Juarez Penitentiary was opened in Merida, Yucatan. Its design followed suit, with five wings radiating in a half circle from an inspection cupola. In 1907 an institution for women was added to the prison system.

During the early twentieth century Belen prison was updated and would henceforth hold only those awaiting trial. The Mexican government bought the Marias Islands in 1905 with the hope of establishing a penal colony there. The penal colony known as Les Tres Marias is comprised of three small island some 75 miles off the Pacific coast. The three islands are named Maria Madre, Maria Magdalena, and Maria Cleotas. By 1925 these islands were considered an integral part of the prison system.

Mexico attempted a variety of prison experiments in the 1930s and 1940s. The work program prevalent in a number of institutions impressed prison observers. All prisoners were required to work in the industrial shop, where they could earn a salary commensurate with the country's minimum wage or higher. Prisoners were expected to pay for food and clothing from their earnings. In addition, 40 percent of their savings were to go toward the reparation of damages caused by their offenses. Another 30 percent was available for the prisoner's family if necessary. The remaining 30 percent was placed in a reserve fund. Supporters of the work program believed that what was most important about the program was that the convicts were forced to atone for their crimes with remunerative compensation. Workers were even allowed to create their own Union of Criminal Workers, although for the most part it was ignored by officials.

The current prison system is made up of both federal and state facilities. The largest federal prison remains the Federal District Penitentiary in Mexico City. The federal system also has four detention centers, sixteen smaller jails, and a women's jail. Every state also has a penitentiary. Complementing these prisons are more than 2,000 municipal jails across Mexico. By 1994 there was a total prison population of almost 100,000, with half of all prisoners awaiting trial or sentencing.

Human Rights regularly target Mexican prisons because of chronic overcrowding, corruption, poor training of guards, poor sanitation, and rampant violence. However, some of these complaints are balanced out in the eyes of at least married prisoners by the introduction of conjugal visiting rights in the 1970s for both sexes. The previously mentioned penal colony in the Marias Islands allowed prisoners to bring their entire families for periods of time.

In 1977 the United States and Mexico agreed to the terms of the Prisoner Transfer Treaty, which allowed nationals in each other's country to return to their country of origin to complete sentences.

In the early 1990s a new building program added an additional 800 prison spaces. In 1991 Mexico opened its first maximum-security prison at Almoloya de Juarez. Other prisons sent major drug traffickers to this modern facility, where the prison's 408 cells were always under surveillance thanks to closed-circuit television and other security devices. Currently the General Directorate for Prevention and Social Re-adaptation administers the prison system under the Ministry of the Interior. In 2003 Mexico had 448 prisons, including 5 federal penitentiaries, 8 federal district prisons, 336 state prisons, and 99 municipal and regional jails. In mid-2000 the prison population stood at 154,765, or 156 per 100,000 of the national population. This has increased substantially over the past few years. In 2003 there were 175,253 prisoners, a rate of 169 per 100,000.

Mexico's prison system has not been able to shake its well-earned reputation for corruption, with most accounts indicating guards and wardens are susceptible to bribery. Most recently conditions in Mexico's federal prisons have come under fire. In January 2005 three guards and three prison administrators were found shot to death less than one mile from the federal penitentiary in Matamoras. This followed on the heels of a riot the previous week in La Palma federal prison near Mexico City that required the intervention of federal troops and police. Authorities suggest the recent murders were in response to the government crackdown on imprisoned gang bosses. In March 2005 an attempt was made to control Mexican prison gangs in a sweep through the Nuevo Laredo Penitentiary. Soldiers found cell phones, a pool table, a disco sound system, and firearms including an AK-47. A number of former drug kingpins lived in relative luxury here.

Sources: LCCS, "Mexico: Prison Conditions," June 1996; Robert Buffington, "Revolutionary Reform: Capitalist Development, Prison Reform, and Executive Power in Mexico," in *The Birth of the Penitentiary in Latin America*, eds. Ricardo D. Salvatore and Carlos Aguirre, 1996, pp. 169–193; Johnston, *Forms of Constraint*, 2000; Walmsley, *WPPL*, 2003; ICPS, Mexico, 2004; Dudley Althaus, "Prison Killings Last Straw for Fox," *Houston Chronicle*, January 21, 2005, A1, A13; Ioan Grillo, "Mexico Prison Sweep Uncovers Surprises," *Houston Chronicle*, March 30, 2005, A1, A6.

MICRONESIA, FEDERATED STATES OF. Four islands make up Micronesia. In 1994 each one had its own prison. In the late 1990s the prison population was estimated at 39, or 34 per 100,000 of the national population.

Source: ICPS, Micronesia, Federated States of, Oceania, 2003.

MIDNIGHT EXPRESS. The book and movie of the same name did for Turkish prisons what the countercultural film *Easy Rider* did for the American South. After watching these films nobody would want to set foot in either region. *Midnight Express* chronicles the 1970 arrest and subsequent imprisonment of American Billy Hayes for drug smuggling. Arrested at Istanbul airport while trying to smuggle two kilos of hashish out of the country, he is subsequently sentenced to the prison fortress of Sagamilcar, where he is beaten and sodomized by a brutal guard. Hayes is initially sentenced to more than four years, but an appeals court later increases the sentence to thirty years. He eventually escapes from the prison in 1975 and successfully flees to Greece and freedom. Critically acclaimed, the film won two Academy Awards in 1978, including Best Screenplay for Oliver Stone. But a number of critics cited the film's unfair portrait of Turkey's prisons, noting the less-than-spotless history of American prisons. Others suggested that Hayes violated the law and deserved prison rather than the accolades for escaping and his lack of contrition.

Sources: Crowther, *Captured on Film*, 1989; Parrish, *Prison Pictures from Hollywood*, 1991.

MILIZIA, FRANCESCO (1725–1798). The Italian author of *Principi di Architettura civile*, published in 1785, articulated a number of penological philosophies that seem modern for their time period. He suggested that prisons are "for detention and not punishment." He also made distinctions between civil and criminal institutions, noting that the most serious offenders should be confined in fortresslike structures characterized by features that convey "darkness, threatening, ruins, terror," in order to suppress criminal activity. According to one source, "Milizia's recipe for civil prisons in 1785 was to provide the deepest shade, cavernous entrances and terrifying inscriptions."

Sources: N. Pevsner, *A History of Building Types* (London: Thames and Hudson, 1976); Johnston, *Forms of Constraint*, 2000.

MILLBANK PRISON. Millbank Prison was built on the marshy grounds on the north bank of the Thames River in 1816. It was considered Great Britain's first centralized effort toward developing a prison system in England prior to the opening of **Pentonville Prison** in 1842. It was built for close to two million dollars, an expense critics compared to building the Taj Mahal Palace in India. **Jeremy Bentham**'s notions on prison management influenced Millbank's design. The prison regime adopted the separate system with silence for the first half of the prison sentence. While little thought was given toward the physical well-being of inmates, efforts were made to educate and reform inmates in preparation for release. Built in the shape of a six-pointed star inside an octagonal wall, the prison was surrounded by moat. Each point of the star was built in the shape of a pentagon from which warders could perpetually monitor prisoners from the center of each pentagon. It has been estimated that the corridors were a total of three miles long and contained 1,000 cells.

Millbank Prison was deemed a colossal failure by the 1840s. Few prisoners were reformed, and the location of the prison in such a damp and gloomy site was detrimental to any chance of rehabilitation. With the opening of Pentonville Prison in 1842, Millbank was downgraded to an ordinary prison, principally used for holding prisoners prior to **transportation** or transfer to other prisons. It was enlarged to hold 1,500 prisoners by ending the separate system. In 1870 it made the transition to military prison and was finally demolished in 1903. Today the Tate Art Gallery resides on this very spot.

Sources: Teeters, *World Penal Systems*, 1944; Babington, *The English Bastille*, 1971; Herber, *Criminal London*, 2002.

MIYAGI PENITENTIARY. Miyagi *sujikan,* or "penitentiary," was one of the first European-style prisons constructed in Japan. Built between 1879 and 1882, it followed a six-wing **radial** design. According to Norman Johnston, it "still retains vestiges of the old moat and feudal castle" that preceded it at this location.

Source: Johnston, *Forms of Constraint*, 2000.

MOABIT PRISON. In the 1840s German architect Karl Busse was sent to England to study British prison models. Upon his return he designed Germany's Moabit Prison and in 1844 work was begun on its construction. Built in the Moabit district of Berlin, it was modeled on **Pentonville Prison**. Moabit conformed to the **radial design**, with four wings connected to a "semicircular inspection center" at its hub. Following the pattern of the **Pennsylvania system**, prisoners worked and lived in isolation and were provided their own individual exercise yards. The construction of Moabit Prison influenced the building of a number of cellular prisons in the German states in the 1840s.

Source: Johnston, *Forms of Constraint*, 2000.

MOLDOVA, REPUBLIC OF. In 1996 the responsibility for the nation's Department of Penitentiary Institutions was transferred from the Ministry of Internal Affairs to the Ministry of Justice. In 2003 Moldova counted 20 penal institutions holding 10,729 inmates, or 297 per 100,000 of the national population. Of these 5 are pre-trial prisons and 12 are prison colonies for adults, including 1 dedicated to women and another for tuberculosis patients. There is also an educational colony for juveniles, another for the rehabilitation of alcoholics, and a national prison hospital. The largest institution is the pre-trial unit at Chisinau, which has space for 1,480. Other units with capacities for more than 1,000 inmates in descending order include Soroca, Cricova, Pruncul, and Branesti. Thanks to a number of amnesties over the past decade, prison numbers have remained stable.

Moldova has experienced a problem staffing the prisons. In 2000 the staff to prisoner ratio stood at 1 to 4. Prognosticators predicted that by 2002 the ratios would be somewhere between 1 to 3.1 and 1 to 4.2. Recent noteworthy developments include the opening of a special prison for lifers at Rezina, a prison colony for former state employees at Lipcani, and a new strict regime correctional colony at Leova. Among the problems that continue to plague the prison system are lack of financial resources, inadequate treatment of tuberculosis patients, overcrowding, and inadequate conditions in holdover units from the Soviet era.

Sources: ICPS, Moldova (Republic of), 2003; Walmsley, *Further Developments in the Prison Systems of Central and Eastern Europe*, 2003.

MONACO. Monaco has one prison located at Pierre Tournier. At last count in 1998 it held 13 prisoners. According to the International Centre for Prison Studies, the prison population is "artificially reduced" because many prisoners serve their sentences in **France**. The prison rate is 39 per 100,000 of the national population, not counting prisoners in France.

Source: ICPS, Monaco, 2004.

MONGOLIA. Into the 1990s Mongolia operated prison camps and correctional-educational colonies. There were detention camps to handle minor offenders and provide rehabilitation through "socially useful labor." Labor projects included public works projects, street cleaning, and building repairs. Individuals participating in this labor regimen are not given wages or food but must purchase food or hope their families will supply victuals. Those serving brief detention of less than 24 hours are held in local jails, as are those awaiting indictments. As of mid-2001 the prison population stood at 6,656 (sentenced prisoners only), a ratio of 256 per 100,000 of the national population. By mid-2003 Mongolia reported 7,871 prisoners held in 28 penal institutions. Prison facilities included 15 central prisons, 13 provincial prisons, and at least 21 pre-trial detention centers. These centers are located in each of the country's twenty provinces, plus at least one other one in the capital of Ulaanbaatar. The Imprisonment General Department is responsible for sentenced prisoners, whereas the police manage pre-trial detainees, all under the direction of the Ministry of Justice. The prison rate was last gauged at 303 per 100,000 of the national population.

Sources: LCCS, "Mongolia: The Penal System," June 1989; Walmsley, *WPPL*, 2003; ICPS, Mongolia, 2004.

MONTENEGRO. In 1994 the Institute for the Executions of Criminal Sanctions was created "to provide a prison administration, independent of prosecutorial and court authorities." It operates under the Ministry of Justice. There are currently three prison facilities. One is a pre-trial facility at Spuz, on the periphery of Podgorica, holding both male and female pre-trial detainees and convicted prisoners serving sentences less than three months. At Spuz there is also a facility dedicated to sentenced prisoners. It has its own separate director and offers a closed unit and a semi-open section. The third facility is a pre-trial prison at Bijelo Polje. It primarily served the courts in the northern region of Montenegro. It holds pre-trial detainees of both genders and sentenced prisoners confined for up to three months.

By most accounts Montenegro's prison standards measure up to European Prison Rules standards covering prison space, food, and sanitation. However, criticism has been leveled at the conditions in isolation cells, which offer inadequate space, light, heating, ventilation, and sanitation facilities.

Prisoners already sentenced are permitted a one-hour visit once every two weeks. There are also accommodations for conjugal visits in the closed section of Spuz Prison. In 2002 285 of the country's 301 prison staff were posted within the active prison. The staff-to-prisoner ratio is typically 1 to 2.5. Prospective prison guards must complete a 16-week training course that was just recently inaugurated.

Among the prison system's most pressing problems is a lack of budgetary resources, lack of drug treatment programs, poorly trained staff, and the challenges of upgrading the neglected prisons from the Yugoslavian era.

In late 2003 Montenegro's three prisons hold 734 prisoners, more than one third of who were pre-trial detainees or remand prisoners. The prison rate is 108 per 100,000 of the national population.

Sources: Walmsley, *Further Developments in the Prison Systems of Central and Eastern Europe*, 2003; ICPS, Serbia and Montenegro: Montenegro, 2004.

MONTESINOS, MANUEL (ACTIVE 1830s). Colonel Manuel Montesinos was one of Spain's most prominent prison reformers. He served as director of Valencia Prison in 1835 and later served as the inspector, or *visitador*, of the General Spanish Prisons. Montesinos instituted a quasi-military regime at Valencia, which held more than 1,500 prisoners. What was novel about his approach was that prisoners acted as inferior officers in the greater system and could earn one-third reductions of their sentences through good behavior and a number of accomplishments. During his tenure prison morale improved. His scheme preceded by several years the similar but better-known regimes inaugurated by **Alexander Maconochie** and **Walter Crofton**. Montesinos ended up resigning after his innovation involving the remission of sentences was repealed. In 1846 he published his views on penal reform in a small booklet.

Sources: Teeters, *World Penal Systems*, 1944; McKelvey, *American Prisons*, 1977.

MOROCCO. After regaining its independence from France in 1956, the Moroccan government sought to reform its criminal and judicial systems. As of the late 1980s the Department of Penitentiary Administration was operated under the Ministry of Justice. By the end of the 1980s there were at least 34 prisons and correctional facilities, with central prisons located in Rabat, Meknes, Fez, Settat, Oujda, Marrakech, Kenitra, Casablanca, and Tagounite. Casablanca had two maximum-security institutions at Prison Ain Borja and Prison Civile; Kenitra maintains one as well. The rest of the prisons are considered medium security, with one juvenile facility in Kenitra. According to **Amnesty International**, Morocco also maintains seven large detention centers. Two are near Casablanca, one outside Mulay Cherif, another close to the Anfa Airport, one near Rabat, another between Rabat and Kenitra, and one near the Alegrian border at Oujda. According to French authorities, other police detention facilities are located in Agudal and on Imam Malik Street in Marrakech. Over the past 20 years most reports indicate that prison populations were sometimes between 5 and 10 times their designed capacities. The most recent reports indicate that there are now 48 prison institutions, including 39 local prisons, 5 agricultural prisons, and various other establishments. In 1999 a new program was introduced to open sites to allow married couples to have intimate meetings. Although the justice minister suggested a movement toward more fines in order to relieve the overcrowded prisons, five years later there had been little progress in this direction. In 2002 the prison population stood at 54,207, equaling 176 per 100,000 of the national population. Just over 40 percent of these were either pre-trial detainees or on remand. According to the International Center for Prison Studies, the official capacity of the prison system as of 2000 was 35,000. All indicators suggest a growing rate of incarceration, from 33,040 prisoners at 135 per 100,000 in 1990 to 48,600 in 1997 at 177 per 100,000 to current figures.

Sources: Amnesty International, *Report of an Amnesty International Mission to the Kingdom of Morocco*, February 10–13 (London: Amnesty International, 1981); "Moroccan Justice

Minister Notes Considerable Progress in Moroccan Prisons," February 6, 1999, www.arab-icnews.com; Walmsley, *WPPL*, 2003; ICPS, Morocco, 2004.

MOUNT PLEASANT FEMALE PRISON. In 1835 New York opened the nation's first separate state prison exclusively for women. It remains so for the next 35 years. The prison, while managed by female matrons, was under the administration of inspectors at **Sing Sing Prison**. Female prisoners were kept busy with a number of domestic tasks, from sewing and button making to trimming hats. Between 1844 and 1847 matron **Elizabeth Farnham** introduced a number of reforms that were considered radical for the day, including the elimination of the silent system. After Farnham resigned, the reform regimen slowly returned to the more punitive roots of the **Auburn system**. Thirty years after the prison opened, the inmate population was at double its designated capacity. When it came time for the state legislature to renovate the structure, it decided to close the prison instead and sent the inmates to other facilities in 1872.

Sources: McKelvey, *American Prisons*, 1977; Lucia Zedner, "Wayward Sisters: The Prison for Women," in *Oxford History of the Prison*, ed. Morris and Rothman, 1998, pp. 295–324.

MOZAMBIQUE. The Prison Department and the National Directorate of Prisons operate Mozambique's prisons under the direction of the Ministry of Home Affairs (maximum-security units) and the Ministry of Justice. At the beginning of 2000 Mozambique held 8,812 prisoners in 27 central and provincial prisons. These are supplemented by 42 open centers and a number of district facilities that are considered branches of the central and provincial institutions. Almost 73 percent of the prisoners were either remand or pre-trial detainees. The national rate was 50 per 100,000 of the national population and prison occupancy was 144 percent of capacity.

Source: ICPS, Mozambique, Africa, 2004.

MURTON, THOMAS G. (1928–1990). Born and raised in Oklahoma, Thomas Murton earned a degree in animal husbandry before moving to Alaska, where he eventually moved up the ranks of the correctional service from jailer to temporary chief of corrections. He is credited with organized the opening of five prisons in Alaska after statehood. He then taught criminology at Southern Illinois University before he was given the opportunity to head up Arkansas's infamous Tucker Prison Farm in 1968 after the superintendent, threatened inmates with a submachine gun, and three wardens were fired during a prison scandal. Initially state officials supported his reforms, including the abolition of flogging and physical torture. Before his arrival a number of punishments had been adopted to enforce discipline beginning in 1962. Many harkened back to a darker era of humankind. Among the punishments were such novelties as inserting needles under fingernails, crushing knuckles and testicles with pliers, beating inmates with a 5-foot leather strap up to 10 times a day, and the so-called Tucker Telephone, which involved stripping the individual, strapping him to a table, and then attaching electrodes to the big toe and penis. The prisoner was then subjected to electrical charges until passing out. When the warden of the larger nearby Cummins Prison Farm resigned over Murton's reforms, having sought elimination of these medieval leftovers, Murton became warden of both prison farms.

Almost from the beginning Murton ran into adversity as he attempted to eliminate the Cummins trustee system, which permitted inmates with special privileges to run roughshod over the prison population. Because of a paucity of public funding the Arkansas Prison System had become one of the worst of the state prison systems. Whereas most prisons operate with a staff-to-prisoner ratio of 1 to 7, the 4,500-acre Tucker and 16,227-acre Cummins prison farms operated with 35 staff for 2,000 inmates, a ratio of almost 1 to 65 (staff was increased to 113 in 1968). The prison system filled the gap by using trusties and mounted inmates to guard convicts at work in the fields. A typical week for prisoners included 14-hour days, 6 days a week, with no remuneration. Corruption and violence had always been an implicit part of the regime.

Murton's discovery that almost 200 prisoners had been listed as escapees set into motion a sequence of events that would gain international attention. The story inspired the 1980 fictional drama *Brubaker*, starring Robert Redford. Murton's penchant for publicity as much as his zeal as a reformer led to his being fired by Governor Winthrop Rockefeller within months of excavations at the farm to look for inmate graves. Although Murton told newspapers he believed that many of the 213 missing men had been murdered, digging uncovered only 3 unmarked graves, and the investigation came to a crashing halt. Murton could point to his vindication two years later, when a federal court decision cited conditions at the Cummins Prison Farm as a violation of the Eighth Amendment protection against cruel and unusual punishment.

Following his Arkansas experience Murton found it impossible to find another corrections post and instead earned a Ph.D. in criminology at the University of California at Berkeley. Assuming he had been blacklisted, he opted for a career in academia teaching criminal justice at the University of Minnesota. Retiring in 1980, he devoted the rest of his life to prison reform while tending his poultry farm.

Sources: Tom Murton and J. Hyams, *Accomplices to the Crime: The Arkansas Prison Scandal* (New York: Grove Press, 1969); K. Wymand Keith, *Long Line Rider: The Story of the Cummins Prison Farm* (New York: McGraw Hill, 1971); Christianson, *With Liberty for Some*, 1998; Sifakis, *Encyclopedia of the American Prison System*, 2003.

MUTUAL WELFARE LEAGUE. Thomas Mott Osborne inaugurated the Mutual Welfare League at **Auburn Prison** in 1913. Inspired by English prime minister William Gladstone's motto, "It is liberty alone that fits men for liberty," upon being selected chairman of the New York commission for the reform of the prison system he began applying his notions of self-government to the adult inmate population at Auburn. The Mutual Welfare League initially consisted of 49 prisoners elected by secret ballot from among the prison's 1,400 inmates. This committee then organized a grievance court and adopted its own disciplinary measures. Following his appointment as warden of **Sing Sing Prison** in 1914, Osborne instituted a Mutual Welfare League there as well. Osborne's "anti-institutional" approach flew in the face of the notoriously punitive Auburn regime. Between 1914 and 1929 Osborne experimented with abandoning prison stripes and nonconstructive work regimes, as well as eliminating the silent system, in an attempt to allow the inmates a sense of responsibility and self-respect. In 1929 a violent escape attempt and subsequent riot took place at Auburn, in which a keeper was killed and the warden and several guards were taken hostage. Following resolution of the conflict, pressure from guards and politicians hastened Osborne's departure and the end of his experiment in prison self-government.

Sources: Christianson, *With Liberty for Some*, 1998; Edgardo Rotman, "The Failure of Reform: United States, 1865–1965," in *Oxford History of the Prison*, eds. Morris and Rothman, 1998, pp. 151–177.

MYANMAR. Information on the prison system of Myanmar (formerly Burma) is hard to come by. In the late 1980s the Ministry of Home Affairs controlled the penal code and the Prisons Department. Although most towns had some type of facility, the system is loosely organized and in poor condition. As of 1987 there were 10 central prisons, 20 district jails, and 10 guardhouses. Rangoon had a facility for juveniles, but none of the institutions apparently employed teachers, social workers, or vocational trainers. The most recent figures for the prison population date back to 1993, when there were 53,195 prisoners, or 118 per 100,000 of the national population. At last report the country maintained 118 prison facilities.

Sources: Kurian, *WEPP*, 1989; Walmsley, *WPPL*, 2003; ICPS, Myanmar, 2004.

N

NAGORNO-KARABAKH. A disputed region within **Azerbaijan**, Nagorno-Karabakh is semi-autonomous and houses at least three penal establishments, including a pre-trial **SIZO** located in the capital city of Stepanakert, a **tyrooma**, or closed prison in Susha, and a mixed regime colony in Fisuali. The inhabitants of this region are mostly ethnic Armenian, and thus this area considers itself an extension of that country. The three institutions are governed either by the Ministry of Security or the Ministry of Internal Affairs. Most recently women and minors were incarcerated in separate facilities in Armenia.

Source: Walmsley, *Further Developments in the Prison Systems of Central and Eastern Europe*, 2003.

NAMIBIA. The Namibia Prisons Service is operated under the Ministry of Prisons and Correctional Services. As of 2002 the thirteen institutions that made up the prison system held 4,814 prisoners. The prisons were considered at 126 percent of their official capacity of 3,822. The prison population was 267 per 100,000 of the national population.

Source: ICPS, Namibia, 2002.

NATIONAL PRISON ASSOCIATION. The National Prison Association organization was formed out of the 1870 **National Prison Congress**. Between 1870 and 1907 this prison reform organization was known as the National Prison Association. In 1908 its name was changed to the more familiar American Correctional Association (ACA). Its first president was Ohio governor and future U.S. president **Rutherford B. Hayes.** Following his stint as U.S. president between 1877 and 1880, Hayes returned to his position with the National Prison Congress, serving as president from 1883 to 1892. From 1870 to 1876 **Enoch Wines** served as secretary.

His son Frederick would follow in his father's footsteps in this position from 1887 to 1890.

Sources: McKelvey, *American Prisons*, 1977; Christianson, *With Liberty for Some*, 1995.

NATIONAL PRISON CONGRESS. Earlier international prison congresses on prison reform had convened in Frankfort-on-Main in 1846, and in Brussels the following year. Several unofficial meetings were held in Paris, London, and Vienna in the 1850s. Of these meetings, the United States was present only at one—the Frankfort Congress in 1846—and represented only by **Louis Dwight**. Little came of these meetings. However, several reformers came to the conclusion that if the United States became more involved, the organization of an international prison reform movement could be jump-started. **Enoch Wines** took the lead in canvassing for representatives to attend a prison congress in Cincinnati, Ohio, in 1870.

In 1870 Ohio governor and future U.S. president **Rutherford B. Hayes** welcomed more than 130 delegates representing 24 states, Canada, and South America meeting in Cincinnati. Among them were judges, wardens, prison chaplains, and governors. A number of papers and presentations were delivered to the eager audience. After considerable discussion among the delegates and presenters, the congress unanimously adopted a Declaration of Principles (see Appendix I).

Among the forty papers and addresses delivered at the congress were several by French and English reformers, including a notable one on the **Irish system** by **Walter Crofton**. However, the majority of speakers represented the United States. Most prominent among the Americans was New Yorker **Zebulon Brockway**, who delivered an address entitled "Ideal for a True Prison System for a State." Although much of what Brockway proposed was controversial, after much discussion most of his recommendations formed the nucleus for the congress's Declaration of Principles. His contributions included, among others, recommendations to create special reformatories for women and the use of an indeterminate system regulated by marks and grades, which could lead to a convict's early release. The congress threw its support behind the principles that defined it—society's responsibility for rehabilitating and reforming criminals; increased emphasis on education, religion, and vocational trades training; aid and supervision of prisoners following discharge; the end of political patronage in selecting staff and personnel; and of course the previously mentioned adoption of the indeterminate sentence.

Following the meeting a number of leaders and prominent figures pledged their support of the **National Prison Association** by joining as charter members. Subsequently the United States Congress passed a resolution inviting prison reformers from around the world to attend an international prison reform congress in London in 1872. Thanks to the First National Prison Congress and the efforts of organizer Enoch Wines, from July 3 to July 13, 1872, in London 400 delegates from 22 different countries attended the International Congress on the Prevention and Repression of Crime, Including Penal and Reformatory Treatment. Both meetings would influence the creation of the International Prison and Penitentiary Congress.

Sources: McKelvey, *American Prisons*, 1977; Christianson, *With Liberty for Some*, 1995.

NATIVE AMERICAN PRISON SYSTEM. In May 2004 federal investigators found a number of human rights abuses in the Native American prison system. According to the U.S. Justice Department, Indian prisons held 2,006 inmates in 2002. Almost 1,400 were men, 300 women, and more than 300 were juveniles of both genders. There are 74 Native American prisons dispersed over 55 million acres of Indian lands in the United States. Investigators have found staffing problems, poor housing, and some facilities without running water, heat, or working toilets. These conditions reached the Interior Department's Bureau of Indian Affairs only after a frustrated employee filmed the scandalous conditions at a number of prisons. Among the findings were raw sewage flowing through a cellblock at the prison on the Fort Belknap reservation in Montana; inmates sleeping on shredded mattresses and juveniles sharing space with adults in Montana's Rocky Boy reservation prison; and at the Crow Reservation prison, also in Montana, male and female prisoners freely mingling outside their cells and forced to take showers using buckets of water.

Sources: Kevin Johnson, "Feds Probe Tribal Prison Deaths," *USA TODAY*, May 21, 2004, 1A; Kevin Johnson, "Former BIA Official Urged Prison Fixes," *USA TODAY*, May 21, 2004, 3A.

NAURU. In 2003 there was one prison holding 6 inmates, or 48 per 100,000 of the national population.

Source: ICPS, Oceania Statistics, 2003.

NEILD, JAMES (1744–1814). James Neild was a retired London jeweler who turned his attention to prison reform in the 1790s. He served stints as justice of the peace and high sheriff of Buckinghamshire before following in **John Howard's** footsteps and embarking on a tour of British prisons and jails. Neild rose to prominence following the 1812 publication of *State of the Prisons in England, Scotland, and Wales*, which chronicled his visits to more than 300 jails. Following his prison tour between 1800 and 1806, he reserved some of his greatest criticism for the state of Scottish jails, which he found little improved since John Howard observed them 30 years earlier.

Sources: Evans, *The Fabrication of Virtue*, 1982; Cameron, *Prisons and Punishment in Scotland from the Middle Ages to the Present*, 1983.

NEPAL. The Nepalese prison system was reorganized in 1953, initiating a reform-oriented regime, which introduced medical treatment, recreational opportunities, and visits from relatives. Today state-supported institutions include a central prison in Katmandu and jails in most district capitals. Despite agreeing to the International Covenant on Civil and Political Rights and the Convention against Torture and Other Cruel, Inhuman, or Degrading Treatment in 1991, state-run prisons have come under attack by human rights activists who claim prisons are characterized by unsanitary and degrading conditions. Nepalese prisons are divided into three categories. At the bottom are the Class C prisons. These are the most numerous and are dedicated to common criminals. In these facilities prisoners are frequently subjected to physical abuse by jail guards. The other two categories hold individuals with political connections or of higher social status. Conditions there are much better than in the Class C prisons. Since no institutions are devoted exclusively to women, females often endure the same insalubrious conditions as their male counterparts. Most communities are not equipped to handle the mentally ill, who are often tossed in with common criminals in local jails. First steps have been taken to address the aforementioned problems by transferring the prison administration and management from the police to the Ministry of Home Affairs beginning in 1990. Currently the Department of Jail Administration is the responsibility of the Home Ministry. In 2002 the country maintained 73 penal institutions, with the capacity to hold 5,000 inmates. That year the prisons were at 142.6 percent of capacity, holding 7,132 prisoners. More than half the prisoners were classified as either pretrial detainees or remand prisoners. However, the prison population rate of 29 per 100,000 of the national population was rather stable. In 1994 the ratio was the same, diminishing to only 25 per 100,000 in 1999.

Sources: Kurian, *WEPP*, 1989; LCCS, "Nepal: The Police System," September 1991; ICPS, Nepal, October 2004.

NETHERLANDS. After **John Howard** visited prisons in Holland in the 1770s, he described them as quiet and clean, with a physician and surgeon appointed to each prison. Besides being impressed by the relative health of the prisoners Howard was also impressed that each convict had his own room, allowing for complete separation. However, this was in stark contrast to the **rasphouses** and **spinhouses** where prisoners worked in a congregate setting. A century earlier **William Penn** noted a similar impression of the houses of correction he visited in the Netherlands. He reportedly used these facilities as a model for the new colony in Pennsylvania.

Between 1847 and 1850 the first cell prison was constructed in Amsterdam as Holland formally adopted the separate confinement model employed by Pennsylvania (although this model was not wholly unfamiliar). Radial prisons based on the **Pennsylvania system** were built in Rotterdam (1866), Groningen (1883), the Hague (1886), and Zutphen (1886). According to prison historian Norman Johnston, "Three true **panopticon** prisons" were opened in 1884, making them "the only fully circular cell houses built in Europe." These were constructed in Arnhem, Haarlem, and Breda.

By the 1940s the Netherlands had three special prisons, including Leeuwarden Prison for men serving less than five years, Rotterdam for women serving the same sentences, and the Hague Prison, dedicated to the tubercular and older prisoners, individuals who refuse military service, and prisoners under observation. Three labor colonies were located at Veenhuizen, Hoorn, and Gorincem (for women). In addition, there were 21 houses of correction, 20 "ordinary" prisons, and 8 local prisons. Until 1935 women were incarcerated in men's prisons.

By the 1980s short-term semi-open prisons included Bankenbosch Prison in Veenhuizen, Ter Peel Prison in Sevenum, Oostereiland in Hoorn, De Raam in Grave, and Westlinge in Heerhugowaard. Prisoners serving longer terms typically serve their time at Esserheem and Nogerhaven prisons in Veenhuizen, Nooderschans in Winschoten, Schutterswei in Almaar, or the Hague Prison.

During the 1990s a number of new prisons were built based on either a **cruciform** or double cruciform design with a security apparatus centrally located. Both Zoetermeer Prison (1996) and Almere (1996) conform to this pattern. Other recent prisons include Rotterdam's De Schie Penitentiary (1988) and Nogerhaven's Veenhuizen Prison (1996).

The National Agency of Correctional Institutions is directed under the Ministry of Justice. In 2004 the prison population stood at 18,242, which was 95 percent of capacity. The country's 79 institutions were capable of holding 19,205 inmates. Almost one third of the current inmates are untried prisoners. The prison population represented 112 per 100,000 of the national population, considerably higher than the 7,397 inmates in 1992, representing 49 per 100,000, and the 13,333 inmates in 1998 reflecting a percentage of 85 per 100,000 of the national population.

According to Peter Tak, the number of prison cells increased from 3,789 in 1980 to 10,059 in 1994—this, in response to a more punitive regime emphasizing longer prison sentences. In addition, the number of suspended prison sentences was drastically reduced. These changes were mostly precipitated by a rise in crime between 1976 and 1984. Subsequently the increase in violent crime in the 1990s led to more serious sentencing options. According to Tak and van Kalmthou, between 1985 and 1997 the Dutch prison population was "among the fastest growing in the world," increasing 123 percent during this period, compared to the U.S. increase of only 116 percent. But the Netherlands incarceration rate of 78 per 100,000 of the national population in 1997 was only one eighth that of the U.S. rate of 648 per 100,000.

Despite a rising prison population, several innovations in prison design have been adopted. Prisons have moved away from the traditional architecture in favor of adding more color to prison interiors. According to Norman Johnston, windows, skylighting, and furniture have also been redesigned to create a softer environment in an attempt to make cell interiors "as normal as possible."

Sources: W. A. Bonger, "Development of the Penal Law in the Netherlands," *Journal of Criminal Law and Criminology* 24, (May–June 1933), pp. 260–270; Teeters, *World Penal Systems*, 1944; Kurian, *WEPP*, 1989; Johnston, *Forms of Contraint*, 2000; Peter J.P. Tak, "Sentencing and Punishment in the Netherlands," pp. 156–161; Peter J.P. Tak and Anton M. Van Kalmhout, "Prison Population Growing Faster in the Netherlands than in the United States," pp. 161–169, and Josine Junger-Tas, "Dutch Penal Policies Changing Direction," pp. 179–188, all in *Penal Reform in Overcrowded Times*, ed. Tonry, 2001; ICPS, Netherlands, October, 2004.

NETHERLANDS ANTILLES. The Prison Service of the Netherlands Antilles operates under the Ministry of Justice. As of 2003 the prison population consisted of 780 prisoners, the majority of whom were in either the largest prison at Bon Futaro (549) or in Pointe Blanche Prison (129). With an official capacity to hold 791 inmates, the prisons were at 85.7 percent of capacity in 2002. The prison population rate is 364 per 100,000 of the national population.

Source: ICPS, Netherlands Antilles, Caribbean, November 2003.

NEW CALEDONIA. The French Ministry of Justice manages the prison system on this French possession. At last count New Caledonia's one prison held 139 prisoners, or 139 per 100,000 of the national population. In 2003 this was considered 164 percent of the official capacity, suggesting little change since 1998.

Source: ICPS, New Caledonia (France), February 2003.

NEWGATE PRISON (ENGLAND). London's Newgate Prison was probably the most famous British prison. More than 700 years old, Newgate Prison was considered one of England's oldest prisons, having originated during the reign of King

John in the thirteenth century. It was named for a gate in the wall that surrounded the medieval city. A number of prisons would be built on this foundation over the years. Newgate Prison was rebuilt several times. In 1423 the prison offered inmates five stories and a dining hall. However, keepers, as the guards were known, continued to torture and rob prisoners. If the guards did not rob the new prisoner, the inmates would. Following the Great Fire of 1666, Newgate was rebuilt six years later. Among the luminaries imprisoned there were **William Penn**, highwayman Jonathan Wild, and *Robinson Crusoe* author Daniel Defoe.

By the early 1700s the prison usually held about 300 prisoners, twice the number it was designed for, with most awaiting trial at the Old Bailey. Like most prisons of this era it was sporadically devastated by plague and typhoid. Attempts were made to remedy the putrid stench caused by lack of ventilation and inadequate water supply by building a windmill on top of the gate in 1752. However, whatever fresh air it could muster provided little improvement. Conditions were not helped by the habit of many prisoners to keep animals as pets. Dogs were prohibited in 1792, but pigs and fowl were not banned until 1814.

Originally Newgate had been closer to a dungeon than a penitentiary, but by the seventeenth century accommodations ranged from well-furnished apartments to dark dungeons. Initiates into the Newgate regime were welcomed into the area reserved for the most common criminals and, unless they could afford to upgrade their digs, served their sentences in the most degrading conditions. However, the less penurious could summon not only a servant, wife, or prostitute but also alcoholic beverages, firewood, and basically anything money could buy. But these very inmates quickly became the object of desire for the impoverished denizens who demanded protection money of them lest their privileges end.

By the late eighteenth century the Old Newgate had become a barrier to the growth of London and was demolished in 1777. A new jail was begun in 1770 near the present-day Old Bailey and was completed ten years later in 1780. That same year it was almost destroyed by fire during the anti-Catholic Gordon Riots. Rioters also demolished the **Fleet Prison, King's Bench Prison**, and the **Clink**.

Newgate was rebuilt once more and by the nineteenth century was still beset by overcrowding and poor sanitation. In 1873 a female ward was added. Built to accommodate 500 prisoners, it was typically at double the capacity, with the average ward measuring 15 by 30 feet and containing between 15 and 30 prisoners. Members of the public were encouraged to pay for tours of the cells. By the early 1850s the only prisoners held here were those awaiting trial or execution. Later efforts were undertaken to improve the structure in the late 1850s. A reminder of the dark ages of the English prison system, Newgate was torn down in 1902. Today the Central Criminal Court resides on the very site of the "English **Bastille**."

Source: Babington, *The English Bastille*, 1972.

NEWGATE PRISON (NEW YORK). Following outbreaks of violence and disorder at the New York City Jail, prison reformer **Thomas Eddy** was enlisted to visit Philadelphia's **Walnut Street Jail** to seek alternatives. Eddy is credited with helping pass legislation that led to the construction of New York's first penitentiary. Eddy was placed in charge of its construction in 1797, and Newgate Prison soon took shape on the Hudson River in what is now New York City's Greenwich Village. Named after its London counterpart, the new prison would follow closely the design of Walnut Street Jail, which featured congregate rooms and workshops along with 14 solitary confinement cells. When completed, the structure stood 2 stories high, with 54 rooms. These 12-foot by 18-foot rooms could hold up to 8 inmates. However, by 1802 Newgate was plagued by the same problems as its model in Philadelphia. After the militia was called out to suppress a bloody riot at the facility, Eddy became convinced that a new remedy was needed. Subsequently, at **Auburn Prison** Eddy would put theory into practice, creating an institution that featured single cells for separate confinement at night and congregate workshops where inmates could work in silence by day. However, authorities took several missteps before fully incorporating this program at Auburn in the 1820s.

Sources: Lewis, *From Newgate to Dannemora*, 1965; Johnston, *Forms of Constraint*, 2000.

NEW ZEALAND. The signing of the Treaty of Waitangi in 1840 brought the inhabitants of the two landmasses that compose New Zealand under British imperial law. Initially, convicts were hanged, flogged, or transported to the Australian penal colonies. However, with the cessation of transportation in 1854, sentences were then punished with penal servitude.

The first attempt at inaugurating a national penal policy occurred with the Secondary Punishment Act of 1854. Under this policy prisoners were forced to work at hard labor on public works projects. Prisoners were prohibited from speaking to each other while at work. The transition to a tenable penal policy made a number of false starts until a decision was made to centralize it in 1876.

The early foundations of the modern penal system are credited to Captain Arthur Hume, who had served as a deputy governor at **Wormwood Scrubs** and **Dartmoor** prison back in England. Under Hume's aegis, the first prison was erected at Tabanaka in New Plymouth in the 1880s; this was followed by Mount Eden at Auckland in 1882. Both prisons adopted the **Pennsylvania system** of separate confinement. In the 1890s Hume continued his reforms outlawing the use of **convict hulks** (1891) and introducing trades training and a classification system. In 1886 the passage of the First Offenders Probation Act heralded the world's first national probation system. In 1893 the Criminal Code Act led to the abolition of solitary confinement and options of imprisonment without hard labor.

Hume was not without his detractors. Above all, his regime was still punitive in nature. Hume was not above reducing rations and opposed abolishing corporal punishment or educating illiterate prisoners. It would take almost a half-century before New Zealand introduced toilets in prisoners' cells. Hume retired in 1909.

Under new direction, New Zealand passed the Crimes Amendment Act of 1910. Influenced by the advances made at the Elmira Reformatory in New York, indeterminate sentencing and a prison board to decide on parole issues were implemented. The period referred to as the New Method era lasted until 1949. During this period emphasis on education, training, and classification led to an improvement in conditions.

During the 1910s and 1920s land was purchased for prison farms, markings were eliminated from prisoner clothing, and up to 70 percent of the prisoners were employed outside the walls. In 1917 the first juvenile facility or **Borstal** was opened.

Over the next half-century a number of reforms were implemented, leading to the adoption of commissaries, a reduction of hours of confinement. During the 1950s newspapers were allowed behind bars and inmate recreation, communal dining, and unsupervised visits were introduced. At the same time efforts were in progress to professionalize the prison service through better wages and training.

With overcrowding became an issue after 1955, headway was made toward creating noncustodial alternatives and the building of detention centers. The introduction of periodic detention, or weekend imprisonment, in 1963 is regarded as one of the nation's most notable innovations and remains a mainstay of New Zealand corrections. However, the rule of silence and bread-and-water misconduct penalties were not abolished until 1961. The Crimes Act of 1961 also abolished the death penalty in favor of life sentences with a 10-year minimum. During the 1960s group therapy and counseling were introduced.

During the 1970s and 1980s increasing recidivism led to a system of collective or "shock" training for the rapidly increasing juvenile population. But its success was limited. The Criminal Justice Act of 1985 pushed for a reduction in the prison population through noncustodial remedies and better parole provisions. However, this was unsuccessful in the long term because many parolees ended up back in prison. Between the 1980s and the mid-1990s emphasis was placed on lengthening sentences for violent offenders.

Today's Department of Corrections is governed under the Ministry of Justice. New Zealand's eighteen prisons house 6,403 prisoners in a system with the designed capacity for 6,462. This represents a 2003 prison population rate of 161 per 100,000 of the national population. This is a minor increase from 2001's 5,955 but is substantially higher than the 1992 population of 4,443, or 129 per 100,000.

Sources: Greg Newbold, *Punishment and Politics: The Maximum Security Prison in New Zealand* (New York: Oxford University Press, 1989); Greg Newbold and Chris Eskridge, "History and Development of Modern Correctional Practices in New Zealand," in *Comparative Criminal Justice*, eds. Fields and Moore, 1996, pp. 453–478; ICPS, New Zealand, Oceania, 2003.

NICARAGUA. Prior to the 1980s, Nicaraguan prisons were "often makeshift in character." Prison guards were members of the Judicial Police. In 1960 a rehabilitation center known as the Centro Penal de Rehabilitacion Social was opened. With the ascendance of the Sandinistas in the 1980s the prison system was expanded and reorganized. By the middle of the decade Nicaragua had nine penitentiaries or public jails, more than twenty detention centers, and holding cells in almost fifty police stations around the country. In 1984 the government estimated the country's prison population at about 5,000, with almost 2,000 charged with cooperating with the Contras and the former regime. However, independent human rights groups such as the Permanent Human Rights Commission claimed that more than 10,000 were imprisoned, the majority of whom were political prisoners. By the end of the decade periodic visits by such groups as the International Committee of the Red Cross indicated about 2,500 prisoners charged with pro-Contra activity. Under the Sandinista regime physical punishment and torture was common in detention centers. Conditions were not much better in the regular prisons and jails, where corruption and poor conditions predominated.

The prison system operates under the direction of the Prison Directorate in the Ministry of Interior. Nicaragua's largest prison is located at Tipitapa on the outskirts of Managua. Most of the prisoners here are linked to Contra activity. Despite President Chamorro's establishment of a National Penitentiary Commission in 1990, human rights groups continue to label the prison system as "disastrous." Although physical abuse had diminished in the penitentiaries, those incarcerated at police stations still report continued torture and physical punishment. Reports continue to target cases of malnutrition, lack of food and clean water, poor clothing, and lack of medical treatment. Because of a low budget for the nation's criminal justice system, more than half the prisoners in 1993 were still awaiting trial. The most recent figures estimate the prison population at 7,198 (1,750 in policy lock-ups), or 143 per 100,000 of the national population, slightly higher than the designated capacity of the prison system.

Sources: Kurian, *WEPP*, 1989; LCCS, "Nicaragua: Prison Conditions," December 1993; ICPS, Nicaragua, January 2004.

NIGER. The prison system is operated under the Ministry of Justice. Estimates in 2002 placed the prison population at around 6,000. This would place the 35 penal institutions at well below their capacity to hold 8,722. If the estimates of the United Nations for 2002 were correct, this would average out to a ratio of 52 per 100,000 of the national population.

Source: ICPS, Niger, Africa, October 2004.

NIGERIA. The origins of the Nigerian prison system can be traced back to its years as a British colony beginning in 1861. Although some evidence suggests that the concept of imprisonment was not unknown to the indigenous Yorubas, who seemed to use it only for debtors, banishment was the traditional method of handling criminal malefactors. By the end of the nineteenth century, prisoners in the Northern Protectorate lived in their own villages and reported to work each morning. Prisons maintained by native or British keepers were in operation throughout Nigeria by 1912. According to T. Asuni, prisoner classification was introduced in 1873 but did not go beyond differentiating between long- and short-term prisoners. Thirteen years' classification was updated to differentiate between juveniles, debtors, felons, and detainees awaiting trial. Vocational training was initiated at this time as well.

Under the direction of Nigeria's first governor, Sir Frederick Lugard, between 1912 and 1930 a two-tiered system of prison administration was inaugurated. At the national level, prisons held offenders convicted under the colonial British court system. Inmates at this level included those sentenced to more than two years, inmates serving less than two-year stints in provincial jails, and divisional facilities for individuals serving less than six months. The second tier included native prisons operated and controlled by native authorities. Native control was tempered by the supervisory control maintained by the country's director of prisons. During this era poorly trained staff and inferior sanitation and health conditions characterized prisons.

Between 1931 and 1945 the prisons saw a decline in population, necessitating the closing of several facilities. At this time movement was made toward separating adults and juveniles, and in 1932 a juvenile institution, similar to a **Borstal**, was opened in Engu. It catered to males under the age of 16. Informal alternatives for this age group included placing them with missionaries and tribal chiefs, for these approaches seemed to have more potential for enabling reform.

A more modern era of prison reform paralleled the tenure of R. E. Dolan as prison director between 1946 and 1954. He brought to the job a wealth of penal experience as a prison administrator from other British colonies. One of his first acts was to have the prison system headquarters moved from Engu to the capitol of Lagos. During the Dolan administration classification of prisoners became official policy; religious and moral training was initiated, as was a more active rehabilitation and educational regime. In 1947 a training school for guards was established and more attention was paid toward improving the quality of staff by sending some prospects for training abroad. A campaign to improve the prisons was initiated, including the creation of an open prison at Kakuri in 1953. In 1968 the dual prison system of federal and local prisons was consolidated.

By 1979, following a period of war and political upheaval, the Nigerian prison system was in dire need of updating. The Prison Administration did not even have its own health service. To make matters worse, because of a lack of infrastructure mentally ill non-offenders were housed with the ordinary prison populations. Prisoners surveyed in the mid-1970s cited a number of suggestions for improvement, including better food, recreational facilities, better housing, less lockups, more vocational and educational opportunities, and the segregation of the most violent offenders.

The Nigerian Prisons Service falls under the control of the Ministry of Internal Affairs. Headquartered in Lagos, it controls some 400 facilities, including regular prisons, special penal facilities, and lockups. In 1975 all Nigeria's 51 prisons came under federal control. Each of Nigeria's states has its own prison headquarters under the command of the assistant directors of prisons. Depending on the size and type of prison, the various institutions themselves are directed by a chief superintendent, superintendent, or assistant superintendent.

By 1990 the prison staff had decreased by 5,000 from its 1983 level. Exacerbating the problems within the system was that between 1975 and 1985 the daily prison population more than doubled to 54,000. Lagos State had the largest population with 6,400. This was followed by Anambra, Borno, and Kaduna, each holding more than 4,000. Smaller inmate populations characterized Kwara, Niger, and Ondo, with less than 1,000 each. By 1989 the prison population had risen to 58,000 in a system designed for a total capacity of 28,000 as a dwindling number of staff members attempted to control the prisons. As the prison system stood poised for the 1990s, it was beset by overcrowding, poor sanitation, lack of toilets and water, malnutrition, and virtually no differentiation between classes of inmates.

Critics have labeled the prisons as "colleges for criminals" and "breeding grounds for crime." Ikoyi Prison serves as a microcosm for what is wrong with the prisons. By the end of the 1980s this institution held 2,000 prisoners who had committed minor offenses but had been waiting for trial for 9 years. Had they been tried and convicted immediately, they would have faced only up to two years' imprisonment. In the 1980s the government turned to periodic amnesties to reduce the prison population. The criminal justice system has proven inadequate, leading to a backlog of cases and filling three fifths of the prisons with pre-trial detainees. Human rights groups have targeted a number of institutions, citing mistreatment of inmates, suicides, and secret detention camps. In 1989 Chief Ebenezer Babatope chronicled the dire conditions inside the Kirikiri maximum-security institution in his memoir *Inside Kirikiri*.

According to figures from 2004 Nigeria had 147 penal facilities, not counting 83 "satellite institutions." With an official capacity to hold 42,681 prisoners, they were operating at almost 100 percent of official capacity, giving the nation a prison population equivalent to 31 per 100,000 of the national population.

Sources: T. Asuni, "Corrections in Nigeria," in *International Corrections*, eds. Wicks and Cooper, pp. 163–181, 1979; allfer.com/country-guide-study/nigeria, June 1991; LCCS, "Nigeria: Crime and Punishment," June 1991; Bernault, ed., *A History of Prison and Confinement in Africa*, 2003; ICPS, Nigeria, 2004.

NORFOLK ISLAND. Australia's Norfolk Island was "discovered" by Captain Cook in 1774. A cursory exploration of Norfolk Island found it uninhabited with an adequate water supply. Its first settlers, including several dozen English convicts, arrived in 1788, becoming part of the population of the larger region of New South Wales (Australia). Norfolk Island's isolation and punitive regime earned the island the reputation as a "living hell."

Norfolk Island was one of England's most dreaded penal colonies in the 1830s. In 1836 **Alexander Maconochie**'s arrival on the island led to one of the most famous prison experiments in the first half of the nineteenth century. Maconochie would earn the moniker the "father of **parole**" for his attempts to introduce the indeterminate sentence here. He was resolute in his belief that offering prisoners better conditions and more perks could lead to a better-behaved population, the so-called carrot-and-stick approach. Like most Victorian reformers Maconochie believed that all things should be moderated with a healthy dose of religion. Maconochie argued that prisoners should not be sentenced to a fixed sentence in the penal colony. Instead, they should be sentenced to a certain amount of work that could be gauged by marks. For example, prisoners could earn marks for good behavior and labor and lose them through poor deportment. Prisoners were encouraged to use their marks to purchase food, clothing, and certain "luxuries," but these would be subtracted from the marks they needed for release.

Maconochie wanted to build a large prison, but constraints imposed by London meant he had to settle for a chapel building instead. However, he used a novel approach to incarceration that would not gain popularity in England until much later in the century, and that was the use of single-cell confinement. According to his plan for the chapel-prison, the building would have two floors. On the bottom floor were twelve solitary cells that could be accessed through a trapdoor from the chapel door above. Also integrated into the design was a removable panel that could on occasion allow convicts to listen to religious services emanating from the chapel. According to prison historian Norman Johnston, the Pentagonal Jail built at Kingston, Norfolk Island, between 1836 and 1848 was one of the first European-built jails to feature "back-to-back cells" that were so "common in the United States."

During Maconochie's tenure on Norfolk Island he carried out some of the most progressive correctional reforms of the nineteenth century. He was considered one of the first reformers to actively endorse a prison policy that prepared prisoners for their return to society by treating them humanely in captivity. Maconochie is credited with introducing the **mark system** of graduated privileges that could result in the ticket-of-leave required for early release. **Walter Crofton** would build on Maconochie's achievement in creating his progressive-stage **Irish system**. The mark system would become the basis of penal treatment in Great Britain and the United States in the 1850s. However, Maconochie's efforts to put his theories into practice when he returned to England in 1849 ended in failure. Appointed governor of the Birmingham Jail in 1849, almost as soon as he implemented the system he was beset by critics who charged him with spending too much time theorizing and not enough time managing the prison, and he was subsequently relieved of his duties.

Sources: Barry, *Alexander Maconochie of Norfolk Island*, 1958; John Hirst, "The Australian Experience: The Convict Colony," in *The Oxford History of the Prison*, eds. Morris and Rothman, 1998, pp. 235–265; Johnston, *Forms of Constraint*, 2000.

NORTHERN IRELAND. *See* IRELAND

NORTHERN MARIANA ISLANDS. This island nation's Division of Corrections operates under the Department of Public Safety. At the end of 2002 there were 123 prisoners housed in the 5 facilities making up the Saipan Prison Complex. The rate of imprisonment is 156 per 100,000 of the national population, an increase over the previous seven years.

Source: ICPS, Northern Marianas Islands, Oceania, 2003.

NORTH KOREA. *See* KOREA, NORTH

NORWAY. Records indicate there have been prisons in Norway since at least the eighteenth century. Fortresses stood in for the traditional prisons at this time and held male prisoners in what is now Oslo, Bergen, Trondheim, and Vardo. In the 1830s a representative from the Department of Justice was selected to examine prisons throughout Western Europe. Following his return a commission prepared a report that favored replacing the aging fortresses with the more in vogue **Pennsylvania system**. In 1841 the commission proposed a building program to construct seven new buildings that would offer 2,100 new cells. Not until 1851 was a cellular prison was built in Oslo. It would be the only such structure completed in Norway in the nineteenth century. Other national prisons were modified to replace large rooms with smaller rooms for confinement. By the end of the 1850s district prisons introduced cellular confinement. Following subsequent investigations abroad in the 1870s, other adaptations were made, and by the new century three central prisons based on the Pennsylvania system, albeit with several progressive modifications, were built in Aakeberg, Akershus, and Trondheim.

Currently the Prison and Probation Department operates out of the Ministry of Justice and Police. Reflecting the low prison populations common to Scandinavia, recent reports indicate a prison population of 2,914 residing in 43 different institutions. This would reflect a ratio of 64 per 100,000 of the national population and an occupancy level of 98.3 percent as of 2003.

Sources: Johnston, *Forms of Constraint*, 2000; ICPS, Norway, Europe, 2003.

NUREMBERG PALACE OF JUSTICE. *See* PALACE OF JUSTICE

OAKUM PICKING. Prior to the prison reform movements of the late nineteenth century the prisoner's lot often included months and years of idleness. A number of prisons, particularly in England, adopted a number of "make work" strategies. Some adopted the **treadmill**, others the **crank**, but perhaps none was more tedious than picking oakum. Oakum picking consisted of unraveling lengths of old tar-soaked rope and then digging out with bare hands the rope's single strands, or oakum. After these strands were tarred they would be used as caulking in wooden ships. However, as the days of wooden ships came to a close, this practice became somewhat obsolete, although there were a number of reports of its persistence as a punishment regime into the twentieth century, well after the abolition of the treadmill and the crank.

Source: DeFord, *Stone Walls*, 1962.

OMAN, SULTANATE OF. Oman's criminal justice system is based on the Islamic legal tradition. During the late 1980s and early 1990s the U.S. Department of State reported cases of prisoner abuse by police; however, in recent years these reports have ceased. Mirroring life in the blazing desert sultanate of Oman, prison conditions are described as harsh, with extreme heat and a lack of proper ventilation. In earlier years prisoners were worked at hard labor under the desert sun, but in 1991 this practice was reportedly discontinued. In 2000 Oman had three penal institutions holding a total of 2,020 inmates, or 81 per 100,000 of the national population.

Sources: LCCS, "Oman: Internal Security," January 1993; ICPS, Oman, Middle East, 2004.

OMSK PRISON. This Siberian prison was located 2,000 miles from Moscow. Here, **Fyodor Dostoyevsky,** wrote his novel *Memoirs from the House of the Dead*, a fictionalized account of his four years at Omsk, incarcerated among prisoners serving sentences mostly for common crimes. Arrested in 1849 for political activities, Dostoyevsky underwent a mock execution before being slapped in fetters and sent on his epic forced sled journey to western Siberia.

Source: Aryeh Neier, "Confining Dissent: The Political Prison," in *The Oxford History of the Prison*, eds. Morris and Rothman, 1998, pp. 350–380.

OSBORNE, THOMAS MOTT (1859–1926). The scion of a prominent Auburn, New York, family, Osborne grew up in the shadow of **Auburn Prison,** one of the most prominent institutions in America. It should not be surprising that he grew up in the thrall and fear of prison escapees, real and imaginary. Osborne embarked on an impressive public career with stints as a successful businessman, town mayor, and trustee of a progressive school for delinquent boys. In the ensuing years he became a frequent visitor to Auburn Prison, where he met and carried on correspondence with a number of inmates. In 1913 he was appointed to convene a state commission on prison reform. After studying every work on penology he could lay his hands on, he decided that his last phase of self-education should include a short incarceration behind prison walls to learn firsthand what the life of a convict entailed.

Shortly after, he was admitted into Auburn as "Tom Brown." He refused to be treated other than as prisoner No. 33,333X, and so he was treated to the full regime of the **silent system.** At the same time he was initiated into the prison subculture—its argot, values, and unwritten codes of behavior.

Following his week of incarceration he wrote *Within Prison Walls*, published in 1914. Osborne reveals in stark detail how penal institutions crush individuality and purposely destroy "the manhood" of inmates. During his short respite in stir, Osborne conjured up a plan for limited self-government among the inmates. In 1914 he would put theory into practice when he was appointed the warden of **Sing Sing Prison.** Here he introduced the **Mutual Welfare League** in an attempt to give inmates a sense of group responsibility and self-worth that would lead to rehabilitation.

However, his constant and vocal criticism of political interference led his growing list of political enemies to mount a campaign against him that led to Osborne's indictment on charges of perjury and neglect of duty. Although he was exonerated and reinstated as warden in 1916, Osborne resigned in 1916. He went on to serve as commanding officer at Portsmouth Naval Prison from 1917 to 1920 and to continue his crusade for prison reform. Osborne founded the Welfare League Association to aid discharged prisoners, as well as the National Society of Penal Information, a repository for data on prison conditions. Both organizations were merged into the Osborne Association.

Sources: Osborne, *Society and Prisons*, 1916; DeFord, *Stone Walls*, 1962; McKelvey, *American Prisons*, 1977.

P

PAKISTAN. Since 1962 Pakistan's prisons have been governed under the regulations and guidelines set by that year's West Pakistan Jail Warden Service Rules. However, according to human rights groups, these guidelines are often neglected, resulting in poor conditions and overcrowding. The Pakistani prison system is divided into provinces, all under the direction of an inspector general of prisons in the Ministry of Law, Justice, Human Rights, and Parliamentary Affairs. A director of prisons oversees the prisons at the district level. At lower levels jail superintendents are in command. At the lowest level are local village lockups. Prison classification includes Class C confinement for common criminals and few amenities; Class B prisons for persons of higher social status, which offers more amenities and better conditions; and Class A prisons for the most prominent offenders. As a rule most prisons do not allow conjugal visits. Juveniles are housed separately in adult prisoners. These juvenile wards confines inmates until they are 21. There are also separate reform institutions dedicated to boys aged 11 to 20. As of 2002 Pakistan's 87 penal facilities held 87,000 inmates, or 59 per 100,000 of the national population. Since 1993 this ratio has remained rather constant in the 50s per 100,000.

Sources: LCCS, "Pakistan: Prisons," April 1994; ICPS, Pakistan, Asia, 2004.

PALACE OF JUSTICE (NUREMBERG). The high-ranking Nazis that were selected for trial at Nuremberg, in Germany, following World War II were held in that city's Palace of Justice. At the time the prisoners were transferred there, two of the prison's wings were still occupied by German felons. The war criminals were held separately in another wing of the prison. But almost immediately there were security concerns. The prison walls had several large gaps, the result of bombing raids during the war. In addition, a number of prison guards and warders in the regular jail included Nazis who had not yet been replaced.

Most of the Nazi leaders were held in six-foot by eight-foot cells on the ground floor of the four-story prison wing closest to the Nuremberg courthouse. Other Nazis awaiting later trials were held in the upper tiers. Each prison cell contained a steel cot with a mattress attached to the wall, a chair, and a card table that could not hold the weight of an adult if one tried to stand on it. Almost hidden in the corner of each cell was a seatless toilet. All the high barred windows were replaced with plexiglass and all electric fixtures removed. The only light provided at night came from "a bare bulb with a metal reflector directed into the cell through a rectangular flap in the thick, solid door." This flap was always open so that guards could observe inmates as well as serve them water and food through it.

All the accused war criminals were held in isolation and were forbidden from speaking with guards and each other. If a guard entered a cell, the prisoner was required to stand up and bow. When the time came for "lights out" at 9:30 P.M., the lamp was left on for surveillance purposes but was redirected at the floor. Each prisoner was allow one-half hour of daily exercise, which mostly consisted of walking single file in the prison yard. Twice a week the prisoners were allowed hot showers.

A chapel was located on the second tier of the prison, as was a dispensary. When Hermann Goering initially entered custody in Mondorf, he carried with him 16 suitcases and a red hatbox. His luggage, according to historian Robert E. Conot, included "his medals, 81,000 marks (equivalent to 20,000 dollars), and enough gold, silver, and precious stones to open a small jewelry store." If this was not odd enough, his toenails and fingernails were "lacquered bright red." At Nuremberg, a separate baggage storage area was set aside for the prisoners, with Goering's taking up "more space than all the others combined." Food was cooked by German prisoners-of-war and served at 7 A.M. A typical day's cooking provided prisoners from 1,500 to 1,800 calories per day. The corpulent Goering reportedly lost two pounds per week on this diet and was reduced to mopping up the last bit of gravy with his bread crust. Despite all the precautions taken to keep the prisoners under surveillance, Goering managed to cheat the hangman by chewing on a cyanide capsule just hours before his scheduled execution.

Sources: Andrus, *I Was the Nuremberg Jailer*, 1969; Conot, *Justice at Nuremberg*, 1983.

PALAU. Palau's Division of Corrections is administered under the Ministry of Justice. There is one main prison at Koror that in 2003 held 103 prisoners, a rate of 523 per 100,000 of the national population.

Source: ICPS, Palau, Oceania, 2003.

PANAMA. Panama established its Department of Corrections in 1940. Earlier the nation's penal facilities were under the direction of the National Police, but they now operate out of the Ministry of Government and Justice. In 1942 Panama reorganized its prison system following recommendations by officials from the Federal Bureau of Prisons of the United States who were conducting a survey of prisons. According to the new classification of prisoners, the Department of Corrections would be responsible for sending convicts either to prison or to other facilities, thereby making a distinction between offenders by age, offense, gender, and mental health.

The most prominent prison has been the so-called Model Jail, or *Carcel Modelo*, in Panama City. Built in 1920, it has earned a reputation for overcrowding. Cells envisioned for 3 inmates held up to 15 by the late 1980s. Overcrowding has led to a number of prisoners being sent to Coiba Penal Colony on the Isle of Coiba. Considered the nation's most punitive facility, it accepted its first prisoners in 1919. Not unlike other penal island facilities, Coiba operates a draconian regime that has been infamous over the years. Prisoners, both pre-trial detainees and convicts, are housed in a handful of camps scattered on the island. The main camp offers opportunities for education and rehabilitation, but most inmates cannot take advantage of this because they are housed too far away. All prisoners regardless of status are required to work. Although a number of convicts work in animal husbandry and farming, they receive little if any remuneration. Those who do receive compensation are skilled craftsmen and mechanics.

There is little in the way of classification at Model Jail, with human rights monitors reporting hardened criminals mixed with first-time offenders. Each provincial capital has a jail, and these jails are often the focus of human rights groups for the same problems that plague the rest of the system. Apparently women receive much better care, with Panama City's Women's Rehabilitation Center, or *Centro Femino de Rehabilitacion*, lauded as a model facility. Nuns, who combine the discipline of trained guards with the humanity of the church clergy, operate this institution. However, the darker part of this phenomenon is that when women are first arrested, they are sometimes forced spend several nights in the Model Jail, where they face the same travails as the men (without the nuns to protect them). During the 1980s Panamanian jails continued to experience poor sanitation, overcrowding, and lack of medical care.

The most severe penalty of incarceration is a 20-year sentence. The most severe imprisonment is *reclusion*, or work at hard labor. The most simple sentence is *prision*, simple imprisonment, which lasts from 30 days to 18 years. But all prisoners can be forced to work whether or not work is a condition in their sentences. In 2003 Panama's 73 prison facilities held 10,630 inmates, an average of 354 per 100,000 of the national population. This figure included 10 central prisons and 63 public jails located in police stations. More than half the prisoners were either pre-trial detainees or remand prisoners. With an official capacity to hold 7,348, by 2003 the system was operating at 144.7 percent.

Sources: Teeters, *World Penal Systems*, 1944; LCCS, "Panama: The Penal System," December 1987; ICPS, Panama, Central America, 2003.

PANOPTICON. Prisons built on a circular or semicircular pattern were inspired by the architectural design of the Panopticon, created by **Jeremy Bentham** and his brother, the naval architect Sir Samuel Bentham, in 1791. According to the Bentham plan, the Panopticon consisted of several stories of outside cells, built in a large circle and facing onto an interior courtyard. Like the hub of the center of the wheel, the center rotunda contained an enclosed guard's station. Bentham envisioned a facility that would improve prison security and further the inmates' attempts at self-reflection. The Benthams hoped that this new plan would lead to better sanitation and humane conditions. Every cell was visible from the central guard tower, allowing for the constant surveillance of all the inmates. Being centrally located, the guard's tower was intended to provide a convenient site for reading sermons and religious instruction to the captive audience.

Although the Benthams' design was never as popular as the **Auburn** and **Pennsylvania** systems, a number of institutions were built on the panopticon model in Europe and the United States. Among them were the semicircular Virginia State Prison, designed by **Benjamin Latrobe**, and built in Richmond in 1800. In 1826 Western State Penitentiary in Pittsburgh, Pennsylvania, adopted this design as well. Its use was short lived, however, and it was soon demolished in favor of the Auburn style. The most successful manifestation of this design in America can be found at Stateville Penitentiary, built in Illinois in 1919.

No true full-circle panopticons were built in England; however, a number of semi-circular or polygonal facilities were constructed in England, Scotland, and Ireland by the 1820s. True examples of the classic panopticon were constructed in Holland in the 1880s, at the Isle of Pines in Cuba, and in Joliet, Illinois, in 1919. Criticism has been directed at the panopticon design because of its tendency to waste space. In addition, although guards can view all prisoners, prisoners can as easily follow the movements of the guards.

Source: Janet Semple, *Bentham's Prison: A Study of the Panopticon Penitentiary* (Oxford: Oxford University Press, 1993).

PAPUA NEW GUINEA. In 1885 the first prison in what was then German New Guinea was opened in Rabaul. Three years later New Guinea became a colony of Great Britain, and in 1889 a prison was established in Hanuabada. Home to more than 700 unique cultures and language groups, New Guinea society is dominated by a tribal culture. As New Guinea became more industrialized in the nineteenth and twentieth centuries, crime patterns began to mirror those of other industrialized societies, broken down in economic terms. With the rural to urban drift many of the ties that bound family and tribe were weakened, necessitating Western social control strategies. Among the most often cited problems faced by Papuan corrections are the cultural conflicts that have arisen with the introduction of Western prison administration. This has been compounded by public animosity toward the entire prison system—including prisons, prisoners, and staff. According to the commissioner of the Corrective Institutions, when he took command in 1985 the correctional staff had not received training in fifteen years. Additionally, there were no classification system, no vocational programs, nor pre- or post-release programs. Among the reforms implemented since then are management and training courses for senior officers and staff and an increased emphasis on prisoner rehabilitation through the involvement of community members, including family members, traditional tribal leaders, church groups, universities, and business organizations. The largest prison is at Bomana, which has an average population of 700 men and 30 women, including those convicted or held on remand, and is guarded by a staff of 200. It is located about 15 miles outside the national capital and the nation's largest city of Port Moresby. One inmate has described Bomana Prison as the nation's "last place," or last place where an individual would want to be. As of 2002 the Papua New Guinea Correctional Services was operating at 87.4 percent of capacity. Its seventeen institutions held a total of 3,302 prisoners, or 66 per 100,000 of the national population. These numbers reflect a declining prison rate. From 1993 through 1998 the average was between 78 and 87 per 100,000.

Sources: Pious B. Kerepia, "Correctional Programmes for Indigenous People," in *Current International Trends in Corrections*, ed. David Biles, 1988, pp. 77–82; ICPS, Papua New Guinea, Oceania, 2002; Reed, *Papua New Guinea's Last Place: Experiences of Constraint in a Postcolonial Prison*, 2003.

PARAGUAY. In 1956 a national penitentiary was opened, though unfinished, at Tacumbu, not far from Asuncion. At that time it could hold all the nation's sentenced males. According to Norman Johnston, its **telephone pole design** was based on Argentina's Carcel de Resistencia. Today the National Penitentiary in Asuncion remains the nation's main correctional institution. Most reports indicate an average population of 2,000. Another prominent facility is the Tacumbu Penitentiary in Villa Hayes, just outside the capital. In 1999 Paraguay had an estimated prison population of 4,088 held in 18 different facilities. Separate institutions are dedicated to women and juveniles, with women confined to the Women's Correctional Institute under the direction of the Sisters of the Good Shepherd. Nationally, anyone sentenced to more than one year in prison is transferred to one of the national penitentiaries in the capital. With an official capacity for 2,707, the prison population is overflowing at 151 percent of occupancy, a rate of 75 per 100,000 of the national population.

Sources: LCCS, "Paraguay: The Prison System," December 1988; ICPS, Paraguay, South America, 1999.

PAROLE. The term *parole* originated from the French expression for giving one's word of honor, or *"parole d'honneur,"* not to escape or pursue certain behaviors, thereby gaining certain concessions or privileges. However, the French usually refer to this innovation as "conditional liberation" rather than parole. Early steps toward the development of parole were taken by the Frenchman Honore Mirabeau, who published a report in 1791 that called the concept of reformation based on such principles labor, segregation, rewards under a mark system, conditional liberation, and aid on discharge. Early traces of parole can also be found in an indenture system for juvenile delinquents in colonial America. By 1825 prisoners could be released and placed in the employment of private citizens to whom they were legally bound.

Historians of parole in the English system trace it back to the **"ticket-of-leave system"** that tempered **transportation** and penal servitude expectations and to the innovations introduced by **Alexander Maconochie** and **Walter Crofton**. Maconochie is most often lauded as the true "father of parole" for his experiments with indeterminate sentencing in the penal colony at Norfolk Island in 1840.

Throughout the eighteenth and nineteenth centuries American prison sentences were definite and final unless reduced by a pardon. In 1817 New York became the first state to pass a good time law. Predicated on the notion that rewards could be more effective than punishment, good time laws were adopted by a number of others states in the nineteenth century. By 1876 **Zebulon Brockway** had established a regime at the **Elmira Reformatory** that is comparable with the present-day parole administration.

Source: F. H. McClintock, "The Future of Parole," in *Prisons Past and Future*, ed. John Freeman, 1978, pp. 123–130.

PATERSON, ALEXANDER (1883–1947). In 1922 Alexander Paterson was appointed England's prison commissioner responsible for the **Borstal** system. Paterson's appointment was considered unique because he had had no affiliation with the prison service prior to his selection. At age 38, he was younger than any of the country's prison service governors. Paterson had long been associated with penal reform, beginning in 1908 when he was consulted for the drafting of the Children's Act. However, while he retained his interest in the treatment of young offenders, he was drawn as well to the larger world of prison reform. During the 1930s and 1940s he won an international reputation for his reform efforts and his drafting, along with Sir Walter Maurice Waller, of the "Minimum Rules for the Treatment of Prisoners," later adopted by the League of Nations. Paterson would decline offers to become the nation's chairman of the Prison Commission, seeking to reform the prison system as "a missionary not an administrator."

Although a number of reforms were passed under his watch, Paterson's most important achievements were in the realm of juvenile offenders. He abhorred a punitive approach to young offenders in favor of eliminating the social and environmental factors that often led to criminality. The 1920s and 1930s saw the influence of reformers such as Paterson reflected in the relaxation of a number of rules in adult institutions, including the end of the **silent system**, better visiting conditions, and the end of separate confinement for the initial months of a sentence as well of a variety of degrading practices such as convict hair-cropping. In 1930 separate confinement was phased out, and by 1936 prisoners were permitted to have tobacco, a privilege that had previously been extended only to those prisoners serving more than four years.

When Paterson took over the Borstal system, all Borstals were closed facilities that were more prisons than reform schools. Paterson's goal was to transform the Borstals following the model set by public schools. He organized the Borstals into "houses." To create a more open climate, staff members were required to make the transition from prison uniforms to civilian clothes. Interhouse games and outdoor recreation were introduced to improve the socialization process. A heavy dose of religion was added to the traditional three R's, which Paterson regarded as fundamental to the character-building process. There were no open Borstals before 1930, but by 1939 four were in operation, as were five new closed facilities. The outbreak of World War II abruptly ended this spurt of activity in 1939.

Sources: Teeters, *World Prison Systems*, 1944; Benjamin Grew, *Prison Governor* (London: Herbert Jenkins, 1958); Sean McConville, "The Victorian Prison: England, 1865–1965," in *Oxford History of the Prison*, eds. Morris and Rothman, 1998, pp. 117–150.

PAUL, GEORGE ONESIPHORUS (ACTIVE 1780–1820). George Paul was the son of a wealthy merchant. As early as 1783 he delivered an address to the Lent Assize arguing that England's entire prison system should be re-evaluated from top to bottom. In a subsequent address he noted such problems as disease and immorality, citing the number of female prisoners impregnated in a recently designed prison. His speeches evidently swayed the sitting of magistrates, and soon plans were underway for a county jail and five **Bridewells** in Gloucester County.

According to Norman Johnston, Paul was "Perhaps the greatest of the local [prison] reformers" of the eighteenth century. During the twenty years following the death of **John Howard**, Paul emerged as England's leading advocate for prison reform. He rose to prominence in 1783 with his efforts to create a county prison system in Gloucestershire. In order to do this he endeavored to initiate a system in which prisoners worked at hard labor with other prisoners by day and slept in solitary confinement at night, a harbinger of the **Auburn system**. He also favored a system of classification, but one that was amenable to both jailers and architectural designers.

Sources: Sidney and Beatrice Webb, *English Prisons under Local Government* (New York: Longmans, 1922); J.R.S. Whiting, *Prison Reforms in Gloucestershire, 1776–1820: A Study of the Work of Sir George Onesiphorus Paul* (London: Phillimore, 1975); Evans, *The Fabrication of Virtue*, 1982; Johnston, *Forms of Constraint*, 2000.

PAZ SOLDAN, MARIANO FELIPE (ACTIVE 1850s). Mariano Felipe Paz Soldan is considered one of Latin America's major prison reformers. A lawyer and former judge in **Peru**, he is remembered for his report detailing his examination of American prisons in the 1850s, *Examen de las Penitenciarias de los Estados Unidos*, published in New York by S.W. Benedict in 1853. When he embarked on a visit to prisons in the United States, Paz Soldan was following in the tradition of foreign luminaries who had been taking the same tour since the beginning of the century, including **Alexis de Tocqueville**, Charles de Beaumont, and even Charles Dickens in 1842. Ten years later Paz Soldan published *Relamento para el servicio interior de la prision penitenciaria de Lima*, a set of regulations for the Lima penitentiary. Although he remained a critic of Peruvian prisons, he also reported his discomfort with the American punishment of the "rain shower," which involved a prisoner's continuous exposure to a heavy shower. However, he later adopted a version of it for the penitentiary in Lima.

After completing his examinations of the **Auburn** and **Pennsylvania** systems, he selected the Auburn as most appropriate for Peru. He saw the solitary confinement of the other system as a needless and expensive budgetary constraint. A product of the racist thinking of his times, Paz Soldan was convinced that Peru's large Indian population would enjoy solitary confinement, and that working in a congregate setting would cure them of what he regarded as their "natural laziness." Together with the prison's architect Maximilano Mimey, he developed a blueprint allowing the construction of Lima Penitentiary to begin in 1856. In 1862 Paz Soldan became the first director of the penitentiary. However, within a few years of its opening the prison suffered from overcrowding, riots, escape attempts, and terrible living conditions leading to disillusionment. By 1867 director Paz Soldan considered the congregate regime he championed a failure.

Source: Carlos Aguirre, "The Lima Penitentiary and the Modernization of Criminal Justice in Nineteenth Century Peru," in *The Birth of the Penitentiary in Latin America*, eds. Salvatore and Aguirre, 1996, pp. 44–77.

PENITENTIARY. The word penitentiary is typically applied to correctional institutions that house serious offenders. The term also refers to a place for penitents. Most sources indicate that the word was first used in conjunction with the **Eastern State Penitentiary** and the ideas of **John Howard**. The word can be traced back to 1790 America, when Quaker prison reformers organized a special cell block at the **Walnut Street Jail** to separate offenders according to the seriousness of their offenses. According to Norman Johnston, American institutions are referred to as either "penitentiaries" or "correctional institutions."

Source: Johnston, *Forms of Constraint*, 2000.

PENITENTIARY ACT OF 1779. Influenced by the work of **John Howard**, Sir William Blackstone and Sir William Eden drafted a comprehensive bill for the creation of places to hold criminals in solitary confinement by night and employed in some type of labor during the day under strict supervision. According to this legislation, religious instruction would also be emphasized. However, initially little came of this act except for the introduction of some of these features in several local jails. It was not long before England witnessed a flurry of county jail construction. John Howard noted that by 1789 more than 40 new local county jails had been built. But only a handful employed the principles of cellular construction, separate confinement and congregate work. Although no actual penitentiaries were built as a result of the Penitentiary Act of 1779, it was a step forward in the movement toward the modern penitentiary. According to one authority, prison experimentation in England proceeded slowly because of the ongoing reliance on **transportation** to its far-flung colonies.

Source: Howard, *John Howard*, 1963.

PENN, WILLIAM (1644–1718). William Penn was among the early Philadelphia Quakers who were opposed to England's "bloody code" of corporal and capital punishment. Penn had been incarcerated for a short stint in England in 1670 for his Quaker leanings. However, because of his high status and connections he was held in an inn rather than a noisome common jail. Such a benign punishment reportedly led Penn to initiate a different penal code for his colony in 1682, emphasizing reform over punishment, and for most crimes substituting imprisonment for physical punishments.

Penn's Great Law of 1682 abolished religious crimes, public punishments, and most capital crimes. But he made his greatest mark as a prison reformer. It had long been customary for jailers to charge prisoners for room and board. Penn ended this practice by affording prisoners free room and board. He introduced a number of other reforms, including putting prisoners to work to pay for their crimes and making all prisoners eligible for bail.

Sources: Gail McKnight Beckman, *The Statutes at Large of Pennsylvania in the Time of William Penn*, vol. 1 (New York: Vantage Press, 1976); Roth, *Crime and Punishment*, 2005.

PENNSYLVANIA PRISON SOCIETY. Formerly established as the **Philadelphia Society for the Alleviation of the Miseries of Public Prisons** in 1787, the Pennsylvania Prison Society is considered the oldest prison aid society in the world. It is credited with inspiring the creation of the **Pennsylvania system**, based on separate confinement, and for the opening of America's "first penitentiary" at Philadelphia's **Walnut Street Jail**. Members of this society visited prisoners in the vicinity of Philadelphia and first turned their efforts toward helping prisoners reform, before later on helping ex-prisoners readjust.

In 1887 the society adopted its current name. In its more than 200-year history the society has dedicated itself to improving prison facilities and the treatment of inmates. Its many achievements have included the adoption of the indeterminate sentence, establishing prison-visiting rights, the removal of mentally ill offenders to proper treatment facilities, separating prisoners by age and gender, and helping create a professional prison staff.

In the early decades of the twentieth century society members were all expected to be graduates of accredited schools of social work. The society still remains active, focusing its attentions on modern challenges such as the death penalty, overcrowding, alternatives to imprisonment, education programs, and other projects. Over the past 160 years the society has published periodicals heralding its mission and achievements. It started in 1845 as the *Journal of Prison Discipline and Philanthropy* before changing its name to the more recognizable *Prison Journal* in 1921. Today the society has almost 600 members representing most facets of society. A board of directors meets 10 times each year to establish the current agenda for prison reform.

Sources: McKelvey, *American Prisons*, 1977; Johnston, *Eastern State Penitentiary*, 1994; Robert Jerrin, "Pennsylvania Prison Society," in *Encyclopedia of American Prisons*, eds. McShane and Williams, 1996, pp. 350–351.

PENNSYLVANIA SYSTEM. In the early years of the nineteenth century American prison reformers championed two prison models. New York established the **Auburn system**, sometimes referred to as the congregate model, which allowed convicts to work in a congregate setting with other inmates by day and then isolated them in solitary cells at night. The model that developed in Pennsylvania became known as the solitary or separate system for the forced separation of prisoners 24/7 for their entire sentence. Prisoners were expected to sleep, work, and eat in their cells. It was intended that by spending their terms in solitary confinement prisoners could reflect on their lives and at the same time through daily labor learn the value of discipline and proper work habits. Detractors of the competing Auburn model noted that though prisoners were forbidden to communicate with each other, by allowing them to work in a congregate setting it was almost impossible to prevent inmates from communicating with each other. In addition, any prisoner suspected of speaking and breaking the silence was cruelly punished. Supporters, according to historian David J. Rothman, could point out that "Pennsylvania, by contrast, would be humane, secure, ordered, and ultimately, successful." However, in the end virtually all state-adopted prison plans were based on the Auburn model. The explanation is rather simple—the Auburn system was cheaper to operate, and congregate workshops brought in more revenue than solitary workers. The Pennsylvania system's two earliest and best exemplars were **Eastern State Penitentiary** at Cherry Hill and Pittsburgh's Western Pennsylvania Prison. In 1913 the real birthplace of the Pennsylvania system at Eastern State Penitentiary made the transition to the Auburn congregate model. However, the legacy of the Pennsylvania system was much more prominent in Europe and South America, where a number of prisons were built on this model. Among the prisons that adopted architect **John Haviland**'s design were China's Beijing Prison (1912), Belgium's Louvain Prison (1860), Japan's Hakodate Prison (1931), London's **Pentonville Prison** (1842), and Russia's Kresty Prison in St. Petersburg (1890), to name just a few of the 300 prisons modeled after Eastern State Penitentiary's radial plan.

Sources: Teeters and Shearer, *The Prison at Philadelphia*, 1957; David J. Rothman, "Perfecting the Prison: United States, 1789–1865," in *Oxford History of the Prison*, eds. Morris and Rothman, 1998, pp. 100–116; Johnston, *Forms of Constraint*, 2000.

PENTONVILLE PRISON. Construction on England's Pentonville Prison began in 1840 and was completed in 1842. Modeled on the separate and **silent system**, it was originally meant to confine convicts awaiting **transportation** to **Australia**. Eleven commissioners were initially appointed to oversee the institution. Hailed as "the Model Prison," it was inspired by **William Crawford's** evaluation of the **Auburn** and **Pennsylvania** systems in America during his visit there. As the newly appointed inspector for English convict prisons, Crawford, while regarded as a man with "little imagination," was also a member of the London Society for the Improvement of Prison Discipline. Following his return to England from Philadelphia, Crawford demonstrated a fondness for the Pennsylvania system, which with some modifications was adopted throughout Great Britain.

Pentonville was designed as a main building consisting of four wings, each one linked to a central area by corridors arranged in fan-shaped radial pattern with a 60-degree angle between them. Cells were constructed on gallery landings on either side of the wings and were described as "cathedral like" because of their high vaulted ceilings and tall stone windows. This prison design was so successful that 54 English prisons were planned on the same pattern by 1848, making Pentonville one of the most copied prisons in the world. A number of European countries built prisons using the Pentonville prototype, including France, Prussia, Austria, Denmark, Sweden, and Holland. A number of these prisons are still in operation.

This prison became well known for its association with the Australian system of deportation. Convicted criminals were first sent to this institution to serve up to 18 months before being shipped to **Australia**. Prisoners were forced to wear masks to prevent any communication or recognition from each other. During the first stage of imprisonment still-masked prisoners exercised by themselves in the yard. In the next stage of the regimen they could mingle with other prisoners (still masked) in the yard, but still in silence. Over time masks were abolished and the exercise yards enlarged.

Following the end of transportation, convicts served their sentences at hard labor at most prisons. At Pentonville prisoners were forced to "grind wind" on the ever-present **cranks**. Following the closure of **Newgate Prison** in 1902, its gallows were moved here. Pentonville was the scene of some of the modern era's most famous executions, including those of Irish nationalist Roger Casement (1916), serial killer John Reginald Christie (1953), and wife-murderer Hawley Crippen (1910).

During the 1940s the prison population diminished, rarely exceeding 750 inmates. However, this did not keep the German Luftwaffe from bombing the prison in 1941, killing 11 prisoners, 2 staff, and 4 family members. The prison was forced to close but reopened in 1946. Over the next two decades Pentonville was beset by overcrowding, housing up to 1,500 prisoners at times. Motions were made to close the aging facility in 1979, but because of the overcrowding problems across the nation, it was kept on line and now on average holds 800 prisoners.

Sources: Robert Stephen Duncan, *Peerless, Priceless Pentonville* (pub. by R.S. Duncan, 2000); Johnston, *Forms of Constraint*, 2000; Her Majesty's Prison Service, compiled by Dave Botten, "H.M. Prison Pentonville, 1842–2000 Plus," 2002.

PERU. Shortly after independence from Spain, Peru began experimenting with various notions of incarceration. By the early 1820s Lima was home to two insalubrious jails: Carcel de Pescaderia and the city jail of Carcel de Cabildo. Before independence from Spain most of the country's jails, referred to as "little hells," or *infiernillos*, were located in bottom floors of municipal buildings. After independence from Spain in 1821, the Peruvian liberator Jose de San Martin hoped the transformation of the Convent of Guadalupe into a new prison would be a step forward for prison reform. It did not live up to expectations, and soon the newly named Carcel de Guadalupe was as malodorous as its predecessors in Lima. In 1822 Peru enacted the first prison bylaws as an independent nation. Among its rules was the elimination of prison fees and separation of inmates by sex and by age, although its rules were impossible to enforce. On the cusp of the new era of prison reform, Peru had a handful of other prisons and centers for temporary confinement. Some were in old military or police barracks; others were old inquisition buildings or fetid sites such as the notorious Presidio de Casas-Matas. By all accounts early nineteenth-century Peruvian jails cared little about sanitation, rehabilitation, or constructive training.

Although Lima considered building a **workhouse** in 1825, it did not come to fruition until 1853. That same year a commission was sent to the United States under the guidance of Mariano Felipe **Paz Soldan**. It returned with recommendations for erecting a penitentiary based on the **Auburn system**. Architecturally the prison at Lima was built like the **Panopticon**. This institution would be completed in 1862. Early on, a prescient Peruvian reformer named Dr. Thomas Lama became its second director. It did not take him long to realize that most of the prisoners were more victims of socioeconomic conditions rather than truly criminal, and he moved toward a more lenient regime favoring mild discipline and moral instruction. When **Enoch Wines** visited Peru in 1879, he described a system based on the Auburn model, favoring cellular separation at night and congregate labor by day. Among its most attractive features was its inexpensiveness, for it was cheaper to implement than the single-celled **Pennsylvania system**. Despite Paz Soldan's preferences, a number of features from the Pennsylvania system were adopted, particularly the strong emphasis on religious teachings. Prisoners who worked were paid according to their contributions and level of ability.

The Lima Penitentiary became a monument to prison reform in Peru, as well as an unhappy reminder of how difficult it is to put theory into practice. By the time it was demolished in the mid-1960s, most individuals referred to it as the *panoptico*, where the most impoverished individuals and political radicals languished in the most hostile conditions.

By the early twentieth century all penal establishments were under the authority of the general inspector of prisoners appointed by the executive branch of government. All prisoners were expected to work in order pay for prison expenses. There was a classification system based on intellectual and physical potential, work background, and aptitude. This was complemented with obligatory religious and moral instruction. Despite attempts at modernization and reform in the 1920s, with the adoption of pseudo-scientific anthropomorphic labs and the organization of an Institute of Criminology, living conditions in Peruvian prisons did not improve.

Youthful offenders as early as the 1940s served sentences in one of three correctional institutions in Lima. Lay officials ran two reformatories for boys, and the facility for young women was operated by the sisters of the Third Order of Saint

Francis of Assisi. As late as the 1940s Peru, unlike most countries, did not have fixed prison sentences. Penitentiary punishments ranged from one to twenty years and were typically served in an agricultural or penal colony or in the central penitentiary. The most serious form of confinement was internment, which refers to sentences of more than twenty-five years.

By the mid-1980s prison conditions began to plummet to intolerable conditions. Many blame the Shining Path insurgency with exacerbating conditions, particularly after it raided the Ayacucho Prison, freeing the majority of its prisoners in the process. Other critics blame the misdirected policy of separating Shining Path prisoners from others, allowing them to create ideological blocks in the prison that just reinforced their goals. This in part contributed to Shining Path prisoner riots at Lima's Lurigancho, El Fronton, and Santa Barbara prisons in 1986. Following the capitulation of the prisoners, guards and army reinforcements killed almost 300 of them.

In 1990 Peru had more than 110 prisons holding 40,000 prisoners, half in Lima's prisons. Manning the prisons was a guard staff of 4,000 former members of the Republican Guards. A survey of the prisons in 1987 revealed that 14 were in good condition, 59 in average condition, and 36 in poor condition. The most important institutions were located in Lima. Among them were Lurigancho Prison, completed in 1968; Canto Grande, completed in the early 1980s; Miguel Castro Prison; and two women's prisons at Santa Barbara and Santa Monica. At Santa Monica more than 150 children were in jail with their mothers in 1992.

In mid-1995 one prisoner reported spending more than four years in a 10-by-6 cell with two other inmates, "taking turns sleeping on the floor curled up like a dog because there were only two cement beds." During this period prisons were designated as either maximum security, catering mostly to terrorists, or reduced security for common criminals. According to reporter Tiffany Woods, the prison housed on a naval base in Callao, not far from Lima, was "in a class of its own." Its notorious isolation blockhouse known as the "Wolf's Lair," or *La Lobera,* had garnered a reputation for brutality second to none. Callao housed the nation's greatest security threats, including Shining Path terrorist leader Abimael Guzman. The mother of one prisoner reported conditions in Callao as "worse than the Holocaust." Reduced-security prisons contrast sharply with the maximum-security ones. According to reports, some inmates are armed and ignore the demands of guards, who, according to Woods, are "often intoxicated on drugs." Other staff members engage in a lucrative drugs and weapons trade behind prison walls.

Peru's largest prison is Lurigancho Prison, outside Lima. Human rights experts report that prostitutes come and go as they please. As a result, AIDS and tuberculosis have spread into the inmate population. But reduced-security prisons are considered luxurious compared to the maximum-security counterparts. Near Puno, 13,000 feet above sea level, is Yanamayo Prison, considered the country's coldest prison. Reports indicate that prisoners are responsible for removing ice from prison patios after spells of subfreezing weather. Many critics blame the conditions of the prison system on the Fujimoro government, citing better conditions in the prison before the administration took over in 1990.

The most recent estimates place the prison population at the end of 1999 at 27,452, reflecting the diminished nature of the terrorist threat. This is a ratio of 107 per 100,000 of the national population.

Sources: LCCS, "Peru: Penal System," September 1992; Carlos Aguirre, "The Lima Penitentiary and the Modernization of Criminal Justice in Nineteenth-Century Peru," in *The Birth of the Penitentiary in Latin America*, eds. Salvatore and Aguirre, 1996, pp. 44–77; Tiffany Woods, "Conditions Are Worse than Holocaust in Peru's Prisons," *Houston Chronicle*, January 5, 1997, 27A; Walmsley, *WPPL*, 2003.

PHILADELPHIA SOCIETY FOR THE ALLEVIATION OF THE MISERIES OF PUBLIC PRISONS. The Philadelphia Prison Society is considered the world's first prison reform organization. The motivating force behind the organization, founded in 1787, was the prominent physician and social reformer **Benjamin Rush**. Rush came to prominence in prison reform circles with his paper *An Inquiry into the Effects of Public Punishment upon Criminals and upon Society*. Some of Philadelphia's most prominent citizens were members of the society, including Benjamin Franklin. The prison reform society endeavored to alleviate the inhumane conditions of places of confinement. Among its goals was to reform malefactors into law-abiding citizens. It was hoped that prisons and jails could be improved if reformers visited them on a regular basis, allowing them to enquire from prisoners their conditions and any current abuse.

Deplorable conditions at Philadelphia's **Walnut Street Jail** spurred the society into action. One of its biggest complaints was the employment of prisoners on work projects outside the prison walls. Prisoners were chained together and dressed in brightly colored uniforms, something considered degrading if not humiliating. While behind bars, prisoners endured inadequate supervision, poor sanitation, and a lack of any meaningful classification of inmates. Outside the walls the malnourished prisoners resorted to begging for food. The efforts of the society to improve prison conditions in 1789 and 1790 led the Pennsylvania state legislature to pass laws utilizing new reforms and in the process establish the first modern penitentiary. It was not long before the society was targeting Pennsylvania's separate confinement system. Since 1887 the society has been known as the Pennsylvania Prison Society. Among its most recent contributions is the preservation of **Eastern State Penitentiary** as a historical site.

Sources: Teeters, *They Were in Prison: A History of the Pennsylvania Prison Society, 1787–1937*, 1937; Alan T. Harland, "The Philadelphia Society for Alleviating the Miseries of Public Prisons," in *Encyclopedia of the American Prison*, eds. McShane and Williams, 1996, pp. 353–354.

PHILIPPINES. While still an American possession during the 1920s the Philippines prison system included 3 large convict facilities and 52 provincial jails under the administration of the insular director of prisons. The main prisons included Manila's large industrial prison called Bilibid, the Iwahig penal colony, and the San Ramon Prison Farm, which was used primarily for indigenous Moros. The total number of prisoners, including those awaiting trial, convicted, and the insane, numbered around 6,500.

Bilibid had been built by the Spanish occupiers in 1865 and was the closest example to a modern penitentiary. Its architecture most closely resembled the **Eastern State Penitentiary** model, with "spokes" of buildings extending out from a central hub containing the main guard tower. Each block of cells held different categories of inmates, such as those condemned to death, and women and men were separated by gender. One feature that is significantly different is the absence of individual cells, a hallmark of the **Pennsylvania system.**

All convicts were required to work. There were a wide variety of industries to keep everyone busy. Both women and men participated. It was hoped that prisoners would be encouraged to follow their prison trades when they got out. Prisoners were divided into four grades. If prisoners were demoted to the third grade, they had to wear the familiar prison-stripe uniforms. Prisoners could earn privileges and release as they successfully navigated the various ranks through industriousness and good behavior.

The penal colony at Iwahig is located on the island of Palawan, which was used as a place of banishment under the Spanish regime. When the islands were taken over by the United States in 1904, the punishment of exile was abolished. Steps were then taken to make the island a colony for first offenders. The 100,000-acre colony held an average of 1,500 to 2,000 prisoners. They were divided into two groups. Colonists were scattered in groups of 30 to 60, each participating in different activities, such as farming, road construction, and animal husbandry. The settlers were prisoners who were allowed to bring their families to live on the island. They lived in separate houses near the administration system. Arrangements were made for the children to attend school nearby.

As of the 1940s the prison system still lagged behind other nations in its lack of procedures for conditional release. Without a system of **parole** and probation, prisoners could only win early release through a pardon for good behavior, a practice that often involved political collusion and corruption.

Following Japanese occupation, a new penal code was promulgated in 1947 based on the positivist notion that criminality was the result of social, environmental, and economic factors as much as it was rooted in the inherited character of the criminal. In 1972 the prison system was reorganized, establishing seven national and regional prisons. Prisoners were segregated by length of sentence. Women and children were accommodated at Mandaluyong in the Rizal Province. Every town maintains its own jail, in most cases a room or two in the local police station. It was estimated that as much as 40 percent of the prison population in the late 1980s were awaiting trial.

By the 1980s the Philippines prison system was plagued by overcrowding. The Bureau of Prisons of the Department of Justice supervises the national prisons. In 1991 local jails came under the control of the Philippine National Police. Today the government operates six correctional institutions and penal farms, the largest of which was the National Penitentiary at Muntinlupa, Rizal Province, outside Manila. This facility is considered the central penitentiary for inmates serving long sentences. It is divided into separate camps for minimum- and maximum-security offenders. Women are housed in the Correctional Institution for Women in Manila. There is a combination prison and penal farm in Zamboanga City, and in Palawan, Mindoro Occidental.

In 2003 a 10-year study of the nation's 600 jails was published. It reported that inmates in more than half the institutions were deprived of basic needs, such as water, food, living space, and adequate shelter. One prison in Manila meant to hold 1,800 held 5,200 prisoners. With a total prison capacity meant for 45,000 prisoners, the more than 70,000 inmates were housed in a system at a rate of 156.4 percent over maximum capacity. The guard-to-prisoner ratio stands at 1 to 10.3. Human rights groups have targeted the prison system on a variety of fronts, including legal abuse, torture, and health concerns.

However, for wealthy prisoners typical prison conditions were no barrier to comfort. A former congressman convicted of raping a minor was sentenced to life in prison at the new Bilibid Prison. The ex-politician had the means and clout to build his own quarters, hire bodyguards, and construct a tennis court. It goes without saying that corruption is a major problem.

Sources: CIA, *World Factbook—Philippines*, www.cia.gov; Choices, "New Judicial Reforms in Philippines Aim to Address Needs of Poor," www.undp.org; Gillin, *Taming the Criminal*, 1931; Kurian, *WEPP*, 1989; LCCS, "The Philippines: The Correctional System," June 1991.

POLAND. Following independence in 1918, Poland rose to the task of centralizing its prison system and organizing the prisons that prior to World War I had been parts of **Russia, Austria,** and **Germany.** In 1922, prisons from Silesia were added to the mix. Initially these facilities added up to 33 large prisons, 70 even larger institutions, 35 small facilities, and 400 "arrest" prisons for detainees. In 1928 new penal legislation was adopted that placed all prisons under the Ministry of Justice and divided prisons into three classes. Class I prisons could house more than 450 inmates and held inmates serving three years or more. Class II prisons held between 150 and 450 prisoners serving sentences of between one and three years. Class III institutions held up to 150 prisoners serving sentences up to one year; all prisons connected to the offices of Justices of the Peace fit in this category as well.

By the 1930s Poland had adopted the **progressive stage system** and confined women and minors to separate facilities. In its earliest stages prison labor was compulsory. On the other hand prisoners enjoyed the protections of insurance policies that covered them in the event of an accident or illness related to work. Through good behavior and progress at work inmates could earn extra privileges such as visitors, more books, longer exercise breaks, and permission to smoke. By 1940 an aftercare program known as "Association of Patronage" was in operation in larger towns. Members of this organization were known as prison curators, who were privileged to visit inmates and help formulate a plan for post-incarceration life.

Under the Communist regime, the Polish penal system was grounded in the penal practices of the neighboring Soviet Union. In 1956 the prison system came under the jurisdiction of the Ministry of Justice through the Main Bureau of Penal Institutions. Every prison institution had a commission that classified inmates and adjusted treatment regimes according to an individual's need. In 1969 Poland adopted a penal code considered one of the most punitive in Europe. Under the Communist government there was little opportunity for prisoners to follow through on appeals related to grievances and questioned documents or even to investigate prison conditions. Compared to the earlier regimes, prisoners suffered from poor medical access and barriers to using libraries. In 1981 it was estimated that there were between 130,000 and 200,000 prisoners, much higher than the United States at that time (350 to 580 per 100,000 versus 212 per 100,000 for the United States).

The establishment of Solidarity in 1980 led to the dissemination of little-known prison conditions to the outside world. In the early 1980s a number of prison hunger strikes and riots led to investigations that revealed a system fraught with routine torture, inadequate diet, poor sanitation, and overcrowding. It has surfaced that in the 1970s an uncodified set of rules and regulations gave prison guards the power to mete out punishment as they saw fit. However, the riots and unrest in the prison system led to some reforms in the early 1990s when the director of the Central Prison Administration oversaw the dismissal of one third of the guards and three quarters of the prison governors. By the middle of 1992 virtually half the prison personnel had been on the job for only two years. However, as late as 1992 human rights groups such as Helsinki Watch reported poor conditions and overcrowding in a number of prisons and that only fifteen prisons could claim their own hospitals. With the decline of prison industries in the post-Soviet era, the budget of the Ministry of Justice vastly diminished. There was little capital for prison construction, and the average facility was almost 100 years old. However, the prison population had demonstrably decreased to 61,329.

In 1993 martial law ended and there arose the question how to handle or disperse the large prison population. Most evidence suggests that political prisoners who had been held without charges were forced into the army or sent to hard labor camps, where military law prevailed over civil law.

A number of amendments to the penal code in the 1990s impacted Polish prisons by reducing the number of pre-trial detainees and introducing community service and suspended sentences for some minor crimes. Between 1995 and 2000 the prison population averaged between 54,000 and 57,000 (140 to 150 per 100,000). However, in 2000 the Minister of Justice asked for more restrictions on bail and heavier sentences for a number of personal felonies. As a result the prison population rose to 70,000 by the end of 2000 and 80,000 in August 2001. This surge gave Poland a prison rate twice higher than Germany's and higher than those of its eastern neighbors the **Czech Republic** and **Slovenia**, but still lower than the **Ukraine**.

At present the Central Board of Prison Service is responsible to the Ministry of Justice. As of 2003 Poland contained 156 prisons, 70 of which were for pre-trial detainees and 86 for those already sentenced. In addition, there are 58 other facilities, including 2 separate facilities for "mothers and children," 14 prison hospitals, and 40 separate lower-security units attached to the previously mentioned prisons. As of 2003 these 210 facilities were 116.4 percent of capacity at 80.093. The largest pre-trial institution is at Warsaw-Bialoleka (1272), followed by Lodz (1008), Gdansk (952), and Radom (907). Thirteen institutions dedicated to sentenced prisoners hold more than 750 each, with the largest at Wronki (1.405), followed by Potulice (1262), and Kaminsk (1255). According to Roy Walmsley, 6 others can hold more than 1,000 each. Approximately two thirds of the prisons were products of the early twentieth century, with only one fifth built since World War II. Outstanding for their decrepitude are Koronwo Prison, built inside a fourteenth-century convent, and Leczyca, a monument to fifteenth-century architecture.

Sources: Edouard Neymark, "The Prisons of Poland," *Journal of Criminal Law and Criminology* 19 (November 1928), pp. 399–407; Edouard Neymark, "The Prisons of Poland," *Howard Journal*, June 1929, pp. 321–327; LCCS, "Poland: Penal System," October 1992; ICPS, Poland, 2003; Walmsley, *Further Developments in the Prison Systems of Central and Eastern Europe*, 2003.

PORT ARTHUR PRISON. Named after Governor George Arthur, Port Arthur Prison was built on a peninsula connected to the penal colony of **Van Diemen's**

Land, modern day Tasmania, by a 400-yard isthmus. Van Diemen's Land was nearly 250 miles off the coast of **Australia.** Its original penitentiary was transformed from its origins as a flourmill in 1850. Surrounded by shark-infested waters and patrolled by guards and attack dogs, the island was considered almost escape-proof. From 1830 to 1877 more than 12,000 out of the 180,000 convicts transported to Australia ended up at Port Arthur. Most prisoners were recidivist offenders who had already served sentences for crimes ranging from murder to petty theft in English or Australian prisons. Belying its malevolent reputation, the prison was rather small, never holding more than 68 inmates at one time. Based on the model prison at **Pentonville,** a silent and separate system was maintained. Even guards were expected to wear slippers while patrolling the corridors. In order to prevent contact between prisoners, inmates were kept in their cells 23 hours a day; there they worked on menial tasks in isolation. They were allowed one hour of exercise each day, but in isolation in 6-by-12-foot outdoor yards built behind each cell. Prisoners saw other inmates only on Sunday, when they were allowed to attend chapel. Port Arthur Prison figured prominently in the 1870s novel *For the Term of His Natural Life,* written by Marcus Clarke. Port Arthur Prison was closed in 1877.

Sources: Robson, *The Convict Settlers of Australia,* 1965; Hughes, *The Fatal Shore,* 1987.

PORTUGAL. Some of the earliest information on Portugal's prison system was gleaned from accounts in the 1930s that lauded the Colonia Penal Agricola de Antonio Maciera near Sentra and Lisbon's recent modern prison. In 1932 noted author V.S. Pritchett complimented the latter prison but was disenchanted with its reliance on the separate system, which was maintained into the 1940s. In 1936 steps were taken toward reorganizing the entire prison system, including new types of punishments, organizing work for prisoners, the training and selection of personnel, preparing prisoners for freedom, and the construction and maintenance of appropriate facilities. By mid-century the more popular forms of incarceration consisted of jails, prisons, and establishments for security, or *establissements de surete.* Prisons were divided into departmental facilities for sentences up to three months, central prisons for longer stints, and penitentiaries for long-term confinement. Following on the heels of the 1936 penal reform agenda, special institutions were created, including hospitals for the mentally ill offender, facilities for juveniles, and workhouses for mendicants and alcoholics, as well as more punitive penal colonies outside the country for political prisoners and recidivists.

In 1936 Portugal implemented a **progressive stage system,** which begins in cellular isolation and progresses to congregate settings in silence by day and solitary accommodations at night, before the prisoner reaches the last stage, which allows association all day. After half the sentence has been served, or at six months, prisoners can earn additional privileges. However, any retrogression during confinement can lead to confinement to a penal colony, isolation, or demotion to a lower stage. During this era minors were kept in separate sections but were often incarcerating for public drunkenness, loitering, and other types of delinquent behavior.

The decree of 1936 reported a capacity to hold up to 500 inmates. Supervision of the prison system was under the Ministry of Justice through the director general of prisons. Prison personnel were hired largely at the discretion of the Ministry of Justice, although increasing emphasis was directed at proper training and the development of an officer-training school. By the late 1980s the Ministry of Justice still presided over the prison administration, which included 39 prisons and three military prisons. Civilian prisons included 12 central facilities, 24 regional prisons, and 3 special institutions. These institutions held more than 8,300 prisoners in 1988, more than 700 over capacity. The overwhelming majority was male, with 475 female adults and 922 under age 21. The central prisons were the largest institutions, capable of holding a total population of almost 5,000. In 1988 the military prisons had capacity for 299 but held only 186. Almost 500 male juveniles were housed in 7 reformatories, and 211 females in 3 separate facilities. Other juveniles were kept in observation and social action centers in Lisbon, Porto, and Coimbra.

The average male sentence in 1990 was six months. The country had an incarceration ratio of 83 per 100,000, similar to the rates in neighboring **Spain** and **France**. During the 1980s human rights monitors reported periodic hunger strikes and other protests over various prisoner grievances. But except for several reports of individual mistreatment, most independent evidence suggests prison conditions were acceptable. Younger prisoners are encouraged to take advantage of opportunities to learn trades and improve educational skills, which could lead to a reduction in sentencing. The Portuguese equivalent to America's **three-strikes legislation** mandates that anyone convicted three times for the same crime should be considered a danger to society and ineligible for parole. These prisoners also served a more punitive prison regimen, with little ability to earn a wage through prison labor.

Currently the General Directorate of Prisons falls under the Ministry of Justice. In 2004 Portugal had 55 prisons, including 17 central prisons, 3 special prisons, and 35 regional facilities. Designed to hold 12,435, they were just above capacity with 13,563 prisoners, or 129 per 100,000 of the national population.

Sources: Teeters, *World Penal Systems*, 1944; LCCS, "Portugal: Penal System," 1993; ICPS, Portugal, 2004.

PRESIDIO. The term *presidio* is derived from the Latin word *praesidium*, which refers to a garrison or fort surrounded by protective walls. Two types of prisoners were sentenced to penal servitude in the presidios, which by most accounts evolved from the use of medieval fortresses and castles as sites of incarceration. Prisoners sentenced to North African presidios were originally referred to as *desterarados*, or "banished men." These prisoners typically performed military services. The other type of prisoner was the *presidiarios*, prisoners condemned to hard labor. With the official abandonment of **galley** servitude in 1748, the numbers of prisoners sentenced to presidios increased substantially.

Most Spanish forced labor prisons were located in port cities. During the 1770s these public works presidios put prisoners to work on public sanitation, canal, and road projects. The term also referred to penal colonies outside Spain, similar to the French use of penal colonies with forced labor. In the 1870s and 1880s **Puerto Rico** mobilized the entire prison population of the presidio at La Puntilla for similar construction projects. **Cuba**'s Presidio prison was a large **panopticon** structure comprising five circular buildings and was regarded a step toward modernity by Cuban prison reformers. However, facilities such as **Peru**'s Presidio de Casas-Matas in Lima was closer to the traditional presidio prison. This deteriorating jail was located inside the Fortress de Callao. By the mid-nineteenth century it was described as a vile facility with little internal vigilance or work opportunities, offering the bare minimum of sanitation, with poor food and ventilation. It was basically 2 underground rooms measuring 7-by-50 yards each, holding between 60 and 200 inmates.

It was common for prisoners to be exchanged between various presidios in the Spanish colonies. This was especially common in North Africa in closer proximity to Spain. Prisoners were also transferred across the Atlantic Ocean to the colonies in the Americas. Many of these prisoners were recidivist deserters. According to historian Ruth Pike, the exchange of "military prisoners between the presidios of North Africa and Spanish America were common." This exchange could also occur in the opposite direction, with military prisoners being shipped from New Orleans and Pensacola to Manila and North Africa.

In the eighteenth century the North African presidios completed the transition into "full-fledged" prisons. Among the most prominent presidios were Presidio del Prado, Madrid, Presidio del Puente de Toledo, Madrid, the Oran Presidio, and the presidio in Havana, Cuba.

Sources: Colin M. MacLachlan, *Criminal Justice in Eighteenth Century Mexico* (Berkeley: University of California Press, 1974); Pike, *Penal Servitude in Early Modern Spain*, 1983; Salvatore and Aguirre, eds., *The Birth of The Penitentiary in Latin America*, 1996.

PRIVATE PRISONS. Historically, private prisons have been viewed as an alternative to traditional government-operated facilities. Ancient Rome had a facility known as the *carcer privatus*, or private prison. Slaves were often imprisoned by their masters, as were "reluctant" debtors who needed to be forcibly convinced to pay their debts. The typical sentence however was short-term. According to criminologist Malcolm Feeler, the first example of private sector involvement in corrections began in the early 1600s, when private entrepreneurs first transported British convicts to the American colonies. During the nineteenth and early twentieth centuries a number of American prisons turned to convict leasing systems to save money. According to historian Larry E. Sullivan, Kentucky had the "first entirely private prison" beginning in 1825 when all of the state's prisoners were leased out. In 1894 Tennessee leased out its entire prison population to a major railroad. By the late 1880s more than a dozen states had leasing contracts with private enterprises. **San Quentin Prison**, built in the 1850s, is considered "the first facility constructed and operated by a private provider." By the end of the twentieth century prisoner leasing had gone out of vogue.

During the 1980s prison privatization found increasing support among American conservatives. Since crime rates were soaring and imprisonment and probation had little impact on recidivism, corrections officials began to look elsewhere for solutions. However, there is little evidence to suggest that the private sector has been more successful at curing recidivism than the public sector. In a 1988 report by the President's Commission on Privatization, recommendations included contracting with outside companies to run prisons at the federal, state, and local levels. The report also noted that "problems of liability and accountability should not be seen as posing insurmountable obstacles to contracting" as long the standards of the American Correctional Association were met.

Today the privatization of prisons refers to "a contract process that shifts public functions, responsibilities, and capital assets, in whole or in part, from the public sector to the private sector. By 2003 private prisons in the United States were operating in 31 states, with a total prison population of 73,497, almost 6 percent of the nation's state inmates. According to one 2005 study, "private prisons held enough inmates nationwide on June 30, 2002, to constitute the third largest state-level prison system behind California and Texas. Arguments citing the benefits of private prisons focus on their lower operational costs, faster and cheaper bed capacity, and better quality of service.

A number of other countries are experimenting with private prisons. Among the most adept has been Australia, which in 1997 housed 11 percent of its total prison population in private institutions compared to only 2 percent of the total American inmates.

A 2000 study by the American Federation of State, County, and Municipal Employees (AFSCME) Corrections United found private prison guards were paid less, had a higher turnover rate, and less training than their public sector counterparts. However, in 2003 the association of Private Correctional and Treatment Organizations (APCTO), representing private prisons in Australia, Canada, France, Great Britain, New Zealand, and South Africa claimed, "private prisons have proven to be an effective strategy for helping states keep their corrections budgets under control."

Among the best-known private correctional firms are Avalon Correctional Services, Inc., CiviGenics, Correctional Systems Corporation, Correctional Systems, Inc., Corrections Corporation of America, Maranatha Corrections LLC, Securicor Custodial Services, Ltd., Pricor, and Wackenhut Corrections Corporation. By the twenty-first century there were at least 184 privately operated facilities holding 132,346 prisoners worldwide. In the United States most of these are located in southern or western states. Most private prisons are "relatively new, with bed capacities of 800 or less, and designed for medium and minimum-security custody inmates." Recent studies suggest that the pace of private prison construction is on the decrease leading to the consolidation of correctional companies.

Sources: Sullivan, *The Prison Reform Movement*, 1990; Malcolm Feeler, "The Privatization of Prisons in Historical Perspective," *Criminal Justice Research Bulletin*, 1991, 6(2):1–10; James Austin and Garry Coventry, *Emerging Issues on Privatized Prisons*, U.S. Department of Justice, February 2001, www.ncjrs.org/pdffiles1/bja/181249; Arie Freiberg, "Three Strikes and You're Out—It's Not Cricket," in *Sentencing and Sanctions in Western Countries*, eds. Tonry and Frase, 2001; www.APCTO.ORG; William D. Bales et al, "Recidivism of Public and Private State Prison Inmates in Florida," pp. 57–82, in *Criminology and Public Policy*, February 2005, 4:1.

PROBATION. Probation was first introduced in the United States in 1841 when a Boston boot maker named John Augustus convinced a judge to grant him custody of a convicted offender for a short period of time. Augustus hoped the individual could demonstrate his rehabilitation by the time he returned to court for sentencing. In 1878 Massachusetts introduced the first statewide probation system. Probation is defined as "the suspension of punishment conditional on there being no further offence for a period during which the offender is placed under personal supervision." According to criminologist Philip Reichel, "Probation in England actually developed in a manner similar to its progression in the United States." The first English resolution in favor of probation was passed in 1879. However, a major difference was not resolved until Britain introduced its first real probation statute with the Probation of Offenders Act of 1907. Unlike American probation, which provided for paid probation officers to supervise children and adults, until 1907 England relied on English magistrates, police officers, and volunteers to supervise probationers. These two models would inspire the spread of various probationary schemes in other parts of the world.

Most European countries did not adopt probation as an alternative to prison until much later in the nineteenth century. France adopted some aspects of probation in 1891 but did not by law formalize probation until 1958. The French system became identified as the "suspended execution of a sentence." This strategy allowed nonrecidivists to receive a five-year suspended sentence the first time they are sentenced to prison for a minor offense. If they commit another offense during this period, they are sent to prison. Other European countries have also adopted certain aspects of probation in creating their own alternatives to the prison sentence.

Latin American countries were influenced by their "historical and legal" affiliations with continental Europe. Most initially adopted some variation of the suspended sentence before later adding supervision to the scheme. A number of Asian and African countries adopted probation during their years as colonies or as semi-independent countries.

Sources: Rupert Cross, *Punishment, Prison, and the Public* (London, 1971); Reichel, *Comparative Criminal Justice Systems*, 2005.

PROGRESSIVE STAGE SYSTEM. According to prison historian Sean Mc-Conville, the notion of "breaking the prisoner's sentence into successively less restrictive and punitive parts," with a scheme of progressive stages originated at Gloucester Prison in 1791. As the British government became involved with the creation of penitentiaries in the nineteenth century, this system was featured at **Millbank** and **Pentonville** prisons.

The progressive stage system has also been touted as the brainchild of the Irishman **Walter Crofton**. It came to prominence in an 1842 speech by an English official relating to penal servitude in Australia. Not surprisingly, it became known as the **Irish system**. According to this strategy, a prisoner was not sentenced to a fixed number of years but instead had the opportunity for release after successfully completing series of stages through good behavior and work. The stages began with strict solitary confinement, before entering the next phase considered the indeterminate stage in a group situation. Finally, the prisoner could earn release under supervision. According to McConville, "This system of inducements and threats, and a period of initial purging and breaking, became the basis of the home-based convict system." The successive stages system found an early application in the penal **transportation** system. Once a convict matriculated through the initial solitary confinement at Pentonville, he would be taught a vocational skill or craft and bombarded with religious sermons. Those who made it this far while demonstrating a good work ethic and proper deportment would still be shipped to **Australia**. However, they were given a ticket-of-release that would grant the conditional release as soon as they reached the penal colony. Those who were noncompliant arrived at the penal colony in shackles and could expect several years at hard labor.

By the late 1870s the progressive stage system dominated the British prison regime as expressed in its slogan "hard bed, hard fare, hard labor." The protocol for passing through the various stages began with a one- to six-month stint in solitary confinement, a reduction from the initial term, which ranged from 18 to 9 months prior to the 1850s. In this phase the convict was virtually separated from the world he once knew—no family items, no news from outside, and no view of the sky or natural world. Prisoners who entered the system in first class spent up to six hours per day in nonconstructive labor such as the **crank**. Prisoners worked outside in the next stage, but only on Sundays. Once qualifying for stage 3, prisoners were given a mattress for the first time. It was not until stage 4 that prisoners could read library books, receive visits, and write letters.

What is often lost in any discussion of the progressive stage system was the fact that only long-sentence prisoners, who represented maybe 2 percent of the prison population in the 1870s, could benefit from the system. Most others were serving between one week and six months anyway, not enough time for most prisoners to pass even through stage 1, let alone experience the elation of reaching stage 4.

Source: Sean McConville, "The Victorian Prison," in *The Oxford History of the Prison*, eds. Morris and Rothman, 1998, pp. 117–150.

PUERTO RICO. Initially Puerto Rico's penal institutions were based on practices that predominated in Spain. In the nineteenth century two forms of incarceration were common. In the more common form, individuals were detained to secure their appearance before the magistrate. In this manner, individuals were held under military guard in the nearest detention facility, usually akin to the municipal jails established in the late eighteenth century. The second form of incarceration prevalent for much of the nineteenth century involved hard labor or torture as penal servitude. Penal torture typically took the form of shackling prisoners in heavy chains for years at a time. Convict labor was often used for road construction projects and the upkeep of other public works. Those sentenced to hard labor were usually familiar with the **presidio** at La Puntilla, built between 1809 and 1820 as a **house of correction**. During Puerto Rico's years as a Spanish colony, which did not end until 1898, little consideration was given to prisoner classification and compartmentalization.

Puerto Rico made new strides toward improving its correctional system when it constructed a new penitentiary at Rio Piedras in 1933. The institution combined an eight-acre farm with a facility offering 332 cells and 12 ward dormitories. Designed as a model institution, it used, according to prison supervisor Martin Ergui, a classification system to separate "the youngest, the reformables, the unreformables, and those convicted of crimes against morals, persons, and property." Heavy emphasis was placed on working, either in horticulture or industrial shops. The intention was that the labor would pay maintenance costs. This prison used a strategy similar to the American **state-use** concept, building furniture, clothing, hats, shoes, and the like, for use in state offices, asylums, hospitals, and other state sponsored institutions.

Puerto Rico's Administration of Correction and Rehabilitation is responsible for 50 prisons with a combined population in 2002 of 14,725, or 378 per 100,000 of the national population.

Sources: Martin Ergui, "Puerto Rican Penitentiary," *Journal of Criminal Law and Criminology* 24 (March–April 1934), pp. 1118–1120; Kelvin Santiago-Valles, *"Subject People" and Colonial Discourses: Economic Transformation and Social Disorder in Puerto Rico, 1898–1947* (Albany: State University of New York Press, 1994); Kelvin Santiago-Valles, "Forcing Them to Work and Punishing Whoever Resisted": Servile Labor and Penal Servitude under Colonialism in Nineteenth-century Puerto Rico," in *The Birth of the Penitentiary in Latin America*, eds. Salvatore and Aguirre, 1996, pp. 123–159; ICPS, Puerto Rico, 2002.

Q

Q CAMP EXPERIMENT. Between 1936 and 1940 a camp on the edge of Essex, England, was the scene of one of the most unique experiments in democratic incarceration. Staffed by a small number of officers, a program was developed to give a workable group of male offenders, who had found it difficult to adjust to conventional society, between the ages of 16 and one half and 25, a sense of shared responsibility. Q Camp was more a therapeutic institution than a model community. However, its most significant feature was its emphasis on mutual partnership. Members were sent there or stayed there only by choice. Together group members designed the type of government they preferred. All the member-participants had been previously labeled behavioral problems elsewhere. None was considered dangerous or psychotic or had a long history of incarceration. Rather, all were selected or referred by probation officers, magistrates, friends or relatives, social agencies, and physicians. The Q-Camp Experiment was cut short by the start of World War II. While it is difficult to gauge the ultimate success of the experiment, it represents and important early therapeutic program designed to treat and study antisocial behavior outside the confines of the traditional prison. The punitive nature of penology in the early twenty-first century suggests that these very same participants would probably have been warehoused in prison somewhere.

Sources: W. David Wills, *The Hawkspur Experiment* (London: Allen and Unwin, 1941); Marjorie E. Camp, ed., "Q Camp, an Epitome of Experiences at Hawkspur Camp," Executive Committee of the Camp, 1943; Teeters, *World Prison Systems*, 1944.

QATAR. The Administration of the Penal and Reformatory Institutions is operated under the Ministry of Interior. In 2000 this small Middle Eastern country had only one prison, which held 570 sentenced prisoners. Of these, 12 percent were women and almost 56 percent were from foreign countries. The prison rate is roughly 95 per 100,000 of the national population.

Source: ICPS, Qatar, 2000.

QUAKERS. According to **Frederick H. Wines**, "The Quakers took up the cause of prison reform and made a religion of it." Following the English Civil War of the mid-1600s, a radical religious movement began what would become known as the Quakers, although they referred to themselves as Friends. The sect was founded by George Fox. The Friends grew quickly as they found acceptance among the middle classes in the 1650s. Their primary recruiting grounds were the prisons. Unrelenting repression meant Quakers were arrested at the slightest pretense, and the fetid cells offered a captive audience for Quaker.

The Quakers first made their mark on prison reform when **William Penn** issued legislation in Pennsylvania and West Jersey in 1682 that abolished corporal punishment, most capital crimes, and the practice of jailers demanding pay for food and lodging in prisons. Quakers remained the dominant group in American prison reform for much of the eighteenth and nineteenth centuries. They played a crucial role in establishing prisoner aid societies such as the **Philadelphia Society for the Alleviation of the Miseries of Public Prisons.** Quaker teacher John Griscom, a member of the New York Society for the Prevention of Pauperism, played an important role in establishing juvenile reform schools. Other prominent Quaker prison reformers included **Elizabeth Fry** and **William Tallack.**

Sources: Wines, *Punishment and Reform*, 1919; DeFord, *Stone Walls*, 1962.

R

RADIAL MODEL. The hub-and-spoke model of prison came to international prominence after architect **John Haviland** designed the **Eastern State Penitentiary** in Philadelphia. Haviland referred to this model in an 1821 letter, noting his preference for its combination of features, including "watching, convenience, economy and ventilation." The popularity of the radial plan lay in its facilitation of better control and observation of the inmates. According to prison expert and Eastern State Penitentiary historian Norman Johnston, where Haviland received his inspiration for the design is unknown. However, by the 1780s a variety of prisons in England and Ireland employed radial features. Architect William Blackburn, who according to Johnston might be considered the "father" of the radial plan, designed a number of these. These structures featured a semi- or fully circular house housing the warden or governor. Cellblocks extended out from the center house, like spokes in a wheel. Johnston describes a radial prison as "any grouping of cell wings emanating from a central point." Although this form of prison predominated internationally into the early 1900s, it never became popular in the United States. Only about 15 percent of American prisons followed this design in the nineteenth century. Its association with the **Pennsylvania system**, and its single-cell confinement limited the appeal of the radial design. The **Auburn system** with its congregate work regimen during the day and solitary-cell confinement at night remained most popular in the United States during this era because Auburn system prisons were less costly to build and operate and the congregate workshops provided enough money to run the prison and at times turn a profit.

Although eighteenth-century British models probably influenced the construction of the Eastern State Penitentiary, only after its adoption in the United States did it find popularity in Europe and elsewhere. The construction of the radial **Pentonville Prison** in 1842 was followed by 30 more in England alone before the end of the century. The popularity of the radial design did not end there. During the 1800s Britain built radial prisons in its colonies in Canada, Australia, Malta, South Africa, Burma, New Zealand, and Hong Kong. By 1910 German states had constructed more than 40 radial prisons. Most Latin American countries preferred this model. Ultimately close to 300 prisons around the world were influenced by the radial model.

Sources: Johnston, *Eastern State Penitentiary*, 1994; Johnston, *Forms of Constraint*, 2000.

RAGEN, JOSEPH EDWARD (1897–1971). Born in Trenton, New Jersey, and with little education, Joseph Ragen rose from deputy sheriff in 1922 to national prominence as one of America's foremost prison reformers beginning in the 1930s. Ragen's first affiliation with the prison system began with a stint as warden of the Illinois State Penitentiary at Menard in 1933. Ragen's acumen for prison management led to his appointment in 1935 as warden of the Illinois State Penitentiary at Stateville. Over more than two decades his name became synonymous with the "world's toughest prison."

When Ragen took over Stateville, he found a prison with an entrenched system of corruption—where prisoners had freedom to move with ease throughout the prison, where liqueur and drug use were rampant, and unauthorized conjugal visits were common. Prison gangs seemed to run the prison with alacrity, and because of improper attire it was often difficult to separate inmates from guards.

Ragen's strategy to gain control of the prison is considered standard operating procedures by prisons to this day. According to criminal justice historian Mark Jones, Ragen introduced a 10-point plan to redeem the system from the inmates, that included (1) eliminating political patronage from the hiring of prison personnel; (2) selecting guards carefully and training them better; (3) Keeping the inmates working; (4) closely regulating all prisoner movements; (5) strictly enforcing restrictions on inmate possessions, including banning the availability of money; (6) granting all prisoners equal treatment; (7) placing main emphasis on security, and secondary emphasis on rehabilitation; (8) prohibiting prison bargaining groups, an approach clearly opposed to **Thomas Mott Osborne**'s theories on self-governance; (9) anticipating trouble and acting proactively; 10) operating the prison with the highest standards of cleanliness and neatness in order to ensure good health and adequate security.

Ragen resigned his position in 1941 when a new administration took office in Illinois. However, after a high-profile escape under the new warden in 1942, Ragen was rehired. According to Jones, Texas prison warden **George Beto** was most influenced by the Ragen model of prison management. Ragen was an opponent of the death penalty and a firm believer in religious instruction and discipline. In the 1960s the Ragen style came into conflict with an era of inmate and staff unionization and a climate of litigation. In 1965 he acceded to requests for his resignation, ending a three-decade career in corrections. Ragen chronicled his career at Joliet and Stateville in his book *Inside the World's Toughest Prison*, published in 1962.

Sources: Ragen and Finston, *Inside the World's Toughest Prison*, 1962; Jacobs, *Stateville*, 1977; Mark Jones, "Joseph Ragen," in *Criminal Justice Pioneers in U.S. History*, ed. Mark Jones, 2005, pp. 210–214.

RASPHOUSE. The rasphouse is most identified with the evolution of the Dutch prison system. In the late 1590s authorities opened a men's **house of detention** in a former monastery in Amsterdam. Here, the theories of progressive humanists were put into practice. Long before the Enlightenment, prescient thinkers endeavored to use punishment and treatment as more than a deterrent; it was used as an avenue on the road to reform and education. This was to be accomplished through strict discipline and hard labor, guided, of course, with a heavy dose of religious education. At the so-called rasphouse, two inmates were required to rasp at least 50 pounds of sawdust per day. Rasping involved the strenuous job of pulverizing logs of dyewood in order to produce a powder for coloring goods. Depending on the workhouse, males convicted of the most serious crimes were expected to rasp from 10 to 12 hours each day (similar to the average workday of the era). During his tour of European prisons in the 1770s, **John Howard** was suitably impressed by the rasphouses. In his reports he noted how men were constantly working in these facilities preparing rough timber for carpenters' workshops. By the end of the sixteenth century the rasphouse in Amsterdam had gained a monopoly on the rasping of wood for the shipbuilding industry. Visitors from throughout Europe visited the rasping house before returning home with favorable reports of how prisoners could be reformed into hard-working members of society and at the same time earn enough money to allow the house of detention to remain self-sufficient.

Sources: Howard, *John Howard*, 1963; Anton M. Kalmthout and Dirk Van Der Landen, "Breda Prison, Holland," in *The State of the Prisons—200 Years On*, ed. Dick Whitfield, 1991, pp. 88–118.

RASPHUYS. *See* RASPHOUSE

READING COUNTY GAOL. England's Reading County Gaol, designed by Gilbert Scott and William Moffatt, resembled a fairytale castle more than a formidable prison. Its façade influenced other prison designs in the 1840s. However, it was often reviled by critics for what Robin Evans described as its "domesticated, toyish castellation," earning it the moniker the "palace prison." Built between 1842 and 1844 for Berkshire County, it was the first prison constructed after **Pentonville Prison.** Its dimensions were modeled after Pentonville, with 247 cells on three to four tiers. According to historian Norman Johnston, initially each cell had its own toilet, gas illumination, and large double windows.

This English prison attained prominence for its association with English prisoner poet **Oscar Wilde,** who was inspired by his experiences here between 1895 and 1897 to write *De Profundis* and the *Ballad of Reading Gaol*. According to one source, prisoners often referred to the prison as "Read, Read, Reading Gaol" because of Chaplain John Field's insistence that prisoners fill their days memorizing passages from the Bible.

Sources: Evans, *The Fabrication of Virtue*, 1982; Johnston, *Forms of Constraint*, 2000.

REFORMATORIES. Inherent in any discussion of the reformatory is its potential to rehabilitate or reform prisoners. Early incarnations of the reformatory were more **house of correction** than prison. Several early examples of the reform school model can be found in sixteenth- and seventeenth-century Europe. However, until the 1800s it was more common for families to discipline their own children. The American reformatory movement between 1870 and 1900 built on the work of **Alexander Maconochie** and **Walter Crofton**. The most prominent example was the **Elmira Reformatory**. Between 1876 and 1913 17 states built reformatories based on the Elmira model. Reformatories were distinct from prisons through their emphasis on education and trades training, grades and marks, indeterminate sentencing, and **parole**.

The most glaring difference between the reformatory and the state prison was a preference for indeterminate sentencing rather than fixed maximum terms, allowing prisoners to earn parole. In addition, reformatories placed inmates in one of three classes based on their accomplishments and behavior.

By 1910 the reformatory movement had peaked. There were a number of explanations for its fall from favor. Some blame the grading system, suggesting it was too complicated to maintain given a revolving door policy in which new prison officials came to office with each new political administration. By the early 1900s most prisons had begun incorporating rudimentary educational and trades training in various incarnations. Others suggest that the reformatories became little more than "junior prisons" where some individuals participated in the training programs while the majority slipped back into the old routines of learning the criminal trades from their peers.

Sources: McKelvey, *American Prisons*, 1977; Roberts, *Reform and Retribution*, 1997.

REMAND PRISONS. Similar to American county jails, these local prisons in England and Wales are used to incarcerate offenders waiting for trial or sentencing or serving very brief sentences. In a number of developing countries budgetary restrictions prohibit separating the untried from the tried. This often creates confusion when attempts are made to determine a prison's population of only convicted prisoners.

Source: Fairchild and Dammer, *Comparative Criminal Justice Systems*, 2001.

RIKERS ISLAND. Rikers Island is considered New York City's largest prison. The island was named after Dutch settler Abraham Rycken, who settled the 415-acre island in the East River in the 1630s. In 1884 the city bought the land from his descendents for $180,000. It has been used as a jail site ever since. Each year more than 130,000 prisoners make their way through Rikers Island under the watchful eyes of a staff composed of 10,000 officers and 1,500 civilians. On average the facility holds about 15,000 at any given time. To give one the perspective of the size of the institution, according to one source Rikers Island holds more prisoners than the entire prison systems in 35 other states. The prison complex is comprised of ten jails dedicated to holding prisoners waiting for trial or unable to make bail, offenders serving less than one year, and those in temporary confinement awaiting transfer elsewhere when there is an opening. Until 1966 access to the island was accomplished only by ferry. Since then access is provided only from Queens over the 4,200-foot Rikers Island Bridge. The prison figured prominently in a recent heist. Apparently artist Salvador Dali donated a painting to the prison when he was unable to keep an appointment with prison art students in the 1960s. It hung in the prisoners' dining hall until 1981, when it was moved to the lobby for security reasons. In March 2003 it was taken and replaced with a forgery. Subsequently three prison guards were charged and convicted for the theft. The painting is still missing.

Sources: "Guards Charged in Dali Theft," news.bbc.co.uk/2/hi/americas/2999430.stm; "Rikers Island," wikipedia.org/wiki/Rikers_Island.

ROBBEN ISLAND. This South African prison rose to prominence as a penal facility for political prisoners such as Nelson Mandela, Walter Sisulu, Govan Mbeki, and Robert Sobukwe. Robben Island, Dutch for "Seal Island," is located 12 kilometers off the coast of Cape Tow. It has been used as a place of detention since the end of the 1600s. According to one source, its first prisoner was a member of the Khoikhoi tribe named Autshumato, who was imprisoned there in 1658. He also is credited with making the first successful escape from the island. Many of the prison's earliest prisoners were Dutch political leaders from the various Dutch colonies, including South Africa and Indonesia. Robben Island was used as an insane asylum and as a leper colony between 1836 and 1931, when it was transformed into a prison. During World War II its strategic location was used as a military headquarters. After the apartheid regime cracked down on dissidents after the Sharpeville Massacre in 1961, a maximum-security prison was opened on the island for government opponents. From 1964 to 1990 Robben Island was a rallying cry for Mandela supporters as prisoners mounted an organized resistance against the governing regime. Although the prison is now closed, it remains a potent symbol of political resistance. Declared a World Heritage Site in 1999, it is a popular tourist destination for those taking the ferry from the Victoria and Albert Waterfront when the weather permits.

Sources: Buntman, *Robben Island and Prisoner Resistance to Apartheid,* 2003; D.M. Zwelonke, *Robben Island* (London: Heinemann, 1973); Florence Bernault, "The Politics of Enclosure in Colonial and Post-colonial Africa," in *A History of Prison and Confinement in Africa,* ed. Bernault, 2003, pp. 1–53.

ROCHEFOUCAULD-LIANCOURT, DUC DE LA. Norman Johnston suggested that Duc de la Rochefoucauld-Liancourt was "the first to have given Europeans knowledge of the Philadelphia prison reforms of the 1790s." Influenced by **John Howard**'s work, this Frenchman wrote a book on his observations of American prisons. Rochefoucauld-Liancourt's book, *The Prison in Philadelphia,* published in 1796, three years after he visited the **Walnut Street Jail,** indicated "Howard's teachings and system were carefully adopted in Philadelphia many years ago." He went on to discuss Pennsylvania legislation influenced by Enlightenment concerns such as replacing the death penalty with solitary confinement. He later was elected president of the French National Assembly.

Source: Albert Krebs, "John Howard's Influence on the Prison System of Europe," in *Prisons Past and Future,* ed. John Freeman, 1978, pp. 35–51.

ROMANIA. The adoption of a new penal code in 1978 reduced the punitive nature of criminal justice that reigned under Communist rule. Besides introducing lighter sentences, the new penal code adopted a more flexible approach toward the treatment of offenders, particularly juvenile offenders. In many cases some rehabilitation regimes superceded prison sentences. Despite such attitudes, a large number of political prisoners remained incarcerated in the 1980s. Following 1978, the penal system offered a variety of new alternatives to traditional incarceration policies. Bail, which had previously been available only to foreigners, was now available for Romanians accused of minor offenses. Although first-time offenders were punished by administrative sanctions and court-ordered fines, courts could also demand corrective labor under the supervision of particular industrial or agricultural businesses and at a reduced salary. Juveniles were often sentenced to "special training institutes" to serve stints in supervised labor.

Since the revolution of 1989 the prison population has risen from 29,000 to 44,000 in 1992. Subsequently the prison population stabilized at about 50,000 prisoners, and at last count in 2001 there were 48,841 prisoners in the nation's 43 penal institutions. A breakdown of the Romanian prison system shows 24 closed-regime prisons (some have semi-open blocks), a women's facility at Targsor, an institution for juvenile offenders at Craiova, 8 maximum-security prisons (both closed and semi-open), a prison dedicated to a semi-open regimen, 5 penitentiary hospitals and 3 juvenile re-education units. Bucharest's Jilava Prison is the only facility that exclusively handles pre-trial detainees and individuals in transit to other institutions. Twelve of the prisons have the capacity to hold more than 1,000 prisoners. Since 1994 new prisons have been opened at Bucharest-Rahova, Arad, and Giurgiu.

Among the explanations for the rising prison population since the end of communism have been the rise in crime accompanying the transition to a market economy, increasing the length of confinement for maximum sentences, and the absence of noncustodial alternatives.

Reports in mid-2001 indicate that 31 out of 35 institutions were overcrowded, with 7 prisons forcing half the prisoners to share beds. As in other central and eastern European countries, it is rare to find a prisoner in a single cell. Many inmates are kept in rooms with the capacity to hold up to 40 prisoners. According to human rights monitors, the food, medical care, and sanitation are at a reasonable level, but drug and alcohol programs are still lacking, and there is little response to HIV and AIDS.

The ratio of staff to prisoners is about 1 to 4.5 prisoners, but this includes management, guards, administrative, and medical staff. In recent years attention has focused on the demilitarization of the prison staff. Prison work is compulsory except when medical problems or lack of work prohibits it. It was estimated that in 2001 less than half the prisoners worked. The General Directorate for Prisons, which falls under the direction of the Ministry of Justice, has made progress in the realm of rehabilitation by offering inmates eleven different educational regimes, ranging from education on legal matters and completion of basic education to professional training.

As of late 2004 Romania operated 45 penal institutions, including 35 prisons, 6 prison hospitals, and 4 facilities for minors. Designed for 38,705 inmates, the prisons held 39,935 in 2004, 103.2 percent of capacity, a ratio of 184 per 100,000 of the national population. Romanian prison officials can point to a number of achievements, including the increased capacity of the prison system and the modernization of facilities. However, overcrowding and a shortage of financial resources continue to plague the system. In addition, there are few noncustodial alternatives to incarceration. Prisons with populations of more than 1,000 are located at Aiud,

Bucharest-Rahova, Colibasi, Craiova, Deva, Gherla Center, Iasi, Margineni, Poarta Alba Central, Timisoara, and Tulcea Center.

Sources: LCCS, "Romania: Penal Code," July 1989; Walmsley, *Further Developments in the Prison Systems of Central and Eastern Europe*, 2003; ICPS, Romania, 2004.

RUGGLES-BRISSE, HUGH EVELYN (b. 1861). Educated at Eton and Oxford, Hugh Ruggles-Brisse began his rise to prominence with his selection to the British Prison Board in 1896. Two years later he was appointed to the prestigious position of chairman of the Prison Commission. On his elevation to commissioner he began the task of dismantling the punitive Victorian prison regime. His support of the Prison Act of 1898 led to the abolition of the **treadmill** and **crank** in favor of productive and constructive labor such as bookbinding, shoemaking, carpentry, tailoring, and other profession that could manufacture goods for government use. This system in many respects would mirror the American **state-use system**.

Soon after taking over the prison system, the new chairman visited American penitentiaries and was particularly impressed by the **Elmira Reformatory**. This visit influenced his decision to reform the English **Borstal system**. One of his first acts was to set up a Borstal in Kent for male offenders between the ages of 16 and 21. His actions led to the birth of the Borstal system, which was consolidated in the Borstal Act, or Prevention of Crime Act of 1908. This act would be modified in 1914 and 1923. He is also credited with introducing the Probation of Offenders Act of 1907, considered Britain's first real probation statute. In 1921 Ruggles-Brisse retired and published *The English Prison System*.

Sources: Shane Leslie, *Sir Evelyn Ruggles-Brisse* (London: Murray, 1938); Ruggles-Brisse, *The English Prison System*, 1985.

RUSH, BENJAMIN (1746–1813). Born to a gunsmith in Byberry, Pennsylvania, and educated at what would later become Princeton University, Benjamin Rush went into medicine as an apprentice while still in his teens. Rush was one of America's most prominent physicians during the eighteenth century and has been accorded the sobriquet "father of American psychiatry." Rush later studied at the University of Edinburgh, receiving his medical degree in 1768. Rush supported the reform efforts of the Pennsylvania **Quakers** and was an ardent foe of the death penalty for any offense. In 1787 he was prominent in the creation of the **Philadelphia Society for Alleviation of the Miseries of the Public Prisons**. Rush was an early proponent of prisoner rehabilitation, diverging from the Quakers when it came to forced labor, which he opposed. A product of the Enlightenment and the utilitarian ethos, he sought to punish better rather than harsher, letting the punishment fit the crime. A signer of the Declaration of Independence and later professor of medicine at the University of Pennsylvania, Rush is also remembered for several of his writings, including an "Enquiry into the Effects of Public Punishments upon Criminals and Society" (1787) and *Medical Inquiries*, which is considered the first manuscript on medical jurisprudence produced in America. His accomplishments overshadow his purported invention of the "mad or tranquilizing chair," which was used at his hospital for subduing out-of-control mental patients. Constructed of heavy wood in the shape of a chair, it had a rather sinister design. A "prisoner" was fastened by straps to the contraption, with handcuffs binding the hands and no support for the legs, so that after being bound by a number of straps, the prisoner found it impossible to move, leading to great pain and swelling in the limbs.

Sources: Teeters and Shearer, *The Prison at Philadelphia, Cherry Hill*, 1957; David Freeman Hawke, *Benjamin Rush: Revolutionary Gadfly* (Indianapolis: Bobbs-Merrill, 1971).

RUSSIA. Russia has one of the largest prison populations per capita in the world, a legacy of the former Soviet Union and its harsh **Gulag** system that began in tsarist Russia. When **John Howard** visited Russia shortly before his death in 1790, he found a highly militarized prison system with little concern for rehabilitation. The Enlightenment response to prison reform made little headway in this vast agricultural country. However, Russia was not much different from other European countries in the seventeenth and eighteenth centuries. Howard's survey of Russian prisons took him to St. Petersburg, Moscow, and Riga; he found all the institutions in deleterious condition. At Moscow's Kaluska Ostrog he witnessed prisoners chained together in small wooden cages. At the military prison at Butyrka he reported 126 prisoners confined to a 29-foot by 26-foot room.

Between 1762 and 1796 Empress Catherine took the first steps toward penal reform, which was considerably influenced by **Cesare Beccaria**'s 1764 work *Essay on Crimes and Punishments*. Catherine is credited with including legislation in the new penal code that would make distinctions between offenders. In 1775 Catherine's efforts led to a reorganization of the provincial prison system. As a result, separate prisons were officially established for children, females, the poor, and minor offenders. Other attempts were made to separate the convicted from the accused, career criminals from the general population, and so forth. Despite these and other proposals, many reform measures went unheeded.

Prison reform efforts in the nineteenth century resulted in a centralization of the prison system in 1802 and the formation of a Russian prison society in 1817. Russian prison planners borrowed from architects such as **John Haviland** but also developed their own models. New Russian prisons were inaugurated in Kharkov and Novgrod, and the Siberian prison colonies were reorganized.

In 1845 Russia abolished the more primitive forms of corporal punishment such as the infamous *knut*, a whip fashioned out of dried rawhide and wires. By the 1870s several Russian universities were offering course materials on "penitentiary science" and a commission was convened to formalize a three-tiered system of confinement. Despite the addition of the magnificent Central Prison at St. Petersburg in 1875, Russian prisons mostly offered dampness and abhorrent conditions, with one observer noting that the new prison was merely a "soul extractor." In the 1890s new prisons were constructed at Vilva, Vladivostok, Ussuriysk, and Chelyabinsk. But by most accounts the tsarist era, which would end in 1917, had demonstrated little in the way of a specific penal policy.

Throughout much of the nineteenth and early twentieth centuries Russia, like other European countries, converted convents, military barracks, and other buildings into prisons in order to save money. Examples included Kherson Prison in the Ukraine, converted from an old arsenal building; Baku in current Azerbaijan, originally a marine barracks; and Perm, an arms factory.

In the 1980s the Soviet Union sentenced 99 percent of convicted criminals to labor camps, supervised by the Main Directorate for Corrective Labor Camps, better known as the **Gulag**. While Soviet authorities asserted the country had a low recidivism rate because of the Gulag system's success, human rights groups lambasted them for their brutal and inhumane conditions. Despite legislation in 1989 to humanize the labor camp system, few changes took place prior to 1991 and the end of the Soviet era.

According to Richard Terrill, in the years and months before the collapse of the Soviet Union there was a spike in the number of assaults on prison guards. As the Soviet Union stood on the edge of the democratic revolution, the common consensus was that the country was experiencing more violent antisocial behavior than in previous years, meaning the prisons contained more violent criminals in the past. Efforts to release most of the political prisoners and decrease the number of white-collar criminals sentenced to prison was successful, but their cells rapidly filled with unheard numbers of murderers, rapists, and other felons.

Between 1993 and 2001 a number of new laws were adopted that were considered major steps in aligning Russia's prison system with prevailing international standards. However, a rising crime problem led to a larger prison population, resulting in overcrowding and deteriorating conditions. For example, one Moscow prison in the mid-1990s held more than 17,000 prisoners in a facility designed for 8,500. Human rights commissions have reported examples of prisoners not receiving their food rations and surviving only thanks to outside help.

Some of the greatest barriers to improving the system in the 1990s were a lack of budget, resources, and legislative support, as well as a poorly trained correctional staff. By the end of 2001 the Russian prison system was managed by a staff of 347,000, a number Roy Walmsley considered a "50% rise on the number recorded in 1994." This figure would equal a staff-to-prisoner ratio of 1 to 2.8. One of the distinctive features of the Russian system is the use of specific staff-prisoner ratios for various types of prisons. By law, pre-trial facilities are expected to maintain a ratio of 1 to 4; corrective colonies, 1 to 6; and educational colonies 1 to 2. A number of policies have been implemented that have led to higher salaries, better staff morale and medical coverage, and better-trained guards. In order to align the system with the recommendations by the Council of Europe, training classes must offer courses on human rights in places of detention.

Following the implementation of new policies in the mid-1990s, much of the Soviet-era leftovers have been abolished, including arbitrary punishment, bans on mail and visitors, head shaving, and physical abuse. By law, prison officials are required to grant religious freedom and protect prisoners who have been threatened with harm.

Russia currently operates four types of facilities. Most numerous are the corrective colonies, or *Ispravitelnie kolonii* (IK), with 737 institutions with the capacity to hold 791,615 inmates. Corrective colonies offer four regimes ranging from very strict, or special, to strict, to general, and to settlements with open regimes. There are 184 pre-trial institutions or SIZOS, which are considered investigative isolation facilities. Educative labor colonies are institutions dedicated to juveniles under the age of 18. Of the 64 institutions dedicated to juveniles, 61 are for boys and 3 for girls. The **tyroomi** hold the system's most dangerous prisoners.

Today Russia's Principal Department of Prison Administration operates under the Ministry of Justice. The Russian Federation has continued the tradition established in the Soviet era of using two basic prison facilities—prisons and labor colonies.

Although conditions are regarded as incredibly harsh, reports indicate that the pre-trial detention centers were even worse off. The failure to implement any meaningful bail system in the mid-1990s left more than 223,000 prisoners languishing in pre-trial detention. In some cases they were held longer than they would have been had they served out the sentence for which they were charged. Of the more than one million prisoners in the prison system in 1994, more than half were held in labor camps.

In 2004 Russia had 1,024 penal institutions, including 760 prison colonies, 194 pre-trial facilities or sizos, 8 prisons, and 62 juvenile colonies. The Russian prison population is reportedly 787,900, or 548 per 100,000 of the national population. According to last reports from 2003 the prisons were under capacity at 90.2 percent. These figures would indicate a decline in Russia's prison population of 688 per 100,000 in 1998 and 638 per 100,000 in 2001. A number of amnesties are in part responsible for diminishing the prison population. *See also* **GULAG**

Sources: LCCS, "Russia: Prisons," July 1996; Morris and Rothman, eds., *The Oxford History of the Prison*, 1998; Terrill, *World Criminal Justice Systems*, 1999; Johnston, *Forms of Constraint*, 2000; Walmsley, *Further Developments in the Prison Systems of Central and Eastern Europe*, 2003; ICPS, Russian Federation, 2004.

RUSSIAN FEDERATION. *See* RUSSIA

RWANDA. Imprisonment and Western concepts of punishment were introduced to Rwanda during the Germany military occupation of the late nineteenth century. By the time the German occupation ended in 1907, Rwanda had adopted standard rules for flogging and other forms of exhibitory punishment. But not until the Belgian rule following World War I were actual detention centers built. Between 1918 and 1922 a number of **houses of detention** had been opened. The Belgians also introduced preventive detention, or house arrest. By the 1940s two types of preventive detention predominated, including detention by a warrant of summons, or *mandat d'amener*, which mandated incarceration up to three days; the other alternative was preventive detention, or *detention preventive*, a very similar device.

Following independence in the 1960s *cachots*, or informal prisons, became the most prominent form of detention. These ranged from a single holding cell within a prison or a small hut, to even a place designated for detention, such as an individual's kitchen. During the 1960s the anti-Tutsi government made the transition from monarchy to republic to a repressive Hutu-dominated government. It was able to keep the numerous Tutu critics in check through a widespread system of cachots and mass arrests. During the late 1970s human rights groups reported a number of violations ranging from arbitrary arrest and detention to forced labor camps, torture, and prohibition of visitors. The death of the nation's president unleashed the unprecedented mass executions of 1994. Later that year the new government arrested suspects, and cachots were holding prisoners in detention by the thousands. The following year, prisons reported holding five times their maximum capacity.

Most prisoners preferred the more informal cachots to the central prisons, where epidemic disease flourished in conditions that left prisoners packed 6 per square meter. The Butare Prison, created for 1,500 prisoners, held 4,000 inmates. During the last 6 weeks of 1994 166 prisoners died there. Things were even worse at Kigali Central Prison, where 5,000 prisoners shared space designed for 1,500, resulting in 50 deaths per week. Despite the promise of Rwandan independence in 1961 and the end of the Tutsi genocide in 1994, the decentralization of the nation's prison system has led to widespread abuse and continuing high levels of violence as the Hutus and Tutsis attempt to come to some type of reconciliation just a decade after the murder of hundreds of thousands innocent Tutsis and moderate Hutus.

As of mid-2002 Rwanda's 18 prisons held 112,000 prisoners. Of these, more than 103,000 were detained on suspicion of having participated in the 1994 genocide. More than 94,000 prisoners were held in a prison system designed to hold 46,700. At 202.4 percent of occupancy as 2002, this represents a rate of 109 per 100,000 of the national population. This figure takes into account only prisoners who are not considered genocide suspects, or almost 7,800 prisoners.

Sources: ICPS, Rwanda, Africa, 2002; Michele D. Wagner, "The War of the Cachots: A History of Conflict and Containment in Rwanda," in *A History of Prison and Confinement in Africa*, ed. Bernault, 2003, pp. 239–270.

S

S-21. Closer to an interrogation and torture facility than a traditional prison, S-21 was the code name for Tuol Sleng Prison, one of Pol Pot's most horrifying institutions. In a period of less than 4 years close to 14,000 men, women, and children were interrogated and tortured by the Khmer Rouge at this secret prison, with only 7 surviving. Located in the Cambodian capital of Phnom Penh, Tuol Sleng was finally closed after Vietnamese troops captured the city in January 1979. Subsequently the building was transformed into the Tuol Sleng Museum of Genocidal Crimes to commemorate the victims. A tour of the museum today would reveal the metal beds and fetters that held soon-to-be-murdered prisoners. Other rooms display torture instruments, paintings by survivors, and hundreds of prisoner mugshots taken before their executions.

S-21 had a maximum capacity for 1,500 prisoners, which was reached in 1977. At other times the population was fewer than 200. Most prisoners were young ethnic Khmer Rouge from the countryside. In his examination of S-21, David Chandler observed that prisoners "were socially and ethnically indistinguishable" from the guards. Guards followed a list of 30 rules, which included prohibitions from talking to prisoners or exhibiting humane behavior.

Sources: Chandler, *Voices from S-21: Terror and History in Pol Pot's Secret Prison*, 1999.

ST. KITTS AND NEVIS. The country's two prisons are operated under the Ministry of Home Affairs. In 1998 these 2 facilities held 135 prisoners, almost 25 percent were either pre-trial detainees or remand prisoners. The island's rate is 338 per 100,000 of the national population.

Sources: ICPS, St. Kitts and Nevis, Caribbean, 1999; Walmsley, *WPPL*, 2003.

ST. LUCIA. In late 1999 St. Lucia's 4 prisons held 365 inmates, almost one third of whom were either pre-trial detainees or on remand. The prisons were reportedly at 278.4 percent, a rate of 243 per 100,000 of the national population.

Sources: ICPS, St. Lucia, Caribbean, 1999; Walmsley, *WPPL*, 2003.

ST. VINCENT AND THE GRENADINES. The Prison Service of St. Vincent and the Grenadines falls under the direction of the Ministry of National Security, the Public Service, Seaport and Airport Development. In 2001 there were two prison facilities holding 302 prisoners. These facilities were considered at 107.9 percent of capacity. The rate of imprisonment was 270 per 100,000 of the national population, a substantial decline from the 390 per 100,000 in 1998.

Sources: ICPS, St. Vincent and Grenadines, Caribbean, 2001; Walmsley, WPPL, 2003.

SAMOA. The Ministry of Police, Prison, and Fire Service falls under the direction of the Police and Prisons Department. At the end of 2003 Samoa's 2 prisons held 281 prisoners, which was considered 108.1 percent of capacity, or 281 per 100,000 of the national population. The two prisons of what was formerly known as Western Samoa include a traditional prison at Tafa'igata, outside Aphia, and the Vaia'ata Prison Farm on Savai'i Island. Both facilities are considered minimum security and have adopted a vocational training regime.

Sources: Kurian, *WEPP*, 1989; ICPS, Samoa, Oceania, 2003.

SAN MICHELE HOSPICE. The utilization of cellular confinement is usually traced back to this juvenile correctional institution established in Rome in 1703. Designed by the architect Carlo Fontana, it was a rectangular structure consisting of 30 cells arranged on three tiers with balconies on each level. Each cell was equipped with a mattress, a latrine set in the wall, an outside window, and a solid door opening onto the balcony. Here young boys were tasked to manufacture products for the Vatican State. Bound to work desks from morning to evening and with leg chains, the young inmates were forbidden to communicate by talking. The inmates were chained to these desks on the ground floor of the prison, where they were expected to eat their meals, say their prayers, and view the punishments of other inmates.

San Michele inspired prison reformers to pursue a variety of reform initiatives, particularly in hygiene. Much planning went into the placement of wall latrines in the cells between two windows to allow for the free passage of air. Similar regard was placed on the importance of bathing and cleaning clothes. Another principle favored by the architect Fontana was the desirability of adequate lighting and visibility for supervision. The structure allowed guards, priests, and officers to monitor the convicts from their quarters even when off duty.

When **John Howard** visited here, he described it as the first correctional establishment for juveniles he had ever seen. At the time he visited it held 200 boys, who were reportedly well cared for and taught trades to prepare them for release. The prison's motto was clearly printed above the front door, stating, "It is of little use punishing the vicious by imprisonment unless you reclaim them—make them virtuous by discipline."

Sources: Howard, *John Howard*, 1963; Norman Johnston, *The Human Cage* (New York: Walker, 1973); Luigi Cajani, "Surveillance and Redemption: The Casa di Correzione of San Michele a Ripa in Rome," in *Institutions of Confinement*, eds. Finzche and Jutte, 1996, pp. 301–324.

SAN QUENTIN PRISON. San Quentin is located near an old Indian village of the same name, some 13 miles from San Francisco. This California institution is one of America's most storied prisons. After California joined the United States in 1850, it was just a matter of time before a state penitentiary was constructed. During the gold rush era beginning in 1849 every manner of criminal flocked to California to make his fortune. A site known as Point Quentin was purchased by the state in 1852, and by 1854 the first cells were completed with the help of inmate labor. By the time the first prison structure, known as the Stones, was opened, its 48 cells were already outnumbered by the 300 prisoners. Designed by Ruben Clark, the prison had a distinctive design that is rare in prison architecture. The upper levels of the prison allowed access to prison cells, but only by balconies located on the exterior of the building. Other additions were made as the prison became more crowded. The prison suffered from overcrowding during its early years, and its leasing of state prisoners resulted in such a high death rate that the Board of Prison Directors took full control of the prison population. The original San Quentin saw use for more than a century. Since it has always been overcrowded, San Quentin has never used the single-cell system.

Almost from its inception San Quentin earned a well-deserved reputation for brutality. According to Kenneth Lamott, its use of a dungeon remained "the shame of San Quentin for eighty years." Physical punishments were even worse, including whipping and the so-called shower bath in which a hard stream of water from a hose is sprayed in the face until "blood bursts from the eyes and ears." In 1900 the prison introduced punishment by straitjacket. Guards would often participate in beating the gagged inmate. According to one source, an inmate spent 139 hours confined in the canvas jacket as its lacing cut into his flesh.

San Quentin's cells measured only 5 feet 11 inches by 9 feet 10 inches. Although these were larger than the typical single cell, they were meant to hold four prisoners each. The cells had no windows, poor ventilation and light, and inadequate sanitation facilities. The treatment of prisoners outside their cells was even worse. Inmates were subjected to floggings and shaming punishments such as the shaving of half a prisoner's head to identify him as a behavioral problem. In 1858 a more "reform"-oriented regime was installed. In this case the new warden tried a less punitive approach by making the transition from flogging to the construction of 14 "dungeon" cells to punish recalcitrant inmates. According to historian Clare McKenna, floggings were reduced from 300 strokes per month in January and February of 1858 to zero in April. In 1873 2 new cell houses were completed, raising the capacity of the prison to 444 (although it held 915).

Prior to 1933 women as well as men were housed at San Quentin, but in the 1950s a women's facility was opened in Tehachapi. In the first decade of the 1900s prisoner classification separated inmates by offense, criminal history, and so forth. The 1930s and 1940s saw a shift toward educational and vocational training under noted warden **Clinton Duffy**. In the 1930s the prison's population peaked at 6,380 prisoners. In 1941 legislation was passed that made San Quentin the receiving prison for all male felony commitments. As a result, a classification center was built there as well.

In the 1950s the prison adopted a rehabilitation scheme based around the indeterminate sentence. The 1960s and 1970s saw a political awakening among the inmates. However, this polarized the various racial and ethnic groups, diminishing the more traditional and stable prison culture. As a result, gangs blossomed based on race. During these years the prison was at the epicenter of the Black Power movement when black inmates killed three correctional officers. Subsequent violent episodes led the prison to construct a high-security "adjustment center" inside the historic prison. By the 1960s San Quentin was the second-largest prison in the United States, holding almost 4,000 prisoners.

San Quentin, or "Q" as it is more commonly known, has held California's most violent and dangerous convicts over the years and is currently the state's only prison housing death row inmates. All state executions occur here as well. Among its current inmates are murderer Scott Peterson, Richard "Night Stalker" Ramirez, and Richard Davis, the killer of Polly Klaas. Earlier prisoners included Charles Manson until 1989, Sirhan Sirhan, the "Red Light Bandit" Caryl Chessman, and Merle Haggard, who began serving a 15-year stint at the age 19.

By the 1990s the prison was functioning as the Northern California Reception Center and also held Level II security inmates (Level IV is the highest security risk). In 2000 it held 5,967 prisoners in various classifications in a prison designed to hold 3,317. 1,500 officers and service workers staff the prison. In April 2005 a team of medical experts declared that the historic prison was too "dangerous to house new or sick inmates," describing it as overcrowded "old, antiquated, dirty, poorly staffed, poorly maintained, with inadequate medical space and equipment." Although there has been talk about closing the institution for years due to its prime waterfront location, opposition has thus far prevented it.

Sources: Lamott, *Chronicles of San Quentin: Biography of a Prison*, 1961; Clare V. McKanna Jr., "The Origins of San Quentin," *California History*, March 1987, pp.49–54; Bookspan, *A Germ of Goodness: The California State Prison System, 1851–1944*, 1991; "Experts: San Quentin Prison Conditions Bad," April 15, 2005, www.wjla.com/news/stories/0405/220727, retrieved 07/30/05.

SÃO TOME E PRINCIPE. The nation's prisons are the responsibility of the Ministry of Justice, State Reform and Public Administration. In mid-2002 this small African country had a central prison and an agricultural unit holding a total of 130 prisoners in space capable of handling 300 inmates. The prison rate is 79 per 100,000 of the national population.

Source: ICPS, São Tome e Principe, Africa, 2002.

SAUDI ARABIA. The director general of public security supervises Saudi Arabian prisons. Although the government asserts that conditions have improved since the adoption of a number of prison reforms in the 1960s, the country is frequently targeted by human rights groups for the poor treatment of prisoners. In 1983 a report by the *Middle East Economic Digest* suggested that prison rooms contain up to 200 prisoners. Although a subsistence level of food is ladled out to prisoners, reports indicate inmates are forced to scrounge it from the floor by hand. It is often necessary to receive supplemental food from family members. A typical cell forces inmates to sleep on a bare floor and provide their own blankets. Sanitation is primitive with a hole in the floor for a privy and little in the way of ventilation. There has been little evidence of any meaningful rehabilitation regime and no provisions for parole, but prisoners are often released for good behavior after serving three quarters of their sentences. Although various reports indicate conditions are not violent or intentionally degrading, **Amnesty International** has reported testimony of torture from political prisoners who have been detained in the offices of the secret police, called the Mubahathat. In 1992 alone human rights groups reported the deaths of 43 political prisoners incarcerated without formal charges. Despite its participation in the Persian Gulf War, the Saudi royal family has showed little inclination toward the modernization of the criminal justice system. According to the most recent estimates of 2000, Saudi Arabia has 30 prison facilities holding 23,720 prisoners. More than half the prisoners are foreigners and almost two thirds are either pre-trial detainees or remand prisoners. The country's rate was estimated at 110 per 100,000 of the national population in 2000.

Sources: LCCS, "Saudi Arabia: Prison Conditions, Human Rights," December 1992; ICPS, Saudi Arabia, Middle East, 2000; Walmsley, *WPPL*, 2000.

SCOTLAND (UK). When prison reformer **John Howard** visited Scotland on his survey in the 1770s, he found at least one jail dating back to the seventeenth century. He described a "bridge jail" from 1684 as a simple "vaulted room" located behind an iron door. Other earlier places of confinement included pits or dungeons in the lowest levels of some of the region's many castles. A variety of names were used to mark these dank rooms, including *spedlins, tantallon, comlongon, direleton,* and *hailes*. Access to these rooms was typically made through a hatch, which led below to a room ranging from 2.5 feet by 7.5 feet to 13 by 22 feet. Toilets were usually provided, but no thought was given to windows or natural light. The first large-scale prison based in part on the **panopticon** model was the Edinburgh **Bridewell** constructed in the mid-1790s.

Scotland's attempts to reform its prison system followed well behind the English movement. Early on, the **Pennsylvania system** was favored. Perth Prison, designed by Thomas Built, started to take shape in 1839, following the familiar **radial** design. Only a handful of prisons were built in the nineteenth century. Barlinnie Prison, built in 1882, could hold almost 1,000 prisoners. Edinburgh Prison, erected in 1920, was designed for 400 inmates; both prisons were influenced by the design of **Wormwood Scrubs,** the first prison built on the **telephone plan model**.

Currently the Scottish Prison Service, under the Ministry of the Scottish Executive, administers Scotland's prison system. As of mid-2004 Scotland's 16 prisons held 6,649 prisoners. Two of the aforementioned facilities are open prisons that are directed by the same governor. With a designated occupancy of 6,186, the prisons were just above capacity, with rate of 130 per 100,000 of the national population.

Sources: Cameron, *Prisons and Punishment in Scotland,* 1983; Johnston, *Forms of Constraint,* 2000; ICPS, Scotland, 2004.

SCREW. This slang for prison guard originated in the mid-nineteenth century. According to Robert Hendrickson, it referred to the brutal nature of early prison guards who were apt to use thumbscrews on misbehaving inmates. Other theories suggest "screw" was originally slang for key. Another source traces the term back to the punishment of the **crank**. Jailers reportedly had the authority to tighten a screw to make the turning of the crank more difficult, hence the expression being "screwed."

Sources: William and Mary Morris, *Morris Dictionary of Word and Phrase Origins*, 2nd ed. (New York: Harper & Row, 1988); Robert Hendrickson, *Encyclopedia of Word and Phrase Origins* (New York: Facts on File, 1997).

SENEGAL. By 1840 French colonial officials had opened the first prison. In 1867 prisons were built at Senegalese trading and military stations in Gorée and Saint-Louis. Confronted with a high rate of delinquency, the administration was faced with a dearth in penal housing. During the 1850s colonial administrators used Saint-Louis Prison to control common urban criminals and itinerant Africans. Throughout the colonial era Senegal possessed inadequate penal institutions and outside of the trading posts most of the native population would seldom be confronted with the phenomenon of the prison.

Slavery was abolished in the colony in 1848. Minors composed a huge part of the freed population—anywhere between 34 and 41 percent by 1881. Beginning in the late 1880s a number of penitentiary schools were established to contend with the problem of juvenile delinquency. Between 1888 and 1903 several penitentiary schools were created as private institutions. From 1916 to 1927 a similar trend created public institutions. The first penitentiary school was opened at Thiès in 1888. In 1916 the agricultural colony of Bambey welcomed more than 100 minors. Most attention was paid toward the discipline of the young prisoners. However, adult prisons continued to hold minors as well. In 1931, for example, Dakar Prison held almost fifty prisoners between the ages of twelve and seventeen.

No group suffered more in prisons than women, since penal law did not separate prisoners by gender, although French law mandated the separation of sexes in 1850. However, Senegalese authorities chose not do so. By the late 1920s separate wards were created inside prisons for women, but according to Dior Konaté, the legislation was rarely enforced. Most reports indicate that women suffered from these conditions until at least 1943. Although proposals to improve prison conditions were bandied about in 1944, there was insufficient financial support to follow through with the proposals. As a result, the physical abuse of women by guards became a regular feature of the colonial prisons. Living conditions were characterized by inadequate ventilation and medical care and by "makeshift wards" jerry-built with hay, clay, and barbed wire. During the colonial period rehabilitation and reformation were not priorities for prison officials in Senegal. The worst conditions were at the two largest prisons in Dakar and St. Louis.

Recent scholarship suggests that postcolonial regimes have done little to improve this situation. According to Dior Konaté, "Today, female quarters do not differ significantly from colonial ones." However, in 1972 penal reform efforts were directed at reducing the discrimination against female prisoners, leading officials to open a prison for women in Rufisque and hire female guards, and at offering educational opportunities for women behind bars. But this is just the beginning.

Currently the prison system is the responsibility of the Ministry of Justice. Recent figures indicate there are 38 penal facilities, with the capacity to hold 2,972 prisoners. However, as in most poor nations, the facilities are typically overcrowded. Most prisoners are confined to prisons adjacent to the more crime-prone urban centers such as Dakar. As of late 2002 there were 5,360 prisoners. The occupancy rate was at 168 percent, with a prison population rate of 54 per 100,000 of the national population.

Sources: Kurian, *WEPP*, 1989; ICPS, Senegal, Africa, 2002; Ibrahima Thioub, "Juvenile Marginality and Incarceration during the Colonial Period: The First Penitentiary Schools in Senegal, 1888–1927," pp. 79–95, and Dior Konaté, "Ultimate Exclusion: Imprisoned Women in Senegal," pp. 155–164, in *A History of Prison and Confinement in Africa*, ed. Bernault, 2003; Walmsley, *WPPL*, 2003.

SEPARATE SYSTEM. Cities as diverse as Amsterdam, Ghent, and Florence at its **Le Stinche** prison maintained the separation of prisoners by gender as early as the fifteenth century. So while **John Howard** became well known as an advocate of separation, he popularized the concept rather than invented it, which many have credited him with doing. Howard's advocacy of separation influenced the separate system developed by Philadelphia's Quakers and is based more on the philosophical precept that separation served best the rehabilitative functions of reflection and self-reformation. Despite his support for separation, Howard also recognized the dangers of protracted isolation.

Sources: Barnes, *The Evolution of Penology in Pennsylvania*, 1968; Christianson, *With Liberty for Some*, 1998.

SERBIA. The Serbian Administration of the Execution of Penitentiary Sanctions is operated under the Ministry of Justice. In late 2003 Serbia had 28 prison facilities, holding 7,487, more than 25 percent of whom were either pre-trial detainees or on remand. With an official capacity to hold 10,184 inmates, the prisons were considered well below capacity at 73.5 percent. Serbia's prisons include two maximum-security prisons at Pozarevac and Valjevo (juveniles), two closed prisons at Nis and Sremska Mitrovica, one female institution at Pozarevac, four open prisons, one closed hospital for both genders in Belgrade, and an educational-corrective institution for both genders in Krusevac. Of these facilities only four were designed for at least 1,000 inmates. The country's current prison population rate of 92 per 100,000 of the national population is lower than rates in a number of eastern and central European countries. Most information suggests that the prison system operated under the European Prison Rules and that there is an absence of overcrowding. The staff-to-prisoner ratio is 1 to 1.9; but excluding management and treatment staff, the security contingent is considered too small.

The Serbian prison system made international news in 2000 following a spate of riots in a handful of prisons involving some 3,000 inmates. Inmates issued a list of demands that included better health care, treatment, and overall conditions. Other demands, interestingly enough, included demands for higher pay for prison staff. These incidents were resolved after negotiations. However, a survey of these prisons the following year by representatives of the Council of Europe found a number of problems persisted. Serbian authorities moved quickly to improve conditions, and measures were taken to follow through on promises made in 2000. The prison system is still plagued by poorly trained personnel, little financial resources, and the overall poor condition of prison facilities.

Sources: ICPS, Serbia, Europe, 2003; Walmsley, *Further Developments in the Prisons Systems of Central and Eastern Europe*, 2003.

SEYCHELLES. The main incarceration facility is a high-security prison operated by the army on Mahé Island. According to **Amnesty International**, prisoners are often forced to labor under "excessively strenuous" conditions. The Prison Division is the responsibility of the Ministry of Social Affairs and Manpower Development. The most recent information from late 1999 indicates a prison population of 157, a rate of 207 per 100,000 of the national average.

Sources: LCCS, "Madagascar: Penal System," August 1994; ICPS, Seychelles, Africa, 1998; Walmsley, *WPPL*, 2003.

SIERRA LEONE. Sierra Leone's prison system was most influenced by the British colonial model. The nation's most prominent prison is Freetown Central Prison. The prison system operates under the Ministry of Social Welfare. Other important facilities are located in Bo, Makeni, Kabala, Kailahun, Sefadu, Mafanta, and Masanki. According to Bankole Thompson, Freetown Central Prison is the only facility that separates inmates by gender. The main emphasis of the current prison regime is the rehabilitation of prisoners through educational and vocational programs. A paucity of resources has made it next to impossible to secure modern equipment and machinery to teach the latest techniques in shoemaking, printing, carpentry, and weaving.

Most prison staff members have an education ranging from elementary school to high school. Policies have been implemented since independence that aim at recruiting high school and university graduates. Armed with the requisite education, recruits have the opportunity to move up through the hierarchy from assistant superintendent, to chief superintendent, and finally to director. The most recent information, dating back to 1989, indicates 16 prisons operating under the Ministry of Social Welfare.

Sources: Kurian, *WEPP*, 1989; Bankole Thompson, "The Criminal Justice System of Sierra Leone," in *Comparative and International Criminal Justice Systems*, ed. Ebbe, 1996, pp. 83–102.

SILENT SYSTEM. *See* AUBURN SYSTEM

SIMSBURY PRISON. According to one of the earliest chroniclers of the Simsbury Prison, this converted copper mine and its caverns became a permanent prison in Connecticut in 1773. Prisoners could expect stints at hard labor in the mines. Following the American Revolution, it became the state prison. Horrendous conditions included the chaining of inmates in badly crowded underground cages. Draconian sentencing that included 10 years for a first burglary only ensured that the prison would be overcrowded. Sometimes more than 30 men were crammed into a single cage measuring 21-feet long, 10 feet wide, and less than 7 feet high.

Source: Richard H. Phelps, *Newgate of Connecticut* (Hartford, CT: American Publishing Company, 1876).

SINGAPORE. Roughly three times the size of Washington, D.C., with a population of almost 4.5 million people, Singapore incarcerates a remarkably high number of people at a rate of 382 per 100,000. What is probably most surprising is the low crime rates that accompany this figure. This can be partly explained by the fact that prisoners in Singapore serve longer sentences compared to prisoners in most countries. In mid-2002 the prison population stood at 16,800, a figure that is 107.1 percent of the occupancy level. The prison-to-staff ratio is 8.8 prisoners per staff member.

Like Australia, Singapore was initially a destination for transportees from Britain. During British rule four prisons were constructed, including a cluster of sheds known as the First Convict Gaol in 1841; the Civil Jail (also known as Her Majesty's Gaol) at Pearl's Hill, built six years later; Her Majesty's Criminal Jail, built in 1882; and Changi Prison in 1936.

In 1872 a Commission of Inquiry into the Prisons suggested that the current prison regime had lost sight of the punitive aspect of prison life. Formerly prisoners worked on various public works projects. The conclusions of the committee led to a new regimen, which revolved strict control within the prison perimeter. Soon the cellular concept was adopted in the construction of the Civil Jail between 1879 and 1882. Later this facility would be renamed Outram Prison, before it was demolished in 1968.

As the colony grew in the twentieth century, so did its crime rate, requiring the construction of a new prison at Changi. Built to hold 568 inmates, it was constructed on a 13-acre site. Its walls measured 3,000 feet long and 24 feet high. During the Japanese occupation of World War II these prisons were used to hold prisoners-of-war. Following the war, several commissions were convened and as a result the former punitive regime was replaced with a regime that favored safe confinement, education, training, religion, and education. Soon a classification system was also adopted. In 1974 the prison system was reorganized once more, and by 1980 more reforms led to better classification and rehabilitation schemes, with a corresponding rise in professionalism.

By the end of the 1980s Singapore used six types of correctional facilities, including 2 maximum-security prisons for males, 3 medium-security prisons for males, 1 female prison, 4 day-release camps, 7 drug treatment centers, and 1 reformative training center for youths between 16 and 21 years of age. There are several prominent facilities, including the Queenstown Remand Prison, which serves as a maximum-security prison as well as a short-term facility for holding individuals awaiting trial and classification. The most secure maximum-security prison is Changi Prison, which is dedicated to those considered least likely to rehabilitate. Inside the Changi Complex political prisoners are housed in the Moon Crescent Center.

Adult prisoners, regardless of institution, are expected to serve their last six months of their sentences in day-release centers. Here they are allowed to work and visit family without supervision. Most drug abusers do go to jail, unlike those convicted of selling drugs. Singapore's Central Narcotics Bureau operates at least six drug rehabilitation centers and one dedicated to anti-inhalant abuse. Individuals testing positive for drugs can be sentenced to up to six months in one of these centers.

The current prison system has 14 prisons and drug treatment centers and has recently made the transition from a paperwork-based system to one that is based on information technology (IT). The IT system reportedly tags each prisoner on admittance, scanning the tag each time the prisoner is admitted, discharged, or transferred and allowing correctional officers to closely monitor their charges inside the prison. The new IT system has improved the efficiency in collecting statistical data.

Typically first-time offenders convicted of minor crimes are allowed to serve their sentences at home, where they are required to wear an electronic device on their ankle to track the movements of the offender. Most reports indicate that this is very economical, since direct supervision is not required in an institutional setting. It also serves the rehabilitative purpose of allowing offenders to continue relationships and employment.

In recent years rehabilitation has become the focus of authorities because of a high recidivism rate. According to reports, three out of four offenders return to crime within five years of release. In response, correctional reformers have suggested selectively erasing the prison records of offenders who were well behaved in prison and were serving time for minor offenses. Rehabilitation efforts have included inmate training in computers and industrial and financial endeavors.

The high-profile case involving American teenager Michael Fay drew international attention to Singapore's use of caning as punishment. The practice originated under the British colonial rulers in the nineteenth century and is now mandatory punishment in some cases, with a legal maximum of twenty-four strokes. Those subjected to this punishment are males between 16 and 50. It is typically administered in conjunction with another penalty, such as imprisonment.

Today the Singapore Prison Service operates fifteen facilities under the direction of the Ministry of Home Affairs. Institutions include four maximum-security, nine medium-security, one low-medium-security, and one minimum-security prison.

Sources: LCCS, Singapore: "Prisons and Rehabilitation Centers," 1990; ICPS, Singapore, Asia, 2004; Singapore Prison Department, www.mha.gov.sg/sps/penahist.html#the, pp. 1–9.

SING SING PRISON. One of America's most fabled prisons, Sing Sing was built on 170-foot cliffs overlooking the Hudson River, some 33 miles from New York City. It was New York's second state prison and as of 2000 it was the second-largest prison in the state after **Clinton Prison** at Dannemora. By most accounts, Sing Sing was named for the indigenous Sint Sinck Indians that once lived in the area. During its 180-year history it has been referred to as Swing Swing for a prison sex scandal in 1988 and as the more appropriate "Bastille on the Hudson." According to Ted Conover, Sing Sing has also introduced such phrases as "the big house" and being sent "up the river" to the lexicon of prison culture.

Sing Sing was built to replace New York City's **Newgate Prison** and to relieve overcrowding at **Auburn Prison**. A 130-acre spot near the town of Mount Pleasant (today it is Ossining) was selected for New York's second state prison because of its proximity to rock quarries for building materials. The community decided to change the name of the community from Sing Sing to Ossining in an attempt to distance the town from the notorious prison. Notorious Auburn warden **Elam Lynds** selected 100 inmates from his prison to construct the new institution. During the construction project prisoners were lodged in nearby fields. Modeled after Auburn Prison, it received its first inmates in 1825. The following year all old Newgate's inmates had been transferred to Sing Sing, or Mount Pleasant, as it was first known. Elam Lynds was selected as its first warden. He would hold this position until 1834, when he was forced to resign. However, under subsequent wardens, Sing Sing gained a reputation for laxity. As a result, Lynds was brought back in 1844 to reintroduce his no-nonsense regime using the lash, straitjackets, and bread-and-water diets. From the start cells were poorly ventilated and damp, despite efforts to the contrary, and for prisoners to speak with each other was relatively easy. In 1828 the entire main building was completed. Almost exactly a century later a building was erected housing a kitchen, a hospital, and a chapel. Although a wall surrounds Sing Sing Prison today, initially the facility was one of the first prisons built without one marking the periphery.

When the **Mount Pleasant Female Prison** opened at Sing Sing in 1839, it was considered the country's first prison specifically for women. In 1877 all women were transferred from Sing Sing and scattered in New York's county facilities.

By the end of the nineteenth century Sing Sing had earned a reputation for brutality and conflict and witnessed a number scandals involving escapes, overcrowding, and various torture techniques. Sing Sing gained further notoriety as the state's death house between 1914 and 1963.

A reform campaign began in the late nineteenth century thanks to the New York Prison Association. In the early 1900s the prison started its own newspaper, the *Star of Hope*, and in 1914 warden **Thomas Mott Osborne** introduced his famous **Mutual Welfare League** experiment. In the 1920s and 1930 warden **Lewis E. Lawes** played an important role in introducing a more reform-oriented regime.

In mid-1994 Sing Sing held more than 1,700 inmates, but with a capacity to hold more than 2,000. Sing Sing is currently classified as a maximum-security institution for men 21 years or older. Within the prison grounds is a medium-security facility called Tappan, a detention center for men 16 years or older, and several health-related units. During the 1930s Warner Brothers filmed several crime films at the prison. To show its appreciation, the movie company built a large gym for prisoners that is still in use today. Ted Conover, who worked as a guard for a short time at Sing Sing, noted that the prison was "unusual for a large max [prison] in that it [had] few vocational or other programs for inmates."

Sources: McKelvey, *American Prisons*, 1977; Christianson, *With Liberty for Some*, 1995; Conover, *Newjack: Guarding Sing Sing*, 2000.

SIZO. SIZO is the Russian acronym for pre-trial institutions, *Sledstvennie Izolatoris*. These institutions are regarded as "investigation isolation units." At last count **Russia** operated 184 of these institutions containing 114,800 inmates, an average of 624 per facility. Among the better-known institutions are Moscow's **Butyrka Prison** and St. Petersburg's Kresty Prison, each capable of holding more than 2,000 prisoners.

Source: Walmsley, *Further Developments in the Prison Systems of Central and Eastern Europe*, 2003.

SLOVAKIA. Slovakia became a separate state in 1993. Its oldest prisons can be traced back to the seventeenth century. Leopoldov originated as fortress before being transformed to a prison in 1855. Ilava was reconstructed from a former monastery during the heyday of the Austro-Hungarian Empire. Between 1865 and 1952 the General Directorate of the Corps of Prison and Court Guard, under the Ministry of Justice, controlled Slovakia's prison system. The same organizational structure exists today. In 2002 the country had 18 institutions capable of holding 9,500. Of these, five were devoted to pre-trial detainees, nine for sentenced prisoners, and four for a combination of sentenced prisoners and pre-trial detainees.

In 2004 the prison system was considered at 93.6 percent of capacity with 8,891 prisons. Almost one third of the prisons were either remand prisoners or pre-trial detainees. These figures represent a significant increase in the prison population. In 2004 the ratio was 165 per 100,000 of the national population. Between 1992 and 2001, numbers ranged from 119 per 100,000 (1992) to 138 per 100,000 in 1995 and 1998. One explanation for the rise and fall of the prison population is the utilization of periodic amnesties to relieve overcrowding or to win votes. For example, President Vaclav Havel issued an amnesty in 1990 that reduced the population to 3,500. But within four years it had almost doubled. In 2001 Slovakia's prison system had the lowest occupancy levels in central and eastern Europe.

Slovakia's largest prisons hold between 600 and 900 prisoners each. These include, in descending order, Banskà Bystrica-Kralova, Hrnciarovce nad Parnou, Leopoldov, Bratislava, Kosice, Kosica-Saca, and Zeliezovce. The most serious offenders are housed at Ilava Prison, Leopoldov, or Ruzomberok.

The most pressing problems include low morale and salaries of prison staff, lack of budgetary resources, inadequate security surveillance, and the lengthening of pretrial detention leading to overcrowding. However, according to Roy Walmsley, "there is a positive atmosphere in the Slovak prison system" as great strides are taken to conform to European Prison Rules.

Sources: Walmsley, *Further Developments in the Prison Systems of Central and Eastern Europe*, 2003; ICPS, Slovakia, Europe, 2004.

SLOVENIA. Slovenia's National Prison Administration, formally created in 1995, operates under the Ministry of Justice. In 2004 the country maintained 13 prisons, including 6 prisons with facilities in 13 different locations, as well as a center for juveniles. Only one of these institutions has been built since World War II. Three prisons are housed in old monasteries, one is in a castle, and two use structures from the nineteenth century. As of mid-2004 the prison population was at 1,170, or 59 per 100,000 of the national population, and an occupancy level of 106.1 percent. Over the past four years these figures have been rather stable.

Slovenia's prison rates are considered similar to **Croatia**'s, but less than those of its western and northern neighbors of Italy, Austria, and Hungary. According to the Council of Europe, Slovenia's low rates can be explained by "the high cultural homogeneity" and dearth of "real metropolitan settlements." Following in the tradition of other central and eastern European countries, single-cell confinement is a rarity. The largest prison, and as of 2000 the only one built since the 1940s, is Dob, built in 1963. A new prison was reportedly under construction in Koper in 2000. While most prisoners are confined in rooms holding up to eight prisoners, one prison reportedly held fourteen in a room measuring 60 meters square, in violation of European Prison Rules. The main barriers to prison reform include overcrowding, staff shortages, and lack of financial support. But these are overshadowed by more bright spots, including the allowance of more visits, more opportunity for home leave, a better educational environment, a 25 percent increase in female staff, and better recruitment of personnel.

Regional prisons holding inmates whose sentences are less than 18 months are located at Koper, Nova Gorica, Ljubljana, Radovljica, Novo Mesto, Ig, Maribor, Murska Sobota, and Rogoza. Central prisons for longer sentences are located at Dob, Ig, and Celje, whereas juveniles of both genders are housed at Radece.

Sources: Walmsley, *Further Developments in the Prison Systems of Central and Eastern Europe*, 2003; ICPS, Slovenia, Europe, 2004.

SLUZEWIEC PRISON. Sluzewiec Prison in Poland was initially constructed to hold prisoners-of-war used to clear the rubble of the once thriving city of Warsaw after World War II. It was designed to be a temporary facility with eight narrow barracks and no sewer system. Rather than being torn down as originally planned, in 1951 the barracks were separated from each other by internal walls and tall wire fences. Surrounded by a high wall, an administration building was constructed on the other side. The facility soon held 1,540 prisoners rather than the several dozen it had been planned for. Sometimes the population exceeded 2,000. Each small cell contained three double-decker beds, with extra inmates sleeping on straw mattresses on the floor. Although there was no internal factory, the prisoners spent most of their time at labor, with a number of businesses employing prisoners springing up in the prison neighborhood. By the 1980s the facility was referred to as a Penal Labor Center for First Offenders, in other words, a minimum-security prison housing nonrecidivists serving up to six years. By the end of the 1980s it contained prisoners serving sentences not to exceed two years. Inmates wear prison clothes stamped with the institution's insignia. In winter they are allowed to wear their own clothes.

Source: Monika Platek, "The Sluzewiec Prison in Warsaw, Poland," in *The State of the Prisons—200 Years On*, ed. Dick Whitfield, 1991; pp. 56–68.

SOLITARY SYSTEM. See SEPARATE SYSTEM

SOLOMON ISLANDS. The Solomon Prison Service administers a prison system that in 1999 held 134 prisoners, mostly in the main prison of Rove in Honiara. There are also three other prisons, or district prisons, which are located at the various police headquarters. In late 1989 two thirds of the prisoners were serving sentences less than three months. Based upon its 1999 population its prisoner ratio was 31 per 100,000 of the national population, substantially less than its 1992 rate of 85 per 100,000, but higher than its 1998 level of 26 per 100,000.

Sources: Kurian, *WEPP*, 1989; ICPS, Solomon Islands, Oceania, 1999; Walmsley, *WPPL*, 2003.

SOLZHENITSYN, ALEXANDER ISAYEVICH (b. 1918). This Soviet dissident was probably the world's most famous prisoner of the twentieth century, although he received his renown following release. Born in Kislovodsk, Russia, he fought against the Germans in World War II, but was arrested for criticizing dictator Joseph Stalin in letters to his brother-in-law in 1945. For this he was imprisoned in a white-collar prison labor camp, or *sharashka,* between 1945 and 1952. He chronicled this experience in his book *The First Circle,* published in 1968. Solzhenitsyn would later serve stints in hard labor camps in the Soviet **Gulag.** He brought this system to world attention with his novel *One Day in the Life of Ivan Denisovich* in 1962 and then with the historical work *The Gulag Archipelago* in three volumes published between 1973 and 1978.

In 1970 he was awarded the Nobel Prize in literature. Four years later he was exiled from his beloved country when the KGB discovered the manuscript for the first volume of *Gulag.* He initially took refuge in Zurich, Switzerland, but moved to the United States, where he settled in Vermont. Following the breakup of the Soviet Union, he had his citizenship restored in 1990, and in 1994 he was repatriated. Despite his reputation as a "liberal" or "radical," he has been derided by some for his blaming Jews, Latvians, Georgians, and other minorities for Russia's troubles in the twentieth century. Besides his well-known prison writings, he published a number of other books, including several plays, political essays, and works on World War I, most prominently his historical novel focusing on the 1914 Battle of Tannenberg entitled *August 1914* (1971).

Source: Thomas, *Alexander Solzhenitsyn,* 1998.

SOMALIA. Prior to 1960 most of Somalia's prisons were relics of the former British and Italian colonial administrations. What facilities existed following independence in 1962 were in terrible condition. The Somali Penal Code of 1962 included an article to reorganize the prison system. This code legislated that all prisoners regardless of age must work on labor projects ranging from prison farms, to construction projects, to road building. In return prisoners would be paid a small salary that could be either saved until release or used in the prison canteens. According to the new legislation juveniles were legally separated from adults. Over the next decade the prison system would grow to include 49 institutions, with the most prominent and best equipped the Central Prison of Mogadishu. Other prominent prisons are located in Hargeisa, Somaliland, in the northwest; Bosasso, Puntland, in the northeast; and Hareryale and Shirloe prisons in the capital city of Mogadishu. In the 1970s East Germany lent a hand in building four modern prisons. But as turmoil increased in subsequent years, particularly opposition to the Siad Barre administration of the late 1970s and early 1980s, existing prisons became so overcrowded that schools, police headquarters, military buildings, and even a section of the presidential palace were transformed into temporary jails. Despite the fall of Siad Barre in 1991, human rights groups continue to target the faltering prisons.

Sources: LCCS, "Somalia: Prison System and Penal System," 1992; ICPS, Somalia, Africa, 2004.

SOUTH AFRICA. The South African prison system was created in the nineteenth century during the expansion of British colonial rule. The development of the prison system in South Africa diverged from other African countries on a number of levels. Although it was influenced by developments in Europe and the Americas, the

Cape Colony was recognized for aiming incarceration more toward offenders of the pass laws than common criminals; thus the development of the prison system has been closely connected to the progressive institutionalization of racial discrimination in the country. During the late nineteenth century settlers' communities in South Africa developed pass laws to control the movement of native Africans and regulate the labor force. Those sentenced to prison often ended up as convict labor for diamond- and gold-mining countries. Between 1916 and the end of apartheid in 1986 more than 17 million blacks were imprisoned for violating pass laws.

In 1911 a consolidated Prisons and Reformatories Act was passed. It stayed in effect until the 1959 Prisons Act, which has undergone several revisions over the past four decades but still remains the basis of South African prison law. The increasing militarization of the South African state began to trickle down to prison officers, who wore uniforms and were assigned ranks. At the same time the prison staff was becoming increasingly militarized, new prohibitions against the media and outside inspections were implemented. The major new prison legislation introduced in 1959 was based on apartheid policy. As a result, the prison became racially segregated. Segregation did not just mean black and white but was also applied to African ethnic groups.

During the 1960s South African jails became home to a growing number of political prisoners leading to charges of human rights abuses by international organizations. With the introduction of a state of emergency in 1985, a large number of anti-apartheid activists were arrested and strict controls were placed on journalists and human rights monitors. The end of the state of emergency, along with the release of Nelson Mandela and other political prisoners from **Robben Island** in 1990, has been followed with a number of democratic reforms. That same year apartheid was abolished in the prison system. In addition, the Prisons Service was disconnected from the Department of Justice and renamed the Department of Correctional Services. Some less punitive sentences were also introduced, including "correctional supervision," a method of reducing an individual's prison sentence. A number of restrictions hampering prison inspectors were also abolished.

Following the release of Mandela and the legitimizing of the African National Congress in the early 1990s, the South African prison system was reorganized and restructured. One of the first steps was changing the name of the Department of Prisons to the Department of Correctional Services. A number of amendments to the Prison Act of 1959 were enacted, including the abolition of apartheid in the prison system. As overcrowding became a problem, a provision was made in 1991 to release on amnesty 57,000 prisoners.

By the mid-1990s the South African Department of Correctional Services operated 234 prisons, including 226 men's prisons; 119 of these had separate wings for women. These units are supplemented by 20 prison farms. Of the nation's 114,000 prisoners in 1995, 22,000 had not yet been sentenced. In 2003 the South African prison administration reported 231 prison facilities holding 180,952 prisoners, a rate of 402 per 100,000 of the national population, up from 280 in 1996.

Sources: E. Rhoodie, *Penal Systems of the Commonwealth: A Criminological Survey against the Background of the Cornerstones for a Progressive Correctional Policy* (Cape Town: Academia, 1967); Dirk Van Zyl Smit, *South African Prison Law and Practice* (Durban: Butterworths, 1992); LCCS, "South Africa: Prison System," May 1996; ICPS, South Africa, 2003.

SOUTH KOREA. *See* KOREA, REPUBLIC OF SOUTH

SOUTH OSSETIA. In 1992, following ethnic clashes in **Georgia**, this region was granted semi-autonomy. At last count there was one penal facility with a staff of eighteen located in the capital of Tskhinvali. As of 2001 the facility held 87 prisoners, which suggests an inadequate staff-to-prisoner ratio. Given these figures, if accurate, the prison rate would be 88 per 100,000 of the national population.

Source: Walmsley, *Further Developments in the Prison Systems of Central and Eastern Europe*, 2003.

SOVIET LABOR CAMPS. *See* GULAGS

SPAIN. Before the advent of the penitentiary, members of the Spanish royalty maintained their own private detention prisons. According to at least one source, Spain did not operate any underground dungeons in the Middle Ages, unlike her continental counterparts. Women were housed in monasteries. The first Spanish leader to express interest in the process of incarceration was King Alfonso XI, who in 1329 came out in favor of the humane treatment of prisoners by their keepers. This included providing clean water for drinking and bathing. However, the tradition of charging prisoners for their accommodations persisted. In order to support the most destitute prisoners poor boxes were passed throughout the countryside to solicit funds for their subsistence. Cells were not segregated by gender until 1519 or by age until 1785.

Throughout the sixteenth century condemned prisoners were sentenced to **galleys,** as was the case in most western European countries. In the middle of the 1700s prisoners were sentenced to work in the mines at Almaden, which led to the establishment of mine-prisons, or *presidios mineros.* Another outgrowth of this development were military prisons built in Oran and Ceuta.

During the eighteenth century the **house of correction** movement had taken root in Spain. Vagrants and transient types were confined in such institutions as the San Fernando House of Correction, or *Casa de Correccion de San Fernando*, built on the **panopticon** model on the outskirts of Madrid. Houses of correction were distinguished from their more punitive counterparts by the separation of the sexes, better sanitation and provisions, and more concern for the sick.

The publication of works by **John Howard** and **Rouchefoucald-Liancourt** at the end of the eighteenth century inspired the creation of Spain's first prisoners' aid society in 1799. According to Norman Johnston, "Penal progress came to Spain relatively late." A number of innovations went unheeded into the nineteenth century as a consequence of political instability.

In the 1820s legislation provided for the labor of inmates on public works projects, but any outside work necessitated that each convict be chained in pairs. A new penal system was inaugurated under the Minister of Patronage beginning in 1834. Prisons fit under three classifications, including *depositos correccionales* for prisoners serving up to two years, *presidios peninsulares* for those serving two to eight years, and *presidios de Africa,* for sentences of more than eight years. Other features of the new system included separation of prisoners less than 18 years of age from older inmates, obligatory labor, military discipline, and the continuous association of prisoners day or night. To sort things out among the prisoners trusties were selected from their ranks.

Several Spanish penologists toured American and European prisons in the nineteenth century. Ramon de la Sagra is credited with founding, on his return to Spain, a society to improve conditions for juveniles and women, and in 1843 he published an atlas showing the main prisons of Europe. Colonel Manuel Montesinos has been credited with introducing the indeterminate philosophy in Spain several years before **Alexander Maconochie**'s achievements in **Australia**. Montesinos has probably not received his due because a lack of support led to the collapse of his system in the 1840s. But as director of the Valencia Prison and later inspector of the General Spanish Prison, he was inspired by **Walter Crofton**'s celebrated **Irish system** to introduce a system that allowed prisoners to earn credits toward reducing their prison terms by half.

Several revisions of the penal code took place in the 1820s and 1830s. In 1834 the prison administration was centralized. The following year Ramon de la Sagra was appointed to visit American and European prisons. In the mid-1840s he led the creation of a prison society and published his *Atlas Carcelario*, which heralded a number of prison models by French and Spanish architects. It appears that de la Sagra favored circular and radial designs; nonetheless political infighting and a lack of budget barred any new construction until the late 1850s. In 1861 a radial prison was completed in Vitoria. Provincial prisons were built in Bilbao (1873), Almeria (1883), Lugo (1887), Albacete (1887), Lérida (1889), San Sebastián (1889), Alicante (1900), Palencia (1900), and Pamplona in 1908. One of the largest prisons built in this era was the five-tiered Madrid Prison, which provided 1,059 cells on five wings.

Jeremy Bentham's **Panopticon** inspired a number of prison plans in the nineteenth century, but no exact replicas were constructed. Closest to the plan was the half-circular Mataro Prison outside Barcelona (1852). Other offshoots of the Panopticon were erected in Maresa in 1859 and Sabadell in 1898. Three more semicircular prisons would be built in the first half of the twentieth century. Spain's Valladolid Prison rose to prominence for its reform regime by 1850. Johnston suggests that it came the closest to replicating the **Ghent Maison de Force**.

Regardless of their sentences, most inmates were allowed to associate in congregate settings at some time during the day. However, communication between Spanish penologists and prison reformer **Enoch Wines** in 1879 suggests "Spain's penal legislation showed a progress far in advance of her penal practice." The Spanish penal system offered a wide variety of sentences, many remarkably punitive. Convicts were sentenced at hard labor for life in the convict prisons of Africa, the Canary Islands, and OutreMer. During their lifetime of servitude they wore a foot-long chain, which extended from a girdle. A variety of other methods of penal servitude were sanctioned at descending levels of sentencing, with the least punitive allowing prisoners to earn money in preparation for release.

Even excluding the terrible conditions of the convict prisons, prison buildings in Spain itself were not much better, with inmates remaining mostly idle in their poorly ventilated dormitories. On top of this was a trustee system that allowed prisoners called *caporaux a verge*, or "sergeants of the birch," to mete out corporal punishment to maintain order. According to one claim, the only reason that recidivism was low was because the police were so inadequate.

According to a survey of world prison systems in 1894, Spain used every possible edifice to house prisoners, so many that although there were 456 correctional institutions, only 166 were actually habitable for this purpose, with most rapidly deteriorating because of age. Spain's most famous destination for transportation was the Ceuta prison colony on the coast of Africa. The citadel prison of Hacho and the "Field Prison" of Presidio del Campo were considered among the most wretched prisons of 1890s Spain.

Under the dictatorship of Francisco Franco little in the way of reliable information was made public. According to official records, there were 12,574 prisoners languishing in Spanish prisons in 1933. However, by the time Franco rose to power in 1939 the number had risen to 100,000. In the following year the prison population more than doubled through the influx of political prisoners and other "enemies of the state." In the 1940s Spain increased the number of penitentiaries from 12 to 27. Following the Spanish Civil War, the Franco regime emphasized that all prisoners should be constructively employed. Several prisons were destroyed during the civil war, including the five-tiered Madrid Prison. Prior to 1950 the radial scheme with the central rotunda was the preferred prison design.

By 1987 Spain's prison population consisted of 17,643 prisoners, 1,486 of whom were women. Almost 9,000 others were being held while awaiting trial. In addition, 7,200 prisoners were ensconced in various other correctional institutions and halfway houses. Persistent complaints have been aimed at overcrowding and poor medical attention. In the late 1970s a series of violent riots brought the delays in sentencing and overcrowding into public focus. During the Franco years, sporadic amnesties, reduced the prison populations. However, the new constitution of 1978 ended these amnesties, leading to a prison construction campaign. By 1984 over one third of all the prisons had been built since 1978. In addition, a number of others had been renovated and updated. By 1987 the country's 47 prisons were mostly located in metropolitan areas, with the largest located in Barcelona and Madrid, each having more than 2,000 inmates.

The General Directorate of Prison Administration is operated under the Ministry of the Interior. As of 2004 Spain held 59,604 prisoners in 77 facilities, a prison population rate of 145 per 100,000 of the national population. More than 25 percent of inmates were foreigners. The official prison occupancy rate was over capacity at 114.1 percent in 2003.

Sources: Arthur Griffiths, *The World's Famous Prisons* (London: Grolier Press, 1908); Klaus Dohrn, "Franco's Prisons," *The Commonweal*, December 31, 1943, pp. 274–276; DeFord, *Stone Walls*, 1962; LCCS, "Spain: Criminal Justice and the Penal System," December 1988; Johnston, *Forms of Constraint*, 2000; ICPS, Spain, 2004.

SPANDAU PRISON. Built in western Berlin by the Allies specifically to house Nazi war criminals sentenced to life in prison at the Nuremberg Trials, Spandau Prison was operated by the four Allied victors of World War II. Spandau was one of only two four-power organizations to exist during the Cold War. The other example was the Berlin Air Safety Center, unrelated to prisons. Each of the four occupying powers of Berlin took alternate control of the prison on a monthly basis. In order to figure out which nation was in control, one needed only look at the position of the flags atop the prison. The flag farthest to the left had control for the month.

At its peak the facility held seven prisoners, including Rudolf Hess, Erich Raeder, Walther Funk, Albert Speer, Baldur von Schirach, Konstantin von Neurath, and Karl Doenitz. The prison was named after the historic Spandau Citadel fortress, which was built nearby. Spandau was demolished in 1987 after the death of Hess in order to preclude its becoming a neo-Nazi monument. The demolished materials were then ground up into powder and unceremoniously deposited in the North Sea. Hess had been its only prisoner during its last eleven years.

Source: Asinah.NET Encyclopedia.

SPINHOUSES. According to Lucia Zedner, the spinhouse or *spinhaus*, opened in Amsterdam in 1645 as the "first prison built for women." In this facility female prisoners spun wool for the Dutch textile industry. This regimen was intended to teach "wayward" women appropriate domestic skills that could be of use for employment once they were back on the streets. Initially it only held poor inmates but over time cells held females that would not heed husbands or parents. Zedner suggests that the spinhouse "remained virtually unique" for its order and gender segregation. Other European countries followed the Dutch model by keeping female prisoners employed in constructive labor such as spinning and sewing, while others sometimes worked in prison services, such as cooking and cleaning. Norman Johnston described the first spinhouse as a "rectangular range of buildings" surrounding an "inner court with covered walkways."

Sources: Lucia Zedner, "Wayward Sisters: The Prison for Women," in *Oxford History of the Prison*, eds. Morris and Rothman, 1998, pp. 295–324; Johnston, *Forms of Constraint*, 2000.

SRI LANKA. By the 1920s Ceylon, the future Sri Lanka, was still an English colony. Its prisons had more in common with **India**'s prisons than the fortresslike institutions that predominated in Great Britain and the United States. Descriptions of these prisons offer a portrait of simple white buildings surrounded by colorful gardens and offering open-air workshops that allowed prisoners to work without enforced silence or much actual confinement. By the late 1920s the prisons were all under the jurisdiction of the Inspector General of Prisons. The only system of prisoner classification was based on length of sentence rather than crimes committed. During this earlier era of prison reform the classification depot was located at the Welikada Prison at Colombo. This also served as a detention facility for short-term offenders. Others incarcerated here were all male first offenders serving séances over two years, all juveniles under twenty-three for first offenses, and all female prisoners serving longer sentences. Other important prisons included Bogambara Prison at Kandy, Mahara, Jaffna, Nagombo, and Anuradhapura.

In 1924 authorities instituted an overhaul of the system. A progressive system of prison industries was introduced based on **state-use** philosophy, predicated on economic production and prisoner rehabilitation. First offenders and special offenders were permitted to earn small wages, and education and medical service standards were considered more than satisfactory. For all prisoners under the age of twenty-four, education was compulsory.

Members of the correctional staff receive training at Colombo's Centre for Research and Training in Corrections, established in 1975. New recruits typically follow a 10-week course of study focusing on such topics as law, human relations, unarmed combat, first aid, and firearms training.

Sri Lanka's prison population was relatively consistent between 1977 and 1985, with an average total of 11,500 new inmates each year. Of those incarcerated in 1985, 75 percent were for minor offenses, with 62 percent serving sentences of less than 6 months. During this period convicted offenders between the ages of 16 and 22 were incarcerated in separate penal institutions and work camps. Since female prisoners represented such a small portion of the overall population, no separate facilities were established for women. As an alternative arrangement each major prison set aside a small women's section replete with female staff officers. Females serving longer than six weeks are housed at Welikade Prison in Colombo. By the end of the 1980s all prisoners serving longer than 6 months were offered vocational training in 22 different trades. All convicted offenders were required to work eight-hour days and were remunerated with wages commensurate with their expertise. In addition to the traditional correctional system, Sri Lanka operates a number of detention camps for individuals arrested under the Prevention of Terrorism Act. Since the escalation of violence involving Tamil terrorists a number of these camps have come under fire for human rights abuses in recent years.

Currently Sri Lanka's Department of Prisons operates under the Ministry of Justice. In mid-2003 the country had 62 institutions, including 3 closed prison, 16 remand prisons, 6 work camps, 2 open prison camps, 1 work release center, 1 juvenile training school, 2 correctional centers for minors, 2 rehabilitation centers for drug addicts, 1 center for correctional research and training, and 28 prison lockups. Its prison population of 19,974 is considered 189.9 percent of capacity. The prison rate is 105 per 100,000 of the national population.

Sources: Gillin, *Taming the Criminal*, 1931; LCCS, "Sri Lanka: Penal Institutions and Trends in Prison Population," October 1988; Kurian *WEPP*, 1989; ICPS, Sri Lanka, Asia, 2003.

STATE OF THE PRISONS IN ENGLAND AND WALES.

John Howard's most famous work, originally entitled *The State of the Prisons in England and Wales; with Preliminary Observations; and an Account of some Foreign Prisons*, was published in March 1777. According to Howard's biographer, its "few literary merits" are attributable to the proofreading by a physician friend named Dr. Aiken. Howard was insistent that the book be published at a low price in order to gain a wider readership.

This book documenting the low state of English (and other European) prisons is divided into three parts. The first part focuses on the main scourges of prisons, including poor food and water, the extortionate fee system, inadequate sanitation, lack of medical care, and the confinement of prisoners together without distinction of gender, offense, and age. The second part of the book summarizes what he calls the "bad customs in prisons," such as the tolerance for gambling and the prisoners' claim to "garnish" from new prisoners. Howard also criticizes overcrowding and private prisons. This section ends with an estimate of the population of prisons in England and Wales. He estimated that in spring 1776, of the 4,084 prisoners then incarcerated, 2,437 were jailed for debt. Penologists and historians regard the third section as the most important part of the book. Entitled "Proposed Improvements in the Structure and Management of Prisons," this section included a number of proposed reforms, among them better prison construction and separate cells, the separation of debtors from felons, workshops for prisoners to help them earn money to support their families, hospitals for each prison, and bathing facilities. It would take another century, but by the end of the nineteenth century the majority of Howard's proposals would be adopted.

Sources: Howard, *John Howard*, 1963; Freeman, ed., *Prisons Past and Future*, 1978.

STATE USE SYSTEM. According to historian Larry E. Sullivan, as early as the 1820s "Most prisons on the **Auburn** model were nothing more than factories that used the lower classes as enforced labor." Later in the century, states still controlled the labor of prisoners as well as profits from sales to outside businesses. Entrepreneurs had long protested the unfair competition of prison-produced goods on the free market. A growing labor movement beginning in the late 1890s pressured the government to prohibit the unfair prison competition on the free market. The states of New Jersey, Pennsylvania, and New York were the first to prohibit the sale of these goods to the public.

In 1887 the federal government stepped in by prohibiting the leasing of inmates. Other federal laws followed. The passage of the Hawes-Cooper Act in 1929 banned the shipping of prison-made goods outside state borders. Six years later the Ashurst-Sumner Act of 1935 prohibited shipping companies from bringing prison-manufactured items into any state in which this violated state law. By the end of the 1930s all states had passed various laws preventing the sale of prison goods on the free market. Prisons that had long depended on various contracting and leasing systems soon found themselves facing huge budget deficits. On the other hand, prisoners once integral cogs in the production of prison goods, soon found themselves languishing with little constructive labor to pass the time. Prisoner idleness soon became a plague for the prison systems, leading to increasing tensions, violence, and escape planning.

Finally a compromise was reached in the early 1940s, which permitted the manufacture and sale of prison goods as long as it was only for the consumption of state agencies. As early as the 1920s several states had already restricted prison labor to state use. The state-use system typically produced furniture, stationary, and publications that did not compete with existing free manufacturers. Despite the compromise, prisoners learned few marketable skills or trades in preparation for outside employment. Other types of prison employment that fell under the purview of state use included building and maintaining public highways.

Sources: Sullivan, *The Prison Reform Movement*, 1990; Roberts, *Reform and Retribution*, 1997.

STATEVILLE PRISON. The Illinois State Penitentiary, near Joliet, better known as Stateville, is one of America's most studied prisons. The prison was built with prison labor between 1916 and 1924. Prison architectural historian Norman Johnston suggests it is "perhaps the most unusual United States prison from an architectural standpoint." Designed by the W. Carbys Zimmerman architectural firm, the prison's most distinct features are its four **panopticon** cell houses surrounding a circular mess hall. These were the only panopticon cell houses built in the United States. Only one remains today. Less known are the underground corridors linking the four units with each other so that in an emergency guards can respond unimpeded by inmates

In later years a large rectangular **Auburn**-style wing was added. Although the original plan called for eight circular cell houses clustered around a central dining hall, a riot broke out in the early 1920s soon after the completion of the first three. Almost immediately the security limitations of such construction was apparent. While the panopticon design was developed for guards to observe inmates at all times, it is often forgotten that the reverse is true as well, allowing prisoners to monitor the movements of the prison staff. Modifications made on the fourth panopticon cell house ameliorated a number security concerns. In any case, by the end of the 1920s this mammoth prison held up to 3,250, two to a cell.

Stateville officially opened in March 1925. It initially was composed of the four panopticons, or "roundhouses," each connected by a corridor leading to a central hub housing the dining hall. In the 1970s three of the roundhouses were demolished and an extensive renovation of the prison took place. Of all the research conducted at Stateville, none has surpassed James B. Jacobs's seminal 1977 study, *Stateville: The Penitentiary in Mass Society*. As the prison enters the twenty-first century, it contends with problems endemic to most modern prisons—gangs, overcrowding, staff training, and employee salaries. *See also* **RAGEN, JOSEPH EDWARD**

Sources: Jacobs, *Stateville,* 1977; McKelvey, *American Prisons*, 1977; Johnston, *Forms of Constraint*, 2000.

STROUD, ROBERT FRANKLIN (1887/1890–1963). Best known as the "Birdman of Alcatraz," Stroud was one of America's most famous prisoners, and contrary to popular conceptions he never tended birds at Alcatraz. Stroud entered the American prison system after killing a man in Alaska at the age of 18. He was sentenced to 12 years in the federal prison at McNeil Island. He was then transferred to **Leavenworth Prison**, where he killed a guard and earned a death sentence. President Woodrow Wilson eventually commuted his sentence to life imprisonment. Stroud would ultimately spend 54 years in prison, mostly in solitary confinement. During his years in isolation at Leavenworth Prison, Stroud earned his moniker "birdman" when he taught himself how to care for and breed small birds. He eventually became a respected authority on birds after the publication of his *Diseases of Canaries* (1933) and *Digest on the Diseases of Birds* (1943).

Within less than 15 minutes in 1942 Stroud was transferred to Alcatraz. He was prohibited from taking any of his birds, books, or experimental equipment with him to the Rock. Under the new regime of warden **James A. Johnston**, Stroud was permitted to communicate with his publisher and conduct research on the history of the federal prison system. When Johnston was replaced with a new warden in 1948, Stroud's perks were ended and he languished in solitary confinement.

No event was more crucial to his rise to prominence and folk hero status as the publication of Thomas Gaddis's 1962 book *The Birdman of Alcatraz*, which almost single-handedly perpetuated the myths of the "Birdman of Alcatraz." The subsequent release of the film by the same name starring Burt Lancaster as Stroud only solidified his status in the minds of the public. However, Stroud was far from the benign naturalist. Most reports indicate he was a predatory sexual psychopath. One critic noted that those who wrote letters in favor of his release after seeing the movie confused Hollywood with reality. As his health diminished in the late 1950s, Stroud was transferred to a federal medical center, where he died in isolation at the age of 76. His study of the federal prison system has never been published.

Source: Jolene Babyak, *Birdman: The Many Faces of Robert Stroud* (Berkeley, CA: Ariel Vamp Press, 1994).

SUDAN. Bedeviled by a civil war over the past 20 years, Sudan remains one of the world's leading abusers of human rights. The Sudan Prison Service is supervised by the director general of prisons, who also directs the nation's central prisons and reformatories. Central prisons include Kober in Khartoum North, Shalla in Al Fashir, Port Sudan on the Red Sea, and Darfur State Prison. During the early 1990s Sudan also had 140 local prisons and detention centers. According to human rights monitors, conditions were poor, with prisoners detained in a variety of fashions. Some were held in shackles, whereas others could go to their homes at night. Shalla Prison was reportedly the most primitive of the institutions. However, it is conceded that most political prisoners "welcomed" a transfer from the abusive security personnel to the confines of a prison.

Provincial officials control the almost four-dozen provincial prisons. These are classified as either Local Class I or Local Class II, both determined by size. Khartoum maintains a training school for guards, and according to reports from the 1980s vocational and literacy programs are mandatory. During the 1980s trusted low-risk prisoners were allowed to take 15-day vacations with their families.

In 2001 **Human Rights Watch** reported that Omdurman Women's Prison was beset with overcrowding, poor sanitation, disease, and the deaths of many children living with their mothers. Pardons have been sporadically issued to relieve the overcrowding, but there are always more than enough prisoners to take the places of those who leave.

At last count Sudan's Department of Prisons was operating 125 prison facilities, among them 4 federal prisons, 26 local government prisons, 46 provincial prisons, 45 open and semi-open prisons, and 4 juvenile reformatories. The total prison population was estimated in 2003 to be about 12,000, which would equal a rate of 36 per 100,000 of the national population. If correct, these figures probably do not include individuals in pre-trial detention, since Walmsley reported that in 1997 there were 32,000 prisoners, or 115 per 100,000 of the national population.

Sources: Kurian, *WEPP*, 1989; LCCS, "Sudan: The Prison System," June 1991; *Human Rights Watch World Report*, 2001; ICPS, Sudan, Africa, 2003; Walmsley, *WPPL*, 2003.

SUPERMAXIMUM PRISONS. The spread of the so-called supermax prison in the U.S. prison system has been linked to the prison violence that predominated in the 1970s and early 1980s, leading to the murders of dozens of guards by inmates throughout the country. The evolution of this institution began with prison authorities first developing procedures to minimize contact between staff and prisoners. Other measures followed, including "locking down" entire prisons for indeterminate periods, thereby leaving prisoners in their cells 24/7, making communal dining rooms and exercise yards redundant. Over time prison administrators came up with the idea of segregating the most dangerous prisoners—gang leaders and sociopaths—in a permanent lockdown environment. It was thought this would make prisons safer for both prisoners and staff. California opened two of the first supermax prisons at Corcoran State Prison in 1988 and then Pelican Bay in 1989. In 1994 the federal prison system fell in step, opening its first supermax in Florence, Colorado. By 2002 more than 42,000 prisoners were housed in these units, with 8,000 in California alone. Most supermax units have a familiar architecture that has cells arranged in lines radiating out like spokes from a control center or hub. By this arrangement prisoners can never see another prisoner unless they are forced to double bunk in a cell. However, double bunking is usually a last resort. Between 1995 and 2002 a dozen prisoners were killed by cellmates when Pelican Bay opted for this because of space limits.

The typical supermax prisoner receives meals through a slot in the steel wall, and all are shackled when leaving the cells. In 2001 inmates at Pelican Bay went on a two-week hunger strike. Nonetheless, they still found themselves ensconced 23 hours a day in spartan concrete cells measuring 7.5 feet by 11 feet. Supermax facilities continue to be at the center of a debate over what constitutes "cruel and unusual" punishment. Claims that they have reduced violence in general prison populations by removing the most troublesome inmates and serving as a deterrent are countered by a number studies that indicate the propensity for high levels of mental illness among supermax inmates. In order to bring about the supermax's abolition, human rights groups have cited the prison system as a violation of the Eighth Amendment. Prisons have responded by limiting visits by outside observers. According to most anecdotal evidence, these prisons appear to create more violent inmates whose impact upon release will unleash more dangerous ex-convicts on the public.

Source: Sasha Abramsky, "Return of the Madhouse: Supermax Prisons are Becoming the High-Tech Equivalent of the Nineteenth-century Snake Pit," www.thirdworldtraveler.com/Prison_System/Return_Madhouse.

SURINAME. The Central Penitentiary Institution operates under the Ministry of Justice and Police. In 2000 there were 1,933 prisoners held in prisons and police lockups. The main facilities included three adult prisons and two juvenile facilities. With a capacity to hold 1,188 prisoners, the facilities held an inmate population at 162.7 percent of official capacity, or 437 per 100,000 of the national population.

Sources: ICPS, Suriname, South America, 2000; Walmsley, *WPPL*, 2003.

SURINGAR, WILLEM HENDRIK (1790–1872). A Netherlands businessman, Willem Suringar earned the reputation as the "Dutch **John Howard.**" Suringar traded his intentions to become a vicar for the life of a businessman. He held several political offices, including local councilor and member of the Provincial States of County Council. Beginning in the 1840s he devoted his life to charity, philanthropy, and prison reform. Among his services on behalf of prisons was his tenure as a member of the Amsterdam Prison Commission. He won the "Golden Prize of Honour" from the Society for Public Welfare for his writing "of an elevating and sustaining book for prisoners on Sundays and feast days." His book, *Zedekundig Handboek*, included a number of stories revolving around prison life, which have been compared to "sermons." A copy of his book was available in every dormitory and shop, but as one prisoner remembered, it was "seldom consulted." As chairman of the Society for Moral Improvement of Prisoners, Suringar lobbied in favor of the **Pennsylvania system** of cellular confinement. He remained a strong proponent of solitary confinement, even for life, into his eighties.

Source: Franke, *The Emancipation of Prisoners*, 1995.

SWAZILAND. The Swaziland Correctional Services operates under the Ministry of Justice and Constitutional Development. At the beginning of 2003 the country reported 3,245 prisoners held in 12 correctional facilities. With an official capacity of 3,130 the prisons are operating at 103.7 percent of capacity, which is 324 per 100,000 of the national population.

Source: ICPS, Swaziland, Africa, 2003.

SWEDEN. By most accounts the first prison was built in Stockholm in 1624. But early jails were typically little more than congregate rooms located in the bottom recesses of castles and fortresses with no thoughts toward rehabilitation. When **John Howard** visited the country, he hoped that the prisons would reflect the cleanliness of Swedish domestic life, but he found rather the opposite. In Stockholm alone he found three prisons featuring convicts chained to walls and living in the most brutal circumstances. At other prisons he was pleased to report that women were employed at needlecraft and that many prisoners were kept industrious at spinning. Sweden did not mitigate the old penalties of the 1734 penal code until 1864 as the country adopted a more humane and progressive regime.

In the 1840s Crown Prince Oscar inaugurated an era of prison reform with the publication of his *Om Straff Och Sraff-Anstalter*, which would later gain a wider audience when translated into French, Norwegian, and English as *On Crimes and Punishments* in 1844. In his book the prince argued against capital punishment while extolling the innovations of the **Walnut Street Jail, Eastern State Penitentiary,** the **Maison de Force** in Ghent. By the late 1840s Sweden had adopted the **Pennsylvania system** for sentences under six years. By the end of the decade Sweden was in the process of completing nine prisons offering 860 cells. However, within a few years the solitary regime of the Pennsylvania system was modified by offering educational and religious instruction to prisoners in a congregate setting outside their cells. In 1847 Gavle Prison was built in a crucifix design. Between 1848 and 1862 prisons were built modeled on a T-shape at Vaxjo (1848), Karlskrona (1851), Kalmar (1852), Gothenburg (1857), Harnosand (1861), and Uppsala in 1862. Central prisons using the traditional radial design were constructed in Malmo in 1871 and in Langholmen in 1878, outside Stockholm.

Sweden's two most important prison reform acts were passed in 1921 and 1945. Legislation adopted in 1921 required separation of long-term felons from other prisoners during their first three years imprisonment. But during this period these inmates each had their own separate cell to work in and one to sleep in. At the same time the government introduced several prison farms, which serve as a transition between prison and release. In 1934 the Schlyter Plan was discussed as a method to "depopulate the prisons."

By the 1940s Sweden had 178 houses of detention dedicated to persons awaiting trial. One of the largest was located in Stockholm, which also housed individuals unable to pay fines. The 34 larger state institutions include central prisons, or *centralfangelser*; prisons, or *strafflangelser*; and crown prisons, or *kronohakten*. Complementing these facilities were special prisons dedicated to minor offenders such as vagabonds, and for recidivists. By 1944 the prison labor policy was more in tune with the American **state-use** policy then in vogue. In 1938 Sweden began experimenting with juvenile facilities similar to the English **Borstals**. Sweden's Prison Act of 1945 introduced a more treatment-oriented approach, by which inmates were treated according to their individual needs.

By the 1950s a number of older prisons were being demolished and replaced with more modern ones. Although the system was considered short on social workers, probation officers, and psychologists, by 1954 an adequate psychiatric facility was in operation at Roxtuna. At the end of the decade it became common for prisoners to be transferred from closed prisons to open ones after three months. At a time when most American prisons banned the reading of local and state newspapers, Swedish prisoners came to expect this as a daily privilege.

During the 1970s a number of steps were taken toward reforming the correctional system. Foremost among the new proposals was an emphasis on noncustodial treatment in favor of day-fines and probation. Sweden utilizes three types of correctional institutions. Remand facilities hold individuals who have been detained or have been arrested and are awaiting trial. Local institutions house prisoners serving sentences of less than one year. These facilities are usually hold between 10 and 40 prisoners at a time. These institutions allow nonrecidivist prisoners to be confined near their hometowns to assist in furloughs and outside work opportunities. Sweden's national correctional institutions are meant to hold individuals sentenced to terms of more than one year. These are typically closed institutions to accommodate a more threatening population. These units are comparatively small, with the largest one at Kumla capable of holding 206 prisoners. Kumla was opened in 1965 and designed to hold 435 inmates behind its imposing 21-foot walls. However, as mentioned previously, it has been remodeled to hold a smaller prison population in keeping with the modern trends toward a less punitive regime.

Today's Swedish Prison and Probation Administration is operated under the Ministry of Justice. The country's 84 penal institutions include 30 remand facilities. Together they hold 6,755 prisoners in a system designed for 6,317. As of 2003 the country had a ratio of 75 per 100,000 of the national population. These figures suggest a growing preference for incarceration or a rising crime problem. In 1992 the national rate was 63 per 100,000, and this figure was rather stable in the 60s per 100,000 until 2003.

Sources: Teeters, ed., *World Penal Systems*, 1944; DeFord, *Stone Walls*, 1962; Morris and Rothman, eds., *Oxford History of the Prison*, 1998; Johnston, *Forms of Constraint*, 2000; Nils Jareborg, "Sentencing Law, Policy, and Patterns in Sweden," in *Penal Reform in Overcrowded Times*, ed. Tonry, 2001, pp. 118–124; ICPS, Sweden, 2003.

SWITZERLAND. During his survey of European prisons **John Howard** wrote glowingly of the separation of prisoners in eighteenth century Swiss **workhouses**. But he found the larger prisons in Lausanne, Berne, Basel, and Zurich less salubrious and more punitive. Howard even reported the more serious offenders being chained to small wagons and forced to clean up street refuse. Although attempts were made to introduce some type of uniformity to the prison system, by the 1940s it still adhered to a decentralized pattern in which each canton contained a penitentiary, several district prisons, and in most cases a reformatory. So, although each Swiss canton had its own prison system, most conformed to the same penal code. Zurich, one of Switzerland's largest cities, offers a microcosm of the canton prison system. In the 1940s Zurich had one penitentiary, several district prisons, a correctional establishment for boys 12 to 20 years old, a **house of correction** targeting alcoholics and public drunkenness, and five educational or prevention-oriented facilities.

By the 1860s Swiss reformers were questioning the placement of youthful offenders with adults. Given that Switzerland is sitting between **France** and **Germany**, both impacted by American prison reform by the 1830s, it is not much of a leap to suggest that the country was influenced by the studies of American houses of refuge conducted by **Alexis de Tocqueville** and Gustave de Beaumont in this era. There is little doubt that the initial success of New York's **Elmira Reformatory** in 1876 did not filter into the landlocked country. Less than 20 years later the Aarburg Reformatory was opened in Canton Aargau, as was the Trachselwald Reformatory in Berne. Similar to the Elmira experiment, these facilities catered to individuals sentenced to imprisonment between the ages of 16 and 20. However, pointing to the construction of the Geneva Penitentiary in the 1820s, historian Norman Johnston argues that the English influence on Switzerland's prisons in the early nineteenth century was most dominant. The larger prisons built in the nineteenth century were either **radial**, like Lenzburg (1859), or **cruciform**, such as Basel (1864), Ticino (1873), Vaud (1887), and Zurich's Regensdorf Prison, completed in 1901.

By the mid-twentieth century Swiss penal treatment included traditional cellular confinement and **Auburn**-style strategies, which included congregate settings by day and solitary confinement by night. Those in cellular confinement are allowed to attend church and classes together, but they must work, eat, and sleep in individual cells. Those who are ill are confined in congregate dormitories but are prohibited from conversing with each other.

The popularity of the indeterminate sentence and conditional release has led to prison sentences divided into three disciplinary classes. Prisoners advance toward the higher class through good behavior. However, violations such as trying to escape, resisting guards, breaking the rule of silence, and faking illness are usually strictly punished with "intensified arrest," which is a reduction of food combined with a stint in a dark cell. When an individual reaches the final stage of reform and can demonstrate a means of support following release, inmates can petition for a probationary release under the monthly watch of a "communal officer." Violation of parole will return the inmate to prison.

In 1895 Switzerland opened a penal colony at Witzwil. Although the plan had support thirty years earlier, it took a sequence of events for it to come to fruition. First, a private experiment to build an agricultural colony on Neuburger Lake failed, allowing the Canton of Berne to purchase the 2,000-acre site. Second, Berne had planned to move the main prison from inside Berne to its outskirts. Both events led to the opening of the colony in 1895. When American penologist John Gillin visited in the 1920s, he found 500 prisoners working on a reclamation project that benefited both the state and the rehabilitation of prisoners through constructive work. Gillin suggested that the prisoners' health improved and that they acquired a number of skills related to scientific farming.

Switzerland has experienced a low imprisonment rate for years, ranging from 42 per 100,000 in 1972 to 88 per 100,000 in 1997. These figures are even low compared to other European countries. However, such was not always the case. In the 1940s the percentage was 150 per 100,000, and more than 120 per 100,000 in the 1920s. Explanation for such high numbers is rather "speculative," according to Killias and his colleagues, who suggest high unemployment and longer prison sentences as possible reasons. The 1980s saw a dramatic increase in prison overcrowding, but this was solved by the next decade through a prison construction program.

Today the Section for the Execution of Sentences and Measures is operated under the Federal Department of Justice and Police. In the second half of 2003 Switzerland's prison population stood at 5,266. As of 1997 the country had 167 prisons with a capacity to hold 6,513. Operating under capacity, the nation's prisons had a population of 72 per 100,000. More than 70 percent of the prisoners are from foreign countries.

Sources: Gillin, *Taming the Criminal*, 1931; Johnston, *Forms of Constraint*, 2000; Martin Killias, Marcelo F. Aebi, André Kuhn, and Simone Ronez, "Sentencing in Switzerland in 2000," in *Penal Reform in Overcrowded Times*, ed. Tonry, 2001, pp. 189–197.

SYRIA. Since the 1980s Syria's penal system has been concerned more with punishment than rehabilitation. Little detailed information is available on prisons. It is known, however, that convicted criminals are kept separate from political prisoners, often in solitary confinement. Health care, food, and access to family visitors in the ordinary prisons were reported as acceptable in the 1980s. However, a much more punitive regime prevailed where political and security prisoners were held, with family visits strictly prohibited. In 1985 **Amnesty International** reported "credible reports of torture, primarily during arrest and interrogation." Several general amnesties in the 1980s targeted only political prisoners who were members of the Muslim Brotherhood, numbering between 200 and 500 members. These amnesties barely made a dent in a prison population that held thousands of other political prisoners.

By 2002 hundreds of political prisoners were held in indeterminate detention under poor conditions, but fewer cases of torture and ill treatment were reported compared to previous years. In June 2002 the Assad regime announced an amnesty reducing by one third the prison sentences imposed on children between the ages of 7 and 18 who had not been convicted of criminal offenses (that these children were incarcerated in the first place suggests a rather draconian juvenile penal system). Sednaya Prison is a major facility holding mostly pro-Iraqi Ba'ath Party, Muslim Brotherhood, and Islamic Liberation Party members. A number of other political detainees are held "incommunicado" at detention centers at Far'Falstin (Palestine Branch) and Far'al-Tahqiq al-'Askari (Military Interrogation Branch). Since most human rights activists target the treatment of political prisoners, there is a dearth of material on criminal prisons and detention. What is known is that there are no safeguards against arbitrary torture and arrest, and that civilian and military prisons, particularly the infamous Tadmor Prison in the Palmyran desert, are off limits to independent observers. There is a woman's prison in Duma. In 1980 reports came out of Syria that more than 1,000 unarmed prisoners were massacred at Tadmor Prison. Information on the modern prison system is scarce. The most recent estimates from 1997 indicate a prison population of at least 14,000, which would average to 93 per 100,000 of the national population.

Sources: *Human Rights Watch World Report*, 2001; *Amnesty International Report*, 2003; ICPS, Syria, Middle East, 2003; Walmsley, *WPPL*, 2003.

T

TAIWAN. The Ministry of Justice governs the Taiwanese prison system. Prisons are centralized under the administration of the Department of Prison and Detention Facilities of the Ministry of Justice. Custodial institutions include prisons, detention houses, and reformatories. Prisons are used to incarcerate individuals serving sentences of more than one year. Those held in temporary custody or serving sentences of less than one year are held in detention houses. Reformatories house juvenile offenders between the ages of 14 and 18, who by law must be held separate from adults.

Taiwan's 16 prisons fall under a number of categories. General types house mostly medium-security prisoners; maximum-security prisons house serious and dangerous offenders at institutions such as Green Island, Taichung, and Hue Lien Prisons; prisons for habitual offenders house prisoners convicted for crimes within five years of serving a previous sentence, most notably the Kao Hsiung Prison; open prisons or branch prison camps house those who are not considered security risks, allowing prisoners to work outside the prison by day and return to the prison at night, such as Wu Ling Prison; and prisons for prisoners with special illness who need to be segregated; for example, prisoners with leprosy are held in Hsing Chuang, and the mentally ill at Tao Yuan.

District courts are provided with a prison and a detention house. Reformatories are located in Taoyuan, Changhua, and Kaohsiung. Every prison is helmed by a warden and is divided into five divisions, consisting of Education and Reform, Work, Health, Guard, and General Affairs. Correctional facilities are well accommodated with well-staffed medical wards, workshops, classrooms, and recreational areas. By law, one quarter of the profits generated by prison farms is distributed to convicts, 40 percent for maintenance of the institution, 10 percent into the national treasury, and the remainder banked for future improvements.

There are three types of juvenile facilities, including youth jails, which house individuals between 14 and 16 years of age, who are serving minimum sentences of five years (Hsing Chu); juvenile reformatories, for those convicted of less serious crimes (among the three institutions is Chang Hua, which also houses females); and juvenile foster homes, which offer a family environment for children under 12, usually convicted of stealing.

Today the Department of Corrections is operated under the Ministry of Justice. In 2004 Taiwan had 86 penal institutions, including 18 detention houses, 18 juvenile and classification houses, 25 prisons, 2 juvenile reformatory schools, 4 vocation-training facilities, 17 drug abstention and treatment centers, and 2 juvenile correctional-educational schools. Altogether these institutions held 56,066 prisoners, or 248 per 100,000 of the national population. This would be considered a decline from the trends of 1999 and 2002.

Sources: Lee-Jan Jan, "Corrections in Taiwan (Republic of China)," *International Journal of Comparative and Applied Criminal Justice* 12, no. 1 (Spring 1988), pp. 95–100; ICPS, Taiwan, Asia, 2004.

TAJIKISTAN. Following Tajikistan's independence from the Soviet Union in the mid-1990s, its system of criminal justice has evolved from its roots in the former system. The prison system is administered under the Ministry of Justice. In subsequent years the country has been targeted by human rights groups for its treatment of political prisoners and restraints on civil liberties. Many political prisoners are ensconced in secret prisons run by the regime. In 2003 Tajikistan had an estimated 10,000 prisoners housed in 18 prisons, a ratio of 161 per 100,000 of the national population.

Sources: LCCS, "Tajikistan: Internal Security," March 1996; ICPS, Tajikistan, Asia, 2003.

TALLACK, WILLIAM (1831–1908). One of the foremost penal reformers of the Victorian era, William Tallack is remembered as a long-serving secretary for the **Howard Association** and for the publication of his *Penological and Preventive Principles* in 1896, recognized as one of the earliest attempts to promote prisons as a device to prevent crime and offer better methods of treatment to offenders. According to Miriam Allen DeFord, as its secretary Tallack was responsible for keeping the Howard Association alive. Tallack was a Quaker and also secretary for the lesser-known Society for the Abolition of Capital Punishment.

Sources: Teeters, *World Penal Systems*, 1944; DeFord, *Stone Walls*, 1962.

TANZANIA. Following World War I, British colonial authorities in Tanzania introduced a penal code that had been perfected in **India** based on English common law. There have been a number of modifications over the past century, mostly relating to minimum sentencing. The adoption of the Preventive Detention Act of 1962 gave the president the power to arrest and imprison anyone considered a national security threat. Although the law limited detention to fifteen days without a hearing or charges, **Amnesty International** has reported cases as long as ten years. The Germans built the first Tanzanian prisons when Tanzania was part of German East Africa prior to World War I. When the British took over, they abolished the more punitive aspects of the former regime and constructed more prisons. One of the first prisons built following independence from Britain was Dar es Salaam's Ukonga Prison, which quickly earned a reputation for poor food and medical care, as well as overcrowding.

As of 2004 the Tanzania Prisons Service fell under the direction of the Ministry of Home Affairs. Most recently the country's 120 prisons were considered almost double their capacity to hold 22,699. Almost half the inmates were either pre-trial detainees or remand prisoners. Tanzania's prison population of 43,244 is equal to 116 per 100,000 of the national population. However, this figure is lower than the prison population trends between 1998 and 2002.

Sources: Kurian, *WEPP*, 1989; ICPS, Tanzania, Africa, 2004.

TELEPHONE POLE DESIGN. Prison historian Norman Johnston describes the telephone pole layout as a design "in which parallel pavilions are connected by one or two corridors." He suggests that this prison scheme "may have been inspired by the **Mettray Colony for Boys** in France. The most prominent early examples of telephone pole style prisons were built at **Wormwood Scrubs** (1874), in Great Britain, and **Fresnes Prison** (1898), outside Paris. By the 1940s the United States had adopted this prison-building scheme. According to Johnston, this prison design was not replicated much internationally because of the smaller size of institutions. The federal penitentiary in Lewisburg, Pennsylvania, was among the earliest American prisons to adopt this design. Architect Alfred Hopkins designed the prison. What distinguished the telephone pole design was the centrality of a long corridor surrounded by cellblocks, dormitories, dining halls, a chapel, shops, schools, and administrative offices, all branching off from the corridor. Cellblocks typically consisted of three or four stories, but with a new emphasis on "openness" facilitated by the introduction of floor-to-ceiling security windows. A number of Latin American countries have built large prisons based on this scheme, including Brazil, Argentina, Venezuela, Paraguay, and Ecuador.

Sources: Johnston, *The Human Cage*, 1973; Johnston, *Forms of Constraint*, 2000.

THAILAND. Among the countries of Asia, Thailand is unique in its response to incarceration. Since Thailand did not have a colonial heritage, it was left free to develop its own criminal justice system. Not until turning to general criminal law reform in the early twentieth century did Thailand borrow from continental traditions, resulting in the Penal Code of 1908.

One of the country's first prisons was Ban-Kwang Central Prison, completed in 1931. Located just outside Bangkok, this prison is usually referred to as the Big Tiger. Nearby is the "Bangkok Hilton," or Central Women's Correctional Institution. The Big Tiger has earned a reputation as one of the worst prisons in the world. Created to hold 4,000 inmates, as of 2004 it held double that. Exacerbating the terrible conditions is a prisoner-to-guard ratio of 25 to 1, which according to Scott Christianson is the highest of any Asian nation.

Currently the Department of Corrections, operating under the Ministry of Interior, is responsible for all offenders outside the juvenile system. Rehabilitation and incarceration centers include prisons, penal institutions, houses of confinement, and a house of relegation. Individuals sentenced to short sentences for minor crimes are placed in houses of confinement, which are considered less severe than imprisonment. There is a central house of confinement as well as 129 temporary houses of confinement, for offenders serving up to three-month sentences or for those unable to pay fines. Under the Habitual Criminal Relegation Act, habitual offenders are confined in the one house of relegation.

The Department of Corrections administers twenty central prisons located throughout the country. Prisoners in these institutions are serving sentences over five years. These inmates are typically transferred from local prisons. Some central prisons contain separate wings for special classes of prisoners such as women or those awaiting death sentences.

Women are imprisoned either in small units attached to the main provincial prisons or in the central women's correctional institution for long-term women offenders. Thailand has 51 provincial prisons and 13 district prisons, responsible for prisoners serving sentences less than five years and prisoners waiting for trial in the provinces.

In addition, there are women's correctional institutions, medical correctional institutions, and open institutions. Thailand has four open institutions. These facilities originated in the mid-1960s as a method of teaching self-discipline and responsibility to selected offenders. These institutions are designed to resemble normal communities on the outside in stark contrast to the brutality of traditional prisons. These have been successful at alleviating overcrowding that became a concern in the 1970s. Besides the open institutions there are more than 30 prison camps used to train prisoners in agricultural work and improve discipline and conduct.

Younger offenders between the ages of 18 and 25 are housed in four youthful offenders institutions and serve between one and ten years. Organized like the **Borstal system**, these facilities offer training and treatment different from the prisons.

In 1972 steps were taken to improve prison staff training with the opening of a training and research center for correctional officers. Here recruits receive comprehensive training prior to joining prison staffs.

By the late 1980s the penal system was made up of 47 regular penal institutions. Of these, seven were central prisons, with the oldest and largest, Khlong Prem Central Prison in Bangkok. Of the regular facilities, 5 are considered regional prisons, 23 prison camps, 7 correctional institutions, 3 reformatories, and a detention home. Smaller facilities are maintained in provincial, metropolitan, and district police stations capable of holding individuals serving up to one-year sentences. A maximum-security facility is located at Nakhon Pathom. The prison camps are located on Ko Tarutao Island in the Strait of Malacca. Youthful offenders are held in Ayutthaya and Bangkok, usually between the ages of 18 and 25 and serving terms less than 5 years. Bangkok maintains the Women's Correctional Institution, and the Medical Correctional Institution for drug addicts and inmates with other medical problems operates to the north of the city in the Pathum Thani Province.

In 2000 measures were taken to relieve the rampant overcrowding and reported human rights abuses. Efforts have been made to better train prison guards and to decrease pre-trial detention time, as well as releasing more prisoners earlier. In 2003 Thailand announced that it aimed to reduce the prison population by 40 percent. One method has been to release compliant inmates with microchip bracelets monitoring their movements. As of 2002 there were more than 257,000 inmates in Thailand, of these 66.46 percent were incarcerated for drug violations. With a prison rate of 403 per 100,000, 23 percent of the inmates were held awaiting either trial or the conclusion of an investigation.

The Thai prison system includes at least 133 facilities and is currently at a capacity of 231 percent. Prisoners outnumber staff members 25.4 to 1, leading to intolerably dangerous conditions. Human rights groups report a number of abuses, including torture. Many of these abuses have targeted minority members from Myanmar or Africa. Much of the physical punishment is reportedly the work of trusties, known as "blue shirts," who are prisoners given special privileges. The prison system is also plagued by corruption, particularly at the local levels. Although heavy leg irons are prohibited by Thai law, there is evidence that they are used, especially on prisoners on death row.

Poor pay and inadequate funding for the prisons, resulting in poor food and water, sanitation, and medical care, have undermined the competence of the correctional guards. Prison staff have been characterized as apathetic victims of a weak chain of command and communication between the prison governor and the chief of the cellblock.

Most recently Bangkok's Bang Kwang maximum-security prison has received much attention as it rapidly becomes a tourist attraction. Located on the outskirts of the city, the prison is home to the nation's death row and more than 8,000 inmates serving sentences of at least 25 years. Recent movies such as the 1999 film *Brokedown Palace* and the book *The Damage Done*, by Australian writer Warren Fellows, brought this visitor practice to the attention of a wider public. Visitors are more often travelers than actual friends or family members. Four days each week visitors are permitted to visit prisoners. They are advised to dress modestly and be respectful to staff. They are allowed to bring food and other gifts to prisoners.

Sources: CIA, World Factbook—Thailand, www.cia.gov/cia/publications/factbook; Dhavee Choosup, "Innovation in the Administration of Criminal Justice in Thailand," in *Innovations in Criminal Justice: In Asia and the Pacific*, ed. Clifford, 1979, pp. 81–97; Amnesty International, "Thailand: Widespread Abuse in the Administration of Justice," June 11, 2002, http://web.amnesty.org; Corrections Forum, "Thailand to Microchip Early-Release Convicts," January/February 2003, http://proquest.umi.com; Christianson, *Notorious Prisons*, 2004; Jennifer Valentino, "Prison in Thailand Draws Tourists," *Houston Chronicle*, October 31, 2004, A23.

THREE PRISONS ACT. *See* UNITED STATES FEDERAL PRISON SYSTEM

TIBET. Prior to the Chinese occupation in 1959, Tibet had only two small prisons, both located in Llhasa. According to one former prisoner from this era, the presence of more than fifteen prisoners in the two facilities would have been viewed as scandalous. Several monasteries were also used as unofficial penal facilities. Following the Chinese invasion, unprecedented numbers of individuals were arrested for protesting the occupation. It should not be surprising that since then the number of penal institutions has multiplied. It is difficult to measure the number of prisoners in Tibet because of the strict control of information by the Chinese.

When several European Union (EU) ambassadors visited Tibet in 1998, they were informed there were three prisons in Tibet, including Drapchi, Llhasa Municipal Prison, the Outridu, and in the Linzhi Prefecture, Pomi Prison. At that time there were an estimated 1,800 prisoners in the 4 facilities. Prisoners in these units reportedly include only those convicted of crimes. Drapchi is dedicated to prisoners serving sentences of more than five years' duration, although there is evidence that others are detained there as well.

In addition to the aforementioned prisons, Tibet has a number of administrative detention centers known collectively as Laojiao. In 1994 the National People's Congress passed legislation replacing the term *Laogai* with the more neutral "prison." Individuals incarcerated in these camps typically have not been sentenced by trial and can be held for three years without legal proceedings or appeals. There are three of these centers in Llhasa, including Yitridu and Trisam. Although unsubstantiated by EU observers, the Chinese claim that re-education through labor incorporated a much freer and independent regime, allowing inmates to work without supervision and with access to unlocked doors. Sentences to these centers can be extended another four years for various reasons.

When individuals are first taken into custody, they are confined in detention centers on the average up to six months. Their only contacts are other cellmates and interrogators. There are also a number of county-level jails, most devoted to Tibetan dissidents. These include Meldrogongkar, Taktse, Toelung, Llhatse, Phenpo, Lhundrup, Tingri, Nyalam, and Lhokla Gongkar. Still others are held in local police lockups.

Source: Tibetan Centre for Human Rights and Democracy, *Behind Bars: Prison Conditions in Tibet*, 1998.

TICKETS-OF-LEAVE. Prisoners sentenced to penal servitude in the Australian colonies could earn freedom, or a ticket-of-leave, in three ways. Rarest of the three was a pardon from the governor, which also included a return to England. Others earned a "conditional release," which bestowed citizenship in the colonies but barred return to England. Finally, the ticket-of-leave granted prisoners freedom from forced labor in the colonies and allowed the former convict to work for wages anywhere in the colonies but still prohibited a return to England. During its early years the ticket-of-leave had to be renewed yearly but could also be revoked at any time.

Considered a precursor to **parole**, in 1801 ticket-of-leave regulations were established by Britain to reward convicts in the Australian penal colonies for good behavior. In the early nineteenth century prisoners in the Australian penal colonies could earn a ticket-of-leave if they were well behaved for anywhere from four to eight years, depending on the type of sentence. According to historian A.G.L. Shaw, between 1825 and 1836 less than one fifth of all prisoners who were qualified by time actually received them. Most prisoners received tickets-of-leave after four years of good conduct while serving a seven-year sentence.

Sources: Shaw, *Convicts and the Colonists*, 1966; Hughes, *Fatal Shore*, 1987.

TIMOR-LESTE. The country formerly known as East Timor had at last count in 2003 at least 320 prisoners. The Timor-Leste Prison Service operates three prisons, including the main facility in Dili, and Gleno and Baucau prisons. In 2003 73 percent of these inmates were pre-trial detainees or remand prisoners. Its prison population rate is 41 per 100,000 of the national population.

Source: ICPS, Timor-Leste, Oceania, 2003.

TOCQUEVILLE, ALEXIS DE (1805–1859). In 1831 French magistrates Alexis de Tocqueville and **Gustave de Beaumont** visited the United States at their own expense to investigate the American prison system for the French government. However, as David J. Rothman noted, "the unexpected spin-off from the mission" was de Tocqueville's classic analysis *Democracy in America*. In penological circles de Tocqueville and his partner are best remembered for the classic 1833 work *On the*

Penitentiary System of the United States, and Its Application in France; With an Appendix on Penal Colonies, and Also, Statistical Notes. According to Norman Johnston, de Beaumont wrote most of the book. In this book published 2 years after their 10-month visit, the authors discussed the attributes of the **Auburn** and **Pennsylvania** systems, singling out **Eastern State Penitentiary** for "the unnecessary expenses" of its construction. The French authors targeted the unrelenting silence of American prisons, comparing them to "catacombs." However, they would more favorably portray the recent reform schools as deserving of European emulation. De Beaumont is credited with playing a role in the establishment of the **Mettray Colony for Boys** in 1840. According to Norman Johnston, this French institution near Tours is considered "the first of the fairly open agricultural colonies for juveniles."

Sources: Johnston, *Eastern State Penitentiary,* 1994; David J. Rothman, "Perfecting the Prison: United States, 1789–1865," in *History of the Prison,* eds. Morris and Rothman, 1998, pp. 100–116; Johnston, *Forms of Constraint,* 2000.

TOGO. The nation's penitentiary administration is the responsibility of the Ministry of Justice. As of 1998 the country operated 12 prisons populated with 2,043 prisoners. More than half are either pre-trial detainees or remand prisoners. The national prison population rate at the end of 1998 was 46 per 100,000 of the national population.

Source: ICPS, Togo, Africa, 1998.

TOLBOOTH (SCOTLAND). Scottish authorities sometimes employed redundant toll houses as places to hold prisoners in small villages, hence the term *tolbooth* would be used to refer to small jails. According to historian Joy Cameron, by the "middle of the seventeenth century the word 'tolbooth' became synonymous with prison." The typical tollbooth started out as a booth at a fair. Here dues and tolls were collected, and anyone who violated fair regulations was detained. Over time tolbooths were transformed into "courts of justice" and places to confine criminals. By the fifteenth century the tolbooth was one of the most prominent buildings in Scottish towns. The best-known tolbooth was located in Edinburgh. Built in 1480, during the next half-century it was transformed into a modest jail, where inmates were held in shackles. However, conditions became so appalling that it was demolished in the 1560s and replaced with a more secure facility. Edinburgh could boast of three tolbooths at one time, one surviving until 1817.

Sources: Cameron, *Prisons and Punishment in Scotland,* 1983; Johnston, *Forms of Constraint,* 2000.

TOMBS PRISON. Constructed in 1838, the Tombs Prison was considered New York City's earliest prison. Since it contained New York City's courts, police, and detention facilities when it opened, the facility was officially referred to as the Halls of Justice. But the sobriquet "the Tombs" seemed to be more fitting because of the appelation's resemblance to a mausoleum. According to Carl Sifakis, it was reportedly modeled on an illustration from John L. Stevens's book on ancient Egypt entitled *Stevens' Travels.* However, because the prison was designed by noted prison architect **John Haviland,** that this was the case is doubtful. According to Norman

Johnston, Egyptian motifs had been popular in architectural circles for years and even inspired the design of Haviland's **Trenton State Prison** several years earlier. In any case, Johnston admits, "Its is not entirely clear what motivated Haviland to choose Egyptian revival for his two final large prisons." The Tombs deserved an early reputation for insalubrity, and as early as 1850 critics were calling for its demolition. It was the site of a number of scandals and successful escapes. In 1900 the Public Schools Association established a school in the prison for younger inmates. According to Miriam Allen DeFord, it was "the first of its kind in an American adult institution." In 1902 a new Tombs Prison was built to replace the harsh and dilapidated facility. The new version of the Tombs was kept open until it was closed because of security and health concerns in 1974.

Sources: DeFord, *Stone Walls*, 1962; Johnston, *Forms of Constraint*, 2000; Sifakis, *Encyclopedia of American Prisons*, 2003.

TONGA. Tonga's prison system is the responsibility of the Ministry of Police, Prisons, and Fire Services. As of mid-2002 the country had 6 prisons capable of holding 139 inmates. These facilities include the main institution at Hu'atolitoli, on the outskirts of Nuku'alofa, and smaller prisons at Haapai, Vava'u, and Niuatoputapu. The main prison is dedicated to those serving sentences exceeding six months. With a low crime rate and no overcrowding, the institutions are reportedly adequately run. It is mandatory for all prisoners to labor on public works projects or on government-owned plantations. In late 2003 the prison population stood at 113, a rate of 106 per 100,000 of the national population.

Sources: Kurian, *WEPP*, 1989; ICPS, Tonga, Oceania, 2003.

TOWER OF LONDON. England's most famous prison was completed in 1097 following the Norman Conquest (1066). During its more than 900-year history it has been used as a prison mostly for political and religious prisoners, a court, and a site for executions. The Tower has sheltered at various times the Crown Jewels, the Crown's armory, state records, the Mint, as well as a military garrison and an animal menagerie. During the thirteenth century the Tower keep became known as the White Tower after its walls were whitewashed. Although cells were built below the keep, prisoners also languished in confinement in other areas of the tower.

In the twelfth century the Tower was one of three prisons serving the London area. The Tower's first recorded prisoner, in 1101, was the bishop of Durham, who was allowed to keep his servants with him. His imprisonment demonstrates the treatment of prisoners according to status of individual and type of crime. In the late 1200s close to 600 Jews were arrested on trumped-up charges of coin-clipping. Almost half were executed, while most of the remainder perished from poor treatment. Some of England's most famous personages have spent time here, ranging from Henry VIII's second wife, Anne Boleyn, to convicted Irish traitor Sir Roger Casement (1916) and World War II traitor William "Lord Haw Haw" Joyce (1945), both of whom were awaiting execution (Casement was executed at **Pentonville Prison**).

All the four towers in the Tower of London were used as prisons at one time or another. For example, King Henry VI was held in Wakefield Tower, where he was murdered in 1471. Prior to her execution Lady Jane Grey was confined in the Beauchamp Tower. Sir Thomas More waited for execution in the Bell Tower in the

1530s. Sir Walter Raleigh was among the luminaries held in the Brick Tower and later spent 13 years in the so-called Bloody Tower, or Garden Tower, prior to his execution.

Sources: R. B. Pugh, "The King's Prisons before 1250," *Transactions of the Royal Historical Society*, 5th series, vol. 5, London, 1955, pp. 1–22; John E. N. Hearsey, *The Tower: Eight Hundred and Eighty Years of English History* (London: MacGibbon and McKee, 1960); Christopher Hibbert, *Tower of London* (New York: Newsweek, 1971).

TRANSDNIESTRIA. *See* TRANSNISTRIA

TRANSNISTRIA. In 1994 this breakaway region within the borders of the Republic of **Moldova** was granted autonomy but not national sovereignty. The local prisons are controlled by provincial authorities without intervention from Moldovan officials. As of 2001 Transnistria had five prisons holding 3,500 prisoners. This would be a rate of 450 per 100,000 of the national population. There is some dispute about these figures. The director of Moldova's prison system reported 500 less prisoners, which would bring the rate down to 385. Transnistria's prisons include Glinoe; Tiraspol (No. 2); Tiraspol (No. 3), which houses female prisoners; an open prison colony outside Tiraspol, which only requires prisoners to spend the nights in the facility; and an educational labor colony for male juveniles at Alexandrovka, also near Tiraspol. According to reports in 1997, this educational colony located in the Camenca district was "regarded as a model prison."

Recent inspections of these facilities indicate problems with overcrowding, lack of beds and space inside the cells, poor ventilation, and inadequate light and sanitary facilities. Several of the institutions had a tuberculosis problem and insufficient medical resources to treat patients. According to prison expert Roy Walmsley, one report indicated some prisoners were wholly dependent on medical care provided by family and friends.

Source: Walmsley, *Further Developments in the Prison Systems of Central and Eastern Europe*, 2003.

TRANSPORTATION. The transportation or banishment of prisoners and other undesirables from society is as old as history. Ancient Rome and Greece adopted this practice, and all the major colonial powers have forcibly relocated citizens to colonies or distant corners of their empires at one time or another. As late as the 1940s Portugal was sending convicts to **Angola.** Holland shipped unwanted residents to the Dutch East Indies, Italy to the island of **Lipari,** and the French first to Madagascar and later French Guiana and the notorious **Devil's Island**. In the 1750s tsarist Russia replaced capital punishment with hard labor in the penal colonies in Siberia.

Transportation has been most readily identified with England's experience in America and **Australia** in the eighteenth and nineteenth century. However, the practice was actually established as a form of bondage more than a century earlier under King James I. By the end of the seventeenth century several other European countries experimented with it as well, but it was only used infrequently by England until 1718.

By the eighteenth century, according to common law, all felonies were capital offenses. The adoption of transportation as an alternative to the gallows gave the British court system the opportunity to mitigate the brutality of England's "bloody code" by pardoning the less serious felons on the condition they accept banishment to America. According to historian A. Roger Ekirch, perhaps one quarter of all immigrants to the colonies in the eighteenth century were transported convicts. Close to 50,000 English convicts were sent to the American colonies between 1718 and the outbreak of the American Revolution in 1775. With hostilities barring the further transportation to America new solutions were considered, since England was once against faced with overcrowded prisons and the concomitant hazards of epidemic disease, prison riots, and escape attempts. The English government toyed with transporting convicts to several regions in Africa, before settling on New South Wales in current-day Australia.

The first convict ship arrived at Botany Bay in 1788. More than 187,000 convicts were sent to Australia, the majority of them after 1815 and the conclusion of the Napoleonic Wars. According to Australian penal historian John Hirst, the mortality rate on the ships could rise as high as 25 percent. Not until the British government began paying transportation shipping contractors for the number of prisoners who arrived alive did the mortality rate dramatically reduce. Hirst suggests that it was "less dangerous to travel to Australia as a convict" after this, "than to sail to the United States as a migrant."

By the 1850s England had built enough prisons and introduced enough prison reforms that the transportation system had become cost-prohibitive and had outlived its usefulness. In 1853 the penal settlement at **Van Diemen's Land** was closed to penal settlement followed by closure of **Norfolk Island** in 1856. Transportation continued to Western Australia until 1867.

In 1791 France became more identified with transportation when the government passed legislation that required all men convicted of a second felony to be transported for life to Madagascar. The Napoleonic Wars broke out, however, and the plan was not used. In 1851 a new leader and a new era saw France revive transportation, this time to **Algeria**, New Caledonia, and French Guiana. In the 1890s Devil's Island came to prominence when Captain Alfred Dreyfus became the first prisoner to be detained there, between 1894 and 1899. Devil's Island was probably the most famous penal colony in the world in its day, as well as the terminus most identified with penal transportation in the popular consciousness.

Sources: A. Roger Ekirch, *Bound for America: The Transportation of British Convicts to the Colonies, 1718–1775* (Oxford: Clarendon Press, 1987); Hughes, *The Fatal Shore*, 1987; Sir Brian Cubbon, "Notes on the History of Transportation," in *Current International Trends in Corrections*, ed. Biles, 1988, pp. 47–50; John Hirst, "The Australian Experience," in *Oxford History of the Prison*, eds. Morris and Rothman, 1998, pp. 235–265.

TREADMILLS. Treadmills, sometimes referred to as treadwheels, have existed since the ancient world. By working lower-body muscles, treadmills could be used to power pumps and mills. The first prison treadmill was designed by the Lowestoft engineer William Cubitt. He was inspired to create the device following a visit in 1818 to the Suffolk County Gaol. Cubitt was almost immediately struck by the crowd of prisoners lounging about just inside the prison gates. A local magistrate evidently noted his disdain and asked the engineer to come up with something to occupy what Cubitt later referred to as "repulsive groups" of prisoners. It was not long before Cubitt devised the human treadmill, which would become a common sight in British prisons into the late nineteenth century.

The device was composed of a series of steps on a giant wheel and was propelled by the climbing motion of prisoners. On the average 200 men and women could replicate the output of a water wheel. Many observers compared it to a very wide paddle wheel, in which workers held on to a bar and climbed the paddle blades. It was similar to ascending stairs for hours at a time. Prisoners had to continue to lift their legs for up to eight hours, the length of treadmill shifts. Officials were pleased with the contraption's dual function as a means of punishing prisoners with a monotonous and degrading form of exercise as well as its practicality as a device to grind corn and raise water. Initially prisoners spent entire days repeating 15-minute shifts on and then being relieved for 15 minutes. More than 50 prisons had adopted this mechanism by 1824.

In 1838 English innovators placed vertical separators between prisoners, so that inmates would be forced to labor in isolation. British writer **Oscar Wilde** noted his stint on a treadmill in his *Ballad of Reading Gaol*, after serving time in 1895. During the nineteenth century attempts were made to introduce the treadmill to America, but to little avail. By the end of the nineteenth century the drudgery and labor-wasting work on the treadmill seemed outdated and counterproductive. Parliament banned treadmills in 1898.

Sources: Babington, *The English Bastille*, 1971; D.H. Shayt, "Stairway to Redemption: America's Encounter with the British Prison Treadmill," *Technology and Culture* 30, no. 4 (1989), pp. 908–938.

TREADWHEEL. *See* TREADMILL

TRENTON STATE PRISON. Architect **John Haviland** designed the New Jersey state prison at Trenton in the early 1830s. New Jersey officials favored the **Pennsylvania system** of separate confinement with labor. Haviland modified his typical **radial** plan to allow for better surveillance of inmates. By the time the prison opened in 1836, only two of the planned five cell houses had been completed. A number of the prison's features were similar to other Haviland prisons. However, he eliminated the individual exercise yards utilized at **Eastern State Penitentiary**, claiming, according to Norman Johnston, "Attached yards increased dampness and prohibited air circulation in the cells." Otherwise Trenton State Prison operated as had the earlier prison, featuring 24-hour confinement. However, similar to other solitary units the system eroded over time as a result of such exigencies as health concerns and overcrowding. Within two years selected prisoners were laboring outside their cells, and soon most cells were holding two prisoners. Prison historian Norman Johnston suggests that Haviland, having learned a great deal from his previous models, "regarded Trenton as his best prison." Trenton State Prison followed the **Auburn** model until it ceased operation in the 1970s. Like Eastern State Penitentiary, Trenton would influence international prison design throughout the nineteenth century.

Source: Johnston, *Forms of Constraint*, 2000.

TRINIDAD AND TOBAGO. The Trinidad and Tobago Prison Service is operated under the Ministry of National Security and Justice. The country's 7 prisons were above capacity at 4,794 inmates, slightly more than the 4,348 they were designed to hold. Almost one third of prisoners are either pre-trial detainees or remand prisoners. The prison population rate of 351 per 100,000 of the national population indicates a decrease from 353 per 100,000 in 1998, but it is significantly higher than the 269 per 100,000 in 1992.

The country's penal code is based on the British legal tradition introduced in 1848. The current correctional system is based on the Prison Service Act of 1965. Of the country's seven prisons, two are maximum-security facilities, which include the Royal Gaol in Port-of-Spain and the Carrera Island prison in the vicinity of Chaguaamas. The Golden Grove Prison outside Arouca is a minimum-security prison. During the late 1980s juveniles under the age of sixteen were committed to industrial schools or orphanages rather than jails.

Sources: Kurian, *WEPP*, 1989; ICPS, Trinidad and Tobago, Caribbean, 1999; Walmsley, *WPPL*, 2003.

TRUSTEE. Spelled variously as "trusty" or "trustee," the term is typically applied to prisoners who are given the authority to manage other inmates. The trustee system was especially prominent in southern prisons maintaining large agricultural plantations. In New Jersey's Trenton State Prison in the 1930s, trusties could be relied on to run errands for guards, pass messages to inmates in cells, and even help with guard duty. They were also adept at selling drugs and other illegal goods. In return they could roam the prison without supervision. Edgardo Rotman has suggested that this "peculiar feature" made the Mississippi prison system more punitive than necessary, arguing that trustees "were every bit as cruel and unyielding as the guards who hired them." In the 1960s, Arkansas prison warden **Thomas Murton** discovered that armed trusties essentially controlled the Tucker Prison Farm. Rewarded with the best food, clothing, and perquisites, trusties were at the top of the prison food chain. They were even allowed to carry weapons to prevent prison escapes. According to Scott Christianson, prison trusties were at one time compared to "kapos in Nazi concentration camps."

Not every trustie experiment turned out to be a failure. In 1885, Michigan State Penitentiary warden Hiram F. Hatch organized a Mutual Aid League that allowed the prisoners to discipline themselves. It was quickly labeled a failure. But **Thomas Mott Osborne** would build on the experiment and create the Mutual Welfare League at **Auburn Prison** in 1914. As warden, he made prisoners responsible for discipline. The success of his scheme led to his appointment as warden of **Sing Sing Prison** where he adopted a similar program. Although it boosted the morale of prisoners, politicians and newspapers denounced the tactics as "coddling" prisoners, and as a result of the vitriolic attacks, Osborne resigned.

Using trusties has been considered a method of cutting expenses since less staff is required. It is also not just an American phenomenon. As early as the seventeenth century, Spanish prisons appointed trusties who received special privileges for acting as night guards and internal police. Called *poteros*, these individuals were trusted with keys so they could lock up new prisoners. There are examples of trusties from prisons throughout the world. For example, a former inmate in Egypt's

Abu-Za'abal prison, an hour from Cairo, reported trusties joining prison guards in the beating and torturing of other prisoners, and Jewish prisoners were sometimes targeted by Muslim trusties in the prison complex's House of Correction. Anne Applebaum has reported that prisoners in the Soviet **Gulags** often worked as trusties to earn better food and work conditions. A number of writers including **Alexander Solzhenitsyn** apparently worked as prisoners and even informed on other prisoners to increase their living standards. In 2002, human rights groups targeted Thailand's prisons for the torture of foreign prisoners by trusties. Accordingly, most human rights standards cite the use of trusties as a contravention of international human rights. In the United States the trustee system has been challenged and diminished by various legislation and administrations averse to allowing prisoners any control over others. It continues to flourish in other countries however.

Sources: Edgardo Rotman, "The Failure of Reform: United States, 1865–1965," in *Oxford History of the Prison*, eds. Morris and Rothman, 1995, pp. 151–177; Christianson, *With Liberty for Some*, 1998; Applebaum, *Gulag*, 2003; "The Abu-Za'abal Prison," www.hsje.org/THE%20ABU-ZA-ABAL%20PRISON, retrieved 07/30/05.

TUCHTHUIZEN. In early modern Europe the Dutch distinguished the prison from other modes of confinement with the term *tuchthuizen*, which translates to "houses of discipline."

Source: Pieter Spierenburg, "The Body and the State," in *Oxford History of the Prison*, eds. Morris and Rothman, 1998, pp. 44–70.

TUNISIA. Tunisia's prison system is operated under the direction of the Ministry of Justice. Recent information is scarce. In 1996 the country had 23,165 prisoners, a rate of 253 per 100,000 of the national population. Tunisia's most prominent prisons include the central prisons at Tunis, Bajah, Bizerte, Qabis, Qafsah, Al Qayrawan, Al Kaf, Safiqis, Susah, and Bardo. Smaller jails operated in more sparsely populated areas. As of 1990 most recidivist prisoners were expected to work at hard labor at the agricultural facility at Jabal Faqirin. First-time and minor offenders are often allowed to serve their sentences in open camps that emphasize rehabilitation. Virtually all the prisons that existed prior to 1990 were constructed during the French colonial period that preceded independence in 1956. Most reports indicate that during the French era most prisoners were valued as cheap labor. Since independence some strides have been made toward reform. Prisoners are provided a number of amenities, including radios, televisions, beds and mattresses, and access to medical care and various educational and vocational programs. Food rations are reportedly barely adequate, and visits by friends and family are very short.

Sources: Kurian, *WEPP*, 1989; ICPS, Tunisia, Africa, 1996; Walmsley, *WPPL*, 2003.

TUOL SLENG PRISON. *See* S-21

TURKEY. Turkey's leaders did not focus on prison reform until the creation of the Turkish Republic in 1923 under Kemal Attaturk. By 1935 Turkey housed almost 35,000 inmates in 362 prisons. Most characteristic of the system at this time was the popularity of small prisons, with the average facility having less than 50 inmates, and with only 6 having more than 500 prisoners at one time. By the 1930s only 3 of the prisons were considered modern, but the majority were initially conceived for other purposes such as barracks, schools, and warehouses. Istanbul's modern institution was built to hold prisoners waiting for trial and includes separate cells for women either waiting for trial or already sentenced, as well as a special block for juvenile offenders. Little progress had been made toward classification of prisoners in Turkey at that time, with some Turkish prisons holding 200 inmates in one large room, regardless of offense. The majority of sentences toward mid-century were rather short, with few serving life sentences.

Compared to most prisons in the Western world in the 1930s, Turkish prisoners enjoyed a wide range of freedom. Without organized programs or constructive regimes, prisoners spent a good part of the day mingling with each other, smoking, talking, eating, or playing games of chance. The prison menu offers only 900 grams of bread per day, but most inmates are able to supplement this with food from friends and relatives.

In 1926 the Turkish penal code was modeled after the Italian penal code. However, the inauguration of solitary imprisonment required too much capital, and related prison reform was tabled until the budget was available. Although the first discussion of prison reform revolved around youthful offenders, the first legislation was directed at adults. In 1933 Bay Sukru Saracoglu was appointed as Minister of Justice, and one of his first acts was to hire a socially aware lawyer named Mutahhar Serif Basoglu to survey the state of Turkish prisons. Influenced by advances in penal reform from the United States, and after voluntarily serving an anonymous stint in prison as had his hero **Thomas Mott Osborne**, Basoglu convinced the minister that an overhaul of the system was in order. Basoglu was sent to Europe to study various prison systems and upon his return was selected as acting general of prisons.

Basoglu's first step was to create a penal colony on Imrali Island, seven miles from the Turkish coast. In 1936 the first 50 prisoners arrived here. Most were young, serious offenders who had already served part of their sentences in Istanbul, but they were selected because of their prison records and had skills that could be of use. Each day served at the colony counted as two; here they could earn a wage in preparation for release and had opportunities to improve their education. The colony saw success in its first year, with the proceeds earned from products cultivated and sold from the colony paying much of its expense. Invigorated by the success of Imrali, Basoglu led similar ventures at Edirne and at a coalmine in Zonguldak.

Today the nation's penal system is operated under the control of the General Directorate of Prisons and Houses of Detention in the Ministry of Justice. Almost every town operates some type of jail; every district maintains at least one. Many of these facilities are deteriorating, having been in use since the Ottoman Empire. Most recently new so-called penitentiary labor establishments have been opened, but these are distinctive only for the availability of labor equipment. Prison labor is mandatory at all institutions. Inmates can send half their prison earnings to family members, with the rest paying for rations or held for release. Turkish prisons have been routinely cited for overcrowding, but the reduction of prison sentences for less serious crimes and the commutation of long sentences in recent years have relieved this problem somewhat. Between 1984 and 1991 the prison population decreased from 46,000 to 10,656. Under a special laws category political prisoners and terrorists are counted separately and in 1991 numbered more than 32,000. A number of hunger strikes over poor conditions in 1989 led to attempts to reform the prisons, resulting in a prison reform bill in 1993 that offered to end corporal punishment, bread-and-water diets, and separate confinement in dark cells. But by the following year none of these reforms had been acted on.

As of 2003 Turkey maintained 562 prison facilities with a designated capacity for 70,320 prisoners. As of 2003 the government reported a prison population of 64,051, or 91.1 percent of capacity, a rate of 92 per 100,000 of the national population. More than half the inmates were pre-trial detainees or remand prisoners. Turkey has seen a dramatic increase in its prison population since 1992, when it recorded a rate of 55 per 100,000 of the national population. *See also* **MIDNIGHT EXPRESS**.

Sources: E. Gueron, "Turkey Plans Better Prisons," *Christian Century* 53 (1936), p. 1508; Teeters, *World Penal Systems*, 1944; LCCS, "Turkey: Penal System," January 1995; ICPS, Turkey, Asia, 2003.

TURKMENISTAN. The country's prison system is administered under the Ministry of Internal Affairs. The most recent information indicates nineteen prisons holding approximately 22,000 prisoners, an estimated rate of 489 per 100,000 of the national population.

Source: ICPS, Turkmenistan, Asia, 2004.

TURNKEY. The term "turnkey" is slang for prison guard. It refers to the guard's main function, which is to control the cell keys and make sure prisoners are in their cells. According to Eric Partridge "turnkey" can be traced back to at least 1821.

Source: Eric Partridge, *A Dictionary of Slang and Unconventional English*, 5th ed. (London: Routledge & Paul, 1961).

TUVALU. Tuvalu's prison system is operated by the Police and Prisons Department. As of 2000 the country reported 6 prisoners in the island's one prison facility, which was designed for 56 inmates. Tuvalu's rate of imprisonment was 56 per 100,000 of the national population.

Sources: ICPS, Tuvalu, Oceania, 2002; Walmsley, *WPPL*, 2003.

TYROOMI. *Tyroomi* refers to Russia's closed prisons. The *tyrooma* regime is utilized for prisoners convicted of the most serious crimes or those individuals regarded as physically dangerous to staff and other prisoners. Many have been transferred from other prisons for disciplinary reasons. In 2001 Russia maintained thirteen tyroomi capable of holding 7,910 inmates.

Source: Walmsley, *Further Developments in the Prison Systems of Central and Eastern Europe*, 2003.

U

UGANDA. Until independence from British rule the main prison in Uganda was Luzira Prison outside Kampala. Jails were also common in other significant towns. Initially prisoners confined to Luzira were separated into a number of categories, including Europeans, Asians, children, women, long-term inmates, and so-called recidivists. In a separate building were punishment rooms and a death row, as well as workshops and a hospital. By the mid-1960s the Ugandan Prison Service maintained thirty prisons, a number of which were devoted to a rehabilitation regime of an industrial or agricultural nature. As the 1960s ended the prisons were controlled by a Prison Service force of 3,000 guards, who answered to the commissioner of prisons.

In the 1970s during the Idi Amin era Ugandan prisons rapidly deteriorated. Reports surfaced that indicated that Langi and Acholi soldiers suspected of opposing the regime were executed at the Makindye and Mutukula military prisons on the periphery of Kampala. However, other prisons were the scenes of even worse carnage, including reports of prisoners turned cannibals in one institution. Conditions continued to decay into the 1980s, with **Amnesty International** reporting overcrowding and political imprisonment being common. However, there were also reports that some guards treated prisoners more humanely, allowing inmates to read, to exercise, and to frequent religious services.

Despite promises by President Museveni to improve prison conditions, by the end of the 1980s prisoners still lived under the most odious conditions imaginable. According to Uganda human rights activists, in 1986 there were 10,000 prisoners in the Murchison Bay Prison, which was built for a capacity of 800 inmates.

Today the Uganda Prisons Service operates under the Ministry of Internal Affairs, which is responsible for central government prisons, and the local government, which directs local government prisons. In mid-2002 there were estimated to be 15,902 held in 45 central government prisons, and 6,000 in 149 local government prisons. Almost two thirds of the prisoners in central government prisons were either on remand or pre-trial detainees. These prisons were at 186.4 percent of capacity. The nation's prison population rate was estimated at 89 per 100,000 of the national population in 2002.

Sources: Julius Lewin, "Uganda's Prison Problem," *Howard Journal*, 1936, pp. 409–410; Julius Lewin, "Crime and Punishment in Africa," *Howard Journal*, Spring 1940, pp. 245–248; Kurian, *WEPP*, 1989; LCCS, "Uganda: Prison System" and "Criminal Justice System," December 1990; ICPS, Uganda, Africa, 2002.

UKRAINE. The country's prison system was the responsibility of the Ministry of Internal Affairs until 1998, when it was placed under the newly created State Department for the Execution of Punishments. As of 2003 there were 180 penal facilities holding 198,386 prisoners. A breakdown of the prison facilities indicates 33 are pre-trial "investigation isolators," or **SIZOs**, 128 corrective labor colonies, 11 educational colonies for juveniles, and 8 facilities dedicated to alcoholics. Two of the SIZOs at Vinnytsia and Zhytomir are regarded as prisons, or *tyroomi*. The corrective labor colonies feature a variety of regimes from maximum security to open institutions. Beginning in 1999 the practice of naming the camps by number was replaced with using individual names. As of 2001 the Ukraine held 35,334 prisoners in pre-trial detention, which would make it the sixth-highest rate in Europe; since then the number has grown from 18 to 21 percent of the prison population. Currently the prison rate is 416 per 100,000 of the national population, almost double the 1991 rate of 231 per 100,000 of the national population. Periodic amnesties have been used to alleviate prison overcrowding.

Overcrowding is a major problem in the prison system. As is customary in Eastern Europe the availability of single cells is virtually nonexistent. The prisons are also plagued by a high rate of HIV and tuberculosis, inadequate budgetary support, and a dearth of work opportunities for prisoners.

In 2001 the prison staff numbered 48,000, an increase of 27 percent since 1996. Basic training reportedly includes a probationary period of one month in prison, followed by 45 days of training school.

Current efforts to improve the prison system have been directed at creating an agricultural farm in each institution, providing better food and medical care, improving lighting and ventilation, and increasing the capacity of the prisons system.

Sources: ICPS, Ukraine, Europe, 2003; Walmsley, *Further Developments in the Prison Systems of Central and Eastern Europe*, 2003.

UNITED ARAB EMIRATES. In 1998 the United Arab Emirates held approximately 6,000 prisoners, of these more than 40 percent were either on remand or pre-trial detainees.

Source: ICPS, United Arab Emirates, Middle East, 1998.

UNITED KINGDOM. *See* ENGLAND AND WALES (UK); SCOTLAND (UK)

UNITED STATES FEDERAL PRISON SYSTEM. Until the late nineteenth century anyone convicted of a federal crime was imprisoned in state institutions because there were no federal prison facilities. This system worked as long as state prisons were permitted to lease out inmates and received boarding fees from the federal government. The number of federal prisoners doubled between 1885 and 1895, and in 1887 Congress stepped in to end the contract leasing of federal prisoners. In response state prisons refused to accept federal prisoners, necessitating the construction of federal penitentiaries.

A number of factors led to the creation of the federal prison system. A rapidly growing population and the promulgation of a number of new federal laws naturally led to more federal prisoners. National outrage over the conditions of state prisons and the horrors of the convict-leasing system that led to the prohibition against leasing federal prisoners led to the creation of federal facilities. In 1891 Congress passed the Three Prisons Act, which authorized the construction of three federal penitentiaries. The first federal prison was built in **Leavenworth**, Kansas, and received its first charges in 1895. Soon followed the U.S. penitentiary at Atlanta in 1902 and **McNeil Island**, Washington, in 1907.

During its first decade the federal prison system became distinct from the state system. By 1930 five federal prisons were in operation. Despite the addition of more federal prisons, the facilities became more overcrowded as the federal criminal justice system created more laws to break. Poor recordkeeping and overcrowding led to the creation of the Federal Bureau of Prisons in 1929.

Sources: Keve, *Prisons and the American Conscience*, 1991; Roth, *Crime and Punishment*, 2005.

UNITED STATES PRISON SYSTEM. There was little need for prisons and the concept of imprisonment in colonial America. Typically, individuals were only detained temporarily as they waited either for court or quick but certain punishments. Incarceration was considered an expensive proposition and a loss of valuable labor, so confinement rarely lasted more than one day. In 1682, almost a century before the outbreak of the American Revolution, the Quakers of Pennsylvania adopted **William Penn**'s *Frame of Government,* which became a blueprint for the colony and perhaps the first example of penal reform in American history. One of the major reforms was the abandonment of the practice of **gaolers** (jailers) charging prisoners for fees, room and board, and other luxuries. The Quaker reformers of Pennsylvania would dominate American prison reform into the nineteenth century.

Prior to 1750 incarceration by statute was rare compared to more common physical and public punishments. Colonial jails held a variety of military and political prisoners; however, sentences were undetermined. Several New England colonies developed versions of the pre-Enlightenment prison, but incarceration did not become an important criminal sanction until the late eighteenth century following the end of the American Revolution. Early jails in post-revolutionary America were utilized to hold debtors and others behind on tax and fine payments. So, initially, jails were considered more a method of coercion to make debtors pay rather than function as a criminal sanction.

In the early eighteenth century American jail conditions mirrored its counterparts in the Western world. Cellular confinement was virtually nonexistent; jails and prisons were little more than large rooms housing together every manner of prisoner—debtors, felons, children, the mentally ill, and the dissolute. A number of prison architectural historians suggest that the roots of the modern prison system are found in the evolution of Philadelphia's **Walnut Street Jail**.

Thanks to reformers like **Benjamin Rush** and **John Howard**, the Walnut Street Jail and the jails that followed it made the transformation from a purely punitive regime to one that emphasized reform, rehabilitation, and, most important, penitence. Rush and others favored introducing single cells to Walnut Street Jail as a way of separating the most dangerous prisoners from the others, eliminating the so-called element of criminal contagion. By the early 1820 two competing prison models had evolved out of the innovations of the Walnut Street Jail. The **Pennsylvania system** that replaced Walnut Street Jail favored 24-hour isolation and labor behind bars. However, the alternative **Auburn Prison** scheme that developed in New York favored cellular isolation at night and congregate labor in strict silence by day. Ultimately, the Auburn scheme became the dominant prison design in the United States. What made it so popular was that congregate labor was more productive than individual labor. Hence, Auburn prisons were more cost-effective—they saved more money and made a profit, the bottom line for any prison administrator.

A new wave of prison reform coincided with the end of the American Civil War in 1865. By the late 1860s America's prisons were plagued by overcrowding. Together with the growing opposition of the labor unions, who opposed the unfair competition prison labor posed to free labor, prison reform was on the horizon. Despite the new environment for reform, the Southern states, so devastated by the war, would end up playing catch up for the next century. Ill-equipped to house prisoners in conventional prisons, most of the Southern states turned to **convict leasing**, agricultural prison camps, and the **chain gang**.

The meeting of the first **National Prison Congress** in Cincinnati, Ohio, in 1870 represented a huge theoretical turning point in penology. Building on the recent experiments with indeterminate sentences and the mark system in Ireland and Australia, the congress adopted a Declaration of Principles (see Appendix I), which is regarded as one of the most progressive documents in the history of nineteenth-century prison reform. Before the end of the century a number of experiments at reform were attempted. New York's **Elmira Reformatory** laid the groundwork for the reformatory movement in 1876 by emphasizing indeterminate sentencing and the **mark system** over the fixed sentence. Between 1877 and 1901 twelve states would create similar reformatories.

One important area that went virtually unnoticed at the National Prison Congress was the incarceration of female offenders. However, in 1874 Indiana opened the nation's first female-run prison. The following year Massachusetts opened a reformatory for women. However, female imprisonment was not a high priority for reformers in the early nineteenth century with so few female prisoners. New York's **Sing Sing Prison** was the first prison to establish a separate wing for women when it established the **Mount Pleasant Female Prison** in the 1830s. Between 1870 and 1935 20 female reformatories were built exclusively for women as female criminality became more of an issue.

During the nineteenth century American prisons adopted such correctional innovations as **probation, parole**, and indeterminate sentencing. Between 1870 and 1904 the country's inmate population grew by 62 percent. No prisons felt the increase more than the country's state prisons. By 1935 the state prison population had grown 162 percent since 1904. Despite the addition of new prisons and the implementation of new progressive experiments, the first decades of the twentieth century suggested the return to an earlier era, placing less emphasis on moral instruction, education, and classification in favor of the more punitive and financially lucrative labor regime of the nineteenth century.

Prior to the 1890s federal prisoners were housed in state prisons. This agreement worked as long as the federal government paid boarding fees and allowed prisons to lease out convict labor. When Congress stepped in and prohibited the leasing of federal prisoners, state prisons refused to accept federal prisoners. As a result, a handful of federal prisons were built and in 1929 the Federal Bureau of Prisons was created.

During the Great Depression the nation's prison population rose from 79 to 137 per 100,000 between 1925 and 1939. By 1933 the country reported 4,300 prison establishments holding 233,632 inmates, more than half in state institutions. Prison industries were especially affected by the growth of the labor union movement between 1915 and 1930. The only prison labor that labor unions approved of was the so-called **state-use** system, in which prison-manufactured goods could be sold only if they did not compete with free manufacturers. By 1940 state-use purchase of prison-built furniture, stationary, and other products was mandatory in 22 states.

With the continued increase of the American prison population in the 1980s and 1990s, prisons responded to a number of problems with new initiatives that are actually rooted in the previous century. Prison privatization was able to flourish in the 1980s because of the growth of anti-union sentiments as prison labor became controversial once more. The Federal Bureau of Prisons opened its first **supermaximum prison** at Florence, Colorado, in 1994. Writer Charles Dickens criticized the solitary confinement of **Eastern State Penitentiary** in the 1840s. Were he alive today, it is unlikely he would respond in like manner to prisons in which prisoners spend 23 hours each day confined in 7-by-12-foot cells. At least 36 states now operate similar institutions. In order to move to an easier regime prisoners must maneuver through a progressive regime not unlike the mark system of the previous century.

Today the United States maintains different prison systems for each level of government. The Federal Bureau of Prisons and state and local authorities all maintain prisons under the direction of the Department of Justice. The United States incarcerates more people than almost any other country. According to Sam Roberts, at the end of 2002, there were 2,166,260 people behind bars. This represents 701 prisoners for every 100,000 American residents. Just seven years earlier the rate was 601 per 100,000. By mid-2003 the picture was even bleaker, with more than two million Americans in prison. This does not include the more than 110,000 juveniles in various custodial facilities and the almost 2,000 prisoners in Native American jails. According to 2000 statistics, the U.S. prison system consisted of 3,365 local jails, 1,558 state institutions, and 146 federal prisons. Since prisons have been a growth industry for several decades in the United States, there is plenty of room in the prison system to accommodate these inmates. At last count there were 715 prisoners for 100,000 of the national population, but the estimated prison occupancy rate was 106 percent. The least crowded institutions are the local jails at 94 percent, followed by state prisons at 110 percent, and federal institutions at 145.9 percent.

Sources: ICPS, United States, 2003; Sam Roberts, *Who We Are Now: The Changing Face of America in the Twenty-first Century* (New York: Henry Holt, 2004); Roth, *Crime and Punishment*, 2005.

UPPER VOLTA. *See* BURKINA FASO

URUGUAY. Very little has been written about the early development of the Uruguayan prison system. By the end of the 1870s official policy clearly sanctioned the humane treatment of prisoners. In 1882 efforts were directed at creating a new penal code. The commission assigned this task first presented a report on the state of contemporary prison systems. The Uruguayan government accepted the commission's recommendation to adopt a combination of the **Pennsylvania** and **Auburn** systems in 1889. Among the most important ingredients of this plan was the emphasis on mandatory work and the inplementation of a gradual system, or **mark system**, that emphasized rewards and penalties during the rehabilitation process. The separate confinement of prisoners was abandoned in 1912 as penitentiary reform gathered momentum.

In its early stages the Uruguayan penal system was administered by the Ministry of Public Instruction and Social Prevention. By the 1940s there were three federal prisons and the Educational Work Colony. Within the latter was a section for the criminally insane. Upon being sentenced to prison, offenders are brought to the prisons of Montevideo, which included Prison No. 1, Prison No. 2, the Establishment for the Correction and Detention of Women, and the Educational Colony of Work. Meanwhile, jails hold those waiting in temporary confinement.

All that have been accused are housed in Prison No. 1 until they receive their sentence. In the meantime they are examined by the Observation Pavilion to classify each person's physical and mental health. Following receiving sentencing, prisoners are confined in Prison No. 2 for the remainder of the sentence. Women were housed separately in the Establishment for the Correction and Detention of Women.

Today the prison system is administered by the Ministry of Interior. Each of the nineteen departments is responsible for maintaining jails to temporarily confine prisoners awaiting trial and sentencing. Prisoners sentenced to prison terms are incarcerated at the three federal prisons or the San Jose de Mayo work colony. The work colony contains maximum-, minimum-, and medium-security units on a parcel of 1,800 acres. One of the three federal prisons is exclusively for women. Uruguay is one of Latin America's most social service–oriented countries, and its work colony is supposed to help rehabilitate prisoners most identified with this lifestyle in preparation for future release. According to recent penal code provisions, inmates in minimum-security facilities can be hired for public works projects, road construction, and quarrying. Work is apparently mandatory for those awaiting trial, but such individuals earn a small wage that is paid upon release.

One noteworthy addition to the prisons system has been the adoption of a pre-release facility for individuals on the cusp of freedom. At this stage they are permitted to have their families with them until release. The facility is located close to the penitentiary, but not too close, separated as it is by a moat.

Sources: Teeters, ed., *World Penal Systems*, 1944; LCCS, "Uruguay: The Criminal Justice System," December 1990; Salvatore and Aguirre, "The Birth of the Penitentiary in Latin America," in *The Birth of the Penitentiary in Latin America*, eds. Salvatore and Aguirre, 1996, pp. 1–43.

UZBEKISTAN. Uzbekistan's General Department of Corrections and Labour is operated under the Ministry of Internal Affairs. In August 2003 the country's 53 prisons held 48,000 prisoners in a system designed for a capacity of 56,300. Uzbekistan's penal institutions included 11 pre-trial detention centers, 1 prison, and

41 prison colonies. Of the 41 prison colonies, 3 were considered medium security, 12 short term, and 1 maximum security. Of the other institutions, 1 was for women, 2 for juveniles, 1 for former law enforcement officials, 1 republican hospital, and 2 tuberculosis colonies. As of mid-2003 the prison rate was 184 per 100,000 of the national population, a decline from 257 per 100,000 in 2002 and 265 per 100,000 in 2000.

Source: ICPS, Uzbekistan, Asia, 2004.

V

VAN DIEMEN'S LAND. Better known today as Tasmania, this island off the Australian coast was first settled by the British as part of New South Wales in 1803 before becoming a separate colony in 1825. It was originally named after Anthony van Diemen, the governor general of the Dutch East India Company and organizer of an expedition in 1642 to map "the remaining unknown part of the terrestrial globe." The leader of the expedition was an Abel Tasman, who ironically sailed by Australia, missing the continent in the process. However, he did come across the island, which he surmised was the mainland, and named it for his sponsor. Two hundred years later the name was changed to the more familiar Tasmania.

Van Diemen's Land would serve as a **transportation** destination for some 65,000 English convicts. In time it acquired a terrible reputation among the convicts. In 1803 the first settlers landed on the island, a party that included 24 convicts and 25 free settlers. Between 1812 and 1817 the white population of New South Wales and Van Diemen's Land increased from 12,471 to 20,379, the majority of whom were convicts. Lieutenant Governor Thomas Davey (1758–1823) governed the island between 1813 and 1816. Van Diemen's Land was not considered a separate colony but part of New South Wales, the eastern portion of Australia.

The appointment of Sir George Arthur (1784–1854) to lead Van Diemen's Land beginning in 1824 was a turning point in the history of the colony, placing it in the hands of what Robert Hughes noted was "the most powerful, skilful, and ruthless figure in the colony." Arthur's resume included military service against Napoleon and service as post commandant of the slave state of British Honduras. His stint in the latter position would come in handy in the convict colony. When Arthur was chosen as lieutenant governor he lobbied the Colonial Office for permission to run the outpost as a separate colony from New South Wales. In 1825 he got his wish, when Van Diemen's Land officially became a separate colony. Arthur directed the colony from 1824 to 1836.

In 1830 Port Arthur was established by Governor George Arthur, for whom the city was named. Arthur endeavored to make the penal colony escape-proof. Arthur proved to be an adept and officious administrator, ruling the island with the help of an informant system. More than 1,700 convicts passed through Port Arthur in its first five years. Upon arrival convicts were issued yellow-dyed clothing, jacket, trousers, ankle boots, waistcoat, cap, and shirt. Next stop was the commissary shop for a blanket, a rug, and a bedtick. Daily rations consisted of three-quarter pound of meat, one and three-quarter pounds of flour or bread, three-quarter pound of vegetables, and one-half ounce of soap. Prison guards fared little better, with daily rations roughly the same as the convicts' except for more soap and the permission to grow fruit and vegetables to supplement their diets.

By 1840 Australian settlers and freemen were so numerous that they had enough support to be taken seriously by government officials. The overwhelming majority opposed convict labor because of the job competition and, furthermore, did not want more criminals being dumped in their colony. In 1840 all transportation to South Wales ceased but would continue in Van Diemen's Land until 1853. *See also* PORT ARTHUR PRISON.

Sources: Hughes, *The Fatal Shore*, 1987; John Hirst, "The Australian Experience: The Convict Colony," in *The Oxford History of the Prison*, eds. Morris and Rothman, 1998, pp. 235–265.

VANUATU. The Vanuatu Prison Services is currently responsible for the operation of four prisons housing 93 inmates. As of mid-2003 the prison rate was 93 per 100,000 of the national population. The four prisons include three located at each of the three district headquarters, and one at Vila. There is also a rehabilitation center in Vanuatu. Since most inmates are incarcerated for public intoxication and related offenses, most offenders serve less than one-month sentences. According to reports from 1989, the prisons were adequate and offered vocational training. There is a minimum-security facility at Pialulub that allows prisoners to cohabitate with their families while they undergo vocational training and then earn a wage.

Sources: Kurian, *WEPP*, 1989; ICPS, Vanautu, Oceania, 2003.

VAUX, RICHARD (1816–1895). Richard Vaux followed in his father Roberts's footsteps by serving as president of Eastern State Penitentiary's Board of Inspectors. Vaux garnered a worldwide reputation as a penologist, educator, and philanthropist, and warden of **Eastern State Penitentiary**. However, his militant approach varied from his father's more compromising strategy. During his lifetime he proved an effective advocate of the solitary **Pennsylvania system**. Not until the 1860s were two men celled together. His book *A Brief Sketch of the Origin and History of the State Penitentiary for the Eastern District of Pennsylvania* was published in 1872.

Sources: Teeters and Shearer, *The Prison at Philadelphia*, 1957; Barnes, *The Evolution of Penology in Pennsylvania*, 1968.

VAUX, ROBERTS (1786–1836). Roberts Vaux was a Quaker and prominent spokesperson for the Philadelphia Prison Society. During his career as a prison reformer he became recognized as a historian, educator, philanthropist, and penologist. He was later appointed as one of the commissioners to construct **Eastern State Penitentiary**. Roberts came to prominence as penal reformer and advocate of the separate system. He was an advocate of solitary confinement but with work and access to books as a method of reforming prisoners. Vaux worked as one of the society's corresponding secretaries. His correspondence with prison reformers in America and Europe is well documented, including his response to **Thomas Eddy**'s inquiries about building his prison in New York.

Sources: Barnes, *The Evolution of Penology in Pennsylvania*, 1968; McKelvey, *American Prisons*, 1977.

VENEZUELA. Little had changed in Venezuelan prisons between the colonial era and the late 1930s. Antonio Guzman Blanco made early attempts at modernization between 1870 and 1887. During Blanco's administration he oversaw the construction a crafts school and legislation was passed (on paper only) directing the erection of regional penitentiaries at San Carlos, Puerto Cabello, and Santiago. However, little construction, let alone reform, was accomplished until 1896, when an act was promulgated that supported the introduction of a system of criminological files, infirmaries, and workshops in each institution. Despite noble intentions, the plans for these three regional penitentiaries went nowhere.

Rather than build new penitentiaries, dictator Juan Vicente Gomez discovered between 1908 and 1935 that old structures filled the same purpose as any proposed facility. Political prisoners and common criminals alike found accommodations in the antiquated Castillo at Puerto Cabello, the Rotunda at Caracas, and the Castillo at Maracaibo, saving the expense of building new prisons for the same purpose. After the fall of the dictatorship in 1935, a model penitentiary was constructed in Caracas, achieving some of the goals set by reformers six decades earlier.

According to the Penal Code of 1964, Article VII, there are six corporal punishments. These include a term in the penitentiary, a prison term, arrest, assignment to a penal colony, confinement in a specific location, and expulsion from the country. Anyone sentenced to a term in the penitentiary must follow a regime of mandatory labor and maximum security. Overcrowding and understaffing have been the continuous bane of the Venezuelan prison system. By the mid-1980s, the average prison housed 15,000 inmates, far above the suggested capacity. The majority of those incarcerated were still awaiting trial. As late as 1989 only 25 percent had been tried and convicted. This has lead to the usual problems associated with the twin afflictions of prison systems worldwide—physical abuse and poor sanitation. The prisons have continued to deteriorate at a time when prison populations have been rising as the result of a spike in crime.

The Venezuelan prison system comprises 25 prisons in three different categories. Seventeen are judicial detention units, and seven are national penitentiaries and jails; the National Institute of Female Orientation in Los Teques completes the triumvirate of facility types.

Civilian members of the Ministry of Justice staff prisons on the inside, whereas National Guard staff provides exterior security. Attempts have been made to separate inmates in the different categories of prisons; however, many of the prisons have become microcosms of sorts by maintaining separate wings for each "type of inmate." For example, the Caracas Prison has a separate wing for homosexuals, and others have units for minors.

During the 1990s a number of attempts were made to "humanize" the prisons. In 1996 the Ministry of Justice closed Catia Prison in Caracas, reportedly the worst of the nation's prisons. Prior to its closure Catia Prison was holding 2,400 prisoners in a jail meant for 700. Overcrowding persists as one of Venezuela's main concerns. With a capacity for 15,000 prisoners, the country's prisons often hold almost twice that number. Inmates at Sabaneta and Ciudad Bolivar are often forced to sleep two and three to a bed. Complicating the crisis is that nearly three quarters of the prisoners have not yet been convicted of a crime and should not even be behind bars. Overcrowding also exacerbates violent conditions that in 1996 alone saw 207 prisoners killed and 1,133 injured, a weekly death toll of 4 prisoners. Weapons ranging from knives and pistols to grenades have been confiscated in recent years. With just one untrained, low-paid guard for 150 inmates, it is not surprising that corruption is rampant. Following several riots and continued prison violence, the government was forced to bring in the National Guard, who reportedly retaliated against the prisoners. In 1996 a fire blamed on National Guardsmen resulted in the death of 25 inmates in La Planta Prison. Following the fire Human Rights Watch–Americas issues a statement that charged Venezuela along with Brazil with having "probably the worst [prison conditions] in the hemisphere."

Although the prisons are deficient in virtually every area, they offer prisoners a liberal visiting policy, with two visiting days each week, one of which is for conjugal visits. Despite long waits to enter the facilities, once inside there are no barriers to physical contact between visitors and prisoners. Over the past decade there has been a noted improvement in prison conditions. In 1994 the prison system held 28,000 prisoners in 32 prisons meant to hold 15,000. By mid-2003 the country had 29 prisons holding 19,554 prisoners, which was considered 97.2 percent of capacity, or 76 per 100,000 of the national population.

Sources: LCCS, "Venezuela: The Prison System" and "Criminal Justice System," December 1990; Mary Matheson, "Hellish Life Provokes Violence in Venezuela Prison," *Houston Chronicle*, October 15, 1994, 23A; Bart Jones, "Guards Acting out of 'Wickedness' Start Fire in Venezuela Jail, Kill 25 Inmates," *Houston Chronicle*, October 24, 1996, 24A; Salvatore and Aguirre, "The Birth of the Penitentiary in Latin America," in *Birth of the Penitentiary in Latin America*, eds. Salvatore and Aguirre, 1996, pp. 1–44; Human Rights Watch, "Prison Conditions in Venezuela," www.hrw.org/advocacy/prisons/venez-sm.htm, 1997; ICPS, Venezuela, South America, 2003.

VIETNAM. Scholars trace Vietnamese prison origins to somewhere between 111 B.C. and A.D. 939, when China ruled the region. Following independence from China in the tenth century, Vietnam continued to base its penal institutions on Chinese models. As early as the fifteenth century a Vietnamese penal code suggested a tradition of moderation and humanitarian treatment toward prisoners. Reports by nineteenth-century visitors indicate that some classification procedures were used in prisons, but little regard was given toward separation by age or offense, in stark contrast to mid-nineteenth-century Western prisons. During the late nineteenth century the French began to replace local institutions. The colonial penal system grew out of the prisoner camps during the subjugation of the country by the French beginning in the 1860s.

Under the French Indochinese prison system, which included Laos, Cambodia, Annam, Tonkin, and Cochin China, the smallest penal facilities were provincial prisons meant to hold between 50 and 100 prisoners, serving less than three years for petty crimes. Larger central prisons were operated in Saigon, Hanoi, Phnom Penh, and Vientiane. The first of these central prisons was *Kham Lon*, or "the Big

Jail," built in Saigon in the early 1860s. In 1898 a second central prison, *Hoa Lo*, or "the Oven," was built outside Hanoi. During the American war in Vietnam Hoa Lo won notoriety as the **Hanoi Hilton**. Hoa Lo was originally designed for up to 600 prisoners, but renovation and overcrowding allowed it to hold 1,430 prisoners by 1933. The main distinction between central and provincial prisons was the professionalism and training of the staff. Whereas central prisons were typically located in urban centers, penitentiaries were positioned in more remote areas in order to alleviate security concerns. The main distinction between the penitentiaries and central prisons was the ethnic diversity of the guards. Central prison guards were predominately ethnic Vietnamese, whereas the penitentiaries were staffed by ethnic minorities from the surrounding regions, such Mnong, Ede, and Jarai tribesmen. According to Peter Zinoman, the "staffing of penitentiaries with minorities was one of the conventional divide-and-rule tactics of the colonial administration."

Supplementing the penitentiaries, central and provincial prisons were civil prisons, supervised by municipal officials and **houses of correction** for juvenile offenders. By the mid-1860s the French were also sending convicts to its penal colonies in New Caledonia, and then in French Guiana. During the last decades of the nineteenth century the French colonial state expanded its control by annexing protectorates in Annam and Tonkin. This led to a new round of prison construction. Annam's first prison was constructed at Lao Bo in 1896. This was followed by Hai Phong Prison in 1904, Cao Bang Penitentiary in 1905, and Thai Nguyen in 1908.Prison construction waxed and waned, slowing down in the 1920s and then rising during the anticolonial strife of the 1930s. During World War II Communist uprisings saw the colonial prison population peak at 30,000 in 1942.

As with other socialist nations, little information is available on the country's modern prisons. According to most sources, there has been little if any construction of new prisons since the French colonial era. The largest and best-known facilities are located at Hoa Lo in Hanoi, which is considered the largest; Haiphong; Nam Dinh; and Chi Hoa in Ho Chi Minh City. It is estimated that the twelve national prisons hold upwards of 40,000 inmates. More than 130 miles south of Ho Chi Minh City is the prison island of Con San. District and provincial capitals typically have some form of detention room or jail. Hanoi, for example has 18 detention centers, each capable of holding 500 individuals awaiting trial. Following the fall of South Vietnam a number of labor camps were built based on the Soviet archetype.

To distinguish with certainty the number and classification of inmates assigned to the various prisons, work camps, and administrative facilities is virtually impossible. It is estimated that each of the forty provincial prisons can hold between 1,000 and 5,000 prisoners. Building on some recent developments in reform a number of provinces have "model prisons," which have been compared to "new economic zones," where prisoners are given the opportunity to work in agricultural production to earn remuneration.

Reports by ex-prisoners indicate that conditions remain harsh and squalid. Days revolve around labor and daily rehabilitation lectures. Visits from friends and family are strictly controlled, with few visits allowed. According to these sources, the prisons are heavily policed, with an estimated one guard for every 250 inmates.

The evolution of re-education camps in Vietnam as a form of social control is an important development in terms of the prison system, although such camps are considered an alternative incarceration. By the late 1980s re-education camps were considered the favored form of social control. The main purpose of these camps was to detain members of certain classes until they accepted assimilation into the new social norms. Its intent was to control the so-called deviant element while at the same time preventing counter-revolution and resistance. The concept of re-education camps was adopted from Chinese Communists and put into practice during the French-Indochina war of the 1950s. Another explanation for the popularity of these institutions was that the transient nature of the early North Vietnamese government in the 1950s made sustaining traditional prisons impossible.

Following the fall of South Vietnam in 1975, these camps began to attract international attention. Although controlled by the Ministry of Interior, they were always regarded as separate from prisons and orthodox penal control. Here rehabilitation was expected to occur through education and socially constructive labor.

Several types of re-education camps emerged in the North and the South after 1975. In the late 1970s the "level-three camp" were most prevalent, but by 1987 only the level-three camp, out of five different levels, was dedicated to its original purpose. In theory, the five levels were conceived in "ascending order of perceived individual recalcitrance and ascending length of incarceration."

Level-three camps were originally designed as collective reformatories directed at ideological thought reform. Since inmates at these camps were better educated, more emphasis was placed on psychological and intellectual strategies in the reform process. Over time these socialist reform camps became more oriented toward permanent incarceration, with the emphasis on re-education through forced labor and political indoctrination. Level-four and level-five camps still exist, but they are mainly as rudimentary detention centers housing individuals deemed future risks to the socialist government.

Human rights groups have targeted Vietnamese prisons since the 1990s. **Human Rights Watch** reported poor conditions, with prisoners detained in dark cells in chains and subject to torture. The Vietnamese government responded with its largest amnesty in 2000, when 12,264 prisoners were released on April 30 to commemorate the reunification of the country on that day in 1975.

The Department of Correctional Services operates under the Ministry of Public Security. The most recent statistics from 1999 indicate a prison population of 55,000, or 71 per 100,000 of the national population.

Sources: LCCS, "Vietnam: Re-education Camps" and "Vietnam: Law Enforcement," December 1987; ICPS, Vietnam, Asia, 1999; Zinoman, *The Colonial Bastille*, 2000; Walmsley, *WPPL*, 2003.

VILAIN, JEAN JACQUES PHILIPPE (1712–1777). Count Vilain came to prominence in the 1770s following his association with the Maison de Force in Ghent. In 1771 Vilain was appointed by the government of Austrian Flanders to come up with a new penal reform policy. He outlined a number of his ideas in 1775 in his book *Mémoire sur les moyens de corriger les malfacteurs et les fainéants à leur propre avantage et de les rendre utiles a l'état*. In this report he argued against corporal punishment in favor of imprisonment with hard labor, labor that would help financially benefit the institution. Vilain's main contribution was taking several ideas that had been used in the past and combining them together in the operation of the Ghent House of Correction beginning in 1775, when he became its director.

According to Norman Johnston, the use of nighttime solitary confinement and separation by gender, age, length of sentence, and criminal predisposition "had never been put into practice all at the same time before."

Sources: Deford, *Stone Walls*, 1962; Johnston, *Forms of Constraint*, 2000.

VILLERME, LOUIS RENE (c. 1820). French physician Louis Rene Villerme was inspired by the writings of **John Howard** and the **Duc de la Rochefoucauld-Liancourt,** and in 1820 he published *Prisons As They Are and As They Should Be.* Dedicating the work to de la Rochefoucauld-Liancourt, Villerme weighs forth on a variety of timely prison issues, such as architecture, hygiene, and morality. He agreed with the aforementioned proponents of solitary confinement for serious crimes and advocated the appointment of inspectors to alleviate draconian prison conditions.

Source: Albert Krebs, "John Howard's Influence on the Prison System of Europe," in *Prisons Past and Future*, ed. Freeman, 1978, pp. 35–51.

VIRGIN ISLANDS (U.S.). The Bureau of Corrections of the U.S. Virgin Islands is operated under the Department of Justice. In 2002 the country held 647 prisoners, a rate of 522 per 100,000 of the national population, up from 356 per 100,000 in 1997 and 402 per 100,000 in 2001.

Source: ICPS, Virgin Islands, USA, 2003.

WAGNITZ, H. B. (c. 1790s). While prison chaplain at Halle Prison in **Germany**, H.B. Wagnitz came under the influence of **John Howard**'s work on prison reform. Wagnitz lobbied to end the more "barbaric" forms of deterrence. He also advocated individualized treatment for inmates, human rights, and preparation of convicts for release through trades training. The year following Howard's death Wagnitz published *Historical Accounts and Observations on the Major Houses of Correction in Germany* in 1791, which he dedicated to "Howard's spirit and those on whom it rests." Wagnitz lobbied for the establishment of so-called seminaries to train prison staff. However, in several important areas his theories conflicted with Howard's— namely, in his support for small portions of food and hard, unproductive labor.

Source: Albert Krebs, "John Howard's Influence in the Prison System of Europe," in *Prisons Past and Future*, ed. Freeman, 1978, pp. 35–51.

WALLA WALLA PRISON. While the site was still a territory, in 1883 legislation was passed to build a prison at Walla Walla. The Washington State Penitentiary, as Walla Walla Prison is formally named, has earned a reputation over the past century as one of America's toughest prisons. Completed in 1887, Walla Walla was Washington's first prison and was one of the first in the Pacific Northwest. Located on the periphery of the town of Walla Walla, the penitentiary held close to 450 inmates by the beginning of the twentieth century. This prison has been the subject of a number of academic studies over the years, most recently by Ines Cardoza Freeman, in *The Joint: Language and Culture in a Maximum Security Prison* (1984), and Charles Stastny and Gabrielle Tyrnauer's *Who Rules the Joint* (1982). Today the prison houses 2,300 inmates in 4 sub-facilities, or separate prisons, each representing a different classification level. The institution sits on a 580-acre site manned by a staff of 553 security personnel and 293 support staff. In 1994 Walla Walla appointed its first woman to run this male institution.

Despite its implementation of a number of reforms, Walla Walla has been targeted by numerous critics over the years. As early the first decades of the twentieth century a progressive regime abolished striped prison uniforms and instituted several other reforms. But by the 1920s serious overcrowding and lack of constructive work led to riots and violence. One prison escape attempt in 1934 was met with public revulsion after it was revealed that guards killed seven inmates in the process with a machine gun. As in most American prisons during the 1940s, patriotism seemed to dim most tensions as hatred was focused on the Axis powers and prisoners were involved in production for the war effort.

By the 1950s Walla Walla returned to normal with a number riots and disturbances. Most prominent was the 1955 takeover of the prison by inmates. This incident was portrayed in the 1967 novel *The Riot* by F. Elli, a convict who participated in the riot. The riot was concluded when negotiations guaranteed that the riot leaders would not be placed in the dreaded wing known as the Growler. This was located in the original prison wing, where few improvements had been made since 1887. As a result, conditions there were almost medieval with an absence of ventilation and water, and with only buckets for toilets.

Conditions changed dramatically in the 1960s and 1970s as the institution adopted a more progressive and professional approach to penology. But the prison never lost its reputation for violence. In the 1970s a number escape attempts, hostage-taking incidents, and fatal stabbings of officers kept the prison in the headlines for the wrong reasons. In the 1970s alone the prison experienced 25 murders, compared to only 3 in the 1960s. Walla Walla was prominent most recently when the state held its first execution in 30 years by hanging, the first use of this form of capital punishment since 1965.

Sources: McKelvey, *American Prisons*, 1977; Richard Morgan and Keith Farrington, "Walla Walla, Washington State Penitentiary," in *Encyclopedia of American Prisons*, eds. McShane and Williams, 1996, pp. 489–493.

WALNUT STREET JAIL. There had been either a city or county prison on Philadelphia's Walnut Street in the years prior to the site's selection as Pennsylvania's first state penitentiary in 1790. The establishment of the Walnut Street Jail was a seminal event in the history of corrections, leading prison authority Negley Teeters to declare it the "cradle of the penitentiary." It was designed by architect Robert Smith in 1771 to perform a dual function as jail and **house of correction**. The Quaker prison reformers who favored a more benevolent penal philosophy inspired its creation. Although its life span from 1773 to 1835 was comparatively short, its impact was felt internationally.

When the prison accepted its first prisoners in 1773, inmates walked through a rather unimposing entrance and after passed through a brace of iron-gated doors into a hall with eight arched rooms. The main building was graced with two two-storied wings, each consisting of five rooms, which overlooked a courtyard. In the original plan each wing was dedicated to different classes of offenders who were warehoused in large rooms. One wing was devoted to misdemeanants and debtors, and on the other side was a wing that housed serious offenders and individuals awaiting trial or sentencing.

In 1790 members of the **Philadelphia Society for Alleviation of the Miseries of Public Prisons**, formed just three years earlier, convinced the state legislature to build a small block of cells inside the Walnut Street prison enclosure. Inspired by the writings of **John Howard**, this new block would be specifically dedicated to keeping the worst convicts confined to solitary cells, where it was intended that they work, sleep, and eat. When the block was completed, it was christened "Penitentiary House." It measured 40 by 25 feet and was built 3 stories high. Each of the block's 16 cells faced out toward a corridor. Construction of the cells was intended to prevent inmates from speaking with each other. However, this goal was never actually achieved. Cells measured 6 by 8 feet and were nine-feet high. High up on each wall was an iron-grated window equipped with louvers that prevented inmates from looking out. Cells were equipped with a mattress on the floor as the only piece of furniture. Each cell was connected to a water tap and privy pipe and stoves in the corridors controlled heat. Prisoners were never permitted to leave their cells. The intent was to ensconce the prisoners in solitude so they could contemplate their crimes. However, despite the noble intentions of the Quaker reformers, recent research indicates that this cellblock was probably only used to punish other prisoners who broke the rules, rather than handling offenders specifically sentenced to solitary confinement.

The real legacy of Walnut Street is twofold. First of all, the new cellblock was built with the specific purpose of housing offenders in solitary isolation at hard labor. Second, the original Walnut Street regimen incorporated a combination of congregate work by day and isolation at night. Hence its reputation as the first penitentiary in the world and the first American adoption of the theory of solitary confinement as a major step on the road to repentance.

Under the direction of **Caleb Lownes** the prison reached such prominence that prison reformers around the world came to observe the various regimens. New York's **Thomas Eddy** would incorporate congregate production by day and solitary confinement by night in the development of the **Auburn system**. By the end of the eighteenth century the prison was beset with overcrowding, violence, and escape attempts. In 1801 Lownes resigned because of various administrative problems.

An 1820 uprising resulted in the calling out of the militia to quell the disorder. The Walnut Street Jail's last years were plagued by overcrowding and turmoil. Prior to the jail's closure in 1835, according to Norman Johnston, one visitor described the Penitentiary House as "badly ventilated and suggested that inmates could converse with occupants of adjacent cells." Its remaining prisoners were transferred to **Eastern State Penitentiary**, the true birthplace of the **Pennsylvania system**.

Sources: Negley Teeters, *The Cradle of the Penitentiary: The Walnut Street Jail at Philadelphia, 1773–1835* (Philadelphia: Pennsylvania Prison Society, 1955); Thorsten Sellin, "Origin of the Pennsylvania System of Prison Discipline," *Prison Journal* 50, no. 1 (Spring/Summer 1970), pp. 19–20; McKelvey, *American Prisons*, 1977; Johnston, *Eastern State Penitentiary*, 1994.

WANDSWORTH PRISON. In 1851 England's Wandsworth opened its first prison. It was designed as a **house of correction** named the Surrey House of Correction and was capable of holding 1,000 prisoners in a regime of solitary confinement and silence. It initially held men and women. The male section was made up of five wings radiating from a central rotunda; the women's wing consisted of three wings. Although there were no **treadmills**, there were 100 **cranks** for prisoners sentenced to hard labor. Women for the most part worked in the laundry. According to Wandsworth rules, men were required to wear masks and women veils. Prison uniforms were marked by the prisoner's number. Males wore brass discs bearing their cell numbers somewhere on the arm; women wore similar accoutrements on their belts. Guards, or warders, addressed prisoners only by their cell numbers. Warders were also required to read all letters before they were sent. Beginning in 1877 Wandsworth was dedicated to holding only short-term prisoners. **Oscar Wilde** was held here during the first six months of his sentence in 1895.

Wandsworth is now considered a category B local prison. In 1989 most of the prison was updated and refurbished. In 2001 it held 1,163 inmates but had the capacity to hold 1,371. The prison regime provides a range of workshop opportunities as well as a "Listener Scheme," which provides help to prisoners at risk of harming themselves. Visits are predicated on the prisoner's sentence. Those on **remand** receive more regular visits. Prisoner's can earn privileges through good behavior. The prison has greatly expanded in recent years and is now the largest in England.

Sources: Babington, *The English Bastille*, 1972; Herber, *Criminal London*, 2002.

WILDE, OSCAR (1854–1900). One of the most famous writer-prisoners of England, Oscar Wilde was tried at the Old Bailey in 1895 and convicted of "committing gross indecency with another man," a statute that had only become law in 1885. He was sentenced to two years' imprisonment at hard labor. He served six months in **Wandsworth Prison** before being transferred to **Reading Gaol**. Upon his release in 1897, his spirit broken, he moved to France for the last three years of his life. Wilde campaigned for prison reform in his last years, particularly the treatment of juvenile offenders in adult prisons. Wilde also targeted the poor food and sanitary conditions that characterized Victorian prisons. He was outspoken in his criticism of the unconstructive "meaningless" work prisoners were expected to take part in. In his famous poem *The Ballad of Reading Gaol*, Wilde reported,

> We tore the tarry rope to shreds
> With blunt and bleeding nails . . .
> We sewed the sacks, we broke the stones.

Despite his legal travails, he is best remembered for his plays *The Importance of Being Earnest* and *A Woman of No Importance*, as well as his poem *The Ballad of Reading Gaol*.

Sources: Cameron, *Prisons and Punishment in Scotland*, 1983; Peter Southerton, *Reading Gaol by Reading Town* (Berkshire Books, 1993).

WINES, ENOCH COBB (1806–1879). One of the pioneers of prison reform in the United States, Wines came to prominence when he was named secretary of the New York Prison Association in 1862. He gradually made the transition from teacher and professor of classical languages to prison reformer in the early 1860s. Together with reformer **Louis Dwight**, the two men focused their criticism on the poor state of the nation's prisons and the preoccupation on prison labor for profit.

Wines and Dwight educated themselves on the plight of the prisons, visiting virtually every penal institution in the Northeast. They compiled a plethora of notes on the state of prisons and in 1867 published *Report on the Prisons and Reformatories of the United States and Canada*. Following the Civil War, Wines came under the spell of **Walter Crofton**'s reform ideas that formed the groundwork for the so-called **Irish system**. He was particularly taken with the idea of individualization of sentencing using degrees of incarceration depending on the offense. Perhaps Wines's greatest accomplishment was his role in the formation of the first **National Prison Association,** which met for the first time in Cincinnati in 1870. Wines served as secretary at each of the National Prison Congresses that took place between 1870 and 1879, and he also served as the first president of the National Prison Association. He continued his campaign for an international congress but died before it could be accomplished. However, his son **Frederick Howard Wines** would more than fill his father's shoes in subsequent years.

Sources: D. Malone, "Enoch Wines," *Dictionary of American Biography* (New York: Charles Scribner's Sons, 1936); T. Eriksson, *The Reformers: An Historical Survey of Pioneer Experiments in the Treatment of Criminals* (New York: Elsevier, 1976).

WINES, FREDERICK HOWARD (1838–1912). The son of prison reformer **Enoch Wines,** Frederick Wines followed in his father's footsteps in his concerns for reforming American prisons. Born in Philadelphia, he graduated Princeton with a seminary degree following the American Civil War. In 1869 he was selected secretary of the newly formed Illinois State Board of Public Charities, a position he would hold for the next three decades. As head of the commission Reverend Wines continued his father's reform efforts. Frederick Wines is credited with participating in the development of the National Conference of Charities and Correction and served as a delegate to the International Penitentiary Congress held in Stockholm.

Frederick Wines is remembered as an advocate of separating criminals from the mentally ill. Among his works was *Punishment and Reformation*, published posthumously in 1919. He lobbied against the use of prisoners as human guinea pigs in prison and questioned the methodology of the so-called criminal anthropologists. Somewhat paradoxically Wines believed some of the tenets of criminal anthropology, including the notion that if one were familiar with criminals through participation in the criminal justice system, one could readily observe "their most obvious and striking characteristics."

Source: Wines, *Punishment and Reformation*, 1919.

WORKHOUSES. The demographic upheaval that followed the collapse of the old feudal order left many peasant agricultural workers unemployed. In the 1530s Henry VIII's dissolution of the monasteries had similar results for the former retainers of the monastic order. As a result, the bakers, gardeners, launderers, and others who serviced the monasteries joined the unemployed masses of agricultural workers. Soon England was awash in vagrants moving from town to town. A new element began to make its presence felt among the transients—the professional criminal. The development of the **house of correction** and the workhouse were early attempts to control this unruly lot in the years before the modern prison.

The workhouse had more in common with the house of correction than with the modern prison. The workhouse movement began as an early attempt to deal with pauperism and the concomitant social problems of poverty. By the sixteenth century those needing society's assistance to survive fell into two groups. On the one hand were the so-called impotent poor who through the calamities of old age, insanity, or various physical disabilities could not support themselves. On the other hand were those who could not find work or wages. However, as the century wore on the latter were stigmatized for their unwillingness to work, rather than for inability to find work. By the 1550s it was automatically assumed that anyone physically fit could be idle only by personal choice. In response, officials promulgated various laws to punish such individuals. According to one 1552 British law, "If any man or woman, able to work, should refuse to labor and live idly for three days," he or she would be punished with the branding of the letter *V* for "vagrant" with a "red hot iron on the breast." In addition, this individual would be "judged the slave for two years of any person who should inform against the idler."

In Elizabethan England "houses of industry" were established to provide labor for the country's idlers. According to workhouse historian Norman Longmate, "It was not until 1652 that the word [*workhouse*] was first used in its modern sense."

In colonial America, according to historian David J. Rothman, "the threat of incarceration at hard labor was to discourage the needy stranger from entering the community, and to punish him should he be appended." Criminal justice historian Harry E. Barnes has suggested that by 1682 the workhouse had become "a true penal institution" in Pennsylvania, "no longer limited to the treatment of the destitute and vagrant classes." **William Penn**'s Great Law of 1682 stipulated, "All prisons shall be workhouses for felons, thiefs [*sic*], vagrants, and loose, abusive and idle persons," ordering a prison to be built in each county.

Like the house of correction, the workhouse was meant to inculcate the rehabilitative value of hard work and industrious work habits. Amsterdam's **rasphouse** was one of the most prominent examples. In this sixteenth-century male institution prisoners rasped a variety of woods in order to produce dyes for textiles. Its female counterpart was the *spinhuis*, where women were engaged in the constructive routines of textile work, such as spinning and sewing. Most sentences to the workhouse were indeterminate in length, with rehabilitation achieved only through work, a prescient notion in its day, particularly when one observes the idleness of prisoners that characterizes modern penology.

Sources: Barnes, *The Evolution of Penology in Pennsylvania*, 1968; Rothman, *The Discovery of the Asylum*, 1971; Norman Longmate, *The Workhouse* (New York: St. Martin's Press, 1974).

WORMWOOD SCRUBS PRISON. According to prison architecture scholar Norman Johnston, England's Wormwood Scrubs should be considered the first prison modeled on the **telephone pole** plan, a design that would not become a standard model for high-security adult prisons until the end of World War II. Designed by architect **Edmund du Cane**, it was the first British facility to break with the **Pentonville** model. The prison was constructed with convict labor and opened its doors to its first 1,244 inmates in 1890, making it Britain's largest prison at that time. Convict labor reportedly saved the administration more than half of what it would have cost using free labor. It was distinguished from the traditional radial design by its layout of four parallel cellblocks connected by a covered passageway. Each block consisted of tiers of 46 cells each. This passageway was open to the weather on one side and intersected each block at midpoint. One could gain entry to shops, the hospital, and other services situated off this passageway. When the prison opened, it had the longest prison tiers in Europe.

Wormwood Scrubs was opened after it became clear that **Millbank Prison** had not met expectations. Until 1902 it held men and women serving short sentences.

Since then it has housed more serious offenders. Convicts had little time for relaxation, since the prison was well supplied with **cranks, treadmills,** and other laborious pastimes.

From 1872 to 1922 prisoners wore uniforms with arrow symbols to make them instantly identifiable. This mark originated around 1700 to identify government stores and was intended to distinguish the prisoner from others in case of an escape. Today the uniform consists of basic blue trousers and shirts.

In 1904 one block of the prison's four parallel blocks was a **Borstal** that separated young offenders from the "corruption" of the adult population. Following World War I, a small section of the prison was turned into a Boys' Prison for London, incorporating a separate regime and governor. Today Wormwood Scrubs still houses the largest prison population in England.

Sources: Babington, *The English Bastille*, 1972; Herber, *Criminal London*, 2002; Johnston, *Forms of Constraint*, 2000.

Y

YEMEN. Directed by the Ministry of the Interior, Yemen's main prisons are located at Sana'a, Al Hudaydah, Ibb, and Dhammar. During the late 1980s conditions in these facilities were described as adequate, offering inmates medical care and allowing radios and newspapers. However, in the late 1980s prison conditions were much worse in southern Yemen. The majority of inmates were considered political prisoners. Estimated at more than 10,000, a number of them have been held incommunicado and were subject to torture. The only bright spot was apparently the better conditions at Al Mansura Prison. The most recent estimates come from 1998, which indicates 83 prison facilities holding 14,000 prisoners.

Sources: Kurian, *WEPP*, 1989; ICPS, Yemen, Middle East, 1998.

YUMA TERRITORIAL PRISON. Yuma Arizona's Territorial Prison received its first seven inmates on July 1, 1876. During its 33-year history a total of 3,069 prisoners, including 29 women, served stints at the prison for crimes ranging from murder and polygamy to larceny, the most common crime. Because of the corruption and ease associated with the granting of pardons and paroles in this era, few prisoners served their entire sentences. More than 100 men died in the prison, mostly from tuberculosis. Despite its reputation as a hellhole a number of reports indicate that the institution was humanely administered, with the harshest punishments consisting of wearing a ball and chain and solitary confinement on a bread-and-water diet.

Prisoners had opportunities to learn to read and write and had access to the prison library, one of the first public libraries in the Arizona Territory. Thanks to one of the first electrical generating plants in the West, the prison had power for lights and for running a ventilator system in the cellblock. The last prisoners left Yuma in 1909, but the building would become home to Yuma Union High School between 1910 and 1914. During the Great Depression homeless families and hoboes found sanctuary behind the former prison walls. Among its most famous wardens was "Tombstone," Arizona's former marshal John Behan.

Sources: John Mason Jeffrey, *Adobe and Iron: The Story of the Yuma Territorial Prison at Yuma* (La Jolla, CA: Prospect Avenue Press, 1969); Cliff Trafzer and Steve George, *Prison Centennial, 1876–1976* (Yuma: Rio Colorado Press, 1978).

Z

ZAIRE. Information is sketchy regarding the prison system in Zaire. Sporadic amnesties and civil war led to the degradation of the prison system during the 1990s. Most prisons date from the pre-independence days before the 1960s. In fact, a number of rural prison camps established to manage political detainees and mass roundups during the troubles of the 1960s have occasionally been pressed back into service. In 1987 an "inspector corps" was inaugurated to oversee prison procedures and conditions. Besides lacking adequate personnel and government support, this inspection unit is hamstrung by its lack of jurisdiction and control over secret detention centers used by security forces for interrogation and detention. Since political prisoners have been traditionally confined incommunicado outside prison walls, there is little information on their treatment as they languish in silence.

In the early 1990s the administration of the prisons was placed under the direction of the Ministry of Justice and Keeper of the Seals. Each of the nation's regional capitals has a central prison, with others located in other major cities. Major prisons are located at Mikala in Kinshasa, Kasapa Prison in Lubumbashi, and the Buluo detention camp. These institutions are supplemented by district prisons, territorial prisons, detention centers, and a number of informal lockups found sporadically throughout smaller towns and villages at the lowest administrative levels. Juvenile facilities are uncommon, with most communities preferring to release youthful offenders to family custodians.

Human rights activists have cited the nation's prisons as being in a state of decay, with limited sanitation. At most prisons, including the central prison at Makala, prisoners reportedly washed out their nonfunctioning toilets by hand. Kitchen facilities, when they did exist, tended to consist of no more than a common pot on an improvised wooden stove. As in other poor countries, overcrowding and corruption are omnipresent, with reports of torture, poor sanitation, and malnutrition commonplace. Other reports suggest that given the theft of meager food rations by prison guards and officials, many prisoners subsist entirely on food and provisions from friends and family. According to one source, the commissioner of justice was impeached in 1977 for selling prison victuals on the black market while prisoners starved. There were reports in 1993 that there was such a deficiency in food supplies at the central prison at Kinshasa that the Red Cross stepped in with food to prevent starvation.

Sources: LCCS, "Zaire: The Prison System," December 1993; *WEPP*; Human Rights Watch, *The Human Rights Watch Global Report on Prisons* (New York: Human Rights Watch, 1993).

ZAMBIA. As of mid-2002 Zambia housed 13,173 prisoners, a prison rate of 124 per 100,000 of the national population. The Prison Service is operated under the Ministry of Home Affairs. In 1990 there were at least 52 penal institutions. By law, adults and juveniles are separated, as are males and females, and first-time offenders from recidivists. There are 12 prisons located in the various provincial capitals, all holding males only. The most serious offenders are imprisoned in the Kabwe Maximum Security Prison. Juvenile offenders are typically placed in the Katambora Reformatory outside Livingstone, and Kasama Prison in the north is dedicated to women serving more than three-month sentences. Reports from the late 1980s indicated overcrowding and unsanitary facilities.

Sources: Kurian, *WEPP*, 1989; Walmsley, *WPPL*, 2003.

ZIMBABWE. Following a 15-year war, Zimbabwe won its independence from Great Britain in 1980 after almost 100 years of colonial rule. At the time of independence there were almost 29,000 prisoners. The majority were freedom fighters that had been incarcerated by the former colonial regime. Their release in 1980 left almost 6,000 inmates who were considered "common criminals." The prison population increased substantially over the next decade in part because of a rising crime rate and a lack of jobs, education, and occupational skills—problems that often accompany the transition from colony to statehood. By the late 1980s Zimbabwean prisons were considered self-sufficient as a result of the productivity of inmate workers. Prison population problems have been most typically controlled through sporadic amnesty programs.

As of mid-2002 Zimbabwe maintained 41 prison facilities holding an estimated 21,000 prisoners. With a designated capacity for 16,000 inmates, the prison system was over capacity by 131.3 percent. The national prison population rate was about 160 per 100,000 of the national population.

Sources: J. G. Mutambikwe, "Crime and Recidivism in Zimbabwe," in *Current International Trends in Corrections*, ed. Biles, 1988, pp. 114–118; ICPS, Zimbabwe, Africa, 2002.

ZUCHTHAUS. A German word for prison, *Zuchthaus* is based on the root *zucht*, meaning "discipline." It refers to the types of prison accommodations used by the German states for long-term prisoners as a cost-saving venture. Prison historian Norman Johnston suggests that the harshest sentences were served in the *zuchthaus*. Although the German states renovated a number of buildings with cellular construction in the nineteenth century, a rising prison population and reservations about the use of solitary confinement resulted in a number of prisoners serving sentences in ancient fortresses, castles, and eighteenth-century facilities into the twentieth century. According to Johnston, German states operated at least 35 *Zuchthauser* in the 1800s. One of the more prominent examples was the Zuchthaus at Insterburg, completed in 1838.

Source: Johnston, *Forms of Constraint*, 2000.

Appendix A Prison Museums

1897 Pauly Jail Museum, Union Springs, AL, USA

Abashiri Prison Museum, Abashiri City, Hokkaido, Japan

Acre Underground Prisoners Memorial Museum, Acre, Israel

Alcatraz, San Francisco, CA, USA

Alton Confederate Prison, Alton, IL, USA

Anamosa State Penitentiary Museum, Anamosa, IA, USA

Andersonville National Historic Site, Andersonville, GA, USA

Andrey Sakharov Museum and Public Center, Moscow, Russia

Barbados Museum, St. Michael, Barbados

Barron County Historic Society Museum / The Dallas Jail, Cameron, WI, USA

Beaumaris Gaol, Beaumaris, Anglesey, UK

Border History Museum, Hexham, Northumberland, UK

Bridge of Sighs, Venice, Italy

Burlington County Prison Museum, Mount Holly, NJ, USA

Capital Punishment Museum / NJ State Corrections Academy, Trenton, NJ, USA

Changi Prison Museum, Changi, Singapore

Clink Prison, South Bank, London

Correctional Service of Canada Museum, Kingston, Ontario, Canada

Crime and Punishment Museum, Ashburn, GA, USA

Cromarty Courthouse Museum, Cromarty, Ross & Cromarty, Scotland

Dachau Concentration Camp Memorial, Dachau, Germany

Debtor's Prison, Accomac, VA, USA

Eastern State Penitentiary Historic Site, Philadelphia, PA, USA

Essex County Jail, Newark, NJ, USA

Folsom Prison Museum, Sacramento, CA, USA

Fort Delaware State Park / Pea Patch Island, Delaware City, DE, USA

Fort Jesus Museum, Mombasa, Kenya

Fremantle Prison, Fremantle, Australia

Fuhlsbuttel Concentration Camp and Prison Memorial, Hamburg, Germany

The Gevangenpoort (prison gate) Museum, Hague, The Netherlands

Grenada, National Museum, St. George's Grenada, West Indies

Guildhall Museum, Rochester, Kent, UK

Gulag Museum, Perm, Russia

Hale Paahoa (stuck in irons house), Lahaina, Maui, Hawaii, USA

Hameenlinna Provincial Prison Museum, Hameenlinna, Finland

Hong Kong Correctional Services Museum, Stanley, Hong Kong

Huron Historic Gaol, Goderich, Ontario, Canada

Hyde Park Barracks Museum, Sydney, Australia

Inverary Jail, Inverary, Argyll, Scotland

Jackson County Jail, Independence, MO, USA

Jedburgh Castle Jail and Museum, Castlegate, Jedburgh, Scotland

Kilmainham Gaol, Kilmainham, Dublin County, Ireland

Kingston Penitentiary / Correctional Service of Canada, Kingston, Ontario, Canada

Langholmen Prison Museum, Stockholm, Sweden

Lincoln Castle, Lincoln, England, UK

Louisiana State Penitentiary Museum, Angola, LA, USA

Mansfield Reformatory, Mansfield, OH, USA

Manzanar National Historic Site, Independence, CA, USA

Miklus Prison, Kosice, Slovakia

Model Prison Museum, Reparto Chacon, Nueva Gerona, Isla de la Juventud, Cuba

Museum of Colorado Prisons / Territorial Prison, Canon City, CO, USA

New York Correction History Society, Albany, NY, USA

Ohio State Reformatory Historic Site, Mansfield, OH, USA

Old Idaho Penitentiary, Boise, ID, USA

Old Jail Art Center, Albany, TX, USA

Old Jail Museum, Allegan, MI, USA

Old Jail Museum, Jim Thorpe, PA, USA

Old Jail Museum, Montgomery County, IN, USA

Old Jail Museum, St. Augustine, FL, USA

Old Lincoln County Jail and Museum, Wincasset, ME, USA

Old Melbourne Gaol, Melbourne, Victoria, Australia

Old Montana Prison, Deer Lodge, MT, USA

Old Monterey Jail, Monterey, CA, USA

Old New-Gate Prison and Copper Mine, East Granby, CT, USA

Old Stone Jail, Goochland, VA, USA

Parkhurt Heritage Museum, UK

Pawiak Prison, Warsaw, Poland

Peter and Paul Fortress, St. Petersburg, Russia
Robben Island, Robben Island, South Africa
San Juan Historical Museum, Friday Harbor, WA, USA
San Quentin Prison Museum, San Quentin, CA, USA
Sodaemun Prison, Sodaemun-Gu, Seoul, South Korea
Squirrel Cage Jail, Council Bluffs, IA, USA
Stirling Old Town Jail, Stirling, Scotland
Studentenkarzer, Heidelburg, Germany
Texas Prison Museum, Huntsville, TX, USA
Tower of London, London, UK
Ushuaia National Prison, Ushuaia, Tierra Del Fuego, Argentina
Wayne County Historic Society Old Jail Museum, Lyons, NY, USA
Westgate Towers Museum, Canterbury, Kent, UK
West Virginia Penitentiary, Moundsille, WV, USA
Wyoming Frontier Prison, Rawlins, WY, USA
Wyoming Territorial Museum, Laramie, WY, USA
York Castle Museum, The Eye of York, York, UK
Yorkshire Law and Order Museums at Ripon, St. Marygate, Ripon, North Yorkshire, UK
Yuma Territorial Prison State Historic Park, Yuma, AZ, USA

Sources: Eastern State Penitentiary Prison Museum Links, www.easternstate.org/links/prison-museum.

Appendix B Some Famous Prisoners and Their Prison History

Archer, Jeffrey, author. Bellmarsh Prison; Hollesley Bay Prison, UK, 2001–2003

Berkman, Alexander, anarchist. Western Penitentiary, USA, 1890s

Bunyan, John. Bedford Jail, England, 1660–1672

Cleaver, Eldridge. Soledad Prison, San Quentin Prison, 1957–1966

Debs, Eugene V., labor organizer. McHenry County Jail, Illinois

De Sade, Marquis. The Bastille, Charenton

Dostoyevsky, Fyodor. Omsk Prison, western Siberia

Gandhi, Mahatma. Yeravda Prison, 1930s

Genet, Jean. Mettray Reformatory, 1925–1929; Fresnes Prison, 1940s

Goldman, Emma, anarchist and political agitator. Blackwell's Island, New York City

Henry, O., author. Ohio State Penitentiary, 1898

Himes, Chester. Ohio State Penitentiary, 1929–1936

Jones, Mary Harris (Mother Jones), union organizer Pratt Jail, West Virginia, 1913

King, Martin Luther. Birmingham City Jail, 1963

Kyi, Aung San Suu. Nobel Peace Prize winner, 1991; Myanmar, house arrest

Ledbetter, Huddie "Leadbelly." Shaw State Prison Farm, Huntsville, TX, 1930s

Levi, Primo, author. Auschwitz Concentration Camp

Little, Malcolm (Malcolm X), Nation of Islam Minister. Charlestown Prison; Concord Reformatory; Norfolk Prison, 1940s

London, Jack, author and "vagrant." Erie County Penitentiary, 1893

Lowell, Robert, poet. Federal prison, 1943–1944

Mandela, Nelson. Robben Island, Danbury, CT; Pollsmoor Prison, 1964–1990

More, Thomas (Lord Chancellor). Tower of London, 1535

Penn, William. Tower of London, 1670

Raleigh, Sir Walter. Tower of London, 1600s

Russell, Bertrand, mathematician, pacifist. Brixton Gaol, 1918

Stroud, Robert, murderer. Leavenworth, Alcatraz, 1910–1963

Thoreau, Henry David. Concord Jail (1 night), 1849

Timmerman, Jacobo, journalist. Sao Paulo Military Prison, Argentina, 1970s

Verlaine, Paul, french poet. Mons Prison, Belgium, 1874–1876

Villon, Francois, troubador. Meung-Sur-Loire dungeon, 1450s

Voltaire. The Bastille, 1717–1718, 1725

Wilde, Oscar, poet. Reading Gaol, Wandsworth Prison

Wilkes, John, English MP. King's Bench Prison, 1760s

Zenger, John Peter, newspaper publisher. New York City Jail, 1734–1735

Appendix C Writings by Prisoners

PRISON POETRY

Aguila, Pancho (Folsom Prison). *Anti-gravity*. Berkeley, CA: Aldebaran Review, 1976.
———. *Hijacked*. Berkeley, CA: Two Windows Press, 1976.
———. *Dark Smoke*. San Francisco: Second Coming Press, 1977.
———. *The Therapeutist and 3rd Hunger Poem*. Berkeley, CA: Artaud's Press, 1978.
———. *Clash*. San Francisco: Poetry for the People, 1980.
Chaplin, Ralph. *Bars and Shadows: The Prison Poems of Ralph Chaplin*. Ridgewood, NJ: N.S. Nearing, 1923.
Chenier, Andre. *Oeuvres Completes*. Ed. Gerard Walter. Paris: Gallimard, 1958.
Donne, John. Devotions upon Emergent Occasions, 1624.
Lowell, Robert. "In the Cage." 1946.
———. "Memories of West Street and Lepke." 1959.
Verlaine, Paul. "Le ciel est, par-dessus le toit." 1875.
Villon, Francois. "Ballade des pendus." 1461.
Wilde, Oscar (Reading Jail). *Ballad of Reading Gaol*. London: L. Smithers, 1898.

AUTOBIOGRAPHY AND OTHER PRISON WRITINGS

Abbott, Jack Henry (Utah State Penitentiary). *In the Belly of the Beast: Letter from Prison*. New York: Random House, 1981.
———. With Naomi Zack. *My Return*. Buffalo, NY: Prometheus Books, 1987.
Algren, Nelson (Texas Jail). *Somebody in Boots*. New York: Farrar, Straus and Giroux, 1935.
Baker, Peter (England). *Time Out of My Life*. London: Heinemann, 1961.
Behan, Brendan. *Borstal Boy*. New York: Knopf, 1959.
Belbenoit, Rene (Devil's Island). *Dry Guillotine: Fifteen Years among the Living Dead*. New York: Blue Ribbon Books, 1938.
———. *Hell on Trial*. New York: Dutton, 1946.
Benton, Roger. *Where Do I Go from Here?* New York: Furman, 1936.
Boethius. *De Consolatione Philosophiae*. Trans. Richard Green. Indianapolis: Bobbs-Merrill, 1962.
Booth, Ernest (San Quentin). *Stealing through Life*. New York: Knopf, 1929.

Braly, Malcolm. *On the Yard*. Boston: Little, Brown and Co., 1967.

Burns, Robert. *I Am a Fugitive from a Georgia Chain Gang!* New York: Vanguard, 1932.

Burroughs, Stephen. *Memoirs of the Notorious Stephen Burroughs of New Hampshire*. New York: Dial Press, 1924.

Chernyshevsky, [Nikolai.] (Peter and Paul Fortress, St. Petersberg). *What Is to Be Done*, 1862.

Chessman, Caryl. *Trial by Ordeal*. Englewood Cliffs, NJ: Prentice-Hall, 1955.

———. (San Quentin). *Cell 2455, Death Row*. Englewood Cliffs, NJ: Prentice-Hall, 1960.

Cleaver, Eldridge *Soul on Ice*. New York: McGraw Hill, 1968.

———. (San Quentin, Folsom, and Soledad Prisons). *Post-prison Writings*. New York: Random House, 1969.

Defoe, Daniel. *The Fortunes and Misfortunes of the Famous Moll Flanders*. New York: Oxford University Press, reprint 1981.

Degras, Henry Ernest. *Gaol Delivery*. London: Longmans Green, 1948.

Deming, Barbara (Albany City, Georgia). *Prison Notes*. New York: Grossman Publishers, 1966.

Dostoyevsky, Fydor Mikhaylovich. *Memoirs from the House of the Dead*. Trans. Jesse Coulson. Ed. Ronald Hingley. Oxford: Oxford University Press, 1990.

Duncan, Lee (Oregon State Prison). *Over the Wall*. New York: Dutton, 1936.

Genet, Jean. *The Thief's Journal*. Trans. Bernard Frechtman. New York: Grove Press, 1964.

Goosen, William (South Africa). *On the Run*. Cape Town: Timmins, 1964.

Grant, John (Norfolk Island). *John Grant's Journey: A Convict's Story, 1803–1811*. Ed. W. S. Hill. London: Heinemann, 1957.

Guerin, Eddie (Devil's Island). *Crime: The Autobiography of a Crook*. London: Murray, 1928.

Hassler, Alfred (Lewisburg, Pennsylvania). *Diary of a Self-Made Convict*. Chicago: Regnery, 1954.

Heckstall-Smith, Anthony. *Eighteen Months*. London: Allan Wingate, 1954.

Himes, Chester (Ohio State Penitentiary). *Cast the First Stone*. 1952.

———. "Head of a Prison Library." *Library Journal* 83, February 15, 1958, pp. 558–560.

Leopold, Nathan. *Life Plus 9 Years*. Garden City, NY: Doubleday, 1958.

Lovelace, Richard. "To Althea, from Prison." 1648.

Lowrie, Donald. *My Life in Prison*. London: Kennerley, 1912.

Macartney, Wilfred F. R. *Walls Have Mouths: A Record of Ten Years' Penal Servitude*. London: Gollancz, 1936.

MacIsaac, John. *Half the Fun Was Getting There*. Englewood Cliffs, NJ: Prentice-Hall, 1968.

Malcolm X [pseudonym of Malcolm Little]. *The Autobiography of Malcolm X*, with assistance by Alex Haley. New York: Grove Press, 1965.

O'Hare, Kate Richards (Jefferson City, Missouri State Penitentiary). *In Prison*. New York: Knopf, 1923.

Raleigh, Sir Walter (Tower of London). *History of the World*. 1614.

Runyon, Tom (Fort Madison, Iowa Penitentiary). *In for Life: A Convict's Story*. New York: Norton, 1953.

Russell, Bertrand (Brixton Prison). *Political Ideals: Roads to Freedom*. 1918.

———. *Introduction to Mathematical Philosophy*. 1919.

Sachs, Albert Louis. *The Jail Diary of Albie Sachs*. London: Harvill, 1966.

Sands, Bill (pseudonym), (San Quentin). *My Shadow Ran Fast*. Englewood Cliffs, NJ: Prentice-Hall, 1964.

———. *The Seventh Step*. New York: New American Library, 1967.

Shakur, Assata [pseudonym of Joanne Chesimard]. (Clinton Women's Correctional Facility). Autobiography. Zed Books, 1987.

Smedley, Agnes (NY City Jail). "Cell Mates." 1920.

Solzhenitsyn, Alexander (Soviet Gulag). *One Day in the Life of Ivan Denisovich, 1962*. First Circle, 1968.

Stroud, Robert ("Birdman of Alcatraz"). *Stroud's Digest of the Diseases of Birds*. Minneapolis: Marcus and Stroud, 1943.

Tannenbaum, Frank (Sing Sing and others). *Walls Shadows: A Study in American Prisons*. New York: Putnam's Sons, 1927.

Tasker, Robert Joyce (San Quentin). *Grimhaven*. New York: Knopf, 1928.

Touhy, Roger (Stateville Penitentiary, Illinois). *The Stolen Years*. Cleveland: Pennington Press, 1959.

Voltaire, Francois-Marie Arovet (Bastille). "Oedipe." 1717.

Zimmerman, Isadore. *Punishment without Crime: The True Story of a Man Who Spent Twenty-four Years in Prison for a Crime He Did Not Commit*. New York: Potter, 1964.

Appendix D Writings by Prison Employees

Duffy, Clinton T. (Warden). *88 Men and 2 Women*. Garden City, NY: Doubleday, 1962.

———. *The San Quentin Story*. Garden City, NY: Doubleday, 1962.

———. *Sex and Crime*. Garden City, NY: Doubleday, 1965.

Eshelman, Byron E. (Chaplain). *Death Row Chaplain*. Englewood Cliffs, NJ: Prentice-Hall, 1962.

Lawes, Lewis Edward. *Life and Death in Sing Sing*. Garden City, NY: Doubleday, Doran, and Co., 1928.

———. *Man's Judgment of Death: An Analysis of the Operation and Effect of Capital Punishment Based on the Facts, Not on Sentiment*. New York: R. Long and R.R. Smith, 1932.

———. (Warden). *Cell 202, Sing Sing*. New York: Farrar and Rinehart, 1935.

———. *Invisible Stripes*. New York: Farrar and Rinehart, 1938.

Leibert, Julius Amos (Rabbi). *Behind Bars: What a Chaplain Saw in Alcatraz*. Garden City, NY: Doubleday, 1965.

Ragen, Joseph E. (Warden). *Inside the World's Toughest Prison*. Springfield, IL: 1962.

Wilson, Donald Powell (Psychologist). *My Six Convicts: A Psychologist's Three Years in Fort Leavenworth*. New York: Rinehart, 1951.

Appendix E Prison Architects and Visionaries

Adam, Robert. Edinburgh Bridewell, 1794.

Alexander, David Asher. **Dartmoor Convict Prison,** 1812; oversaw expansion of **Maidstone Prison** in 1817.

Aranguren, Tomas. Madrid model prison, 1877.

Atwood, Thomas Ware. Bath Prison, 1773.

Averlino, Antonio. Author of *Treatise on Architecture*, c. 1560s.

Azevedo, Francisco de Paula Ramos de. **Carandiru Prison,** Sao Paulo, Brazil, 1920.

Baltard, Louis Pierre. Published *Architectonographie des prisons*, France, 1829.

Bentham, Jeremy. Panopticon. 1790.

Blackburn, William. Suffolk County Jail at Ipswich, 1790; Gloucester House of Correction at Northleach, 1791; Liverpool Borough Jail, 1787; Bury Saint Edmunds Jail, 1805.

Blouet, Guillaume Abel. Mettray Colony for Boys, Tours, France, 1840.

Bullfinch, Charles. Charlestown State Prison, MA, 1805.

Bunge, Ernesto. Buenos Aires Penitentiary, 1877.

Busse, Karl. Moabit Prison, Berlin, 1840s.

Byfield, George. Cambridge County Jail, 1807.

Carr, John. Wakefield House of Correction, 1770; York Castle Women's Prison, 1780; Northallerton House of Correction, 1788.

Clark, Ruben. **San Quentin Penitentiary,** California, 1852.

Crawford, William. Ohio Penitentiary, Columbus, 1835.

Cray, John. **Auburn Prison,** 1817.

Dance, George. **Newgate Prison,** 1770; Giltspur Street Compter, 1787.

Demetz, Frederic-Auguste. **Mettray Colony for Boys,** Tours, France, 1840.

Dobson, John. Carlisle County Gaol, 1825; Morpeth County Gaol, 1828.

Du Cane, Edmund. Wormwood Scrubs, 1891.

Ducpetiaux, Edouard. Tongres Prison, Belgium, 1830s and 1840s.

Eames, William. **Leavenworth Prison,** Kansas, 1906.

Fontana, Carlo. Hospice of San Michele, Rome, 1704.

Gandy, James. Lancaster County Gaol, 1821.

Gilbert, Emile. Mazas Prison, Paris, 1850; St. Petersburg central prison, Russia, 1892.

Goodwin, Francis. Derby County Gaol, 1827.

Harrison, Thomas. Chester County Gaol, 1800.

Haviland, John. **Eastern State Penitentiary,** Cherry Hill, 1829; Trenton State Prison, 1836; **"Tombs" Prison,** New York City, 1838; Rhode Island Penitentiary, 1834; Western Penitentiary, Pittsburgh, 1826.

Henderson, Walcott. Fremantle Prison, Australia, 1855.

Hillyer, William. Newport Bridewell, 1775; Moulsham County Gaol, 1773.

Hopkins, Alfred. Federal Prison at Lewisburg, Pennsylvania, 1932; Wallkill Prison, Wallkill, New York, 1932.

Hopper, Thomas. Fisherton Anger County Gaol, 1818; Springfield County Gaol, 1822; Ilford House of Correction, 1831.

Howard, John. **Bedford County Gaol,** 1773.

Jappeli, Giuseppe. Padua Prison, Kingdom of Lombardy and Venice, 1824.

Jebb, Joshua. **Pentonville Prison,** 1842.

Jefferson, Thomas. Virginia Penitentiary at Richmond, 1800.

Jijuruo, Ogawa (Japanese). Peking First Prison, China, 1912.

Johnson, Clarence. Minnesota State Prison, Stillwater, 1914.

Labrouste, Pierre-Francois-Henri. French architect, 1801–1875.

Latrobe, Benjamin. Virginia Penitentiary at Richmond, 1800.

Le Bas, Hippolyte. Petite Roquette Prison, Paris, 1836.

Lecointe, Jean Francois. Mazas Prison, Paris, 1850.

Lenci, Sergio. Italian architect, 1960s.

Maconochie, Alexander. **Norfolk Island,** Australia, 1840.

Metzelaar, J. F. Arnhem Prison, Holland, 1884.

Milizia, Francesco. *Principi di Architettura Civile,* 1785.

Mimey, Maximiliano. Lima Penitentiary, Peru, 1862.

Moser, Jean. Lenzburg Prison, Switzerland, 1864.

Nash, John. Hereford House of Correction, 1796.

Normand, Alfred. Rennes Prison, France, 1879.

Oliveira, Manoel de. Rio de Janeiro House of Correction, 1856.

Orridge, John, and Thomas Fowell Buxton. Bury Saint Edmunds Gaol, 1819; Huntingdon Gaol, 1828.

Palmer, Robert. Hertford County Gaol, 1776.

Paz Soldan, Mariano. Peru, 1860s.

Poussin, Francisque-Henri. **Fresnes**-les-Ringis, Paris, 1898.

Powers, William. **Kingston Penitentiary,** Canada, 1835.

Sanmicheli, Michele. San Pancrazio **lazaretto,** Verona, Italy, 1539.

Schinlel, Karl Friedrich. Zuchthaus at Insterburg, Germany, 1838.

Schirmer, Heinrich Ernst. Oslo Prison, Norway, 1851.

Smirke, Sir Robert. **Millbank Penitentiary**, 1821; Lincoln Castle Gaol, 1830; St. Johns New-foundland, 1831.

Smith, Robert. **Walnut Street Jail**, 1773.

Soane, John. Norwich County Gaol, 1793.

Strickland, William. Western Penitentiary, Pittsburgh, 1818.

Thorigny, Robert de. Mont-Saint-Michel chatelet, 1100s.

Torija, Antonio Torres. Mexico City federal prison, 1885.

Trojan, E. von. Plzen Prison, Bohemia (Czech Republic), 1878.

Tyrwhitt, Thomas. Dartmoor Convict Prison, 1809.

Vaucher-Cremieux, Samuel. Switzerland, 1800s.

Vaudremer, Emile. Sante Prison, Paris, 1867.

Viollet-le-Duc, Eugene Emmanuel. Pierrefonds, c. 1800s.

Wagner, Gyula. Szeged, Hungary, 1884; Budapest Prison, 1896.

Watson, John, with John Carr. Wakefield House of Correction, 1770.

Wyatt, James. Petworth House of Correction, 1788.

Young, Thomas. Leavenworth Prison, Kansas, 1906.

Zimmerman, W. Carbys. Illinois State Penitentiary, Joliet (Stateville), 1924.

Sources: Evans, *The Fabrication of Virtue*, 1982; Johnston, *Forms of Constraint*, 2000; Johnston, *Eastern State Penitentiary*, 1994.

Appendix F United States Federal Correctional Institutions (FCIs)

FCI Allenwood, White Deer, Pennsylvania
FCI Ashland, Ashland, Kentucky
FCI Bastrop, Bastrop, Texas
FCI Beaumont, Beaumont, Texas
FCI Beckley, Beckley, West Virginia
FCI Big Spring, Big Spring, Texas
FCI Butner, Butner, North Carolina
FCI Coleman, Coleman, Florida
FCI Cumberland, Cumberland, Maryland
FCI Danbury, Danbury, Connecticut
FCI Dublin, Dublin, California
FCI Edgefield, Edgefield, South Carolina
FCI Elkton, Elkton, Ohio
FCI El Reno, El Reno, Oklahoma
FCI Englewood, Littleton, Colorado
FCI Estill, Estill, South Carolina
FCI Fairton, Fairton, New Jersey
FCI Florence, Florence, Colorado
FCI Forrest City, Forrest City, Arkansas
FCI Fort Dix, Fort Dix, New Jersey
FCI Gilmer, Glenville, West Virginia
FCI Greenville, Greenville, Illinois
FCI Jesup, Jesup, Georgia
FCI La Tuna, Anthony, New Mexico
FCI Lompoc, Lompoc, California

FCI Loretto, Loretto, Pennsylvania

FCI Manchester, Manchester, Kentucky

FCI Marianna, Marianna, Florida

FCI McKean, Bradford, Pennsylvania

FCI Memphis, Memphis, Tennessee

FCI Miami, Miami, Florida

FCI Milan, Milan, Michigan

FCI Morgantown, Morgantown, West Virginia

FCI Oakdale, Oakdale, Louisiana

FCI Otisville, Otisville, New York

FCI Oxford, Oxford, Wisconsin

FCI Pekin, Pekin, Illinois

FCI Petersburg, Petersburg, Virginia

FCI Phoenix, Phoenix, Arizona

FCI Ray Brook, Ray Brook, New York

FCI Safford, Safford, Arizona

FCI Sandstone, Sandstone, Minnesota

FCI Schuylkill, Minersville, Pennsylvania

FCI Seagoville, Seagoville, Texas

FCI Sheridan, Sheridan, Oregon

FCI Talladega, Talladega, Alabama

FCI Tallahassee, Tallahassee, Florida

FCI Terminal Island, Terminal Island, California

FCI Texarkana, Texarkana, Texas

FCI Three Rivers, Three Rivers, Texas

FCI Tucson, Tucson, Arizona

FCI Victorville, Adelanto, California

FCI Waseca, Waseca, Minnesota

FCI Yazoo City, Yazoo City, Mississippi

Appendix G Standard Minimum Rules for the Treatment of Prisoners

PART I: RULES OF GENERAL APPLICATION

Basic Principle

1. There shall be no discrimination on grounds of race, color, sex, language, religion, political or other opinion, national or social origin, property, birth or other status.

2. It is necessary to respect the religious beliefs and moral precepts of the group to which the prisoner belongs.

Register

1. In every place where prisoners are imprisoned there shall be kept a bound registration book with numbered pages in which shall be entered in respect of each prisoner received:

    (a) Information concerning his identity

    (b) The reasons for his commitment

    (c) The day and hour of his admission and release

Separation of Categories

1. The different categories of prisoners shall be kept in separate institutions or parts of institutions taking account of their sex, age, criminal record, the legal reason for their detention and the necessities of their treatment.

Accommodation

1. Where sleeping accommodation is in individual cells or rooms, each prisoner shall occupy by night a cell or room by himself.

2. Where dormitories are used, they shall be occupied by prisoners carefully selected as being suitable to associate with one another in those conditions.

3. In all places where prisoners are required to live or work,

    (a) The windows shall be large enough to enable the prisoners to read or work by natural light, and shall be constructed that they can allow the entrance of fresh air whether or not there is artificial ventilation.

4. The sanitary installations shall be adequate to enable every prisoner to comply with the needs of nature when necessary and in a clean and decent manner.

5. Adequate bathing and shower installations shall be provided so that every prisoner may be enabled and required to have a bath or shower, at a temperature suitable to the climate, as frequently as necessary for general hygiene according to season and geographical region, but at least once a week in a temperate climate.

Personal Hygiene

1. Prisoners shall be required to keep their persons clean, and to this end they shall be provided with water and with such toilet articles as are necessary for health and cleanliness.

Clothing and Bedding

1. Every prisoner who is not allowed to wear his own clothing shall be provided with an outfit of clothing suitable for the climate and adequate to keep in good health. Such clothing shall in no manner be degrading or humiliating.

2. Every prisoner shall, in accordance with local or national standards, be provided with a separate bed, and with separate and sufficient bedding which shall be clean when issued, kept in good order and changed often enough to ensure its cleanliness.

Food

1. Every prisoner shall be provided by the administration at the usual hours with food of nutritional value adequate for health and strength, of wholesome quality and well prepared and served.

2. Drinking water shall be available to every prisoner whenever he needs it.

Exercise and Sport

1. Every prisoner who is not employed in outdoor work shall have at least one hour of suitable exercise in the open air daily if the weather permits.

2. Young prisoners, and others of suitable age and physique, shall receive physical and recreational training during the period of exercise. To this end space, installations and equipment should be provided.

Medical Services

1. At every institution there shall be available the services of at least one qualified medical officer who should have some knowledge of psychiatry. The medical services should be organized in close relationship to the general administration of the community or nation. They shall include a psychiatric service for the diagnosis and, in proper cases, the treatment of states of mental abnormality.

2. Sick prisoners who require specialist treatment shall be transferred to specialized institutions or to civil hospitals. Where hospital facilities are provided in an institution, their equipment, furnishings and pharmaceutical supplies shall be proper for the medical care and treatment of sick prisoners, and there shall be a staff of suitable trained officers.

3. The services of a qualified dental officer shall be available to every prisoner.

4. In women's institutions there shall be special accommodation for all necessary pre-natal and post-natal care and treatment. Arrangements shall be made wherever practicable for children to be born in a hospital outside the institution. If a child is born in prison, this fact shall not be mentioned in the birth certificate.

5. The medical officer shall see and examine every prisoner as soon as possible after his admission and thereafter necessary, with a view particularly to the discovery of physical and mental illness and the taking of all necessary measures; the segregation of prisoners suspected of infectious or contagious conditions: the noting of physical or mental defects

which might hamper rehabilitation, and the determination of the physical capacity of every prisoner to work.

Discipline and Punishment

1. Discipline and order shall be maintained with firmness, but with no more restriction than is necessary for safe custody and well-ordered community life.

2. No prisoner shall be punished except in accordance with the terms of such law or regulation, and never twice for the same offence.

3. No prisoner shall be punished unless he has been informed of the offence against him and given a proper opportunity of presenting his defence. The competent authority shall conduct a thorough examination of the case.

4. Corporal punishment, punishment by placing in a dark cell, and all cruel, inhuman or degrading punishments shall be completely prohibited as punishment for disciplinary offences.

5. Punishment by close confinement or reduction of diet shall never be inflicted unless the medical officer has examined the prisoner and certified in writing that he is fit to sustain it.

Instruments of Restraint

1. Instruments of restraint, such as handcuffs, chains, irons and straitjackets, shall never be applied as punishment. Furthermore, chains or irons shall not be used as restraints. Other instruments of restraint shall not be used except in the following circumstances:

   (a) As a precaution against escape during a transfer

   (b) On medical grounds by direction of the medical officer

   (c) By order of the director, if other methods fail, in order to prevent a prisoner from injuring himself or others or from damaging property.

Information and Complaints by Prisoners

1. Every prisoner on admission shall be provided with written information about the regulations governing the treatment of prisoners of his category, the disciplinary requirements of the institution, the authorized methods of seeking information and making complaints, and all such other matters as are necessary to enable him to understand both his rights and his obligations and to adapt himself to the life of the institution.

2. If a prisoner is illiterate, the aforesaid information shall be conveyed to him orally.

3. Every prisoner shall have the opportunity each weekday of making requests or complaints to the director of the institution or the officer authorized to represent him.

4. Every prisoner shall be allowed to make a request or complaint, without censorship as to substance but in proper form, to the central prison administration, the judicial authorities through approved channels.

Contact with the Outside World

1. Prisoners shall be allowed under necessary supervision to communicate with their family and reputable friends at regular intervals, both by correspondence and by receiving visits.

2. Prisoners who are foreign nationals shall be allowed reasonable facilities to communicate with the diplomatic and consular representatives of the State to which they belong.

3. Prisoners shall be kept informed regularly of the more important items of news by the reading of newspapers, periodicals or special institutional publications, by hearing wireless transmissions, by lectures or by any similar means as authorized or controlled by the administration.

Books

1. Every institution shall have a library for the use of all categories of prisoners, adequately stocked with both recreational and instructional books, and prisoners shall be encouraged to make full use of it.

Religion

1. If the institution contains a sufficient number of prisoners of the same religion, a qualified representative of that religion shall be appointed or approved. If the number of prisoners justifies it and conditions permit, the arrangement shall be on a full-time basis.

2. Access to a qualified representative of any religion shall not be refused to any prisoner. On the other hand, if any prisoner should object to a visit of any religious representative, his attitude shall be fully respected.

Retention of Prisoners' Property

1. All money, valuables, clothing and other effects belonging to a prisoner which under the regulations of the institution he is not allowed to retain shall on his admission to the institution be placed in safe custody.

2. On the release of the prisoner all such articles and money shall be returned to him except in so far he has been authorized to spend money or send any such property out of the institution, or it has been found on hygienic grounds to destroy any article of clothing.

Notification of Death, Illness, Transfer, Etc.

1. Upon the death or serious illness of, or serious injury to a prisoner, or his removal to an institution for the treatment of mental affections, the director shall at once inform the spouse, if the prisoner is married, or the nearest relative and shall in any event inform any other person previously designated by the prisoner.

2. A prisoner shall be informed at once of the death or serious illness of any near relative. In case of the critical illness of a near relative, the prisoner should be authorized, whenever circumstances allow, to go to the bedside either under escort or alone.

Removal of Prisoners

1. When the prisoners are being removed to or from an institution they shall be exposed to public view as little as possible, and proper safeguards shall be adopted to protect them from insult, curiosity and publicity in any form.

2. The transport of prisoners in conveyances with inadequate ventilation or light, or in any way which would subject them to unnecessary physical hardship, shall be prohibited.

Institutional Personnel

1. The prison administration, shall provide for the careful selection of every grade of the personnel, since it is on their integrity, humanity, professional capacity and personal suitability for the work that the proper administration of the institution depends.

2. The personnel shall possess an adequate standard of education and intelligence.

3. Before entering on duty, the personnel shall be given a course of training in their general and specific duties and be required to pass theoretical and practical tests.

4. In an institution for both men and women, the part of the institution set aside for women shall be under the authority of a responsible woman officer who shall have the custody of the keys of all that parts of the institution.

5. No male member of the staff shall enter the part of the institution set aside for women unless accompanied by a woman officer.

6. Officers of the institutions shall not, in their relations with the prisoners, use force except in self-defense or in cases of attempted escape, or active or passive physical resistance to an order based on law and regulations. Officers who have recourse to force must use no more than is strictly necessary and must report the incident immediately to the director of the institution.

Source: Selected from the First United Nations Congress on the Prevention of Crime and the Treatment of Offenders, Geneva, 1955, and approved by the Economic and Social Council by its resolutions 663 C (XXIV) of 31 July 1957 and 2076 (LXII) of 13 May 1977.

Appendix H   Selections from Alcatraz Prison Regulations

UNITED STATES PENITENTIARY ALCATRAZ, 1956

30. CELLHOUSE RULES: Caps are never worn in the cellhouse. You may smoke in your cell, in the Library or in A-Block, but not elsewhere in the cellhouse. DO NOT SMOKE OR CARRY LIGHTED CIGARETTES OR PIPES ON THE GALLERIES OR FLATS IN THE CELLHOUSE AT ANY TIME. WALK—DO NOT RUN when moving from one place to another.

Upon entering the cellhouse, remove your cap and walk directly and quietly to your cell. Loud talking, loitering or visiting on the galleries, stairs or aisles is not permitted. Don't enter any other inmate's cell at any time.

When you talk in the cellhouse, talk quietly. Don't create a disturbance. Keep your cell neat and clean and free from trash and contraband. Keep your property neatly arranged on your shelves. . . . Don't paste or tack anything on the walls or shelves in your cell. Keep the floor and the bars of the cell-front free from dust and dirt. The only articles permitted on the cell floor are shoes, slippers, trashbaskets, drawing boards and musical instruments. . . .

At the wake-up bell in the morning you must get out of bed and put on your clothes. Make up your bed properly with your pillow at the end near the bars, blankets tucked neatly under the mattress, and extra blankets folded neatly at the foot of the bed. Sweep your cell and place the trash in the trash basket. Don't attempt to flush trash down the toilet. Don't sweep trash or dirt onto the gallery or off the gallery.

At 9:30 P.M. lights out, retire promptly. All conversations and other noises must cease immediately. . . .

Loud talking, shouting, whistling, singing or other unnecessary noises are not permitted. You are permitted to hold QUIET conversations and to play games QUIETLY with your adjoining neighbors ONLY.

33. DINING ROOM RULES: Meals are served three times a day in the dining room. Do not exceed the ration. Do not waste food. Do not carry food from the dining room.

Wear standard uniform.

Conduct yourself in a quiet, orderly manner. You may converse in normal tones with persons near you. Boisterous conduct will not be tolerated in the dining room.

Observe the ration posted on the menu board and take all that you wish to eat within the allotted amounts, but you must eat all you take.

You may go to the coffee urn on your side of the dining room only when no other inmate is there. Do not go to the urn for purpose of visiting with others.

Do not pass or exchange food, cigarettes, notes or any other items anywhere in the dining room.

You will be given ample time to eat but no loitering will be permitted.

Shortages of silverware at the table must be reported to the Officer before beginning to eat. . . .

40. AUDITORIUM RULES: When preparing to attend religious services or movies, in the Auditorium, you must remove everything from your pockets except your handkerchief and eyeglasses and eyeglass case. All other items will be classed as contraband. There is no smoking permitted in the Auditorium and you are not permitted to wear or carry caps, coats, jackets, cushions, blankets or pillows. . . .

If you have poor vision, and wish to sit in the front seats tell the Officer who is directing the seating.

After being seated, remain in your seat until the Officer directs you to leave. Loud talking, pushing or boisterous conduct is forbidden.

In general, you are expected to conduct yourself in an orderly manner, with proper consideration for the rights of others.

Leaving the Auditorium before the end of the program is permitted only in emergencies. . . . You will not be able to return to the auditorium. . . .

49. SPECIAL PURCHASES: There is no commissary at Alcatraz. The institution supplies all your needs. You are not allowed to have anything sent to you from home, friends or relatives. You may be allowed to purchase certain items such as textbooks, correspondence courses, musical instruments, or magazine subscriptions. All such purchases must be listed on your property card by the cellhouse Officer. . . .

50. TOBACCO: Pipe and cigarette tobacco is available from the dispensers at the West-End of the cellhouse. Take what you need for immediate use, not to exceed six packs altogether. Don't hoard tobacco. Don't waste tobacco.

Cigarettes: One pack of cigarettes may be issued to each inmate in good standing, each Monday, Wednesday, and Friday evening. Inmates who are restricted or on report will not receive cigarettes. You are not permitted to have more than 3 packs (60 cigarettes) at any one time. If you are found to have in excess of 60 cigarettes at any one time, all will be confiscated and you will be placed on a disciplinary report.

Matches: Matches and cigarette papers are distributed during bathlines. Do not accumulate more than 10 books of matches nor more than two of the 150-paper size books of cigarette papers. . . .

Source: "Institution Rules and Regulations," Alcatraz: Inmate Regulations, 1956, www.bop.gov/ipapg/ipaalcarule.

Appendix I National Prison Congress Declaration of Principles (1870)

1. Establishing reformation, not vindictive suffering, as the purpose of penal treatment
2. Making classifications on the basis of the **mark system**, patterned after the **Irish system**
3. Rewarding good conduct
4. Helping prisoners realize that their destiny is in their own hands
5. Removing the chief obstacles to prison reform, namely: the political appointment of prison officials and the instability of management
6. Providing job training for prison officials
7. Replacing fixed sentences with indeterminate sentences; removing the gross disparities and inequities in prison sentences and demonstrating the futility of repeated short sentences
8. Establishing religion and education as the most important agencies of reformation
9. Using prison discipline that gained the will of prisoners and conserved their self-respect
10. Making industrious freemen rather than orderly and obedient prisoners as prison's aim
11. Urging full provision for industrial training
12. Abolishing the system of contract labor in prison
13. Establishing small prisons and separate institutions for different type of offenders
14. Laws striking against the so-called "higher-ups" in crime, as well as against the lesser operatives
15. Indemnifying prisoners who later were discovered to be innocent
16. Revising laws relating to the treatment of insane criminals
17. Making more judicious exercise of pardoning power
18. Establishing a system for the collection of uniform penal statistics
19. Developing more adequate prison architecture, providing sufficiently for air and sunlight, as well as for prison hospitals, schoolrooms, and such
20. Establishing central prison management within each state
21. Facilitating the social training of prisoners through proper associations and abolishing the silence rule

22. Making society at large realize its responsibility for crime conditions

23. "In the official administration of such a [prison] system and in the voluntary cooperation of citizens, therein, the agency of women may be employed with excellent effect."

Source: This is a summary, or abridgement, of the Declaration of Principles adopted at the **National Prison Congress** meeting in Cincinnati in 1870.

Appendix J The Mutual Welfare League

1. The League is a prison system not imposed arbitrarily by the prison authorities, but one, which is desired and requested by the prisoners themselves.
2. There must be no attempt on the part of the prison administration to control the result of the League elections.
3. Membership in the League must be common to all prisoners; any other basis is false and will not attain the desired object—universal responsibility.
4. Under the League better discipline is secured because the prisoners will co-operate with the authorities when precious privileges are granted through the League.
5. Under the League all privileges are utilized as means of obtaining responsibility for the good conduct of the prison community.
6. The open courts of the League mean better conduct and fewer punishments.
7. The League has proved to be the most effective agent of stopping the drug traffic and combating unnatural vice.
8. The League, when properly handled by prison authorities, can largely increase the output of work and improve its quality.

Source: Osborne, *Prisons and Common Sense*, 1924.

Appendix K   Plan for a Penitentiary Inspection House, by Jeremy Bentham

Before you look at the plan, take in words the general idea of it.

The building is circular.

The apartments of the prisoners occupy the circumference. You may call them, if you please cells.

These cells are divided from one another, and the prisoners by that means secluded from all communication with each other, by partitions in the form of radii issuing from the circumference towards the center, and extending as many feet as shall be thought necessary to form the largest dimension of the cell.

The apartment of the inspector occupies the center: you may call it if you please the inspector's lodge.

It will be convenient in most, if not in all cases, to have a vacant space or area all around, between such center and such circumference. You may call it if you please the *intermediate* or *annular* area.

About the width of a cell may be sufficient for a *passage* from the outside of the building to the lodge.

Each cell has in the outward circumference, a *window*, large enough, not only to light the cell, but through the cell, to afford light enough to the correspondent part of the lodge.

An iron grating, so light as not to screen any part of the cell from the inspector's view, forms the inner circumference of the cell.

Of this grating, a part sufficiently large opens, in form of a *door*, to admit the prisoner at his first entrance: and to give admission at any time to the inspector or any of his attendants.

To cut off from each prisoner the view of every other, the partitions are carried on a few feet beyond the grating into the intermediate area: such projecting parts I call the *protracted partitions*.

Source: Jeremy Bentham, *Panopticon; or, The Inspection-House, Containing the Idea of a New Principle of Construction . . .* , (Dublin, London: T. Payne, 1791).

Appendix L   General Prison Argot and Slang

A big day: visiting day at the penitentiary

Across the street (SQ):   warden's office

Alligator bait (ST):   bad food

Anchorite: hermit who has retired from the world for religious reasons

Annie Oakley (ST):   free ticket or pass

Anoint (ST):   to whip or flog

Anus bandit (ST):   convicted sodomist

Balloon juice (ST):   idle talk

Band house (ST):   jail or prison

Bank (ST):   solitary

Barbering (ST):   conversation

Bark (ST):   the skin

Bate sohar **(Hebrew):**   prison

Belch (ST):   complaint

Belly robber (ST):   cook or person responsible for feeding prisoners

Biblebacks (WW):   religious prisoners viewed by other prisoners as insincere

Big house: the prison

Big muddy (WW):   prison gravy

Big pasture (U.S. West):   prison

Big red (WW):   segregation unit, includes death row

Big time (WW):   long prison sentence; serving sentence in an adult institution

Big yard: general population of a large prison

Bikboi (Papua NG):   big boy or senior gang mate

Binkie: prison-made syringe

Bit (ST):   prison sentence

Bit (WW):   short sentence

Bit asiri (Babylonian):   imprisonment of foreign prisoners

Bit kili (Babylonian):   prison

Blanket asses (WW):   derogatory for Native American prisoners

Bones: dominoes

Boneyard (SQ):   trailers reserved for conjugal visits

Boo coo (WW):   plenty

Book (ST):   life sentence

Box: police station or jail

Bread snatchers (Scotland):   affectionate reference to a prisoner's children

Bull (1890s):   prison guard

Bum pay (WW):   someone who does not pay debts in prison

Bundle of time (ST):   long prison sentence

Bunker (Netherlands):   slang for a small high-security cellblock at the high-secuity
          Den Haag Prison

Buried deep (WW):   prisoners spending a long stint in the hole

Bush parole (ST):   escape from prison

Bush parole (WW):   to hide in bushes after escaping prison

Cake and wine (WW):   to dine on bread and water

Calaboose (U.S. West):   prison

Calaboza (Spanish):   dungeon

Can: police station or jail

Carcel (U.S. West):   prison

Carcer (Roman):   prison

Car wash (WW):   shower in Eight Wing

Cat-o'-nine tails: whip with nine leather lashes or "tails"

Cellie: cellmate

Chain, The (WW):   bus that brings inmates to jail

Charms: exercise routine emphasizing chest and arms

Chester: child molester

Chiva: heroin

Chokey (19th c. Dartmoor):   three days' bread and water

Circus bees (ST):   body lice

Circus squirrels (ST):   body lice

Clavo (SQ):   drugs, a large stash of narcotics

College: penitentiary

Corner (ST):   place of solitary confinement

County hotel (U.S. West):   county jail

Cracker: low-class white prisoner

Crankster gangster: usually a white inmate that abuses meth, known as "crank"

Crush (ST):   to escape from prison

Crush out (ST):   to break out of jail using violence

Cupid's itch (ST): venereal disease

Czar (ST): prison warden

Dance hall: death house of penitentiary; where inmate paces cell

Deep freeze (W): in solitary confinement

Deportatio **(Roman):** banishment

Desmoterion **(Greek):** place of chains

Diesel therapy: form of punishment involving the transfer of a prisoner from county jail to county jail in an attempt at breaking the inmate. Sources indicate this often works because each new jail confronts the inmate with a new hostile environment

Dirty towell (ST): prison barbershop

Double sawbuck (ST): twenty-dollar bill: twenty-year sentence

Driving irons: lifting weights

Ducket (SQ): money, or pass that allows an inmate to walk from one place to another in the prison

Dug out (ST): heavy eater

Dutch act (ST): to commit suicide in prison

Eat your duck (ST): get on your way

Es'e: mexican equivalent of "dude"

Fall togs (ST): clothing supplied by attorney for court appearance

Featherwood: female version of Peckerwood

Fin (ST): Five-year sentence or five-dollar bill

Fish: new men in jails or prisons

Flat tire (WW): prisoner who is missing a foot or leg, or has a limp

Fools parade (Dartmoor): single-file circular walk that served as the only exercise

Frajo (SQ): Hispanic term for cigarette

Frustrating the parole board (ST): committing suicide in prison

Fry: LSD

Gaol or jail: from the Latin word *cavea* or cave. Used in British colonies by the 1640s. By 1776 jail replaced gaol in American colonies

Garbage hounds (ST): heavy eaters who enjoy prison food

Gladiator school: violent prison

Going back to the line (SQ): being sent back to general population from a more serious confinement

Going to the holes (SQ): being sent to a segregated unit with the worst criminals

Gone to Korea: rhyming slang for gonorrhea

Greasing (WW): eating

Guns: massive arm muscles

Hack: prison guard

Hap meri (Papua NG): half woman, or male prisoner who consents to anal penetration

Her Majesty's bad bargains (19th c. Dartmoor): soldier prisoners

Hit your house (SQ): cell search

Hitch (ST): prison sentence

Hog pen (WW): control room manned by guards

Hole: solitary confinement

Hoosegow (ST): jail

Hot-spot: electric chair

Hot-squat: electric chair

House (SQ): cell

Hummer (WW): fake arrest by guard

Hump (ST): middle of prison sentence

Humps: non-filter Camel cigarettes

Indian Reservation (WW): wherever several cells containing Native Americans are clustered together

In the car: refers to individuals involved in drug action, as in "So, I hear you're in the car."

Ink: tattoos

Iron pile (SQ): weightlifting area in prison yard

Istikbal (Egypt): reception center or holding facility

Jockey diet (Dartmoor): three days' bread and water

Jolt (ST): prison sentence

Jug (ST): solitary, jail, or prison; derived from *jusgado*

Jusgado **(U.S. West):** court or tribunal; jail

Kalabus (Papua NG): prison

King: warden of penitentiary

Lagged (19th c. Dartmoor): arrested

Lagging (19th c. Dartmoor): period of prison sentence

Lames (SQ): stupid people

Latuminae **(Roman):** quarry prison

Life on the installment plan: indeterminate sentence

Liman (Egypt): Arabic term used to describe the nation's three maximum-security facilities

Lock down: when an entire prison population is locked in cells for extensive time periods, usually as a result of escapes or riots

Long duckets (SQ): lots of money

Lus bodi (Papua, NG): or "loose body," a prisoner to whom no one claims a relationship

Made it (ST): granted parole

Makin' horse hair bridles (U.S. West): prison; convict pastime of making intricate bridles while serving time

Man (ST): prison guard

Mat cat (Vietnam):   inmates who served prison food; named after macaque, monkeys, noted for "snacking" while gathering food

Motorcycle soup (Vietnam):   sour broth conducive to flatulence later heard in latrines

Munman (Papua NG):   month man, convict with less than a year's sentence left to serve

One-Fifteen (SQ):   a disciplinary write-up

One-Twenty-Eight (SQ):   disciplinary warning, but not as severe as one-Fifteen

Ordinary (UK):   prison chaplain

Pad (SQ):   cell

Parole dust (WW):   fog a prisoner uses to obscure an escape attempt

Peacock note (Vietnam):   five-year sentence reflecting the peacock on Bank of Indochina's five-piaster bill

PC: protective custody

Peckerwood: respected white convict but considered derogatory if used by inmate of another race

Penitentiary agent (ST):   public defender

Pin: to be on lookout for guards while associates are violating rules

Phoenix dance (Vietnam):   strip search of body

***Phylake* (Greek):**   prison

Plex: being in a confused state, as in "why you plexin?"

Pruno (SQ):   illicit wine made from prunes

Punks (SQ):   homosexual prisoners

Puttin on the ugly: developing a prison persona, e.g. muscles, tattoos, attitude

Quack (ST):   prison doctor

Quare fellow (Irish):   condemned man

Quod (19th c. Dartmoor):   prison

Raisin jack (SQ):   illicit raisin wine made in the cell

Returning the mat (Vietnam):   release from prison

Road dog: someone you hang out with, former jail partner or friend

Rocket fuel: methamphetamines used for injection

Saw Buck (ST):   Ten-dollar bill or 10-year sentence

Sel (Papua NG):   prison cell

Settled (ST):   imprisoned

Shake down: thorough search of a convict's cell by a guard

Shank (SQ):   knife or similar homemade weapons

Shooting kites (SQ):   writing or mailing letters

Short eyes: child molester

Skookum house (U.S. West):   prison

Slop (SQ):   food

Snout (Dartmoor): tobacco

State issue (SQ): basically anything from the state department of corrections, including uniform

Stir (U.S. East Coast, U.S. Midwest): penitentiary

Streets (SQ): outside world

Strip you out (SQ): body search by police

Surveillant (France): most senior uniformed staff grade

Swim (WW): to survive in prison

Tacks (SQ): tattoos

Taking in the croaker (19th c. Dartmoor): fooling the prison doctor, malingering

The man (SQ): prison guard

Trip over the Alps (Dartmoor): four-year wait for privileges

Trusty: prisoners with special privileges earned through good behavior

Turnkey (UK): prison warder or guard

Up the river (ST): any prison

V (ST): five dollars or five-year sentence

Vinculum (Roman): chaining

Vollzug (Germany): prison

Wake up (ST): day of release from prison

Walker (WW): prisoner who cannot sit still in cell

Walking sentence: individuals sentenced to incarceration, but there is no room

Wangang (Papua NG): one gang or gang mates

Wetkot (Papua NG): wait court, or prisoner on remand

Woof tickets: as in selling woof tickets, inferring that an inmate is making a loud display of fearlessness

Yiaman (Papua NG): year man, or convict with more than a year left to serve

Yoked: very muscular

Zoo (ST): prison or jail

Notes:
WW refers to Walla Walla Prison.
Papua NG refers to Papua New Guinea.
ST refers to Stateville Prison.

Sources: Ragen and Finston, *Inside the World's Toughest Prison*, 1962; Adams, *Western Words*, 1968; Maurer, *Language of the Underworld*, 1981; Cardozo-Freeman, *The Joint: Language and Culture in a Maximum Security Prison*, 1984; Middle East Watch, *Prison Conditions in Egypt*, 1992; Hendrickson, *Happy Trails*, 1994; James, *A Glimpse of Dartmoor Prison*, 1995; Zinoman, *The Colonial Bastille*, 2001; Reed, *Papua New Guinea's Last Place*, 2003; Prison Dictionary, www.downtimemovie.com/home/dic, retrieved July 21, 2005; Guests of the State, www.phrases.org.uk/bulletin_board/29/messages/350.

Appendix M French Prison Slang from Devil's Island

Bagnard: prisoner serving time in a bagne

Bagne: prisons or penal colonies where sentences of hard labor are served; derived from the Italian *bagno*, where convicts were kept below sea level

Camelote: shoddy goods, originated from the French *coesmelot,* which stands for a dealer in odds and ends

Cavale: to beat it from the police; first used by Victor Hugo and stems from the Latin word *cabalus*

Condamne: convict

Dodou: local French Guianan prostitutes

Doublage: law requiring convicts sentenced to hard labor to live in French Guiana for a time equal to their sentence

Evasion: escape

Fort-a-bras: aggressive, dominant prisoners

Gourbi: from the Arabic term meaning "primitive shelter"; later in 1840s temporary shelter for soldiers

Libere: an ex-con completing the requirements of doublage

Mec: originally referred to a pimp but made the transition to buddy, pal, and guy among the lower-class French

Mome: young passive member of homosexual relationship

Plan: suppositories used to hide contraband; probably originated from *plan d'evasion,* or plan of escape

Relegue: type of prisoner sent to French Guiana but not convicted, with a long history of minor crimes and required to serve an indeterminate sentence

Tafia: moonshine rum derived from crushed sugar cane

Transporte: convict transported to penal colony

Vieux blanc: an old white man, or an ex-convict who stayed in the colony after
it was closed as a penal colony

Sources: Henri Charriere, *Papillon*, New York: William and Morrow, 1970; Miles, *Devil's Island: Colony of the Damned*, 1988.

Appendix N Soviet Slang from the Gulags

Balanda: prison soup

Beskonvoinya: prisoner with right to travel in different camp divisions without an armed guard

Blatnoi slovo: thieves' jargon

Bushlat: prisoner's work jacket

Dezhurnaya/dnevalnyi: individual who stays in barracks during the day to clean and to suppress theft

Dokhodyaga: "goner" or individual on edge of death

Dom Svidanii: "House of Meetings" where prisoners were allowed to meet with relatives

Etap: prisoner transport

Katorga: forced labor; term originated in tsarist Russia

Kontslager: Russian for "concentration camp"

Maloletki: juvenile prisoners

Mamka: female prisoner; one who has a child while in prison

Nadziratel: prison camp guards

Sharashka: special prisons where scientists and others worked on secret projects

Starosta: literally means "elder"; responsible for keeping order in prisons

Suki: translates as "bitch," directed at prisoners who collaborate with officials

Vagonki: double-decker bunks meant to hold four prisoners

Zek: a gulag prisoner

Zona: the physical concentration camp behind the barbed wire

Source: Applebaum, *Gulag*, 2003.

Bibliography

Adams, Ramon F. 1968. *Western Words: A Dictionary of the American West.* Norman: University of Oklahoma Press.

American Correctional Association. 1983. *The American Prison: From the beginning . . . A Pictorial History.* College Park, MD: American Correctional Association.

Americas Watch. 1989. *Prison Conditions in Brazil.* New York: Human Rights Watch.

———. 1990. *Prison Conditions in Jamaica.*

———. 1991a. *Prison Conditions in Mexico.*

———. 1991b. "Prison Conditions in Puerto Rico." *A Human Rights Watch Short Report* 3, no. 6 (May 1991).

Amnesty International. 1981. *Report of an Amnesty International Mission to the Kingdom of Morocco.* London: Amnesty International.

Andrus, Burton C. 1969. *I Was the Nuremberg Jailer.* New York: Coward-McCann.

Applebaum, Anne. 2003. *Gulag: A History.* New York: Doubleday.

Babington, Anthony. 1971. *The English Bastille: A History of Newgate Gaol and Prison Conditions in Britain, 1188–1902.* New York: St. Martin's Press.

Bailey, Victor, ed. 1981. *Policing and Punishment in Nineteenth Century Britain.* New Brunswick, NJ: Rutgers University Press.

Barnes, Harry Elmer. 1968 reprint. *The Evolution of Penology in Pennsylvania: A Study in American Social History.* Montclair, NJ: Patterson Smith.

Barry, John Vincent. 1958. *Alexander Maconochie of Norfolk Island: A Study of a Pioneer in Penal Reform.* Melbourne, Australia: Oxford University Press.

Bates, Sanford. 1936. *Prisons and Beyond.* New York: Macmillan Company.

Bateson, Charles. 1959. *The Convict Ships, 1787–1868.* Glasgow: Brown, Son & Ferguson.

Beaumont, Gustave de, and Alexis de Tocqueville. 1964 reprint. *On the Penitentiary System in the United States and Its Application in France.* Carbondale: Southern Illinois Press.

Bentham, Jeremy. 1995. *The Panopticon Writings,* edited and introduced by Miran Bozovic. London: Verso.

Bernault, Florence, ed. 2003. *A History of Prison and Confinement in Africa.* Portsmouth, NH: Heinemann.

Biles, David, ed. 1988. *Current International Trends in Corrections.* Annandale, Australia: Federation Press.

Binny, John, and Henry Mayhew. 1968 reprint. *The Criminal Prisons of London and Scenes of Prison Life*. New York: Reprints of Economic Classics.

Blomberg, Thomas G., and Karol Lucken. 2000. *American Penology: A History of Control*. New York: Aldine De Gruyter.

Bookspan, Shelley. 1991. *A Germ of Goodness: The California State Prison System, 1851–1944*. Lincoln: University of Nebraska Press.

Buntman, Fran. 2003. *Robben Island and Prisoner Resistance to Apartheid*. Cambridge: Cambridge University Press.

Branch-Johnson, W. 1917. *The English Prison Hulks*. London: Christopher Johnson Publishers.

Brockway, Zebulon. 1968 reprint. *Fifty Years of Prison Service: An Autobiography*. Montclair, NJ: Patterson Smith.

Cameron, Joy. 1983. *Prisons and Punishment in Scotland from the Middle Ages to the Present*. Edinburgh: Canongate.

Campbell, Charles. 1993. *The Intolerable Hulks: British Shipboard Confinement, 1776–1857*. Bowie, MD: Heritage Books.

Cardoza-Freeman, Inez. 1984. *The Joint: Language and Culture in a Maximum Security Prison*. Springfield, IL: Charles C. Thomas.

Carlie, Michael K., and Kevin I. Minor. 1992. *Prisons around the World: Studies in International Penology*. Dubuque, IA: Wm. C. Brown Publishers.

Chadha, Kukkum. 1983. *The Indian Jail: A Contemporary Document*. New Delhi: Vikas Publishing House.

Chancellor, Henry. 2001. *Colditz: The Untold Story of World War II's Great Escapes*. New York: William Morrow.

Chandler, David. 1999. *Voices from S-21: Terror and History in Pol Pot's Secret Prison*. Berkeley: University of California Press.

Christianson, Scott. 1998. *With Liberty for Some: 500 Years of Imprisonment in America*. Boston: Northeastern University Press.

———. 2004. *Notorious Prisons: An Inside Look at the World's Most Feared Institutions*. London: Lyons Press.

Clifford, William, ed. 1979. *Innovations in Criminal Justice in Asia and the Pacific*. Canberra: Australian Institute of Criminology.

Collins, Philip. 1962. *Dickens and Crime*. London: Macmillan.

Conot, Robert E. 1983. *Justice at Nuremberg: The First Comprehensive Dramatic Account of the Trial of the Nazi Leaders*. New York: Harper and Row.

Conover, Ted. 2000. *Newjack: Guarding Sing Sing*. New York: Random House.

Coxe, William. 1781. *Account of the Prisons and Hospitals in Russia, Sweden, and Denmark*. London: T. Cadwell.

Crowther, Bruce. 1989. *Captured on Film: The Prison Movie*. London: B.T. Batsford.

DeFord, Miriam Allen. 1962. *Stone Walls: Prisons from Fetters to Furloughs*. Philadelphia: Chilton.

Dikotter, Frank. 2002. *Crime, Punishment, and the Prison in Modern China*. New York: Columbia University Press.

Drapkin, Israel. 1989. *Crime and Punishment in the Ancient World*. Lexington, MA: Lexington Books.

Duffy, Clinton T. 1950. *The San Quentin Story*. New York: Doubleday and Co.

Early, Pete. 1992. *The Hot House: Life inside Leavenworth Prison*. New York: Bantam.

Eaton, Joseph W. 1964. *Prisons in Israel: A Study of Policy Innovation*. Pittsburgh: University of Pittsburgh Press.

Ebbe, Obbe, ed. 1996. *Comparative and International Criminal Justice Systems: Policing, Judiciary, and Corrections*. Boston: Butterworth-Heinemann.

Egypt, Ministry of Interior. 1925. *Note on the History of Prisons in Egypt since the Foundation of Cairo*. Cairo: Government Press.

Englebarts, Rudolf. 1972. *Books in Stir: A Bibliographic Essay about Prison Libraries and about Books Written by Prisoners and Prison Employees*. Metuchen, NJ: Scarecrow Press.

Erickson, Gladys. 1957. *Warden Ragen of Joliet*. New York: E.P. Dutton.

Evans, Robin. 1982. *The Fabrication of Virtue: English Prison Architecture, 1750–1840*. Cambridge: Cambridge University Press.

Fairchild, Erika, and Harry R. Dammer. 2001. *Comparative Criminal Justice Systems*. 2nd edition. Belmont, CA: Wadsworth Publishing.

Fellows, Warren. 1999. *The Damage Done: Twelve Years of Hell in a Bangkok Prison*. London: Mainstream Publishing.

———. 2000. *4000 Days: My Life and Survival in a Bangkok Prison*. New York: St. Martin's Press.

Fields, Charles B., and Richter H. Moore Jr. 1996. *Comparative Criminal Justice: Traditional and Non-traditional Systems of Law and Control*. Prospect Heights, IL: Waveland Press.

Finzsch, Norbert, and Robert Jutte, eds. 1996. *Institutions of Confinement: Hospitals, Asylums, and Prisons in Western Europe and North America, 1500–1950*. Cambridge: Cambridge University Press.

Foucault, Michel. 1995 edition; 1977. *Discipline and Punish: The Birth of the Prison*. New York: Vintage Books.

Fox, Lionel W. 1952. *The English Prisons and Borstal Systems*. London: Routledge and Kegan Paul.

Franke, Herman. 1995. *The Emancipation of Prisoners: A Socio-Historical Analysis of the Dutch Prison Experience*. Edinburgh: Edinburgh University Press.

Franklin, H. Bruce. 1989. *Prison Literature in America: The Victim as Criminal and Artist*. Expanded edition. New York: Oxford University Press.

Freeman, John, ed. 1978. *Prisons Past and Future: In Commemoration of the Bi-centenary of John Howard's The State of the Prisons*. London: Heinemann.

Gillin, John Lewis. 1931. *Taming the Criminal*. New York: Macmillan Company.

Gosselin, Luc. 1982. *Prisons in Canada*. Montreal: Black Rose Books.

Hayes, Billy, with William Hoffer. 1977. *Midnight Express*. New York: Popular Library.

Hendrickson, Robert. 1994. *Happy Trails: A Dictionary of Western Expressions*. New York: Facts on File.

Herber, Mark. 2002. *Criminal London: A Pictorial History from Medieval Times to 1939*. Chichester, UK: Phillimore.

Hopkins, Alfred. 1930. *Prisons and Prison Building*. New York: Architectural Book Publishing.

Howard, D.L. 1958. *The English Prisons*. London: Christopher Johnson.

———. 1963. *John Howard: Prison Reformer*. New York: Archer House.

Howard, John. 1789. *An Account of the Principal Lazarettos in Europe*. London: J. Johnson, C. Dilly, T. Cadell.

———. 1792. *State of the Prisons in England and Wales*. 4th edition. London: J. Johnson, C. Dilly, T. Cadell.

Hughes, Robert. 1987. *The Fatal Shore: The Epic of Australia's Founding*. New York: Alfred A. Knopf.

Human Rights Watch. 1992. *Prison Conditions in Egypt*. New York: Human Rights Watch.

———. 1993. *Global Report on Prisons*. New York: Human Rights Watch.

———. 1994. *Prison Conditions in South Africa*. New York: Human Rights Watch.

———. 1995. *Prison Conditions in Japan*. New York: Human Rights Watch.

———. 1998. *Behind Bars in Brazil*. New York: Human Rights Watch.

Ignatieff, Michael. 1978. *A Just Measure of Pain: The Penitentiary in the Industrial Revolution, 1750–1850*. New York: Pantheon.

International Centre for Prison Studies. World Prison Brief Online. www.kcl.ac.uk/depsta/rel/icps/worldbrief/world_brief_background.

Jacobs, James B. 1977. *Stateville: The Penitentiary in Mass Society*. Chicago: University of Illinois Press.

James, Trevor. 1995. *A Glimpse of Dartmoor Prison*. Devon, UK: Peninsula Press.

Johnston, James A. 1937. *Prison Life Is Different*. Boston: Houghton Mifflin.

———. 1949. *Alcatraz Island and the Men Who Live There*. New York: Charles Scribner's Sons.

———. 1973. *The Human Cage: A Brief History of Prison Architecture*. New York: Walker and Company.

———. 1994. *Eastern State Penitentiary: Crucible of Good Intentions*. Philadelphia: Philadelphia Museum of Art.

———. 2000. *Forms of Constraint: A History of Prison Architecture*. Urbana: University of Illinois Press.

Jones, Mark. 2005. *Criminal Justice Pioneers in U.S. History*. Boston: Pearson Allyn and Bacon.

Kennan, George. 1891. *Siberia and the Exile System*. New York: Century Company.

Keve, Paul W. 1991. *Prisons and the American Conscience: A History of U.S. Federal Corrections*. Carbondale: Southern Illinois University Press.

Kurian, George Thomas, ed. 1989. *World Encyclopedia of Police Forces and Penal Systems*. New York: Facts on File.

Lamott, Kenneth. 1961. *Chronicles of San Quentin: Biography of a Prison*. New York: David McKay.

Lawes, Lewis Edward. 1928. *Life and Death in Sing Sing*. New York: Doubleday and Sons.

———. 1932. *Twenty Thousand Years in Sing Sing*. New York: R. Long and R.R. Smith.

Lewis, Orlando. 1967. *The Development of American Prison Customs, 1776–1845*. Montclair, NJ: Patterson Smith.

Lewis, W. David. 1965. *From Newgate to Dannemora: The Rise of the Penitentiary in New York*. Ithaca, NY: Cornell University Press.

Library of Congress Country Studies. lcweb2.loc.gov/cgi-bin/query.

Maestro, Marcello. 1973. *Cesare Beccaria and the Origins of Penal Reform*. Philadelphia: Temple University Press.

Maurer, David W. 1981. *Language of the Underworld*, collected and edited by Allan W. Futrell and Charles B. Wordell. Lexington: University of Kentucky Press.

Mayhew, Henry, and John Binny. 1971. *Criminal Prisons of London*. London: Frank Cass & Co. (orig. published 1862).

McAllister, Matthew. 2004. *Blinded by the Sunlight: Emerging from the Prison of Saddam's Iraq*. New York: HarperCollins.

McConville, Sean. 1981. *A History of English Prison Administration, 1750–1877*. London: Routledge and Kegan Paul.

McKelvey, Blake. 1977. *American Prisons*. Montclair, NJ: Patterson Smith.

McShane, Marilyn D., and Frank P. Williams III, eds. 1996. *Encyclopedia of American Prisons*. New York: Garland Publishing.

Miles, Alexander. 1988. *Devil's Island: Colony of the Damned*. Berkeley, CA: Ten Speed Press.

Mohanty, Amarenda, and Narayan Hazary. 1990. *Indian Prison System*. New Delhi: Ashish Publishing House.

Morris, Norval, and David J. Rothman, eds. 1995. *The Oxford History of the Prison: The Practice of Punishment in Western Society*. Paperback edition. New York: Oxford University.

Morris, Rosamund. 1976. *Prisons*. London: B.T. Batsford.

Muncie, John, and Richard Sparks, eds. 1991. *Imprisonment: European Perspectives*. New York: St. Martin's Press.

Newman, Graeme, ed. 1999. *Global Report on Crime and Justice*. New York: Oxford University Press.

Osborne, Thomas Mott. 1916. *Society and Prisons*. New Haven, CT: Yale University Press.

————. 1924. *Prisons and Common Sense*. New York: Lippincott.

————. 1969. *Within Prison Walls*. Montclair, NJ: Patterson Smith (orig. published 1914).

Parish, James Robert. 1991. *Prison Pictures from Hollywood*. Jefferson, NC: McFarland.

Pears, Edwin. 1872. *Prisons and Reformatories at Home and Abroad*. London, I.P.P.C. Congress.

Peters, Edward M. "Prison Before Prison." In *Oxford History of Prison*, eds. Morris & Rothman. New York: Oxford University Press, pp. 3–43.

Philip, Cynthia Owen, ed. 1973. *Imprisoned in America: Prison Communications, 1776 to Attica*. New York: Harper and Row.

Phillips, Charles, and Alan Axelrod. 1996. *Cops, Crooks, and Criminologists: An International Biographical Dictionary of Law Enforcement*. New York: Facts on File.

Pierson, George W. 1938. *Tocqueville and Beaumont in America*. Oxford: Oxford University Press.

Pike, Ruth. 1983. *Penal Servitude in Early Modern Spain*. Madison: University of Wisconsin Press.

Pugh, Ralph B. 1968. *Imprisonment in Medieval England*. Cambridge: Cambridge University Press.

Rafter, Nicole H. 1985. *Partial Justice: Women in State Prisons, 1800–1935*. Boston: Northeastern University Press.

Ragen, Joseph E., and Charles Finston. 1962. *Inside the World's Toughest Prison*. Springfield, IL: Charles C. Thomas.

Reed, Adam. 2003. *Papua New Guinea's Last Place: Experiences of Constraint in a Postcolonial Prison*. New York: Berghahn Books.

Reichel, Philip L. 2002. *Comparative Criminal Justice Systems: A Topical Approach*. 3rd edition. Upper Saddle River, NJ: Prentice Hall.

————. 2005. *Comparative Criminal Justice Systems: A Topical Approach*. 4th edition. Upper Saddle River, NJ: Prentice Hall.

Reid, Patrick R. 1952. *The Colditz Story*. London: Hodder and Stoughton.

Rienits, Rex. 1977. *Convict Life in Australia*. Sydney: Paul Hamlyn.

Roberts, John W. 1997. *Reform and Retribution: An Illustrated History of American Prisons*. Lanham, MD: American Correctional Association.

Robinson, Louis W. 1921. *Penology in the United States*. Philadelphia: John C. Winston.

Robson, L. L. 1965. *The Convict Settlers of Australia*. Melbourne: Melbourne University Press.

Roth, Mitchel P. 2005. *Crime and Punishment: A History of the Criminal Justice System*. Belmont, CA: Wadsworth.

Rothman, David J. 1971. *The Discovery of the Asylum: Social Order and Disorder in the New Republic*. Boston: Little, Brown and Company.

————. 1980. *Conscience and Convenience: The Asylum and Its Alternatives in Progressive America*. Boston: Little, Brown.

Rounds, Delbert. 2000. *International Criminal Justice: Issues in a Global Perspective*. Boston: Allyn and Bacon.

Ruggles-Brisse, Sir Hugh Evelyn. 1985. *The English Prison System*. New York: Garland.

Ryder, Chris. 2000. *Inside the Maze: The Untold Story of the Northern Ireland Prison Service*. London: Methuen.

Salvatore, Ricardo D., and Carlos Aguirre, eds. 1996. *The Birth of the Penitentiary in Latin America: Essays on Criminology, Prison Reform, and Social Control, 1830–1940*. Austin: University of Texas Press.

Saunders, Trevor. 1991. *Plato's Penal Code: Controversy and Reform in Greek Penology*. Oxford: Clarendon Press.

Sellin, Thorsten. 1934. *Pioneering in Penology*. Philadelphia: University of Pennsylvania Press.

Seymour, James D., and Richard Anderson. 1998. *New Ghosts, Old Ghosts: Prisons and Labor Reform Camps in China*. Armonk, NY: M.E. Sharpe.

Shaw, A.G.L. 1966. *Convicts and the Colonies: A Study of Penal Transportation from Great Britain and Ireland to Australia and Other Parts of the British Empire*. London: Faber and Faber.

Sifakis, Carl. 1982. *The Encyclopedia of American Crime*. New York: Facts on File.

———. 2003. *The Encyclopedia of American Prisons*. New York: Checkmark Books.

Singh, Indra J. 1979. *Indian Prison: A Sociological Inquiry*. New Delhi: Concept Publishing.

Speed, P.F. 1977. *Police and Prisons*. London: Longman.

Spens, Iona, ed. 1994. *Architecture of Incarceration*. London: Academy Editions.

Stockdale, Eric. 1977. *A Study of Bedford Prison, 1660–1877*. London: Phillimore.

Sullivan, Larry E. 1990. *The Prison Reform Movement: Forlorn Hope*. Boston: Twayne Publishers.

Teeters, Negley K. 1937. *They Were in Prison*. Philadelphia, Chicago: The John C. Winston Company.

———, ed. 1944. *World Penal Systems: A Survey*. Philadelphia: Pennsylvania Prison Society.

———. 1946. *Penology from Panama to Cape Horn*. Philadelphia: University of Pennsylvania Press.

———. 1955. *The Cradle of the Penitentiary: The Walnut Street Jail at Philadelphia, 1773–1835*. Philadelphia: Pennsylvania Prison Society.

Teeters, Negley, and John D. Shearer. 1957. *The Prison at Philadelphia, Cherry Hill*. New York: Columbia University Press.

Terrill, Richard J. 1999. *World Criminal Justice Systems: A Survey*. Cincinnati: Anderson Publishing Company.

Thomas, D.M. 1998. *Alexander Solzhenitsyn: A Century in His Life*. New York: St. Martin's Press.

Thomas, J.E., and Alex Stewart. 1978. *Imprisonment in Western Australia: Evolution, Theory, and Practice*. Nedlands: University of Western Australia Press.

Tibetan Centre for Human Rights and Democracy. 1998. *Behind Bars: Prison Conditions in Tibet*. New Delhi: Indraprastha Publishing.

Tonry, Michael, ed. 2001. *Penal Reform in Overcrowded Times*. Oxford: Oxford University Press.

Tonry, Michael, and Richard S. Frase, eds. 2001. *Sentencing and Sanctions in Western Countries*. New York: Oxford University Press.

Topping, C.W. 1930. *Canadian Penal Institutions*. Chicago: University of Chicago Press.

Vagg, Jon. 1994. *Prison Systems: A Comparative Study of Accountability in England, France, Germany, and the Netherlands*. Oxford: Clarendon Press.

Vansina, Jan. 2003. "Confinement in Angola's Past." In *A History of Prison and Confinement in Africa*, ed. Florence Bernault, pp. 55–68. Portsmouth, NH: Heinemann.

Voyce, Arthur. 1955. *The Moscow Kremlin*. Berkeley: University of California Press.

Wachsmann, Nikolaus. 2004. *Hitler's Prisons: Legal Terror in Nazi Germany*. New Haven, CT: Yale University Press.

Walmsley, Roy. 1996. *Prison Systems in Central and Eastern Europe: Progress, Problems, and the International Standards*. Helsinki: European Institute for Crime Prevention and Control.

———. 2003. *Further Developments in the Prison Systems of Central and Eastern Europe: Achievements, Problems, and Objectives*. Helsinki: European Institute for Crime Prevention and Control.

Whitfield, Dick, ed. 1991. *The State of the Prisons—200 Years On*. London: Routledge Press.

Whitney, Janet. 1936. *Elizabeth Fry, Quaker Heroine*. Boston: Little, Brown and Company.

Wicker, Tom. 1975. *A Time to Die: The Attica Prison Revolt*. New York: Quadrangle Books.

Wicks, Robert J., and H.H.A. Cooper, eds. 1979. *International Corrections*. Lexington, MA: Lexington Books.

Wines, Frederick H. 1919. *Punishment and Reform*. New York: Thomas Y. Crowell.

World Prison Population List (fifth edition). www.homeoffice.gov.uk/rds/pdfs2/r234.pdf.

Wu, Hongda Harry. 1992. *Laogai—the Chinese Gulag*. Boulder, CO: Westview Press.

Wylie, Donovan, ed. 2004. *The Maze*. London: Granta Books.

Zinoman, Peter. 2001. *The Colonial Bastille: A History of Imprisonment in Vietnam, 1862–1940*. Berkeley: University of California Press.

Index

About the Author

MITCHEL P. ROTH is Associate Professor of Criminal Justice at Sam Houston State University. He is author of a number of books including *Historical Dictionary of Law Enforcement* (Greenwood, 2001).